W9-BCK-455

Fodor's

VIENNA'S
25 BEST

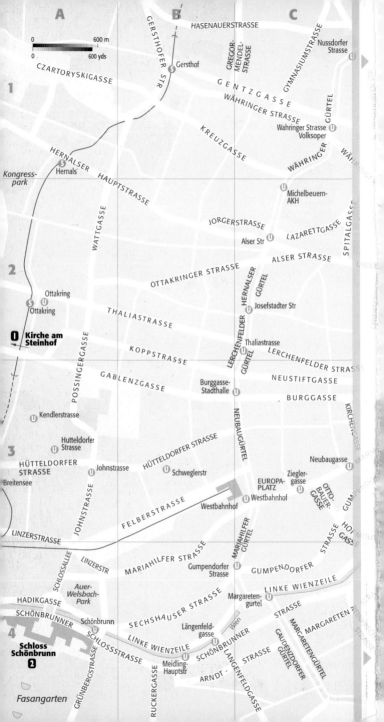

Top 25 locator map
(continues on inside
back cover)
←

Fodor's
VIENNA'S **25 BEST**

by Louis James

Fodor's Travel Publications
New York • Toronto •
London • Sydney • Auckland
www.fodors.com

About This Book

KEY TO SYMBOLS

✚	Map reference to the accompanying fold-out map and Top 25 locator map	🚢	Nearest riverboat or ferry stop
✉	Address	♿	Facilities for visitors with disabilities
☎	Telephone number	✋	Admission charges: Expensive (over €10), Moderate (€5–€10) and Inexpensive (€5 or less).
⏰	Opening/closing times		
🍴	Restaurant or café on premises or nearby	↔	Other nearby places of interest
🚆	Nearest railway station	❓	Other practical information
Ⓤ	Nearest *U-Bahn* station	➤	Indicates the page where you will find a fuller description
🚌	Nearest bus route	ℹ	Tourist information

ORGANIZATION

This guide is divided into six chapters:

- Planning Ahead, Getting There
- Living Vienna—Vienna Now, Vienna Then, Time to Shop, Out and About, Walks, Vienna by Night
- Vienna's Top 25 Sights
- Vienna's Best—best of the rest
- Where To—detailed listings of restaurants, hotels, shops and nightlife
- Travel Facts—practical information

In addition, easy-to-read side panels provide extra facts and snippets, highlights of places to visit and invaluable practical advice.

The colours of the tabs on the page corners match the colours of the triangles aligned with the chapter names on the contents page opposite.

MAPS

The fold-out map in the wallet at the back of this book is a comprehensive street plan of Vienna. The first (or only) grid reference given for each attraction refers to this map. **The Top 25 locator map** found on the inside front and back covers of the book itself is for quick reference. It shows the Top 25 Sights, described on pages 26–50, which are clearly plotted by number (**1**–**25**, not page number) across the city. The second map reference given for the Top 25 Sights refers to this map.

Contents

Planning Ahead

WHEN TO GO

Most of the important festivals and events are held in spring and summer. The main opera and concert seasons kick-off in autumn. Some prime attractions (such as the Lipizzaners and the Vienna Boys Choir) take a summer break from about July to September and may be on tour some months.

TIME

Vienna is one hour ahead of the UK, six hours ahead of New York and nine hours ahead of Los Angeles.

AVERAGE DAILY MAXIMUM TEMPERATURES

JAN	FEB	MAR	APR	MAY	JUN	JUL	AUG	SEP	OCT	NOV	DEC
34°F	37°F	48°F	59°F	66°F	73°F	79°F	77°F	68°F	59°F	45°F	39°F
1°C	3°C	9°C	15°C	19°C	23°C	26°C	25°C	20°C	15°C	7°C	4°C

Spring (March to May) is rainy and sometimes fairly cool until mid-April.

Summer (June to August), every year seems to get hotter!

Autumn (September to October) is the most pleasant time to visit when it is not too hot and mostly dry.

Winter (November to February) can be bitterly cold, often with heavy snow from late December.

If you suffer from migraines or circulation problems you may be affected by the *Föhn* wind blowing off the Alps.

WHAT'S ON

February *Opernball* (Opera Ball): The highlight of the social calender.

March *Osterklang Wien*: Sacred music for Easter in St. Stephen's, the Musikverein and elsewhere.

March–June & September–December Equestrian ballet, by the Lipizzaners (► 38).

April *Frühlingsfestival* (mid-Apr to mid-May): Concerts in the Musikverein and Konzerthaus.

May *Maifest* (1 May): Celebrations mostly in the Prater. The Socialist march through town looks increasingly self-conscious.

Spring Marathon (mid-May): Schönbrunn to the Rathaus.

Wiener Festwochen (May to mid-Jun): Arts festival.

June *Klangbogen Wien* (Jun–Sep): Chamber music and some jazz.

Open-air festival (end Jun): Music, cabaret and theatre on the Danube Island.

July *Jazz Festival* (Jun–Jul): Jazz ensembles at the Opera House and the Volkstheater.

Opera on Film (Jul–Aug): Opera films on a screen in front of the Rathaus.

Mozart at Schönbrunn (Jul–Aug): Mozart opera against a backdrop of the fake Roman ruins in the park at Schönbrunn.

October *Vienna Film Festival.*

Wien Modern (Oct–Nov): One of the biggest festivals of contemporary music.

November–December *Christkindlmarkt* (mid-Nov to 24 Dec): A Christmas fair in front of the Rathaus.

'Mozart and Friends': Concert house series devoted to the works of Mozart and his contemporaries.

New Year *Die Fledermaus*: At the State Opera.

VIENNA ONLINE

www.austria-tourism

An easy to navigate site that gives information on all types of holidays in Austria, including car, motorcycle and hiking itineries. Other features include a listing of events, weather forecasts, water temperatures in the lakes, plus webcam pictures of towns, landscapes and buildings.

www.vienna.at

Available in German or English, this site offers diverse general information on the city from politics and culture to urban development and the environment. The restaurant and eaterie listings are rather brief.

www.info.wien.at

A site pullulating with images of Vienna and with entertainingly delivered information on sightseeing, eating out, culture, and more. Useful for locating theatre booking offices and (in some cases) booking online. The 72-hour itinerary is a good tour for first-time visitors and those with limited time.

www.vienneseball.org

Details on how to join a party (organized by the Johann Strauss society of Great Britain) for one of the celebrated Vienna winter balls. It includes history of the balls, instructions about etiquette for participants and much more.

www.hungrymonster.com

A fun site for those interested in international cuisine, including Viennese.

www.falter.at

Look under 'Wien, wie es isst' for details of recommended restaurants (German only).

www.tourist-net.co.at/.../coffee

This general tourist site for Austria has some nice material about Vienna's coffee-houses and a useful listing of some of the better known and most characteristic. Currently in German, but an English version is promised shortly.

GOOD TRAVEL SITES

www.fodors.com

A complete travel-planning site. Research prices and weather; book air tickets, cars and rooms; pose questions to fellow travellers; and find links to other sites.

www.oeamtc.at

Invaluable for motorists, this site (only in German) informs about the current state of traffic on Austrian roads, roadworks, weather conditions and much more. The visuals will help non-German speakers.

CYBERCAFÉS

BIGNET.cafe
🚑 H6 ✉ Hoher Markt 8–9 ☎ 533 2939
🕐 Daily 10am–midnight

Coffeeshop Company
🚑 H6 ✉ Rabensteig 8
☎ 532 8361
🕐 Mon–Sat 7am–11pm, Sun 10am–11pm

g-zone
🚑 G5
✉ Universitätsstrasse 11
🕐 Mon–Fri 10am–11pm, Sat–Sun 2pm–11pm

Internetcafe Surfland
🚑 H6 ✉ Krugerstrasse 10 ☎ 512 7701 🕐 Daily 10am–11pm

Getting There

ENTRY REQUIREMENTS

Visitors from the UK, EU countries, the US and Canada need a passport (valid for at least six months) but do not need a visa.

ARRIVING

Vienna International Airport is 19km (12 miles) east of the city at Schwechat. Recently extended, the airport has extensive shopping facilities, restaurants, bars, newsstands and car rental desks. Vienna is also served by good rail and bus links from other European countries.

96km (60 miles) 64km (40 miles) 32km (20 miles) Vienna

MONEY

The euro (€) is the official currency of Austria. Notes in denominations of 5, 10, 20, 50, 100, 200 and 500 euros, and coins in denominations of 1, 2, 5, 10, 20 and 50 cents, and 1 and 2 euros, were introduced in 2002.

€10

€50

€200

€500

ARRIVING BY AIR

For arrivals information at Vienna International Airport ☎ 7007 22233 (24 hours). The convenient option for transport to the city is the Vienna Airport Lines bus (☎ 93000/2300) to and from UNO-City, Schwedenplatz, Südbahnhof and Westbahnhof (20–30 minutes, €6). The CAT express train (www.cityairporttrain.at) to Wien Mitte costs €9 and runs between 5.30am and 11.30pm; the journey lasts 16 minutes. The S-Bahn (Schnellzug) rapid transit service is slower (32 minutes) but cheaper (€3) and runs from the Flughafen via Wien Mitte and Wich Nord to Floridsdorf. Timetables of the above services are shown on the website of Flughafen Wien. Taxis from the airport cost between €35 and €45.

ARRIVING BY TRAIN

The international stations are the Westbahnhof and the Südbahnhof. Confusingly, trains do not necessarily only go south from the Südbahnhof or west from Westbahnhof. Check your departure station carefully. Franz-Josefs-Bahnhof is for trains to northern Austria. For train information and bookings ☎ 05-717 (24 hours) ☎ 93000 22222 (lost and found). Vienna is about three hours by train from Budapest and five hours from Prague.

ARRIVING BY CAR

Vienna is reached from Bavaria/Salzburg via the West Autobahn (A1); from the south it is reached from Graz and the Italian border via the South Autobahn (A2); and from the Hungarian border it is reached via the East Autobahn (A4). Currently there are motorway tolls in Austria, Italy and Hungary but none in Germany.

Avoid taking your car into the old city centre where underground parking is expensive and above-ground difficult and complicated.

ARRIVING BY BUS

International bus lines arrive at Endbergstrabe 202 (☎ Wein 798 2900) or Arsenalstrabe (☎ Wein 796 8552), depending where you are coming from.

ARRIVING BY BOAT

May to September, cruise ships run on the Danube between Passau (Germany) and Vienna. Ships dock at the *Donaudampschiffsgesellschaft* (DDSG) berth near the Reichsbrücke (close to U1 Vorgartenstrasse) ☎ 588 88-0.

GETTING AROUND

Vienna is covered in an overlapping network of *U-Bahn* (underground trains), *Strassenbahn* (trams) and buses. Newsagents (*Tabaktrafik*) sell tickets for public transport. Main *U-Bahn* and *S-Bahn* (rapid transit railway) stations have ticket counters. A single journey card must be validated at the entrance to the *U-Bahn*, or on a tram or bus, using the stamping machines. It can be used for one unbroken ride, including changes of line, from *U-Bahn,* to tram, to bus, and is valid one hour from stamping. Taxis are usually white and can be hired at the taxi ranks in the city and at the larger public transport terminals. Officially it is not allowed to hail them in the street, but some will stop for you. For more information on getting around ➤ 91–92.

INSURANCE

EU nationals receive reduced cost medical treatment with form E111—obtain this form before you go. Full health and travel insurance is still advised. US travellers should check their health cover before departure and buy a supplementary policy if necessary.

VACCINATIONS

Some wooded areas of Austria are home to *Zecken*, a kind of tick whose bite can transmit encephalitis, which in a few cases proves fatal. Enquire at the Austrian consulate about inoculation.

VISITORS WITH DISABILITIES

Facilities have improved in museums and some other major sights, but access is not always guaranteed. Older trams and buses remain impossible for anyone in a wheelchair, but most U-Bahn stations are now better equipped with escalators and elevators. The visitors service website (http:/info.wien. at) gives the detailed status of transport, hotels, sights, museums and more.

Living
Vienna

Vienna Now

Dinner dance in the Volksgarten

Movie buffs will recall the powerful evocation of Vienna in Carol Reed's classic film from Graham Greene's screenplay of *The Third Man*. This was Vienna immediately following World War II, a bleak, sinister place divided by the zones of the four allied powers, where crime and the black market flourished. It could hardly have been more different than the city's traditionally marketed image of civilized, carefree pleasures. *The Third Man* is a reminder that the glitzy surface of today's Vienna is the culmination of sixty years hard work and good governance. It is also a reminder that behind the candy floss façade of elegant Strauss waltzers, prancing

NEIGHBOURHOODS

• Many Viennese remain for generations in the same city district (*Bezirk*). This continuity has given each district an individual profile (known as *Grätzel-Kultur*): The Josefstadt is well-to-do, intellectual and Bohemian; Hietzing is middle class and populated by the higher bureaucrats; Ottakring is heavily immigrant, while Favoriten remains largely working class. The Inner City with it churches, offices, luxury shops and restaurants is where the Viennese work and show themselves off. Around the periphery are the Heurigen villages where they take their leisure from spring to autumn. In winter they retreat to the warmth of the neighbourhood coffee-houses.

Lipizzaners and idyllic *Heurigen* evenings with Schrammel music lurk other Viennese worlds of the past and present.

Sunset on the Danube

Set strategically at the heart of Central Europe (east of Prague), Vienna has developed into a sophisticated modern metropolis, shrewdly—and for the most part tastefully—adapting its sumptuous imperial heritage to the requirements of modern living. With its relatively small population of around 1.6 million, Vienna might at first glance seem to be living entirely from service industries and tourism. While it is true that these are the biggest employers (around 75 per cent of the workforce), there are still substantial numbers of small firms in the city,

VIENNESE DIALECT

• Viennese dialect is sophisticated and has a long tradition on stage and in cabaret, even in verse. Vivid, but impenetrable to outsiders, it is both a colourful assertion of identity and a means whereby the Viennese can shelter his private sphere in a city full of tourists and new arrivals.

FÖHN

• Suddenly the waitresses are forgetful and brusque, the ambulance sirens ring in the streets and cars begin colliding on the Ringstrasse. It is as if a curse has been put on the city—but it's only the warm *Föhn* wind blowing from the Alps—and making everyone wish they were somewhere else.

11

Above: *Street art in Vienna*

although large, Austria-wide concerns mostly have their head offices here (nearly half of Austrian industry is directed from Vienna). Metal working, production of food and drink and printing are the most significant activities. At the same time the country's financial sevices are predominantly located in Vienna, which also has a small stock exchange dominated by national and international institutional investors.

From Habsburg times, Vienna has always been the core of government and bureaucracy, but also of display and lavish spending on culture. The long-serving Social Democratic administration of the city has access to funds both in its capacity as one of the nine Federal States and as the nation's showcase, attracting Central Goverment largesse. A period of 'museum millions' has just ended, resulting in the refurbishment, with no expense spared, of existing galleries like the Albertina and the Akademie der Bildenden Künste, and the creation of a gigantic new Museums Quartier, a temple raised to Modernism in painting and architecture, that includes a location devoted to cybernetics.

LOCAL PATRIOTISM

• The Viennese exhibit strong local patriotism, coupled with a conservatism that ensures each new architectural project is greeted with cries of scorn. It was ever so: The critics complained of the opera on its completion in 1869 that it looked like an 'elephant lying down to digest its dinner'.

Music flourishes as never before, with one festival following another; concert series feature a roll-call of the many great composers associated with the city, from Mozart and Beethoven through Brahms and Bruckner to Mahler, Berg and Schönberg. The *fin de siècle* critic Karl Kraus said Vienna's streets 'were paved with culture as those of other cities are covered with asphalt', and he could be describing Vienna today.

Looking to the future, Vienna is benefiting from the eastward expansion of the EU, as it has already profited from the fall of the Iron Curtain. However, the likely benefits are tempered by trades unionists' fears of an influx of cheap labour

Above left: View from the neoclassical columns of the Gloriette in the grounds of the Schönbrunn Palace
Above: The Hundertwasser Haus, a block of fifty flats designed by Friedensreich Hundertwasser and built in 1983–85

MUST BE TIME FOR A MEAL

● An anstonishing 4,000 eateries cater to the Viennese need for meals at all times of day. Extracurricular consumption includes at least one 'coffee-pause' in the morning, and maybe a *Jause* (a hefty snack of bread, charcuterie and cheese) to stave off hunger pangs between serious eating. The locals cheerfully joke about 'suicide by knife and fork', being no more perturbed by this prospect than they were by the abuse of medieval moralists (and the poet Schiller) who compared them to the Phaeacians, a gluttonous and pleaure-loving people featured in Homer's *Odyssey*.

13

Above: *Live performance in a Viennese nightclub*

and from the new EU members. What they mean is cheap, highly skilled labour, more of a threat than the controllable semi- and unskilled labour provided hitherto by the Southern Slavs on the basis of need, not competition. On the other hand, many a young banker, manager or entrepreneur now ventures out from Vienna to do a stint in Hungary, Poland or the Czech Republic, perhaps returning with a Slav or Hungarian wife in tow. In this way, a very ancient tradition is renewed, as the pages of the Vienna telephone book confirm.

With considerable aplomb, modern Vienna has tackled problems that have almost lamed cities like New York and London. Yes, there are traffic jams, and yes, prices and unemployment have risen sharply since the introduction of the euro and the onset of the 2002–3 recession. Yet Vienna remains a city where accommodation (unlike London) is still generally within the reach of the lower paid, where crime (unlike in many major cities) is minimal. It is clean, unpolluted and has an efficient infrastructure with smoothly functioning public transport—an easy city to live in.

LONG LIVE THE TRAM

• Vienna's red and cream tramcars are icons with the same resonance as London's double-decker buses. They are clean, slow, safe and avoid the jams, and are also democratic; rich and poor alike use them. You can hold a party on an 'oldtimer' from the Vienna Tram Museum as it trundles round the town.

Visitors to Vienna will appreciate the considerable energy that has been expended on creating new attractions. The revitalized museums now have excellent bookshops and better cafés. No wonder that Vienna is a firm tourist favourite, a lively cosmopolitan city where sophisticated modernity coexists with unalloyed nostalgia and a strongly local vernacular culture that's unique on the Continent.

Above left: *The Vienna International Centre, also known as UNO City, one of the headquarters of the United Nations, built in 1979*
Above: *Diners in the Baroque vaulted Esterhazykeller*

FACTS AND FIGURES

- The non-Austrian population of Vienna stands at more than 16 per cent, excluding an estimated 60,000 illegal residents.
- The population of Vienna is 1.6 million.
- Of the 185,000 Jewish-Viennese who lived here before World War II, 50,000 died in the Holocaust.
- Vienna's coat of arms is a white fesse cross on a red background, a symbol derived from a motif on 13th-century coins.
- The current Austrian national anthem (Land of Mountains, Land of Rivers) is doubtfully attributed to Mozart.

Vienna Then

MUSICAL NOTES

Music has reverberated within the walls of Vienna since the days when the Minnesänger (poets of chivalry) performed at the Babenberg court in the 13th century. Members of the Habsburg dynasty were patrons of Gluck, Haydn, Mozart and Beethoven, among others. Key musical dates include:
1782 Mozart's opera *The Abduction from the Seraglio* premieres at the Court Theatre.
1792 Beethoven settles in Vienna.
1828 In June, Franz Schubert completes Die Winterreise song cycle. He dies 19 November, age 31.
1867 Johann Strauss Junior's *On the Beautiful Blue Danube* is performed by the Vienna Male Choral Society; it flops.
1897 Gustav Mahler becomes director of the Vienna opera, initiating a period of imaginative productions.

5th–1st century BC The Celtic Boier tribe settles on the site of today's Belvedere Palace.

15BC The Romans conquer the area.

AD400–791 The Romans withdraw. Charlemagne creates the *Ostmark* (Eastern Region of his empire).

881 The Salzburg annals recall a battle *ad Weniam*—the first reference to the name *Wien* (Vienna).

1156 Austria becomes a Babenberg dukedom and Vienna the ducal residence.

1278 640 years of Habsburg rule begins.

1421 Pogrom against the Viennese Jews. Two hundred are burnt alive.

1517 The advent of Lutheranism in Vienna.

1521 The Spanish and German realms of the Habsburgs, ruled by Charles V, are divided. Charles' brother, Ferdinand I, takes Austria.

1529 The first Turkish siege of Vienna.

1551 The Jesuits are invited to the city. The Counter-Reformation begins.

1683 The second, unsuccessful Turkish siege.

1805– 1815	Napoleon's troops occupy Vienna. After his defeat, the Congress of Vienna imposes order on Europe.
1848	Revolutions against Habsburg absolutist rule take place. 18-year-old Franz Joseph becomes emperor.
1867	Austro-Hungarian Empire is formed.
1916	Franz Joseph dies. The Habsburg Empire is dissolved in 1919.
1922	Vienna becomes one of the Federal States of the Republic of Austria.
1934	Civil War breaks out. Clerico-Fascist dictatorship under Engelbert Dollfuss follows.
1938	Hitler invades Austria.
1945– 1955	Vienna is under joint allied control until the State Treaty restores a free Austrian state.
1995	Austria joins the European Union.
2000	The far right Freedom Party joins the government coalition, amid international controversy.
2003	After new elections, the Conservatives and the Freedom Party resume their coalition.

From left to right:
*The crown of Rudolf II;
figurine of Mozart;
statue of the Empress
Elisabeth;
cupola and statuary in the
Hofburg complex*

THE RINGSTRASSE

On Christmas Day 1857 Emperor Franz Joseph ordered the demolition of the city bastions and the creation of a great boulevard around the city. The Ringstrasse symbolized an era of wealth, industry and modernization.

THE *ANSCHLUSS* (1938)

After the *Anschluss*—the annexation of Austria to Germany by Adolf Hitler—many Viennese went into exile, and artistic and academic talent was lost through Austrian-born Adolf Eichmann's campaign to make Vienna *judenrein* (Jew-free).

17

Time to Shop

There are always limits to how much a visitor can integrate into a local style and these are reached quite quickly with 'Tracht' (traditional costume), found in shops all over the city. But you do not

SHOPPING CULTURE HAS CHANGED

Time was when Viennese shopkeepers called all the shots, but much has changed. Despite a long rearguard action by retailers, shopping hours have been greatly liberalized: No longer do sad crowds mill around the windows of closed shops on Saturday afternoons; no more do bookstore assistants crouch over the tills, glaring suspiciously at browsers. And for those who want to shop till they drop, there are now several constantly expanding shopping malls. The biggest is the aptly named Shopping City Sud. An alternative is the Ringstrassen Galerien.

need to go the whole hog of 'Dirndlkleid' or 'Lederhosen': The more restrained Steirer-Jacke (Styrian jacket with decorative edgings) or the marvellously enduring Loden overcoats, or even a smart Austrian hat can still look good when you get home.

Austrians are good at designing charming ornaments, some admittedly bordering on kitsch. Typical are the models of animals and birds that occur in different materials. Decorative enamel influenced by the Wiener Werkstätte, the leading producer of which is Michaela Frey, is also attractive, while petit point (for ladies' purses and handbags) is another item that makes a nice present. Porcelain comes from two great names: Augarten in Vienna and the Gmundner Keramik from Upper Austria. The latter, with its wavy green motifs is vernacular, while the Augarten is formal and aristocratic.

Vienna has plenty of local delicacies. The famous Sachertorte (a chocolate cake invented in 1832) can be shipped anywhere for you from the Sacher shop, likewise the rival *Imperialtorte*. Then there are the Mozart Kugel (gold-wrapped spherical chocolates filled with marzipan and

Below: *Window shopping in the elegant Freyung Arcade*

nougat) and the Mozart Thaler (the same, but shaped like coins). These are the trademark Austrian chocolates, but many other *chocolatiers* produce something just as good. Austrian wine remains much underrated (the whites, such as *Grüner Veltliner* or *Riesling* from the Wachau, are recommended) and the *Sekt* is better than its reputation as the poor man's champagne. *Obstler* (schnaps made from various fruits), is an Austrian speciality much prized by connoisseurs.

Nothing gives a better flavour of a country than its music. Naturally Vienna offers a huge selection of CDs (including rare performances) of the great Austrian composers, as well as Johann Strauss, the indigenous art form of operetta (Lehár, Kálmán) and 'Schrammel music' from the Heurigen. Austrian Broadcasting (ORF) has produced a comprehensive anthology of *Wiener Lied,* featuring singers like Walter Berry and Angelika Kirchschlager. A fascinating collector's item is the ORF CD of the music of ethnic minorities in Austria, '*Hausgemacht*'.

SHOPPING AREAS

Vienna shopping can roughly be divided into luxury, middle market and cheap. The three sides of the rectangle comprising Kohlmarkt, Graben and Kärntner Strasse offer upmarket Austrian goods and international designer labels. Mariahilfer Strasse is Vienna's Oxford Street, with the last of the big stores (good for household and clothing). Cheapest of all is the flea-market (*Flohmarkt*) at the west end of the Naschmarkt each Saturday morning. Lots of bargains!

Out and About

MORE IDEAS...

River Trips

River Danube trips organized by the DDSG-Blue Danube Schiffstundfahrten.
✉ Schiffstation Reichsbrücke ☎ 588 80-440; www.ddsg-blue-danube.at

Walking

Walking in the Wienerwald is a favourite Viennese pastime. The Information Bureau in the City Hall dispenses maps with routes for walkers.
✉ Friedrich-Schmidt-Platz 1 ☎ 525 50

Cycling

A good way to see Vienna (May–Sep) is with a three-hour bike tour organized by Pedal Power. Bikes are provided. The meeting point is the Ferris wheel in the Prater ☎ 729 7234

INFORMATION

LAXENBURG

🚌 Bus 267 from Südtirolerplatz
🚆 From Südbahnhof
🕐 Museum: Sun 10–12 (longer hours for exhibitions).
Franzensburg: daily 10–12, 2–5 (☎ 02236 71226)
www.laxenburg.at

GUMPOLDSKIRCHEN

🚌 Bus from Baden

ORGANIZED SIGHTSEEING

Vienna's most intriguing sights are best visited on foot. The Vienna Tourist Information Bureau (✉ Albertinaplatz 1 ☎ 24 555 🕐 Daily 9–7) has a pamphlet with a choice of guided walks, covering anything from Hundertwasser sights to

'Vienna Underground'. For information in English ☎ 894 5363. Companies offering sightseeing trips include Vienna Sightseeing Tours (✉ Graf-Starhemberg-Gasse 25 ☎ 712 4683) and Cityrama Sightseeing ✉ Börsegasse 1 ☎ 534 13-0). A city tour on an old-time tram starts from Otto Wagner Pavilion on Karlsplatz Pre-booking is required (☎ 7909–105 🕐 May–Sep Sat 11.30, 1.30, Sun and hols 9.30, 11.30, 1.30).

EXCURSIONS

LAXENBURG

About 15km (9 miles) south of Vienna is the moated 18th-century Laxenburg castle. Highlights include the 19th-century neo-Gothic Frazensburg folly and the re-creation of a medieval dungeon, complete with the model of a knight in chains.

GUMPOLDSKIRCHEN

Close to Baden (Road 12 southwest of Vienna) is the wine village of Gumpoldskirchen, whose main street is full of *Heurigen* (▶ 66). The region produces some good white wines (Zierfandler, Rotgipfler and Neuburger).

DÜRNSTEIN

This attractive town is on the edge of the wine-growing region of Wachau. Richard I (the Lionheart) was imprisoned here in 1192. According to legend, his minstrel, Blondel, roamed Europe in search of him, playing outside castle windows

until one day the king responded. The ransom raised for the king's release was used to build up Vienna. The main feature of Dürnstein is the 18th-century monastery and church built by Matthias Steinl.

BADEN

A geological fault where the eastern edge of the Alps meets the Vienna Basin is responsible for the mineral springs at Baden, first exploited by the Romans. The now-sleepy town became a fashionable spa during the Biedermeier period (1815–1848). Mozart wrote his sublime *Ave Verum* chorus for the choir of the parish church. The town is full of Joseph Kornhäusel's neo-Classical architecture. A tram (Lokalbahn) runs from Oper to Baden (25km/16 miles).

HEILIGENKREUZ

This abbey, whose name 'Holy Cross' is derived from the fragment of the True Cross preserved in a tabernacle on the main altar, was founded in 1133 by the Cistercians. The church has a lovely Gothic nave, and later baroque features include a Trinity Column in the courtyard.

INFORMATION

DÜRNSTEIN

🚉 From Franz-Josefs-Bahnhof

🚢 Contact the DDSG at Schiffstation, Reichsbrücke (☎ 588 80–585; central booking 58 880–0)

BADEN

🚊 Lokalbahn (tram) from Oper

🎭 Operetta performances Jul to mid-Sep; Beethoven festival Sep

HEILIGENKREUZ

☎ 02782 840 97

🚌 Bus 365 from Südtirolerplatz

🕐 Daily 10–5; tours 5 times daily from 10am

🎭 Thirteen Babenbergs (the pre-Habsburg dynasty) are buried at Heiligenkreuz.

Above left: *Walking through the woods in Baden is a favourite pastime*

Above: *The elaborate Trinity Column (1714), in Baden's Hauptplatz, backed by 18th-century buildings*

21

Walks

INFORMATION

Distance 3km (1.8 miles)
Time 2 hours (without museums)
Start point ★ Burgtor
🔲 G6
🚇 U1, U2, U4
🚋 Tram: 1, 2 to Burgring
End point Michaelertor of the Hofburg
🔲 G6
🚇 U3
🍴 Self-service Markt-Restaurant Rosenberger (✉ Maysedergasse 2, behind Sacher). Good cafés on Graben, in Kärntner Strasse and Naglergasse.

THROUGH THE INNER CITY

Start at the Burgtor on the Ringstrasse. Walk through the Arch (Burgtor), commemorating Napoleon's defeat, into the Heldenplatz. On your right stands the Neue Hofburg, containing museums and the National Library. Continue through the Hofburg arches (► 37) into the main courtyard (In der Burg), where you'll find the entrance to the Imperial Apartments and, via the Swiss Gate (Schweizertor) on the south side, access to the Burgkapelle and the treasuries (Weltliche und Geistliche Schatzkammer). Continue on through the Michaelertor onto Michaelerplatz, and turn right for Josefsplatz.

Head along Augustinerstrasse, past the Augustinian Church (► 39) and the Albertina (► 56) on the right. Turn left after Hotel Sacher into Kärntner Strasse, Vienna's premier shopping street. Turn right down Annagasse, past the baroque Annakirche (► 52), then left into Seilerstätte and left again into Himmelpfort-gasse, passing the Winter Palace of Prince Eugene of Savoy (► 55).

At Kärntner Strasse again turn right and continue to Stephansplatz and St. Stephen's Cathedral (► 45). Opposite is the Haas-Haus (1990), by Hans Hollein. Its upper-floor bar and restaurant affords a fine view of the cathedral, which is ironic given that the building itself is controversial for having blocked that same view from the Graben. Walk west along the Graben past the Plague Column and St. Peter's Church (► 42). Continue west along picturesque Naglergasse to the southwestern edge of Am Hof.

Above: *Looking across Vienna's Stephansplatz, past the ultra-modern Haas-Haus towards St. Stephen's Cathedral*

Proceed along the Heidenschuss through the Freyung (► 40), and turn left through the Ferstel Arcade. Emerging on Herrengasse, walk back to the Hofburg's Michaelertor.

THE RINGSTRASSE

Walk west from Schwedenplatz, then follow the Ring southwards. On your right, in Schlickplatz, is the Rossauer Kaserne, originally a barracks built in 'Windsor Castle style'. Almost immediately on your left is Theophil Hansen's graceful Börse (Stock Exchange), a symphony of mellow red brickwork and silver-grey stone. Walk on through Schottentor: On your right you will pass the Votivkirche (➤ 53), then the neo-Renaissance university, both by Heinrich Ferstel. On your left you pass the monument to Andreas von Liebenberg (who was mayor during the 1683 Turkish siege), before reaching the Burgtheater (➤ 33) opposite the new City Hall (➤ 32). Walk on past the Parliament (by Theophil Hansen) on your right; to the left is a park, the Volksgarten (➤ 58), in which are monuments to the Empress Elisabeth and Franz Grillparzer (Austria's greatest dramatic poet), and the mock-antique Theseum.

Continuing east on the Ring you pass the Natural History Museum (Naturhistorischers Museum), the Museum of Art History (➤ 34) and the monument to Maria Theresa (➤ 59). Pass Schillerplatz, with its statue of the poet in front of the Academy of Fine Arts (➤ 35), and continue until you reach the junction at Oper with the Opera House on your left.

Proceed along the right side (southeast) of the Ring past the Hotel Imperial (➤ 86), then past Schwarzenbergplatz and into the Stadtpark (➤ 58). Leave the Stadtpark near the Museum of Applied Art (➤ 49). Cross the Ring to Georg-Coch-Platz and walk past Otto Wagner's Austrian Post Office Savings Bank (➤ 60), then follow the Ring to the left and back to Schwedenplatz.

INFORMATION

Distance 3km (1.8 miles)
Time 2.5 hours
Start/end point
★ Schwedenplatz
➕ H6
🚇 U1, U4
🚊 Tram 1, 2
🍴 Café Landtmann next to Burgtheater, favourite haunt of Sigmund Freud

Above: Vienna's early French Renaissance-style State Opera House on the Ringstrasse

23

Vienna by Night

Above: *St Charles' Church (Karlskirche) illuminated at night*
Centre: *Tables outside a bar in the nightlife district*
Right: *The Parliament building on the Dr-Karl-Lueger-Ring*

BALMY EVENINGS

Exploiting five and a half months of mild to warm weather, revellers in Vienna can linger at café or restaurant tables on the pavement outside, or in *Heurigen* gardens, until late into the evening. A restaurant extension is known as a *Schanigarten* from the nickname of the first person to erect one on the Graben in 1754. In summer there are also major open-air events: among them the jazz festival on the Donau-Insel, the opera films in front of the Rathaus and the son et lumiére at the Belvedere Palace.

New *Szenelokale* (trendy or 'in' bars and restaurants) open every year in Vienna. These are concentrated in certain areas—the best known is the so-called *Bermudadreieck* (Bermuda Triangle) to the west of Schwedenplatz. Here you will find intimate bars, or noisy ones with live music, as well as places offering 'fifty types of beer' or vintage wines by the glass. There are also ethnic eateries and a few chichi restaurants with their hip or Bohemian clientele.

Less self-consciously chic and utterly charming is the Spittelberg area, a good example of inner city revival. Here you can sit in an 18th-century courtyard, or on a street flanked by baroque and Biedermeier façades, enjoying Austrian regional or ethnic cooking, or check out the many bars and Italian-style cafés. A fun night atmosphere has developed in the area from Stephansdom to Am Hof and between Josefstädterstrasse and Laudongasse in the Josefstadt, a region frequented by intellectuals and the well-to-do.

An entire culture revolves around the wine-taverns of Vienna's peripheral villages, Grinzing Heiligenstadt, Salmannsdorf and Neustift am Walde being the best known. Many may prefer this to the bustle of the city; here you can sip white wine in the peace of a *Heurige* (➤ 66) garden and tuck into a *Heurigen* pork roast.

Perhaps the greatest evening pleasure is entirely gratis, namely walking around the floodlit monuments of the Inner City—especially the Stephansdom and the Hofburg's Michaelertor.

VIENNA's
top 25 sights

The sights are shown on the maps on the inside front cover and inside back cover, numbered **1**–**25** from west to east across the city

25

Kirche am Steinhof

HIGHLIGHTS

- Remarkable acoustics
- Sloping floor that focuses attention on the altar
- Perfect visibility from every angle
- Gold baldachin over the altar
- Stoop with running water
- Short benches for easy access and exit
- Spangled ceiling
- Glass-mosaic windows
- Angels on portico
- Sts. Leopold and Severin on external columns

INFORMATION

- A6; Locator map off A2
- Baumgartner Höhe 1, Penzing
- 910 60–20031
- Organized tours (in German) Mon–Fri from 3pm, Sat–Sun and hols from 10am. Telephone for an appointment to visit
- Buses 47A, 48A
- None
- Expensive (tours in German); expensive (tours in English)
- Telephone for times of tours in English

The weird and wonderful Steinhof Church was built for mental patients in 1907. The interior is clinically white with special fittings, full of wonders from Secession artists—most notably Kolo Moser's glass-mosaic windows.

Functionalism Great churches tend to be long on awe-inspiring atmosphere, and Otto Wagner's church, appropriately, evokes sentiment. At the same time, it is functional, and creates an aesthetic, religious and practical environment appropriate for dealing with people who are mentally ill.

Exterior features The façade is striking: the copper cupola, with its lovely patina, rises behind the two squared columns on which sit St. Leopold and St. Severin, patron saints of Lower Austria. The portico has four columns topped by massive copper angels by Othmar Schimkovitz in front of an impressive arched, stained-glass window.

The interior A number of features enhance the brightness of the light-flooded interior. A false ceiling in the cupola imitates a star-studded sky, and a vast, colourful glass mosaic covers the wall behind the altar, while Kolo Moser's fabulous windows in the crossing of the vault and above the side altars are also glass mosaic. The overall effect is luxurious, and yet Wagner's design is also highly functional. The short oak benches were positioned in a spacious semicircle to facilitate the removal of ill patients, and running water was used in the stoop to minimise the risk of infection. Attention was also paid to heating, ventilation and acoustics.

Schloss Schönbrunn

Schönbrunn is a cold if imposing palace, which was designed to show how many rooms a great monarch could afford. Yet Maria Theresa (1740–80) made it a cheerful home for her 12 surviving children.

Pacassi's palace The original designs for an imperial residence in the hunting park with the beautiful spring (Schönbrunn) were made by Johann Bernhard Fischer von Erlach in 1695, and were intended to rival Versailles. Only part of it was built when, between 1744 and 1749, Maria Theresa's court architect, Nikolaus Pacassi, revamped the design. His symmetrical, immensely long palace is a vast corridor of gilded and crimson displays—Japanese, Italian, Persian and Indian works of art, ceiling frescos celebrating the Habsburgs and 18th-century furniture and porcelain. The palace looks out on a park with immaculate parterres and hedges and a vista of ornamental pools and fountains.

The park The 18th-century gardens were later partially restyled by Adrian van Steckhoven. The modern park now also contains a spectacular glass and iron palm house and a zoo.

HIGHLIGHTS

- Coach museum (right of main entrance)
- Chapel with fresco by Daniel Gran
- Oriental panels, Vieux-Lacque Room
- Mirrors and frescoed ceiling in Great Gallery
- Indian and Persian miniatures
- Imperial embroidery
- Chinoiserie
- Park with statues and the original 'Schönet Brunn'

INFORMATION

www.schoenbrunn.at

🔲 C/D8/9/10; Locator map A4

✉ Schönbrunner Schlosstrasse 47

☎ 81 113-239

🕐 Palace Apr–end Oct daily 8.30–5.30; Nov–end Mar 9–4.30. Coach museum 9–6.30. Zoo 9–6.30 or until sunset. Park 6–sunset

🍴 Café and Tyrolean Restaurant

Ⓢ Schönbrunn

🚌 Bus 10A; trams 10, 58

♿ Good

👜 Tour expensive

❓ Palace tours only: Grand Tour (40 rooms); Imperial Tour (22 rooms). Occasional concerts; performances in Schlosstheater

Schlosstheater,
Schönbrunn

27

The Narrenturm

HIGHLIGHTS

- 1820s apothecary's shop
- Specimens in formaldehyde
- Abnormal skeletons
- Diseased lungs
- The world's best kidney and gallstone collection

INFORMATION

✚ G5; Locator map D2

✉ Spitalgasse 2, then follow signs to Courtyard 13

☎ 406 8672/2

◷ Sep–Jul Wed 3–6, Thu 8–11, first Sat of month 10–1. Closed on hols

Ⓠ Schottentor

Ⓔ Trams 5, 43, 44

♿ None

🖐 Moderate

❓ Tours by arrangement

You may find it bizarre or gruesome but you won't forget a visit to this 18th-century, circular Fool's Tower, now home to a museum. Be prepared for its gruesome medical chamber of horrors.

Utopian design The Narrenturm is a strange cylindrical building with a circular inner courtyard divided in half by an extra wing. It was built by Isidore Canevale in 1784 on the orders of Emperor Joseph II, who had also founded the Vienna General Hospital in the same grounds. Each of its five floors had 28 centrally heated cells for mental patients, called fools in the parlance of the day; however, not everyone here was actually mad. The emperor reprimanded one aristocrat, Count Seilern, for shutting his son in here because the young man refused to wed the bride selected for him.

Piece of cake The Viennese have always had an irreverent attitude to the Fool's Tower, calling it the Emperor Joseph's *Gugelhupf* because it is supposed to resemble the locally prized pound cake. Unpopular politicians with ill-thought-out policies are often said to 'belong in the *Gugelhupf*'.

Museum The Narrenturm was used as an asylum until 1866; subsequently it housed a store and provided living quarters for medical staff. It is now the Museum for Pathological Anatomy, and contains a large collection of medical curiosities.

Aesculapian snake on museum door

Josephinum

Aspiring military surgeons pored over life-like anatomical wax models here, preparing for a career on the battlefields of the Empire. Joseph II had seen first hand the terrible suffering caused by medical ineptitude.

Wax models The museum for the history of medicine, commonly called the Josephinum after its founder Emperor Joseph II, was a pioneering institution in Austria. No expense was spared in providing teaching materials so that the students would be fully prepared for their humanitarian work for the wounded. The most impressive of these are the 1,200 wax models used for teaching anatomy. They were made between 1775 and 1785 in Florence under the direction of Felice Fontana and Paolo Mascagni, and are considered the finest examples of this obscure form of educational art outside Florence itself.

Other collections Teaching ceased in the 19th century. In 1920 Max Neuburger's medical collection was added to the wax models. The present collection includes memorabilia of Semmelweis, Billroth and other famous surgeons, as well as mememtoes of Sigmund Freud. Since 1996 the world's largest museum of endoscopy has been here also.

Art-nouveau steps Leaving the neo-classical building by its splendid wrought-iron gate you will shortly reach Strudlhofgasse, which leads to the double-flighted Strudlhofstiege (Strudlhof Steps). This graceful art-nouveau stairway with lanterns and wells was designed in 1910 by Theodor Jäger. The steps are especially attractive at night, when the stairway lanterns throw a soft light on the silvery stone.

HIGHLIGHTS

- Fine wrought-iron gates
- Library with coffered ceiling and Corinthian columns
- Anatomical wax figures by Felice Fontana
- Memorabilia of great surgeons
- Collection of medical instruments
- Endoscopy museum

INFORMATION

- G5; Locator map D2
- Währinger Strasse 25
- 4277-63401
- Mon–Fri 9–3, first Sat of month 10–2
- Trams 37, 38, 40, 41, 42 from Schottentor
- Moderate
- The Narrenturm (► 28)
- Tours on request in advance

Above: A life-size wax anatomical model made by Florentine craftsmen

29

Servitenkirche

HIGHLIGHTS

- Wrought-iron screen (1675)
- Death of St. Juliana Falconieri sculpture
- Martyrdom of St. John Nepomuk sculpture
- Lourdes grotto
- Cupola with frescos of Assumption/Crowning of Mary
- B Moll's carved pulpit
- 15th-century crucifix
- Rococo ironwork

Cupola frescos

INFORMATION

- ✚ G5; Locator map D2
- ✉ Servitengasse 9
- ☎ 317 6195-0
- 🕐 Daily 8am–10pm
- Ⓜ U4 Rossauer Lände
- 🚊 Tram D
- ♿ Access easy
- 🎟 Free

The Servite Church is closely associated with the Servite St. Peregrine. Peregrine bread rolls are sold in Vienna from 6 April to 6 May, ever since a local baker honoured this saint (who gave bread to the poor) by contributing to the same cause.

Origins of the church Emperor Ferdinand II allowed the Servite nuns to settle in Vienna in the 17th century. Their church was begun in 1656, outside the city walls, to a design by Carlo Canevale; but the money ran out on the death of the order's patron, the imperial general Ottavio Piccolomini. The rich and exciting interior decoration was completed in 1677. The church is an impressive example of a baroque design that predates the second Turkish siege of 1683. It was also the city's first church to contain an oval nave.

Church interior Most of the superb stucco work is by Giovanni Bussi and Giovanni Barbarino. Upon entering the church you will see fabulous stuccolustro chapels to the right and left under the towers; the sculptures show respectively the death of St. Juliana Falconieri, who founded the Servite order, and the martyrdom of St. John Nepomuk, a vicar-general of Prague who was drowned in the Vltava river by order of King Wenceslas IV.

St. Peregrine Off the main church to the right is the chapel of St. Peregrine. He suffered from foot ailments, and his shrine has traditionally attracted the similarly afflicted—among them the composer Joseph Haydn.

Sigmund Freud Museum

Some of this century's most influential ideas came from the tenant of apartment No. 5, Berggasse 19. Whether you think of Freud as a cantankerous authoritarian or as a genius, it is interesting to see the place where his work began.

Sigmund Freud 1856–1939 Recognized as the founder of modern psychoanalysis, Freud was none the less typically Viennese, playing tarock (a card game still popular with the older generation), visiting Café Landtmann (➤ 61) and taking a daily constitutional along the entire length of the Ringstrasse. Like many other gifted Jewish Viennese, Freud opted for medicine, partly because it was a profession in which discrimination was not the barrier that it could be in the army and bureaucracy. He pursued a career at the University of Vienna, where he became an Associate Professor in 1902.

Theories Freud's most controversial theory was that infantile sexual impulses were at the root of adult neuroses. Adler and Jung—the other famous early psychoanalysts, and contemporaries of Freud's—parted company with him over this. However, many now-mainstream concepts started with Freud—for example, division of the personality into id and ego, and the ideas of sublimation and the Oedipus complex. Although many academics still accept Freud's dogmas as axiomatic, his critics believe that he doctored his evidence. For them, doctrinaire psychoanalytic theory is the most stupendous intellectual confidence trick of the 20th century. The Viennese writer Karl Kraus, also a contemporary of Freud's, remarked: 'Psychoanalysis is the disease of which it purports to be the cure'.

HIGHLIGHTS

- Freud's hat and cane
- Antiquities collected by Freud on his travels
- Photographs of Freud and contemporaries
- Part of Freud's book collection
- Original writings
- Video room

Freudiana elsewhere

- Bust of Freud in Vienna University's courtyard
- Plaque at the picturesque spot where the role of dreams first occurred to Freud (✉ Bellevue Höhe, Himmelstrasse, 19th District 🚌 Buses 38A and 39A, both to last stop)

INFORMATION

www.freud-museum.at
✚ G5; Locator map D2
✉ Berggasse 19
☎ 319 1596
🕐 Jul–end Sep daily 9–5; Oct–end Jun 9–6
Ⓜ U2 Schottentor
🚋 Tram D
♿ Few
🍴 Moderate

Neues Rathaus

The 'new' City Hall (Neues Rathaus), built between 1872 and 1883 by architect Friedrich Schmidt, is possibly the finest neo-Gothic building in all Vienna. Certainly, the debating chamber would not disgrace a small independent nation.

Inspiration The great buildings along the Ringstrasse, built between the 1860s and 1880s, exemplify the values of Liberalism—industrial modernization, democracy and capitalist enterprise. It is typically Viennese that this vision of the future was expressed in historic symbols. Schmidt chose, as his model, town halls typical of medieval Flanders. The main model for the Vienna Rathaus was the Brussels City Hall.

Inside and out The huge façade with its traceried arches over the arcades, faces the Ringstrasse; above the arches are loggias and imposing balustrades adorned with statues. Rising from the middle is the 98-m (321-ft) tower topped by a 3.4-m (11-ft) copper statue. Inside the grand staircase, noble promenades and richly decorated halls are a spectacle; don't miss the City Council Chamber and the (Ceremonial Hall).

HIGHLIGHTS

Outside, in Rathauspark
- Statues of Babenberg rulers 976–1246
- Monument to Socialist Chancellor/President Karl Renner
- Opera films in summer; Christmas Fair (Christkindlmarkt) in winter

Inside
- The Arkadenhof (arcaded coutyard)
- *Festsaal*
- Roter Salon (mayor's reception room)
- Heraldic rooms

INFORMATION

- G6; Locator map D2
- Friedrich-Schmidt-Platz 1
- 52 550
- Tours: Mon–Fri 1pm; or phone to book
- Rathauskeller
- U2 Rathaus
- Trams 1 and 2 on the Ringstrasse, D, J
- Few
- Tour: moderate
- Burgtheater (➤ 33)
- Visits by tour only (apply at Schmidthalle). The Rathaus is a starting point for other tours, a general information centre and a concert venue

Bust of President Karl Renner in Rathauspark

Burgtheater

The heavily subsidized Burgtheater is Austria's national theatre in all but name. Coruscating plays by Thomas Bernhard (d1989), ridiculing Austria's complacency and exposing its half-submerged Nazi past, have provoked the outrage the author anticipated.

Origins The name is taken from the court theatre that stood on the edge of the Hofburg (on Michaelerplatz) from the time of Maria Theresa (1741) until 1888. Mozart's *Marriage of Figaro* was premièred there in 1786.

Architecture This neo-Renaissance building by Karl von Hasenauer and Gottfried Semper opened in 1888, but it was soon altered; so much attention in the design had been paid to architectural proportion and so little to function that some of the boxes faced away from the stage and the acoustics were appalling. An anecdote at the time claimed that 'In the Parliament you can't hear anything, in the Rathaus you can't see anything and in the Burgtheater you can neither see nor hear anything'.

Decorative plan Inside and out, the Burgtheater is a symbolic celebration of the history of drama from ancient times. On the central façade are monuments to the world's greatest playwrights. On the ceremonial stairways that rise through the two wings towards the auditorium are busts of the great Austrian and German dramatists whose works are performed here. Gustav Klimt, his brother Ernst and Franz Matsch decorated the ceilings above the stairway with frescos depicting the history of theatre. Oil portraits of famous Viennese actors and actresses hang on the walls of the curving ground-floor foyer.

HIGHLIGHTS

Exterior
- View from the Rathaus across Ringstrasse
- Busts of famous dramatists
- Frieze of Dionysius and Ariadne
- Apollo and the Muses of Comedy and Tragedy

Interior
- Ceremonial stairway, busts of dramatists
- *Thespiskarren*, Gustav Klimt
- *Globe Theatre, London*, Gustav Klimt
- *Theatre at Taormina*, Gustav Klimt
- *Medieval Mystery Theatre*, Ernst Klimt
- *Molière's Le Malade Imaginaire*, Ernst Klimt

INFORMATION

www.burgheater.at
- G6; Locator map D2
- Dr-Karl-Lueger-Ring
- 51444-4140
- Guided tours daily (telephone for times). Closed 24 Dec, Good Friday, Jul and Aug except for tours
- U2 Schottentor
- Trams 1 and 2 on the Ringstrasse
- Good
- Moderate
- Neues Rathaus (➤ 32)
- Visits by tour only

Kunsthistorisches Museum

HIGHLIGHTS

- *Theseus and Centaur,* Antonio Canova
- *The Apotheosis of the Renaissance,* Mihály Munkácsy
- Hans Makart's allegories of art above the stairwell

In the collections

- 2,000BC blue faience hippopotamus, Egyptian Collection
- *Gemma Augustea,* Roman imperial cameo
- Cellini gold salt cellar
- *Madonna in the Meadow,* Raphael
- *Conversion of St. Paul,* Francesco Parmigianino
- *Infanta Margareta Teresa,* Velázquez
- *The Tower of Babel,* Brueghel

INFORMATION

www.khm.at
- G6/7; Locator map D3
- Maria-Theresien-Platz/Burgring 5
- 52 524-0
- Tue–Wed, Fri–Sun 10–6, Thu 10–9. Closed 1 May, 1 Nov
- Café upstairs
- U2 Babenberger Strasse, Volkstheater
- Trams 1 and 2 on the Ringstrasse D, J
- Good
- Moderate
- Frequent lectures and special exhibitions

Here in the Museum of Art History you'll find the Habsburgs' fabulous art collection, acquired over several centuries (especially by the emperor Rudolf II and Archdukes Leopold Wilhelm and Ferdinand II). However, it's virtually impossible to see it all in a day.

Origins The German architect Gottfried von Semper planned to continue the sweep of the Neue Hofburg and build a parallel wing on the other side of the Heldenplatz; both wings were to extend across the Ringstrasse, creating a gigantic Imperial Forum of museums. The Museum of Art History and the Natural History Museum facing it are the partial realization of this attempt to bring together the widely dispersed Habsburg treasures. The Museum of Art History contains collections of paintings, Egyptian artefacts, sculpture, decorative art, coins and medals.

Architectural decoration Both the Museum of Art History and the Natural History Museum opposite are principally the work of Gottfried von Semper; their interiors are by Karl Hasenauer. Between the museums lies a park that is dominated by a monument to Maria Theresa (1740–1780). Inside the Museum of Art History, marble and stucco are interspersed with murals; most notable is the ceiling fresco above the main landing, Mihály Munkácsy's *Apotheasis of Art.* Note the dome, which has medallions of collector-emperors. Hasenauer planned showrooms appropriate to their contents; the Egyptian collection, for example, is ornamented with columns from Luxor, a present from the Khedive to the Emperor Franz Josef.

Akademie der Bildenden Künste

In 1907, Adolf Hitler was denied entry to the Academy of Fine Arts for his poor rendering of human heads. He tried a second time and was rejected by the academy's architecture professor, Otto Wagner, because he lacked the requisite academic qualifications. He later turned to politics!

The building The academy was completed in 1876 by one of the greatest architects of the Ringstrassen era, Theophil Hansen, whose other work includes the classical Parliament, the Stock Exchange and numerous neo-Renaissance palaces. In the middle of the square in front is a statue of the poet Friedrich Schiller (1759–1805). Along the façade are figures from antiquity associated with the fine arts; on the back are allegorical frescos by August Eisenmenger, the academy's Professor for Painting in the late 19th century. Founded in 1692 by the painter Peter von Strudel, the academy numbers among its alumni the painter Friedensreich Hundertwasser, whose spectacular multi-coloured house at Löwengasse, 3rd District is a tourist attraction, and Fritz Wotruba, designer of an extraordinary modern church (▶ 53).

The interior Anselm Feuerbach's ceiling fresco, *Downfall of Titans*, dominates the Basilical Hall; the collection of Dutch Masters is renowned and the graphic art collection is superb.

HIGHLIGHTS

- *Last Judgement*, Hieronymus Bosch
- *Views of Venice*, Antonio Guardi
- *Family in a Courtyard*, Pieter de Hooch
- *Sketches for Banqueting House, Whitehall*, Rubens

INFORMATION

www.akbild.ac.at
- G7; Locator map D3
- Schillerplatz 3
- 58816-225
- Tue–Sun 10–4. Closed 1 May, Corpus Christi and the following Fri, 1–2 Nov
- U1, U2, U4 Karlsplatz/Oper
- Trams 1 and 2 on the Ringstrasse
- Few
- Moderate

Statue at the Academy of Fine Arts

Secession Building

HIGHLIGHTS

- Three gorgons over the doorway
- Inscription *Ver Sacrum* (Sacred Spring)
- Dome of gilded laurel leaves
- Picturesque sculpted owls
- Vast flower tubs on tortoise stands
- Statue: *Mark Antony in a Chariot Drawn by Lions* (1900), Arthur Strasser
- *Beethoven Frieze* (1902), Gustav Klimt

INFORMATION

www.secession.at

- ✚ G7; Locator map D3
- ✉ Friedrichstrasse 12
- ☎ 587 5307
- 🕐 Tue–Sun 10–6 (Thu until 8)
- 🍴 Summer café beside the building
- Ⓜ U1, U2, U4 Karlsplatz
- 🚌 Bus 59A
- ♿ Few
- 💷 Inexpensive
- ↔ Akademie der Bildenden Künste (➤ 35), Karlskirche (➤ 46)

In a gesture of defiance towards the art establishment, this exhibition building of revolutionary design was built under the windows of the Academy of Fine Arts. Their motto is inscribed over the main entrance: 'To every age its art, to art its freedom'.

Vienna Secession In 1897, frustrated with the increasing conservatism of academic painting in Vienna and its stranglehold over the art market, a group of young artists broke away to form the subsequently famous 'Vienna Secession'. The elected head of the Vienna Secession was the painter Gustav Klimt, whose *Beethoven Frieze*—an allegorical interpretation of the themes of the Ninth Symphony conceived as a homage to the composer—can be seen here.

Jugendstil Like other artists of the day, Klimt had begun his career working in the conventional genre of historical painting (exemplified by his work for the Burgtheater, ➤ 33). The Secession's style was associated with Jugendstil, the German version of art nouveau. It is sensuous and decorative, and achieves its best effects in architecture and stained glass (➤ 60).

The exhibition hall The breakaway artists needed a hall both to exhibit their own works and to display avant-garde art from abroad. In 1898, Joseph Maria Olbrich completed the cube-like, towered and windowless Secession Building with a glass roof that provided daylight. The Viennese dubbed it the 'golden cabbage' because of its gilded dome of entwined laurel leaves. Inside, innovative, movable partitions make the display space more flexible.

Hofburg

It is said that the Habsburgs never finished their great projects; the Hofburg (the former imperial residence), like St. Stephen's Cathedral (► 45) and the Habsburg Empire itself, is an example of their unfinished business.

Ages of the Hofburg The first fortress was built in 1275 on the site that later became the Schweizerhof. This building is named after the 18th-century Swiss Guards at the Burg and, with the Schweizertor (Swiss Gate), is the oldest surviving section of the Hofburg, built in the mid-16th century. The other Renaissance wings are the Amalienburg and, to the north, the beautiful Stallburg, where the famous dancing horses, the Lipizzaners, are stabled.

Baroque Much of the richest architecture is 17th- and 18th-century baroque. Italian architects built the wing named after Emperor Leopold I (Leopoldinischer Trakt) in 1681. Under Charles VI and Maria Theresa, Johann Bernhard Fischer von Erlach and his son, Josef Emanuel, worked on the sumptuous Hofbibliothek (the Court, now National Library; 1726) and the Reitschule (1735, ► 38). Their rival, Lukas von Hildebrandt, began the Reichskanzleitrakt, which housed the officials of the Holy Roman Empire. It was altered and completed by Fischer von Erlach in 1730.

19th and 20th centuries The area bordering Michaelerplatz, which includes the State Apartments, was built in the 19th century to an earlier design in baroque style. The huge Neue Hofburg was finished only in 1913, shortly before the demise of the dynasty itself. It was to have been part of the Imperial Forum (► 34).

HIGHLIGHTS

- Burgkapelle (chapel)
- Schatzkammer (Treasury)
- Sisi Museum
- State Apartments (Kaiserappartments)
- Prunksaal in Hofbibliothek
- Tableware Museum (Silberkammer)

INFORMATION

www.hofburg-wien.at
- G6; Locator map D2
- State Apartments: Innere Burghof, Kaisertor. Hoflbibliothek, Burgkapelle: Josefsplatz 1
- 533 7570
- State Apartments and Tableware Museum daily 9–5. Sisi Museum daily 9–5. Library May–end Oct Mon–Wed, Fri, Sat 10–4, Thu 10–7, Sun and hols 10–2; Nov–end Apr Mon–Sat 10–2. Treasury Mon, Wed–Sun 10–6; closed 1 May, 1 Nov. Burgkapelle Tue–Thu 1.30–3.30, Fri 1–3; mass Sun and church hols 9.15am (obtain tickets Fri before). Vienna Boys Choir Sep–end Jun
- U3 Herrengasse
- Hopper 3A to Habsburgergasse
- Few
- Expensive (where charged)
- Tours of State Apartments daily on the hour 10–4

Spanische Hofreitschule

HIGHLIGHTS

**Movements in the haute
école**

- *Capriole*: a leap into the
  air in which the hind legs
  are extended at the
  height of the jump
- *Levade*: the horse rears
  up in a slow, controlled
  manner
- *Piaffe*: trotting on the
  spot, often between two
  pillars
- *Croupade*: a leap with
  the legs under the body

INFORMATION

www.srs.at

- G6; Locator map D3
- Josefsplatz
- Performances Feb–end
  Jun, Sep–end Oct Sun
  10.45am and some
  evenings. 'Morning training' Mon–Fri 10–noon.
  Closed public hols
- ☎ 533 9031
- U3 Herrengasse
- Hopper 3A to
  Habsburgergasse
- Few
- Expensive
- Tickets for morning training: purchase on the day
  at Michaelerplatz 1.
  Tickets for performances:
  online at the above website or at some ticket
  agencies in Vienna. Tours
  with visits to the stables
  ☎ 533 90 31.

The 'airs above the ground', the ancient practice of cavalry skills in which the horses were trained to fight by leaping and kicking at their riders' commands, are still rehearsed and performed here in the baroque Spanish Riding School.

The building The Reitschule was constructed in 1735 by Josef Emanuel Fischer von Erlach for Karl VI, the father of Maria Theresa. Inside, two viewing galleries supported on columns ring the all-white space where the all-white Lipizzaner horses perform. It is called the Spanish Riding School because the horses originally came from Spain; the stud, established in 1580 at Lipica in Slovenia, gave its name to the Lipizzaners.

The performance The horses dance the quadrille, the gavotte, and the latest addition to their repetoire, the Viennese waltz showing the *haute école*, the most refined dressage techiques derived from the battle tactics of the Middle Ages. The *Capriole* is a leap into the air in which the hind legs are extended at the height of the jump. In the *Levade* the horse rears up in a slow, controlled manner. In the *Piaffe* the horse trots on the spot, and in the *Croupade* the horse leaps with its legs tucked up under its body.

Popular The performances (*Vorführungen*) are very popular and are often reserved long in advance. If you haven't made a reservation you may be able to watch the morning training session (*Morgenarbeit*) instead. Although there is no music, and the chandeliers used during performances remain unlit, the training session still shows the horses in action and the beauty of the Winter Riding School itself.

Augustinerkirche

The historic Church of St. Augustine, the 'parish church' of the Habsburg court, can seem bleak and forbidding. In its Loreto Chapel are preserved the hearts of members of the imperial family. On Sundays Vienna's best-sung masses cheer things up.

Origins The Gothic church is said to have been founded by Friedrich 'the Handsome' of Habsburg (1289–1330) in fulfillment of a vow he made when imprisoned by the Bavarian king. In the Counter-Reformation, the Augustinians of the adjacent monastery formed the *Totenbrüderschaft* (Brotherhood of the Dead), which visited prisoners and buried executed criminals. A famous Augustinian was the fiery preacher Abraham a Sancta Clara (1644–1709), who criticized the Viennese for their licentiousness in sermons that were liberally sprinkled with violent images and anti-Semitism. The pulpit stands on the spot from which he preached.

Architectural features The original clock in the tower was a gift from the Hungarian Count Nadasdy, who lived in the house opposite and thought it would be convenient to check the time from his window.

Interior The interior was 're-gothicized' by Ferdinand von Hohenberg in the late 18th century. Notable features are the marble cenotaph (1805) by Antonio Canova for Marie Christine, the favourite daughter of Maria Theresa (1740–1780), and the rococo organ on which Brückner composed his Mass no. 3. The St. George Chapel is dedicated to a Habsburg order similar to the Teutonic Knights and is the burial place of distinguished servants of the dynasty.

HIGHLIGHTS

- Clock tower
- Canova's tomb for Marie Christine
- Baroque pews
- Pulpit marking where Abraham a Sancta Clara preached
- Silver urns with Habsburg hearts, in Loreto Chapel
- Graves of Habsburg dignitaries

Art from dissolved churches

- *Vision of Mary Magdalene*, J. M. Rottmayr
- Stucco figures of Sts. Augustine and Ambrose
- *Deposition from the Cross*, Johann Auerbach

INFORMATION

- ✚ G/H6; Locator map E3
- ✉ Augustinerstrasse 3 (entrance Josefsplatz)
- ☎ 533 7099; for music programme 533 6963
- ◎ Mon–Sat 10–6, Sun 1–6 (and for morning sung mass)
- 🍴 Ancient Augustinerkeller (entrance from the Albertina)
- Ⓠ U1, U2, U4 Oper/Karlsplatz
- 🚌 Hopper 3A to Albertinaplatz
- ♿ None 🎟 Free
- ↔ Hofburg (► 37)

Freyung

This irregularly shaped square acquired its name (meaning 'asylum') as a result of its association with the adjacent Benedictine monastery, which until 1848 had the right to give asylum to fugitives from justice.

HIGHLIGHTS

Freyung
- Section of medieval cobbles in the northeast corner
- Hildebrandt's Palais Kinsky, Freyung 4

Schottenkirche and Prelacy Museum
- Gothic wing altar, Master of the Scots 1469–1480
- *Assumption,* Tobias Pock, and *St. Sebastian,* Joachim von Sandart
- High altar (Ferstel) with glass mosaic
- Tomb of Count Starhemberg

Palais Ferstel
- Danube Fountain

INFORMATION

- G6; Locator map D2
- Schottenkirche and Prelacy Museum: Freyung 6. Palais Ferstel: Freyung 2
- Schottenkirche: 534 98. Museum: 534 98600
- Schottenkirche usually 7am–9pm. Museum Mon–Sat 10–5, Sun 10.30–1
- Café Central in Palais Ferstel
- U2 Schottentor
- Hopper IA
- Few
- Inexpensive

Freyung Eighteenth-century paintings show a lively scene, with stallholders, jugglers and clowns. Baroque palaces still rim the square.

Schottenkirche The Abbey Church of the 'Schotten' Benedictines, dominating the east side of the square, was called Scottish because the Latin name for Ireland was *Scotia maior.* The 15th-century Gothic altarpiece, now in the Prelacy Museum in the Schottenstift, shows the earliest extant view of Vienna.

Palais Ferstel This structure is not actually a palace but a complex named after its architect. Inside, a glass-roofed arcade lined with gift shops leads from the Freyung to Herrengasse ('Street of the Lords'). Formerly the seat of The Vienna Stock Exchange.

Obizzi Palace

This picturesque little palace once belonged to Count Ernst Rüdiger von Starhemberg, who defended the city during the Turkish siege of 1683. As battles raged outside, lead cannonballs were cast in its fireplace.

History of the palace There was a dwelling here in the 11th century, possibly the successor to a Roman building. The irregular shape of the palace earned it the nickname 'Harp House'. The Starhembergs owned it for over a century from 1580 and added a storey. The baroque façade and another floor were added by Ferdinand Obizzi, who commanded the city militia in 1690. Narrowly escaping demolition in 1901, it was repurposed as home of a clock museum on an order from the city council in 1917.

The Clock Museum (Uhrenmuseum) The first of its kind in the world, this museum covers three floors and houses more than 3,000 exhibits from the 15th to the 20th centuries. Many are unique, including an amazingly complicated astronomical clock—one of its hands requires 20,904 years to make one complete revolution!

HIGHLIGHTS

- Courtyard fountain with Roman trough
- Mechanism of the clock from the Old Town Hall
- Augsburg standing clock
- Nürnberg sand clock
- Onion clock by Isaac Roberts
- Astronomical clock
- Hussar-figure clock
- Rowboat clock
- Clock set in a picture of a landscape with waterfall

INFORMATION

- ✚ H6; Locator map E2
- ✉ Schulhof 2 (alley flanking Am Hof church)
- ☎ 533 2265
- 🕐 Tue–Sun 9–4.30
- 🚇 U1, U3 Stephansplatz
- 🚌 Hopper 2A
- ♿ None
- 💶 Moderate
- ❓ Tours (minimum 8 persons)

Peterskirche

INFORMATION

- ✚ H6; Locator map E2
- ✉ Petersplatz 6
- ☎ 533 64 33
- ⏲ Mon–Fri 6.30am–7pm, Sat–Sun 7.30am–7pm
- Ⓤ U1, U3 Stephansplatz
- 🚌 Hopper 2A
- ♿ None
- 💰 Free
- ↔ Stephansdom (▶ 45)

The most striking aspect of the lovely baroque St. Peter's Church is the way the architects, Gabriele Montani and Lukas von Hildebrandt, fitted it into a space so narrow that it looks almost as if it had been poured into a mould.

Origins of the church It is thought that the first Christian sanctuary of Vienna (then Vindobona) was built on this site in late Roman times. A 1906 marble plaque on the east wall outside attributes the refounding of the church to Charlemagne, but this is not true. Because of St. Peter's historical significance, the Emperor Leopold I took a personal interest in the building of a new church on this site; he was present at the laying of the foundation stone in 1702, when a trench collapsed injuring members of the imperial retinue. Hildebrandt took over Montani's work shortly afterwards, and Franz Jänggl extended the choir and completed the towers between 1730 and 1733.

The interior The external effect of compression and harmonious unity is continued in the interior, which is subordinated to the 56-m (183-ft) diameter dome. There is striking ornamentation; note the trompe-l'œil effects in the choir by Antonio Galli-Bibiena, who was famous for his illusionist stage settings. Gilded stucco to the right as you face the altar depicts the martyrdom of St. John Nepomuk, a saint venerated in Central Europe. No less dazzling is the pulpit by Matthias Steinl. All the theatricality of high baroque art is exuberantly manifested here.

The exterior Niches on the façade show statues of the apostles, and the inscription above the middle door reads: 'What I vow to the Lord for my salvation that will I fulfil'.

Altes Rathaus

Once a private house, the Old City Hall was confiscated after an unsuccessful anti-Habsburg uprising and donated to the city council in 1316. The Habsburgs continually suppressed the civic rights of the Viennese up to the 19th century.

The price of dissent Until 1309 the building was owned by Otto Haymo. After he led an unsuccessful anti-Habsburg uprising, Duke Friedrich 'the Handsome' confiscated the house and seven years later it was given to the city.

History Several extensions of the hall were added during the 14th and 15th centuries. Its Gothic core dates from 1457. At the end of the 17th century it acquired baroque elements, most notably the façade, which shows the influence of Johann Bernhard Fischer von Erlach. The Vienna Council sat in this building until 1885. It is now mostly municipal offices and the Bezirksmuseum (District Museum) for the 1st District, the old town (Innenstadt).

Sights in and around The baroque façade of the former Bohemian Court Chancellery across the street at Wipplingerstrasse 7 was mainly the work of Johann Bernhard Fischer von Erlach in 1714. Upstairs in the City Hall (Stiege 3) is the Museum of Austrian Resistance active during World War II, with its archive. Located in a courtyard is Georg Raphael Donner's beautiful *Andromeda Fountain* (1745). At the rear, in Salvatorgasse, is a fine Renaissance portal to the Salvatorkapelle (the Chapel of the Saviour); originally the City Hall chapel, it now belongs to the Old Catholic Community—those who rejected the 1870 doctrine of papal infallibility.

HIGHLIGHTS

Old City Hall
- Portals with J. M. Fischer's 1781 allegories
- Relief with city coat of arms, corner Stoss in Himmel
- Alberto Camesina's baroque stucco, 1713
- Museum of Austrian Resistance
- Old Town District Museum
- *Andromeda Fountain*, Georg Raphael Donner, in courtyard
- Renaissance doorway to Salvatorkapelle

Bohemian Chancellery
- Baroque portals with Atlas figures
- Coats of arms of Bohemia, Moravia, and Silesia on wall
- Lorenzo Mattielli's allegorical figures

INFORMATION

- ✚ H6; Locator map E2
- ✉ Wipplingerstrasse 6–8
- ☎ 53436-90319
- 🕐 City Hall Mon, Wed, Sat 9am–11am, Sun 10–noon. Museum of Austrian Resistance Mon, Wed–Thu 9–5 (appointment required). District museum Wed, Fri 3–5
- Ⓤ U1, U4 Schwedenplatz
- 🚌 Hopper 3A
- ♿ None 🍴 Moderate

Kapuzinergruft/Kaisergruft

HIGHLIGHTS

The church
- Bronze of Marco d'Aviano
- Statues of four emperors
- Marble altar by Hildebrandt
- *Pietà*, by Peter Strudel and Matthias Steinl

The crypt
- Tomb of Charles IV
- Double tomb of Franz Stephan and Maria Theresa
- Tombs of Franz Joseph and Elisabeth
- Bust of the last emperor, Karl, and coffin of the last empress, Zita

INFORMATION

www.kaisergruft.at
- H6; Locator map E3
- Tegetthoffstrasse 2
- 512 6853
- Church daily 9.30–3.30. Crypt daily 9.30–3.30
- U1, U3 Stephansplatz
- Hopper 3A
- None
- Church free; crypt moderate

Deceased emperors' hearts are preserved in the Augustinian Church (► 39), their embalmed entrails in St. Stephen's (► 45), and their bodies here in the Capuchin Crypt, a shrine for pilgrims and loyalists.

The Capuchins and their church The Franciscan Capuchins came to Austria in the reign of Duke (later Emperor) Matthias (1612–1619), whose wife, Empress Anna, founded their monastery in 1618. The preacher Marco d'Aviano, friend and adviser to Emperor Leopold I, was Vienna's most celebrated Capuchin. Famously intrepid, he went into battle with the imperial forces against the Turkish army, which was besieging Vienna in 1683. He died in the city in 1699 and is buried in one of the church's side chapels.

Simplicity The building is in accord with the austere precepts of the Capuchins. Almost the only decoration is a tasteless 1936 fresco of St. Francis of Assisi and a cross on the façade. Inside is the Kaiserkapelle (Emperor Chapel), with wooden statues of emperors Matthias and Ferdinand II, III and IV. The Chapel of the Cross has an altar by Lukas von Hildebrandt and a very moving *pietà* (Mary embracing the dead Christ), with weeping angels and women by Peter Strudel and Matthias Steinl (1717).

Habsburg resting place The first emperor and empress to be buried in the crypt were Matthias and his wife Anna. Since then 138 members of the Habsburg family have been interred here, along with Maria Theresa's governess. The simple copper coffin of Joseph II, which contrasts with the elaborate baroque tombs, is a reminder of its occupant's distaste for religious excess.

Stephansdom

St. Stephen's Cathedral has been the spiritual focus of the Viennese people since the Middle Ages—it's huge 'Pummerin bell' rings in the New Year. The great South Tower is affectionately known as the Steffl ('Little Steve').

Ornamentation From the three preceeding Romanesque churches on this site, only the Giant's Door and Heathen Towers (so called because a pagan shrine was supposed to have been here) have survived as part of the Gothic church. Note the striking yellow, green and black chevrons of the tiled roof and a representation of the Habsburg double-headed eagle. Against the north external wall is the pulpit marking the spot where Giovanni Capistrano (1386–1456) preached fiery sermons against the Turks. The cathedral is considered a symbol of endurance, having undergone numerous stages of repair due to the ravages of the Turks, the Napoleonic French and the Allies. All the Federal States contributed to the cathedral's restoration after World War II.

Inside Anton Pilgram's late Gothic pulpit with portraits of the fathers of the church is near the entrance. Above the organ loft of the north aisle is a sculpted self-portrait of Pilgram holding a square and compass. The Gothic vaulting in the Albertine Choir (1304–1340) is especially beautiful. Tobias Pock's 1647 baroque altar painting shows the martyrdom of St. Stephen. In the north apse is the exquisite Wiener Neustädter Altar (1447). In the south apse is the magnificent marble tomb of Friedrich III (1440–1493).

HIGHLIGHTS

- Pilgram's pulpit
- Tomb of Prince Eugene of Savoy, Kreuzkapelle
- Johann Pock statues of Saints Sebastian, Leopold, Florian and Rochus
- Nicolas van Leyden's tomb of Friedrich III
- *Man of Sorrows* crucifix

INFORMATION

- ✚ H6; Locator map E2
- ✉ Stephansplatz 3
- ☎ 5155 23767
- ◷ Daily 6am–10pm. Climbing the tower 9–6
- Ⓢ U1, U3 Stephansplatz
- 🚍 Bus 1A
- ♿ Good
- 🎫 Cathedral free; tour of choir moderate
- ↔ Peterskirche (► 42)
- ❓ Separate tours of cathedral and catacombs

Nave and high altar, St. Stephen's

Karlskirche

St. Charles's Church is one of Europe's finest baroque buildings. The symbolism in the two exotic columns at the front, modelled on Trajan's Column in Rome, illustrates Habsburg secular power and spiritual legitimacy.

Origins In 1713 Vienna was hit by the last of many plagues; Emperor Charles VI vowed to dedicate a church to St. Charles Borromeo, who succored the people during the 1576 Milan plague. Begun in 1716, it is the masterpiece of Johann Bernhard Fischer von Erlach, who died in 1723 leaving his son, Joseph Emanuel, to complete it in 1739.

Paean in stone The two columns at the front symbolize the Pillars of Hercules in the Mediterranean, a reference to the Spanish realm (by then lost) of the other Habsburg line. Their spiralling friezes show the life of Charles Borromeo. The columns are also emblems of the Emperor's motto, '*Constantia et fortitudine*'). The russet, gold and white interior creates a harmonious tranquillity.

HIGHLIGHTS

Exterior

- Angels flanking external steps
- Frieze in pediment: *The Ending of the 1713 Plague*
- Statues above pediment: St. Charles Borromeo with allegories of religion
- Two Trajan columns chronicling the life of St. Charles Borromeo and emblematic of Charles VI

Inside the church

- *Assumption of St. Charles Borromeo*
- *Apotheosis of Charles Borromeo*, J. M. Rottmayr
- *Christ and the Centurion*, Daniel Gran
- *Assumption of Mary*, Sebastiano Ricci
- *The Healing of the Man with the Palsy*, Giovanni Pellegrini
- Carved pulpit with rocaille and floral decoration

INFORMATION

- ✚ H7; Locator map E3
- ✉ Karlsplatz
- ☎ 504 6187
- 🕐 Mon–Fri 7.30–7, Sat 9–7
- Ⓤ U1, U2, U4 Karlsplatz
- 🚌 Bus 4A
- ♿ Good 🚻 Free
- ❓ Tours: audio guides available. Live sacred music Jun–Sep: Sun 7.30pm

Wien Museum Karlsplatz

Although housed in a drab 1950s-style building, the Viennese History Museum is one of Europe's best city museums, and its well-displayed contents bring the Viennese palimpsest vividly to life.

Origins The city's first historical museum was founded in 1887 and occupied several rooms in the newly built City Hall. Many plans were made for a purpose-built museum but the council gave the go-ahead only in 1953. The characterless design of the structure—its banality made more striking by its juxtaposition with the baroque architecture of St. Charles's Church next door—aroused considerable anger among Viennese patriots, although it had its defenders.

Museum collection Vienna's history, topography, art and culture are explored in the many works of art and architectural relics, and in the early city plans, reconstructions of interiors like Adolf Loos's living room and Franz Grillparzer's Biedermeier apartment and beautifully made period models of the city.

Sweeping view The ground floor spans prehistory (Hallstatt culture) up to and including medieval times. On the first floor are exhibits of the baroque period and Enlightenment. The material relating to the time of the Turkish siege of Vienna (weapons and a portrait of Turkish commander Kara Mustafa) is especially interesting. The second floor covers the Congress of Vienna (1814–1815), the Biedermeier era (1815–1848), the revolution of 1848 and Vienna at the beginning of the 20th century, with examples of the art, artefacts and designs of the Vienna Secession (▶ 36), and the later Austrian Expressionism movement.

HIGHLIGHTS

- Edouard Fischer's maquette of old town, 1854
- Franz Xavier Messerschmidt's grotesque busts
- Augustin Hirschvogel's plan of Vienna, 1548
- *View of the Siege of Vienna* (1683), Franz Geffels
- Portrait of Kara Mustafa, the Turkish commander in 1683
- Johann Höchle's paintings of the final Napoleonic campaign
- *Stephansplatz (*1834), Rudolf von Alt
- Reconstructed apartment of playwright Franz Grillparzer
- Reconstructed sitting room in architect Adolf Loos' house
- *Anna Moll, Writing,* Carl Moll

INFORMATION

www.wienmuseum.at
- H7; Locator map E3
- Karlsplatz
- 505 8747
- Tue–Sun 9–6
- Café
- U1, U2, U4 Karlsplatz
- Bus 4A; tram 62, 65
- Good
- Moderate
- Karlskirche (▶ 46)

47

Schloss Belvedere

INFORMATION

www.belvedere.at
- H/J7/8; Locator map E4
- Lower Belvedere and Orangery: Rennweg 6; Upper Belvedere: Prinz-Eugen-Strasse 27
- 79 55 71 34
- Lower and Upper Belvedere Tue–Sun 10–6. Closed 1 May, 1 Nov and 13 Jun
- Café in Upper Belvedere
- Tram 71 (Lower Belvedere) and D (Upper Belvedere)
- Moderate Good
- Tours: each open day

After St. Stephen's Cathedral (► 45), the restored Belvedere Palace is Vienna's most important landmark. It was built in the early 18th century for Prince Eugene of Savoy, the most successful general in Austria's history.

Schloss Belvedere, staircase

Origins Lukas von Hildebrandt constructed the Lower Belvedere (Unteres Belvedere) between 1714 and 1716. The magnificent Upper Belvedere (Oberes Belvedere), designed to house the prince's fabulous art collection, went up between 1721 and 1723.

Palace in history Emperor Josef II installed the Imperial Picture Gallery in the Upper Belvedere. Franz Ferdinand, the heir to the throne, lived here from 1894 until his assassination in 1914. In 1955 the Austrian State Treaty ending the Allied occupation was signed in the Marble Hall.

Museums The Lower Belvedere displays Austrian baroque art; the adjacent Orangery showcases medieval art. The Austrian Gallery in the Upper Belvedere contains 19th- and 20th-century Austrian paintings and sculpture, except for the Modern Gallery, which houses European works.

Museum für Angewandte Kunst

A striking example of experiments with minimalist display techniques at the Museum of Applied Art is the projection of silhouettes of chairs against a white screen which emphasizes the beauty of the individual designs.

Forerunner Established in 1864, and originally named the Museum of Art and Industry, the MAK was the first museum of its kind in Europe. The initiative came from art historian Rudolf Eitelberger, who had been much impressed by London's South Kensington Museum, later the Victoria and Albert Museum.

Decorative The beautiful 1871 neo-Renaissance building by Heinrich Ferstel combines architecture with applied art—its façade is ornamented with impressive sgrafito and majolica portrait medallions of famous artist-craftsmen.

The interior Inside, a glass-enclosed entrance hall is surrounded by the arcades of higher storeys. In the 1990s, an extension built between 1907 and 1909 was connected to the main part with a steel and glass passageway. On the north side is the University of Applied Arts.

The collections The amazingly rich collections include a fine selection of Jugendstil, Biedermeier and Thonet furniture from Austria. There is a section devoted to artefacts from the East (textiles, carpets, ceramics), and another part contains European decorative art, including both Venetian and Bohemian glass, Meissen porcelain, and jewellery. The display of works by leading artists of the Wiener Werkstätte on the first floor alone is worth the visit.

HIGHLIGHTS

- Atrium (entrance hall), with Renaissance-style arcades
- 16th-century Egyptian silk carpet
- 15th-century Buddha head
- Intarsia table from Old University (1735)
- Meissen bear by J. G. Kirchner (1735)
- Bohemian glass
- Lobmeyr glass (Vienna)
- Biedermeier sofa with red covering (1830), by J. Danhauser
- Thonet bentwood furniture
- Furniture and artefacts by the Wiener Werkstätte

INFORMATION

www.mak.at
- J6; Locator map F2
- Stubenring 5
- 711 360; recorded information 112 8000
- Tue 10–midnight, Wed–Sun 10–6. Closed 1 May, 1 Nov
- Elegant café
- U3 Stubentor
- Trams 1 and 2 on Ringstrasse
- Schnellbahn to Landstrasse
- Good
- Moderate
- Tours: audio-guide. Frequent special exhibitions, often avant-garde

49

Heeresgeschichtliches Museum

HIGHLIGHTS

- Ornate Byzantine façade
- Life-size statues of Austria's greatest generals

First floor
- Montgolfier balloon
- *Portrait of Wallenstein*, J. Van Dyck
- Turkish tent
- *The Battle of Aspern*, J. P. Krafft

Ground floor
- 'To the Unknown Soldier' (1916), Albin Egger Lienz
- Car in which Archduke Franz Ferdinand was assassinated
- Bloodstained uniform of Archduke Franz Ferdinand
- Tank park

INFORMATION

www.hgm.or.at

☩ J9; Locator map F4

✉ Arsenal, Ghegastrasse Objekt 18

☎ 79 561-603 70

🕐 Mon–Thu, Sat–Sun 9–5. Closed public hols

🍴 Café

🚌 Bus 13A to Südbahnhof; trams O, D, 18 to Südbahnhof

🚆 Schnellbahn to Südbahnhof

♿ Few 🖩 Moderate

❓ Tours: audio-guide

The huge military complex known as the Arsenal and Museum of Military History is notable for its exotic pseudo-Byzantine architecture and for the collection inside, which provides visitors with a fascinating insight into Vienna's imperial history.

Riotproof After the revolution of 1848, during which the old town armoury Am Hof was plundered, leading Ringstrassen architects were commissioned to design a riot-proof arms factory and depot. This state-of-the-art complex was built with eight fortress-like barracks along its perimeter; by 1854 the facilities it enclosed were like those of an entire city within a city. The task of constructing it created jobs at a time of social unrest and unemployment. After World War II, part of the complex was rebuilt, and part is now occupied by state-owned theatre workshops and the central telephone exchange, as well as the Museum of Military History.

Collection Themed sections include the Thirty Years War (1618–1648), the Napoleonic Wars and the Austrian Navy (in existence until 1918). Particularly gruesome is the bloodstained tunic Archduke Franz Ferdinand, heir to the Habsburg throne, was assassinated in—this event triggered the start of World War I.

VIENNA's
best

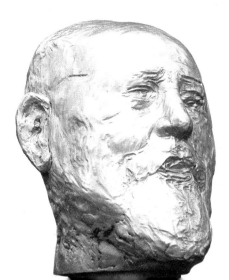

51

Churches

ANTON BRUCKNER

The composer Anton Bruckner gave a recital on the organ in the Piaristenkirche in 1861 as part of his examination for a teaching post at the Music Conservatory. A long silence followed his second piece, during which the composer sat nervously with bowed head. The silence was broken by the senior examiner, who remarked in an awed whisper, 'He should be examining us!'

Jesuitenkirche

ANNAKIRCHE

An intimate little gem of baroque architecture with Daniel Gran's ceiling fresco of the Immaculate Conception. In the side-chapel is a beautiful Gothic carving of Mary, Jesus and St. Anne by Veit Stoss of Nürnberg.

✚ H6 ⊠ Annagasse 3B ☎ 512 4797 ◷ Daily 6am–7pm
Ⓡ U1, U3 to Stephansplatz

FRANZISKANERKIRCHE

Built next to a home for repentant prostitutes, whom Viennese burghers were encouraged to marry, this church later became the Franciscan monastery. The most notable feature is the illusionist architecture of Andrea Pozzo's high altar picture.

✚ H6 ⊠ Franziskanerplatz 4 ☎ 512 4578
◷ Mon–Sat 6am–5.45pm, Sun 7am–5.30pm Ⓡ U1, U3 to Stephansplatz

JESUITENKIRCHE

Andrea Pozzo designed the interior of this extremely ornate church in the early 18th century; it replaced a church built by the Jesuits soon after they had constructed the adjacent university, over which they gained control in 1622. From this base the Jesuits drove forward the Counter-Reformation in Vienna.

✚ H6 ⊠ Dr-Ignaz-Seipel-Platz 1 ☎ 512 5232
◷ Daily 7am–6.30pm Ⓡ U3 to Stubentor

MARIA AM GESTADE

Danube boatmen once worshipped in this 14th-century Gothic church built on the former river bank (*Gestade*). The nave is not exactly aligned with the choir because the site was so small. The graceful spire, with its filigree decoration, is a landmark. The church was the centre of a 19th-century religious revival by the Moravian preacher Clemens Maria Hofbauer, later patron saint of the city, whose tomb is here.

✚ H5/6 ⊠ Salvatorgasse 12 ☎ 533 2282 ◷ Daily (rear nave)
6.30am–6pm. Access to choir on request Ⓡ U1, U4 to Schwedenplatz

MICHAELERKIRCHE

In the crypt of St. Michael's Church are mummified corpses in coffins, the lids of which have warped and lifted. Parts of this richly decorated building date to the late 13th century. Karl Georg Merville's dramatic stucco over the high altar depicts the fall of the angels, a theme continued in the sculpture by Lorenzo Mattielli over the portico.

🔲 G6 ✉ Michaelerplatz 1 ☎ 533 8000 🕐 Daily 6.30am–7pm 🚇 U3 to Herrengasse 🚌 Bus 2A to Michaelerplatz

PIARISTENKIRCHE (MARIA TREU)

This lesser-known work by the great Lukas von Hildebrandt was built in 1716 for the Piarist teaching order. The marvellous rococo frescos (1752–1753), depicting biblical scenes, are Vienna's finest example of the work of Franz Anton Maulbertsch.

🔲 F6 ✉ Jodok-Fink-Platz–Piaristengasse 43 ☎ 405 04 25 🕐 For mass or by appointment 🚋 Tram J to Theater in der Josefstadt

RUPRECHTSKIRCHE

St. Rupert's, Vienna's oldest surviving church built in the 11th century, was once patronized by salt merchants landing their wares on the Danube shore. A remaining portion of medieval stained glass in the choir shows the crucifixion, complemented by a vivid modern stained-glass window of the baptism of Christ.

🔲 H6 ✉ Ruprechtsplatz ☎ 535 6003 🕐 Mon–Fri 10–1, Easter–Oct 🚇 U1, U4 to Schwedenplatz

VOTIVKIRCHE

This huge neo-Gothic church was built to commemorate Franz Josef's escape from an assassination attempt in 1853. Its chapels are dedicated to Austrian regiments. Note the Renaissance sarcophagus of Count Salm, defender of Vienna in the Turkish siege of 1529.

🔲 G5 ✉ Rooseveltplatz 8 ☎ 406 1192-0 🕐 Daily 9–4 🚇 U2 🚋 Trams 1, 2 to Schottentor

WOTRUBA KIRCHE

This extraordinary modern church, designed by the sculptor Fritz Wotruba, seems to have been built with randomly jumbled concrete blocks and lit by arbitrarily placed narrow glass panels.

🔲 Off map to southwest ✉ Georgsgasse/Rysergasse (Mauer, 23rd District) ☎ 888 6147 🕐 Thu–Fri 2–4, Sat 2–8, Sun 9–5 🚌 Bus 60A; tram 60 from Hietzing-Mauerer Lange Gasse, then walk

Ruprechtskirche

MODERN SANCTUARY

Fritz Wotruba went into exile in Switzerland before World War II and was one of the few of Austria's artistic and academic élite to return. He worked on his 'Cyclopean church', now known as the Wotruba Kirche, for ten years starting in 1966, aiming to create a sanctuary for meditation with modern materials. He died in 1976, a year before his very personal architectural statement was completed.

Palaces

In the Top 25
🔟 **OBIZZI PALACE** (➤ 41)

AUSTRIAN THEATRE MUSEUM

This is in the Lobkowitz Palace and gives an overview of drama in Austria from the 19th century onwards. Models of opera stage-sets designed by the Secession artist Alfred Roller are on view; he helped Gustav Mahler revolutionise opera production. The loveliest room is the Eroica-Saal where Beethoven first conducted and played several of his works.

KINSKY-PALAIS

One of Lukas von Hildebrandt's masterworks built in 1716, with a slim, elegant façade that overlooks the Freyung. Try to get a look at the ceremonial staircase inside and also its ceiling fresco, *Apotheosis of a War Hero*, which flatters Count Philipp von Daun, the military commander who first owned the palace.

➕ G6 ✉ Freyung 4 ☎ 532 4200 🕐 Mon–Fri 10–6, Sat 10–5, Sun noon–5 🚇 U2 to Schottentor 🚋 Trams 1, 2

LOBKOWITZ-PALAIS

This noble palace was built between 1685 and 1687 by Giovanni Tencala for the powerful Dietrichstein family, but the present impressive façade is by Johann Bernhard Fischer von Erlach. After the Lobkowitzes acquired it in 1753, it became the centre for social and artistic life; Beethoven's Eroica Symphony was given its first performance here in 1804, and during the Congress of Vienna many famous balls were held. 'The congress dances, but it doesn't progress', quipped Prince de Ligne. The Austrian Theatre Museum is now here.

➕ H6 ✉ Lobkowitzplatz 2 ☎ 512 8800 🕐 Tue–Sun 10–5, Wed 10–8pm 🚇 U1, U2, U4 to Karlsplatz/Oper 🎫 Moderate

SCHÖNBORN-BATTHYÁNY PALAIS

The Hungarian Bán (Governor) of Croatia, Adam Batthyány, commissioned Johann Bernhard Fischer von Erlach's most impressive palace, built in 1698. The long monumental façade is enlivened with reliefs of a triumphal procession in antiquity and with allegories of wisdom and fame. Reliefs above the side-window show Hercules taming the Bull of Minos and scenes from Roman mythology.

➕ G6 ✉ Renngasse 4 🚫 Not accessible to the public 🚇 U2 🚋 Trams 1, 2 to Schottentor

SCHWARZENBERG-PALAIS

In 1716, Prince Schwarzenberg bought an unfinished palace by Lukas von Hildebrandt and then commissioned Johann Bernhard Fischer von Erlach, and later his son Josef Emanuel, to complete what is now one of Vienna's best hotels (➤ 86); it is still owned by the family. The grand sweep up to the portico was conceived by the younger Fischer, who

Grand entrance of the Schönborn-Batthyány Palais

The front of the Kinsky-Palais

also installed Vienna's first steam-driven motor to pump water for the fountains. The Schwarzenbergs' neighbour and rival, Prince Eugene of Savoy, had to postpone his great Belvedere project (▶ 48) until he had persuaded the Schwarzenbergs to sell a vital piece of adjacent land.
www.palais-schwarzenberg.com 🔢 H7 ✉ Schwarzenbergplatz 9 ☎ Hotel/restaurant: 798 4515 🚊 Tram D to Schwarzenbergplatz

TRAUTSON-PALAIS
Smaller yet elegant, this is another palace designed by Fischer von Erlach the elder, built in 1710, and was the headquarters of Maria Theresa's Hungarian Lifeguards. It is now the Ministry of Justice.
🔢 G6 ✉ Museumstrasse 7 🕐 Not accessible to the public Ⓤ U2, U3 to the Volkstheater

PRINZ-EUGEN-WINTERPALAIS
The two greatest architects of their age—Johann Bernhard Fischer von Erlach and Lukas von Hildebrandt—both worked on the Winter Palace of Eugene (1695–1698), although the former was careful to claim the credit for it. You can see the fabulous ceremonial stairway and, during special exhibitions, the frescos of Apollo and Hercules, symbolizing Prince Eugene of Savoy's many talents.
🔢 H6 ✉ Himmelpfortgasse 8 ☎ 51 433 🕐 Vestibule: Mon–Thu 8–4, Fri 8–3.30 Ⓤ U1, U3 to Stephansplatz 🎫 Free

WITTGENSTEIN HAUS
Ludwig Wittgenstein, one of the most famous philosophers of the 20th century, designed this austere house for his sister in the 1920s. The house reflects its creator's intellect; built in the Bauhaus style, it is curious rather than architecturally appealing.
🔢 K6 ✉ Parkgasse 18 ☎ 713 3164 🕐 Mon–Fri 9–noon, 2–6 Ⓤ U3 to Rochusgasse 🎫 Free ❓ Accessible for functions of the Bulgarian Cultural Institute

SCHWARZENBERG FAMILY
The influential Schwarzenbergs had vast estates in Bohemia and palaces in Austria. They supplied the Habsburgs with senior clerics, generals, politicians and administrators. The current Prince Schwarzenberg is said to have ironically thanked Queen Elizabeth II for 'bombing his palace into a hotel'—hotel-keeping paid for restoring his mansion after the war. After the 1989 'Velvet Revolution' in Prague he acted as adviser to the Czech President Václav Havel.

Museums & Galleries

In the Sigmund Freud Museum

ALBERTINA

Louis Montoyer built this gallery between 1801 and 1804 to house the magnificent collection of drawings, engravings and watercolours assembled by Duke Albert of Sachsen-Teschen. Rebuilt and reopened in 2003.

www.albertina.at 🔁 H6 ✉ Albertinaplatz 1 ☎ 53 483-0 🕐 Daily 10–6, Wed 10–9 🚇 U1, U2, U4 to Karlsplatz/Oper 💶 Moderate

BESTATTUNGSMUSEUM

In this Burial Museum, devoted to the undertaker's art, exhibits include photographs of dressed corpses seated on chairs, a stiletto for stabbing the dead through the heart to ensure against being buried alive and a coffin bell-pull for use in such an emergency.

🔁 H8 ✉ Goldeggasse 19 ☎ 5019 54227 🕐 By appointment Mon–Fri noon–3pm 🚋 Tram D to Upper Belvedere 💶 Inexpensive

ERZBISCHÖFLICHES DOM UND DIÖZESANMUSEUM

The Cathedral Museum's most celebrated item is a portrait of Duke Rudolf IV, but there are also fine medieval woodcarvings and paintings by masters such as Lukas Cranach and Franz Anton Maulbertsch.

www.dommuseum.at 🔁 H6 ✉ Stephansplatz 6, Stiege 1/1 ☎ 5155 23560 or 5155 23689 🕐 Tue–Sat 10–5 🚇 U1, U3 to Stephansplatz 💶 Moderate

JEWISH MUSEUM

Here you'll find thought-provoking exhibitions of Judaica. Not far away on the Judenplatz is Rachel Whiteread's famous Holocaust Memorial.

www.jmw.at 🔁 H6 ✉ Dorotheergasse 11 ☎ 535 0431 🕐 Sun–Fri 10–6, Thu 10–8 🚇 U1, U3 to Stephansplatz 💶 Moderate

IMPERIAL FUNITURE DEPOT

Fascinating panorama of furniture made by craftsmen patronized by the Habsburgs from the time of Maria Theresa onwards.

www.hofmobiliendepot.at 🔁 F7 ✉ Andreasgasse 7 ☎ 524 3357 🕐 Tue–Sun 10–6 🚇 U3 to Neubaugasse 💶 Moderate

DUKE RUDOLF IV

The likeness of Rudolf IV (1339–1365) in the Cathedral Museum, painted in his last year by a Bohemian master, is claimed as the first individual royal portrait in the German territories. Rudolf, called 'the Founder', initiated the South Tower of the Stephansdom and founded the University of Vienna in 1364. He also forged documents tracing his line back to Julius Caesar, and awarded himself several impressive titles.

LIPIZZANER MUSEUM WIEN

Photographs, antique tack, uniforms and videos and displays on the training of the Lipizzaners, plus a peek at the horses in their stalls.
www.lipizzaner.at ⊞ G6 ⊠ Stallburg/Hofburg Reitschulgasse 2 ☎ 533 7811 ⏰ Daily 9–6. Tours by arrangement ⨀ U3 to Herrengasse 🚋 Moderate

TECHNISCHES MUSEUM

Here you can explore the inventions and technical development of Austria from earliest times.
www.technischesmuseum.at ⊞ D8 ⊠ Mariahilfer Strasse 212 ☎ 899 98 ⏰ Mon–Sat 9–6, Sun 10–6 🚋 Tram 52, 58 🚋 Moderate

SECULAR AND SACRED TREASURIES (SCHATZKAMMER: HOFBURG, ➤ 37)

The insignia and crown (AD962) of the Holy Roman Emperor, a mid-15th-century Burgundian goblet, the Imperial Cross (c1024) and the so-called 'Sword of Charlemagne' (late 9th century) are the stars here.
⊞ G6 ⊠ Schweizerhof ☎ 533 60 46 ⏰ Wed–Mon 10–6 ⨀ U3 to Herrengasse 🚋 Hopper 2A to Michaelerplatz 🚋 Moderate

WIENER STRASSENBAHNMUSEUM

You can join a round trip on a vintage tram starting from Karlsplatz and visit the Tramway Museum.
⊞ L8 ⊠ Erdbergstrasse 109 ☎ 790 9437 ⏰ Sat–Sun 9–4, May–end Oct ⨀ U3 to Erdberg, then a short walk 🚋 Inexpensive

MUSEUM QUARTER (MUSEUMS QUARTIER WIEN)

Museums located in this quarter occupying the former imperial stables include the Kunsthalle (currently holding shows of contemporary art in Karlsplatz) and the Museum of Modern Art. The new Leopold Collection has a fine assemblage of works by Gustav Klimt, Egon Schiele and other artists of the period.
www.mqw.at ⊞ G7 ⊠ Museumsplatz 1 ☎ 523 5881 ⨀ U2 to Museums Quartier

REFORMING EMPEROR

Emperor Joseph II sometimes carried rationalism to extremes—as when he decreed that coffins be reusable, with exit flaps for the corpses. However, he founded both the General Hospital, with its revolutionary 'Fool's Tower' (➤ 28), and the Josephinum (➤ 29). The Vienna Medical School, founded under Maria Theresa, subsequently became world famous, especially for its introduction of new diagnostic techniques.

The grandeur of the Heeresgeschichtliches Museum

Parks & Gardens

Ferris wheel on the Prater

THE BIG WHEEL

The giant Ferris wheel on the Prater, built in 1896 by Englishman Walter Basset, was where Harry Lime met his old friend in the film *The Third Man*. The wheel rotates at 75cm (29in) per second and offers great views across the city.

🕐 19 Feb–30 Apr 1 Oct and Oct–13 Nov daily 10am–10pm; 1 May–30 Sep 11am–8pm; 26 Dec–8 Jan 9.30am–11pm

---

In the Top 25
2 SCHÖNBRUNN PARK (▶ 27)

AUGARTEN

Joseph II opened these gardens to the public in 1775 (much to the irritation of the upper classes, who had walked in them by invitation).
➕ H4 ✉ Obere Augartenstrasse 1 ☎ Porcelain Museum 21 124-18 🕐 Porcelain Museum Mon–Fri 9.30–6. Park daily 6am–dusk 🚋 Tram N from Schwedenplatz 💰 Inexpensive (tours of museum)

BURGGARTEN

The vast Jugendstil glasshouse built by Friedrich Ohmann in 1907 replaced the earliest glass and iron structure in Vienna (1826).
➕ G6/7 ✉ Burgring/Opernring 🕐 Apr–end Sep daily 6am–10pm; Oct–end Mar 6am–8pm 🚋 Trams 1, 2 to Burgring

PRATER

The former imperial hunting grounds were opened to the public in 1766, and now include a chestnut avenue, a fairground and other leisure facilities.
➕ K5–N8 ✉ Praterstern 🕐 Funfair Mar–end Oct daily 8am–midnight 🚇 U1 to Praterstern 🚋 Tram O 💰 Moderate (all attractions)

STADTPARK

Laid out in 1863 on the old River Wien causeway, the park is packed with monuments to the composers and artists of 19th-century Vienna (▶ 59).
➕ H/J6/7 ✉ Stubenring 🕐 Daily 8am–dusk 🚇 U3 to Stubentor, U4 to Stadtpark 🚋 Trams 1, 2

VOLKSGARTEN

Dominated by the Doric Theseus-Tempel, Volksgarten is an oasis of tranquillity in the heart of the city.
➕ G6 ✉ Dr-Karl-Renner-Ring 🕐 Daily May–end Sep 6am–10pm; Oct–end Apr 6am–9pm 🚇 U3 to Volkstheater 🚋 Trams 1, 2

Relaxing in the Burggarten

Statues & Monuments

DONNER FOUNTAIN
This is a copy of Georg Raphael Donner's
Providentia Fountain, which stands in the Baroque
Museum of the Belvedere (▶ 48). Maria Theresa
disapproved of the nude figures. The water nymphs
symbolize the rivers that form the borders of Lower
Austria.
H6 ⊠ Neuer Markt 🚇 U1, U3 to Stephansplatz

HENRY MOORE SCULPTURE
Henry Moore gave his *Hill Arches* sculpture to the
city in 1978 on the condition that it was sited on the
Karlsplatz.
H7 ⊠ Karlsplatz 🚇 U1, U2, U4 to Karlsplatz

JOHANN STRAUSS MONUMENT
The favourite statue of the Viennese Waltz King
represents him with unrestrained, and gilded,
sentimentality.
H7 ⊠ Stadtpark 🚋 Trams 1, 2 to Weihburggasse

LUEGER MONUMENT
Vienna's most famous mayor (1897–1910) was also
notoriously anti-Semitic.
H6 ⊠ Dr-Karl-Lueger-Platz 🚇 U3 to Stubentor

MONUMENT TO EMPRESS ELISABETH
Erected following the assassination of the popular
empress by an anarchist in Geneva in 1898.
G6 ⊠ Volksgarten (Burgtheater end) 🚋 Trams 1, 2 to
Burgtheater

MONUMENT TO FRANZ-JOSEPH
Austria's penultimate and longest-reigning monarch
(1848–1916) is shown in his military uniform, to
which he had a sentimental attachment.
G6 ⊠ Burggarten 🚋 Trams 1, 2 to Burgring

MONUMENT TO MARIA THERESA
The great reforming empress (1740–1780) is shown
enthroned and surrounded by her generals and
ministers.
G6 ⊠ Burgring 🚋 Trams 1, 2 to Burgring

MONUMENT TO THE VICTIMS OF FASCISM
Directly opposite the Albertina stands Austrian
sculptor Alfred Hrdlickla's moving memorial to those
tortured and killed in the Nazi period.
H6 ⊠ Albertinaplatz 🚇 U1, U2, U4 to Oper

MOZART MONUMENT
Austria's greatest composer is portrayed as 19th-
century people liked to imagine him.
G6 ⊠ Burggarten 🚋 Trams 1, 2 to Burgring

*Strauss monument in
the Stadtpark*

WAR MEMORIAL

The Viennese, who had been
treated horrifically by the
Russian liberation army in
1945, were not pleased by the
heroically represented figure
in the middle of the Russian
Liberation Monument in the
Schwarzenbergplatz–officially
it is 'The Unknown Soldier'.
More appropriate names for it
were immediately found,
typically 'The Unknown
Plunderer' or 'The Unknown
Rapist'.

Jugendstil & Secession

ANKERUHR

Every hour, a single figure from Austrian history revolves across the face of the Anchor Clock; then they all appear in sequence daily at noon.
⊞ H6 ✉ Hoher Markt 10–11 🚇 U1, U4 to Schwedenplatz

ARTARIA HAUS

Max Fabiani's Artaria House is one of the most striking Jugendstil buildings in the city.
⊞ H6 ✉ Kohlmarkt 9 🚇 U3 to Herrengasse

ÖSTERREICHISCHES POSTSPARKASSENAMT

The functionalism of Otto Wagner's Austrian Post Office Savings Bank (built 1910–1912) made it seem far in advance of its time.
⊞ J6 ✉ Georg-Coch-Platz 🕐 Mon, Wed, Fri 8–3, Thu 8–5.30
🚇 U1, U4 to Schwedenplatz 🚊 Trams 1, 2 on the Ring

JOSEF HOFFMANN VILLA COLONY ON THE HOHE WARTE

It is worth the 20-minute tram ride to see these elegant villas.
⊞ G1 ✉ Steinfeldgasse/Wollergasse 🚊 Tram 37 to last stop

KARLSPLATZ PAVILIONS

Otto Wagner, the great Secession architect, designed the City Transit Railway. The finest stations are the two on Karlsplatz (1898) and the emperor's own at Schönbrunn.
⊞ H7 ✉ Karlsplatz 🕐 Tue–Sun 9–noon. Closed 1 Nov–31 Mar
🚇 U1, U2, U4 to Karlsplatz

LOOS HAUS

Adolf Loos designed this building specifically for a fashionable tailor. It is now a bank with an exhibition area. Because of its plain façade it was known as the 'house without eyebrows', but it is very luxurious inside.
⊞ G6
✉ Michaelerplatz 3 🕐 Mon–Tue, Wed, Fri 8–3, Thu 8–5.30
🚇 U3 to Herrengasse
🚌 Hopper 2A to Michaelerplatz

JUGENDSTIL

In German-speaking lands, art nouveau was known as Jugendstil (youth style). Vienna developed its own closely related style, Secession —so called because its proponent artists 'seceded' from the conservative Association of Fine Arts in 1897 (► 36). Josef Hoffman was one of the leaders, and founded a guild for applied artists called the Wiener Werkstätte.

Secession style at Karlsplatz station

Coffee Houses

Wax model of Peter Altenberg in the Café Central

COFFEE AND CAKES

Coffee houses flourished in early 20th-century Vienna, when writers and artists used them for discussion, and as workplaces, unofficial banks and postboxes. A few that retain the traditional atmosphere are listed here. All serve a bewildering range of coffees. Freshly baked apfelstrudel is a typical accompaniment, and most places offer a simple menu of hot dishes.

BRÄUNERHOF

An old-fashioned café, with famously cantankerous waiters, this place is very pleasant, and there is a wide choice of newspapers.

H6 ✉ Stallburggasse 2 ☎ 512 3893 ⏰ Mon–Fri 8am–9pm, Sat 8am–7pm, Sun 10am–7pm 🚍 Hopper 2A to Habsburgergasse

CAFÉ MUSEUM

The original, spartan design was by Adolf Loos: today's minimalist furnishings still justify the nickname Café Nihilismus.

G7 ✉ Friedrichstrasse 6 ☎ 586 5202 ⏰ Mon–Sat 8am–midnight, Sun 10–midnight 🚇 U1, U2, U4 to Karlsplatz/Oper

CAFÉ CENTRAL

The lifelike figure seated near the entrance is Peter Altenberg, wittiest chronicler of early 20th-century Viennese life, and a regular patron.

G6 ✉ Herrengasse 14 ☎ 533 3764-26 ⏰ Mon–Sat 8am–10pm, Sun 10–6 🚇 U3 to Herrengasse

DEMEL

A confectioner with an imperial tradition, and a must on every tourist's itinerary (▶ 67).

G6 ✉ Kohlmarkt 14 ☎ 535 1717-39 ⏰ Daily 10–7 🚇 U3 to Herrengasse

HAWELKA

Bohemians, literati and night-owls frequent this cramped café. March 2005 Josefine Hawelka prepared her dumplings for the last time, went to bed and never woke up. She was 92.

H6 ✉ Dorotheergasse 6 ☎ 512 8230 ⏰ Mon, Wed–Sat 8am–2am, Sun 4pm–2am 🚇 U1, U3 to Stephansplatz

LANDTMANN

An elegant Ringstrassen café with a cellar where there's fringe theatre and a pleasant summer terrace.

G6 ✉ Dr-Karl-Lueger-Ring 4 ☎ 241 00–111 ⏰ Daily 7.30am– midnight 🚍 Trams 1, 2 to Burgtheater/Rathaus

The famous Café Demel

Attractions for Children

MÄRCHENBÜHNE 'DER APFELBAUM'

Fairy tales are enacted with puppets at the Apple-Theatre for Fairy Tales. Periodic performances are given in English (check by phone).

www.maerchenbuehne.at ➕ F7 ✉ Kirchengasse 41 ☎ 5231 72920 🕙 Performances Sat 3, 4.30 (irregularly at other times as well) 🚇 U3 to Neubaugasse 💷 Moderate

HAUS DES MEERES

The House of the Sea aquarium is in a World War II bomb shelter. There's plenty for young visitors to shudder at, including piranhas and sharks.

➕ F7 ✉ Esterhazypark ☎ 587 1417 🕙 Daily 9–6 🚇 U3 to Neubaugasse 💷 Moderate

KALEIDOSKOP KULTIPLEX IM PRATER

A high-tech experience with interactive and virtual reality activities.

➕ K5 ✉ Zufahrtsstrabe 140 ☎ 720 14 04 🕙 Mon, Thu, Sat 1–8, Fri 1–10, Sun 10–7 🚇 U1 to Praterstern 🚋 Tram 0

KINDERFREIBAD, AUGARTEN

If your kids are aged 6–15, you can leave them in this super-vised swimming pool while you see the Augarten (► 58).

➕ H4 ✉ Augarten, Karl-Meissl-Gasse entrance ☎ 332 4258 🕙 Mon–Fri 10–6 🚌 Bus 5a from Nestroyplatz 🚋 Tram 5 to Wallensteinplatz 💷 Free

Prater in the dark

PRATER

The world-famous amusement park has many diversions; the Ferris wheel (the Riesenrad) is among the most popular.

➕ K5 ✉ Praterstern 🕙 Mar–end Oct daily 8am–midnight 🚇 U1 to Praterstern 🚋 Tram 0

WIENER EISLAUFVEREIN

You could combine a visit to the Vienna Ice-skating Club (► 80) with child-friendly Sunday lunch at the Hotel Inter-Continental Wien (► 86).

➕ H7 ✉ Lothringerstrasse 22 ☎ 713 6353 🕙 Oct–end Mar Sat–Mon 9–8, Tue, Thu, Fri 9–9, Wed 9–10 🚇 U4 to Stadtpark 💷 Moderate 🛈 Disco Tue, Fri

FUN FOR THE YOUNG

Kids can have fun just getting around Vienna on the horse-drawn *fiacres* (cabs) and on the tram. The more exotic and impressive sights on the adult itinerary (such as the Hofburg and Schönbrunn) are also bound to please.

ZOO (TIERGARTEN) IN SCHÖNBRUNN

The former imperial menagerie is now Vienna's zoo.

www.zoovienna.at ➕ C9 ✉ Schönbrunn Park ☎ 877 9294 🕙 Summer daily 9–6.30 (until 4.30 rest of year) 🚇 U4 to Schönbrunn 💷 Moderate

VIENNA
where to...

Best in Town

PRICES

Expect to pay per person for a meal, excluding drink:

€   up to €36
€€ €36–65
€€€ over €65

NEUE WIENER KÜCHE

Nouvelle cuisine arrived late in the city. The man chiefly responsible for its introduction was Werner Matt, a Tyrolean chef who came to the Hilton in the 1970s. As a result, *Selbstmord mit Gabel und Messer* (suicide with a knife and fork) subsided. Menus grew shorter, and the city's kitchens began to use more fresh produce to reduce flour, fat and deep-frozen ingredients.

IM PALAIS SCHWARZENBERG (€€€)

The view of the gardens of the palace is splendid. So is the food. Try the stuffed guinea fowl in white port sauce or the medallions of venison.
🔛 H7 ⊠ Schwarzenbergplatz 9 ☎ 798 4515/600 ⏰ Daily noon–2, 6–11 🚋 Trams D, 1, 2 to Schwarzenbergplatz

KERN'S BEISEL (€€)

A wonderful place to experience honest Austrian cooking, with friendly service. A major plus is the wide selection of Austrian wines by the glass and spirits (there is a small bar at the back). Unpretentious restauranteurship at its best.
🔛 H6 ⊠ Kleeblattgasse 4 (corner Tuchlauben) ☎ 533 9188 ⏰ Mon–Fri 11.30–4, 6–10 🚇 U1, U3 to Stephansdom

KORSO BEI DER OPER (€€€)

Many consider this elegant restaurant in the Hotel Bristol the best in town, with the finest Viennese cuisine.
🔛 H7 ⊠ Mahlerstrasse 2 ☎ 5151 6546 ⏰ Sun–Fri noon–3pm, 7pm–1am. Closed Sun lunch Jul 🚇 U1, U2, U4 to Oper

PLACHUTTA HIETZING (€€€)

If you want to sample the famous *Wiener Tafelspitz* (boiled beef) at its most luxurious, as well as other beef specialities, this is the place. The atmosphere is ultra-Viennese and the restaurant is in the gracious suburb of Hietzing close to Schönbrunn.
🔛 B8 ⊠ Auhofstrasse 1 ☎ 877 7087 ⏰ Daily 11.30–3, 6–10.30 🚇 U4 to Hietzing 🚋 Trams 58, 10 to Kennedy Brücke

STEIRERECK IM STADTPARK (€€€)

A distinguished restaurant in stunning new premises famous for the delicacy of its *Neue Wiener Küche* and its well-chosen wine list.
🔛 J7 ⊠ Am Heumarkt 2 ☎ 713 3168 ⏰ Mon–Fri 11.30–4.30, 7–midnight 🚇 U3 to Rochusgasse

RESTAURANT MEINL AM GRABEN (€€€)

A discreet gourmet-stop in the only remaining branch of quality grocer Meinl. The best of Austrian cooking in an informal atmosphere; fabulous wines.
🔛 H6 ⊠ Graben 19 ☎ 532 3334-6000 ⏰ Mon–Wed 8–midnight, Thu–Fri 8.30–midnight, Sat 9–midnight 🚇 U3, U1 to Stephansplatz

ZU EBENER ERDE UND ERSTER STOCK (€€)

The Spittelberg area has many goodish eateries but this is the best. Viennese cooking with a light touch and much attention to seasonal specialities like asparagus. Very good wine list. The posher restaurant part is upstairs, while the lower part is less pretentious; good atmosphere in both.
🔛 G6 ⊠ Burggasse 13 ☎ 523 6254 ⏰ Tue–Fri noon–2.30, 6–midnight, Sat 6–midnight 🚇 U3 to Volkstheater

Other Viennese Restaurants

BEIM CZAAK (€)
A traditional Beisl tucked away in a quiet corner of the Innere Stadt. Viennese cuisine, but with emphasis on its Czech origins (dumplings to the fore!).
✚ H6 ✉ Postgasse 15 ☎ 513 7215 🕐 Mon–Sat 11–midnight 🚇 U1, U4 to Schwedenplatz

BEI MAX (€€)
Carinthian noodles are a speciality at this haunt of actors and writers; other regional dishes available.
✚ G6 ✉ Landhausgasse 2, corner of Herrengasse ☎ 533 7359 🕐 Mon–Fri 11–11 🚇 U3 to Herrengasse

ECKEL (€€€)
A charming restaurant in a series of *Stüberln* (annexes), offering recipes from grandfather Eckel's legendary cookbook. Superb service.
✚ F2 ✉ Sieveringer Strasse 46 ☎ 320 3218 🕐 Tue–Sat noon–2.30, 6–10.30 🚋 Tram 38 from Schottentor to Billroth Strasse, then walk or bus 39A

FIGLMÜLLER (€€)
Always crowded, but good value, with huge schnitzels and a choice of wines by the glass. No beer. New branch at Bächerstrabe 6.
✚ H6 ✉ Wollzeile 5 ☎ 512 6177 🕐 Daily 11–10.30 🚇 U1, U3 to Stephansplatz

OSWALD UND KALB (€€)
Favoured haunt of media glitterati. The speciality wine is Styrian Schilcher, made from indigenous grapes.
✚ H6 ✉ Bäckerstrasse 14 ☎ 512 1371 🕐 Daily 6pm–midnight 🚇 U3 to Stubentor

SALM BRÄU (€)
Bustling beer cellar in a former monastery. Good value hot and cold food and great beer, some brewed on the premises.
✚ J7 ✉ Rennweg 8 ☎ 799 5992 🕐 Daily 11am–11pm 🚋 Tram 71 from Schwarzenbergplatz

WRENKH (€€)
Exquisite vegetarian cuisine like wild rice risotto with mushrooms, and Greek fried rice with vegetables, sheep's cheese and olives.
✚ H6 ✉ Bauernmarkt 10 ☎ 533 1526 🕐 Daily 11.30–3, 8–11 🚇 U1, U3 to Stephansplatz

ZU DEN 3 HACKEN (€€)
Good service and a noisy, convivial atmosphere. Some of the cooking has a Styrian flavour.
✚ H6 ✉ Singerstrasse 28 ☎ 512 5895 🕐 Mon–Sat 11am–11pm 🚇 U1, U3 to Stephansplatz

ZUM HERKNER (€€)
Excellent Viennese food carrying on the tradition of the restaurant's celebrated late owner.
✚ B3 ✉ Dornbacher Strasse 123 ☎ 485 4386 🕐 Mon–Fri 11am–10pm 🚋 Tram 43 from Schottentor to last stop

ZUM SCHWARZEN KAMEEL (€€–€€€)
For a charming Viennese lunch, try the Jugendstil Black Camel.
✚ H6 ✉ Bognergasse 5 ☎ 533 8125 🕐 Mon–Sat noon–2.30, 6–10.30 🚇 U1, U3 to Stephansplatz

THE *BEISL*

Most restaurants that offer genuine Viennese cooking are carrying on the *Beisl* tradition: honest food, cooked and served in unpretentious surroundings. The word is of Yiddish origin (in the past, tavern keepers were often Jewish). Prosperity, tourism and the profit motive have transformed some *Beisls* into expensive restaurants, but many hold to tradition and keep prices fair. Typical dishes include *Tafelspitz* (boiled beef), *Zwiebelrostbraten* (beefsteak with crispy onions) and *Beuschel* (chopped lung in sauce). Liver is also popular.

Heurigen

HEURIGEN

A *Heurige* is a tavern in its own vineyard in the Wienerwald (Viennese Woods), traditionally selling only the current year's (*heuer*) wine. A selection of *Heurigen* from four different villages in the northern suburbs are given here. When open, a *Heurige* is *ausg'steckt*, indicated by a bunch of fir-twigs hung outside the door. The basic wine is *Gemischter Satz*, a tindery white blend of local grapes. Roast meats, cheeses and salads are served in most *Heurigen*, although some in Grinzing and Heiligenstadt are full-scale restaurants. The atmosphere is quintessentially Viennese–nostalgic, even maudlin after everyone has had a few glasses. Above all it's *gemütlich* (cosy), with *Schrammelmusik* (named after the 19th-century Schrammel brothers) played on fiddle, guitar and accordion.

GRINZING

ALTER BACH-HENGL (€€)
This is a typical, family-run *Heurige*, with garden tables in summer, Schrammel music, hot and cold buffets and *Gemischter Satz* to drink.
🔢 F1 ✉ Sandgasse 7–9
☎ 320 2439 🕐 4pm–midnight 🚋 Tram 38 from Schottentor to end stop

REINPRECHT (€–€€)
A 300-year-old former monastery.
🔢 F1 ✉ Cobenzlgasse 22
☎ 320 1471
🕐 3pm–midnight. Closed Jan–mid-Feb 🚋 Tram 38 to last stop, then a short walk

HEILIGENSTADT

Heiligenstadt is the village where Beethoven lived at the time he was going deaf, and his lodgings at Probusgasse 6 are now a museum.

FEUERWEHR-WAGNER (€€)
Pleasant, intimate and rustic; very popular in winter.
🔢 F1 ✉ Grinzingerstrasse 53
☎ 320 2442 🕐 4pm–midnight 🚇 U4, U6 🚌 Bus 38A from Heiligenstadt Station

MAYER AM PFARRPLATZ (€€)
One of the best *Heurigen* in Heiligenstadt. There are several rooms and a large garden.
🔢 G1 ✉ Heiligenstädter Pfarrplatz 2 ☎ 370 1287
🕐 4pm–midnight. Closed Christmas to mid-Jan 🚇 U4, U6
🚌 Bus 38A from Heiligenstadt Station

ZIMMERMANN (€€)
An oasis off the beaten track near the Beethoven House where the composer's tragic *Heilgenstädter Testament* was written in 1802.
🔢 G1 ✉ Armbrustergasse 5
☎ 370 2211 🕐 Mon–Sat 5pm–2am 🚇 U4, U6
🚌 Bus 38A from Heiligenstadt Station

NEUSTIFT AM WALDE

FUHRGASSL-HUBER (€€)
One of the most congenial taverns in this village's long main street. The same family also runs an excellent pension close by (▶ 88).
🔢 C1 ✉ Neustift am Walde 68
☎ 440 1405
🕐 2pm–midnight 🚇 U6
🚌 Bus 35A from Nussdorfer Strasse

BUSCHENSCHANK WEINGUT WOLFF (€)
Large traditional *Heurige* that is also cosy in winter.
🔢 C1 ✉ Rathstrasse 44–46
☎ 440 2335 🕐 Daily 11am–1am 🚇 U6 🚌 Bus 35A from Nussdorfer Strasse

STAMMERSDORF

FEITZINGER (€)
In an area seldom visited by tourists, this tavern has pleasant rustic interiors and serves an excellent house wine.
🔢 Off map to northeast
✉ Stammersdorfer Strasse 115
☎ 292 9642 🕐 Mar–end Nov Mon–Sun 1pm–midnight. Closed Wed 🚋 Tram 31 from Schottenring to last stop

Quick Bites

AUGUSTINERKELLER (€€)
Good Austrian and Viennese food, plus local wines. A bit touristy.
🔲 H6 ✉ Augustinerstrasse 1 ☎ 533 1026 🕐 Daily 11–midnight 🚇 U1, U2, U4 to Oper

DURAN SANDWICHES (€)
Rival to Trzesniewski (► below) with a big selection of open sandwiches.
🔲 H6 ✉ Rotenturmstrasse 11 ☎ 533 7115 🕐 Mon–Fri 8.30–9, Sat 9–2 🚇 U4, U1 to Schwedeplatz
Also at:
Schwedenplatz 2

ESTERHAZYKELLER (€)
The Esterhazys gave free wine to the populace here during the 1683 Turkish siege. The wine is no longer free but it's still very good value, as is the simple food.
🔲 G6 ✉ Haarhof 1 (off Wallnerstrasse) ☎ 533 3482 🕐 Mon–Fri 11–10, Sat–Sun 4–10 🚇 U3 to Herrengasse

MELKER STIFTSKELLER (€)
An echoing baroque cellar that serves very acceptable food.
🔲 G6 ✉ Schottengasse 3 ☎ 533 5530 🕐 Tue–Sat 5pm–midnight 🚇 U2 to Schottentor

NORDSEE (€–€€)
Not just fish and chips. You'll find a wide range of seafood dishes and sandwiches with fish fillings. Self-service.
🔲 H6 ✉ Kohlmarkt 6 ☎ 533 5966 🕐 Mon–Fri 10am–9pm, Sat–Sun 10am–8pm 🚇 U1, U3 to Stephansdom
Also at:
Kärntner Strasse 25, Neubaugasse 9, Mariahilfer Strasse 84, and others

SOUPKULTUR (€)
Choice of eight fresh soups, salad and freshly squeezed juices.
🔲 G5 ✉ Wipplingerstrabe 32 ☎ 532 4628 🕐 Mon–Thu 11.30–6, Fri 11.30–4 🚋 Trams 1, 2, to Börse

TRZESNIEWSKI (€)
Lots of open sandwiches, with toppings of fish, meat, vegetables, poultry and eggs from free-range chickens.
🔲 H6 ✉ Dorotheergasse 1 ☎ 512 3291 🕐 Mon–Fri 8.30–7.30, Sat 8–5 🚇 U1, U3 to Stephansplatz
Also at:
Galleria, Landstrasse Hauptstrasse 97–101, Mariahilfer Strasse 95, Am Meiselmarkt, and others

ZWÖLF-APOSTEL-KELLER (€)
A student hang-out. Very atmospheric cellars on three levels.
🔲 H6 ✉ Sonnenfelsgasse 3 ☎ 512 6777 🕐 4.30pm–midnight 🚇 U1, U3 to Stephansplatz

MARKETS

NASCHMARKT
Everything from truffles to oysters. On Saturday you can combine a visit to this food market with one to the flea market at the western end.
🔲 G7 ✉ Wienzeile, Kettenbrückgasse 🕐 Mon–Fri 6am–6.30pm, Sat 6am–5pm 🚇 U4 to Kettenbrückengasse

NO-FRILLS FOOD

Cynics say that the favourite dish of a Viennese is a big one. The new self-service restaurants, however, offer much more flexibility in terms of portion size and in range of food (although the cuisine remains Austrian). Vienna's many ancient wine vaults also offer local wines and modestly priced food in a convivial and romantic setting. (A 15th-century writer remarked that more of Vienna was below ground than above it.) Sandwich bars offer open-sandwiches, a speciality here, and markets always have stands selling snacks and delicacies.

Coffee Houses

See Vienna's Best
(► 61) for
BRÄUNERHOF
CAFÉ MUSEUM
CAFÉ CENTRAL
HAWELKA
LANDTMANN

COFFEE IN CAFÉS

It is said the Viennese go to coffee houses to be alone, for which they need people around them. You can linger for hours and be asked to pay only when the waiter is going off shift. It is also a place to meet friends and exchange some of the gossip that is the motor of Viennese life. Some establishments offer billiards or a card game of Italian origin called tarock. Hot food is usually offered at very modest prices, and the standard dishes—typically such things as schnitzel or apfelstrudel—are always available.

CAFÉ MINISTERIUM (€)

Slightly down-at-heel café that's cosy for hot and filling lunches in winter.

➕ H6 ✉ Georg-Coch-Platz 4
☎ 512 9225 🕐 Mon–Fri
7am–11pm (breakfast until
11am) 🚇 U1, U4 to
Schwedenplatz 🚋 Trams 1, 2
on Ringstrasse

DIGLAS (€€)

Diglas was re-established as a café in the 1990s by the grandson of the original owner. Founded in 1923, it was a comparative latecomer to the coffee-house scene. Its most famous regular customer was the composer Franz Lehár.

➕ H6 ✉ Wollzeile 10
☎ 512 5765 🕐 Daily
7am–11pm 🚇 U1, U3 to
Stephansdom

DOMMAYER (€€)

Vienna's oldest music café is the venue for matinée performances by the female ensemble Wiener Walzermädchen and other groups, as well as drama troupes. Close to Schönbrunn.

➕ B8 ✉ Auhofstrasse 2
(Hietzing) ☎ 877 5465
🕐 Daily 7am–midnight
🚇 U4 to Hietzing

EILES (€)

Situated in a mainly residential area, this is a congenial, old-fashioned establishment with window seats and niches. Small menu at midday.

➕ G6 ✉ Josefstädter
Strasse 2 ☎ 405 3410
🕐 Mon–Fri 7am–10pm, Sat–
Sun, hols 8am–10pm 🚋 Tram J
to Josefstädter Strasse

PRÜCKEL (€€)

The long tradition of cabaret performances continues in the cellar, but Prückel also has piano music on Monday, Wednesday and Friday evenings.

➕ H6 ✉ Stubenring 24
☎ 512 6115
🕐 8.30am–10pm 🚇 U3 to
Stubentor

SCHWARZENBERG (€€)

This is the oldest of the elegant Ringstrassen cafés, opened in 1861 when the boulevard was still under construction. There is a choice of newspapers, including foreign ones, and there are sybaritic touches, like the large selection of cigars for sale.

➕ H7 ✉ Kärntner Ring 17
☎ 512 8998-13 🕐 Sun–Fri
7am–midnight, Sat
9am–midnight 🚋 Trams 1, 2
to Schwarzenbergplatz

TIROLERHOF (€)

Coffee houses were originally for men only, but this one had an exclusively female clientele as early as 1910. Now mixed, it is still a favourite among women.

➕ H6 ✉ Führichgrasse 8
(Albertinaplatz) ☎ 512 7833
🕐 Mon–Sat 7am–9pm, Sun,
hols 9–8 🚇 U1, U2, U4
to Oper

Konditoreien

AIDA (€)

It's cramped, but the coffee and cakes are good.

H6 ✉ Stock-im-Eisen-Platz 2 ☎ 512 2977 🕑 Mon–Sat 7am–8pm, Sun 9am–8pm 🚇 U1, U3 to Stephansplatz

Also at:
Bognergasse 3, Rotenturmstrasse 24, Wollzeile 28, and others

DEMEL (€€–€€€)

Founded in 1776 close to the now-demolished Burgtheater on Michaelerplatz, Demel nearly folded twice, the second time because of the revolution in 1848. Christoph Demel took over in 1857, and it remained in the family until Anna Demel's death in 1956. The staff were traditionally recruited from a convent in Währing and decked out in black uniforms with white frills. The lavish interior is a restoration dating from the 1930s (➤ 61).

G6 ✉ Kohlmarkt 14 ☎ 535 1717 🕑 Daily 10–7 🚇 U3 to Herrengasse

GERSTNER (€€–€€€)

A distinguished Konditorei that lures shoppers from Kärntner Strasse. Light lunches (expensive).

H6 ✉ Kärntner Strasse 13–15 ☎ 512 4963-77 🕑 Mon–Sat 8.30–8, Sun 10–6 🚇 U1, U3 to Stephansplatz

HEINER (€€)

The branch overlooking Kärntner Strasse is excellent, but the little Biedermeier interior of Heiner in the Wollzeile is irresistible; a doll's house atmosphere. The cakes and pastries are really superb and the coffee good; fine handmade chocolates, too. Special goodies for diabetics are available.

H6 ✉ Kärntner Strasse 21–3 ☎ 512 6863 🕑 Mon–Sat 8.30–7.30, Sun 10–7.30 🚇 U1, U3 to Stephansplatz

Also at:
H6 ✉ Wollzeile 9 ☎ 512 2343 🕑 Mon–Sat 8.30–7, Sun 10–7 🚇 U1, U3 to Stephansplatz

KONDITOREI LEHMANN (€€)

Elegant, but so popular that it's hard to get a seat. Good sandwiches as well as a large selection of pastries made on the premises.

H6 ✉ Graben 12 ☎ 512 1815 🕑 Mon–Sat 8.30–7 🚇 U1, U3 to Stephansplatz

KONDITOREI OBERLAAER STADTHAUS (€€)

Cognoscenti assert that this relative newcomer to the city centre is the best Konditorei of all. The premises are more spacious than many, and a light lunch is also available.

H6 ✉ Neuer Markt 16 ☎ 513 2936 🕑 Daily 8–8 🚇 U1, U3 to Stephansplatz

SLUKA (€€)

Another candidate for the title of Vienna's best, with mouth-watering pastries and light lunches.

G6 ✉ Rathausplatz 8 ☎ 405 7172 🕑 Mon–Fri 8–7, Sat 8–5.30 🚋 Tram J to Stadiongasse

PASTRY SHOPS

The Konditorei is another Viennese speciality, and pastry-makers have always been highly esteemed for their skills. The most distinguished in the city, Demel, was rewarded with the title KK Hof-Zuckerbäckerei (Imperial and Royal Confectioners). Zuckerbäcker were so much a part of the Viennese psyche that elaborate, over-ornamented architecture was referred to by locals as Zuckerbäckerstil, what would be called 'wedding-cake style' in English.

International Fare

Apart from the Nordsee chain (► 67), there are a growing number of possibilities for serious fish eaters. For the freshest and best, you have to be prepared to dig deep in the pocket. The pizza trade expands even faster than hamburger joints in this part of the world, and there is now a good choice of places in central Vienna serving oven-fresh pizzas. There are even, in a city of mainly meat-eaters, some vegetarian restaurants.

ASIAN

AKAKIKO (€€)

Better value than many Japanese restaurants. The bonus here is the delightful roof terrace.
🚹 F7 ⊠ Mariahilfer Strasse 40–48 (5th floor of Gerngross store) ☎ 524 0616 🕓 Daily 10.30–midnight 🚇 U3 to Neubaugasse

GREEN COTTAGE (€€)

Close to Naschmarkt, this Chinese restaurant is remarkably successful at creatively mingling European and Asiatic styles of cooking in an extremely creative menu. The ingredients (such as fillet of lamb or beef) may seem very Viennese, but the spicy gastronomic experience is made in Sichuan.
🚹 G7 ⊠ Kettenbrückengasse 3 ☎ 586 6581 🕓 Mon–Sat 6–11.30 🚇 U4 to Kettenbrückengasse

LUCKY PAVILLON (€€)

There are many Chinese restaurants in Vienna, one more dispiriting than another. This is an exception, and the dim sum is good.
🚹 J6 ⊠ Löwengasse 21 ☎ 712 6293 🕓 11.30–3, 5.30–11.30 🚋 Tram N

ROYAL SHERE PUNJAB (€€)

It is a promising sign that this Indian haunt is patronized by members of the small Indian community and is slightly off the tourist track. The dishes are heavily spiced and there is a very moderately priced midday buffet.
🚹 G-H7 ⊠ Paulanergasse 8 ☎ 952 8416 🕓 Mon–Sat 11.30–3, 6–10.30 🚋 Tram 65 or Baden Lokalbahn from Oper to Paulanergasse

SAFRAN (€€€)

If the need for a curry overwhelms you, this dignified restaurant with a wide range of Indian specialities will suit.
🚹 G5 ⊠ Garnisongasse 10 ☎ 407 4234 🕓 Daily 11.30–3, 6–11.30 🚋 Trams 40, 41, 42 from Schottenton to Schwarzspanierstrasse

TOKORI (€€)

This minute bar in Leopoldstadt has made a name for itself among sushi connoisseurs.
🚹 H5 ⊠ Franz-Hochedlinger-Gasse 2 ☎ 214 8940 🕓 Mon–Sat noon–3, 6–11 🚇 U1, U4 to Schwedenplatz, then cross Salztorbrücke

EAST EUROPEAN

BODULO (€€€)

A Croatian restaurant that serves fresh fish, simply prepared. Worth the trek out to Hernals.
🚹 C4 ⊠ Hernalser Hauptstrasse 204 ☎ 486 4311 🕓 Tue–Sat 11.30–3, 5.30–11, Sun 11.30–3, 5.30–10 🚋 Tram 44 from Schottentor to last stop

ILONA-STÜBERL (€€)

Excellent value; stuffed cabbage, goulash and other Hungarian fare.
🚹 H6 ⊠ Bräunerstrasse 2 ☎ 533 9029 🕓 Daily noon–11 🚇 U1, U3 to Stephansplatz

KORNAT (€€–€€€)

This Croatian restaurant serves fish flown in fresh from the Dalmatian coast with wines from Hvar and Korcula.

✚ H6 ✉ Marc-Aurel-Strasse 8 ☎ 535 6518 🕔 Mon–Sat 11.30–3, 6–11.30 🚇 U1, U4 to Schwedenplatz

MEDITERRANEAN

ACHILLEUS (€€)
All the old Greek favourites, from *mezedes* to calamaris and *paidakia* (lamb cutlets).

✚ H6 ✉ Köllnerhofgasse 3 ☎ 512 8328 🕔 Mon–Sat 11–3, 5.30–midnight, Sun 11.30–4 🚇 U1, U3 to Stephansplatz

BODEGA ESPAÑOLA (€)
A taste of Spain in the heart of Vienna's 4th district. *Tapas* like *pinchos de pollo con arroz* (skewers of grilled chicken on rice) to wash down with a good choice of Spanish wines.

✚ H8 ✉ Belvedergasse 10 ☎ 504 5500 🕔 Tue–Sat 6–1am 🚋 Tram D

RESTAURANT HUMMERBAR (€€€)
Vienna's most renowned fish restaurant with the famous *Hummerbar* (lobster bar). Downstairs is a more modest Turkish restaurant.

✚ H7 ✉ Mahlerstrasse 9 ☎ 512 8843 🕔 Mon–Sat noon –midnight 🚇 U1, U2, U4 to Oper

ITALIAN

CANTINETTA ANTINORI (€€€)
One of Vienna's oldest Italian restaurants owned by the Antinori family, who produce their own wines and olive oil.

✚ H6 ✉ Jasomirgottstrasse 3–5 ☎ 533 7722 🕔 Daily

11.30–1am 🚇 U1, U3 to Stephansplatz

DA BIZI (€–€€)
A self-service system allows you to assemble the menu of your choice.

✚ H6 ✉ Rotenturmstrasse 4 ☎ 513 3705 🕔 Daily 11am–11.30 🚇 U1, U3 to Stephansplatz

É TRICAFFÉ (€€)
The lastest thing on the Italian scene—a cooperation with Italy's Harry's Bar. Italian delicacies to consume here or to buy.

✚ H6 ✉ Rotenturmstrabe 25 ☎ 533 8990 🕔 Mon–Sat 8–midnight, Sun 10–midnight 🚇 U1, U3 to Stephansdom

LA GRAPPA (€–€€)
An oasis of Tuscan cooking offering seasonal specialities besides such exotica as smoked swordfish.

✚ H8 ✉ Argentinierstrasse 26 ☎ 503 4598 🕔 Mon–Fri 11.30–3, 6–midnight 🚋 Tram D to Prinz-Eugen-Strasse

NOVELLI BACARO CON CUCINA (€€€)
When you're tired of pizza and pasta, look to this lovely restaurant with superb Italian fare and wines to match.

✚ H6 ✉ Bräunerstrasse 11 ☎ 513 4200 🕔 Mon–Sat 12–2, 6–11 🚇 U1, U3 to Stephausplatz

RIEGI (€€€)
Said to be the best Italian restaurant in Vienna, with a famed wine list, and no pizzas.

✚ G6 ✉ Schauflergasse 6 ☎ 532 9126 🕔 Tue–Sat noon–3, 6–midnight 🚇 U3 to Herrengasse

FOOD FROM AROUND THE WORLD

Although Vienna has had a large international community since the 1970s, the choice of non-Viennese cooking is not as great as you might expect in a capital city. True, the pizza and pasta is ubiquitous, and the number of Chinese and Japanese restaurants is growing; yet there are surprisingly few French restaurants of repute, the Greek and Spanish selection is disappointing, and the cuisines of some other territories are virtually unknown. The list here reflects the relative choice available.

Ten Best Shops

BARGAINS HARD TO FIND

When Austria entered the European Union in 1995, it was expected that prices would fall as a result of more penetration into a previously cartel-ridden and monopolists market. In some areas (chiefly where food is concerned) this has happened, but in luxury goods, prices are oriented to Munich or London and there are no bargains. A tip is to try and buy non-exclusive goods outside the Innere Stadt, where prices are higher because the rents are high and many customers are well-to-do.

ALTMANN & KÜHNE

The maker of Vienna's best chocolates and the most creative candy.

🚪 H6 ✉ Graben 30
☎ 533 0927 🕐 Mon–Fri 9–6.30, Sat 9–5 🚇 U1, U3 to Stephansplatz

CHEGINI

A distinguished women's fashion shop noted for its impeccable taste and selection. There is another branch at Plankengasse 4.

🚪 H6 ✉ Kohlmarkt 7
☎ 533 2058 🕐 Mon–Fri 9.45–6, Sat 10–5 🚇 U1, U3 to Stephansplatz

DOBLINGER

Mecca for music-lovers and performers: sheet music, books, instruments and CDs.

🚪 H6 ✉ Dorotheagasse 10
☎ 515 03 🕐 Mon–Sat 10–5.30 🚇 U1, U3 to Stephausdom

DUFT UND KULTUR

Lovely smells to sweeten any room of the house from Africa and the Orient.

🚪 H6 ✉ Tuchlauben 17
☎ 532 3960 🕐 Mon–Sat 10–6 🚇 U1, U3 to Stephausdom

E. BRAUN & CO

The bed and table linens were once sold to the Habsburg court. Also sells men's and women's clothing.

🚪 H6 ✉ Graben 8
☎ 512 5505 🕐 Mon–Fri 9.15–6, Sat 9.15–5 🚇 U1, U3 to Stephansplatz

FREYTAG O. BERNDT

Travel bookshop stocking English titles, especially books on Central Europe. Unrivalled selection of maps and street plans.

🚪 H6 ✉ Kohlmarkt 9
☎ 533 8685 🕐 Mon–Fri 9–6.30, Sat 9–5 🚇 U3 to Herrengasse

GEORG RUZICZKA

Schnaps is an Austrian speciality. This shop has the most fascinating selection of local products—brandies, grappas and rarities like Burgenland 'Uhudler' wine.

🚪 G7 ✉ Naschmarkt 57
☎ 585 7318 🕐 Mon–Fri 9–6, Sat 8.30–5 🚇 U4 to Kettenbrückengasse

KNIZE

Exclusive men's tailors also notable for the 1913 façade and the interior designed by Adolf Loos.

🚪 H6 ✉ Graben 13
☎ 512 2119 🕐 Mon–Fri 9.30–6, Thu 9.30–8, Sat 9.30–5 🚇 U1, U3 to Stephansplatz

STEFFL

Futuristic shop interior arising from the ashes of the old Steffl, and now full of top labels. Also a floor devoted to cosmetics. Media café, bar and restaurant.

🚪 H6 ✉ Kärntner Strasse 19
☎ 514 310 🕐 Mon–Fri 9.30–7, Sat 9.30–5 🚇 U1, U3 to Stephansplatz

UNGER UND KLEIN

The best selection of wines from Lower Austria, Styria and Burgenland.

🚪 H5 ✉ Gölsdorfgasse 2
☎ 532 1323 🕐 Mon–Fri 9–6, Sat 11–2pm 🚇 U1, U4 to Schwedenplatz

Antiques & Art Galleries

C. BEDNARCZYK
Specialist in 18th-century pieces. Paintings, glass, porcelain and silver.
➕ H6 ✉ Dorotheergasse 12 ☎ 512 4445 ⏰ Mon–Fri noon–6, Sat 10–1 🚇 U1, U2, U4 to Oper

DOROTHEUM
An auction house founded in the 18th century in an old convent. You can find everything from the worthless to the priceless, some items marked for direct sale.
➕ H6 ✉ Dorotheergasse 17 ☎ 515 60-268 ⏰ Art auctions: Thu 2.30. Exhibitions of objects: Mon–Fri 10–6 🚇 U1, U2, U4 to Oper

ERNST HILGER
Contemporary Austrian art. Eleven special exhibitions each year.
➕ H6 ✉ Dorotheergasse 5 ☎ 512 5315 ⏰ Mon–Fri noon–6, Sat 10–1 🚇 U1, U3 to Stephansplatz

GALERIE HEIKE CURTZE
This gallery sells work by some of Austria's leading modern artists.
➕ H6 ✉ Seilerstätte 15 ☎ 512 9375 ⏰ Tue–Fri 3–7, Sat 11–2 🚇 U1, U3 to Stephansplatz

GALERIE HOFSTÄTTER
Contemporary Austrian art, and art nouveau.
➕ H6 ✉ Bräunerstrasse 7 ☎ 512 3255 ⏰ Mon–Fri 10–6, Sat 10–12.30 🚇 U1, U3 to Stephansplatz

GALERIE NÄCHST ST. STEPHAN
Avant-garde art from Austria and abroad.
➕ H6 ✉ Grünangergasse 1 (runs between Singerstrasse and Schulerstrasse) ☎ 512 1266 ⏰ Tue–Fri 10–6, Sat 11–2 🚇 U1, U3 to Stephansplatz

GALERIE NEBEHAY
Author, scholar and collector Christian Nebehay is a leading expert on Klimt and Schiele. His shop also sells old prints and antiquarian books, as well as his own (very useful) books on his specialist field—early 20th-century art.
➕ H6 ✉ Annagasse 18 ☎ 512 1801 ⏰ Mon–Fri 10–6, Sat 10–noon 🚇 U1, U2, U4 to Oper

GRITA INSAM
International avant-garde painting.
➕ H6 ✉ Köllnerhofgasse 6 ☎ 512 5330 ⏰ Tue–Fri 2–6, Sat 11–2 🚇 U1, U3 to Stephansplatz

RAUMINHALT
An unusual shop devoted to decorative objects and furniture of the last five decades. Plastic is particularly well represented with the 1950s a speciality.
➕ F6 ✉ Schleifmühlgasse 13 ☎ 409 9892 ⏰ Mon–Fri 10–7, Sat 10–3 🚋 Tram J to Lederergasse

WIENER INTERIEUR
Compact shop specializing in fine examples of smaller Jugendstil (➤ 60) and art-deco objects.
➕ H6 ✉ Dorotheergasse 14 ☎ 512 2898 ⏰ Mon–Fri 10–6, Sat 10–1 🚇 U1, U4, U2 to Oper

FAMOUS ART GALLERY

Galerie Nächst St Stephan (✉ Grünangergasse 1 ☎ 512 1266) was started in 1954 by the distinguished preacher Otto Mauer, who was devoted to reconciling the modern artist and the conservative Church. His gallery was the focus for discussion for liberal Catholics, including some who went on to lead the conservative Volkspartei (People's Party) in government in 2001. Church hierarchs admired Mauer's capacity for opening up a dialogue with intellectuals and the young, but feared any diminution of the Church's power.

China, Glass & Home Furnishings

FINE CHINA

Since the 18th century or earlier, Vienna has produced a large quantity of objets d'art. The Secession (➤ 36), founded in 1897, was followed by the Wiener Werkstätte—its applied-art branch—and this gave renewed impetus to the creation of beautiful and functional items. The porcelain industry stretches back to the Habsburgs' encouragement of craft industries in the 18th century. The glassware from Lobmeyr, on the other hand, is the product of the 19th-century Historicism Movement, which fostered imitations of Renaissance and baroque models.

AUGARTEN

Porcelain with floral designs produced in Vienna at the factory in the park of the same name (➤ 58).

➕ H6 ✉ Stock-im-Eisen-Platz 3–4 ☎ 512 1494 🕐 Mon–Fri 9–6, Sat 9–12.30 🚇 U1, U3 to Stephansplatz

WIENER PORZELLANFABRIK

You can also buy Augarten porcelain direct from the factory. Seconds sell at a 20 per cent discount.

➕ H4 ✉ Wiener Porzellanmanufaktur, Obere Augartenstrasse 1 ☎ 211 2418-18 🕐 Mon–Fri 9–6, Sat 9–noon 🚋 Tram N

BACKHAUSEN

The inheritor of the Secession tradition has an extensive range of Wiener Werkstätte, along with Liberty patterns (patterns of the English Arts and Crafts Movement sold by Liberty of London). Considered by many as Vienna's best home furnishing store.

➕ H7 ✉ Schwarzenbergstrabe 10 ☎ 514 04 🕐 Mon–Fri 9–6, Sat 9–5 🚋 Trams 1, 2, D to Schwarzenbergplatz

KERAMIK AUS GMUNDEN

Gmunden in the Salzkammergut produces interesting ceramics with a touch of rusticity—green wavy lines on a white background—that is not to everyone's taste but is certainly exotic.

➕ H6 ✉ Kärntner Strasse 10 (Kärntner Durchgang) ☎ 512 5824 🕐 Mon–Fri 9–6, Sat 9.30–5 🚇 U1, U3 to Stephansplatz

J. & L. LOBMEYR

The famous glassware is still made to the 19th-century neo-baroque and neo-Renaissance design. Above the shop is a small exhibition of J. & L. Lobmeyr's early work.

➕ H6 ✉ Kärntner Strasse 26 ☎ 512 0508 🕐 Mon–Fri 9–6, Sat 9–5 🚇 U1, U3 to Stephansplatz

RASPER & SÖHNE

A highly respected emporium for glass, porcelain and cutlery, although some of the styles are an acquired taste.

➕ H6 ✉ Habsburgergasse 1A ☎ 534 33-0 🕐 Mon–Fri 9.30–6, Thu 9.30–8, Sat 9.30–5 🚇 U1, U3 to Stephansplatz

ROSENTHAL

The name needs no introduction for lovers of German-made china and glass.

➕ H6 ✉ Kärntner Strasse 16 ☎ 512 3994 🕐 Mon–Fri 9.15–6, Sat 9.15–5 🚇 U1, U3 to Stephansplatz

WOKA

If you're looking for something with the flavour of the Wiener Werkstätte to take home, a reproduction lamp from this high quality workshop—in business since 1978—may be the answer. Great style.

➕ H6 ✉ Singerstrasse 16 ☎ 513 2912 🕐 Mon–Fri 10–6, Sat 10–5 🚇 U1, U3 to Stephansplatz

Clothing

ADONIS
Young and fashionable leisurewear for men.
✚ H6 ✉ Kohlmarkt 11 ☎ 533 7035 🕐 Mon–Fri 9–6, Sat 9.30–5 🚇 U1, U3 to Stephansplatz

ALEXANDER
Expensive, stylish, international sportswear and other clothing for both sexes.
✚ H6 ✉ Rauhensteingasse 10 (between Himmelpfortgasse and Weihburggasse) ☎ 512 3946 🕐 Mon–Fri 9.30–6, Thu 9.30–8, Sat 9.15–5 🚇 U1, U3 to Stephansplatz

CASETTA-PAJOR
Good women's suits, plus a large selection of accessories.
✚ J6 ✉ Landstrasser Hauptstrasse 1B ☎ 713 5118 🕐 Mon–Fri 9–6, Sat 9–5 🚇 U3 to Wien Mitte/Landstrasse Hauptstrasse

CHANEL
The famous name.
✚ H6 ✉ Kohlmarkt 5 ☎ 536 18 🕐 Mon–Fri 9.30–6, Thu 9.30–8, Sat 10–5 🚇 U1, U3 to Stephansplatz

LODEN-PLANKL
The famous loden coats, which are well set off by a Tyrolean hat, are made with a technique using pressed felt. They are very stylish and warm and not so folkish that you cannot wear them outside Austria. But they do not come cheap.
✚ G6 ✉ Michaelerplatz 6 ☎ 533 8032 🕐 Mon–Fri 9.30–6, Sat 9.30–4 🚇 U3 to Herrengasse, 2A to Michaelerplatz

MODUS VIVENDI
Wide selection of quality knitwear for the whole family, both made-to-measure and off the peg.
✚ F7 ✉ Schadekgasse 4 ☎ 587 2823 🕐 Mon–Sat 9.30–5.30 🚇 U3 to Neubaugasse

PEEK & CLOPPENBURG
Good selection of men's clothing in this well-known store. Just the place for an emergency purchase of a suit or shirt.
✚ G7 ✉ Mariahilferstrasse 26–30 ☎ 525 61 🕐 Mon–Fri 9.30–7, Sat 9–5 🚇 U3 to Neubaugasse

RESI HAMMERER
Here you'll find *Trachtenmode* as well as haute couture. The owner skied on the Austrian national team.
✚ H6 ✉ Kärntner Strasse 29–31 ☎ 512 6952 🕐 Mon–Fri 9.30–6, Thu 9.30–8, Sat 9.30–5 🚇 U1, U3 to Stephansplatz

TOSTMANN TRACHTEN
The place to go for a gift with a *Tracht* look. Departments for men, women and children.
✚ G5 ✉ Schottengasse 3A (Melkerhof) ☎ 533 5331 🕐 Mon–Fri 9–6.30, Sat 9–5 🚇 U2 to Schottentor

TUREK
The main store of 13 with a big selection of designer label casual wear, including Diesel, Fornatina, G-Star and Levi.
✚ F7 ✉ Mariahilferstrasse 24 ☎ 523 1756 🕐 Mon–Fri 9.30–7, Sat 9.30–5 🚇 U3 to Neubaugasse

TRACHTENMODE
The basis of traditional Austrian dress is peasant and hunting costume. Women wear dirndls–dresses with full skirts and lace blouses that have a tight, revealing bodice –perhaps topped by a stylishly cut velvet jacket. Men wear green cloth jackets with braided cuffs and lapels, sometimes with buttons made from antlers. With its rural origins, and its rather showy Austrianness, *Trachtenmode* has definite right-wing associations. Still, it remains the uniform of the bourgeoisie and to some extent the nobility as well.

Shoes, Leather & Lingerie

COSTLY LEATHER

Fashion items such as leather goods are expensive in Vienna. The best selections and prices are found at chain stores like Humanic, in the vast shopping mall on the southern outskirts of the city (✉ Shopping City Süd, Vösendorf 🚌 Ikea bus from the Oper).

ANTONELLA

A large selection of shoes crammed into a small space.
🟥 H6 ✉ Führichgasse 4 ☎ 512 4173 🕐 Mon–Fri 9.30–6, Sat 9.30–5 🚇 U1, U3 to Stephansplatz

BALLY

One of several branches in Vienna of the first-rate shoe shop.
🟥 H6 ✉ Kärntner Strasse 9 ☎ 512 1461 🕐 Mon–Fri 9–6, Thu 9–8, Sat 9–5 🚇 U1, U3 to Stephansplatz

BOUTIQUE ANASTASIA

Handbags and all sorts of leather accessories for the fashion conscious.
🟥 H6 ✉ Spiegelgasse 4 ☎ 512 0240 🕐 Mon–Fri 9.30–6, Sat 9.30–5 🚇 U1, U3 to Stephansplatz

DERBY-HANDSCHUHE

Devoted entirely to gloves. The fact that this store remains in business may have something to do with Viennese winters.
🟥 H6 ✉ Plankengasse 5 ☎ 512 5703 🕐 Tue–Fri 10–6, Sat 10–noon 🚇 U1, U3 to Stephansplatz

GEA

Shoes in a laid-back style. A local speciality is the Waldviertler ankle boot.
🟥 H6 ✉ Himmelpfortgasse 26 ☎ 512 1967 🕐 Mon–Fri 10–6, Sat 10–5 🚇 U1, U3 to Stephansplatz

HUMANIC

Famous throughout the country for its surreal TV advertisements, this large chain offers a wide range of shoes at slightly less daunting prices than those of smaller shops.
🟥 H6 ✉ Kärntner Strasse 51 ☎ 512 5892 🕐 Mon–Fri 9.30–6, Sat 9.30–5 🚇 U1, U3 to Stephansplatz

PALMERS

Austria's most exotic lingerie comes from this chain, which is famous for its high-profile billboard advertising. The reasonable prices are very welcoming.
🟥 H6 ✉ Graben 14 ☎ 532 4058 🕐 Mon–Fri 9–6.30, Sat 9–5 🚇 U1, U3 to Stephansplatz

ROBERT HORN

A cult shop offering fine leather briefcases, handbags, wallets and lots more for the chic man or woman about town.
🟥 H6 ✉ Bräunerstrasse 7 ☎ 512 2507 🕐 Mon–Fri 10–1, 2–6, Sat 10–5 🚇 U1, U3 to Stephansplatz

SZÁSZI HÜTE

A traditional hatmakers—one of a dying bred of shop. Attentive personal service.
🟥 G7 ✉ Manahilferstrabe 4 (entrance at No. 6) ☎ 522 5652 🕐 Mon–Fri 9.30–6, Sat 9.30–5 🚇 U2 to Babenbergerstrabe

WOLFORD

Having been in business for over 50 years, this respected company's chic clothes still manages to retain a worldwide reputation.
🟥 H6 ✉ 1 Gonzagagasse 11 ☎ 535 9900 🕐 Mon–Fri 9–6, Sat 10–5 🚇 U2, U4 to Shottenring

Books & Music

ARCADIA OPERA SHOP

The shop for serious
opera buffs, staffed
by enthusiasts. Next to
the opera.
🕇 H7 ✉ Kärntner Strasse 40
☎ 513 9568 🕔 Mon–Fri
9.30–6, Sat 9.30–5 🚇 U1, U2,
U4 to Oper

BRITISH BOOKSHOP

An institution in Vienna.
Large selection of books
in English, plenty of
Austriaca and stacks of
novels and history
books. Good summer
sales bargains. Also at
Mariahilferstrabe 4.
🕇 H6 ✉ Weihburggasse 24–6
☎ 512 1945 🕔 Mon–Fri 9–6,
Sat 9–5 🚋 Trams 1, 2 to
Weihburggasse

EMI AUSTRIA

Solid selection in all
departments; especially
strong on opera and
classical music.
🕇 H6 ✉ Kärntner Strasse 30
☎ 512 3675-0 🕔 Mon–Fri
9.30–6, Sat 9.30–5 🚇 U1, U2,
U4 🚋 Trams 1, 2 to
Oper/Karlsplatz

FRICK

Primarily literature,
with a small English
department. Paperbacks
and children's books are
strong points.
🕇 H6 ✉ Graben 27 ☎ 533
9914 🕔 Mon–Fri 9–6, Sat 9–5
🚇 U1, U3 to Stephansplatz

GALERIE WOLFRUM

The specialist shop for
art books, with an
excellent print
department. Very
knowledgeable staff.
🕇 H6 ✉ Augustinerstrasse 10
☎ 512 5398 🕔 Mon–Fri
9.15–6, Sat 9.15–5 🚇 U1, U2,
U4 to Oper

GEORG PRACHNER

The best shop for books
on architecture and the
decorative arts, with
material on Viennese art
and architecture.
🕇 H6 ✉ Kärntner Strasse 30
☎ 512 8549-0 🕔 Mon–Fri
9.30–6, Sat 9.30–5 🚇 U1, U2,
U4 to Oper

GRAMOLA

For opera lovers and
those in search of
historic performances
on CD.
🕇 H6 ✉ Graben 16 ☎ 533
5034 🕔 Mon–Fri 9.30–6, Sat
9.30–5 🚇 U1, U3 to
Stephansplatz

HINTERMAYER BÜCHERMARKT

Lots of bargains at this
bookshop with some
English titles.
🕇 G6 ✉ Herrengasse 5
☎ 533 7928 🕔 Daily 10–6
🚇 U3 to Herrengasse
Also at:
🕇 F7 ✉ Neubaugasse 29
☎ 523 0225 🚇 U3 to
Neubaugasse

ROCK-SHOP

A paradise for vinyl
collectors. Oldies from
the 1950s to the 1970s,
mostly singles hits.
🕇 J5 ✉ Taborstrasse 70
☎ 216 8993 🕔 Mon–Fri 9–6,
Sat 9–5 🚋 Tram N from
Schwedenplatz to Heinestrasse

SHAKESPEARE & CO

Plenty of trendy books
from America. The local
owners know their stuff.
Contemporary and
classic literature are
well stocked.
🕇 H6 ✉ Sterngasse 2
☎ 535 5053 🕔 Mon–Wed, Fri
9–7, Thu 9–8, Sat 9–5 🚇 U1,
U4 to Schwedenplatz

BOOK TRADE

Austria imposes Value Added
Tax (*Mehrwertsteuer*) on
books, which makes foreign
paperbacks very expensive.
Expect prices at least 50 per
cent above what you'd pay for
a book in your own home
town, and even more for
newspapers. Austria's own
publishing industry suffers
from the small size of the local
market, and from the
dominance of big German
firms, ever ready to scoop up
promising Austrian authors for
their lists.

That Special Present

VIENNESE GOOD TASTE

Part of the legacy of the Biedermeier and Jugendstil eras in Vienna is a talent for making simple things pleasing. This is reflected in the city's large choice of gifts, small artefacts and clever design ideas, as well as in the skill with which they are packaged and presented. Sometimes, the style promises more than the substance delivers (this is what the Viennese call a *Schmäh*). At its best, however, Viennese design achieves a seductive combination of beauty and practicality.

ENGEL & HOFF

This unusual shop sells the last cry in stylish handbags made from glass fibre, and mostly in dazzling colours.
🔢 H6 ✉ Bäckerstrasse 7 ☎ 513 1184 🕔 Mon 1–6, Tue–Fri 10.30–6 🚇 U1, U3 to Stephamsdom

HAAS & HAAS

A stylish gift shop that stocks candles, dried flowers and delicate ornaments. Café on the premises.
🔢 H6 ✉ Stephansplatz 4 ☎ 512 9770 🕔 Mon–Fri 9–7.30, Sat 9–5 🚇 U1, U3 to Stephansplatz

KÖCHERT

Jewellers to the royal and imperial court since 1814, this reputable shop is elegant and restrained.
🔢 H6 ✉ Neuer Markt 15 ☎ 512 5828 🕔 Mon–Fri 9–6, Sat 9–5 🚇 U1, U3 to Stephansplatz

KULT O TREND

A small shop with an interesting selection of jewellery, including many alternative designs.
🔢 G6 ✉ Teinfaltstrabe 3 ☎ 532 1476 🕔 Mon–Fri 9.30–6, Sat 9.30–5 🚋 Trams 1, 2 to Burgheater

MANNER FABRIKSVERKAUF

Locally produced Neopolitan wafers sold in attractive gift packs, plus Ildefonso chocolates.
🔢 D5 ✉ Wilheminestrasse 6 ☎ 488 22 🕔 Mon–Thu 9–5, Fri 9–2 🚋 Tram 44 from Schottentor

MARIA STRANSKY

Petit-point reticules, purses and spectacle cases.
🔢 G6 ✉ Burgpassage 2, Hofburg ☎ 533 6098 🕔 Mon–Fri 9–6, Sat 9–5 🚇 U3 to Herrengasse 🚌 Hopper 2A to Michaelerplatz

MATERNS NATURBLUMENSALON

Beautiful artificial-flower posies, plus a good selection of plants and cut flowers.
🔢 G6 ✉ Herrengasse 10 ☎ 533 5460 🕔 Mon–Fri 8–6, Sat 8–5 🚇 U3 to Herrengasse

METZGER

Honey cake and candles.
🔢 H6 ✉ Stephansplatz 7 ☎ 512 3433 🕔 Mon–Fri 9–6, Sat 9–5 🚇 U1, U3 to Stephansplatz

ÖSTERREICHISCHE WERKSTÄTTEN

The wide range of glass ornaments and gifts, with Secessionist (► 36) designs and attractive enamel make lovely gifts, but be prepared for the aggressive sales people.
🔢 H6 ✉ Kärntner Strasse 6 ☎ 512 2418 🕔 Mon–Fri 9.15–6, Sat 9.15–5 🚇 U1, U3 to Stephansplatz

SPITTELBERG MARKET

Local handicrafts are sold at Spittleberg Market on Saturdays from April to November, and daily just before Christmas.
🔢 G7 ✉ Spittelberggasse 🕔 About 10am–dusk 🚋 Tram 49 from Dr-Karl-Renner-Ring to Stiftgasse

Food & Drink

ANKER

Fresh bread, excellent cakes and pastries. There are central branches in many U-Bahn stations, on Schwedenplatz, Hoher Market and other destinations. Branches at train termini have longer hours and Sunday opening. Many have a counter for a snack or even *Kaiserfrühstuck* (Emperor's breakfast).
🕓 Mon–Fri 7.30–6, Sat 8–5

DEMMERS TEEHAUS

The genuine Chinese or Indian teas available here will please those who are dispirited by the tea bag and hot water that is sold as 'tea' in cafés. There is a tea salon upstairs. Several branches.
➕ G5 ✉ Mölker Bastei 5
☎ 533 5995 🕓 Mon–Wed, Fri 9–6.30, Thu 9–8, Sat 9–5
🚇 U2 to Schottentor
🚋 Trams 1, 2

JULIUS MEINL AM GRABEN

A fine grocer with a superb delicatessen counter and a very expensive restaurant (► 64) with different hours from the shop.
➕ H6 ✉ Graben 19
☎ 532 3334 🕓 Mon–Fri 8.30–7, Sat 8–5 🚇 U1, U3 to Stephansplatz

NATURKOST ST. JOSEF

The organic food range here includes items such as South American quinoa.
➕ F7 ✉ Zollergasse 26
☎ 526 6818 🕓 Mon–Fri 8–6.30, Thu 8–8, Sat 8–5
🚇 U3 to Neubaugasse

NATURPRODUKTE WALLNER

If you like a sense of well-being, you will appreciate the whole and organic foods, alternative beauty therapies and baby food sold here. There are several branches throughout the city.
➕ G8 ✉ Wiedner Hauptstrasse 66 ☎ 586 0671
🕓 Mon–Fri 9–6, Sat 9–5
🚋 Trams 62, 65

SCHÖNBICHLER

The Viennese come here to buy their English marmalade, tea, Scotch whisky and Christmas pudding.
➕ H6 ✉ Wollzeile 4
☎ 512 1868 🕓 Mon–Fri 8.30–6, Sat 8.30–5 🚇 U1, U3 to Stephansplatz

VINOTHEK ST. URBAH–KELLEREI

You will find a good selection of wines here, and many at reasonable prices.
➕ H6 ✉ Am Hof 11
☎ 532 28-35 🕓 Mon–Fri 9.30–6, Sat 9.30–5 🚇 U1, U3 to Stephansplatz

VINOTHEK VINISSIMO

Some 400 different Austrian wines can be bought here. Since the 1980s, when it was found that glycol had been added to wines to make them sweeter, Austrian wine has had the strictest product regulations in Europe and its quality is often overlooked.
➕ G7 ✉ Windmühlgasse 20
☎ 586 4888 🕓 Mon–Fri 10–6, Sat 10–5 🚇 U2 to Babenberger Strabe

---

WHERE TO BUY YOUR SACHERTORTE

The origin of Sachertorte is so hotly disputed that there have been lawsuits between rival claimants. Those who want authenticity buy at Sacher (✉ Philharmonikerstrasse 4 ☎ 514 56-853 🕓 Mon–Sat 9am–11pm, Sun 3pm–6pm. They will also mail). The Hotel Imperial (► 86) also offers (to a different recipe) an Imperial Torte. On the other hand, you can buy a perfectly acceptable Sachertorte for much less at any branch of Aida (► 69).

Sports

SPORTING CULTURE

The Viennese are not great sportsmen; those who are, flee to the mountains for skiing (Semmering and the Annaberg in Lower Austria are a couple of hours away). However, the Socialist-run Vienna of the 1920s *Rotes Wien* made conspicuous efforts to develop an *Arbeiterkultur* (workers' culture) in contradistinction to middle-class pursuits. This included physical culture, and many of the city's pools date from this period. An example of this is Amalienbad (✉ Reumannplatz 23 ☎ 607 4747 ◷ Tue–Sun 7.30–8), an architecturally intriguing pool and building with marvellous art deco designs.

WIENER STADTHALLE (HALLE C)

Major municipal sports complex with an ice rink and Olympic-sized swimming pool.
✚ E7 ✉ Vogelweidplatz 14 ☎ 981 000 ◷ Mon–Fri 1.30–5, Sat–Sun, hols 8–noon, 1–5 Ⓤ U6 🚋 Tram 49 to Burggasse/Stadthalle/Urban-Loritz-Platz

BOWLING

BRUNSWICK BOWLING
✚ D4 ✉ Schumanngasse 107 ☎ 486 4361 🚋 Tram 42 from Schottentor to Hildebrandgasse

BOWLINGHALLE PRATER
✚ K6 ✉ Prater Hauptallee 124 ☎ 728 0709 🚋 Tram N from Schwedenplatz to last stop

CYCLING

PEDAL POWER
Delivery, pick-up and map with self-guided tour suggestions. Group tours of the city.
✚ J5 ✉ Ausstellungsstrasse 3 ☎ 729 7234 Ⓤ U1 to Praterstern 🚋 Tram 0

GOLF

CITY & COUNTRY GOLF CLUB AM WIENERBERG
In the southern suburbs of Vienna.
✚ Off map at G10 ✉ Gutheil Schoder-Gasse 9 ☎ 661 23 🚌 Bus 16A to Gutheil Schoder-Gasse

THE VIENNA GOLF CLUB
More demanding socially than in terms of sporting skills.
✚ N8 ✉ Rennbahnstrasse 65A, Freudenau ☎ 728 9564-0; fax 728 5379 ◷ 7.30am–dusk 🚌 Bus 77A from Rennweg/Ungargasse

HORSE RACING

Racing attracts people from all classes. Flat races, hurdling and trotting races are held at Freudenau and Krieau from spring to autumn.
✚ N8 ✉ Rennbahnstrasse 65, Freudenau ☎ 728 9535; fax 728 95 17 🚌 Bus 77A from Rennweg/Ungargasse

ICE SKATING

WIENER EISLAUFVEREIN
Open-air rink.
✚ H7 ✉ Lothringerstrasse 22 ☎ 713 6353 ◷ Oct–Mar Sat–Mon 9–8, Tue, Thu, Fri 9–9, Wed 9–10 Ⓤ U4 to Stadtpark

WATERSPORTS

STRANDBAD ALTE DONAU
River swimming in the 'old' arm of the Danube, which is now bypasssed.
✚ H7 ✉ Arbeiterstrandbadstrasse 91 ☎ 263 6538 ◷ Sep–Mar Mon–Tue, Thu–Sat 9am–9pm, Wed 9am–10pm, Sun, hols 9am–8pm 🚋 Trams D, 71

FRITZ EPPEL
Boats for rental.
✚ L3 ✉ Wagramer Strasse 48A ☎ 263 3530 Ⓤ U1 to Alte Donau

SEEPFERDCHEN
Rents out boats and also has a restaurant.
✚ K1 ✉ An der Oberen Alten Donau 20 ☎ 272 1664 Ⓤ U6 to Floridsdorf

Theatre

AKADEMIETHEATER
Sister-theatre to the Burgtheater, the superb Akademietheater has a generally, but not exclusively, modern repertoire of serious plays and a number of translated works. Often overlooked in favour of the more famous Burgtheater, the Viennese like it for its inimate atmosphere.
🚩 H7 ✉ Lisztstrasse 1
☎ 514 44-4140 🚇 U4 to Stadtpark

BURGTHEATER
If you speak German, try to include a visit. Otherwise, join a tour to see the Gustav and Ernst Klimt frescoes (➤ 33).
🚩 G6 ✉ Dr-Karl-Lueger-Ring 2 ☎ 51 444 🚋 Trams 1, 2 to Burgtheater, Rathaus

INTERNATIONAL THEATRE
A small theatre known for good entertainment. It sometimes has a surprise hit on its hands —for example, that most challenging of dramas, *The Mousetrap*, proved as popular in Vienna as in London.
🚩 G5 ✉ Porzellangasse 8
☎ 319 6272 🚋 Tram D to Schlickgasse

KAMMERSPIELE
This subsidiary stage of the Theater in der Josefstadt puts on plays, lighter fare—often comedies and farces, not infrequently recycled London West End hits.
🚩 H6 ✉ Rotenturmstrasse 20
☎ 427 00 🚇 U1, U4 to Schwedenplatz

ODEON
Former home to the Serapiom mime group, the Odeon now goes in for avant-garde or folkeristic/ethnic music and dance shows.
🚩 H5 ✉ Taborstrasse 10
☎ 216 5127 🚋 Tram N from Schwedenplaatz to Karmehterplatz

THEATER IN DER JOSEFSTADT
Once the powerhouse of the famous player-director, Max Reinhardt, who co-founded the Salzburg Festival, this theatre, built in 1788, was remodelled in neo-Classical style by Joseph Kornhäusel in the 1820s and is especially close to Viennese hearts. Particularly striking are the ornate chandeliers. Outside, plaques honour Reinhardt and Hugo von Hofmannsthal, the latter a leading 20th-century dramatist and the librettist for several operas by Richard Strauss. Jugendstil drama is still played and promoted here constantly.
🚩 F6 ✉ Josefstädterstrasse 26 ☎ 427 00 🚋 Tram J

VIENNA'S ENGLISH THEATRE
This theatre presents solid productions of mainstream drama from England and America, given a bit of pep by visiting stars. Thoroughly worthy and occasionally heights-scaling.
🚩 F6 ✉ Josefsgasse 12
☎ 402 1260 🚇 U2 to Lerchenfelderstrasse

OUTRAGE AND EXCELLENCE

From 1986 until 1999, the Burgtheater–the flagship of Austrian drama–was under the direction of Claus Peymann, a German whose radical productions and prejudiced political statements were inimical to the Austrian establishment. Resignations ensued when he imported 80 German actors, and although his contract was renewed, his application for Austrian citizenship was turned down. He was known for his challenging and imaginative productions of contemporary drama and the classics, and for nurturing the talent of Thomas Bernhard, Austria's greatest contemporary writer. His successor, after a successful spell at the Volkstheater, has adopted a lower profile.

Opera, Operetta & Musicals

THE MUSICAL TRADITION

Music has been part of the city's culture from earliest times. In the mid-18th century Haydn and then Mozart began to displace the long-dominant Italians in public esteem. The 19th century was also rich in musical talent, some of it imported (Beethoven, Brahms) but much home-grown (Schubert, Bruckner, Hugo Wolf, Strauss father and son and Mahler). Later, Arnold Schönberg pioneered the 12-tone system, while his erstwhile-pupils, such as Alban Berg and Anton von Webern, made the 'Second Viennese School' world famous.

ETABLISSEMENT RONACHER

This marvellous old variety theatre, with an exotic late 19th-century interior, has reopened after a long period of darkness. Its programme remains unpredictable—from a spectacular *à la* André Heller to a Broadway musical.
➕ H6 ✉ Seilerstätte 9
☎ 514 110 Ⓜ U1, U3 to Stephansplatz

RAIMUND THEATER

Named for the great comedian and dramatist, Ferdinand Raimund (1790–1836), the theatre stages operettas and musicals. Built in 1893, it has an alarmingly precipitous stacking of gallery seats.
➕ E8 ✉ Wallgasse 18–20
☎ 599 77 Ⓜ U3 to Westbahnhof

SCHÖNBRUNNER SCHLOSSTHEATER

In the rococo theatre where Haydn and Mozart once conducted, the Wiener Kammeroper performs lighter opera and operettas throughout July and August.
➕ C8 ✉ Schloss Schönbrunn (main entrance) ☎ 711 55-158
Ⓜ U4 to Schönbrunn

STAATSOPER

The State Opera reopened in 1955 with a performance of Beethoven's *Fidelio*; appropriately enough, the last performance before it closed in 1944 was Wagner's *Götterdämmerung* (*Twilight of the Gods*).

It remains one of the world's top opera stages.
➕ H7 ✉ Opernring 2
☎ 51 444 Ⓜ U1, U2, U4 to Oper

THEATER AN DER WIEN

Original owner Emanuel Schikaneder, librettist for Mozart's *Magic Flute*, complained that he had written 'such a good piece, but Mozart ruined it all with his music'. A shrewd impresario, Schikaneder would have appreciated the theatre's success with such musicals as *Cats*, which ran for 11 years.
➕ G7 ✉ Linke Wienzeile 6
☎ 588 300 Ⓜ U1, U2, U4 to Karlsplatz

VOLKSOPER

Even though it's in the uncongenial area of the Gürtel (Ring Road), the Volksoper is no poor relation of the Staatsoper. It may not have the budget to engage prima donnas, but its Mozart performances are solid and often inspired. The tickets cost less, too.
➕ F4 ✉ Währinger Strasse 78
☎ 51 444 Ⓜ U6 to Volksoper
🚋 Trams 40, 41 42

WIENER KAMMEROPER

A seed-bed for talent for the Volksoper, Staatsoper or abroad. The programme includes many lesser-known operas, sometimes abridged. Small, intimate space.
➕ H6 ✉ Fleischmarkt 24
☎ 512 0100-77 Ⓜ U1, U4 to Schwedenplatz

Orchestral Music

ARNOLD SCHÖNBERG CENTER
Not only a concert hall, but also an archive library and exhibition hall dedicated to the founder of Vienna modernism.

🚋 H7 ✉ Schwarzenbergplatz 6 ☎ 712 1888 🚊 Trams 1, 2 to Schwarzenbergplatz

BÖSENDORFER SAAL
A venue for chamber-music concerts named after Vienna's most celebrated dynasty of piano-makers.

🚋 H8 ✉ Graf-Starhemberg-Gasse 14 ☎ 504 6651 🚇 U1 to Taubstummengasse 🚊 Trams 62, 65

KONZERTHAUS
Opened in 1913, the building contains three concert halls: the Grosser Saal, for orchestral performances; and the Mozartsaal and the Schubertsaal for chamber music, modern music and Lieder evenings. In summer there are twice-weekly selections of Mozart's music, played by musicians dressed in period costume.

🚋 H7 ✉ Lothringerstrasse 20 ☎ 242 002 🚇 U4 to Stadtpark

KURSALON
The Strauss summer festival takes place inside the Kursalon in the Stadtpark (originally a place where bourgeois park visitors could sample the health-giving spa water).

🚋 H7 ✉ Johannesgasse 33 ☎ 513 2477 🚇 U4 to Stadtpark

MUSIKVEREIN
The Musikverein is famous for its superb acoustics and sumptuous gilded interior (caryatids to the right and left of you). The Wiener Philharmoniker's New Year's Day Concert is broadcast from here and the orchestra's Sunday concerts are a Viennese institution. During the week there are orchestral concerts in the Great Hall, and chamber music in the Brahmssaal.

🚋 H7 ✉ Bösendorferstrasse 12 ☎ 505 8190 🚇 U1, U2, U4 to Karlsplatz

PALACES
The city's summer music festival, Wiener Musik-Sommer, offers graceful chamber music in some lovely baroque palaces, among them Palffy, Auersperg and Schwarzenberg.

RADIO KULTURHAUS
The Radio Symphonie-orchester (and other ensembles) supplies varied classical music that is generally very good.

🚋 H8 ✉ Argentinierstrasse 30A ☎ 5017 0377 🚌 Bus 13A

URANIA
Max Fabiani's interesting late Jugendstil building, built between 1904 and 1912, on the Danube Canal has been recently restored. A multicultural peformance centre.

🚋 J6 ✉ Uraniastrasse 1 ☎ 712 6191-94 🚇 U1, U4 to Schwedenplatz

MUSICAL TASTE
The Musikverein—the concert hall for the Society of the Friends of Music—was founded in the 19th century. Mainstream Viennese taste is conservative: 'The popularity of Brahms', wrote one critic, 'is due largely to his music being exactly suited to Viennese tastes, not too hot and not too cold; it eschews excitement and seldom commits the unforgivable sin of being boring'. But there has always been a radical element. The greatest scandal in the Musikverein's history occurred in 1913 when pro- and anti-modernists began fighting at a Schönberg concert.

HANS DER MUSIK
Vienna's interactive sound museum is well worth a visit. The approach is practical and participatory, so visitors get to compose their own waltz, conduct, or even play instruments. A far cry from musty notes in glass cases and faded water-colours on walls. A good restaurant and café provides refreshment.

🚋 H6 ✉ Seilersträtte ☎ 30 516 48-0; www.hdm.at 🕐 Daily 10–10 🚊 Trams 1, 2, to Schwarzenbergplatz

83

Jazz & Nightspots

NIGHT MUSIC

You can now hear most types of jazz regularly in Vienna. In summer there is a jazz festival held partly in the hallowed Staatsoper (► 82), and there is an open-air festival on the Donau-Insel (Danube Island) in July. Performances generally start at 9pm but check the current *Wien Programm* (available at all Tourist Information Bureaux). The night scene has grown livelier and the Bermuda Dreieck (Bermuda Triangle, ► 24) is a magnet for gilded youth. You will find there idiosyncratic bars, trendy restaurants, discos, beer cellars, live music and cabaret.

ARENA

A music and arts centre that includes jazz in its avant-garde repertoire.
✚ L8 ✉ Baumgasse 80
☎ 798 8595 🕐 May–Sep daily from 2pm (4pm in winter)
🚇 U3 to Erdberg

CAFÉ CONCERTO

Jazz, blues, country and ethnic music at this colourful venue.
✚ E6 ✉ Lerchenfelder Gürtel 53 ☎ 406 4795 🕐 Tue–Sat 7pm–2am; events from 9pm
🚋 Tram 46 from Schottentor

JAZZLAND

Traditional jazz from some of the best bands in town in an ancient cellar under the Ruprechtskirche (► 53).
✚ H5 ✉ Franz-Josefs-Kai 29
☎ 533 2575 🕐 Mon–Sat 7pm–1am 🚇 U1, U4

NIGHTFLY'S CLUB

A cosy cellar bar where you'll hear golden oldies, from Glenn Miller to Frank Sinatra.
✚ H6 ✉ Dorotheergasse 14
☎ 512 9979 🕐 Winter–Spring Mon–Sat 8pm–3am. Summer Mon–Sat 6pm–3am
🚇 U1, U3 to Stephansplatz

PAVILLON IM VOLKSGARTEN

A favoured venue in an attractive setting, with an open-air dance floor.
✚ G6 ✉ Burgring 2 ☎ 532 0907 🕐 May–Sep daily 11am–2am 🚇 U3 🚋 Trams 1, 2 to Dr-Karl-Renner-Ring/Bellaria Strasse

ROTER ENGEL

'The Red Angel' exemplifies the best of the Bermuda Dreieck. It calls itself a *Wein und Liederbar* (wine and song bar) and serves drinkable wines with cheeses. It also has folk and rhythm and blues evenings.
✚ H6 ✉ Rabensteig 5
☎ 535 4105 🕐 Sun–Wed 4pm–2am, Thu–Sat 4pm–4am
🚇 U1, U4 🚋 Trams 1, 2 to Schwedenplatz

SZENE WIEN

Visiting rock bands and dance companies perform at this co-operative established by politically engaged musicians. Wear your leather jackets.
✚ Off map at L10
✉ Hauffgasse 26 ☎ 749 3341 🕐 Generally 8pm
🚋 Tram 71 to Kopalgasse from Schwarzenbergplatz

U4

An enduring and continually fashionable dance club with live music most nights. Next door is a luxurious bar.
✚ E9 ✉ Schönbrunner Strasse 222 ☎ 815 8307
🕐 10pm–5am 🚇 U4 to Meidlinger Hauptstrasse

VORSTADT

Look for an interesting mixture of jazz, ethnic music, and cabaret.
✚ E6 ✉ Herbststrasse 37
☎ 493 1788 🕐 Generally 8pm 🚌 Bus 48A from Dr-Karl-Renner-Ring to Kirchenstetterngasse

WUK

Arts centre with café and restaurant, and also performance art, dance and DJ nights.
✚ G5 ✉ Währinger Strasse 59 ☎ 408 7224 🕐 Times vary, phone for details 🚋 Trams 40, 41, 42 from Schottentor

Connoisseurs' Vienna

AMERICAN KÄRNTNER BAR (LOOS–BAR)

This famously tiny bar is a late-night watering hole designed by Modernist Adolf Loos.

🚇 H6 ✉ Kärntner Durchgang (off Kärntner Strasse 10) ☎ 512 3283 🕐 Summer daily 6pm–4am; rest of year Sun–Wed midnight–4am, Thu–Sat midnight–5am 🚇 U1, U3 to Stephansplatz

HARMER'S BAR

The head of the Upper Austrian Kapsreiter brewery opens his glorious valuted cellar just once a week. Enjoy.

🚇 D5 ✉ Ottakringer Strasse 120 ☎ 488 1624 🕐 Thu from 7pm 🚋 Tram J

KRAH KRAH

Some 55 different brands of beer, and hefty black-bread sandwiches.

🚇 H6 ✉ Rabensteig 8 ☎ 533 8193 🕐 Daily 11am–2am 🚇 U1, U4 to Schwedenplatz

LIECHTENSTEIN MUSEUM

A superbly renovated palace displays this noble family art collection. The slickest museum in town.

🚇 G4 ✉ Fürstengasse 1 ☎ 319 5767-0 🕐 Wed–Mon 9–8 🚋 Tram D to Bauernfeldplatz

LOBAU

Although topless bathing is unlikely to raise an eyebrow, nudity remains the province of enthusiasts for FKK (*Freikörperkultur*—naturism). The Lobau is a naturist area on the Neue Donau (Danube) southeast of the city.

🚇 Off map at N6 ✉ Neue Donau 🚇 U1 to Kaisermühlen, then Bus 91A to the Zum Roten Hiasl inn

NASCHMARKT

Vienna's gourmet market is a must to visit—sample its wares in the many small restaurants.

🚇 G7 ✉ Between the Linke and Rechte Wienzeile 🚇 U4 to Kettenbruckengasse

ÖSTERREICHISCHES FILMMUSEUM

The dedicated Austrian Film Museum has kept this shrine to the movies alive. Pay the low membership fee, then a modest entrance charge.

🚇 H6 ✉ Albertina-Augustinerstrasse 1 ☎ 533 7054-0 🕐 Programmes at entrance 🚇 U1, U2, U4 to Oper

SALZAMT

This designer restaurant continues to draw artists and cultural trendies. An added bonus is that the food is good, too.

🚇 H6 ✉ Ruprechtsplatz 1 ☎ 533 5332 🕐 Daily 5pm–1am 🚇 U1, U4 to Schwedenplatz

SCHAU SCHAU

Custom-made glasses by a master of the art: rims of acetate, buffalo-horn, metal and 18-karat gold moulded in styles from the classical to the decidedly outré. A shopping haunt of the 'promis' and 'glitterati' on the Viennese social scene.

🚇 H6 ✉ Rotenturmstrasse 11 ☎ 533 4584 🕐 Mon–Fri 8.30–6 🚇 U1, U4 to Schwedenplatz

WELL-KEPT SECRETS

Geheimtips–things that the initiates prefer to keep to themselves–are by definition inclined to be ephemeral. This page describes what might be called perennial *Geheimtips*–places that have established themselves as having something special to offer. They give a flavour of the Vienna beyond the superficial glitter it so willingly displays for tourists.

THE GAY AND LESBIAN SCENE

Look into the stylish Café Savoy (✉ Linke Wienzeile 36 ☎ 586 7348) with an opulent interior or the Café Berg (✉ Bergasse 8 ☎ 319 5720), a long established café adjacent to a bookshop (Löwenherz) with gay and feminist literature. More information on the gay and lesbian scene appears in the monthly publications that are available at most gay venues around the city.

Luxury Hotels

PRICES

Expect to pay the following prices per night for a double room with breakfast:

€€€ over €218
€€ €109–218
€ €65–109

SACHER HOTEL

Sacher was once famous for its *chambres séparées,* where aristocrats 'entertained' dancers. It was founded in 1876 by the son of the cook to Prince Metternich and carried on by his formidable, cigar-smoking widow, Anna, who ruled her hotel and guests with an iron rod. Just after World War I, Anna single-handedly held off a mob of rioting workers, but she also had a strong social conscience and fed the poor from the kitchen.

BRISTOL (€€€)

Old-fashioned elegance on the Ringstrasse. Its restaurant, Korso bei der Oper (➤ 64), is one of the best in Vienna. 140 rooms.
➕ H7 ✉ Kärntner Ring 1 ☎ 515 16-0; fax 515 16-550; www.westin.com/bristol Ⓜ U1, U2, U4 to Oper

IM PALAIS SCHWARZENBERG (€€€)

In the Fischer von Erlachs' palace (➤ 54), this is probably the most elegant address in the city. Lovely restaurant (➤ 64). 44 rooms.
➕ H7 ✉ Schwarzenbergplatz 9 ☎ 798 4515; fax 798 4714; www.palais-schwarzenberg.com 🚊 Tram D to Prinz EugenStrasse

IMPERIAL (€€€)

This former palace on the Ringstrasse is also the official State Hotel where visiting dignitaries stay. Hitler lodged here just after the *Anschluss.* 138 rooms.
➕ H7 ✉ Kärntner Ring 16 ☎ 501 10-0; fax 501 10-410; www.luxurycollection.com/imperial Ⓜ U1, U2, U4 to Karlsplatz 🚊 Trams 1, 2 to Schwarzenbergplatz

INTERCONTINENTAL WIEN (€€€)

You'll find a bit more than chain-hotel efficiency here. The Vier Jahreszeiten restaurant is superb. 453 rooms.
➕ H7 ✉ Johannesgasse 28 ☎ 711 22-0; fax 713 4489; www.vienna.intercontinental.com Ⓜ U4 to Stadtpark

MARRIOTT VIENNA (€€€)

The post-modern architecture harmonizes well with its surroundings. Excellent business facilities and 313 rooms.
➕ H6 ✉ Parkring 12A ☎ 515 18-0; fax 515 18-6736; www.marriott.com/vieat Ⓜ U3 to Stubentor

PLAZA–HILTON WIEN (€€€)

An attractive hotel built in neo-Secessionist style with all modern comforts and 218 rooms.
➕ G5 ✉ Schottenring 11 ☎ 313 90-0; fax 313 90-22009; www.hilton.com Ⓜ U2 🚊 Trams 1, 2 to Schottenring

RADISSON SAS-PALAIS HOTEL (€€€)

Distinguished hotel famous for solid service and its excellent restaurant, La Siècle im Ersten. 247 rooms
➕ H6 ✉ Palais Heckel von Donnersmarck, Weihburggasse 32, Parkring 16 ☎ 515 17-0; fax 512 2216; www.radissonsas.com Ⓜ U3 to Stubentor

RENAISSANCE WEIN (€€€)

This luxury hotels is slightly impersonal but a plus is the indoor pool. Near the Meidling Hauptstrasse. 309 rooms.
➕ E9 ✉ Ullmannstrasse 71 ☎ 891 02-0; fax 891 02-300; www.renaissancehotels.com/viehw Ⓜ U4 to Meidling Hauptstrasse

SACHER (€€€)

The 108 rooms are not generous, but Sacher is Vienna's most celebrated hotel—and not only because of the cake.
➕ H6 ✉ Philharmonikerstrasse 4 ☎ 514 56-0; fax 514 56-810; www.sacher.com Ⓜ U1, U2, U4 to Oper

Hotels of Local Character

ALTSTADT VIENNA (€€)
Small but refined (37 rooms), the beautifully furnished upper floors of this 18th-century house are an informal, friendly breakfast-only hotel.
✚ F7 ✉ Kirchengasse 41
☎ 526 3399-0; fax 523 4901; www.altstadt.at 🚌 Bus 48A from Dr-Karl-Renner-Ring

ALTWIENERHOF (€€)
This one is for food lovers; bargain rates, in view of the fine restaurant. The 26 rooms have an opulent belle-époque look.
✚ E8 ✉ Herklotzgasse 6
☎ 892 6000; fax 892 6000-8; www.altwienerhof.at 🚇 U3, U6 to Westbahnhof

DAS TRIEST (€€€)
Terence Conran meets Wiener Modern. This post-modern conversion of an old coaching inn has an excellent restaurant. 72 rooms.
✚ G7 ✉ Wiedner Hauptstrasse 12 ☎ 58 918; www.dastriest.at 🚋 Trams 62, 65 to first stop on Wiedner Hauptstrasse

GARTENHOTEL GLANZING (€€)
A peaceful 1920s cube-like villa softened by climbing vines. Far from the centre. 14 rooms
✚ D2 ✉ Glanzinggasse 23
☎ 470 4272; fax 470 4272-14; www.gartenhotel-glanzing.at 🚌 Bus 35A to Krottenbachstrasse

HOTEL AM SCHUBERTRING (€€)
Adolf Loos-style bar and 39 pleasant rooms. Much patronized by visiting musicians. No restaurant.
✚ H7 ✉ Schubertring 11
☎ 717 02-0; fax 713 9966; www.schubertring.at 🚋 Trams 1, 2 to Schwarzenbergplatz

HOTEL RÖMISCHER KAISER (€€)
A modest baroque palace in the old city. Delightful—all crimson fabrics and chandeliers. No restaurant. 24 rooms.
✚ H6 ✉ Annagasse 16
☎ 512 7751-0; fax 512 7751-13; www.hotel-romischer-kaiser.at 🚇 U1, U3 to Stephansplatz

KAISERIN ELISABETH (€€)
This 63-room hotel has a whiff of imperial nostalgia; popular with regular Vienna visitors. A good choice if you want to be immersed in the Altstadt atmosphere.
✚ H6 ✉ Weinburggasse 3
☎ 515 26-0; fax 515 26-7; www.kaiserinelisabeth.at 🚇 U1, U3 to Stephansplatz

KÖNIG VON UNGARN (€€)
An 18th-century building next to the Figarohaus. Rooms ring an airy, glassed-in courtyard. Prestigious restaurant. 33 rooms.
✚ H6 ✉ Schulerstrasse 10
☎ 515 84-0; fax 515 84-8; www.kvu.at 🚇 U1, U3 to Stephansplatz

MERCURE GRAND HOTEL BIEDERMEIER WIEN (€€)
This period townhouse, with Biedermeier furniture is an oasis of tranquillity. 203 rooms.
✚ J7 ✉ Landstrasser Hauptstrasse 28, Ungargasse 13 ☎ 716 71-0; fax 716 71-503; www.accor.com 🚇 U3, U4 to Wien Mitte, Landstrasser Hauptstrasse

CHARM AND COMFORT

The formula of most luxury hotels does not differ much from country to country. More unusual is the individual environment that not only bears the stamp of the owner's persona but exploits the particular characteristics of the local culture. In Vienna such hostelries often occupy a baroque or Biedermeier building, so that the hotel combines all the charm of the original with all the comforts of modernity.

Mid-Range & Budget Accommodation

IN SEARCH OF GOOD VALUE

Other than youth hostels, there is very little inexpensive accommodation in Vienna. At the same time, there are still hotels with less than friendly service that nevertheless charge the (high) going rate. The Viennese themselves remark darkly that the world of hotels is under the eternal sway of the mythical 'King Nepp' (from *neppen*, meaning to overcharge). Few escape his tyrannous rule, but there are several (some of which are listed here) that do try hard to offer value for money and friendly service.

HOTEL JÄGER (€€)

A welcoming 18-room hotel in a large villa with nice garden. Ideal for families but far from the city centre.
➕ C4 ✉ Hernalser Hauptstrasse 187 ☎ 486 6620; fax 486 6620-8; www. hoteljaeger.at 🚊 Tram 43 from Schottentor or Schnellbahn to Hernals

HOTEL-PENSION ARENBERG (€€)

A Best Western hotel; unpretentious and friendly with 22 rooms.
➕ J6 ✉ Stubenring 2 ☎ 512 5291; fax 513 9356; www.arenberg.at 🚊 Trams 1, 2 to Stubenring

HOTEL-PENSION MUSEUM (€€)

Art lovers and academics are attracted to this old-fashioned pension with 15 large rooms. Close to the Kunsthistorisches Museum.
➕ G6 ✉ Museumstrasse 3 ☎ 523 5127; fax 523 4426-30; www.tiscover.com/hotelpension. museum 🚇 U3 to Volkstheater

HOTEL WANDL (€€)

Popular hotel with 138 rooms next to Peterskirche in a partly 12th-century building.
➕ H6 ✉ Petersplatz 9 ☎ 534 55-0; fax 534 55-77; www.hotel-wandl.com 🚇 U1, U3 to Stephansplatz

KUGEL (€)

Extremely good value near the lively Spittelberg neighbourhood, which is full of open-air restaurants in summer. 38 rooms.
➕ G7 ✉ Siebensterngasse 43 ☎ 523 3355; fax 523 3355-5;

www.hotelkugel.at 🕐 Closed early Jan–early Feb 🚊 Tram 49 from Dr. Karl-Renner-Ring

PENSION AM OPERNECK (€)

In this seven-room bed and breakfast, they bring breakfast to your room.
➕ H6 ✉ Kärntner Strasse 47 ☎ 512 9310; fax 512 9310-20 🚇 U1, U2, U4 to Oper

PENSION LANDHAUS FUHRGASSL-HUBER (€€)

Located in a wine village by the Vienna Woods. With its peasant-style furniture and a summer courtyard, this one is special. 38 rooms
➕ C1 ✉ Rathstrasse 24, Neustift am Walde ☎ 440 3033; fax 440 2714; www.fuhrgassl-huber.at 🚌 Bus 35A from junction Krottenbach/Silberstrasse. Tram 38 from Schottentor

PENSION NOSSEK (€€)

Good location in the heart of the city; the pedestrianized area ensures quiet. The 26 rooms range from spacious to compact. Pleasant service. Reserve well in advance.
➕ H6 ✉ Graben 17 ☎ 533 7041; fax 535 3646 🚇 U1, U3 to Stephansplatz

PENSION PERTSCHY (€€)

Pleasant and friendly, this pension is just off the Graben. The 50 rooms are spacious with period furniture.
➕ H6 ✉ Habsburgergasse 5 ☎ 534 49-0; fax 534 49-49; www.pertschy.com 🚇 U1, U3 to Stephansplatz

VIENNA
travel facts

ESSENTIAL FACTS

Customs regulations
- Duty-free limits for non-European Union visitors are: 200 cigarettes or 250g of tobacco or 50 cigars; 2 litres of wine and 1 litre of spirits.

Electricity
- The voltage is 220V AC and two-pin plugs are used.

Etiquette
- Titles are important; if you know which one to use (eg *Herr Doktor*), use it. Address the waiter as *Herr Ober*, the waitress as *Fräulein*.

Money matters
- Credit cards are accepted by most hotels, leading shops, and more expensive restaurants.
- Bankomat machines giving cash against international credit or debit cards with PIN numbers are plentiful in the centre.

National holidays
- 1 Jan, 6 Jan (Epiphany), Easter Monday, 1 May, Christi Himmelfahrt (Ascension Day), Whit Monday Corpus Christi (Thu after Whitsun), 15 Aug (Assumption of the Virgin), 26 Oct (National Day), 1 Nov (All Saints), 8 Dec (Annunciation), 24–26 Dec (everything closes from midday on Christmas Eve).

Opening hours
- Shops: Mon–Fri 9–6; Sat 9–5 (food shops may open earlier). Retailers have the option of Saturday opening, but outside the main shopping areas, some remain closed from noon. Most shops open 9–6 on the four Saturdays before Christmas.
- Banks: Mon–Wed, Fri 8–12.30, 1.30–3; Thu 1.30–5.30. In the centre some stay open at lunch.
- Offices: Mon–Fri 8–4, but may close earlier on Friday.

Places of worship
- The Tourismus Pastoral office issues a booklet with details of services for all Christian denominations and Judaism, and where confession in foreign languages may be made ✉ Stephansplatz 6, 6th floor room 670 ☎ 515 52-335; www.virc.at
- Anglican: Christ Church ✉ Jaurésgasse 17–19 ☎ 714 8900
- Islamic: Islamic Community of Faith ✉ Bernardgasse 5 ☎ 526 3122
- Jewish: City Synagogue ✉ Seitenstettengasse 4 ☎ 532 1884
- Vienna Community Church ✉ Reformierte Stadtkirche, Dorotheergasse 16 ☎ 505 5233
- Methodist: ✉ Sechshauser Strasse 56 ☎ 604 5347
- Roman Catholic (in English and other languages): St. Augustin ✉ 1 Augustinerstrasse ☎ 533 7099

Student travellers
- There are nine youth hostels. You need an International Youth Hostel Federation membership card, obtainable on the spot.
- Österreichischer Jugendherbergsverband (Austrian Youth Hostel Association) ✉ Schottering 28 ☎ 533 5353
- From 1 July to 30 September, student hostels in the city become *Saison Hotels*: information from Academia Hotels ✉ Pfeilgasse 3A, A-1080 ☎ 401 7620. There are rooms for students at the Kolping Movement Centre: Kolpingfamilie ✉ Bendlgasse 10–12 ☎ 813 5487

GETTING AROUND

Integrated system

- Maps and information about the transport network can be obtained at the Wiener Linien information office at the Karlsplatz end of Opern Passage ☎ 790 9100 and 0810/22 2324
- Buy tickets for the U-Bahn, Strassenbahn (trams), buses or S-Bahn from newsagents or at the counters in main U-Bahn and S-Bahn stations. An easy one to find is at the Karlsplatz end of the Opern Passage, at the entrance to U1, U2, U4.
- A single journey card must be validated at the entrance to the underground, or on a tram or bus, using the stamping machines. It can be used for one unbroken ride, including changes of line, or changes from U-Bahn, to tram, to bus. Valid one hour from stamping.
- Penalties for travelling without a valid ticket are heavy and checks quite frequent.

Types of ticket

- Excursion or season tickets are valid on all parts of the network and even on suburban buses (up to the city boundary).
- Individual tickets are much more expensive per ride, and the machines dispensing them on trams are complicated.
- Good-value monthly or weekly tickets allow unlimited travel all over the network for their duration. No photo is required.
- *8 Tage-Karte* (8 strips), each valid for 24 hours' travel all over the network. If there are two or more of you, validate one strip per person.
- You can buy blocks of tickets for single rides, as well as 24-hour and 72-hour time tickets (useful for weekend visitors).
- Time tickets and the *8 Tage-Karte* must be validated once at the commencement of the period of use and are then good for the period stipulated.
- *Wien-Karte* is a 72-hour card with discounts on entry charges to many sights.

U-Bahn

- There are five lines. Oddly there is U1, U2, U3, U4 and U6 but no U5. U2 follows a semi-circular route around the Ringstrasse and is now being extended at each end.
- The U-Bahn maps found on platforms are colour-coded and also show connections to other forms of transport. Be careful to note the end-stop of the direction you want; this will be shown on the illuminated sign of the appropriate platform.
- Three lines (U1, U2, U4) meet at the Oper/Karlsplatz.
- Main stations have lifts and escalators.
- You may take bicycles into designated cars (except during rush hour).
- The S-Bahn (*Schnellbahn*) is a rapid transit railway bringing commuters from the suburbs to the major traffic connections of the city.

Trams/buses

- The route is clearly marked at the tram stop and on a card inside. Check you are travelling in the right direction.
- Bus routes fill the gaps between the mostly radial tram lines. Night buses on main routes run every 30 minutes from

Schwedenplatz after 12.30am until around 5am. A supplement is payable.

- The small hopper buses (1A, 2A and 3A) have circular routes through the Inner City with stops at or near virtually all places of interest. They run only during normal working hours.

Taxis

- Cabs are efficient and not unreasonably expensive by Austrian standards.
- You can order a cab by phone ☎ 31 300 (airport taxi), 40 100 or 60160
- Tips are 10 per cent.
- There are supplements for late-night or weekend rides, plus per head and per piece of luggage.
- Taxis ordered by telephone usually arrive in about five minutes in the city centre and inner suburbs.

MEDIA & COMMUNICATIONS

Newspapers & magazines

- Foreign newspapers are available from newsstands in the city centre (open normal business hours), and from the Südbahnhof and Westbahnhof newsstands (open until 10pm).
- *Falter* (in German) is a mixture of comprehensive listings and agitprop. Its film section includes the programme of the Österreichisches Filmmuseum (► 85).
- *The Observer* and *The Independent* usually arrive Sunday afternoon, other Sunday papers on Monday.

Post offices

- Post offices are open Mon–Fri 8–noon and 2–6.

- There are 24-hour post offices at the following:
  ✉ Fleischmarkt 19 ☎ 513 8350
  ✉ Südbahnhof ☎ 501 810
  ✉ Westbahnhof ☎ 892 3260
- Stamps are sold at post offices and at *Tabak Trafik* shops.

Radio & television

- All foreign films shown on Austrian TV are dubbed, as are foreign TV series.
- There is news in English and in French every morning on the radio (on Österreich 1) at 8am.

Telephones

- Telephone cards are sold in *Tabak Trafik* shops (newsagents) and at post offices. Some telephones in the Kohlmarkt/Graben area take credit cards.
- To call Vienna from the UK dial 00431. To call the UK from Vienna, dial 0044.
- To call Vienna from the US dial 00431. To call the US from Vienna, dial 001.
- Directory assistance: Austria and Germany ☎ 118 877, everywhere else ☎ 0900 11 8877

EMERGENCIES

Embassies & consulates

- Australia ✉ Mattiellistrasse 2–4 ☎ 506 74
- Canada ✉ Laurenzerberg 2 ☎ 5313 830 00
- Ireland ✉ Rotenturmstrasse 16–18 ☎ 715 4246
- New Zealand ✉ Argentinierstrabe 20A ☎ 318 8505 (consulate general)
- UK ✉ Jaurésgasse 10 ☎ 7161 35151
- US ✉ Boltzmangasse 16 ☎ 313 39 (embassy) or ✉ Gartenbaupromenade 2 (next to Marriott Hotel) ☎ 31 339-3005 (consulate)

Emergency phone numbers
- Ambulance ☎ 144
- Doctor on call ☎ 141
- Dentist ☎ 512 2078
- Fire ☎ 122
- Police ☎ 133
- ÖAMTC (breakdown service equivalent to AA) ☎ 120
- Foreign language assistance for bureaucratic problems ☎ 0900/97 0200 (premium line)

Lost property
- Report loss or theft to the nearest police station.
- Lost Property Bureau ⊠ Wasagasse 22 ☎ 313 10-37251 🕒 Mon–Fri 8–noon
- Railway Lost Property: for all lost and found enquiries ☎ 930 00-35656 or 930 00-22222
- Vienna Transport System Lost Property ☎ 790 943-500

Medical treatment
- Vienna General Hospital (Allgemeines Krankenhaus) ⊠ Währinger Gürtel 18–20 ☎ 40 400-1964
- The Barmherzige Brüder (Brothers of Mercy) treat patients for free at their hospital ⊠ Mohrengasse 9 (2nd District) ☎ 211 21-0

Medicines
- Pharmacies are normally open Mon–Fri 8–noon, 2–6, Sat 8–noon.
- English-speaking pharmacists: Internationale Apotheke ⊠ Kärntner Ring 17 ☎ 512 2825; Schweden-Apotheke, Pharmacie Internationale, ⊠ Schwedenplatz 2 ☎ 533 2911

Sensible precautions
- Lock valuables in your hotel safe and don't carry large amounts of cash. Crime is low in Vienna, but high season pickpockets are busy.
- Avoid the main railway stations at night and the red-light district along the Gürtel.

LANGUAGE

Monday, Tuesday, Wednesday, Thursday, Friday, Saturday, Sunday
Montag, Dienstag, Mittwoch, Donnerstag, Freitag, Samstag, Sonntag

1 eins		11 elf	
2 zwei		12 zwölf	
3 drei		13 dreizehn	
4 vier		14 vierzehn	
5 fünf		15 fünfzehn	
6 sechs		16 sechzehn	
7 sieben		17 siebzehn	
8 acht		18 achtzehn	
9 neun		19 neunzehn	
10 zehn		20 zwanzig	

yes/no ja/nein
please bitte
thank you (very much) danke (schön)
I'm sorry verzeihung
excuse me, please entschuldigen Sie, bitte
do you speak English? sprechen Sie englisch?
I do not understand ich verstehe nicht
how much does that cost? wieviel kostet das?
do you take credit cards? darf ich mit Kreditkarte zahlen?
good night gute Nacht
good morning guten Morgen *or* (more usually) Grüss Gott
good afternoon guten Abend
today/tomorrow heute/morgen
here/there hier, da/dort
when/where wann/wo
right/left rechts/links

Index

Fodor's
vienna's 25 best

Author and Edition Reviser *Louis James*
Managing Editors *Apostrophe S Limited*
Cover Design *Tigist Getachew, Fabrizio La Rocca*

Copyright © Automobile Association Developments Limited 1996, 1999, 2002, 2004, 2006

This book was formerly titled *Fodor's Citypack Vienna*

ISBN 1-4000-1639-8

FOURTH EDITION

ACKNOWLEDGMENTS
The Automobile Association would like to thank the following agencies and libraries for their assistance in the preparation of this title.
Austrian National Tourist Office 27b, 38, 48b; Stockbyte 5
Geostock/Photodisc/Getty Images cover (blurred statue)
The remaining photographs are held in the Association's own library (AA WORLD TRAVEL LIBRARY) and were taken by C Sawyer; with the exception of 54 which was taken by M Adelman; 58b which was taken by P Baker; 1t, 2, 4, 6, 7, 8c, 9cl, 10b, 12c, 13t, 14/15, 19t, 23, 33, 39, 40t, 42, 45b, 46b, 48t, 62, 89b which were taken by D Noble and 8cl, 8bl, 8bc, 8/9, 9b, 11t, 12/13, 14c, 15c, 16c, 16/17, 17c, 18c, 18/19, 19c, 21, 24cb, 24cr, 25, 29, 31, 41b, 46t, 50t, 51t, 52, 56, 57, 58b, 61t, 61b, 63, 89t which were taken by M Siebert.

IMPORTANT TIP
Time inevitably brings changes, so always confirm prices, travel facts, and other perishable information when it matters. Although Fodor's cannot accept responsibility for errors, you can use this guide in the confidence that we have taken every care to ensure its accuracy.

SPECIAL SALES
This book is available for special discounts for bulk purchases for sales promotions or premiums. Special editions, including personalized covers, excerpts of existing books, and corporate imprints, can be created in large quantities for special needs. For more information, write to Special Markets/Premium Sales, 1745 Broadway, MD 6–2, New York, NY 10019 or email specialmarkets@randomhouse.com.

Color separation by Keenes, Andover
Printed in Hong Kong by Hang Tai D&P Limited
10 9 8 7 6 5 4 3 2 1

A02353
Maps © Automobile Association Developments Limited, 1996, 1999, 2002, 2004, 2006
Fold out map © MAIRDUMONT / Falk Verlag 2005
Transport map © Communicarta Ltd, UK

DESTINATIONS COVERED IN THIS SERIES
• Amsterdam • Bangkok • Barcelona • Beijing • Berlin • Boston • Brussels & Bruges •
• Chicago • Dublin • Florence • Hong Kong • Las Vegas • Lisbon • London • Los Angeles •
• Madrid • Melbourne • Miami • Milan • Montréal • Munich • Naples • New York •
• Orlando • Paris • Prague • Rome • San Francisco • Seattle • Shanghai • Singapore •
• Sydney • Tokyo • Toronto • Venice • Vienna • Washington DC •

CADOGAN Dana Facaros & Michael Pauls

Florence
Siena Pisa Lucca

W9-BCK-460

Cadogan Guides
27–29 Berwick Street, London W1V 3RF
email: guides@cadogan.demon.co.uk

Distributed in the USA by
The Globe Pequot Press
6 Business Park Road, PO Box 833, Old Saybrook,
Connecticut 06475–0833

Copyright © Dana Facaros and Michael Pauls 1994, 1998
Updated by Nicky Swallow 1998

Illustrations designed by Biljana Lipic and
Adrian McLaughlin
Book and cover design by Animage
Cover photographs by Travel Library/Daniel Cilia (front) and Ellen Rooney (back)
Maps © Cadogan Guides, drawn by Map Creation Ltd

Series Editor: Rachel Fielding
Editing: Dominique Shead and Samantha Batra
Proofreading: Lorna Horsfield
Indexing: Dorothy Frame
Production: Rupert Wheeler Book Production Services

ISBN 1–86011–034–7
A catalogue record for this book is available from the British Library

The author and publishers have made every effort to ensure the accuracy of the information in this book
at the time of going to press. However, they cannot accept any responsibility for any loss, injury or
inconvenience resulting from the use of information contained in this guide.

Printed and bound in Finland, by WSOY.

About the Authors

This guide is Dana and Michael's 20th for Cadogan, and their 12th on Italy. For three years they and their children lived in a tiny Umbrian hilltop village. They then moved to a remote French village in the Lot, but now live in southeast Ireland.

Acknowledgements

Special thanks to Nicky Swallow for updating this edition. The publishers would like to thank Biljana Lipic and Adrian McLaughlin for designing the photographs, Lorna Horsfield for proofreading, and Map Creation for the maps.

And a big thank-you to Siena Colegrave for lending her name to the city.

Please help us to keep this guide up to date

We have done our best to ensure that the information in this guide is correct at the time of going to press. However, places and facilities are constantly changing, standards and prices in hotels and restaurants fluctuate. We would be delighted to receive any comments concerning existing entries or omissions, as well as suggestions for new features. Authors of the best letters will receive a copy of the Cadogan guide of their choice.

Contents

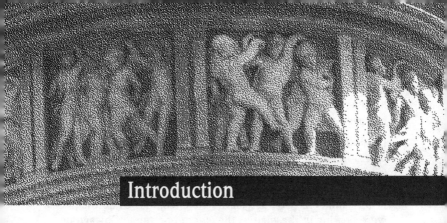

Introduction

Once there were four cities, bearing names as rich and resonant as rare flowers. Although close to one another in many ways, each blossomed in different forms and hues, and in the very springtime of modern western civilization, they astounded the world.

And so these hothouse blooms of Tuscany slip easily into the realm of fairytale or myth. Pictures crowd the imagination: bold Pisa, the first city off the mark, a maritime republic that sent its entire fleet off to the First Crusade with banners flapping and its bishop at the prow, sailing back with holds full of Arabic mathematics and sciences, and enough plunder to erect a Field of Miracles; lovely Siena, starry queen of all hilltowns, city of bankers and elegant storybook art, where the inhabitants annually gathered in their sublime conch shell of a piazza to punch each other in the nose; gentle, urbane Lucca, the medieval city of silk and candy-striped churches, enclosed in green garden walls. Then there's that most precocious Renaissance genius, Florence, first and foremost in a hundred fields, yet full of contradictions: where Dante's house was set ablaze by political rivals and a friend had to brave the flames to rescue the manuscript of the *Inferno*, where Brunelleschi could weave a dome of perfect beauty, only to have to enter a contest to be able to design its lantern.

The stories of Florence, Siena, Pisa and Lucca are especially alive because the sets are still there, nearly intact. It's as if at the height of their respective golden ages these four cities decided they themselves were works of art, *città dell'arte* according to the wonderful Italian expression, and coated themselves with a varnish. Sprawl, suburbia and progress have been kept at the gate and within these inner sanctums nothing has been allowed to change, at least on the surface.

Linger over a glass of Chianti in a quiet little out-of-the-way piazza in any of these cities, watching another day of sun soak into bricks and stones that have soaked in seven or eight centuries of suns and witnessed all that transcendent brilliance, beauty and creativity, and all the violence, too: when the juices were flowing in these cities they were not unlike Chicago in the Roaring Twenties. Fat cat merchants and bankers wrote their own laws. Political factions and gangsters made the streets so dangerous that the big bosses lived high up in Manhattanish skyscrapers. Rather than work together as neighbours, Florence, Siena, Pisa and Lucca constantly clobbered one another and did all they could to drag all the great powers of Europe into the fray. Betrayals, conspiracies, intrigues and vendettas were the order of the day, and if you had any scruples you could read Machiavelli to put your mind at ease. A Medici could order a work from Botticelli one minute, and have a political nuisance rubbed out the next. The juices were flowing, and it doesn't seem quite fair that we have a lot of the same troubles today, but no Fra Angelicos or Donatellos to compensate.

But these varnished, pickled and potted Tuscan cities compensate for a lot in themselves. 'I went to sleep at dawn in Tuscany,' wrote Hilaire Belloc in a poem that ends:

> This sleep I swear shall last the length of day;
> Not noise, not chance, shall drive this dream away;
> Not time, not treachery, not good fortune—no,
> Not all the weight of all the wears of the world.

Travel

By Air

From London Heathrow there are daily Alitalia and British Airways flights to the international airport at **Pisa**, and there are daily flights from Gatwick to **Florence** with Meridiana (twice daily Mon–Fri, once a day Sat and Sun). From Ireland, there are direct flights most weeks from Dublin and Cork to Milan on either Alitalia or Aer Lingus, from where you can pick up a connecting flight to Florence. Keep your eye open for bargains and charters in the papers.

The carriers listed below have a variety of **discounts** if booked in advance. PEX (or APEX) fares have fixed arrival and departure dates, and the stay in Italy must include at least one Saturday night. Children under the age of two usually travel free, and both British Airways and Alitalia offer cheaper tickets on some flights for students and those under 26. Alitalia in particular often has promotional perks like rental cars (Jetdrive), or discounts on domestic flights within Italy, on hotels, or on tours. British Airways do a fly-drive package to Pisa and Florence.

main carriers

Alitalia: London, ✆ (0171) 602 7111; Dublin, ✆ (01) 677 5171

British Airways: London, ✆ (0345) 222 111 (central British number); Belfast,
    ✆ (01849) 422 888 (airport); Dublin, ✆ (1 800) 626 747

Aer Lingus: Belfast, ✆ (01232) 232 270; Dublin, ✆ (01) 844 4777

Meridiana: London, ✆ (0171) 839 2222

discounts and special deals

Italflights, London, ✆ (0171) 405 6771

Italia nel Mondo, London, ✆ (0171) 828 9171

Italy Skybus, London, ✆ (0171) 373 6055

Italy Sky Shuttle, London, ✆ (0181) 748 1333

Budget Travel, Dublin, ✆ (01) 661 1866

United Travel, Dublin, ✆ (01) 288 4346

students and youth travel

Besides saving 25 per cent on regular flights, people under 26 have the choice of flying on special discount charters from:

Campus Travel, 52 Grosvenor Gardens, London SW1, ✆ (0171) 730 3402; with branches at most UK universities.

STA Travel, 86 Old Brompton Road, London SW7 3LH or 117 Euston Road, NW1 2SX, ✆ (0171) 361 6161 and many other branches in the UK.

USIT, Aston Quay, Dublin 2, ✆ (01) 679 8833; Belfast, ✆ (01232) 324 073, and other cities. Ireland's largest student travel agents.

By Train

From London's Victoria Station it's about 24 hours by train to Florence, and will set you back around £163 second-class return, £257 first-class; if you go by Eurostar on the London–Paris leg of the journey, add another £100–150 for a second-class return and up to £392 for first-class. Tickets are valid for two months, and you can stop off on the way as much as you like. These trains require reservations and a *couchette*, and if you take along a good book to read are a fairly painless way of getting there. Order tickets from the **International Rail Centre**, Victoria Station, London SW1. There is a number, ✆ (0990) 848 848, but, unfortunately, the operatives on the other end of the line are not allowed to divulge any information regarding fares over the phone, which means that you will have to book your tickets in person. For information about the London–Paris leg call Eurostar, EPS House, Waterloo Station, London SE1, ✆ (0345) 881 881.

Discounts are available for families and for children, and anyone under 26, eligible for **BIJ** discount tickets. They are valid for two months and allow unlimited stopovers. They can be bought throughout Europe at student offices (CTS in Italy) in main railway stations. If you have a Senior Citizen Railcard, another £5 will get you a Rail Europe Senior Card, good for 30 per cent off Italian fares. Within Italy itself there are several other discount tickets and passes available (*see* p.9), which you can obtain from CIT (Italian State Railways), Marco Polo House, 3–5 Landsdowne Rd, Croydon, Surrey, ✆ (0891) 715 151 or from Wasteels, adjacent to Platform 2, Victoria Station, London SW1V 1JT, ✆ (0171) 834 7066.

By Coach

Usually more expensive than a charter, the coach is the last refuge of airplane-phobic bargain-hunters. The journey time from London to Florence is 26–27 hours; the return full fare is around £136. For Siena, change at Florence and take a SITA bus from the other side of Florence station (1hr). Change at Florence for Lucca and Pisa onto a Eurolines coach, although it's quicker to take the train. There are, again, discounts for students, senior citizens and children and off-peak travel. Contact **National Express** at Victoria Coach Station, London SW1, ✆ (0990) 808 080, for times and bookings.

From the United States, the major carriers fly only to Rome or Milan, though British Airways has just begun a new New York–London–Pisa service called the Manhattan Express that departs at 9pm and has you in Florence by 4pm the next day. Your travel agent may find a much cheaper fare from your home airport to your Italian airport by way of London, Brussels, Paris, Frankfurt or Amsterdam. From Canada only Alitalia flies direct to Italy (Toronto/Montréal to Rome/Milan).

To be eligible for PEX (or APEX) fares, you'll have to have fixed arrival and departure dates, and stay in Italy for at least a week but not more than 90 days. SUPERPEX, the cheapest normal fares available, must be purchased at least 14 days (or sometimes 21 days) in advance and there are penalties to pay if you change your flight dates. At the time of writing the lowest mid-week SUPERPEX between New York and Rome in the off-season is $696 midweek, $756 weekend, rising up into the $900 zone in summer; from Canada low season fares start at around $900 and move up to $1250. To sweeten the deal, Alitalia in particular often has promotional perks like rental cars (Jetdrive), or discounts on domestic flights within Italy, on hotels, or on tours. Ask your travel agent. Children under the age of two usually travel for free and both British Airways and Alitalia offer cheaper tickets on some flights for students and the under-25s.

major carriers

Alitalia: US, ✆ (800) 223 5730, Canada, ✆ (416) 363 1348

Lufthansa: US, ✆ (800) 645 3880, Canada, ✆ (800) 563 5954

Delta: US, ✆ (800) 241 4141

Air Canada: Canada, ✆ (800) 555 1212; US, (800) 776 3000

KLM: US, ✆ (800) 374 7747; Canada, ✆ (800) 361 5330

TWA: US, ✆ (800) 892 4141

British Airways: US, ✆ (800) 247 9297; Canada, ✆ (800) 668 1055

charters, discounts and special deals

New Frontiers, US, ✆ (800) 366 6387. Canada, in Montréal, ✆ (514) 526 8444.

Travel Avenue, US, ✆ (800) 333 3335.

Air Brokers International, US, (800) 883 3273. Discounter.

Council Charter, US, ✆ (800) 223 7402. Charter specialists.

Last Minute Travel Club, US, (800) 527 8646. Annual membership fee gets you cheap standby deals.

Encore Travel Club, US, (800) 444 9800. Scheduled flight discount club.

student and youth travel

STA Travel, in the **US**, New York City, ☎ (212) 627 3111; outside New York, ☎ (1 800) 777 0112. In **Australia**, Sydney, ☎ (02)9212 1255; elsewhere, ☎ (1 800) 637 444.

Council Travel, 205 E 42nd St, New York, NY 10017, ☎ (800) 743 1823. Major specialist in student and charter flights; branches all over the US.

Travel Cuts, 187 College St, Toronto, Ontario M5T 1P7, ☎ (416) 979 2406. Canada's largest student travel specialists; branches in most provinces.

by rail

For information on Italian rail passes and special deals, contact **CIT Tours Corporation**, 15 West 44th Street, 10th Floor, New York, NY 10036, ☎ (212) 730 2400, ✉ (212) 730 4300. From elsewhere, ☎ (800) 248 8687. In **Canada** CIT tours are based at: 1450 City Counsellors, Suite 750, Montreal, Quebec H3A 2E6, ☎ (514) 845 9101.

Getting There from Australia and New Zealand

The only direct flights (well, via Bangkok) are Alitalia's flights from Sydney or Melbourne to Rome and Quantas's from Perth to Rome; there are none at all from New Zealand, but indirect flights on Alitalia, Quantas, British Airways, and Thai Airways. Ask your travel agent about other indirect flights, although weigh the price savings against any car hire or other deals offered by Alitalia. Prices in low season (Nov–Mar) average around $2000 (NZ$2500), and are $3000 (NZ$3300) at other times. If you can pick up a bargain to London, it may work out cheaper to take that and find a discount flight from there (*see* above).

major carriers

Alitalia: Sydney, ☎ (02) 9247 1308

Thai Airways: Australia, ☎ (1 800) 422 020; Auckland, ☎ (09) 377 3886

British Airways: Sydney, ☎ (02) 9258 3300; Auckland, ☎ (09) 356 8690

Singapore Airlines: Sydney, ☎ (02) 9236 0144; Auckland, ☎ (09)379 3209

Quantas: Sydney, ☎ (02) 957 0111; Auckland, ☎ (09) 357 8900

discounts and special deals

Flight Centres, Sydney ☎ (02) 9241 2422; Melbourne, ☎ (03) 650 2899, Auckland, ☎ (09) 309 6171; Christchurch, ☎ (03) 379 7145 and other branches.

Brisbane Discount Travel, in Brisbane, ✆ (07) 3229 9211.

UTAG Travel, Sydney, ✆ (02) 9956 8399 and branches in other Australian cities.

Budget Travel, Auckland, toll free ✆ (0 800) 808 040.

STA, toll free in Australia, ✆ (800) 637 444; Auckland, ✆ (09) 366 6673.

rail travel

For information on Italian rail passes (and throughout Europe), contact **CIT**, 123 Clarence St, Sydney, ✆ (02) 9299 4574; remember some must be purchased before you leave.

Passports and Customs Formalities

To get into Italy you need a valid **passport**. EU citizens do not need visas; US, Canadian and Australian nationals do not need visas for stays of up to three months. If you mean to stay longer than three months in Italy you will have to get a *permesso di soggiorno*. For this you will need to state your reason for staying, be able to prove a source of income and have medical insurance. After a couple of thoroughly exasperating days filling out forms at some provincial *questura* office, you should walk out with your permit.

According to Italian law, you must **register with the police** within eight days of arriving. If you check into a hotel this is done automatically. If you come to grief in the mesh of rules and forms, you can at least get someone to explain it to you in English by calling the Rome Police Office for Visitors, ✆ (06) 4686 ext. 2987.

EU nationals over the age of 17 can now import a limitless amount of goods for their personal use. If you're coming or going from a non-EU country, you'll have to pass through **Italian Customs.** How the frontier police manage to recruit such ugly, mean-looking characters to hold the submachine guns and drug-sniffing dogs from such a good-looking population is a mystery, but they'll let you alone if you don't look suspicious (sadly, not being Caucasian is often grounds for 'suspicion') and haven't brought along more than 150 cigarettes or 75 cigars, a litre of hard drink or three bottles of wine, a couple of cameras, a movie camera, 10 rolls of film for each, a tape recorder, radio, record-player, one canoe less than 5.5m, sports equipment for personal use, and one TV (though you'll have to pay for a licence for it at Customs). US citizens may return with $400 worth of merchandise—keep your receipts.

Getting Around

Tuscany has an excellent network of railways and highways and byways, and you'll find getting between Florence, Siena, Pisa and Lucca fairly easy—unless one union or another takes it into its head to go on strike (to be fair, this rarely happens during the main holiday season). There's plenty of talk about passing a law to regulate strikes, but don't count on it happening soon. Instead learn how to recognize the word in Italian: *sciopero* (SHO-PER-O) and be prepared to do as the Romans do when you hear it—quiver with resignation. There's always a day or two's notice in advance, and usually strikes last only 12 or 24 hours—but long enough to throw a spanner in the works. Keep your ears open.

Transport to and from the Airports

Pisa's international airport, Galileo Galilei, © (050) 500707, 3km to the south, is linked to the city by train, or city bus no. 5 which arrives at Piazza Stazione in front of the main station on the south side of the Arno. A special train service runs from Pisa airport to the central Santa Maria Novella station in Florence (1hr, daily every 1–2hrs); you can call the air terminal in the station for flight information, © 216073. There is a SITA bus service to Florence which fills in the gaps in the train service: information from the airport or on © (055) 483561.

Florence's Vespucci airport is no longer dinky; the runway was lengthened in 1996, and it is now bustling with more international traffic than Pisa. It is 6km outside the city at Peretola, © 373498, flight information © 3061700 (recorded message) and is connected by a regular bus service to Santa Maria Novella station (15mins). A taxi ride from Florence airport to the centre of town will cost about L25,000 plus relevant surcharges.

airlines in Florence

Alitalia: Lungarno Acciaioli 10/12r, © 27881; Piazza dell'Oro 1, © 1478 65643 (flight inquiries), © 1478 65642 (international reservations), @ 2788400.

British Airways: no longer have an office in Florence. For information and reservations they have a toll-free number: © 47812266, or use their office at Pisa airport (*see* below).

Meridiana (for London, Gatwick) Lungarno Vespucci 28/R, © 32961, @ 2302046/2314.

TWA: Via dei Vecchietti 4, © 2396856, @ 214634.

airlines in Pisa

Alitalia: Via Puccini 21, © 48025/6/7, @ 48028.

British Airways: Società Aeroporto Toscana, Galileo Galilei Airport, © 501838.

Train information from anywhere in Italy, ✆ 147888088, open 7am–9pm.

Florence, Siena, Pisa and Lucca are linked by regular trains, so in theory it is possible to do a whistle-stop rail tour of all four cities in one day, but that would not leave a great deal of time for the sights! Florence is the central transport node for Tuscany and harder to avoid than to reach. The central station is **Santa Maria Novella** ✆ 2352061, for reservations. Many long-distance trains arriving at night use **Campo di Marte** station (served by bus nos. 6, 12 and 20, or 91 at night).

There are trains roughly every hour between Florence and Siena (97km, 1½hrs)—the journey takes a little longer if you have to change at Empoli. Pisa, 81km from Florence, is on the main Florence–Livorno line with one or two trains every hour (55mins). Lucca can be reached from Florence hourly via the Florence–Pistoia–Viareggio line (78km, 80mins). The journey from Pisa to Lucca (24km) takes only 25 minutes. To travel from Siena to Lucca, you could go via either Florence or Pisa (125km, 2hrs).

Train fares have increased greatly over the last couple of years and only those without extra supplements can still be called cheap. Italy's national railway, the FS (*Ferrovie dello Stato*) is well run and often a pleasure to ride. Possible FS unpleasantnesses you may encounter, besides a strike, are delays and crowding (especially at weekends and in the summer). Tickets may be purchased not only in the stations, but at many travel agents. Reserve a seat in advance (*fare una prenotazione*). The fee is small and can save you hours standing. On the upper echelon trains, reservations are mandatory. Do check when you purchase your ticket in advance that the date is correct; tickets are only valid the day they're purchased unless you specify otherwise.

Be sure you ask which platform (*binario*) your train arrives at; the big permanent boards posted in the stations are not always correct. Always remember to stamp your ticket (*convalidare*) in the not-very-obvious machine at the head of the platform before boarding the train. Failure to do so will result in a fine. If you get on a train without a ticket you can buy one from the conductor, with an added 20 per cent penalty. You can also pay a conductor to move up to first class if there are places available.

There is a strict hierarchy of trains. A *Regionale* travels shortish distances, and tends to stop at all the stations. There are only a few *Espressi* trains left in service, but they are in poor condition, and mostly service the long runs from the south. No supplement is required. *Intercity* trains link Italian cities, with minimum stops. Some carry an obligatory seat-reservation requirement (free in this case), and all have a supplement. The true Kings of the Rails are the super-swish and super fast (Florence–Rome in 1½ hours) *Eurostars*. These make very few stops, have both first- and second-class carriages, and carry a supplement which includes an obligatory seat reservation. So, the faster the train, the more you pay.

The FS offers several passes. A flexible option is the 'Flexi Card' which allows unlimited travel for either four days within a month (L206,000), 8 days within a month (L287,000), or 12 days within a month (L368,000) plus supplements and seat reservations on Eurostars. Another ticket, the *Kilometrico* gives you 3000 kilometres of travel, made on a maximum of 20 journeys and is valid for two months (2nd class L206,000, 1st class L338,000 plus supplements); one advantage is that it can be used by up to five people at the same time. However, supplements are payable on Intercity trains. Other discounts, available only once you're in Italy, are 15 per cent on same-day return tickets and three-day returns (depending on the distance involved), and discounts for families of at least four travelling together. Senior citizens (men 65 and over, women 60) can also get a *Carta d'Argento* ('silver card') for L44,000 entitling them to a 20 per cent reduction in fares. A *Carta Verde* bestows a 20 per cent discount on people under 26 and costs L44,000.

Refreshments on routes of any great distance are provided by bar cars or trolleys; you can usually get sandwiches and coffee from vendors along the tracks at intermediary stops. Station bars often have a good variety of take-away travellers' fare; consider at least investing in a bottle of mineral water, since there's no drinking water on the trains. Besides trains and bars, Italy's stations offer other facilities. All have a *deposito bagaglio* (or computerized lockers) where you can leave your bags for hours or days for about L5000 a day. The larger ones have porters (who charge L3000 per piece) and luggage trolleys; major stations have an *albergo diurno* ('day hotel', where you can have a shower, shave and haircut), information offices, currency exchanges open at weekends, hotel reservation services, kiosks with foreign papers. You can also arrange to have a rental car awaiting you at your destination—Avis, Hertz, and Maggiore provide this service.

By Bus

The four cities are also well served by bus. From Florence SITA buses go to Siena, LAZZI to Lucca and Pisa and CLAP to Lucca; SITA buses run between Siena and Pisa; TRA-IN buses operate from Siena covering Siena province.

It's possible to reach nearly every city, town and village in Tuscany from Florence, which is wonderfully convenient—once you know which of several bus companies to patronize. The tourist office has a complete list of destinations, but here are some of the most popular.

SITA (near the station, Via S. Caterina da Siena 15, ✆ 483651, or ✆ (166) 845010 for a 24-hour recorded message): towns in the Val d'Elsa, Chianti, Val di Pesa, Mugello and Casentino; Arezzo, Bibbiena, Castelfiorentino, Certaldo, Consuma, Figline Valdarno, Firenzuola, Marina di Grosseto, Montevarchi, Poggibonsi (for San Gimignano and Volterra), Pontassieve, Poppi, Pratovecchio, Scarperia, **Siena**, Stia, Vallombrosa.

LAZZI (Piazza Stazione 47r, ✆ 351061 Mon–Fri; ✆ (166) 845010 24-hour recorded message): along the Arno to the coast, including Calenzano, Cerreto Guidi, Empoli, Forte dei Marmi, Livorno, **Lucca**, Marina di Carrara, Marina di Massa, Montecatini Terme, Montelupo, Montevarchi, Pescia, **Pisa**, Pistoia, Pontedera, Prato, Signa, Tirrenia, Torre del Lago, and Viareggio.

CAT (Via Fiume 2r, ✆ 283400): Anghiari, Arezzo, Caprese, Città di Castello, Incisa Valdarno, Sansepolcro.

CLAP (Piazza Stazione 15r, ✆ 283734): **Lucca**.

CAP (Via Nazionale 13, ✆ 214637): Borgo S. Lorenzo, Impruneta, Incisa Valdarno, Montepiano, Prato.

COPIT (Piazza S. Maria Novella, ✆ 214637): Abetone, Cerreto Guidi, Pistoia, Poggio a Caiano, Vinci.

RAMA (Lazzi Station, ✆ 2398840): Grosseto.

Within the cities buses are the traveller's friend. Most cities label routes well; all charge flat fees for rides within the city limits and immediate suburbs, at the time of writing around L1200. Bus tickets must always be purchased before you get on, either at a tobacconist's, a newspaper kiosk, in many bars, or from ticket machines near the main stops. Once you get on, you must 'obliterate' your ticket in the machines in the front or back of the bus; controllers stage random checks to make sure you've punched your ticket. Fines for cheaters are about L50,000, and the odds are about 12 to 1 against a check, so you may take your chances according to how lucky you feel. If you're good-hearted, you'll buy a ticket and help some overburdened municipal transit line meet its annual deficit.

By Taxi

Taxi metres will start at L4300 plus extras, adding L1450 per km. There is a minimum charge of L7000. Each piece of baggage will cost extra, and there are surcharges for trips outside the official city limits (Fiesole, for example), trips between 10pm and 6am, and trips on Sundays and holidays.

For this tour of the art cities, you're probably better off not driving at all: parking is impossible (Florence and Siena both have traffic-free central zones), traffic impossible, deciphering one-way streets, signals and signs impossible. However, given these difficulties, a car does give you the freedom and possibility of making your way through Tuscany's lovely countryside.

Be prepared, however, to encounter some of the highest fuel costs in Europe and drivers who look at motoring as if it were a video game. The Italians, from 21-year-old madcaps or elderly nuns, turn into aggressive starfighters once behind the wheel, whose mission is to reach their destination in a certain allotted time (especially around lunch or dinner, if they think the pasta is already on the boil) regardless of minor nuisances such as other cars, road signs, traffic signals, solid no-passing lines, or blind curves on mountain roads. No matter how fast you trip along on the *autostrade* (Italy's toll motorways, official speed limit **130km/ 80miles** per hour), someone will pass you going twice as fast.

If you aren't intimidated, buy a good road map of Italy or a more detailed one of Tuscany (the Italian Touring Club produces excellent ones). Many petrol stations close for lunch in the afternoon, and few stay open late at night, though you may find a 'self-service' where you feed a machine nice smooth L10,000 and L50,000 notes. Autostrada tolls are high—for example, to drive on the A1 from Florence to Milan will cost you L30,000. The rest stops and petrol stations along the motorways are open 24 hours. Other roads—*superstrade* on down through the Italian grading system—are free of charge. The Italians are very good about signposting, and roads are almost all excellently maintained—some highways seem to be built of sheer bravura, suspended on cliffs, crossing valleys on enormous piers—feats of engineering that will remind you, more than almost anything else, that this is the land of the ancient Romans. Beware that you may be fined on the spot for speeding, a burnt-out headlamp, etc; if you're especially unlucky you may be slapped with a *super multa*, a superfine, of L150,000 or more. You may even be fined for not having a portable triangle danger signal (pick one up at the frontier or from an ACI office for L2500).

The **Automobile Club of Italy** (ACI) is a good friend to the foreign motorist, and although they no longer offer free breakdown service, their prices are fair. They can be reached from anywhere by dialling 116—also use this number if you have an accident, need an ambulance, or simply have to find the nearest service station. If you need major repairs, the ACI can make sure the prices charged are according to their guidelines. Local ACI addresses are:

Florence: Viale Amendola 36, ✆ (055) 24861.
Lucca: Via Catalani 59, ✆ (0583) 582627.
Pisa: Via San Martino 1, ✆ (050) 47333.
Siena: Viale Vittorio Veneto 47, ✆ (0577) 49001.

Hiring a car is fairly simple if not particularly cheap. Italian car rental firms are called *autonoleggi*. There are both large international firms through which you can reserve a car in advance, and local agencies, which often have lower prices. Air or train travellers should check out possible discount packages; nearly all require the driver to be at least 21, or 25 for powerful cars. Average car hire is L160,000 a day for a Fiat Punto. Rates become more advantageous if you take the car for a week with unlimited mileage. Some essential numbers:

Florence: Most firms are in easy walking distance of the station. **Avis**, Borgo Ognissanti 128r, ✆ 213629; **Europcar**, Borgo Ognissanti 53r, ✆ 290438; **Hertz**, Via M. Finiguerra 33, ✆ 2398205; **Maggiore-Budget**, Via M. Finiguerra 31r, ✆ 294578; **Program**, Borgo Ognissanti 135, ✆: 282916; **Italy by Car**, Borgo Ognissanti 134r, ✆ 287161.

Pisa Airport: Hertz, ✆ 49187; **Maggiore-Budget**, ✆ 42574; **Avis**, ✆ 42028; **Program** (the most economical), ✆ 500296.

By Carriage

The **carozze** of Florence are now used only by tourists. Negotiate times and dates before you begin: prices can be as high as L150,000 per hour.

By Motorbike or Bicycle

The means of transport of choice for many Italians; motorbikes, mopeds and Vespas can be a delightful way to get between the cities and see the countryside. You should only consider it, however, if you've ridden them before—Italy's hills and aggravating traffic make it no place to learn. Helmets are compulsory. Hire costs for a *motorino* (moped) range from about L35,000 per day; Vespas (scooters) are somewhat more (from about L45,000).

Italians are keen cyclists as well, racing drivers up the steepest hills; if you're not training for the Tour de France, consider the region's hills well before planning a bicycling tour—especially in the hot summer months. Bikes can be transported by train in Italy, either with you or within a couple of days—apply at the baggage office (*ufficio bagagli*). Hire prices range from about L20,000 per day, and to buy one costs upwards of L250,000, either in a bike shop or through the classified ad papers which are put out in nearly every city and region. Alternatively, if you bring your own bike, do check the airlines to see what their policies are on transporting them.

Practical A–Z

Winter can be an agreeable time to visit the indoor attractions of the cities and avoid crowds, particularly in Florence, where it seldom snows but may rain for several days at a time.

Average Temperatures in °C (°F)

	January	April	July	October
Florence	6 (42)	13 (55)	25 (77)	16 (60)
Siena	5 (40)	12 (54)	25 (77)	15 (59)

Average Monthly Rainfall in mm (in)

	January	April	July	October
Florence	61 (3)	74 (3)	23 (1)	96 (4)
Siena	70 (3)	61 (3)	21 (1)	112 (4)

Courses for Foreigners

The **Italian Institute**, 39 Belgrave Square, London SW1X 8NX, ℘ (0171) 235 1461, or 686 Park Avenue, New York, NY 10021, ℘ (212) 879 4242, is the main source of information on courses for foreigners in Italy. Graduate students should also contact their nearest Italian consulate to find out about scholarships—apparently many go unused each year because no one knows about them.

One obvious course to take, especially in this linguistically pure land of Dante, is **Italian language and culture**: there are special summer classes offered by the Scuola Lingua e Cultura per Stranieri of the University of Siena, with special classes in August for teachers of Italian. Similar courses are held in Florence—sometimes there seem to be more American students than Florentines in the city. The following have courses all year round:

British Institute, Piazza Strozzi 1, ℘ (055) 284031, ✆ (055) 287056, runs courses on Florentine art and history. The school is at Via Tornabuoni 2, ℘ 284033.

Centro Fiorenza, Via di Santo Spirito, ℘ (055) 287148, offers history, literature and art at both basic and advanced levels. Also offers cooking courses.

Scuola Lorenzo de' Medici, Via dell'Alloro 14r, ℘ (055) 287143, has classes in language and art.

Centro Linguistico Italiano Dante Alighieri, Via de' Bardi 12, ℘ (055) 2342984, specializes in language courses.

Music courses complement the regions' numerous music festivals: Siena's Accademia Musicale Chigiana, Via di Città, offers master classes for instrumentalists and conductors.

Art-lovers can take a course on medieval art at Florence's Università Internazionale dell'Arte, in the Villa Tornabuoni, Via Incontri 3; courses are offered from October to April in history of art, restoration and design, while the Istituto per l'Arte e il Restauro, in Palazzo Spinelli, Borgo Santa Croce 10, holds workshops in art restoration.

A Taste of Florence, Via Taddea 31, ℗ (055) 292578: American cook, Judy Witts, has lived in Florence for many years, and her knowledge of the local food and culture is extensive. Courses are run from her home near the central market in Florence, and the day starts with a shopping session, progressing to the kitchen. Groups are limited to six, and most courses run for a day or a week.

Capezzana Wine and Culinary Centre, Via Cappezana 100, 59011 Loc. Seano, Carmignano, ℗ 8706005: this wine- and olive oil-producing estate some 30 km from Florence hosts courses designed for food professionals, skilled cooks and those involved with food and wine. Accommodation is available in a wing of the villa.

Disabled Travellers

Recent access-for-all laws in Italy have improved the once dire situation: the number of ramps and stair lifts has increased a hundredfold in the past few years, and nearly every hotel has one or two rooms for the disabled—although most of the older ones don't have a lift, or one large enough for a chair. And you could get stuck in unexpected places—Florence, visited by zillions of tourists, is embarassingly lacking in accessible loos. Long flights of steps in front were designed to impress on the would-be worshipper the feeling of going upwards to God—another raw deal for the disabled.

Specialist Organization in Italy

CO.IN (Consorzio Cooperative Integrate), Via Enrico Giglioli 54a, 00169 Rome, ℗ (6) 23267504, ℗ (6) 23267505. Their tourist information centre (open Mon–Fri 9–5) offers advice and information on accessibility.

Specialist Organizations in the UK

Holiday Care Service, 2nd floor, Imperial Buildings, Victoria Rd, Horley, Surrey RH6 9HW, ℗ (01293) 774535, for travel information and details of accessible accommodation and care holidays.

RADAR (Royal Association for Disability and Rehabilitation), 12 City Forum, 250 City Road, London EC1V 8AF, ℡ (0171) 250 3222. They publish *Holidays and Travel Abroad: a Guide for Disabled People* (£3.50), listing hotels with facilities, specialist tour operators, self-catering apartments and more.

Royal National Institute for the Blind, 224 Great Portland Street, London W15 5TB, ℡ (0171) 388 1266. Its mobility unit offers a 'Plane Easy' audio-cassette with advice for blind people travelling by plane. It will also advise on finding accommodation.

Tripscope, The Courtyard, Evelyn Road, London W4 5JL, ℡ (0181) 994 9294, offers practical advice and information on every aspect of travel and transport for elderly and disabled travellers. On request, information can be provided by letter or tape.

Some Specialist Organizations in the USA and Canada

American Foundation for the Blind, 15 West 16th Street, New York, NY 10011, ℡ (212) 620 2000; toll free ℡ 800 2323 5463. The best source of information in the USA for visually impaired travellers.

Mobility International USA, PO Box 10767, Eugene, OR 97440, ℡ (503) 343 1284, ℻ (503) 343 6812. Practical advice and information; $20 membership fee.

SATD (Society for the Advancement of Travel for the Disabled), 347 5th Ave, Suite 610, NY 10016, ℡ (212) 447 7284, offers advice on all aspects of travel for the disabled, on an ad hoc basis for a $3 charge, or unlimited to members ($45, concessions $25).

Jewish Rehabiliation Hospital, 3205 Place Alton Goldbloom, Montréal, Quebec, H7V 1R2, ℡ (514) 688 9550, ext 226. Can post guidebooks and information.

Travel Information Service, MossRehab Hospital, 1200 West Tabor Road, Philadelphia, PA 19141, ℡ (215) 456 96 00. Telephone information service supplying travel advice to people with disabilities.

Embassies and Consulates

Australia: Via Alessandria 215, Rome, ℡ (06) 852721

Britain: Lungarno Corsini 2, Florence, ℡ (055) 284133

Canada: Via Zara 30, Rome, ℡ (06) 8415341

Ireland: Largo Nazareno 3, Rome, ℡ (06) 6782541

New Zealand: Via Zara 28, Rome, ✆ (06) 440 2928

US: Lungarno Amerigo Vespucci 38, Florence, ✆ (055) 2398276.

Festivals

Although festivals in Florence, Siena, Pisa and Lucca are often more show than spirit (though there are several exceptions to the rule), they can add a note of pageantry or culture to your holiday. Some are great costume affairs, with roots dating back to the Middle Ages, and there are quite a few music festivals, antique fairs and, most of all, festivals devoted to food and drink.

Traditional festivals in **Florence** date back centuries. Easter Sunday's *Scioppio del Carro*, or 'Explosion of the Cart', commemorates Florentine participation in the First Crusade in 1096. The Florentines were led by Pazzino de' Pazzi, who upon returning home, received the special custody of the flame of Holy Saturday, with which the Florentines traditionally relit their family hearths. To make the event more colourful, the Pazzi constructed a decorated wooden ox cart to carry the flame. They lost the job after the Pazzi conspiracy in 1478, and since then the city has taken over the responsibility. In the morning, a firework-filled wooden float is pulled by a long procession of trumpeters, flag throwers, drummers and dignatories dressed in Renaissance costume from Porta a Prato to the cathedral, where, at 11am, during the singing of the Gloria, it is ignited by a model dove that descends on a wire from the high altar.

On a Sunday in late May, there's the *Festa del Grillo* (cricket festival) in the Cascine; Michelangelo was thinking of its little wooden cricket cages when he mocked Ammanati's gallery on the cathedral dome. June is the time of the three matches of *Calcio Storico in Costume* (historical football in 16th-century costume) in the Piazza Santa Croce, played by 27-man teams from Florence's four quarters, in memory of a defiant football match played in Piazza Santa Croce in 1530, during the siege by Charles V. Flag-throwing and a parade in historical costume are part of the pre-game ceremonies. The *Festa delle Rificolone* on 7 September is one of Florence's livelier festivals, with a parade of floats followed by a party in the streets. The best fireworks are reserved for the day of Florence's patron, San Giovanni (24 June).

Florentines adore cultural events. The big summer festival is the *Estate Fiesolana*: from late June–August the old Roman theatre is the site of concerts, ballet, theatre and films, for reasonable prices. The *Maggio Musicale Fiorentino*, the city's big music festival, spans from late April to the beginning of July and brings in big-name concert stars. Events take place in the Teatro Comunale, Corso Italia 12 (just off Lungarno Vespucci, ✆ 27791 or 2779236 for ticket information). There's usually some kind of music in the Piazza della Signoria during the summer, with a free concert for the closing of the *Maggio Musicale* festival (late June/early July), and a free ballet a few days later. Other events happen, but irregularly. Look out for posters. The **summer season** of the Teatro Comunale (opera, concerts and ballet) takes place in the Boboli Gardens, the Teatro Comunale and, during festival time only, the Teatro della Pergola (Via della Pergola 18, © 2479651). In May, don't miss the Iris Festival up at Piazzale Michelangelo.

An excellent season of top-rate chamber-music concerts and recitals is put on by the *Amici della Musica*, October–May. These normally take place at Teatro della Pergola, Via della Pergola 12/32, © 2479651. The *ORT* (*Orchestra Regionale Toscana*), based in Florence, plays regularly in Florence and in Tuscany (Pisa, Lucca, Siena, Pistoia, Livorno), December–May. Information on © 242767. The Flower Show is held in the Parterre, near Piazza Libertà, 25 April–1 May.

On 2 July and 16 August Italy's best-known festival is held in **Siena**—the *Palio*, the famous horse race run in the Campo when ten of the local neighbourhoods (or *contrade*) compete furiously against each other (*see* p.232). **Pisa** holds the *Gioco del Ponte* and historic procession on the last Sunday in June (*see* p.282) and the historic regatta and lights festival of San Ranieri on 16–17 June, when the banks of the Arno glimmer with tens of thousands of bulbs. Folklore displays are in order for San Sisto (6 August). Every four years in June Pisa is the site of the Old Maritime Republics' boat race (next 1999), a race between old sea rivals Pisa, Venice, Genoa and Amalfi. The Feast of San Paolino, **Lucca**'s patron saint, is celebrated on 12 July with the offering of a votive candle and the blessing of the *palio* or banner followed by a crossbow contest between the city's three districts in the evening.

Calendar of Events

January

6   Epiphany, or *La Befana,* is a children's festival in Italy, and a public holiday. In **Pisa**, the Befana appears in the form of costumed parachutists who land in the piazzas bringing presents to the children.

February

Sundays   Carnival time in Viareggio (province of **Lucca**) with huge parades of elaborate floats on consecutive Sundays in February, the last being the high point.

March

19   San Giuseppe, **Siena** (with rice fritters) and Torrita di Siena, with a donkey race and tournament.

April

Good Friday   Way of the Cross candlelight procession, Gràssina, near **Florence** and **San Grimiano** (**Siena** province).

Easter Sunday   *Scoppio del Carro,* procession with musicians and flag throwers, **Florence**.

confirm dates   Museum Week, with free admission to all municipal museums, **Florence**. Ask at the Tourist Office for confirmation of dates.

25 April–1 May   Flower show at the Parterre, **Florence**.

End   Flower show, **Lucca**.

May

Early Sunday   The *1000 Miglia* vintage car race passes through **Florence**.

Early Sunday   Flower show, Greve (province of **Florence**).

All month   Iris Festival, **Florence**.

Late Sunday   *Cantine Aperte,* wine estates throughout Tuscany throw open their doors for tastings and tours.

Ascension Day   Cricket Festival, Parco dell Cascine, **Florence**, with floats, and crickets sold in little cages.

May and June   Maggio Musicale Fiorentino, **Florence**.

June

16–17   *Festa di San Ranieri*—lights festival and historic regatta, **Pisa**.

3 weekends   *Calcio in Costume*, Renaissance football game, **Florence**.

24   St John the Baptist's Day, with fireworks, **Florence**.

25   *Gioco del Ponte*, a traditional bridge tug-of-war game with a cart in the middle, **Pisa**.

Last Sunday   San Donato in Poggio (**Florence** province), *La Bruscellata*, a week of dancing and old love songs around a flowering tree.

July

Early July–August	*Estate Fiesolana*—music, cinema, ballet and theatre, in **Florence**.
2	*Palio*, since 1147, **Siena**.
12	Feast of San Paolino, **Lucca**, with parades and games.
End July–mid-August	Puccini Opera Festival, Camaiore (province of **Lucca**). Spectacular lakeside setting for performances of Puccini's operas.
16, 17, 18 July	Pistoia Blues. Excellent blues festival in Pistoia, province of **Florence**.
July	Week of concerts associated with the Chigiana music school.
July/August	*Incontri in Terra di Siena,* three weeks of international chamber-music concerts in Pienza, Sinalunga and Montepulciano, all in **Siena** province.

August

First weekend	Traditional thanksgiving festival in honour of San Sisto, **Pisa**.
16	*Palio*, **Siena**.

September

First Sunday	Processions; lantern festival, **Florence**.
13–14	Feast of Santa Croce, **Lucca**; candlelit procession in honour of the *Volto Santo* (11th-century crucifix) followed by a fair the next day in Piazza San Michele.
End	Grape festival, Impruneta (near **Florence**), with food and wine stalls, and a parade of floats.
Sept–Dec	Opera and ballet season at the Teatro Comunale, **Florence**.

November

22	Santa Cecilia, patroness of music, celebrated with concerts in **Siena**.

December

13	Santa Lucia, celebrated with a pottery fair in **Siena**.

Emergencies, ✆ 113

You can insure yourself against almost any mishap—cancelled flight, stolen or lost baggage, and health—for a price. National health services in the UK and Australia have reciprocal health care agreements with Italy (pack an E-111 form). Citizens of other countries should check their current policies to see if they provide cover while abroad, and under what circumstances, and judge whether a special traveller's insurance policy is required. Travel agencies sell policies, as well as insurance companies, but they are not cheap.

Minor illnesses and problems that crop up in Italy can usually be handled free of charge in a public hospital clinic or *ambulatorio*. If you need minor aid, Italian pharmacists are highly trained and can probably diagnose your problem; look for a *farmacia* (they all have a list in the window with details of which ones are open during the night and on holidays). Extreme cases should head for the *Pronto Soccorso* (First Aid Service). Italian doctors are not always great linguists; contact your embassy or consulate for a list of English-speaking doctors.

Medical Emergencies

Florence: for an ambulance or first aid, Misericordia, Piazza del Duomo 20, ✆ 21 2222. Doctor's night service, ✆ 287788. The general hospital Santa Maria Nuova, in Piazza S. M. Nuova, ✆ 27581, is the most convenient. Tourist Medical Service, 24 hours a day, is staffed by English- and French-speaking physicians at Via Lorenzo il Magnifico 59, ring first on ✆ 475411. There is a pharmacy open 24 hours every day in S. Maria Novella Station, also Molteni, Via Calzaiuoli 7r and Taverna, Piazza S. Giovanni 20r, by the Baptistry.

Siena: ambulance, ✆ 118; hospital ✆ 585111; doctor's night service ✆ 586466/118; Farmacia Centrale, Via Banchi di Sotto 2, ✆ 286109.

Pisa: Farmacia dell'Ospedale, Via Roma ✆ 592111.

Frequent travellers have noted a steady improvement over the years in the cleanliness of Italy's public conveniences; there are fewer holes in the ground, and loo paper is more generally on offer, although as ever you will only find them in places like train and bus stations and bars. If you can't find a public loo, go into the nearest bar; they are legally obliged to let you use their *bagno*. In stations, motorway rest stops and the smarter cafés, there are washroom attendants who expect a few hundred lire. Don't confuse the Italian plurals: *signori* (gents), *signore* (ladies).

Libraries

Florence: British Institute Library, Lungarno Guicciardini 9, ℗ 284032, open 9.45–1 and 3–6.30, closed Sat and Sun. There are so many other libraries in Florence that one, the Biblioteca del Servizio Beni Librari, Via G. Modena 13, ℗ 4382266, does nothing but dispense information on all the others.

Pisa: Biblioteca Provinciale, Via Betti, ℗ 929482.

Lucca: Biblioteca Statale, 12 Via Santa Maria Orlandini, ℗ 41271.

Lost Property and Towed Cars

In Italian lost property is *oggetti smarriti* or *oggetti ritrovati*. The main office in Florence is at Via Circondaria 17b, ℗ 3283942. There are three pounds for **towed-away cars**, but they have a central phone number, ℗ 308249, where they will tell you where your car has been taken. The main pound (open 24 hours) is the *Depositeria Comunale* on Viale Strozzi at the Tourist Bus Park (on the west side of the Fortezza Da Basso). Alternatively, your car could be taken to Via Arcovata 6 (bus 23, 33 to Viale Corsica), open Mon–Sat 7am–9pm, or, less likely, to the car park at the Parterre (near Piazza Libertà), open Mon–Sat 7am–1am, and Sun 7am–8pm.

Maps

The best maps are *Firenze Piantà* (Touring Club Italiano, 1:12,500) and *Firenze* (Litografia Artistica, 1:9000); *Siena City Plan* (Freytag and Berndt, 1:5000); *Pisa City Plan* (Freytag and Berndt, 1:8000); *Lucca Città Piantà* (Studio F.M.B., 1:6000).

Money

It's a good idea to bring some Italian lire with you; unforeseen delays and unexpected public holidays may foul up your plans to find a bank open when you arrive. **Traveller's cheques** or Eurocheques remain the most secure way of financing your holiday in Italy; they are easy to change and an insurance against unpleasant surprises. **Credit cards** (American Express, Diner's Club, Mastercard, Access, Eurocard, Barclaycard, Visa) are accepted in most hotels, restaurants, shops and most petrol stations (possibly not in single-pump operations in the middle of the country). If you have a PIN number you can use the many **cash-point machines**. Do not be surprised if you are asked to show identification when paying with a credit card.

There's been a lot of loose talk about knocking three noughts off the Italian lira, but Italy will go on to the Euro before that happens; until then, everybody can be a 'millionaire'. It can, however, be confusing to visitors unaccustomed to dealing with rows of zeros, and more than once you'll think you're getting a great deal until you recount the zeros on the price tag. Some unscrupulous operators may try to take advantage when you're changing money, so do be careful. **Notes** come in denominations of L500,000, L100,000, L50,000, L10,000, L5000, L2000 and L1000; coins are in L500, L200, L100, L50.

Money can be sent to Italy through Thomas Cook travel agents, Western Union and American Express, or by having someone at home telexing the amount to an Italian bank for you to go and pick up. Technically, it shouldn't take more than a couple of days to arrive (but it always does). Make sure the telex includes the number of your passport, ID card, or driver's licence, or the Italians may not hand over the cash.

Banking Hours

Banks are usually open 8.30am–1.20pm, and for one hour in the afternoon (3–4 or 4–5pm). They are closed on Saturdays, Sundays and national holidays. Some are worth visiting for their space-capsule doors alone.

American Express in Florence: Via Dante Alighieri 22R, ✆ 50981, just off Piazza della Repubblica; and Via Guicciardini 49R, PO Box 617, ✆ 288751. The Via Guicciardini office only offers change facilities.

Official Holidays

The Italians have cut down somewhat on their official national holidays, but note that every town has one or two holidays of its own—usually the feast day of its patron saint. Official holidays, shown on transport timetables and museum opening hours etcetera, are treated the same as Sundays.

1 January   New Year's Day—*Capodanno*.

6 January   Epiphany, better known to Italians as the day of *La Befana*—
                      a kindly witch who brings the *bambini* the toys Santa Claus
                      or *Babbo Natale* somehow forgot.

Easter Monday   Usually pretty dull.

25 April	Liberation Day—even duller.
1 May	Labour Day—lots of parades, speeches, picnics, music and drinking.
15 August	Assumption, or *Ferragosto*—the biggest of them all. Woe to the innocent traveller on the road or train!
1 November	All Saints', or *Ognissanti*—liveliest at the cemeteries.
8 December	Immaculate Conception of the Virgin Mary—another dull one.
25 December	Christmas Day.
Boxing Day	*Santo Stefano*.

Opening Hours and Museums

Most of Tuscany closes down at 1pm until 3 or 4pm, to eat and properly digest the main meal of the day, although things are now beginning to change in the cities. Many more shops in the centre of town now stay open during lunch. Afternoon working hours are from 4 to 7, often from 5 to 8 in the hot summer months.

Food shops shut on Wednesday afternoons in the winter. They close on Saturday afternoons only from the end of June to the beginning of September. Sunday opening is becoming more usual, particularly for shops in the centre of town. Bars are often the only places open during the early afternoon and sometimes on a Sunday. (For **bank** opening hours, *see* p.23.)

Churches have always been a prime target for art thieves and as a consequence are usually locked when there isn't a sacristan or caretaker to keep an eye on things. All churches, except for the really important cathedrals and basilicas, close in the afternoon at the same hours as the shops, and the little ones tend to stay closed. Always have a pocketful of L100, L200 and L500 coins to batten the light machines in churches, or what you came to see is bound to be hidden in ecclesiastical shadows. Some churches now have light machines that accept only L1000 notes, but the light-up time rarely lasts more than a minute. Don't do your visiting during services, and don't come to see paintings and statues in churches the week preceding Easter—you will probably find them covered with mourning shrouds.

Most **museums** are open all day from 9am to 7pm and tend to close on a Monday and often Sunday afternoons as well. Some are now open until 10pm. Many are magnificent, many are run with shameful neglect, and many have been closed for years for 'restoration'. Expect to pay between L4000 and L8000 for museum entrance; expensive ones run to L10,000 and L12,000 (Ufizzi, Accademia). The good news is that state-run museums and monuments are free if you're under 18 or over 60 (bring ID).With an estimated one work of art per inhabitant, Italy has a hard time financing the preservation of its national heritage, and if there's something you really want to see, you would do well to enquire at the tourist office whether it's open or 'temporarily' closed before setting out.

Packing

You simply cannot overdress in Italy. Now, whether or not you want to try to keep up with the natives is your own affair and your own heavy suitcase—you may do well to compromise and just bring a couple of smart outfits for big nights out. It's not that the Italians are very formal; they simply like to dress up with a gorgeousness that adorns their cities just as much as those old Renaissance churches and palaces. The few places with dress codes are the major churches and basilicas (no shorts or sleeveless shirts), and the smarter restaurants.

After agonizing over fashion, remember to pack small and light: transatlantic airlines limit baggage by size (two pieces are free, up to 1.5m in height and width; in second class you're allowed one of 1.5m and another up to 110cm). Within Europe limits are by weight: 20 kilos (44lbs) in second class, 30 kilos (66lbs) in first. You may well be penalized for anything bigger. If you're travelling mainly by train, you'll especially want to keep bags to a minimum: jamming big suitcases in overhead racks isn't much fun.

Never take more than you can carry, but do bring the following: any prescription medicine you need, an extra pair of glasses or contact lenses, a pocket knife and corkscrew (for picnics), a torch (for dark frescoed churches and hotel corridors), a travel alarm (for those early trains) and a pocket Italian-English dictionary (for flirting and other emergencies). You may want to invest in earplugs. Your European electric appliances will work in Italy; just change your plug to the two-prong variety or buy a travel plug; American appliances need transformers as well.

Photography

Film and developing are much more expensive than they are in the USA or UK. You are not allowed to take pictures in most museums and in some churches. Most cities now offer one-hour processing if you need your pics in a hurry.

Police/Emergency, ✆ 113

There is a fair amount of petty crime in the cities—purse snatchings, pickpocketing, minor thievery of the white-collar kind (always check your change) and car break-ins and theft—but violent crime is rare. Nearly all mishaps can be avoided with adequate precautions. Scooter-borne purse-snatchers can be foiled if you stay on the inside of the pavement and keep a firm hold on your property; pickpockets most often strike in crowded buses and gatherings; don't carry too much cash or keep some of it in another place. Be extra careful in train stations, don't leave valuables in hotel rooms, and park your car in garages, guarded car parks, or on well-lit streets, with temptations like radios, cassettes, etc., out of sight. Purchasing small quantities of cannabis is legal although what a small quantity might be exactly is unspecified, so if the police don't like you to begin with, it will probably be enough to get you into big trouble.

Once the scourge of Italy, political terrorism has declined drastically in recent years, mainly thanks to special squads of the *carabinieri*, the black-uniformed national police, technically part of the Italian army. Local matters are usually in the hands of the *polizia urbana*; the nattily dressed *vigili urbani* concern themselves with directing traffic and handing out parking fines. You probably will not have anything to do with the *guardia di finanza*, the financial police, who spend their time chasing corrupt politicians and their friends (unless they catch you leaving a bar or restaurant without a receipt!).

Florence: the *Ufficio Stranieri*, in the *questura*, Via Gallo 81, ✆ 49771, (open Mon–Fri 8.30–12, and Tues–Thurs) handles most foreigners' problems, and usually has someone around who speaks English. Good for residents' permits.

Siena: the *Ufficio Stranieri* is at Piazza Jacopo della Quercia (open Mon–Sat 10–12, and Wed 4.30–6.30).

The postal service in Italy is both the least efficient and the most expensive in Europe, and disgracefully slow; if you're sending postcards back home you often arrive there before they do. If it's important that it should arrive in less than a week, send your letter *Espresso* (Swift Air Mail) for a L3600 supplement, or *Raccomandata* (registered delivery) for a L4000 supplement. Stamps (*francobolli*) may also be purchased at tobacconists (look for a big black T on the sign), but you're bound to get differing opinions on your exact postage. Mail to the UK goes at the same rate as domestic Italian mail, but it's still twice as much to send a letter from Italy to Britain as vice versa (L800). Airmail letters to and from North America can quite often take up to two weeks. This can be a nightmare if you're making hotel reservations and are sending a deposit—faxing or telephoning ahead is far more secure if time is short.

Ask for mail to be sent to you in Italy either care of your hotel or addressed *Fermo Posta* (poste restante: general delivery) to a post office, or, if you're a card-holder, to an American Express office. When you pick up your mail at the *Fermo Posta* window, bring your passport for identification. Make sure that your mail is sent to the proper post office; the **Posta Centrale** is often the easiest option.

The Italian post achieves Gormenghastian levels of inscrutabilty if you try to send a package overseas. Packages have to be of a certain size, under a certain weight to be sent in certain ways, and must have a flap open or be sealed with string and lead. You're best off taking it to a stationer's shop (*cartoleria*) and paying them to wrap it—they usually know what the postal demons are going to require.

Main Post Offices

Florence: Via Pellicceria, near Piazza della Repubblica, open Mon–Sat 8.15–7, ✆ 214145; telegram office open Mon–Sat 8.15–7, or ✆ 160. **E-Mail Services**: you can send e-mail, use the internet or fax from Internet Train, Via dell'Oriulo 25r or Via Guelfa 24a, ✆/✉ 214794; they are also agents for the **Swiss Post International** if you want to avoid the nitpicking slowpokes in the Posta Italiana.

Siena: Piazza Matteotti 37, ✆ 41482.

Pisa: Piazza Vittorio Emanuele II, ✆ 23288.

Lucca: 2 Via Vallisneri, ✆ 46669.

Telephones

> **To call Italy** from abroad, dial ✆ 00 39 followed by the area prefix— omitting the first 0.

Like many things in Italy, telephoning can be unduly complicated and usually costs over the odds to boot. Public phones will accept L100, L200 and L500 coins, as well as phone cards. These cost L5000, L10,000 and L15,000 and are available in tobacconists, stationers (*cartolerie*), bars and newsstands. A digital display will indicate the money you have put in or how much credit is left on your card. When you hear the beep it is usually too late to put any more money in, so keep an eye on the display. If your credit on the phone card runs out, insert another one when you hear a beep. The cards are the best option for long-distance phoning and are available from tobacconist shops for L5000 and L10,000. Hotels and bars sometimes have metered telephones. If you want to reverse charges (call collect), you can call from a phone box; dial ✆ 172 followed by the country code and you will be connected to an international operator.

Tourist Offices

For more information before you go, write to the Italian National Tourist Office:

UK: 1 Princes Street, London W1R 8AY, ✆ (0171) 408 1254

Ireland: 47 Merrion Square, Dublin 2, ✆ (01) 766397

USA: 630 Fifth Avenue, Suite 1565, New York, NY 10111, ✆ (212) 245 4822

500 N. Michigan Avenue, Chicago, Ill. 60611, ✆ (312) 644 0990

12400 Wiltshire Blvd, Los Angeles, California 90025, ✆ (310) 820 0098

Canada: 1 Place Ville Marie, Suite 1914, Montreal, Québec, ✆ (514) 866 7667

Australia: c/o the Italian Embassy, 61–69 Macquerie St, Sidney 2000, NSW, ✆ (02) 9247 8442

New Zealand: c/o the Italian Embassy, 36 Grant Rd, Thomdon, Wellington, ✆ (04) 736 065

For detailed information, write directly to any of the city tourist offices. These are usually very helpful in sending out lists of flats or villas to hire, or lists of agents who handle the properties.

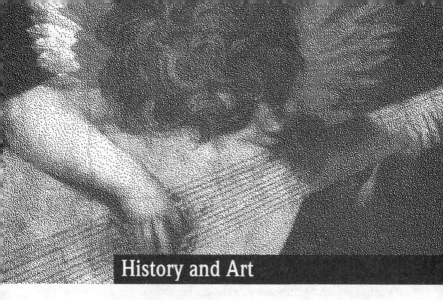

History and Art

At times, the history of Tuscany has been a small part of a bigger story—Rome's, or modern Italy's. However, in the crucial eras of the Middle Ages and the Renaissance each of the city states had a complex history of its own; these are covered in detail under each city.

City Origins

Florence, Siena and Pisa all originated with the first baby steps, or rather stomps, of the Roman empire. As southern Etruria, the old Etruscan heartland, shrivelled and died under Roman misrule in the 4th and 3rd centuries BC, northern Etruria, colonised by Romans, became more prosperous, and important new cities appeared: Lucca, Pisa, Florence, and to a lesser extent, Siena. After the fall of Rome, these cities limped through the various wars and barbarian invasions; only Lucca, the late Roman and Gothic capital of Etruria, managed to keep out the nastiest brutes of all, the bloodthirsty Lombards (AD 568). By this time, low-lying Florence had practically disappeared, while the remnants of the other towns survived under the control of local barons, or occasionally under their bishops. Feudal warfare and marauding became endemic.

By the 9th century, things were looking up. Florence had re-established itself, and built its famous baptistry. The old counts of Lucca extended their power to become counts of Tuscany, under the Attoni family, lords of Canossa. As the leading power in the region, they made themselves a force in European affairs. In 1077, the great Countess Matilda, allied with the Pope, humbled Emperor Henry IV at Canossa—the famous 'penance in the snow' during the struggles over investiture. Perhaps most important of all was the growth of the maritime city of Pisa, which had cleverly allied itself with the Normans as they devoured all of south Italy and Sicily, at the expense of the Byzantines and Muslims. Pisa's bold conquests over Muslim fleets in Palermo and North Africa made her the mistress of the western Mediterranean by the 1080s, giving Tuscany a new window on the world, building wealth through trade and inviting new cultural influences from France, Byzantium and the Muslim world.

Medieval *Comuni*

By 1000, with the new millennium, all of northern Italy was poised to rebuild the civilization that had been lost centuries before. In Tuscany, as elsewhere, increasing trade had created a rebirth of towns, each doing its best to establish its independence from local nobles or bishops, and to increase its influence at the expense of its neighbours. Thus a thousand minor squabbles were played out against the background of the major issues of the day; first came the conflict over investiture in the 11th century, evolving into the endless factional struggles of **Guelphs** and **Ghibellines** after the year 1215 (*see* **Topics**, p.55). Throughout, the cities were forced to choose sides between the partisans of the popes and those of the emperors. The Ghibellines' brightest hours came with the reigns of strong Hohenstaufen emperors **Frederick I Barbarossa** (1152–90) and his grandson **Frederick II** (1212–46), both of whom spent much time in Tuscany. An early Guelph wave came with the papacy of **Innocent III** (1198–1216), most powerful of the medieval pontiffs, and the Guelphs would come back to dominate Tuscany after the invasion of Charles of Anjou in 1261. Florence and Lucca were mainstays of the Guelphs, while Pisa and Siena usually supported the Ghibellines.

In truth, it was every city for itself. By 1200, most towns had become free *comuni*; their imposing public buildings can be seen to this day. All the trouble they caused fighting each other (at first with citizen militias, later increasingly with the use of hired *condottieri*) never troubled the booming economy. Florence and Siena became bankers to all Europe, beginning their fierce rivalry—Florentine bankers collaborated to finance kings and other great men with Europe's first gold coin, the florin (1252); Sienese bankers raked in huge profits by holding the leases and collecting the debts for the popes and the Curia. Great building programmes went up, beginning with the Pisa cathedral complex in the 1100s, while the now tamed and urbanized nobles built fantastical skyscraper skylines of tower-fortresses in the cities. Above all, it was a great age for culture, the age of Dante (b. 1265) and Giotto (b. 1266). Another feature of the time was the 13th-century religious revival, dominated by the figure of **St Francis of Assisi**.

The Background of the Renaissance

Florence, biggest and richest of the Tuscan cities, increased its influence all through the late 1200s and 1300s, in spite of the humiliating defeat at the hands of Siena in 1260 at the battle of Monteaperti (all of the Sienese captains were for razing arrogant Florence, once and for all, but their commander, a turn-coat Florentine gangster named Farinata degli Uberti, surprised all by standing up and announcing that, even if he had to stand alone, he would defend Florence for as long as he lived; the Sienese were so surprised they let Farinata have his way and lost their chance of ever becoming *numero uno* in Tuscany). The Sienese had cause to regret their clemency nine years later, when Florence soundly defeat them at the battle of Colle Val d'Elsa; in 1298, they even took most of Siena's business away when the city's leading bank, the Tavola dei Bonsignori, collapsed. Left the undisputed financial centre of Europe, Florence gobbled up Prato and

Pistoia, and finally won a seaport with the capture of declining Pisa in 1406. This set the stage for the relative political equilibrium of Tuscany during the early Renaissance, the height of the region's wealth and artistic achievement.

The **Wars of Italy**, beginning in 1494, put an end to Renaissance tranquillity. Florence was once more lost in its internal convolutions, twice expelling the **Medici**, while French and Spanish imperial armies marched over Tuscany. When the dust had cleared, the Republic of Siena, which had dared to side with the French, had been extinguished, and with the rest of Tuscany came under the rule of the Grand Duke **Cosimo I** (1537–74), the Medici propped on a newly made throne by Emperor Charles V. Only the tiny duchy of Lucca kept its independence.

The Modern Era

Though maintaining a relative independence, Tuscany had little to say in Italian affairs. Cosimo I proved a vigorous ruler, though his successors gradually declined in ability. By 1600 it didn't matter. The total exhaustion of the Florentine economy kept pace with that of the Florentine imagination. By 1737, when the Medici dynasty became extinct, Tuscany was one of the torpid backwaters of Europe. It had no chance to decide its own destiny; the European powers agreed to bestow Tuscany on the House of Lorraine, cousins to the Austrian Habsburgs. Surprisingly enough, the Lorraines proved able and popular rulers, especially during the rule of the enlightened, progressive Peter Leopold (1765–90).

The languor of Lorraine was interrupted by Napoleon, who invaded central Italy twice and established a Kingdom of Etruria from 1801 to 1807. Austrian rule then returned after 1815, continuing the series of well-meaning, intelligent Grand Dukes. By now, however, the Tuscans and the rest of the Italians wanted something better. In the tumults of the Risorgimento, one of the greatest and kindest of the Lorraines, Leopold II, saw the writing on the wall and allowed himself to be overthrown in 1859. Tuscany was almost immediately annexed to the new Italian kingdom. Since then, the region has followed the history of modern Italy. The head start that Tuscany gained under the Lorraine dukes allowed it to keep up economically with northern Italy. Florence had a brief moment of glory (1865–70) as capital of Italy, awaiting the capture of Rome. Since then, the biggest affair was World War II; the Germans based their Gothic Line on the Arno, blowing up all but one of Florence's bridges, and all of Pisa's.

Stendhal once wrote: 'Ask the Florentines what they are, and they will respond by telling you what they were.' Tuscany's separate sense of identity has spared it most of the convulsions that have shaken Italy in recent years—the corruption and bribe scandals have mostly happened elsewhere, in Sicily, Rome and Milan.

The Tuscany of the 1990s has concentrated on safeguarding its tremendous patrimony of art and architecture while trying to create new jobs and investments to reignite the spark that made the region the wealthiest and most innovative in Europe 800 years ago.

Art and Architecture

Etruscans, Romans and Dark Ages

Although we have no way of knowing what life was like for the average Etruscan, their tomb sculptures and paintings convince us that they were a talented, likeable people. Almost all their art derives from the Greek; the Etruscans built classical temples (unfortunately of wood, with terracotta embellishments, so little survives), carved themselves sarcophagi decorated with scenes from Homer, and painted their pottery in red and black after the latest styles from Athens or Corinth. They excelled at portrait sculpture, and had a remarkable gift for capturing personality, sometimes seriously, though never heroically, often with an entirely intentional humour, and usually the serene smiles of people who truly enjoyed life.

Etruscan art, as in Florence's archaeology museum, is often maddening; some of the works are among the finest productions of antiquity, while others—from the same time and place—are more awkward and childish. Their talent for portraiture, among much else, was carried on by the Romans, and they bequeathed their love of fresco painting to the artists of the Middle Ages and Renaissance, who of course weren't even aware of the debt. Once you have introduced yourself to the art of the Etruscans, you will find it interesting to reconsider all that came later—in Tuscany especially, you will find subtle reminders of this enigmatic people.

After destroying the Etruscan nation, the Romans also began the extinction of its artistic tradition; by the Empire, there was almost nothing left that could be called distinctively Etruscan. Artistically, neither Florence, Siena, Pisa nor Lucca contributed much under the Empire. In the chaos that followed, there was little room for art. What painting survived followed styles current in Byzantium, a stylization that lingered into the 13th century in Tuscan panel painting.

The Middle Ages

In both architecture and sculpture, the first influence came from the north. Lombard masons filled Tuscany with simple Romanesque churches, although it wasn't long before two distinctive Tuscan forms emerged: the Pisan style, characterized by blind rows of colonnades, black and white zebra stripes, and lozenge-shaped designs; and the 'Tuscan Romanesque' which developed around Florence, notable for its use of dark and light marble patterns and simple geometric patterns, often with intricate mosaic floors to match (the Baptistry and San Miniato in Florence are the chief examples). In the cities in between, such as Lucca, there are interesting variations on the two different styles, often carrying an element like stripes or arcades to remarkable extremes. Siena was perhaps the most receptive to Gothic styles from the north, but adapted to an Italian sensibility that produced not only churches but unique public buildings such as the Palazzo Comunale, all of good siena-coloured brick.

From the large pool of talent working on Pisa's great cathedral complex in the 13th century emerged Italy's first great sculptor, **Nicola Pisano**, whose Baptistry pulpit, with its naturalistic figures, derived from ancient reliefs, finally broke away from the stiff hieratic figures of Byzantium. His even more remarkable son, **Giovanni Pisano**, prefigures Donatello in the expressiveness of his statues and the vigour of his pulpits; his façade of Siena cathedral, though altered, is a unique work of art. **Arnolfo di Cambio**, a student of Nicola Pisano, became chief sculptor-architect of Florence during its building boom in the 1290s, designing its cathedral and Palazzo Vecchio with a hitherto unheard-of scale and grandeur.

Painting at first lagged behind the new realism and more complex composition of sculpture. The first to depart from Byzantine stylization, at least according to the account in Vasari's *Lives of the Artists* (*see* **Topics**, p.53), was **Cimabue**, in the late 1200s, who forsook Greek forms for a more 'Latin' or 'natural' way of painting. Cimabue found his greatest pupil, **Giotto**, as a young shepherd, chalk-sketching sheep on a piece of slate. Brought to Florence, Giotto soon eclipsed his master's fame (artistic celebrity being a recent Florentine invention) and achieved the greatest advances on the road to the new painting with a plain, rather severe approach that shunned Gothic prettiness while exploring new ideas in composition and expressing psychological depth in his subjects. Even more importantly, Giotto through his intuitive grasp of perspective was able to go further than any previous artist in representing his subjects as actual figures in space. In a sense Giotto actually invented space; it was this, despite his often awkward and graceless draughtsmanship, that so astounded his contemporaries. His followers, **Taddeo** and **Agnolo Gaddi** (father and son), **Giovanni da Milano**, and **Maso di Banco** filled Florence's churches with their own interpretations of the master's style. In the latter half of the 1300s, however, there also appeared the key figure of **Andrea Orcagna**, the most important Florentine sculptor, painter and architect of his day. Inspired by the more elegant style of **Andrea Pisano**'s Baptistry doors, Orcagna broke away from the simple Giottesque forms for a more elaborate, detailed style in his sculpture, while the fragments of his frescoes that survive have a vivid dramatic power which undoubtedly owes something to the time of the Black Death and social upheavals in which they were painted.

Siena never produced a Vasari to chronicle its accomplishments, though they were considerable; in the 13th and 14th centuries, Siena's Golden Age, the city's artists, like its soldiers, rivalled and often surpassed those of Florence. For whatever reason, it seemed purposefully to seek inspiration in different directions from Florence; at first from central Italian styles around Spoleto, then, with prosperity and the advent of **Guido da Siena** in the early 1200s, to the more elegant line and colour of Byzantium. Guido's work paved the way for the pivotal figure of **Duccio di Buoninsegna**, the catalyst who founded the essentials of Sienese art by uniting the beauty of Byzantine line and colour with the sweet finesse and new human warmth of western Gothic art. With Duccio's great followers **Pietro** and **Ambrogio Lorenzetti** and **Simone Martini**, the Sienese produced an increasingly elegant and rarefied art, almost oriental in its refined stylization. They were less innovative than the Florentines, though they brought the 'International Gothic' style—flowery and ornate, with all the bright tones of May—to its highest form in Italy. Simone Martini introduced the Sienese manner to Florence in the early 1400s, where it influenced most notably the work of **Lorenzo Monaco**, **Masolino**, and the young goldsmith and sculptor, **Ghiberti**.

The Renaissance

Under the assaults of historians and critics over the last two centuries, the term 'Renaissance' has become a vague and controversial word. Nevertheless, however you choose to interpret this rebirth of the arts, and whatever dates you assign to it, Florence inescapably takes the credit for it. This is no small claim. Combining art, science and humanist scholarship into a visual revolution that often seemed pure sorcery to their contemporaries, a handful of Florentine geniuses taught the Western eye a new way of seeing. Perspective seems a simple enough trick to us now, but its discovery determined everything that followed, not only in art, but in science and philosophy as well.

Leading what scholars used self-assuredly to call the 'Early Renaissance' is a triumvirate of three geniuses: **Brunelleschi**, **Donatello** and **Masaccio**. Brunelleschi, neglecting his considerable talents in sculpture for architecture and science, not only built the majestic dome of Florence cathedral, but threw the Pandora's box of perspective wide open by mathematically codifying the principles of foreshortening. His good friend Donatello, the greatest sculptor since the ancient Greeks, inspired a new generation of both sculptors and painters to explore new horizons in portraiture and three-dimensional representation. The first painter to incorporate Brunelleschi and Donatello's lessons of spatiality, perspective and expressiveness was the young prodigy Masaccio, who along with his master Masolino painted the famous Brancacci Chapel in the Carmine, studied by nearly every Florentine artist down to Michelangelo.

The new science of architecture, sculpture and painting introduced by this triumvirate ignited an explosion of talent unequalled before or since—a score of masters, most of them Tuscan, each following the dictates of his own genius to create a remarkable range of themes and styles. To mention only the most prominent: **Lorenzo Ghiberti**, who followed Donatello's advice on his second set of Baptistry doors to cause a Renaissance revolution; **Leon Battista Alberti**, who took Brunelleschi's ideas to their most classical extreme in architecture, creating new forms in the process; **Paolo Uccello**, one of the most provocative of artists, who according to Vasari drove himself bats with the study of perspective and the possibilities of illusionism; **Piero della Francesca**, who explored the limits of perspective and geometrical forms to create the most compelling, haunting images of the quattrocento; **Fra Angelico**, who combined Masaccio's innovations and International Gothic colours and his own deep faith to create the most purely spiritual art of his time; **Andrea del Castagno**, who made use of perspective to create monumental, if often restless figures.

And still more: **Benozzo Gozzoli**, whose enchanting springtime colours and delight in detail are a throwback to the International Gothic; **Antonio** and **Piero Pollaiuolo**, sons of a poultryman, whose new, dramatic use of line and form, often violent and writhing, would be echoed in Florentine Mannerism; **Fra Filippo Lippi**, a monk like Fra Angelico but far more earthly, the master of lovely Madonnas, teacher of his talented son **Filippino Lippi**; **Domenico Ghirlandaio**, whose gift of easy charm and flawless technique made him society's fresco painter; **Andrea del Verrocchio**, who could cast in bronze, paint, or carve with perfect detail; **Perugino** (Pietro Vannucci) of Umbria, who painted the stillness of his native region into his landscapes and taught the young Raphael; and finally **Sandro Botticelli**, whose highly intellectual, but lovely and melancholy, mythological paintings are in a class of their own.

Some of Donatello's gifted followers were **Agostino di Duccio**, **Benedetto da Maiano**, **Desiderio da Settignano**, **Antonio** and **Bernardo Rossellino**, **Mino da Fiesole** and perhaps most famously, **Luca della Robbia**, who invented the coloured terracottas his family spread throughout Tuscany. The leading sculptor in Siena, **Jacopo della Quercia**, also left a number of works elsewhere, especially the lovely tomb of Ilaria del Carretto in Lucca (1408). A few decades later Lucca produced its own great sculptor, **Matteo Civitali**.

The 'Early Renaissance' came to a close near the end of the 1400s with the advent of **Leonardo da Vinci**, whose unique talent in painting, only one of his hundred interests, challenged the certainty of naturalism with a subtlety and chiaroscuro that approaches magic. One passion, however, obsessed the other great figure of the 'High Renaissance', **Michelangelo Buonarroti**: his consummate interest was the human body, at first graceful and serene as in most of his Florentine works, and later, contorted and anguished after he left for Rome.

Mannerism

Michelangelo left in Florence the seeds for the bold, neurotic avant-garde art that has come to be known as Mannerism. The first conscious 'movement' in Western art can be seen as a last fling amid the growing intellectual and spiritual exhaustion of 1530s Florence, conquered once and for all by the Medici. The Mannerists' calculated exoticism and exaggerated, tortured poses, together with the brooding self-absorption of Michelangelo, are a prelude to Florentine art's remarkably abrupt turn into decadence and prophesy its final extinction. Foremost among the Mannerist painters are two surpassingly strange characters, **Jacopo Pontormo** and **Rosso Fiorentino**, who were not in such great demand as the coldly classical **Andrea del Sarto** and **Bronzino**, consummate perfectionists of the brush, both much less intense and demanding. There were also charming reactionaries working at the same time, especially **Il Sodoma** and **Pinturicchio**, both of whom left their best works in Siena. In sculpture **Giambologna** and to a lesser extent **Bartolommeo Ammannati** specialized in virtuoso *contrapposto* figures, each one more impossible than the last. In sculpture, too, Siena shied away from Florentine exaggeration, as in the work of Jacopo della Quercia's chief disciple, **Vecchietta**.

With the advent of Giambologna and Ammannati's contemporary, **Giorgio Vasari**, Florentine art lost almost all imaginative and intellectual content, and became a virtuoso style of interior decoration perfectly adaptable to saccharine holy pictures, portraits of newly enthroned dukes, or absurd mythological fountains and ballroom ceilings. In the cinquecento, with plenty of money to spend and a long Medici tradition of patronage to uphold, this tendency soon got out of hand. Under the reign of Cosimo I, indefatigable collector of *pietra dura* tables, silver and gold gimcracks, and exotic stuffed animals, Florence gave birth to yet another artistic phenomenon—one that modern critics call kitsch.

The Rest Compressed

In the long, dark night of later Tuscan art a few artists stand out—the often whimsical architect and engineer, **Buontalenti**; **Pietro Tacca**, Giambologna's pupil with a taste for the grotesque; the charming Baroque fresco master **Pietro da**

Cortona. Most of Tuscany, and particularly Florence, chose to sit out the Baroque—almost by choice, it seems, and we can race up to the 19th century for the often delightful 'Tuscan Impressionists' or *Macchiaioli* ('Splatterers'; the best collection is in the Modern Art section of the Pitti Palace); and in the 20th century **Ottone Rosai**, the master of the quiet Florentine countryside.

Artists' Directory

This includes the principal architects, painters and sculptors whose works are found in this book. The works listed are far from exhaustive, bound to exasperate partisans of some artists and do scant justice to the rest, but we have tried to include only the best and most representative works that you'll find in our regions.

Agostino di Duccio (Florentine, 1418–81). A precocious and talented sculptor, his best work is in the Malatesta Temple at Rimini—he was exiled from Florence after being accused of theft (**Florence**, Bargello).

Alberti, **Leon Battista** (Florentine, b. Genoa 1404–72). Architect, theorist, and writer, also a sculptor and painter. His greatest contribution was recycling the classical orders and the principles of Vitruvius into Renaissance architecture. (**Florence**, Palazzo Rucellai, façade of S. Maria Novella, SS. Annunziata).

Allori, **Alessandro** (1535–1607). Florentine Mannerist painter, prolific follower of Michelangelo and Bronzino (**Florence**, SS. Annunziata, S. Spirito, Spedale degli Innocenti).

Ammannati, **Bartolommeo** (1511–92). Florentine architect and sculptor. Restrained, elegant in building (**Florence**, S. Trínita bridge, courtyard of Pitti Palace); neurotic, twisted Mannerist sculpture (**Florence**, Fountain of Neptune, Villa di Castello).

Andrea del Castagno (*c*. 1423–57). Precise, dry Florentine painter, one of the first and greatest slaves of perspective. Died of the plague (**Florence**, Uffizi, S. Apollonia, SS. Annunziata).

Angelico, **Fra (or Beato)** (Giovanni da Fiesole, *c*. 1387–1455). Monk first and painter second, but still one of the great visionary artists of the Renaissance (**Florence**, S. Marco—spectacular Annunciation and many more; **Fiesole**, S. Domenico).

Arnolfo di Cambio (born in Colle di Val d'Elsa; *c*. 1245–1302). Architect and sculptor, pupil of Nicola Pisano and a key figure in his own right. Much

Masters and Students: the Progress of the Renaissance

The purpose of this chart is to show who learned from whom, an insight into some 300 years of artistic continuity.

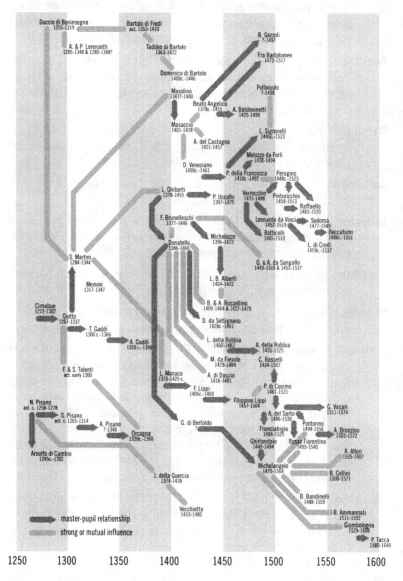

Duccio di Boninsegna
1255-1319

Bartolo di Fredi
act. 1353-1410

A. & P. Lorenzetti
1285-1348 & 1280-1348?

Taddeo di Bartolo
1363-1422

B. Gozzoli
?-1497

Fra Bartolomeo
1472-1517

Domenico di Bartolo
1400c.-1446

Pollaiuolo
?-1498

Masolino
1383?-1440

Beato Angelico
1378c.-1455

A. Baldovinetti
1425-1499

Masaccio
1401-1428

L. Signorelli
1445c.-1523

A. del Castagno
1421-1457

Melozzo da Forlì
1438-1494

D. Veneziano
1400c.-1461

P. della Francesca
1410c.-1492

Perugino
1448c.-1523

L. Ghiberti
1378-1455

P. Uccello
1397-1475

Verrocchio
1435-1488

Pinturicchio
1454-1513

Raffaello
1483-1520

F. Brunelleschi
1377-1446

Leonardo da Vinci
1452-1519

Sodoma
1477-1549

Michelozzo
1396-1472

Botticelli
1445-1510

Beccafumi
1486c.-1551

Donatello
1386-1466

L. di Credi
1459c.-1537

S. Martini
1284-1344

G. & A. da Sangallo
1443-1516 & 1455-1537

L. B. Alberti
1404-1472

Memmi
1317-1347

B. & A. Rossellino
1409-1464 & 1427-1479

Cimabue
1272-1302

D. da Settignano
1428c.-1461

Giotto
1267-1337

T. Gaddi
1300 c.-1366

L. della Robbia
1400-1482

A. Gaddi
1350 c.-1396

A. della Robbia
1435-1525

M. da Fiesole
1429-1484

C. Rosselli
1434-1507

F. & S. Talenti
act. early 1300

L. Monaco
1370-1425 c.

A. di Duccio
1418-1481

F. Lippi
1406c.-1469

P. di Cosimo
1461-1521

N. Pisano
act. c. 1258-1278

Filippino Lippi
1457-1504

G. Vasari
1511-1574

G. Pisano
act. c. 1265-1314

A. Pisano
?-1348

G. di Bertoldo
?

A. del Sarto
1486-1530

Pontormo
1494-1556

A. Bronzino
1503-1572

Orcagna
1320c.-1368

Franciabigio
1484-1525

Arnolfo di Cambio
1245c.-1302

Ghirlandaio
1449-1494

Rosso Fiorentino
1495-1540

A. Allori
1535-1607

J. della Quercia
1374-1438

Michelangelo
1475-1564

B. Cellini
1500-1571

B. Bandinelli
1488-1559

Vecchietta
1410-1480

B. Ammannati
1511-1592

Giambologna
1529-1608

P. Tacca
1580-1640

➤ master-pupil relationship

➤ strong or mutual influence

1250   1300   1350   1400   1450   1500   1550   1600

of his best sculpture is in Rome, but he changed the face of Florence as main architect to the city's greatest building programme of the 1290s (**Florence**, cathedral and Palazzo Vecchio).

Baldovinetti, Alesso (Florentine, 1425–99). A delightful student of Fra Angelico who left few tracks; most famous for fresco work in **Florence** (SS. Annunziata, Uffizi, S. Niccolò sopr'Arno, S. Miniato).

Bandinelli, Baccio (1488–1559). Florence's comic relief of the late Renaissance; supremely serious, vain, and so awful it hurts—of course he was court sculptor to Cosimo I (**Florence**, Piazza della Signoria and SS. Annunziata).

Bartolo di Fredi (Sienese, active *c.* 1353–1410). Student of Ambrogio Lorenzetti, a genuine pre-Raphaelite soul, entirely at home in the Sienese trecento (Pinacoteca in **Siena**).

Bartolommeo, Fra (*c.*1472–1517) Florentine painter, master of the High Renaissance style (**Florence**, San Marco, Pitti Palace)

Beccafumi, Domenico (*c.* 1486–1551). Sienese painter; odd mixture of Sienese conservatism and Florentine Mannerism (**Siena**, Pinacoteca, Palazzo Pubblico, cathedral pavement).

Benedetto da Maiano (Florentine, 1442–97). Sculptor, specialist in narrative reliefs (**Florence**, S. Croce, Strozzi Palace, Bargello).

Bigarelli, Guido (13th century). Talented travelling sculptor from Como, who excelled in elaborate and sometimes bizarre pulpits (**Pisa** Baptistry).

Botticelli, Sandro (Florentine, 1445–1510). Though technically excellent in every respect, and a master of both line and colour, there is more to Botticelli than this. Above every other quattrocento artist, his works reveal the imaginative soul of the Florentine Renaissance, particularly the great series of mythological paintings (**Florence**, Uffizi). Later, a little deranged and under the spell of Savonarola, he reverted to intense, though conventional religious paintings. Almost forgotten in the philistine 1500s and not rediscovered until the 19th century, many of his best works are probably lost (**Florence**, Accademia).

Bronzino, Agnolo (1503–72). Virtuoso Florentine Mannerist with a cool, glossy hyper-elegant style, at his best in portraiture; a close friend of Pontormo (**Florence**, Palazzo Vecchio, Uffizi, S. Lorenzo, SS. Annunziata).

Brunelleschi, Filippo (1377–1446). Florentine architect, credited in his own time with restoring the ancient Roman manner of building—but really deserves more credit for developing a brilliant new approach of his own (**Florence**, Duomo cupola, Spedale degli Innocenti, S. Spirito, S. Croce's Pazzi Chapel, S. Lorenzo). Also a sculptor (he lost the competition for the Baptistry doors to Ghiberti), and one of the first theorists on perspective.

Buontalenti, Bernardo (1536–1608). Late Florentine Mannerist architect and planner of the new city of Livorno, better known for his Medici villas (**Artimino**, also the fascinating grotto in **Florence's** Boboli Gardens, and Belvedere Fort, Uffizi Tribuna).

Cellini, Benvenuto (1500–71). Goldsmith and sculptor. Though a native of Florence, Cellini spent much of his time in Rome. In 1545 he came to work for Cosimo I and to torment Bandinelli (*Perseus*, Loggia dei Lanzi; also works in the Bargello). As famed for his catty *Autobiography* as for his sculpture.

Cimabue (*c.* 1240–1302). Florentine painter credited by Vasari with initiating the 'rebirth of the arts'; one of the first painters to depart from the stylization of the Byzantine style (**Florence**, mosaics in Baptistry, Crucifix in Santa Croce; **Pisa**, cathedral mosaic).

Civitali, Matteo (Lucchese, *c.* 1435–1501). Sweet yet imaginative sculptor, apparently self-taught. He would be much better known if all of his works weren't in Lucca (**Lucca**, cathedral, Guinigi Museum).

Daddi, Bernardo (active 1290–*c.* 1349). Florentine master of delicate altarpieces (**Florence**, Orsanmichele, S. Maria Novella's Spanish chapel).

Desiderio da Settignano (Florentine, 1428/31–61). Sculptor, follower of Donatello (**Florence**, S. Croce, Bargello, S. Lorenzo).

Dolci, Carlo (Florentine, 1616–86). Unsurpassed Baroque master of the 'whites of their eyes' school of religious art (**Florence**, Palazzo Corsini).

Domenico di Bartolo (Sienese, *c.* 1400–46). An interesting painter, out of the Sienese mainstream; the unique naturalism of his art is a Florentine influence. (Spedale di Santa Maria della Scala, Pinacoteca in **Siena**).

Domenico Veneziano (Florentine 1404–61). Painter, teacher of Piero della Francesca; master of perspective with few surviving works (**Florence**, Uffizi).

Donatello (Florentine, 1386–1466). The greatest Renaissance sculptor appeared as suddenly as a comet at the beginning of Florence's quattrocento. Never equalled in technical ability, expressiveness, or imaginative content, his works influenced Renaissance painters as much as sculptors. A prolific worker, and a quiet fellow who lived with his mum, Donatello was the perfect model of the early Renaissance artist—passionate about art, self-effacing, and a little eccentric (**Florence**, Bargello—the greatest works including the original *St George* from Orsanmichele, *David* and *Cupid Atys*, also at San Lorenzo, Palazzo Vecchio, and the Cathedral Museum; **Siena**, cathedral, baptistry).

Duccio di Buoninsegna (d. 1319). One of the first and greatest Sienese painters, Duccio was to Sienese art what Giotto was to Florence; ignored by Vasari, though his contributions to the new visual language of the Renaissance are comparable to Giotto's (**Siena**, parts of the great Maestà in the Cathedral Museum, also Pinacoteca; **Florence**, altarpiece in the Uffizi).

Francesco di Giorgio Martini (Sienese, 1439–1502). Architect—mostly of fortresses—sculptor and painter, his works are scattered all over Italy (**Siena**, Cathedral, Pinacoteca).

Franciabigio (Florentine, 1482–1525). Most temperamental of Andrea del Sarto's pupils but only mildly Mannerist (**Florence**, Poggio a Caiano and SS. Annunziata).

Gaddi, **Taddeo** (*c.* 1300–*c.* 1366). Florentine; most important of the followers of Giotto. He and his son **Agnolo** (d. 1396) contributed some of the finest trecento fresco cycles (notably at S. Croce, and S. Ambrogio, **Florence**).

Gentile da Fabriano, **Francesco di** (*c.*1360–1427). Master nonpareil of the International Gothic style, from Fabriano in the Marches. Most of his work is lost (Uffizi, **Florence**).

Ghiberti, **Lorenzo** (1378–1455). Goldsmith and sculptor. The first artist to write an autobiography was naturally a Florentine. He would probably be better known had he not spent most of his career working on the doors for the Florence Baptistry after winning the famous competition of 1401 (also statues at Orsanmichele **Florence**; **Siena** Baptistry).

Ghirlandaio, **Domenico** (Florentine, *c.* 1448–94). The painter of the quattrocento establishment, master of colourful, lively fresco cycles (with the help of a big workshop) in which he painted all the Medici and Florence's banking elite. A great portraitist with a distinctive, dry, restrained style (**Florence**, Ognissanti, S. Maria Novella, S. Trínita, Spedale degli Innocenti).

Giambologna (1529–1608). A Fleming, born Jean Boulogne; court sculptor to the Medici after 1567 and one of the masters of Mannerist virtuosity— also a man with a taste for the outlandish (**Florence**, Loggia dei Lanzi, Bargello, Villa della Petraia; **Pratolino**, the *Appennino*).

Giotto (*c.* 1266–1337). Shepherd boy of the Mugello, discovered by Cimabue, who became the first great Florentine painter—and recognized as such in his own time. Invented an essential and direct approach to portraying narrative fresco cycles, but is even more important for his revolutionary treatment of space and of the human figure. (**Florence**, S. Croce, cathedral campanile, Horne Museum, S. Maria Novella).

Giovanni da Milano (14th century). An innovative Lombard inspired by Giotto (**Florence**, S. Croce).

Giovanni di Paolo (d. 1483). One of the best of the quattrocento Sienese painters; like most of them, a colourful, often eccentric reactionary who continued the traditions of the Sienese trecento (**Siena**, Pinacoteca).

Giovanni di San Giovanni (1592–1633). One of Tuscany's more prolific, but winning Baroque fresco painters (**Florence**, Pitti Palace, Villa della Petraia).

Gozzoli, Benozzo (Florentine, d. 1497). Learned his trade from Fra Angelico, but few artists could have less in common. The most light-hearted and colourful of quattrocento artists, Gozzoli created enchanting frescoes at **Florence**, Medici chapel and **Pisa**, Camposanto.

Guido da Siena (13th century) One of the founders of Sienese painting, still heavily Byzantine in style; little is known about his life (**Siena**, Palazzo Pubblico, Pinacoteca).

Leonardo da Vinci (1452–1519). We could grieve that Florence's 'universal genius' spent so much time on his scientific interests and building fortifications, and that his meagre artistic output was largely unfinished or lost. All that is left in Tuscany is the *Annunciation* (**Florence**, Uffizi) and also models of all his gadgets at his birthplace, Vinci. As the pinnacle of the Renaissance marriage of science and art, Leonardo requires endless volumes of interpretation. As for his personal life, Vasari records him buying up caged birds in the market-place just to set them free.

Lippi, Filippino (Florentine, 1457–1504). Son and artistic heir of Fra Filippo. Often seems a neurotic Gozzoli, or at least one of the most thoughtful and serious artists of the quattrocento (**Florence**, S. Maria Novella, S. Maria del Carmine, Badia, Uffizi).

Lippi, Fra Filippo (Florentine, d. 1469). Never should have been a monk in the first place. A painter of exquisite, ethereal Madonnas, one of whom he ran off with (the model, at least, a brown-eyed nun named Lucrezia). The pope forgave them both. Lippi was a key figure in the increasingly complex, detailed painting of the middle 1400s (**Florence**, Uffizi).

Lorenzetti, Ambrogio (Sienese, d. 1348). He could crank out golden Madonnas as well as any Sienese painter, but Lorenzetti was also a great innovator in subject matter and the treatment of landscapes. Created the first and greatest of secular frescoes, the *Allegories of Good and Bad Government* in **Siena's** Palazzo Pubblico, while his last known work, the 1344 *Annunciation* in Siena's Pinacoteca is one of the 14th century's most revolutionary treatments of perspective.

Lorenzetti, Pietro (Sienese, d. 1348). Ambrogio's big brother, and also an innovator, standing square between Duccio di Buoninsegna and Giotto; one of the precursors of the Renaissance's new treatment of space (**Siena**, S. Spirito). Both Lorenzettis seem to have died in Siena during the Black Death.

Lorenzo di Credi (1439–1537). One of the most important followers of Leonardo da Vinci, always technically perfect if occasionally vacuous (**Florence**, Uffizi).

Lorenzo Monaco (b. Siena 1370–1425). A monk at S. Maria degli Angeli in Florence and a brilliant colourist, Lorenzo forms an uncommon connection between the Gothic style of Sienese painting and the new developments in early Renaissance Florence (**Florence**, Uffizi, S. Trínita).

Martini, Simone (Sienese, d. 1344). Possibly a pupil of Giotto, Martini took the Sienese version of International Gothic to an almost metaphysical perfection, creating luminous, lyrical, and exquisitely drawn altarpieces and frescoes perhaps unsurpassed in the trecento (**Siena**, Palazzo Pubblico; **Pisa**, Museo S. Matteo; **Florence**, Uffizi).

Masaccio (Florentine, 1401–c. 1428). Though he died young and left few works behind, this precocious 'shabby Tom' gets credit for inaugurating the Renaissance in painting by translating Donatello and Brunelleschi's perspective onto a flat surface. Also revolutionary in his use of light and shadow, and in expressing emotion in his subjects' faces (**Florence**, S. Maria del Carmine, S. Maria Novella; **Pisa**, Museo S. Matteo).

Maso di Banco (Florentine, active 1340s). One of the more colourful and original followers of Giotto (**Florence**, S. Croce).

Masolino (Florentine, d. 1447). Perhaps 'little Tom' also deserves much of the credit, along with Masaccio, for the new advances in art at the Carmine in **Florence**; art historians dispute endlessly how to attribute the frescoes. It's hard to tell, for this brilliant painter left little other work behind to prove his case.

Matteo di Giovanni (Sienese, 1435–95). One Sienese quattrocento painter who could keep up with the Florentines; a contemporary described him as 'Simone Martini come to life again' (**Siena**, Pinacoteca, Cathedral pavement, S. Agostino, S. Maria della Neve).

Memmi, **Lippo** (Sienese, 1317–47). Brother-in-law and assistant of Simone Martini (**Siena**, S. Spirito).

Michelangelo Buonarroti (Florentine, 1475–1564). Born in Caprese (now Caprese Michelangelo) into a Florentine family of the minor nobility come down in the world, Michelangelo's early years and artistic training are obscure; he was apprenticed to Ghirlandaio, but showing a preference for sculpture was sent to the court of Lorenzo de' Medici. Nicknamed Il Divino in his lifetime, he was a complex, difficult character, who seldom got along with mere mortals, popes, or patrons. What he couldn't express by means of the male nude in paint or marble, he did in his beautiful but difficult sonnets. In many ways he was the first modern artist, unsurpassed in technique but also the first genius to go over the top (**Florence**, Medici tombs and library in San Lorenzo, three works in the Bargello, the *Pietà* in the Museo del Duomo, the *David* in the Accademia, Casa Buonarroti, and his only oil painting, in the Uffizi).

Michelozzo di Bartolomeo (Florentine, 1396–1472). Sculptor who worked with Donatello (as in **Florence's** Baptistry), he is better known as the classicizing architect favoured by the elder Cosimo de' Medici (**Florence**, Medici Palace, Chiostro of SS. Annunziata, library of San Marco; Villas at **Trebbio** and **Cafaggiolo**).

Mino da Fiesole (Florentine, 1429–84). Sculptor of portrait busts and tombs; like the della Robbias a representative of the Florentine 'sweet style' (**Fiesole**, cathedral; **Florence**, Badia, Sant'Ambrogio).

Nanni di Banco (Florentine, 1384–1421). Florentine sculptor at the dawn of the Renaissance (**Florence**, Orsanmichele, Porta della Mandorla).

Orcagna, Andrea (Florence, d. 1368). Sculptor, painter and architect who dominated the middle 1300s in Florence, though greatly disparaged by Vasari, who destroyed much of his work. Many believe he is the 'Master of the Triumph of Death' of Pisa's Camposanto (**Florence**, Orsanmichele, S. Croce, S. Maria Novella, *Crucifixion* in refectory of S. Spirito, also often given credit for the Loggia dei Lanzi).

Perugino (Pietro Vannucci, Perugia, *c.* 1450–1523). Perhaps the most distinctive of the Umbrian painters; created some works of genius, along with countless idyllic nativity scenes, each with its impeccably sweet Madonna and characteristic blue-green tinted background (**Florence**, Uffizi, S. Maddalena dei Pazzi, Cenacolo di Foligno).

Piero della Francesca (*c.*1415–1492). Painter, born at Sansepolcro, and one of the really unique quattrocento artists. Piero wrote two of the most important theoretical works on perspective, then illustrated them with a lifetime's work reducing painting to the bare essentials: geometry, light and colour. In his best work his reduction creates nothing dry or academic, but dreamlike, almost eerie scenes similar to those of Uccello. And like Uccello or Botticelli, his subjects are often archetypes of immense psychological depth, not to be fully explained now or ever (**Florence**, Uffizi).

Piero di Cosimo (Florentine, 1462–1521). Painter better known for his personal eccentricities than his art, which in itself is pretty odd. Lived on hard-boiled eggs (**Florence**, Uffizi; **Fiesole**, S. Francesco).

Pietro da Cortona (1596–1699). The most charming of Tuscan Baroque painters; his best is in Rome, but there are some florid ceilings in the Pitti Palace (**Florence**).

Pinturicchio (Perugia, 1454–1513). This painter got his name for his use of gold and rich colours. Never an innovator, but as an absolute virtuoso in colour, style and grace no one could beat him. Another establishment artist, especially favoured by the popes, and like Perugino, he was slandered most vilely by Vasari (**Siena**, Piccolomini Library).

Pisano, Andrea (b. Pontedera, *c.* 1290–1348). Artistic heir of Giovanni and Nicola Pisano and teacher of Orcagna; probably a key figure in introducing new artistic ideas to **Florence** (Baptistry, south doors). Not related to the other Pisani.

Pisano, Nicola (active *c.* 1258–78). The first great medieval Tuscan sculptor really came from down south in Apulia, which was then enjoying a flowering of classically-oriented art under Emperor Frederick II. created a little Renaissance all his own, when he adapted the figures and composition of ancient reliefs to make his wonderful pulpit reliefs in **Siena** and **Pisa**'s Baptistry. His son **Giovanni Pisano** (active *c.* 1265–1314) carried on the tradition, notably in the façade sculptures at **Siena** cathedral (also great relief pulpits in **Pisa** cathedral).

Pollaiuolo, Antonio (Florentine, d. 1498). A sculptor, painter and goldsmith whose fame rests on his brilliant, unmistakable line; he occasionally worked with his less gifted brother **Piero** (**Florence**, Uffizi and Bargello).

Pontormo, Jacopo (Florentine, b. Pontormo, 1494–1556). You haven't seen pink and orange until you've seen the work of this determined Mannerist eccentric. After the initial shock, though, you'll meet an artist of real genius, one whose use of the human body as sole means for communicating ideas is equal to Michelangelo's (**Florence**, S. Felicità—his *Deposition*—and Uffizi).

Quercia, Jacopo della (Sienese, 1374–1438). Sculptor who learned his style from Pisano's cathedral pulpit; one of the unsuccessful contestants for the Florence baptistry doors. Maybe Siena's greatest sculptor, though his most celebrated work, that city's Fonte Gaia, is now ruined (**Lucca**, cathedral *tomb of Ilaria del Carretto* **Siena**, Baptistry).

Raphael (Raffaello Sanzio, 1483–1520). Born in Urbino in the Marches, Raphael spent time in Città di Castello, Perugia, and Florence before establishing himself in Rome. Only a few of the best works of this High

Renaissance master remain in the region; those are in the Pitti Palace and Uffizi, **Florence**.

Robbia, Luca della (Florentine, 1400–82). Greatest of the famous family of sculptors; he invented the coloured glaze for terracottas that we associate with the della Robbias, but was also a first-rate relief sculptor (the *cantorie* in **Florence's** cathedral museum).

His nephew **Andrea della Robbia** (1435–1525) and Andrea's son Giovanni (1469–1529) carried on the blue and white terracotta sweet style in innumerable buildings across Tuscany.

Rosselli, Cosimo (Florentine, 1434–1507). Competent middle-of-the-road Renaissance painter who occasionally excelled (**Florence**, S. Ambrogio).

Rossellino, Bernardo (1409–64). Florentine architect and sculptor best known as the planner and architect of the new town of Pienza. Also a sculptor (**Florence**, S. Croce, S. Miniato). His brother **Antonio Rossellino** (1427–79) was also a talented sculptor (**Florence**, S. Croce).

Rossi, Vicenzo de' (1525–87). Florentine Mannerist sculptor of chunky male nudes (**Florence**, Palazzo Vecchio).

Rosso Fiorentino (Giovanni Battista di Jacopo, 1494–1540). Florentine Mannerist painter, he makes a fitting complement to Pontormo, both for his tortured soul and for the exaggerations of form and colour he used to create gripping, dramatic effects. Fled Italy after the Sack of Rome and worked for Francis I at Fontainebleau. (**Florence**, Uffizi and S. Lorenzo).

Salviati, Francesco (Florentine, 1510–63). Friend of Vasari and a similar sort of painter—though much more talented. Odd perspectives and decoration, often bizarre imagery (**Florence**, Palazzo Vecchio and Uffizi).

Sangallo, Giuliano da (Florentine, 1443–1516). Architect of humble origins who became the favourite of Lorenzo de' Medici. Often tripped up by an obsession, inherited from Alberti, with making architecture conform to philosophical principles (**Poggio a Caiano**; **Florence**, S. Maddalena dei Pazzi).

Il Sassetta (Stefano di Giovanni; active *c.* 1390–1450). One of the great Sienese quattrocento painters, though still working in a style the

Florentines would have found hopelessly reactionary; an artist who studied Masaccio but preferred the Gothic elegance of Masolino. His masterpiece, the Borgo Sansepolcro polyptych, is dispersed through half the museums of Europe.

Il Sodoma (Giovanni Antonio Bazzi, 1477–1549). Born in Piedmont, but a Sienese by choice, he was probably not the libertine his nickname, and Vasari's biography, suggest. An endearing, serene artist, who usually eschewed Mannerist distortion, he got rich through his work, then blew it all feeding his exotic menagerie and died in the poorhouse (**Siena**, Pinacoteca and S. Domenico).

Spinello Aretino (Arezzo, late 14th century–1410). A link between Giotto and the International Gothic style; imaginative and colourful in his compositions (**Florence**, S. Miniato; **Siena**, Palazzo Pubblico).

Tacca, Pietro (1580–1640). Born in Carrara, pupil of Giambologna and one of the best early Baroque sculptors (**Florence**, Piazza SS. Annunziata fountain).

Taddeo di Bartolo (Volterra, 1363–1422). The greatest Sienese painter of the late 1300s—also the least conventional; never a consummate stylist, he often shows a remarkable imagination in composition and treatment of subject matter (**Siena**, Palazzo Pubblico, S. Spirito;).

Talenti, Francesco (early 14th century). Chief architect of **Florence** cathedral and campanile after Arnolfo di Cambio and Giotto; his son **Simone** made the beautiful windows in Orsanmichele (and perhaps the Loggia dei Lanzi) in **Florence**.

Torrigiano, Pietro (1472–1528). Florentine portrait sculptor, famous for his work in Westminster Abbey and for breaking Michelangelo's nose (**Siena**, cathedral).

Uccello, Paolo (Florentine, 1397–1475). No artist has ever been more obsessed with the possibilities of artificial perspective. Like Piero della Francesca, he used the new technique to create a magic world of his own; contemplation of it made him increasingly eccentric in his later years. Uccello's provocative, visionary subjects (*Noah* fresco in S. Maria Novella, and *Battle of San Romano* in the Uffizi, **Florence**) put him up with Piero della Francesca and Botticelli as the most intellectually stimulating of quattrocento artists.

Vasari, Giorgio (Arezzo, 1511–74). Florentine sycophant, writer and artist; *see* p.53–4. Also a fair architect (**Florence**, Uffizi, Corridoio, and Fish Loggia).

Il Vecchietta (Lorenzo di Pietro, 1412–80). Sienese painter and sculptor, dry and linear, part Sienese Pollaiuolo and part Donatello (**Siena**, Loggia della Mercanzia, Baptistry).

Verrocchio, Andrea del (1435–88). Florentine sculptor who worked in bronze; spent his life trying to outdo Donatello. Also a painter, a mystic alchemist in his spare time, and interestingly enough the master of both Botticelli and Leonardo (Uffizi, S. Lorenzo, Orsanmichele, Palazzo Vecchio, and Bargello, **Florence**).

Topics

Death was on everyone's mind when the Great Plague rolled through Italy in 1348. In art, the most striking memories of those harrowing days are the powerful frescoes by the Master of the Triumph of Death in Pisa's Campo Santo; in literature, no account surpasses Boccaccio's introduction to his masterpiece, the *Decameron*, the 'Human Comedy' that complements the *Divine Comedy* of his fellow Florentine.

Boccaccio, the son of a prosperous banker, was the first great writer from the urban middle class. Born either in Florence or in the Florentine town of Certaldo in 1313, he spent much of his youth in the literate, art-loving court of Robert of Anjou in Naples. He returned to Florence shortly before 1348, when the sight of the bodies of plague victims piled in the street sent deep cracks into his belief about the divinely ordered medieval cosmos that he had been reared on and loved in the *Divine Comedy*. Boccaccio's great feat would be to disenchant Dante's world in the most entertaining way possible.

He takes a detached view of the great theatre of life from the very beginning of *The Decameron*. Despite the Church's claims that the plague was 'a punishment signifying God's righteous anger at our iniquitous way of life', Boccaccio notes that in fact it was a highly contagious disease that had come out of the East, and that fate and chance alone seemed to spare some Florentines while others were struck down whether they responded to the plague by praying for deliverance, hiding out, or living riotously as if there would be no tomorrow.

His ten young storytellers gather in Santa Maria Novella and escape the plague for a country villa, where they pass the days by telling tales. These stories sparkle with a secular, spunky vitality and sense of humour that is fresh and new; sex, for the first time in literature, becomes a pleasurable end in itself. Fate and chance, however, decide most of the plots and outcomes of the hundred tales they tell; with few exceptions, the belief in the just outcome of human endeavour is an illusion.

In his old age Boccaccio wrote exclusively in Latin and earned himself a reputation as one of the great humanists of the 14th century, regretting the frivolity of the *Decameron* in his old age. As Giuliano Procacci wrote, 'He put himself in the position of a calmly objective recorder of life's dramas and chances; it was a difficult and exhausting mental standpoint, and a new one, demanding nervous energy and courage. Is it any wonder that Boccaccio too, in his premature old age, should have sought comfort and refuge in study and piety?'

For a century after Boccaccio Florence led the world in humanistic thought. The horrors of the plague were forgotten as victories in diplomacy and the battlefield, a hitherto unknown prosperity, and tremendous strides in architecture, art and science made the city radiate confidence. The fatalism of the *Decameron* seemed unduly pessimistic by the end of the 15th century. The humanists were keenly aware of Florence's special destiny, as described by Leonardo Bruni in his proud, patriotic *Laudatio Florentinae Urbis* or in Coloccio Salutati's 'What city, not merely in Italy but in the whole world, is stronger within the circle of its walls, prouder in palaces, richer in temples, more lovely in buildings...Where is trade richer in its variety, abler in subtle understandings? Where are there more famous men?'—brave new words before the mass neurotic religious revival orchestrated by Savonarola and the return of the wrath of God as the prime mover. Even Pico della Mirandola, the most optimistic of humanists, himself fell under the fanatic's spell.

Florence was never the same, and the repercussions were dire: for a city that practically invented humanism to toss its books and art in the proto-Ayatollah's bonfire of the vanities cast long shadows onto everyone's future. Don't forget that only in the 20th century has the *Decameron* been translated complete with all the naughty bits.

The First Professional Philistine

Many who have seen Vasari's work in Florence will be wondering how such a mediocre painter should rate so much attention. Ingratiating companion of the rich and famous, workmanlike over-achiever and tireless self-promoter, Vasari was the perfect man for his time. Born in Arezzo, in 1511, a fortunate introduction to Cardinal Silvio Passerini gave him the chance of an education in Florence with the young Medici heirs, Ippolito and Alessandro. In his early years, he became a fast and reliable frescoist gaining a reputation for customer satisfaction—a real innovation in an age when artists were increasingly becoming eccentric prima donnas. In the 1530s, after travelling around Italy on various commissions, he returned to Florence just when Cosimo I was beginning his plans to remake the city in the image of the Medici. It was a marriage made in heaven. Vasari became Cosimo's court painter and architect, with a limitless budget and a large group of assistants, the most prolific fresco machine ever seen in Italy—painting over countless good frescoes of the 1300s along the way.

But more than for his paintings, Vasari lives on through his book, the *Lives of the Artists*, a series of exhaustive biographies of artists. Beginning with Cimabue, Vasari traces the rise of art out of Byzantine and Gothic barbarism, through Giotto and his followers, towards an ever-improving naturalism, finally culminating in the great age of Leonardo, Raphael, and the divine Michelangelo, who not only mastered nature but outdid her. Leon Battista Alberti gets the credit for drafting the first principles of artistic criticism, but it was Vasari who first applied such ideas on a grand scale. His book, being the first of its kind, and containing a mine of valuable information on dozens of Renaissance artists, naturally has had a tremendous influence on all subsequent criticism. Art critics have never really been able to break out of the Vasarian straitjacket.

Much of Vasari's world seems quaint to us now: the idea of the artist as a kind of knight of the brush, striving for Virtue and Glory, the slavish worship of anything that survived from ancient Rome, artistic 'progress' and the conviction that art's purpose was to imitate nature.

But many of Vasari's opinions have had a long and mischievous career in the world of ideas. His blind disparagement of everything medieval—really the prejudice of his entire generation—lived on until the 1800s. His dismissal of Sienese, Umbrian and northern artists—of anyone who was not a Florentine—has not been entirely corrected even today. Vasari was the sort who founded academies, a cheerful conformist who believed in a nice, tidy art that went by the book. With his interior decorator's concept of Beauty, he created a style of criticism in which virtuosity, not imagination, became the standard by which art was to be judged; history offers few more instructive examples of the stamina and resilience of dubious ideas.

A Florentine Puzzle

In a city as visually dry and restrained as Florence, every detail of decoration stands out. In the Middle Ages and Renaissance, Florentine builders combined their passion for geometry with their love of making a little go a long way; they evolved a habit of embellishing buildings with simple geometrical designs. Though nothing special in themselves—most are easily drawn with a compass and straight edge—in the context of Florence they stand out like mystic hieroglyphs, symbols upon which to meditate while contemplating old Florence's remarkable journey through the Western mind.

The city is full of them, incorporated into façades and mosaics, windows and decorative friezes. Here are eight of them, a little exercise for the eye while tramping the hard pavements of Florence. Your job is to find them. Some are really obvious, others obscure. For no. 6 you should be able to find at least three examples (two across the street from each other) and if you're clever you'll find not only no. 5, a rather late addition to the cityscape, but also the medieval work that inspired it. Don't worry too much about the last one. But if you're an art historian or a Florentinophile, it's only fair that you seek out this hard one too. Answers can be found on the last page of the index.

4

Guelphs and Ghibellines

One medieval Italian writer claimed that the great age of factional strife began with two brothers of Pistoia, named Guelf and Gibel. Like Cain and Abel, or Romulus and Remus, one murdered the other, starting the seemingly endless troubles that to many seemed a God-sent plague, meant to punish the proud and wealthy Italians for their sins. Medieval Italy may in fact have been guilty of every sort of jealousy, greed and wrath, but most historians trace the beginnings of this party conflict to two great German houses, Welf and Waiblingen.

To the Italians, what those barbarians did across the Alps meant little; the chroniclers pinpoint the outbreak of the troubles to the year 1215, when a politically prominent Florentine noble named Buondelmonte dei Buondelmonti was assassinated by his enemies while crossing the Ponte Vecchio. It was the tinder that ignited a smouldering quarrel all over Italy, particularly in Tuscany. The atmosphere of contentious city-states, each with its own internal struggles between nobles, the rich merchant class and the commons, crystallized rapidly into parties. In the beginning, at least, they stood for something. The Guelphs, largely a creation of the newly wealthy bourgeois, were all for free trade and the rights of the free cities; the Ghibellines from the start were the party of the German emperors, nominal overlords of Italy who had been trying to assert their control ever since the days of Charlemagne. Naturally, the Guelphs found their protector in the emperors' bitter temporal rivals, the popes. This brought a religious angle into the story, especially with the advent of the heretical Emperor Frederick II.

Everything about this convoluted history confirms the worst suspicions of modern behaviourist scientists. Before long, the labels Guelph and Ghibelline ceased to have any meaning. In the 13th and 14th centuries, the emperors and their Ghibelline allies helped the Church root out heretical movements like the Patarenes, while the popes schemed to destroy the liberty of good Guelph cities, and incorporate them into the Papal State. In cities, like Florence, where the

Guelphs won a final victory, they themselves split into parties, battling with the same barbaric gusto. Black was the Ghibelline colour, white the Guelph, and cities arranged themselves like squares on a chessboard. When one suffered a revolution and changed from Guelph to Ghibelline, or vice versa, of course its nearest enemies would soon change the other way. Often the public buildings give us a clue as to the loyalties of a city in any given time. Simple, squared crenellations are Guelph (as in Florence's Palazzo Vecchio, or in a score of other town halls); ornate 'swallow-tail' crenellations are the mark of the Ghibelline. Siena was a generally Ghibelline city, but its great Palazzo Pubblico was built with square crenellations during a Guelph interlude under the rule of the Council of the Nine.

The English, like many uninvolved European nations, looked on all this with bewilderment. Edmund Spenser, in glosses to his *Shepheards' Calendar* (1579), wrote this fanciful etymology: 'when all Italy was distraicte into the Factions of the Guelfes and the Gibelins, being two famous houses in Florence, the name began through their great mischiefes and many outrages, to be so odious or rather dreadfull in the peoples eares, that if theyr children at any time were frowarde and wanton, they would say to them the Guelfe or the Gibeline came. Which words nowe from them (as may thinge els) be come into our vsage, and for Guelfes and Gibelines, we say *Elfes* and *Goblins.*'

The Heresy of Science

The starry Galileo, with his woes

Childe Harold's Pilgrimage, Byron

Frankly, Galileo deserves better in his home town of Pisa than the dusty bits and bobs displayed at his old address, now loftily known as the Domus Galileana. Born in 1564, son of a blue-blooded Pisan mother and Vincenzo Galilei, a brilliant musical theorist whose ideas gave rise to the invention of opera, the young Galileo was nurtured in the lofty intellectual environment of Late Renaissance Tuscany. His father introduced him early to the Medici academies, where he was drawn irresistibly to mathematics from an early age—one thing he did was calculate the precise dimensions of the circles of hell, according to the information provided in the *Inferno*. His real mission, however, as it developed over the years, was far more serious: to overthrow Aristotelian science.

Before Galileo was appointed professor of mathematics at Pisa (1589) and Padua (1592), all scientific learning came from books arguing for or against Aristotle's writings. Galileo taught that you could learn much more by studying nature, and in the process became the founding father of experimental physics—he showed that air had weight by weighing a pig's bladder full of air, then puncturing it to show the difference; he defied the Aristotelian concept of opposites in nature by inventing the principle of the thermometer, demonstrating that hot and cold were merely relative aspects of the same phenonemon, which he called temperature; he debunked Aristotle's precept that heavy bodies had a tendency to fall and light ones to rise with his famous experiment at the Leaning Tower, when he dropped variously sized balls and bullets and weights simultaneously and they all hit the ground at once. His celebrated experiment with the inclined plane established the first principles of dynamics.

In 1609, news reached Galileo of a Dutch spectacle-maker who had made a pipe with lenses that enabled one to see ships far out to sea. Galileo quickly put together one of his own with a convex lens in front, and a concave lens behind, that he soon improved to make the first telescope—with a magnification power of 30. Even so, when Galileo pointed his instrument at the heavens, it was an incredible revelation: he was the first man ever to see the surface of the moon, the moons of Jupiter, what appeared to be ears on Saturn (his telescope was too weak to discern the rings), the phases of Venus, the uncountable stars in the Milky Way, and sunspots, although the last discovery permanently affected his eyesight. In 1610 he published all his discoveries in a little book called *Sidereus Nuncius*, 'The Starry Messenger'. He became an instant celebrity. Cosimo de' Medici made him Grand Ducal mathematician and philosopher with a salary of a thousand florins a year. The Jesuit astronomers in Rome received him as a hero; a certain Cardinal Barberini looked through Galileo's magic tube and wrote him a fulsome eulogy called, prophetically, 'Dangerous Flattery'.

Galileo (along with many Jesuits) had long believed in Copernicus's *De revolutionibus Orbium Coelestium* (1543) and its theory that the earth revolved around the sun, a belief confirmed in Galileo's mind by his discoveries through the telescope. However, by 1615, so many theologians thought that the theory was inconsistent with biblical teachings that, in spite all of Galileo's energetic efforts in Rome, *De revolutionibus* was placed on the Index of prohibited books until it could be amended with a statement that it was an unproved hypothesis. The Holy Office then forbade Galileo from teaching it.

When the same Cardinal Barberini who wrote the eulogy to Galileo became Pope Urban VIII in 1624, the 60-year-old scientist thought the chance had come to break the silence that was killing him. He went to Rome and asked to discuss Copernicanism in a new book, emphasizing to the Pope that it was to the glory of the Catholic Church to promote learning. Urban permitted Galileo to write, as long as he fairly stated the case for the Ptolemiac system as well, because, the Pope added, as God was not constrained by human logic, any arguments based on what appeared to be physical evidence to the human mind were fallible.

Galileo spent the next five years writing (in Italian, instead of the usual Latin) the first-ever book of popular science, a witty and lively masterpiece called the *Dialogue on the Two Chief Systems of the World*, in which three characters (a Copernican, an Aristotelian and an amateur) discuss the two systems, with the Copernican clearly winning the argument. At the end of the book the trapped Aristotelian falls back on the Pope's argument, to which all the characters submit. Although at first greeted with enthusiasm, the *Dialogue* was soon withdrawn by the Pope, who believed he had been duped. A special commission he set up agreed with him: that although Galileo followed the Pope's conditions to the letter, he was advocating an unproved hypothesis as the truth and disobeying the order from the Holy Office of 17 years ago not to teach Copernicanism. In the famous Inquisition trial he was accused of relapsing—a much worse crime than heresy—and made to recant his belief that the earth moved, although, legend has it, with the famous aside:'*eppur si muove*!', 'But it does move!'

The Inquisition was lenient with the old man, first placing him under house arrest in Siena, and then in his villa at Arcetri, just outside Florence. There he wrote (or rather dictated, as he was going blind) his even more influential *The Two New Sciences* (1638), on the mathematical study of motion and the strength of materials, a work that became the basis for the study of physics as a science. He died in 1642, if not a martyr, at least a hero to science.

Yet as much as Galileo accomplished, his conviction that mechanistic explanations were exclusively true created a whole new set of idols, holy scriptures and diehard inquisitors in the name of a new god called Science. It is no small irony that, 350 years after Galileo's death, most physicists today would admit that actually the Pope had been right all along; the more they find out, the more the universe shows itself unconstrained by human logic, stranger not only than anyone ever thought, but stranger than anyone could even imagine.

Hermes Trismegistus

As you pass through the main portal of Siena cathedral, the figure before you on the famous marble pavement comes as a surprise—Hermes Trismegistus, someone rarely seen in art, though a mysterious protagonist in a great undercurrent of Renaissance thought. 'Thrice-great Hermes', mythical author of a series of mystic philosophical dialogues from the 2nd century AD, had a profound influence on Greek and Arabic thought, gradually becoming associated (correctly or not) with the Egyptian god Thoth, inventor of writing and father of a deep mystical tradition that continues to this day. In the 1400s, the Hermetic writings were introduced in the West, largely the work of Greek scholars fleeing the Ottoman conquest of Constantinople and Trebizond. They made quite a splash. Marsilio Ficino, the Florentine humanist and friend of Cosimo de' Medici, completed the first Latin translation of the Hermetic books in 1471—Cosimo specifically asked him to put off his translations of Plato to get this more important work finished!

To the men of the Renaissance, Hermes was a real person, an Egyptian prophet, who lived in the time of Moses and was perhaps his teacher. They saw, revealed in the Hermetic books, an ancient, natural religion, prefiguring Christianity and complementary to it—and in fact much more fun than Christianity, for the magical elements in it were entirely to the taste of neo-Platonists like Ficino. From a contemporary point of view, the recovery of Hermes Trismegistus was one of the main intellectual events of the century, a century that witnessed a tremendous revival of natural magic, alchemy and astrology.

The memorable Hermes in Siena is surrounded by a bevy of ten sibyls: those of Cumae and Tivoli (the Italians), Delphi, Libya, the Hellespont, Phrygia and the rest. These ladies, part of a pan-Mediterranean religious tradition even older than Hermes Trismegistus, are far more common in Tuscan religious iconography (as in the Baptistry and Santa Trínita in Florence, or most famously on Michelangelo's Sistine Chapel ceiling), for the belief that they all foretold the birth of Christ.

Leaning Towers

This isn't a subject the Italians like to discuss. They will be happy to sell you all the little plastic souvenirs you want of the most celebrated of the species—the one in Pisa—but a mention of the other dozens of listing landmarks scattered around Bologna, Venice, Ravenna, Rovigo and Rome makes them uneasy. Italians, of course, rightfully think of themselves as the most skilled engineers on this planet. They built the Roman roads and aqueducts, the Pantheon, the domes of Florence cathedral and St Peter's, the biggest in the world. They invented concrete. Today their *autostrade* zoom through mile-long tunnels and skim over deep valleys on stilts, remarkable *tours de force* of engineering that would make the Romans proud. They have built more railway tunnels, perhaps, than the rest of Europe put together. Why can't they keep their towers from drooping?

The key to the answer is in Pisa, where the campanile stands 54.5m high and is 4.5m out of true. The greatest lean is in the first three storeys of the tower; above, there is an attempt to curve the tower back towards perpendicular by slightly changing the pitch of the columns and raising the galleries on the lower side. From the beginning, nearly everyone swallowed Vasari's explanation for this: that the architects, Guglielmo and Bonanno, noticed the subsidence in the foundations once the third storey had been completed, and endeavoured to right the tilt.

Yet for centuries there has been a dark undercurrent of thought that claims Pisa's tower was intentionally built to lean. Goethe thought so, and architects who have carefully measured the foundation stones came to the same conclusion. There is damning technical evidence in the change in the lengths of the colonnades, most noticeable at the top storey, that would have only been necessary to a tower meant to tilt, not one that was being corrected after accidental subsidence; the line of the soffit of the staircase has been measured to show a deliberate slope meant to throw the weight of the campanile off the overhanging side.

A certain Professor Goodyear, who wrote over a hundred years ago, exposed the whole business as what he called 'symmetrophobia'—not really a fear of the symmetrical, but more a disdain for it. Italy's medieval master builders, not yet squeezed into the Renaissance straitjacket of monumental symmetry, could still be playful now and then, and had the subtle skill to build a token in stone to remind all who saw it that life itself is full of growth and curves and spirals and energy and that nothing alive comes in those uniform straight lines, squares and true circles that were all too soon to dominate architecture in the West.

The Italians of today do not like this explanation any better; they brusquely reject any suggestion that their ancestors could have been tempted away from the perpendicular on a whim. You can judge for yourself at Pisa—that campanile simply would not look right without its tilt.

Trends in Taste

I took a quick walk through the city to see the Duomo and the Battistero. Once more, a completely new world opened up before me, but I did not wish to stay long. The location of the Boboli Gardens is marvellous. I hurried out of the city as quickly as I entered it.

Goethe, on Florence in *Italian Journey*

Goethe, the father of the Italian Grand Tour, on his way from Venice to Rome, did not have much time for the city that likes to call itself 'The Capital of Culture'. Like nearly every traveller in the 18th and early 19th centuries, he knew nothing of Giotto, Masaccio, Botticelli, or Piero della Francesca; it was Roman statues that wowed him, the very same ones that the modern visitor passes in the corridors of the Uffizi without a second glance. Shelley managed to write pages on his visits to the museum without mentioning a single painting.

Some Tuscan attractions never change—the Leaning Tower, Michelangelo's *David*, the villas, the gardens and the cheap wine. Others have gone through an amazing rise or fall in popularity, thanks in part to John Ruskin, whose *Mornings in Florence* introduced the charms of the Romanesque architecture, Giotto, and the masters of the trecento; for him Orcagna was the master of them all (but in the 18th century, the Giottos in Santa Croce were whitewashed over, while many works of Orcagna had been destroyed earlier, by Vasari). Botticelli went from total obscurity in the 18th century to become the darling of the Victorians. Livorno and Viareggio on the coast, and Bagni di Lucca near the Garfagnana, used to have thriving English colonies—no more. But Tuscany itself used to be a very different place, where they used to play a betting game called *pallone*, somewhere between lawn tennis and jai alai; where in 1900 a herd of 150 camels, introduced by Grand Duke Ferdinand II in 1622, roamed the Pisan Park of San Rossore; where, as Robert and Elizabeth Browning found, the rent for a palazzo used to be laughably cheap.

But the story of the Venus de' Medici is perhaps the most instructive. The statue is a pleasant, if unremarkable Greek work of the 2nd century BC, but for two centuries it was Florence's chief attraction; the minute visitors arrived in Florence they would rush off to gaze upon her; those prone to write gushed rapturously of her perfect beauty. Napoleon kidnapped her for France, asking the great neoclassical sculptor Canova to sculpt a replacement; afterwards the Venus was one of the things Florence managed to get back, though her reign was soon to be undermined—Ruskin called her an 'uninteresting little person'. Since then she has stood forlornly in the Tribunale of the Uffizi, unnoticed and unloved.

Some things don't change. Over a hundred years after Goethe's blitz tour of Florence, Aldous Huxley had no time for the city, either: 'We came back through Florence and the spectacle of that second-rate provincial town with its repulsive Gothic architecture and its acres of Christmas card primitives made me almost sick. The only points about Florence are the country outside it, the Michelangelo tombs, Brunelleschi's dome, and a few rare pictures. The rest is simply dung when compared to Rome.'

Tuscany on Wheels

Tuscans have always loved a parade, and to the casual reader of Renaissance history, it seems they're forever proceeding somewhere or another, even to their own detriment—during outbreaks of plague, holy companies would parade through an afflicted area, invoking divine mercy, while in effect aiding the spread of the pestilence. They also had a great weakness for allegorical parade floats. During the centuries of endless war each Tuscan city rolled out its war chariot or battle wagon, called the *carroccio*, invented by a Milanese bishop in the 11th century. A *carroccio*, drawn by six white oxen, was a kind of holy ship of state in a hay cart; a mast held up a crucifix while a battle standard flew from the yard-arm, there was an altar for priests to say Mass during the battle and a large bell to send signals over the din to the armies. The worst possible outcome of a battle was to lose one's *carroccio* to the enemy, as Fiesole did to Florence. One is still in operation, in Siena, rumbling out twice a year for the Palio.

Medieval clerical processions, by the time of Dante, became melded with the idea of the Roman 'triumph' (*trionfo*); in Purgatory, the poet finds Beatrice triumphing with a cast of characters from the Apocalypse. Savonarola wrote of a *Triumph of the Cross*; Petrarch and Boccaccio wrote allegorical triumphs of virtues, love and death. More interesting, however, are the secular Roman-style triumphs which were staged by the Medici, especially at Carnival (the name of which, according to Burckhardt, comes from a cart, the pagan *carrus navalis*, the ship of Isis, launched every 5 March to symbolize the reopening of navigation). You can get a hint of their splendour from the frescoes at Poggio a Caiano; the best artists of the day would be commissioned to design the decorations—two particularly famous *trionfi* in Florence celebrated the election of the Medici Pope Leo X.

Two lovely memories of Florence's processions remain. One is Gozzoli's fairy-tale frescoes in the chapel of the Medici palace, of the annual procession staged by the Compagnia de' Re Magi, the most splendid and aristocratic of pageants. The other comes from the Florentine Carnival, famous for its enormous floats, in which scenes from mythology were portrayed to songs and music. One year, for the masque of Bacchus and Ariadne, Lorenzo de' Medici composed the loveliest Italian poem to come out of the Renaissance, with the melancholy refrain:

> *Quanto è bella giovinezza,*   How fair is youth,
> *Che si fugge tuttavia!*   How fast it flies away!
> *Chi vuol esser lieto, sia:*   Let him who will, be merry:
> *Di doman non c'è certezza.*   Of tomorrow nothing is certain.

Florence

63

Fine balm let Arno be;
The walls of Florence all of silver rear'd,
And crystal pavements in the public way...

14th-century madrigal by Lapo Gianni

'*Magari!*'—If only!—the modern Florentine would add to this
vision, to this city of art and birthplace of the Renaissance, built by
bankers and merchants whose sole preoccupation was making
more florins. The precocious capital of Tuscany began to slip into
legend back in the 14th century, during the lifetime of Dante; it
was noted as different even before the Renaissance, before
Boccaccio, Masaccio, Brunelleschi, Donatello, Leonardo da Vinci,
Botticelli, Michelangelo, Machiavelli, the Medici...

> *This city of Florence is well populated, its good air a*
> *healthy tonic; its citizens are well dressed, and its women*
> *lovely and fashionable, its buildings are very beautiful, and*
> *every sort of useful craft is carried on in them, more so*
> *than any other Italian city. For this many come from dis-*
> *tant lands to see her, not out of necessity, but for the*
> *quality of its manufactures and arts, and for the beauty*
> *and ornament of the city.*

Dino Compagni in his *Chronicle* of 1312

According to the tourist office, in 1997, 685 years after Dino, a
grand total of over 2,500,000 Americans, Germans, French,
Britons (the top four groups), as well as Spanish, Brazilians,
Egyptians, and some 800,000 Italians spent at least one night in a
Florentine hotel. Some, perhaps, had orthodontist appointments.
A large percentage of the others came to inhale the rarefied air of
the cradle of Western civilization, to gaze at some of the loveliest
things made by mortal hands and minds, to walk the streets of new
Athens, the great humanist 'city built to the measure of man'.
Calling Florence's visitors 'tourists', however, doesn't seem quite
right; 'tourism' implies pleasure, a principle alien to this dour,
intellectual, measured town; 'pilgrims' is perhaps the better word,
cultural pilgrims who throng the Uffizi, the Accademia, the
Bargello to gaze upon the holy mysteries of our secular society,
to buy postcards and replicas, the holy cards of our day.

Someone wrote a warning on a wall near Brunelleschi's Santo Spirito, in the Oltrarno: '*Turista con mappa/alla caccia del tesoro/ per finire davanti a un piatto/di spaghetti al pomodoro*' (Tourist with a map, on a treasure hunt, only to end up in front of a plate of spaghetti with tomato sauce). Unless you pack the right attitude, Florence can be as disenchanting as cold spaghetti. It only blossoms if you apply mind as well as vision, if you go slowly and do not let the art bedazzle until your eyes glaze over in dizzy excess (a common complaint, known in medical circles as the Stendhal syndrome). Realize that loving and hating Florence at the same time may be the only rational response. It is the capital of contradiction; you begin to like it because it goes out of its way to annoy.

Florentine Schizophrenia

Dante's *Vita Nuova*, the autobiography of his young soul, was only the beginning of Florentine analysis; Petrarch, who was the introspective 'first modern man', was a Florentine born in exile; Ghiberti was the first artist to write an autobiography, Cellini wrote one of the most readable; Alberti invented art criticism; Vasari invented art history; Michelangelo's personality, in his letters and sonnets, looms as large as his art. In many ways Florence broke away from the medieval idea of community and invented the modern concept of the individual, most famously expressed by Lorenzo de' Medici's friend, Pico della Mirandola, whose *Oration on the Dignity of Man* tells us what the God on the Sistine Chapel ceiling was saying when he created Adam: '…And I have created you neither celestial nor terrestrial, neither mortal nor immortal, so that, like a free and able sculptor and painter of yourself, you may mould yourself entirely in the form of your choice.'

To attempt to understand Florence, remember one historical constant: no matter what the issue, the city always takes both sides, vehemently and often violently, especially in the Punch and Judy days of Guelphs and Ghibellines. In the 1300s this was explained by the fact that the city was founded under the sign of Mars, the war god; but in medieval astronomy Mars is also connected with Aries, another Florentine symbol and the time of spring blossoms. (The Annunciation, at the beginning of spring, was Florence's most important festival and original New Year's Day.) One of the city's oldest symbols is the lily (or iris), flying on its oldest gonfalons. Perhaps even older is its *marzocco*, originally an equestrian statue of Mars on the Ponte Vecchio, later replaced by Donatello's grim lion.

Whatever dispute rocked the streets, Great Aunt Florence often expressed her schizophrenia in art, floral Florence versus stone Florence, epitomized by the irreconcilable differences between the two most famous works of art in the city:

Botticelli's graceful, enigmatic *Primavera* and Michelangelo's cold perfect *David*. The 'city of flowers' seems a joke; it has nary a real flower, nor even a tree, in its stone streets; indeed, all effort has gone into keeping nature at bay, surpassing it with geometry and art. And yet the Florentines were perhaps the first since the Romans to discover the joys of the countryside. The rough, rusticated stone palaces, like fortresses or prisons, hide charms as delightful as Gozzoli's frescoes in the Palazzo Medici. Luca della Robbia's dancing children and floral wreaths are contemporary with the naked, violent warriors of the Pollaiuolo brothers; the writhing, quarrelsome statuary in the Piazza della Signoria is sheltered by the most delicate and beautiful loggia imaginable.

After 1500, all of the good, bad and ugly symptoms of the Renaissance peaked in the mass fever of Mannerism. Then, drifting into a debilitating twilight of *pietra dura* tables, gold gimcracks, and interior decoration, Florence gave birth to the artistic phenomenon known as kitsch—the Medici Princes' chapel is an early kitsch classic, and remains one of the heaviest baubles in the solar system. Since then, worn out perhaps, or embarrassed, this city built by merchants has kept its own counsel, expressing its argumentative soul in overblown controversies about traffic, art restoration, and the undesirability of fast-food counters and cheap pensions. We who find her fascinating hope she some day comes to remember her proper role, bearing the torch of culture instead of merely collecting tickets for the culture torture.

History

The identity of Florence's first inhabitants is a matter of dispute. There seems to have been some kind of settlement along the Arno long before the Roman era, perhaps as early as 1000 BC; the original founders may have been either native Italics or Etruscans. Throughout the period of Etruscan dominance, the village on the river lived in the shadow of *Faesulae*—Florence's present-day suburb of Fiesole was then an important city, the northernmost member of the Etruscan Dodecapolis. The Arno river cuts across central Italy like a wall. This narrow stretch of it, close to the mountain pass over to Emilia, was always the most logical place for a bridge.

Roman Florence can claim no less a figure than **Julius Caesar** for its founder. Like so many other Italian cities, the city began as a planned urban enterprise in an underdeveloped province; Caesar started it as a colony for his army veterans in 59 BC. The origin of the name—so suggestive of springtime and flowers—is another mystery. First it was *Florentia*, then *Fiorenza* in the Middle Ages, and finally *Firenze*. One guess is that its foundation took place in April, when the Romans were celebrating the games of the Floralia.

The original street plan of *Florentia* can be seen today in the neat rectangle of blocks between Via Tornabuoni and Via del Proconsolo, between the Duomo and Piazza della Signoria. Its forum occupied roughly the site of the modern Piazza della Repubblica, and the outline of its amphitheatre can be traced in the oval of streets just west of Piazza Santa Croce. Roman *Florentia* never really imposed itself on the historian. One writer mentions it as a *municipia splendidissima*, a major town and river crossing along the Via Cassia, connected to Rome and the thriving new cities of northern Italy, such as Bononia and Mediolanum (Bologna and Milan). At the height of Empire, the municipal boundaries had expanded out to Via de' Fossi, Via S. Egidio, and Via de' Benci. Nevertheless, Florentia did not play a significant role either in the Empire's heyday or in its decline.

After the fall of Rome, Florence weathered its troubles comparatively well. We hear of it withstanding sieges by the Goths around the year 400, when it was defended by the famous imperial general Stilicho, and again in 541, during the campaigns of Totila and Belisarius; all through the Greek–Gothic wars Florence seems to have taken the side of Constantinople. The Lombards arrived around 570; under their rule Florence was the seat of a duchy subject to the then Tuscan capital of Lucca. The next mention in the chronicles refers to Charlemagne spending Christmas with the Florentines in the year 786. Like the rest of Italy, Florence had undoubtedly declined; a new set of walls went up under Carolingian rule, about 800, enclosing an area scarcely larger than the original Roman settlement of 59 BC. In such times Florence was lucky to be around at all; most likely throughout the Dark Ages the city was gradually increasing its relative importance and strength at the expense of its neighbours. The famous Baptistry, erected some time between the 6th and 9th centuries, is the only important building from that troubled age in all Tuscany.

By the 1100s, Florence was the leading city of the County of Tuscany. **Countess Matilda**, ally of Pope Gregory VII against the emperors, oversaw the construction of a new set of walls in 1078, this time coinciding with the widest Roman-era boundaries. Already the city had recovered all the ground lost during the Dark Ages, and the momentum of growth did not abate. New walls were needed again in the 1170s, to enclose what was becoming one of the largest cities in Europe. In this period, Florence owed its growth and prosperity largely to the textile industry—weaving and 'finishing' cloth not only from Tuscany but wool shipped from as far afield as Spain and England. The capital gain from this trade, managed by the *Calimala* and the *Arte della Lana*, Florence's richest guilds, led naturally to an even more profitable business—banking and finance.

The Florentine Republic Battles with the Barons

In 1125, Florence once and for all conquered its ancient rival Fiesole. Wealth and influence brought with them increasing political responsibilities. Externally the city often found itself at war with one or other of its neighbours. Since Countess Matilda's death in 1115, Florence had become a self-governing *comune*, largely independent of the emperor and local barons. The new city republic's hardest problems, however, were closer to home. The nobles of the county, encouraged in their anachronistic feudal behaviour by representatives of the imperial government, proved irreconcilable enemies to the new merchant republic, and Florence spent most of the 12th century trying to keep them in line. Often the city actually declared war on a noble clan, as with the Alberti, or the Counts of Guidi, and razed their castles whenever they captured one. To complicate the situation, nobles attracted by the stimulation of urban life—not to mention the opportunities for making money—often moved their entire families into Florence itself. They brought their country habits with them, a boyish eagerness to brawl with their neighbours on the slightest pretext, and a complete disregard for the laws of the *comune*. Naturally, they couldn't feel secure without a little urban castle of their own, and before long Florence, like any prosperous Italian city of the Middle Ages, featured a remarkable skyline of hundreds of tower-fortresses, built as much for status as for defence. Many were over 60m in height. It wasn't uncommon for the honest citizen to come home from a hard day's work at the bank, hoping for a little peace and quiet, only to find siege engines parked in front of the house and a company of bowmen commandeering the children's bedroom.

But just as Florence was able to break the power of the rural nobles, those in the town also eventually had to succumb. The last tower-fortresses were chopped down to size in the early 1300s. But even without the nobles raising hell, the Florentines found new ways to keep the pot boiling. The rich merchants who dominated the government, familiarly known as the *popolo grosso*, resorted to every sort of murder and mayhem to beat down the demands of the lesser guilds, the *popolo minuto*, for a fair share of the wealth; the two only managed to settle their differences when confronted by murmurs of discontent from what was then one of Europe's largest urban proletariats. But even beyond simple class issues, the city born under the sign of Mars always found a way to make trouble for itself. Not only did Florentines pursue the Guelph–Ghibelline conflict with greater zest than almost any Tuscan city; according to the chronicles of the time, they actually started it. In 1215, men of the Amidei family murdered a prominent citizen named Buondelmonte de' Buondelmonti over a broken wedding engagement, the spark that touched off the factionalist struggles first in Florence, then quickly throughout Italy.

Guelphs and Ghibellines

In the 13th century, there was never a dull moment in Florence. Guelphs and Ghibellines, often more involved with some feud between powerful families than with real political issues, cast each other into exile and confiscated each other's property with every change of the wind. Religious strife occasionally pushed politics off the front page. In the 1240s, a curious foreshadowing of the Reformation saw Florence wrapped up in the **Patarene heresy**. This sect, closely related to the Albigensians of southern France, was as obsessed with the presence of Evil in the world as John Calvin—or Florence's own future fire-and-brimstone preacher, Savonarola. Exploiting a streak of religious eccentricity that has always seemed to be present in the Florentine psyche, the Patarenes thrived in the city, even electing their own bishop. The established Church was up to the challenge; St Peter Martyr, a bloodthirsty Dominican, led his armies of axe-wielding monks to the assault in 1244, exterminating almost the entire Patarene community.

In 1248, with help from Emperor Frederick II, Florence's Ghibellines booted out the Guelphs—once and for all, they thought, but two years later the Guelphs were back, and it was the Ghibellines' turn to pack their grips. The new Guelph regime, called the *primo popolo*, was for the first time completely in the control of the bankers and merchants. It passed the first measures to control the privileges of the turbulent, largely Ghibelline nobles, and forced them all to chop the tops off their tower-fortresses. The next decades witnessed a series of wars with the Ghibelline cities of Tuscany—Siena, Pisa and Pistoia, not just by coincidence Florence's habitual enemies. Usually the Florentines were the aggressors, and more often than not fortune favoured them. In 1260, however, the Sienese, reinforced by Ghibelline exiles from Florence and a few imperial cavalry, destroyed an invading Florentine army at the **Battle of Monteaperti**. Florence was at the Ghibellines' mercy. Only the refusal of Farinata degli Uberti, the leader of the exiles, to allow the city's destruction kept the Sienese from putting it to the torch—a famous episode recounted by Dante in the *Inferno*. (In a typical Florentine gesture of gratitude, Dante found a home for Uberti in one of the lower circles of hell.)

In Florence, a Ghibelline regime under Count Guido Novello made life rough for the wealthy Guelph bourgeoisie. As luck would have it, though, only a few years later the Guelphs were back in power, and Florence was winning on the battlefield again. The new Guelph government, the *secondo popolo*, earned a brief respite from factional strife. In 1289, Florence won a great victory over another old rival, Arezzo. This was the **Battle of Campaldino**, where the Florentine citizen army included young Dante Alighieri. In 1282, and again in 1293, Florence tried to clean up an increasingly corrupt government with a series of reforms. The

1293 *Ordinamenti della Giustizia* once and for all excluded the nobles from the important political offices. By now, however, the real threat to the Guelph merchants' rule did not come so much from the nobility, which had been steadily falling behind in wealth and power over a period of two centuries, but from the lesser guilds, which had been completely excluded from a share of the power, and also from the growing working class employed in the textile mills and the foundries.

Despite all the troubles, the city's wealth and population grew tremendously throughout the 1200s. Its trade contacts spread across Europe, and crowned heads from London to Constantinople found Florentine bankers ready to float them a loan. About 1253 Florence minted modern Europe's first gold coin, the *florin*, which soon became a standard currency across the continent. By 1300 Florence counted over 100,000 souls—a little cramped, even inside the vast new circuit of walls built by the *comune* in the 1280s. It was not only one of the largest cities in Europe, but certainly one of the richest. Besides banking, the wool trade was also booming: by 1300 the wool guild, the *Arte della Lana*, had over 200 large workshops in the city alone.

Naturally, this new opulence created new possibilities for culture and art. Florence's golden age began perhaps in the 1290s, when the *comune* started its tremendous programme of public buildings—including the Palazzo della Signoria and the cathedral; important religious structures, such as Santa Croce, were under way at the same time. Cimabue was the artist of the day; Giotto was just beginning, and his friend Dante was hard at work on the *Commedia*.

As in so many other Italian cities, Florence had been developing its republican institutions slowly and painfully. At the beginning of the *comune* in 1115, the leaders were a class called the *boni homines*, made up mostly of nobles. Only a few decades later, these were calling themselves *consules*, evoking a memory of the ancient Roman republic. When the Ghibellines took over, the leading official was a *podestà* appointed by the emperor. Later, under the Guelphs, the *podestà* and a new officer called the *capitano del popolo* were both elected by the citizens. With the reforms of the 1290s Florence's republican constitution was perfected—if that is the proper word for an arrangement that satisfied few citizens and guaranteed lots of trouble for the future. Under the new dispensation, power was invested in the council of the richer guilds, the *Signoria*; the new Palazzo della Signoria was designed expressly as a symbol of their authority, replacing the old Bargello, which had been the seat of the *podestà*. The most novel feature of the government, designed to overcome Florence's past incapacity to avoid violent factionalism, was the selection of officials by lot from among the guild members. In effect, politics was to be abolished.

Business as Usual: Riot, War, Plagues and Revolution

Despite the reforms of the *Ordinamenti*, Florence found little peace in the new century. As if following some strange and immutable law of city-state behaviour, no sooner had the Guelphs established total control than they themselves split into new factions. The radically anti-imperial **Blacks** and the more conciliatory **Whites** fought each other through the early 1300s with the same fervour they both had once exercised against the Ghibellines. The Whites, who included Dante among their partisans, came out losers when the Blacks conspired with the pope to bring Charles of Valois' French army into Florence; almost all the losing faction were forced into exile in 1302. Some of them must have sneaked back, for the chronicles of 1304 record the Blacks trying to burn them out of their houses with incendiary bombs, resulting in a fire that consumed a quarter of the city.

Beginning in 1313, Florence was involved in a constant series of inconclusive wars with Pisa, Lucca and Arezzo, among others. In 1325, the city was defeated and nearly destroyed by the great Lucchese general **Castruccio Castracani** (*see* **Lucca**). Castruccio died of a common cold while the siege was already under way, another instance of Florence's famous good luck, but unfortunately one of the last.

The factions may have been suppressed, but fate had found some more novel disasters for the city. One far-off monarch did more damage to Florence than its Italian enemies had ever managed—King Edward III of England, who in 1339 found it expedient to repudiate his foreign debts. Florence's two biggest banks, the Bardi and the Peruzzi, immediately went bust, and the city's standing as the centre of international finance was gravely damaged.

If anything was constant throughout the history of the republic, it was the oppression of the poor. The ruling bankers and merchants exploited their labour and gave them only the bare minimum in return. In the 14th century, overcrowding, undernourishment and plenty of rats made Florence's poorer neighbourhoods a perfect breeding ground for epidemics. Famine, plagues and riots became common in the 1340s, causing a severe political crisis. At one point, in 1342, the Florentines gave over their government to a foreign dictator, Walter de Brienne, the French-Greek 'Duke of Athens'. He lasted only for a year before a popular revolt ended the experiment. The **Black Death** of 1348, which was the background for Boccaccio's *Decameron*, carried off perhaps one half of the population. Coming on the heels of a serious depression, it was a blow from which Florence would never really recover.

In the next two centuries, when the city was to be the great innovator in Western culture, it was already in relative decline, a politically decadent republic with a stagnant economy, barely holding its own among the turbulent changes in trade and diplomacy. For the time being, however, things didn't look too bad. Florence found enough ready cash to buy control of Prato, in 1350, and was successful in a defensive war against expansionist Milan in 1351. Warfare was almost continuous for the last half of the century, a strain on the exchequer but not usually a threat to the city's survival; this was the heyday of the mercenary companies, led by *condottieri* like **Sir John Hawkwood** (Giovanni Acuto), immortalized by the equestrian 'statue' in Florence's cathedral. Before the Florentines made him a better offer, Hawkwood was often in the employ of their enemies.

Throughout the century, the Guelph party had been steadily tightening its grip over the republic's affairs. Despite the selection of officials by lot, by the 1370s the party organization bore an uncanny resemblance to some of the big-city political machines common not so long ago in America. The merchants and the bankers who ran the party used it to turn the Florentine Republic into a profit-making business. With the increasingly limited opportunities for making money in trade and finance, the Guelph ruling class tried to make up the difference by soaking the poor. Wars and taxes stretched Florentine tolerance to breaking point, and finally, in 1378, came revolution. The **Ciompi Revolt** (*ciompi*—wage labourers in the textile industries) began in July, when a mob of workers seized the Bargello. Under the leadership of a wool-carder named Michele di Lando, they executed a few of the Guelph bosses and announced a new, reformed constitution. They were also foolish enough to believe the Guelph magnates when they promised to abide by the new arrangement if only the *ciompi* would go home. Before long di Lando was in exile, and the ruling class firmly back in the seat of power, more than ever determined to eliminate the last vestiges of democracy from the republic.

The Rise of the Medici

In 1393, Florentines celebrated the 100th anniversary of the great reform of the *Ordinamenti*, while watching their republic descend irresistibly into oligarchy. In that year **Maso degli Albizzi** became *gonfaloniere* (the head of the *Signoria*) and served as virtual dictator for many years afterwards. The ruling class of merchants, more than a bit paranoid after the Ciompi revolt, were generally relieved to see power concentrated in strong hands; the ascendancy of the Albizzi family was to set the pattern for the rest of the republic's existence. In a poisoned atmosphere of repression and conspiracy, the spies of the *Signoria*'s new secret police hunted down malcontents while whole legions of Florentine exiles plotted against the republic in foreign courts. Florence was almost constantly at war. In 1398 she defeated an attempt at conquest by Giangaleazzo Visconti of Milan. The imperialist policy of the Albizzi and their allies resulted in important territorial gains, including the conquest of Pisa in 1406, and the purchase of Livorno from the Genoese in 1421. Unsuccessful wars against Lucca finally disenchanted the Florentines with Albizzi rule. An emergency *parlamento* (the infrequent popular assembly usually called when a coming change of rulers was obvious) in 1434 decreed the recall from exile of the head of the popular opposition, **Cosimo de' Medici**.

Perhaps it was something that could only have happened in Florence—the darling of the plebeians, the great hope for reform, happened to be the head of Florence's biggest bank. The Medici family had their roots in the Mugello region north of Florence. Their name seems to suggest that they once were pharmacists (later enemies would jibe at the balls on the family arms as 'the pills'). For two centuries they had been active in Florentine politics; many had acquired reputations as troublemakers; their names turned up often in the lists of exiles and records of lawsuits. None of the Medici had ever been particularly rich until **Giovanni di Bicci de' Medici** (1360–1429) parlayed his wife's dowry into the founding of a bank. Good fortune—and a temporary monopoly on the handling of the pope's finances—made the Medici Bank Florence's biggest.

Giovanni had been content to stay on the fringe of politics; his son, **Cosimo** (known in Florentine history as '**il Vecchio**', the 'old man') took good care of the bank's affairs but aimed his sights much higher. His strategy was as old as Julius Caesar—the patrician reformer, cultivating the best men, winning the favour of the poor with largesse and gradually, carefully forming a party under a system specifically designed to prevent such things. In 1433 Rinaldo degli Albizzi had him exiled, but it was too late; continuing discontent forced his return only a year later, and for the next 35 years Cosimo would be the unchallenged ruler of Florence. Throughout this period, Cosimo occasionally held public office—this was done by lottery, with the electoral lists manipulated to ensure a majority of Medici supporters at all times. Nevertheless, he received ambassadors at the new family palace (built in 1444), entertained visiting popes and emperors, and made all the important decisions. A canny political godfather and usually a gentleman, Cosimo also proved a useful patron to the great figures of the early Renaissance—including Donatello and Brunelleschi. His father had served as one of the judges in the famous competition for the Baptistry doors, and Cosimo was a member of the commission that picked Brunelleschi to design the cathedral dome.

Cosimo did oversee some genuine reforms; under his leadership Florence began Europe's first progressive income tax, and a few years later the state invented the modern concept of the national debt—endlessly rolling over bonds to keep the republic afloat and the creditors happy. The poor, with fewer taxes to pay, were also happy, and the ruling classes, after some initial distaste, were positively delighted; never in Florence's history had any government so successfully muted class conflict and the desire for a genuine democracy. Wars were few, and the internal friction negligible. Cosimo died in August 1464; his tomb in San Lorenzo bears the inscription *Pater patriae,* and no dissent was registered when his 40-year-old son **Piero** took up the boss's role.

Lorenzo the Magnificent

Piero didn't quite have the touch of his masterful father, but he survived a stiff political crisis in 1466, outmanoeuvring a new faction led by wealthy banker Luca Pitti. In 1469 he succumbed to the Medici family disease, the gout, and his 20-year-old son **Lorenzo** succeeded him in an equally smooth transition. He was to last for 23 years. Not necessarily more 'magnificent' than other contemporary princes, or other Medici, Lorenzo's honorific reveals something of the myth that was to grow up around him in later centuries. His long reign corresponded to the height of the Florentine Renaissance. It was a relatively peaceful time, and in the light of the disasters that were to follow, Florentines could not help looking back on it as a golden age.

As a ruler, Lorenzo showed many virtues. Still keeping up the pretence of living as a private citizen, he lived relatively simply, always accessible to the voices and concerns of his fellow citizens, who would often see him walking the city streets. In the field of foreign policy he was indispensable to Florence and indeed all Italy; he did more than anyone to keep the precarious peninsular balance of power from disintegrating. The most dramatic affair of his reign was the **Pazzi conspiracy**, an attempt to assassinate Lorenzo plotted by Pope Sixtus IV and the wealthy Pazzi family, the pope's bankers and ancient rivals of the Medici. In 1478, two of the younger Pazzi attacked Lorenzo and his brother Giuliano during Mass at the cathedral. Giuliano was killed, but Lorenzo managed to escape into the sacristy. The botched murder aborted the planned revolt; Florentines showed little interest in the Pazzis' call to arms, and before nightfall most of the conspirators were dangling from the cornice of the Palazzo Vecchio.

Apparently, Lorenzo had angered the pope by starting a syndicate to mine for alum in Volterra, threatening the papal monopoly. Since Sixtus failed to murder Lorenzo, he had to settle for excommunicating him, and declaring war in alliance with King Ferrante of Naples. The war went badly for Florence and, in the most memorable act of his career, Lorenzo walked into the lion's cage, travelling to negotiate with the terrible Neapolitan, who had already murdered more than one important guest. As it turned out, Ferrante was only too happy to dump his papal entanglements; Florence found itself at peace once more, and Lorenzo returned home to a hero's welcome.

In other affairs, both foreign and domestic, Lorenzo was more a lucky ruler than a skilled one. Florence's economy was entering a long, slow decline, but for the moment the banks and mills were churning out just enough profit to keep up the accustomed level of opulence. The Medici Bank was on the ropes. Partly because of Lorenzo's neglect, it came close to collapsing on several occasions—and it seems that Lorenzo blithely made up the losses with public funds. Culturally, he was fortunate to be nabob of Florence at its most artistically creative period; future historians and Medici propagandists gave him a reputation as an art patron that is entirely undeserved. His own tastes tended towards bric-a-brac, jewellery, antique statues and vases; there is little evidence that he really understood or could appreciate the scores of great artists around him. Perhaps because he was too nearsighted to see anything very clearly, he did not ever commission an important canvas or fresco in Florence (except for Luca Signorelli's mysterious *Pan*, lost in Berlin during the last war). His favourite architect was the hack Giuliano da Sangallo.

The Medici had taken great care with Lorenzo's education; he was brought up with some of the leading humanist scholars of Tuscany for tutors and his real interests were literary. His well-formed lyrics and winsome pastorals have earned him a place among Italy's greatest 15th-century poets; they neatly reflect the private side of Lorenzo, the retiring, scholarly family man who enjoyed life better on one of the many rural Medici villas than in the busy city. In this, he was perfectly in tune with his class and his age. Plenty of Florentine bankers were learning the joys of country life, reading Horace or Catullus in their geometrical gardens and pestering their tenant farmers with well-meant advice.

Back in town, they had thick new walls of rusticated sandstone between them and the bustle of the streets. The late 15th century was the great age of palace building in Florence. Following the example of Cosimo de' Medici, the bankers and merchants erected dozens of palaces (some of the best can be seen around Via Tornabuoni). Each one turns blank walls and iron-barred windows to the street. Historians always note one very pronounced phenomenon of this period— a turning inward, a 'privatization' of Florentine life. In a city that had become a republic only in name, civic interest and public life ceased to matter so much. The very rich began to assume the airs of an aristocracy, and did everything they could to distance themselves from their fellow citizens. Ironically, just at the time when Florence's artists were creating their greatest achievements, the republican ethos, the civic soul that had made Florence great, began to disintegrate.

Savonarola

Lorenzo's death, in 1492, was followed by another apparently smooth transition of power to his son **Piero**. But after 58 years of Medicean quiet and stability, the city was ready for a change. The opportunity for the malcontents came soon enough, when the timid and inept Piero allowed the invading King of France, **Charles VIII**, to occupy Pisa and the Tuscan coast. A spontaneous revolt chased Piero and the rest of the Medici into exile, while a mob sacked the family's palace. A new regime, hastily put together under **Piero Capponi**, dealt more sternly with the French (*see* p.113) and tried to pump some new life into the long-dormant republican constitution.

The Florence that threw out the Medici was a city in the mood for some radical reform. Already, the dominating figure on the political stage was an intense Dominican friar from Ferrara named **Girolamo Savonarola**. Perhaps not surprisingly, this oversophisticated and overstimulated city was also in the mood to be told how wicked and decadent it was, and Savonarola was happy to oblige. A spellbinding revival preacher with a touch of erudition, Savonarola packed as many as 10,000 into the Duomo to hear his weekly sermons, which were laced with political sarcasm and social criticism. Though an insufferable prig, he was also a sincere democrat. There is a story that the dying Lorenzo called Savonarola to his bedside for the last rites, and that the friar refused him absolution unless he 'restored the liberty of the Florentines', a proposal that only made the dying despot sneer with contempt.

Savonarola also talked Charles VIII into leaving Florence in peace. Pisa, however, took advantage of the confusion to revolt, and the restored republic's attempts to recapture it were in vain. Things were going badly. Piero Capponi's death in 1496 left Florence without a really able leader, and Savonarolan extremists became ever more influential. The French invasion and the incessant wars that followed cost the city dearly in trade, while the Medici, now in Rome, intrigued endlessly to destroy the republic. Worst of all, Savonarola's attacks on clerical corruption made him another bitter enemy in Rome—none other than **Pope Alexander VI** himself, the most corrupt cleric who ever lived. The Borgia pope scraped together a league of allies to make war on Florence in 1497.

This war proceeded without serious reverses for either side, but Savonarola was able to exploit it brilliantly, convincing the Florentines that they were on a moral crusade against the hated and dissolute Borgias, Medici, French, Venetians and Milanese. The year 1497 was undoubtedly the high point of Savonarola's career. The good friar's spies—mostly children—kept a close eye on any Florentines who were suspected of enjoying themselves, and collected books, fancy clothes and works of art for the famous **Bonfire of Vanities**. It was a climactic moment in the history of Florence's delicate psyche. Somehow the spell had been broken; like the deranged old Michelangelo, taking a hammer to his own work, the Florentines gathered the objects that had once been their greatest pride and put them to the torch. The bonfire was held in the centre of the Piazza della Signoria; a visiting Venetian offered to buy the whole lot, but the Florentines had someone hastily sketch his portrait and threw that on the flames, too.

One vanity the Florentines could not quite bring themselves to part with was their violent factionalism. On one side were the *Piagnoni* ('weepers') of Savonarola's party, on the other the party of the *Arrabbiati* ('the angry'), including the gangs of young delinquents who would demonstrate their opposition to piety and holiness by sneaking into the cathedral and filling Savonarola's pulpit with cow dung. A Medicean party was also gathering strength, a sort of fifth column sowing discontent within the city and undermining the war effort. Three times, unsuccessfully, the exiled Medici attempted to seize the city with bands of mercenaries. The Pisan revolt continued, and Pope Alexander had excommunicated Savonarola and was threatening to place all Florence under an interdict. In the long hangover after the Bonfire of Vanities, the Florentines were growing weary of their preacher. When the *Arrabbiati* won the elections of 1498, his doom was sealed. A kangaroo court found the new scapegoat guilty of heresy and treason. After some gratuitous torture and public mockery, the very spot where the Bonfire of Vanities had been held now witnessed a bonfire of Savonarola.

Pope Alexander still wasn't happy. He sent an army under his son, Cesare Borgia, to menace the city. Florence weathered this threat, and the relatively democratic 'Savonarolan' constitution of 1494 seemed to be working out well. Under an innovative idea, borrowed from Venice and designed to circumvent party strife, a public-spirited gentleman named **Piero Soderini** was elected *gonfaloniere* for life in 1502. With the help of his friend and adviser, **Niccolò Machiavelli**, Soderini kept the ship of state on an even keel. Pisa finally surrendered in 1509. Serious trouble returned in 1512, and once more the popes were behind it. As France's only ally in Italy, Florence ran foul of Julius II. Papal and Spanish armies invaded Florentine territory, and after their gruesome sack of Prato, designed specifically to overawe Florence, the frightened and politically apathetic city was ready to submit to the pope's conditions—the expulsion of Soderini, a change of alliance, and the return of the Medici.

The End of the Republic

At first, the understanding was that the Medici would live in Florence strictly as private citizens. But **Giuliano de' Medici**, son of Lorenzo and current leader, soon united the upper classes for a rolling back of Savonarolan democracy. With plenty of hired soldiers to intimidate the populace, a rigged *parlamento* in September 1512 restored Medici control. The democratic Grand Council was abolished; its new meeting hall in the Palazzo Vecchio (where Leonardo and

Michelangelo were to have their 'Battle of the Frescoes') was broken up into apartments for soldiers. Soldiers were everywhere, and the Medicean restoration took on the aspect of a police state. Hundreds of political prisoners spent time undergoing torture in the Palazzo Vecchio's dungeons, among them Macchiavelli.

Giuliano died in 1516, succeeded by his nephew **Lorenzo, Duke of Urbino**, a snotty young sport with a tyrant's bad manners. Nobody mourned much when syphilis carried him off in 1519, but the family paid Michelangelo to give both Lorenzo and Giuliano fancy tombs. Ever since Giuliano's death, however, the real Medici boss had been not Lorenzo, but his uncle Giovanni, who in that year became **Pope Leo X**. The Medici, original masters of nepotism, had been planning this for years. Back in the 1470s, Lorenzo il Magnifico realized that the surest way of maintaining the family fortunes would be to get a Medici on the papal throne. He had little Giovanni ordained at the age of eight, purchased him a cardinal's hat at 13, and used bribery and diplomacy to help him accumulate dozens of benefices all over France and Italy.

For his easy-going civility (as exemplified in his famous quote: 'God has given us the papacy so let us enjoy it'), and his patronage of scholars and artists, Leo became one of the best-remembered Renaissance popes. On the other side of the coin was his criminal mismanagement of the Church; having learned the advantages of parasitism, the Medici were eager to pass it on to their friends. Upper-class Florentines descended on Rome like a plague of locusts, occupying all the important sinecures and rapidly emptying the papal treasury. Their rapacity, plus the tremendous expenses involved in building the new St Peter's, caused Leo to step up the sale of indulgences all over Europe—disgusting reformers like Luther and greatly hastening the onset of the Reformation.

Back in Florence, Lorenzo Duke of Urbino's successor Giulio, bastard son of Lorenzo il Magnifico's brother the murdered Giuliano, was little more than a puppet; Leo always found enough time between banquets to manage the city's affairs. Giulio himself became pope in 1523, as **Clement VII**, thanks largely to the new financial interdependence between Florence and Rome, and now the Medici presence in their home city was reduced to two more unattractive young bastards, Ippolito and Alessandro, under the guardianship of Cardinal Silvio Passerini. As Leo had done, Clement attempted to run the city from Rome, but high taxes and the lack of a strong hand made the new Medici regime increasingly precarious; its end followed almost immediately upon the sack of Rome in 1527. With Clement a prisoner in the Vatican and unable to intervene, a delegation of Florentine notables discreetly informed Cardinal Passerini and the Medicis that it was time to go. They took the hint, and for the third time in less than a century Florence had succeeded in getting rid of the Medici.

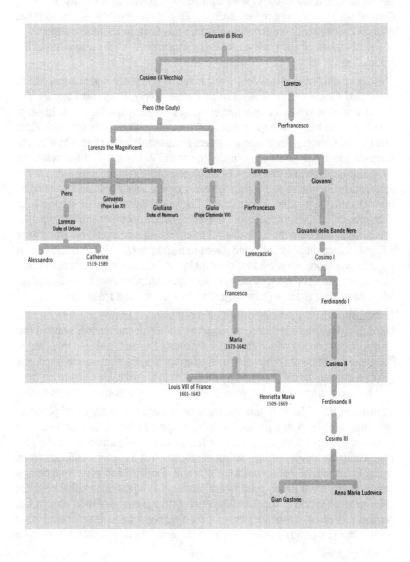

Giovanni di Bicci

Cosimo (il Vecchio)

Lorenzo

Piero (the Gouty)

Pierfrancesco

Lorenzo the Magnificent

Giuliano

Lorenzo

Giovanni

Piero

Giovanni
(Pope Leo X)

Giuliano
Duke of Nemours

Giulio
(Pope Clemente VII)

Pierfrancesco

Lorenzo
Duke of Urbino

Giovanni delle Bande Nere

Alessandro

Catherine
1519-1589

Lorenzaccio

Cosimo I

Francesco

Ferdinando I

Maria
1573-1642

Cosimo II

Louis VIII of France
1601-1643

Henrietta Maria
1509-1669

Ferdinando II

Cosimo III

Gian Gastone

Anna Maria Ludovica

The new republic, though initiated by the disillusioned wealthy classes, soon found radical Savonarolan democrats gaining the upper hand. The Grand Council met once more, and extended the franchise to include most of the citizens. Vanities were cursed again, books were banned and carnival parades forbidden; the Council officially pronounced Jesus Christ 'King of the Florentines', just as it had done in the heyday of the Savonarolan camp meetings. In an intense atmosphere of republican virtue and pious crusade, Florence rushed headlong into the apocalyptic climax of its history.

This time it did not take the Medici long to recover. In order to get Florence back, the witless Clement became allied to his former enemy, **Emperor Charles V**, a sordid deal that would eventually betray all Italy to Spanish control. Imperial troops were to help subdue Florence, and Clement's illegitimate son Alessandro was to wed Charles' illegitimate daughter. The bastards were closing in. Charles' troops put Florence under siege in December 1529. The city had few resources for the struggle, and no friends, but a heroic resistance kept the imperialists at bay all through the winter and spring. Citizens gave up their gold and silver to be minted into the republic's last coins. The councillors debated seizing little Catherine de' Medici, future Queen of France, but then a prisoner of the republic, and dangling her from the walls to give the enemy a good target. Few artists were left in Florence, but Michelangelo stayed to help with his city's fortifications (by night he was working on the Medici tombs in San Lorenzo, surely one of the most astounding feats of fence-straddling in history; both sides gave him safe passage when he wanted to leave Florence, and again when he decided to return).

In August of 1530, the Florentines' skilful commander, Francesco Ferruccio, was killed in a skirmish near Pistoia; at about the same time the republic realized that its mercenary captain within the walls, Malatesta Baglioni, had sold them out to the pope and emperor. When they tried to arrest him, Baglioni only laughed, and directed his men to turn their artillery on the city. The inevitable capitulation came on 12 August; after almost 400 years, the Florentine republic had breathed its last.

At first, this third Medici return seemed to be just another dreary round of history repeating itself. Again, a packed *parlamento* gutted the constitution and legitimized the Medici takeover. Again the family and its minions combed the city, confiscating back every penny's worth of property that had been confiscated from them. This time, however, was to be different. Florence had gone from being a large fish in a small Italian pond to a minuscule but hindersome nuisance in the pan-European world of papal and imperial politics. Charles V didn't much like republics, or disorderly politicking, or indeed anyone who might conceivably say no to him. The orders came down from the emperor in Brussels; it was to be Medici for ever.

Cosimo I: the Medici as Grand Dukes

At first little was changed; the shell of the republican constitution was maintained, but with the 20-year-old illegitimate **Alessandro** as 'Duke of the Florentine Republic'; the harsh reality was under construction on the height above the city's west end—the Fortezza da Basso, with its Spanish garrison, demanded by Charles V as insurance that Florence would never again be able to assert its independence. If any further symbolism was necessary, Alessandro ordered the great bell to be removed from the tower of the Palazzo Vecchio, the bell that had always summoned the citizens to political assemblies and the mustering of the army.

In 1537, Alessandro was treacherously murdered by his jealous cousin Lorenzaccio de' Medici. With no legitimate heirs in the direct line, Florence was in danger of falling under direct imperial rule, as had happened to Milan two years earlier, upon the extinction of the Sforza dukes. The assassination was kept secret while the Medici and the diplomats angled for a solution. The only reasonable choice turned out to be 18-year-old **Cosimo de' Medici**, heir of the family's cadet branch. This son of a famous mercenary commander, Giovanni of the Black Bands, had grown up on a farm and had never been involved with Florentine affairs; both the elder statesmen of the family and the imperial representatives thought they would easily be able to manipulate him.

It soon became clear that they had picked the wrong boy. Right from the start, young Cosimo had a surprisingly complete idea of how he meant to rule Florence, and also the will and strength of personality to see his commands carried out. No one ever admitted liking him; his puritanical court dismayed even the old partisans of Savonarola, and Florentines always enjoyed grumbling over his high taxes, going to support 'colonels, spies, Spaniards, and women to serve Madame' (his Spanish consort Eleanor of Toledo).

More surprising still, in this pathetic age when bowing and scraping Italians were everywhere else losing both their liberty and their dignity, Cosimo held his own against both pope and Spaniard. To back up his growing independence, Cosimo put his domains on an almost permanent war footing. New fortresses were built, a big fleet begun, and a paid standing army took the place of mercenaries and citizen levies. The skeleton of the old republic was revamped into a modern, bureaucratic state, governed as scientifically and rationally as any in Europe. The new regime, well prepared as it was, never had a severe test. Early in his reign Cosimo defeated the last-ditch effort of the republican exiles, unreconstructed oligarchs led by the banker Filippo Strozzi, at the **Battle of Montemurlo**, the last threat ever to Medici rule. Cosimo's masterstroke came in 1557, when with the help of an imperial army he was able to gobble up the entire Republic of Siena.

Now the Medicis controlled roughly the boundaries of modern Tuscany; Cosimo was able to cap off his reign in 1569 by purchasing from the Pope the title of Grand Duke of Tuscany.

Knick-knacks and Tedium: the Later Medici

For all Cosimo's efforts, Florence was a city entering a very evident decline. Banking and trade did well throughout the late 16th century, a prosperous time for almost all of Italy, but there were very few opportunities for growth, and few Florentines interested in looking for it. More than ever, wealth was going into land, palaces and government bonds; the old tradition of mercantile venture among the Florentine élite was rapidly becoming a thing of the past. For culture and art, Cosimo's reign turned out to be a disaster. It wasn't what he intended; indeed the Duke brought to the field his accustomed energy and compulsion to improve and organize. Academies were founded, and research underwritten. Cosimo's big purse and his emphasis on art as political propaganda helped change the Florentine artist from a slightly eccentric guild artisan to a flouncing courtier, ready to roll over at his master's command.

Michelangelo, despite frequent entreaties, always refused to work for Cosimo. Most of the other talented Florentines eventually found one excuse or another to bolt for Rome or even further afield, leaving lapdogs like **Giorgio Vasari** to carry on the grand traditions of Florentine art. Vasari, with help from such artists as Ammannati and Bandinelli, transformed much of the city—especially the interiors of its churches and public buildings. Florence began to fill up with equestrian statues of Medici, pageants and plaster triumphal arches displaying the triumphs of the Medici, sculptural allegories (like Cellini's *Perseus*) reminding us of the inevitability of the Medici and, best of all, portraits of semi-divine Medici floating up in the clouds with little Cupids and Virtues.

It was all the same to Cosimo and his successors, whose personal tastes tended more to engraved jewels, exotic taxidermy and sculptures made of seashells. But it helped hasten the extinction of Florentine culture and the quiet transformation of the city into just another Mediterranean backwater. Cosimo himself grew ill in his later years, abdicating most responsibility to his son **Francesco** from 1564 to his death ten years later. Francesco, the genuine oddball among the Medici, was a moody, melancholic sort who cared little for government, preferring to lock himself up in the family palaces to pursue his passion for alchemy, as well as occasional researches into such subjects as perpetual motion and poisons—his agents around the Mediterranean had to ship him crates of scorpions every now and then. Despite his lack of interest, Francesco was a capable ruler, best known for his founding of the port city of Livorno.

Later Medici followed the general course established by other great families, such as the Habsburgs and Bourbons—each one was worse than the last. Francesco's death in 1587 gave the throne to his brother, **Ferdinando I**, founder of the Medici Chapels at San Lorenzo and another indefatigable collector of bric-a-brac. Next came **Cosimo II** (1609–21), a sickly nonentity who eventually succumbed to tuberculosis, and **Ferdinando II** (1621–70), whose long and uneventful reign oversaw the impoverishment of Florence and most of Tuscany. For this the Medici do not deserve much blame. A long string of bad harvests, beginning in the 1590s, plagues that recurred with terrible frequency as late as the 1630s, and general trade patterns that redistributed wealth and power from the Mediterranean to northern Europe, all set the stage for the collapse of the Florentine economy. The fatal blow came in the 1630s, when the long-deteriorating wool trade collapsed with sudden finality. Banking was going too, partly a victim of the age's continuing inflation, partly of high taxes and lack of worthwhile investments. Florence, by mid-century, found itself with no prospects at all, a pensioner city drawing a barely respectable income from its glorious past.

With **Cosimo III** (1670–1723), the line of the Medici crossed over into the realm of the ridiculous. A religious crank and anti-Semite, this Cosimo temporarily wiped out free thought in the universities, allowed Tuscany to fill up with nuns and Jesuits, and decreed fantastical laws like the one that forbade any man to enter a house where an unmarried woman lived. To support his lavish court and pay the big tributes demanded by Spain and Austria (something earlier Medici would have scorned), Cosimo taxed what was left of the Florentine economy into an early grave. His heir was the incredible **Gian Gastone** (1723–37). This last Medici, an obese drunkard, senile and slobbering at the age of 50, has been immortalized by the equally incredible bust in the Pitti Palace. Gian Gastone had to be carried up and down stairs on the rare occasions when he ever got out of bed (mainly to disprove rumours that he was dead); on the one occasion he appeared in public, the chronicles report him vomiting repeatedly out of the carriage window.

As a footnote on the Medici there is Gian Gastone's perfectly sensible sister, **Anna Maria Ludovica**. As the very last surviving Medici, it fell to her to dispose of the family's vast wealth and hoards of art. When she died, in 1743, her will revealed that the whole bundle was to become the property of the future rulers of Tuscany—whoever they should be—with the provision that not one bit of it should ever, ever be moved outside Florence. Without her, the great collections of the Uffizi and the Bargello might long ago have been packed away to Vienna or to Paris.

Post-Medici Florence

When Gian Gastone died in 1737, Tuscany's fate had already been decided by the great powers of Europe. The Grand Duchy would fall to **Francis Stephen**, Duke of Lorraine and husband-to-be of the Austrian Empress Maria Theresa; the new duke's troops were already installed in the Fortezza da Basso a year before Gian Gastone died. For most of the next century, Florence slumbered peacefully under a benign Austrian rule. Already the first Grand Tourists were arriving on their way to Rome and Naples, sons of the Enlightenment like Goethe, who never imagined anything in Florence could possibly interest him and didn't stop, or relics like the Pretender Charles Edward Stuart, 'Bonnie Prince Charlie', Duke of Albany, who stayed two years. Napoleon's men occupied the city for most of two decades, without making much of an impression.

After the Napoleonic Wars, the Habsburg restoration brought back the Lorraine dynasty. From 1824 to 1859, Florence and Tuscany were ruled by **Leopold II**, that most useful and likeable of all Grand Dukes. This was the age when Florence first became popular among the northern Europeans and the time when the Brownings, Dostoevsky, Leigh Hunt and dozens of other artists and writers took up residence, rediscovering the glories of the city and of the early Renaissance. Grand Duke Leopold was decent enough to let himself be overthrown in 1859, during the tumults of the Risorgimento. In 1865, when only the Papal State remained to be incorporated into the Kingdom of Italy, Florence briefly became the new nation's capital. King Vittorio Emanuele moved into the Pitti Palace, and the Italian Parliament met in the great hall of the Palazzo Vecchio.

It was really not meant to last. When the Italian troops entered Rome in 1870, Florence's brief hour as a major capital was at an end. Not, however, without giving the staid old city a memorable jolt towards the modern world. In an unusual flurry of exertion, Florence finally threw up a façade for its cathedral, and levelled the picturesque though squalid market area and Jewish ghetto to build the dolorous Piazza della Repubblica. Fortunately, the city regained its senses before too much damage was done. Throughout this century, Florence's role as a museum city has been confirmed with each passing year. The hiatus provided by World War II allowed the city to resume briefly its ancient delight in black-and-white political epic. In 1944–5, Florence offered some of the most outrageous spectacles of Fascist fanaticism, and also some of the most courageous stories of the Resistance—including that of the German consul Gerhard Wolf, who used his position to protect Florentines from the Nazi terror, often at great personal risk.

In August 1944, the Allied armies were poised to advance through northern Tuscany. For the Germans, the Arno made a convenient defensive line, requiring that all the bridges of Florence be demolished. All were, except for the Ponte Vecchio, saved in a last-minute deal, though the buildings on either side of it were destroyed to provide piles of rubble around the bridge approaches. After the war, all were repaired; the city had the Ponte Santa Trinità rebuilt stone by stone exactly as it was. No sooner was the war damage redeemed, however, than an even greater disaster attacked Florence's patrimony. The flood of 1966, when water reached as high as 6.5m, did more damage than Nazis or Napoleons; an international effort was raised to preserve and restore the city's art and monuments. Since then the Arno's bed has been deepened under the Ponte Vecchio and 6m earthen walls have been erected around Ponte Amerigo Vespucci; video screens and computers monitor every fluctuation in the water level. If a flood happens again, Florence will have time to protect herself. Far more insoluble is the problem of terrorism, which touched the city, in May 1993, when a bomb attack destroyed the Gregoriophilus library opposite the Uffizi and damaged the Vasari Corridor. Florence, shocked by this intrusion from the outside world into its holy of holies, repaired most of the damage in record time with funds which were raised by a national subscription.

Careful planning has saved the best of Florence's immediate countryside from a different sort of flood—post-war suburbanization—but much of the other territory around the city has been coated by an atrocity of suburban sprawl, some of the most degraded landscapes in all Italy. The building of a new airport extension, which the Florentines hope will help make up some of the economic ground they've lost to Milan, may also include the building of a whole new business city, a new Florence, nothing less than 'the greatest urban planning operation of the century' they say, with some of the old audacity of Brunelleschi. There are plans for an underground, and perhaps even a new high-speed train between Milan and Rome that would pass under Florence in a tunnel. Ideas there are, but getting them past the city's innate factionalism and its own mania for perfectionism has proved to be a mountain of a stumbling block.

Meanwhile Florence works hard to preserve what it already has. Although new measures to control the city's bugbear—the traffic problems of a city of 400,000 that receives 7 million visitors a year—have been enacted to protect the historic centre, pollution from nearby industry continues to eat away at monuments—Donatello's statue of St Mark at Orsanmichele, perfectly intact 50 years ago, is now a mutilated leper. Private companies, banks, and even individuals finance 90 per cent of the art restoration in Florence, with techniques invented by the city's innovative Institute of Restoration. Increasingly copies are made to replace original works. Naturally, half the city is for them, and the other half, against.

Florence is one of the best Italian cities to get around; best, because nearly everything you'll want to see is within easy walking distance and large areas in the centre are pedestrian zones; there are only a few hills, and it's hard to lose your way for very long.

Just a few years ago the traffic problem in Florence was one of the grimmest and most carcinogenic in Italy; a walk along the Lungarno or the remaining streets where the traffic is now channelled will demonstrate that Dante didn't have to go far to find Purgatorio. But in 1988, with great fanfare and howls of protest, Florence attempted to do something about the cars that were choking it to death by greatly enlarging the limited access zone, the *zona a traffico limitato*, which the Florentines, with clenched teeth, somehow pronounce as ZTL. The ZTL restrictions apply Mon–Sat 7.30am–6.30pm. Outside these hours, the relevant areas are accessible. These hours are extended to include Friday, Saturday, and Sunday evenings during the summer. Access to hotels on arrival and departure is permitted. Within ZTL only buses, taxis, and cars belonging to residents are permitted. This new regulation was followed by whole areas, especially around Piazza della Signoria and the Duomo, becoming totally traffic-free zones. The only danger in these areas is the odd ambulance or police car, the speeding mopeds (all of which you can usually hear) and the deadly silent bicycle. The car parking situation in the city has improved a little in the past years. The safest places to park are underground at the Parterre (near Piazza Libertà) where you will get a discount and loan of a bicycle on production of a hotel receipt, the Fortezza da Basso, the biggest and perhaps the most convenient, or under the station. Otherwise there are smaller car parks (marked by blue lines) throughout the city either with a metre or manned by an attendant. If you don't want to pay, take your chances on a side street, but be careful; if you park illegally, you may not find your car when you return. In this case, contact the car pound (*see* p.22).

Just to make life difficult, Florence has two sets of address numbers on every street—red ones for business, blue for residences; your hotel might be either.

by bus

City buses (ATAF) can whizz or inch you across Florence, and are an excellent means of reaching sights on the periphery. Most lines begin at Santa Maria Novella station, and pass by Piazza del Duomo or Piazza San

Marco. ATAF supply a useful route map for their buses. These are available at the information/ticket booth at the station, tourist offices, some bars, and at ATAF's central office in Piazza della Stazione, ✆ 5650222. Ticket prices: L1500 for 60mins, L2500 for 3hrs, L6000 for 24hrs. The most useful buses for visitors are listed below.

6: Via Rondinella–Duomo–Piazza San Marco–Piazza Unità–Soffiano

7: Station–Duomo–San Domenico–Fiesole

10: Station–Duomo–S. Marco–Ponte a Mensola–Settignano

11: Viale Calatafimi–S. Marco Piazza–Independenza Station–Porta Romana–Poggio Imperiale

11A: Viale Calatafimi–Duomo–Porta Romana–Poggio Imperiale

13: Station–Ponte Rosso–Pza. Libertà–Viale Mazzini–Piazzale Michelangelo–Porta Romana

14C: Rovezzano–Duomo–Station–Careggi

17: Cascine–Station–Duomo–Via Lamarmora–Salviatino (for the youth hostel)

25: Station–S. Marco–Piazza Libertà–Via Bolognese–Pratolino

28: Station–Via R. Giuliani–Castello–Sesto Fiorentino

37: Station–Ponte alla Carraia–Porta Romana–Certosa del Galluzzo

38: Porta Romana–Pian del Giullari (you need to book this from the telephone near the bus stop at Porta Romana)

As part of the campaign against city smog, a fleet of Lilliputian electric buses, routes B, C and D, have recently been introduced. These mainly serve the centre, often taking circuitous routes 'round the houses', and are a good way of seeing some of the sights if you've had enough walking. Details of routes are on the ATAF maps.

by taxi

Taxis in Florence don't cruise; you'll find them in ranks at the station and in the major piazze, or else ring for a radio taxi, ✆ 4798 or 4390.

bicycle and scooter hire

Hiring a bike can save you tramping time and angst, but watch out for cars and pedestrians. You can hire a motorbike at **Alinari**, Via Guelfa 85r, ✆ 280500 or Via dei Bardi 35, ✆ 2346436; **Motorent**, Via S. Zanobi 9r, ✆ 490113 and **Florence by Bike**, Via della Scala 12r, ✆ 264035; mountain bikes only can be hired from **Promoturist**, Via Baccio Bandinelli 43, ✆ 701863. For **car hire** in Florence, see p.12.

The head office is a bit out of the way, near Piazza Beccaria on Via Manzoni 16, ✆ 290832 (*open Mon–Sat 8.30–1.30*). There is now a branch of the Via Manzoni office in the centre of town: Via Cavour 1r, ✆ 290832 (*open Nov–Feb Mon–Fri 8.15–1.45, and Mar–Oct Mon–Sat 8.15–7.15, Sun 8.15–1.45*). There's also a very genial booth outside the station, at the end of the bus ranks, ✆ 212245 (*open all year Mon–Sat 8.15–7.15, plus Sun 8.15–2 in the summer*). There's an office in Fiesole at Piazza Mino 37, ✆ 598720 (*open all year 8.30–1.30*). A new office is situated at Borgo Santa Croce 29/r, ✆ 234 0444/226 4524 (*open from 8.15–7.15 and from 8.15–1.30 on Sundays in summer*).

There is no end of places to help you find a hotel (*see* **Where to Stay**, p.327) but these tourist offices usually cannot help.

Florence Walks

Florence

250 metres
250 yards

N

Cenacolo di Sant' Apollonia

VIA SAN GALLO
VIA XXVII APRILE
VIA SAN ZANOBI
VIA GUELFA
VIA NAZIONALE
VIA CAVOUR
VIA RICASOLI
VIA DE' GINORI
VIA TADDEA
VIA PANICALE
Piazza del Mercato Centrale
VIA DELL'ARIENTO
BORGO LA NOCE
VIA SANT'ANTONINO
VIA FAENZA
V.D. MELARANCIO

Lazzi Buses
Stazione Centrale
Sita Buses
Piazza della Stazione
Cenacolo di Foligno
Piazza dell' Unità Italiana
Medici Chapels
San Lorenzo
Piazza Madonna
Palazzo Medici-Riccardi

Cappella degli Spagnuoli
VIA DELLA SCALA
VIA DEI PANZANI
VIA DE' CONTI
VIA DE' MARTELLI
VIA DE' PUCCI

VIA DELLE BELLE DONNE
VIA DELL' ALBERO
VIA DEI BANCHI
GIGLIO
Biblioteca Laurenziana

Santa Maria Novella
Piazza Santa Maria Novella
VIA DE' CERRETANI
Duomo
Museo dell'Opera del Duomo

BORGO OGNISSANTI
VIA DEI FOSSI
Croce del Trebbio
Palazzo Antinori
Piazza di San Giovanni
Baptistry
Piazza del Duomo
Santa Margherita de' Cerchi

Ognissanti
VIA DEGLI AGLI
VIA DE' PECORI
San Gaetano
VIA D. CAMPIDOGLIO
VIA DELLE OCHE
Dante's House
VIA DEL CORSO
Bargello

LUNGARNO AMERIGO VESPUCCI
VIA DEI PORCELLANA
San Pancrazio
VIA ROMA
VIA DANTE ALIGHIERI
San Martino

PONTE AMERIGO VESPUCCI
Palazzo Rucellai
VIA DELLA SPADA
Piazza della Repubblica
VIA SPEZIALI
Arte della Lana
Orsanmichele
Badia

LUNGARNO SODERINI
Piazza Goldoni
VIA D. VIGNA NUOVA
Palazzo Corsini
VIA STROZZI
Palazzo Strozzi
VIA CALIMALA
VIA CONDOTTA
Palazzo Gondi
San Firenze

Piazza di Cestello
VIA DEL PARIONE
Post Office & Telephones
Palazzo Davanzati
Mercato Nuovo
Piazza della Signoria
Palazzo Vecchio

San Frediano in Cestello
LUNGARNO CORSINI
Piazza S. Trinita
Santa Trinita
VIA PORTA ROSSA
Palazzo di Parte Guelfa
Loggia dei Lanzi

Porta San Frediano 100m
PONTE ALLA CARRAIA
SS. Apostoli
VIA DELLE TERME
VIA LAMBERTESCA
Uffizi

Piazza del Carmine
Ponte Santa Trinita
VIA DI S. SPIRITO
LUNG. ACCIAIOLI
Piazzale degli Uffizi

Santa Maria del Carmine
LUNG. GUICCIARDINI
BORGO SAN JACOPO
Ponte Vecchio
Museum of the History of Science
LUNG. DIAZ

VIA S. MONACA
Santo Spirito
Piazza S. Felicità
Fiume

VIA SANT'AGOSTINO
Piazza Santo Spirito
VIA DE' GUICCIARDINI
Santa Felicità
LUNGARNO TORRIGIANI
PONTE ALLE GRAZIE

Casa Guidi
Piazza San Felice
COSTA DI SAN GIORGIO
Museo Bardini

VIA MAGGIO
BORGO TEGOLAIO
Piazza dei Pitti
Grotta di Buontalenti
Piazza dei Mozzi

VIA ROMANA
VIA DE' BARDI
Palazzo dei Mozzi

La Specola Museum
Pitti Palace
Kaffeehaus
Amphitheatre
Belvedere Fort

Boboli Gardens
Neptune Fountain

Porcelain Museum and Giardino del Cavaliere

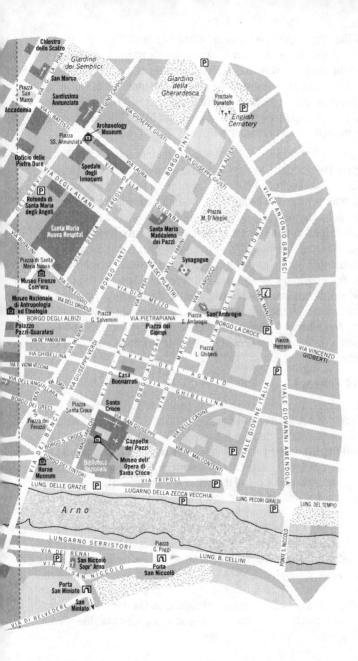

Now that the Florentines have dismissed most of the traffic from their historic centre, the city is extremely pleasant to tackle on foot—the only real way to absorb its beauties and contradictions. The attractions are so dense that none of the nine walks we've divided it up into should cause any fallen arches, except perhaps Walk IX, a tramp through the Oltrarno, but blame the Medici and their mastodontic Pitti palace for that.

The other eight walks more or less have themes—the Cathedral complex (Walk I); the two great churches of the preaching orders, Franciscan Santa Croce (VIII) and Dominican Santa Maria Novella (V), a walk which also includes the Medici palace and tombs; Piazza della Signoria and the Uffizi, the centre of civic life (II); the early medieval core of Florence, where Dante once lived (III); mercantile banking Florence (IV). Walks VI and VII encompass the northeast side with a grab-bag of Florentine essentials: the Accademia, Fra Angelico's San Marco, Brunelleschi's Spedale degli Innocenti, Santissima Annunziata and the Archaeology Museum. At the end comes the Oltrano (IX), literally the area 'beyond the Arno', and a list of peripheral attractions just outside the centre including the most magnificent views over Florence from the surrounding hills.

Highlights of Florence

Florence's museums, palaces and churches contain more good art than perhaps any European city, and to see it all comfortably would take at least three weeks. If you have only a few days, the highlights will take up all your time—the **Cathedral** and **Baptistry**, the paintings in the **Uffizi** and the sculptures in the **Bargello**. Stop for a look at the eccentric **Orsanmichele**, and see the Arno from the **Ponte Vecchio**, taking in some of the oldest streets in the city. If your heart leans towards the graceful lyricism of the 1400s, don't miss the **Cathedral Museum** and the Fra Angelicos in **San Marco**; for the lush virtuosity of the 1500s, visit the **Pitti Palace**'s Galleria Palatina. The churches **Santa Maria Novella** and **Santa Croce** are galleries in themselves, containing some of the greatest Florentine art; **Santa Maria del Carmine** has the restored frescoes of Masaccio and company. Devotees of the Michelangelo cult won't want to miss the Medici Chapels and library at **San Lorenzo** or *David* in the **Accademia**. When the stones begin to weary, head for the oasis of the **Boboli Gardens**. Finally, climb up to beautiful, medieval **San Miniato,** with its enchanting view over the city.

Florence's 'secondary' sights are just as interesting. You could spend a day walking around old **Fiesole**, or 15 minutes looking at Gozzoli's charming fresco in the **Palazzo Medici-Riccardi**. The **Palazzo Vecchio** has more, but less charming, Medici frescoes. You can see how a wealthy medieval Tuscan merchant lived at the **Palazzo Davanzati**, while the **Museum of the History of Science** will tell you about the scientific side of the Florentine Renaissance; **Santa Trínita**, **Santo Spirito**, **Ognissanti** and the **Annunziata** all contain famous works from the Renaissance. The **Casa Buonarroti** has some early sculptures of Michelangelo; the **Archaeology Museum** has even earlier ones by the Etruscans, Greeks and Egyptians; the Pitti Palace's **Museo degli Argenti** overflows with Medicean jewellery and trinkets. Take a bus or car out to Lorenzo il Magnifico's villa at **Poggio a Caiano**, or to the Medicis' other garden villas: **La Petraia** and **Castello**, or **Pratolino**.

There are three museums nearer the present with 19th- and 20th-century collections: the **Galleria d'Arte Moderna** in the Pitti Palace, the **Collezione della Ragione** and the **Photography Museum** in the Palazzo Rucellai.

Florence in a Weekend

If you have only a weekend in Florence, concentrate on **Walk I** (Piazza del Duomo), **Walk II** (Piazza della Signoria and the Uffizi) and **Walk III** (Medieval Florence), especially the often neglected Bargello—the Uffizi of Renaissance sculpture. When too much art begins to make your head spin, get on top of the city—several possibilities are mentioned in **Peripheral Attractions**.

Street Furniture

Although at first glance Florence's streets seem austere and severe, there's plenty of interesting detail to look out for besides the obvious monuments—don't keep your eyes at street level. If you look up, the buildings reveal intricate stone carvings, gargoyles, wrought-iron work and frescoes. After dark, you often see amazing ceilings and chandeliers through the tall windows of the *piano nobile* when the lights are lit inside; Italians tend not to draw their curtains. Rooftop terraces and gardens are always a delight, especially in spring and summer when they are a riot of flowers. Some of them seem to be so precariously perched, you expect them to come tumbling down at any given moment.

If you find doorways into grand buildings open, step inside if you dare; there's often a spectacular courtyard or hidden garden waiting to be discovered. Even when they are closed, these doors, often immensely thick with all sorts of decorations or great studs in them, can be worth a glance. Don't forget the doorbells—there are some wonderful little wrought-iron gargoyles about. The names on the buzzers of the flats, or on the shop signs of the butcher's or furniture restorer's or doctor's offices, are often the very same that shine in Florence's chronicles.

All over the city, both inside and outside buildings, you'll see plaques testifying to the flood of 1966. These are erected at the level to which the water rose at that particular point, and it's quite shocking to stand under one and realize that the brown water of the Arno would have been way over your head. In many areas, the façades of the buildings also bear a faded water mark (at least those which have not been painted in the last 30 years).

Look out for little stone arches at about chest level worked into the sides of some buildings. Many of these have now been filled in, but they were once used for dispensing wine by the glass. Another curiosity are the faded 'R' signs to be found next to the door on some buildings; these date from the war, and marked *rifiugi* or bomb shelters.

Start: *Piazza del Duomo*

Finish: *Orsanmichele*

Walking time: *a morning or afternoon*

I: Piazza del Duomo

Florence's holy centre is in many way the key to the city, and essential to understanding everything that comes after.

Lunch/Cafés

Perche Nò, Via dei Tavolini 19r. Very good ice cream in 1940s surroundings.

Da Pennello, Via Dante Alighieri 4r, ✆ 294848. Very popular and lively, where you can go for great antipasti and large plates of different types of pasta (closed Mon, around L40,000).

Antico Caffè dei Ritti, Via dei Lamberti 9r, ✆ 291583 A busy, above-average *tavola calda* serving a wide variety of hot and cold dishes, sandwiches and desserts to eat in or take away. *Primi* from L8000, *secondi* from L11,000 and salads from L8000. Takeaway is about 25% cheaper.

Bar Manaresi, Via de Lamberti 16r. Many say that the best coffee in Florence is to be had here.

Cantinetta da Verazzano, Via dei Tavolini 18/20r, ✆ 2398132. A wine bar and bakery belonging to the eponymous wine estate in Chianti. It serves a selection of excellent wines from L3000 per glass, and interesting sandwiches and snacks from L5000. It can be very crowded at lunchtime. Closed Sun.

Piazza della Repubblica has three historic and elegant bars, now more popular with tourists than Florentines; all three have an atmosphere of dated elegance:

Gilli del 1733, Piazza della Repubblica 39r, ✆ 213896. Dates back to 1733, when the Mercato Vecchio still occupied this area; its two panelled back rooms are especially pleasant in winter.

Giubbe Rosse, Piazza della Repubblica 13–14r. Its chandelier-lit interior has changed little since the turn of the century when it was the rendezvous of Florence's *literati*.

Paszkowski, Piazza della Repubblica 6r, ✆ 210236.

Robiglio, Via Tosinghi 11r. An old-fashioned pasticceria and bar serving superb pastries.

Vinaio, Via dei Cimatori. One of those typically Florentine 'hole in the wall' wine bars where you stand in the street to sip a glass of Chianti and munch on a sandwich.

Tour groups circle around the three great spiritual monuments of medieval Florence like sharks around their prey, preyed on in turn by postcard vendors,

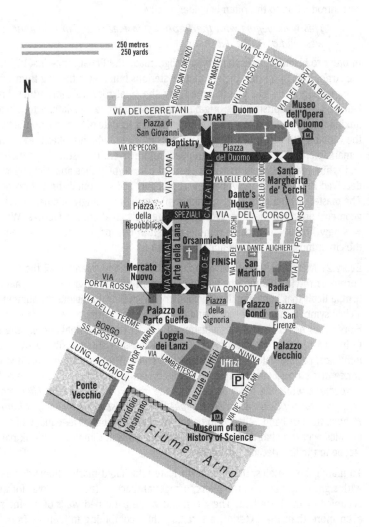

Florence Walk I: Piazza del Duomo

250 metres
250 yards

N

VIA DEI CERRETANI

VIA DEL PUCCI

BORGO SAN LORENZO

VIA DE'MARTELLI

VIA RICASOLI

VIA DEI SERVI

VIA BUFALINI

Duomo

START

Museo
dell'Opera
del Duomo

Piazza di
San Giovanni

Baptistry

VIA DE'PECORI

Piazza
del Duomo

VIA ROMA

VIA DELLE OCHE

Santa
Margherita
de' Cerchi

VIA DELLO STUDIO

CALZAIUOLI

Dante's
House

VIA DEL CORSO

Piazza
della
Repubblica

VIA
SPEZIALI

VIA DEI CERCHI

VIA DANTE ALIGHIERI

VIA DEL PROCONSOLO

Orsanmichele

VIA CALIMALA

Arte della Lana

FINISH

San
Martino

VIA DE'

Mercato
Nuovo

Badia

VIA
PORTA ROSSA

VIA CONDOTTA

VIA DELLE TERME

Palazzo di
Parte Guelfa

Piazza
della
Signoria

Palazzo
Gondi

Piazza
San
Firenze

BORGO
SS.APOSTOLI

LUNG. ACCIAIOLI

Loggia
dei Lanzi

V. D. NINNA

Palazzo
Vecchio

VIA POR S. MARIA

VIA LAMBERTESCA

Uffizi

P

VIA DE' CASTELLANI

Ponte
Vecchio

Corridoio
Vasariano

Piazzale D. Uffizi

Museum of the
History of Science

Fiume Arno

portrait painters, and horses and carriages touting for custom. An occasional street musician serenades the human carnival from a hundred nations, milling about good-naturedly, while ambulances of a medieval first-aid brotherhood stand at the ready in case anyone swoons from ecstasy or art-glut. As bewildering as it often is, however, the Piazza del Duomo and the adjacent Piazza di San Giovanni are the best introduction to this often bewildering city.

> This walk begins with the **Baptistry** in Piazza di San Giovanni at the west end of Piazza del Duomo.

In order to begin to understand what magic made the Renaissance first bloom by the Arno, look here; this ancient and mysterious building is the egg from which Florence's golden age was hatched. By the quattrocento Florentines firmly believed their baptistry was originally a Roman temple to Mars, a touchstone linking them to a legendary past. Scholarship sets its date of construction between the 6th and 9th centuries, in the darkest Dark Ages, which makes it even more remarkable; it may as well have dropped from heaven. Its distinctive dark green and white marble facing, the tidily classical pattern of arches and rectangles that deceived Brunelleschi and Alberti, was probably added around the 11th century. The masters who built it remain unknown, but their strikingly original exercise in geometry provided the model for all of Florence's great church façades. When it was new, there was nothing remotely like it in Europe; to visitors from outside the city it must have seemed almost miraculous.

Every 21 March, New Year's Day on the old Florentine calendar, all the children born over the last 12 months would be brought here for a great communal baptism, a habit that helped make the baptistry not merely a religious monument but a civic symbol, in fact the oldest and dearest symbol of the republic. As such the Florentines never tired of embellishing it. Under the octagonal cupola, the glittering 13th- and 14th-century gold-ground mosaics show a strong Byzantine influence, perhaps laid by mosaicists from Venice. The decoration is divided into concentric strips: over the apse, dominated by a 8.5m figure of Christ, is a *Last Judgement*, while the other bands, from the inside out, portray the *Hierarchy of Heaven*, *Story of Genesis, Life of Joseph, Life of Christ* and the *Life of St John the Baptist*, the last band believed to be the work of Cimabue. The equally beautiful mosaics over the altar and in the vault are the earliest, signed by a monk named Iacopo in the first decades of the 1200s.

To match the mosaics, there is an intricate tessellated marble floor, decorated with signs of the Zodiac; the blank, octagonal space in the centre was formerly occupied by the huge font. The green and white patterned walls of the interior, even more than the exterior, are remarkable, combining influences from the ancient world and modern inspiration for something entirely new, the perfect source that architects of the Middle Ages and Renaissance would ever strive to match. Much of the best design work is up in the **galleries**, not accessible, but partially visible from the floor.

The baptistry is hardly cluttered; besides a 13th-century Pisan-style baptismal font, only the **Tomb of Anti-Pope John XXIII** by Donatello and Michelozzo stands out. This funerary monument, with scenographic marble draperies softening its classical lines, is one of the great prototypes of the early Renaissance. But how did this Anti-Pope John, deposed by the Council of Constance in 1415, earn the unique privilege of a fancy tomb in the baptistry? Why, it was thanks to him that Giovanni di Bicci de' Medici made the family fortune as head banker to the Curia.

The Gates of Paradise

Historians used to pinpoint the beginning of the 'Renaissance' as the year 1401, when the merchants' guild, the Arte di Calimala, sponsored a competition for the baptistry's north doors. The **South Doors** (the main entrance into the baptistry) had already been completed by Andrea Pisano in 1330, and they give an excellent lesson on the style of the day. The doors are divided into 28 panels in quatrefoil frames with scenes from the life of St John the Baptist and the eight Cardinal and Theological Virtues—formal and elegant works in the best Gothic manner.

The celebrated competition of 1401—perhaps the first ever held in the annals of art—pitted the seven greatest sculptors of the day against one another. Judgement was based on trial panels on the subject of the *Sacrifice of Isaac*, and in a dead heat at the end of the day were the two by Brunelleschi and Lorenzo Ghiberti, now displayed in the Bargello. Ghiberti's more classical-style figures were eventually judged the better, and it was a serendipitous choice; he devoted nearly the rest of his life to creating the most beautiful bronze doors in the world while Brunelleschi, disgusted by his defeat, went on to build the most perfect dome. Ghiberti's first efforts, the **North Doors** (1403–24), are contained, like Pisano's, in 28 quatrefoil frames. In their scenes on the Life of Christ, the Evangelists, and the Doctors of the Church, you can trace Ghiberti's progress over the 20 years he worked in the increased depth of his compositions, not only visually but dramatically; classical backgrounds begin to fill up the frames, ready to break out of their Gothic confines. Ghiberti also designed the lovely floral frame of the doors; the three statues, of John the Baptist, the Levite and the Pharisee, by Francesco Rustici, were based on a design by Leonardo da Vinci and added in 1511.

Ghiberti's work pleased the Arte di Calimala, and they set him loose on another pair of portals, the **East Doors** (1425–52), his masterpiece and one of the most awesome achievements of the age. Here Ghiberti (perhaps under the guidance of Donatello) dispensed with the small Gothic frames and instead cast 10 large panels that depict the Old Testament in Renaissance high gear, reinterpreting the forms of antiquity with a depth and drama that have never been surpassed. Michelangelo declared them 'worthy to be the Gates of Paradise', and indeed it's hard to believe these are people, buildings and trees of bronze and not creatures frozen in time by some celestial alchemy. The doors (they're actually copies— some of the original panels, restored after flood damage, are on display in the Museo dell'Opera del Duomo) have been cleaned recently, and stand in gleaming contrast to the others which still carry the grime of centuries. In 1996 copies of Andrea Sansovino's marble statues of Christ and John the Baptist (1502) and an 18th-century angel were installed over the doors. The originals had begun to fall to bits in 1974; they too are now in the Museo dell'Opera.

Ghiberti wasn't exactly slow to toot his own horn; according to him, he personally planned and designed the Renaissance on his own. His unabashedly conceited *Commentarii* were the first attempt at art history and autobiography by an artist, and a work as revolutionary as his doors in its presentation of the creative God-like powers of the artist. It is also a typical exhibition of Florentine pride that he should put busts of his friends among the prophets and sibyls that adorn the frames of the East Doors. Near the centre, the balding figure with arched eyebrows and a little smile is Ghiberti himself.

> *For all its importance and prosperity, Florence was one of the last cities to plan a great cathedral or* **Duomo**. *Work began in the 1290s, with the sculptor Arnolfo di Cambio in charge, and from the beginning the Florentines attempted to make up for their delay with sheer audacity. 'It will be so magnificent in size and beauty', according to a decree of 1296, 'as to surpass anything built by the Greeks and Romans'. In response Arnolfo planned what in its day was the largest church in Catholicism; he confidently laid the foundations for an enormous octagonal crossing 44.5m in diameter. He died before working out a way to cover it, leaving future architects the job of designing the biggest dome in the world.*

Beyond its presumptuous size, the cathedral of Santa Maria del Fiore shows little interest in contemporary innovations and styles; a visitor from France or England in the 1400s would certainly have found it somewhat drab and architecturally primitive. Visitors today often don't know what to make of it as they circle its grimy, ponderous bulk (this is one of the very few cathedrals in Italy that you can walk completely around). Instead of the striped bravura of Siena or the elegant colonnades of Pisa, they behold an astonishingly eccentric green, white and red pattern of marble rectangles and flowers—like Victorian wallpaper, or as one critic better expressed it, 'a cathedral wearing pyjamas'. On a sunny day, the cathedral under its sublime dome seems to sport festively above the dun and ochre sea of Florence; in dismal weather it sprawls morosely across its piazza like a beached whale tarted up with a lace doily front.

The fondly foolish **façade** cannot be blamed on Arnolfo. His original design, only one-quarter completed, was taken down in a late 16th-century Medici rebuilding programme that never got off the ground. The Duomo turned a blank face to the world until the present neo-Gothic extravaganza was added in 1888. Walk around to the north side to see what many consider a more fitting door, the **Porta della Mandorla** crowned with an Assumption of the Virgin in an almond-shaped frame (hence *Mandorla*) made by Nanni di Banco in 1420.

> *Yet if this behemoth of a cathedral, this St Mary of the Floral Wallpaper, was created for no other reason than to serve as a base for its dome, it would be more than enough.* **Brunelleschi's dome,** *more than any landmark, makes Florence Florence.*

Many have noted how the dome repeats the rhythm of the surrounding hills, echoing them with its height and beauty; from those city streets fortunate enough to have a clear view, it rises among the clouds with all the confident mastery, proportions, and perfect form that characterize the highest aspirations of the Renaissance. But if it seems miraculous, it certainly isn't divine; unlike the dome of the Hagia Sophia, suspended from heaven by a golden chain, Florence's was made by man—one man, to be precise.

Losing the competition for the baptistry doors was a bitter disappointment to Filippo Brunelleschi. His reaction was typically Florentine; not content with being the second-best sculptor, he turned his talents to a field where he thought no one could beat him. He launched himself into an intense study of architecture and engineering, visiting Rome and probably Ravenna to snatch secrets from the ancients. When proposals were solicited for the cathedral's dome in 1418, he was ready with a brilliant *tour de force*. Not only would he build the biggest, most beautiful dome of the time, but he would do it without any need for expensive supports while work was in progress, making use of a cantilevered system of bricks that could support itself while it ascended—surpassing the technique of the ancients with a system far more simple than that of the Pantheon or Hagia Sophia. To the Florentines, a people who could have invented the slogan 'form follows function' for their own tastes in building, it must have come as a revelation; the most logical way of covering the space turned out to be a work of perfect beauty. Brunelleschi, in building this dome, put a crown on the achievements of Florence. After 500 years it is still the city's pride and symbol.

The best way to appreciate Brunelleschi's genius is by touring inside the two concentric shells of the dome (*see* p.104), but before entering, note the eight marble ribs that define its octagonal shape; hidden inside are the three huge stone chains that bind them together. Work on the balcony around the base of the dome, designed by Giuliano da Sangallo, was halted in 1515 after Michelangelo commented that it resembled a cricket's cage. As for the **lantern**, the Florentines were famous for their fondness for Doubting Thomas, and here they showed why. Even though they marvelled at the dome, they still doubted that Brunelleschi could construct a proper lantern, and forced him to submit to yet another competition. He died soon after, and it was completed to his design by Michelozzo.

*After the façade, the austerity of the **Duomo interior** is almost startling.*

There is plenty of room; contemporary writers mention 10,000 souls packed inside to hear the hellfire and brimstone sermons of Savonarola. Even with that in mind, the Duomo hardly seems a religious building—more a Florentine building, with simple arches and counterpoint of grey stone and white plaster, full of old familiar Florentine things. Near the entrance, on the right-hand side, are busts of Brunelleschi and Giotto. On the left wall, posed inconspicuously, are the two most conspicuous monuments to private individuals ever erected by the Florentine Republic. The older one, on the right, is to **Sir John Hawkwood**, the famous English *condottiere* whose name the Italians mangled to Giovanni Acuto, a legendary commander who served Florence for many years and is perhaps best known to English speakers as the hero of *The White Company* by Arthur Conan Doyle. All along, Hawkwood had the promise of the Florentines to build him an equestrian statue after his death; it was a typical Florentine trick to pinch pennies and cheat a dead man—but they hired the greatest master of perspective, Paolo Uccello, to make a fresco that looked like a statue (1436). Twenty years later, they pulled the same trick again, commissioning another great illusionist, Andrea del Castagno, to paint the non-existent equestrian statue of another *condottiere*, Niccolò da Tolentino. A little further down, Florence commemorates its own secular scripture with Michelino's well-known fresco of Dante, a vision of the poet and his *Paradiso* outside the walls of Florence. Two singular icons of Florence's fascination with science stand at opposite ends of the building: behind the west front, a bizarre clock painted by Uccello, and in the pavement of the left apse, a gnomon fixed by the astronomer Toscanelli in 1475. A beam of sunlight strikes it every year on the day of the summer solstice.

For building the great dome, Brunelleschi was accorded a special honour—he is one of the few Florentines to be buried in the cathedral. His tomb may be seen in the **Excavations of Santa Reparata** (*the stairway descending on the right of the nave; open 10–5, closed Sun; adm*). Arnolfo di Cambio's cathedral was constructed on the ruins of the ancient church of Santa Reparata, which lay forgotten until 1965. Excavations have revealed not only the palaeo-Christian church and its several reconstructions, but also the remains of its Roman predecessor—a rather confusing muddle of walls that have been tidied up in an ambience that resembles an archaeological shopping centre. A coloured model helps explain what is what, and glass cases display items found in the dig, including the spurs of Giovanni de' Medici, who was buried here in 1351. In the ancient crypt of Santa Reparata are 13th-century tomb slabs, and in another section there's a fine pre-Romanesque mosaic pavement.

There is surprisingly little religious art—the Florentines for reasons of their own have carted most of it off into the Cathedral Museum. The only really conventional religious decorations are the hack but scarcely visible frescoes high in the dome (some 90m up), mostly the work of Vasari. As you stand there squinting at them, try not to think that the cupola weighs an estimated 25,000 tons. In the central apse, there is a beautiful bronze urn by Ghiberti containing relics of the Florentine St Zenobius. Under the dome are the doors to the two sacristies, under terracotta lunettes by Luca della Robbia; the *Resurrection* over the north sacristy is one of his earliest and best works. He also did the bronze doors, with tiny portraits on the handles of Lorenzo il Magnifico and his brother Giuliano de' Medici, targets of the Pazzi conspiracy in 1478.

Murder in the Cathedral

On 28 April 1478, at the moment of the elevation of the Host, Francesco Pazzi, Florentine banker to the Pope, and his bravo Bandini jumped the Medici brothers, leading an attack carefully conceived with Sixtus IV and the King of Naples. Pazzi plunged his dagger 21 times into the handsome Giuliano, while Lorenzo, cape wrapped around one arm as a shield, sword unsheathed, fought off his aggressors, leaping over the then-extant choir screen and taking refuge with his supporters behind the bronze door. He had only a scratch on his neck; his friend Ridolfi sucked it, in case of poison. At the same time, another intriguer, the archbishop of Pisa, Francesco Salviati, who hated Lorenzo for not making him archbishop of Florence, failed in his attempt to capture and seize power in the Palazzo Vecchio. His body was soon seen dangling from the window, joined shortly after by that of Francesco Pazzi and all their co-conspirators, hanged or defenestrated without trial, to the cheers of the pro-Medici mob. Sandro Botticelli was given the job of painting their likenesses on the walls of the Palazzo Vecchio, so all Florence could witness their infamy.

The cultivated, refined Lorenzo then demonstrated the vindictiveness that was an integral part of the Medici character. The mutilations and executions without trial of over a hundred people suspected to have been involved in the plot continued for days, for months; those who fled abroad were relentlessly tracked down. The body of Jacopo, the chief of the Pazzi clan, was exhumed, dragged mockingly through the streets and thrown into the Arno, then fished out again, and cudgelled until the bones were broken into tiny bits, before being tossed back into the river. When Lorenzo had finished, the entire Pazzi clan had been annihilated, their goods were confiscated, and Lorenzo the Magnificent, conveniently relieved of his popular brother, was the undisputed master of Florence.

> *A door on the left aisle near the Dante fresco leads up into **the dome*** (open daily 8.30–12.30 and 2.30–5.30; closed Sun; adm).

The complicated network of stairs and walks between the inner and outer domes (not too difficult, if occasionally claustrophobic and vertiginous) was designed by Brunelleschi for the builders, and offers an insight on how thoroughly the architect thought out the problems of the dome's construction, even inserting hooks to hold up scaffolding for future cleaning or repairs; Brunelleschi installed restaurants to save workers the trouble of descending for meals. There is also no better place to get an idea of the dome's scale; the walls of the inner dome are 3.6m thick, and those of the outer dome 1.8m. These provide enough strength and support to preclude the need for further buttressing.

From the gallery of the dome you can get a good look at the lovely **stained glass** by Uccello, Donatello, Ghiberti and Castagno, in the seven circular windows, or *occhi*, made during the construction of the dome. Further up, the views through the small windows offer tantalizing hints of the breathtaking panorama of the city from the marble lantern. The bronze ball at the very top was added by Verrocchio, and can hold almost a dozen people when it's open.

> *There's no doubt about it; the dome steals the show on Piazza del Duomo, putting one of Italy's most beautiful bell towers in the shade both figuratively and literally. The dome's great size—111m to the bronze ball— makes **Giotto's Campanile** look small, though 85m is not exactly tiny.*

Giotto was made director of the cathedral works in 1334, and his basic design was completed after his death (1337) by Andrea Pisano and Francesco Talenti. It is difficult to say whether they were entirely faithful to the plan. Giotto was an artist, not an engineer. After he died, his successors realized that the thing, then only 11m high, was about to tumble over, a problem they overcame by doubling the thickness of the walls.

Besides its lovely form, the green, pink and white campanile's major fame rests with Pisano and Talenti's **sculptural reliefs**—a veritable encyclopaedia of the medieval world view with prophets, saints and sibyls, allegories of the planets, virtues and sacraments, the liberal arts and industries (the artist's craft is fittingly symbolized by a winged figure of Daedalus). All of these are copies of the originals now in the Cathedral Museum. If you can take another 400 steps or so, the terrace on top offers a slightly different view of Florence and of the cathedral itself (*open daily, summer, 9–7.30, winter 9–5.30; adm*).

> *The most striking secular building on the Piazza del Duomo is the* **Loggia del Bigallo**, *south of the baptistry near the beginning of Via de' Calzaiuoli.*

This 14th-century porch was built for one of Florence's great charitable confraternities, the Misericordia, which still has its headquarters across the street and operates the ambulances parked in front; in the 13th and 14th centuries members courageously nursed and buried victims of the plague. The Loggia itself originally served as a lost and found office, although instead of umbrellas it dealt in children; if unclaimed after three days they were sent to foster homes. In the 15th century the Misericordia merged with a similar charitable confraternity called the Bigallo, and works of art accumulated by both organizations over centuries are displayed in the diminutive but choice **Museo del Bigallo**, located next to the loggia at Piazza San Giovanni 1 (*closed temporarily at the time of writing, © 215440*). The most famous picture here is the fresco of *Madonna della Misericordia*, featuring the earliest known view of Florence (1342); other 14th-century works (by Bernardo Daddi, Niccolò di Pietro Gerini, and sculptor Alberto Arnoldi) portray the activities of the brotherhood, members of which may still be seen wearing the traditional black hoods that preserve their anonymity.

> *East of the Loggia del Bigallo, between Via dello Studio and Via del Proconsolo, is a stone bench labelled 'Sasso di Dante'—***Dante's Seat***, where the poet would sit and take the air, observing his fellow citizens and watching the construction of the cathedral. From here walk around*

*the central apse of the cathedral and enter the **Museo dell'Opera del Duomo** under a bust of Cosimo de' Medici at Piazza del Duomo 9 (open summer 9–8, winter 9–6; closed Sun; adm).*

This museum is one of Florence's finest, and houses both relics from the actual construction of the cathedral and the masterpieces that once adorned it. The first room is devoted to the cathedral's sculptor-architect Arnolfo di Cambio and contains a drawing of his ornate, sculpture-filled façade that was but a quarter completed when the Medici had it removed in 1587. Here, too, are the statues he made to adorn it: the unusual Madonna with the glass eyes, Florence's original patron saints, Reparata and Zenobius, and nasty old Boniface VIII, who sits stiffly on his throne like an Egyptian god. There are the four Evangelists, including a St John by Donatello, and a small collection of ancient works—Roman sarcophagi and an Etruscan cippus carved with dancers.

Two small rooms nearby contain materials from the construction of the dome— wooden models, tools, brick moulds and instruments—as well as Brunelleschi's death mask. Also on the ground floor are several hack Mannerist models (one by dilettante Giovanni de' Medici) proposed in the 1580s for the cathedral, reminders that the façade could have been much, much worse. The Florentines were never enthusiastic about the worship of relics, and long ago they shipped San Girolamo's jaw-bone, John the Baptist's index finger and St Philip's arm across the street to this museum; note the 16th-century *Libretto*, a fold-out display case of saintly odds and ends, all neatly labelled.

On the landing of the stairs stands the *Pietà* that Michelangelo intended for his own tomb. The artist, increasingly cantankerous and full of *terribilità* in his old age, became exasperated with it and took a hammer to the arm of the Christ—the first known instance of an artist vandalizing his own creation. His assistant repaired the damage and finished part of the figures of Mary Magdalene and Christ. According to Vasari, the hooded figure of Nicodemus is Michelangelo's self-portrait.

Upstairs, the first room is dominated by the two **Cantorie**, two marble choir balconies with exquisite bas-reliefs, made in the 1430s by Luca della Robbia and Donatello. Both works rank among the Renaissance's greatest productions. Della Robbia's delightful horde of laughing children dancing, singing and playing instruments is a truly angelic choir, Apollonian in its calm and beauty, perhaps the most charming work ever to have been inspired by the forms of antiquity. Donatello's *putti*, by contrast, dance, or rather race, through their quattrocento decorative motifs with Dionysian frenzy. Even less serene is his statue of *Mary Magdalene*, surely one of the most jarring figures ever sculpted, ravaged by her own piety and penance, her sunken eyes fixed on a point beyond this vale of tears. Grey and weathered prophets by Donatello and others stand along the white walls. These originally adorned the façade of the campanile. According to Vasari, while carving the most famous one, the bald *Habbakuk* (nicknamed *lo Zuccone*, 'baldy'), Donatello would mutter 'Speak, damn you. Speak!' The next room contains the original panels on the *Spiritual Progress of Man* from Giotto's campanile which was made by Andrea Pisano.

The last room is dedicated to works removed from the Baptistry, especially the lavish silver altar (14th–15th century), made by Florentine goldsmiths, portraying scenes from the life of the Baptist. Antonio Pollaiuolo used the same subject to design the 27 needlework panels that once were part of the priest's vestments. There are two 12th-century Byzantine mosaic miniatures, masterpieces of the intricate, and a *St Sebastian* triptych by Giovanni del Biondo that may well be the record for arrows; the poor saint looks like a hedgehog. Usually this room also contains four panels from Ghiberti's 'Gates of Paradise', which are being restored one by one and make fascinating viewing close up.

> *Of all the streets that radiate from the Piazza del Duomo, the straight, pedestrian-only* **Via de' Calzaiuoli** *is the one most people almost intuitively turn down, the Roman street that became the main thoroughfare of medieval Florence, linking the city's religious centre with the Piazza della Signoria. Widening of this 'Street of the Shoemakers' in the 1840s has destroyed much of its medieval character, and the only shoe shops to be seen are designer-label. Its fate seems benign, though, compared with what happened to the Mercato Vecchio, in a fit of post-Risorgimento 'progress' that converted it into the* **Piazza della Repubblica***, a block to the right along Via Speziali.*

On the map, it's easy to pick out the small rectangle of narrow, straight streets around Piazza della Repubblica; these remain unchanged from the little *castrum* of Roman days. At its centre, the old forum deteriorated through the Dark Ages into a shabby market square and the Jewish ghetto, a piquant, densely populated quarter known as the Mercato Vecchio, the epitome of the picturesque for 19th-century tourists but an eyesore for the movers and shakers of the new Italy, who tore down its alleys and miniature *piazze* to create a fit symbol of Florence's reawakening. They erected a triumphal arch to themselves and proudly blazoned it with the inscription: 'THE ANCIENT CITY CENTRE RESTORED TO NEW LIFE FROM THE SQUALOR OF CENTURIES'. The sad result of this well-intentioned urban renewal, the Piazza della Repubblica, is one of the most ghastly squares in Italy, a brash intrusion of ponderous 19th-century buildings and parked cars. Just the same it is popular with locals and tourists alike, full of outdoor cafés, something of an oasis among the narrow, stern streets of medieval Florence.

> *From Piazza della Repubblica the natural flow of street life will sweep you down to the* **Mercato Nuovo**, *the old Straw Market, bustling under a beautiful loggia built by Grand Duke Cosimo in the 1500s.*

Although you won't see more than a wisp of straw these days, vendors hawk leather bags and belts, scarves, stationery, toys, umbrellas, embroidered linens and knick-knacks. In medieval times this was the merchants' exchange, where any merchant who committed the crime of bankruptcy was publicly spanked before being carted off to prison; in times of peace it sheltered Florence's battle-stained *carroccio*—the ox cart every medieval city took with it to war, bearing an altar and banners, that served to rally the troops. Florentines often call the market the '*Porcellino*' (piglet) after the large bronze boar erected in 1612, a copy of the ancient statue in the Uffizi. The drool spilling from its mouth reminds us that unlike Rome, Florence is no splashy city of fountains. Rub the piglet's shiny snout, and supposedly destiny will one day bring you back to Florence. The pungent aroma of the tripe sandwiches sold nearby may give you second thoughts.

> *From the Mercato Nuovo take Via Porta Rossa back to Via de' Calzaiuoli and turn left. There is a wonderfully eccentric church here that looks like no other church in the world:* **Orsanmichele** *rises up just on your left in a tall, neat, three-storey rectangle.*

It was built on the site of ancient San Michele ad Hortum (popularly reduced to 'Orsanmichele'), a 9th-century church located near a vegetable garden, which the *comune* destroyed in 1240 in order to erect a grain market; after a fire in 1337 the current market building (by Francesco Talenti and others) was erected, with a loggia on the ground floor and emergency storehouses on top where grain was kept against a siege.

The original market had a pilaster with a painting of the Virgin that became increasingly celebrated for performing miracles. The area around the Virgin became known as the Oratory, and when Talenti reconstructed the market, his intention was to combine its secular and religious functions; each pilaster of the loggia was assigned to a guild to adorn with an image of its patron saint. In 1380, when the market was relocated, the entire ground floor was given over to the church, and Francesco Talenti's talented son Simone was given the task of closing in the arcades with lovely Gothic windows, which were later bricked in.

Orsanmichele is most famous as a showcase of 15th-century Florentine sculpture; there is no better place to get an idea of the stylistic innovations that succeeded one another throughout the decades. Each guild sought to outdo the others by commissioning the finest artists of the day to sculpt their patron saints and create elaborate canopied niches to hold them. Continuing to the left on Via de' Lamberti you can see Donatello's *St Mark*, patron of the linen dealers and used-cloth merchants. Finished in 1411, it is believed to be the first free-standing marble statue of the Renaissance.

The niches continue around Via dell'Arte della Lana, named after the Wool Merchants' Guild, the richest after that of the bankers. Their headquarters, the **Palazzo dell'Arte della Lana** is linked by an overhead arch with Orsanmichele; built in 1308, it was restored in 1905 in a delightful William Morris style of medieval picturesque. The first statue on this façade of Orsanmichele is *St Eligio*, patron of smiths, by Nanni di Banco (1415), in a niche embellished with the guild's emblem (black pincers) and a bas-relief below showing one of this rather obscure saint's miracles—apparently he shod a horse the hard way, by cutting off its hoof, shoeing it, then sticking it back on the leg. The other two statues on this street are bronzes by Ghiberti, the Wool Guild's *St Stephen* (1426) and the Exchange Guild's *St Matthew* (1422), the latter an especially fine work in a classical niche. On the Via Orsanmichele façade stands a copy of Donatello's famous *St George* (the original now in the Bargello) done in 1417 for the Armourers' Guild; the dramatic predella of the saint slaying the dragon, also by Donatello, is one of the first-known works making use of perspective. Next are the Stonecutters' and Carpenters' Guild's *Four Crowned Saints* (1415, by Nanni di Banco), inspired by Roman statues. Nanni also contributed the Shoemakers' *St Philip* (1415), while the next figure, *St Peter*, is commonly attributed to Donatello (1413). Around the corner on Via Calzaiuoli stands the bronze *St Luke*, patron of the Judges and Notaries, by Giambologna, a work of 1602 in a 15th-century niche, and the *Doubting of St Thomas* by Andrea del Verrocchio (1484), made not for a guild but the Tribunal of Merchandise, who like St Thomas always wanted to be certain before making a judgement. In the rondels above some of the niches are terracottas of the guilds' symbols by Luca della Robbia.

Orsanmichele's dark **interior** (*open 8–12 and 3–6.30*) is ornate and cosy, with more of the air of a guildhall than a church. It makes a picturebook medieval setting for one of the masterpieces of the trecento: Andrea Orcagna's beautiful Gothic **Tabernacle**, a large, exquisite work in marble, bronze and coloured glass framing a contemporary painting of the Madonna (either by Bernardo

Daddi or Orcagna himself), replacing the miraculous one, lost in a fire. The Tabernacle was commissioned by survivors of the 1348 Black Death. On the walls and pilasters are faded 14th-century frescoes of saints, placed as if members of the congregation; if you look at the pilasters on the left as you enter and along the right wall you can see the old chutes used to transfer grain from the storeroom above.

Start: *Piazza della Signoria*
Finish: *Palazzo Davanzati*
Walking time: *one full day plus an evening*

II: Piazza della Signoria

This walk takes in the essentials of Florence's genius—the show-case of her civic virtue, the masterpieces of her greatest painters and marvels of Brunelleschi's heirs in science and engineering.

Lunch/Cafés

Antico Fattore, Via Lambertesca 1–3r, ℘ 2381215. Simple fare at fair prices.

Caffé delle Carozze, Piazza del Pesce. Excellent ice-cream shop with seats outside in summer.

Pasquini, Via Val di Lamona 2/r, ℘ 218995, closed Sun. This diminutive, but elegant trattoria is always crowded at lunchtime.

Rivoire, Piazza della Signoria 5, ℘ 214412. This beautiful and old-fashioned *caffè* serves superb cakes and sandwiches in elegant surroundings looking over the square up to the Palazzo Vecchio. Very expensive.

Buca dell'Orafo, Volta de' Girolami 28r. Home-made pasta in a friendly atmos-phere, frequented both by Florentines and tourists (closed Mon, around L40,000).

Tripe Stand, Mercato Nuovo. Be bold. Do as the Florentines do, and have a hot tripe or *lampredotto* (intestines) sandwich with *salsa verde* from the stand on the southwest corner of the market.

---

*Italian city builders are renowned for effortlessly creating beautiful squares, but it's an art where the Florentines are generally all thumbs. Only here, in the city's civic stage, the **Piazza della Signoria**, did they achieve a grand, meaningful space, although not by design—in the 13th century the victorious Guelphs knocked down the hated Ghibelline quarter that stood here, and no one wanted to rebuild on the tainted land. Still, the piazza is an antidote to the stone gullies of the centre, a showcase for the sombre fortress of the **Palazzo Vecchio** and a lively gathering of some of the best and worst of Florentine sculpture. The whole makes a fine backdrop to open-air concerts and ballet in the summer. Banks and insurance companies share the rest.*

Although the Piazza della Signoria currently serves as Great Aunt Florence's drawing-room-cum-tourist-overflow-tank, in the old days it saw the public assem-blies of the republic, which in Florence meant that the square often degenerated into a battleground for impossibly inscrutable internecine quarrels. These could be

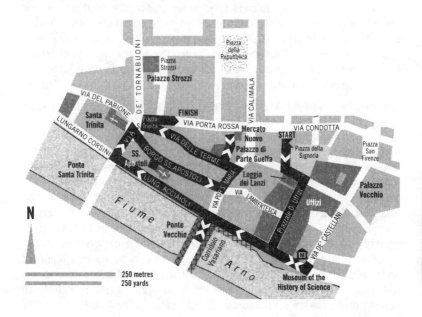

stirred up to mythic levels of violence; in the 14th century a man was eaten by a crowd maddened by a political speech. Such speeches were given from the *arringhiera*, or oration terrace in front of the Palazzo Vecchio, a word which gave us 'harangue'. It was in the Piazza della Signoria that Savonarola ignited his notorious Bonfire of Vanities in 1497, and here, too, the following year, the disillusioned Florentines ignited Savonarola himself. A small plaque in the pavement marks the exact spot, not far from Ammannati's fountain.

If, on the other hand, trouble came from without, the Florentines would toll the famous bell in the tower of the Palazzo Vecchio, and the square would rapidly fill with the gonfalons of the citizens' militia and the guilds. 'We will sound our trumpets!' threatened the French King Charles VIII, when the Florentines refused to shell out enough florins to make him and his army go away. 'And we will ring our bell!' countered the courageous republican Piero Capponi—a threat that worked; Charles had to settle for a smaller sum. When Alessandro de' Medici was restored as duke of Tuscany three years later, one of his first acts was to smash the bell as too potent a symbol of Florence's liberty.

Having a citizens' militia, as opposed to depending on foreign mercenaries, answered one of Machiavelli's requirements for a well-governed state. Training was taken fairly seriously; to build up their endurance, the republic's citizens played a ball game similar to rugby, believed to be descended from a Roman sport. Known these days as *Calcio in Costume*, it is played again every June in Piazza Santa Croce, and it's good fun to watch the usually immaculate Florentines in their Renaissance duds mixing it up in the dirt (fighting is more than permitted, as long as it's one to one).

Since the 1970s and 80s a different kind of battle has been waged in this piazza, spiced with good old-fashioned Florentine factionalism. At stake is the future of the Piazza della Signoria itself. In 1974, while searching for signs of the original paving stones, the Soprintendenza ai Beni Archeologici found, much to their surprise, an underground medieval kasbah of narrow lanes, houses and wells—the ruins of Ghibelline Florence, built over the baths and other portions of Roman and Etruscan *Florentia*. During the excavations, the remains of Roman dyeing vats were also found, an indication that Florence was associated with textiles even back then. The *comune* ordered the excavations filled in; from the city's point of view, the piazza, essential to the essential tourist trade, was untouchable. In the 80s, the communal government fell, and the excavations were reopened on the portion of the piazza near the Loggia. There are proposals to excavate the rest of the square, much to the horror of the *comune*, and to create eventually an underground museum similar to the one in Assisi. For now, the pavement of Piazza Signoria is complete—no gaping holes.

> *Generally of a lower key than a political harangue was the* parlamento, *a meeting of eligible male citizens to vote on an important issue (usually already decided by the bosses). On these occasions, the Florentines heard speeches from the platform of the graceful three-arched* **Loggia dei Lanzi**, *also known as the Loggia della Signoria or the Loggia dell'Orcagna, after Andrea Orcagna, the probable architect.*

Completed in 1382, when pointed Gothic was still the rage, the loggia with its lofty round arches looks back to classical antiquity and looks forward to the Renaissance; it is the germ of Brunelleschi's revolutionary architecture. If the impenetrable, stone Palazzo Vecchio is a symbol of the republic's muscle and authority, the Loggia dei Lanzi is a symbol of its capacity for beauty. Unfortunately there are plans to put in a railing of some kind around it 'to protect the statues'; one hopes that the traditionalists squawk loud enough to keep it open.

The loggia received its name 'of the lances' after the Swiss lancers, the private bodyguard of Cosimo I. It was Cosimo who, in 1545, was responsible for the most famous sculpture sheltered in the arcade, Cellini's *Perseus*: not by commissioning it from the volatile Cellini, but by scoffing, saying a life-sized bronze statue was impossible, infuriating Cellini, who proved him wrong, although it took 10 years, and cost his health and the roof of his house which caught fire as he stoked the furnace to melt the bronze. The result, his masterpiece, is a Mannerist *tour de force* with its attention to detail and expressive composition, graceful and poised atop the gruesome bleeding trunk, eyes averted from the horrible head with its petrifying eyes. The subject was a hint to the Florentines, to inspire their gratitude for Grand Ducal rule which spared them from the monstrosity of their own unworkable republic. Another gamble was behind Giambologna's *Rape of the Sabines* (1583): he took a rough block of marble all the other sculptors in Florence had rejected as impossible, on the bet that he could do something with it. Its curious shape 'liberated', as Michelangelo would say, became an old man, a young man and a woman spiralling upwards in a fluid *contrapposto* convulsion, one of the first sculptures designed to be seen from all sides: the title was stuck on after its completion. The loggia also shelters Giambologna's less successful *Hercules and Nessus*, a chorus line of six Roman vestal wallflowers, and several other works that contribute to the rather curious effect, especially at night, of people at a wild party frozen into stone by Medusa's magical gaze.

The first two statues placed in the square were carried there by republican enthusiasm. Donatello's *Judith and Holofernes* was hauled from the Medici palace and placed here in 1494 as a symbol of the defeat of tyranny. Michelangelo's *David* was equally seen as the embodiment of republican triumph (when it was finished in 1504, the Medici were in exile), though it is doubtful whether Michelangelo himself had such symbolism in mind, as the statue was intended to stand next to the cathedral, only to be shanghaied to the Piazza della Signoria by eager republican partisans. It was replaced by a copy in 1873 when the original was relocated (with much pomp, on a specially built train) to safekeeping at the Accademia. Later Florentine sculptors attempted to rival the *David*, especially the awful Baccio Bandinelli, who managed to get the commission to create a pendant to the statue and boasted that he could surpass Il Divino himself. The pathetic result, *Hercules and Cacus*, was completed in 1534; as a reward, Bandinelli had to listen to his arch-enemy Cellini insult the statue in front of their patron, Cosimo I. An 'old sack full of melons' he called it, bestowing the sculpture's alternative title.

Another overgrown victim of the chisel stands at the corner of the Palazzo Vecchio. Ammannati's **Neptune Fountain** (1575) was dubbed *Il Biancone* ('Big Whitey') almost as soon as it was unveiled; Michelangelo pitied the huge block of marble Ammannati 'ruined' to produce Neptune, a lumpy, bloated symbol of Cosimo I's naval victories, wearing a silly crown of anti-pigeon spikes as he stands arrogantly over a low basin and a few half-hearted spurts of water, pulled along by four struggling sea steeds, mere hobby-horses compared with Big Whitey himself.

The last colossus in Piazza della Signoria is the *Equestrian Monument to Cosimo,* by Giambologna (1595), the only large-scale equestrian bronze of the Late Renaissance. The scheme on the panels below the statue depicts scenes of Cosimo's brutal conquest of Siena, and of the 'Florentine Senate' and the Pope conferring the Grand Dukedom on Cosimo. Directly behind Cosimo stands the **Tribunale di Mercanzia**, built in the 14th century as a commercial court for merchants of the guilds and adorned with heraldic arms. To the left of this (no. 7) is a fine, 16th-century contribution, the **Palazzo Uguccioni**, very much in the spirit of High Renaissance in Rome, and sometimes attributed to a design by Raphael.

> *When Goethe made his blitz-tour of Florence, the **Palazzo Vecchio** (also called the Palazzo della Signoria) helped pull the wool over his eyes. 'Obviously,' wrote the great poet, 'the people . . . enjoyed a lucky succession of good governments'—a remark which, as Mary McCarthy wrote, could make the angels in heaven weep.*

But none of Florence's chronic factionalism mars Arnolfo di Cambio's temple of civic aspirations, part council hall and part fortress. In many ways, the Palazzo Vecchio is the ideal of stone Florence: rugged and imposing, with a rusticated façade that was to inspire so many of the city's private palaces, yet designed according to the proportions of the Golden Section of the ancient Greeks. Its dominant feature, the 94m tower, is a typical piece of Florentine bravado, for long the highest point in the city.

The Palazzo Vecchio occupies the site of the old Roman theatre and the medieval Palazzo dei Priori. In the 13th century this earlier palace was flattened along with the Ghibelline quarter, and in 1299, the now ascendant Guelphs called upon Arnolfo di Cambio, master builder of the cathedral, to design the most impressive 'Palazzo del Popolo' (as the building was originally called) possible, with an eye to upstaging rival cities. The palace's unusual trapezoidal shape is often, but rather dubiously, explained as Guelph care not to have any of the building touch land once owned by Ghibellines. One doubts that even in the 13th century real estate realities allowed such delicacy of sentiments; nor does the theory explain why the tower has swallowtail Ghibelline crenellations, as opposed to the square Guelph ones on the palace itself. Later additions to the rear of the palace have obscured its shape even more, although the façade is essentially as Arnolfo built it, except for the bet-hedging monogram over the door hailing Christ the King of Florence, put up in the nervous days of 1529, when the imperial army of Charles V was on its way to destroy the last Florentine republic; the inscription replaces an earlier one left by Savonarola. The room at the top of the tower was used as prison for celebrities and dubbed the *alberghetto*; inmates of the 'little hotel' included Cosimo il Vecchio before his brief exile, and Savonarola, who spent his last months, between torture sessions, enjoying a superb view of the city before his execution in the piazza below.

> *Today the Palazzo Vecchio serves as Florence's city hall, but nearly all of its* **historical rooms** *are open to the public* (open 9–7, Sun 8–1; closed Thurs; adm L10,000).

With few exceptions, the interior decorations date from the time of Cosimo I, when he moved his Grand Ducal self here from the Medici palace in 1540. To politically 'correct' its acres of walls and ceilings in the shortest amount of time, he turned to his court artist Giorgio Vasari, famed more for the speed at which he could execute a commission than for its quality. On the ground floor of the palazzo, before you buy your ticket, you can take a gander at some of Vasari's more elaborate handiwork in the **Courtyard**, redone for the occasion of Francesco I's unhappy marriage to the plain and stupid Habsburg Joanna of Austria in 1565.

Vasari's suitably grand staircase ascends to the largest room in the palace, the vast **Salone dei Cinquecento**. The *salone* was added at the insistence of Savonarola for meetings of the 500-strong Consiglio Maggiore, the reformed republic's democratic assembly. Art's two reigning divinities, Leonardo da Vinci and Michelangelo, were commissioned in 1503 to paint the two long walls of the *salone* in a kind of Battle of the Brushes to which the city eagerly looked forward. Sadly, neither of the artists came near to completing the project; Leonardo managed to fresco a section of the wall, using the experimental techniques that were to prove the undoing of his *Last Supper* in Milan, while Michelangelo only completed the cartoons before being summoned to Rome by Julius II, who required the sculptor of the *David* to pander to his own personal megalomania.

In the 1560s Vasari removed what was left of Leonardo's efforts and refrescoed the entire room as a celebration of Cosimo's military triumphs over Pisa and Siena, complete with an apotheosis of the Grand Duke on the ceiling. These wall scenes are inane, big and busy, crowded with men and horses who appear to have all the substance of overcooked pasta. The sculptural groups lining the walls of this almost uncomfortably large room (the Italian parliament sat here from 1865 to 1870 when Florence was the capital) are only slightly more stimulating; even Michelangelo's *Victory*, on the wall opposite the entrance, is more virtuosity than vision: a vacuous young idiot posing with one knee atop a defeated old man still half-submerged in stone, said to be a self-portrait of the sculptor, which lends the work a certain bitter poignancy. The neighbouring, muscle-bound duet, *Hercules and Diomedes* by Vicenzo de' Rossi, was probably inevitable in this city obsessed by the possibilities of the male nude.

Beyond the *salone*, behind a modern glass door, is a much more intriguing room, although it's not much bigger than a closet. This is the **Studiolo of Francesco I**, designed by Vasari in 1572 for Cosimo's melancholic and reclusive son, where he would escape to brood over his real interests in natural curiosities and alchemy. The little study, windowless and more than a little claustrophobic, has been restored to its original appearance, lined with allegorical paintings by Vasari, Bronzino and Allori, and bronze statuettes by Giambologna and Ammannati, their refined, polished, and erotic mythological subjects part of a carefully thought-out 16th-century programme on Man and Nature. The lower row of paintings conceals Francesco's secret cupboards where he kept his most precious belongings, his pearls and crystals and gold.

After the *salone* a certain fuzziness begins to set in. Cosimo I's propaganda machine in league with Vasari's fresco factory produced room after room of self-glorifying Medicean puffery. The first rooms, known as the **Quartiere di Leone X**, carry ancestor worship to extremes, each one dedicated to a different Medici: in the first Cosimo il Vecchio returns from exile amid tumultuous acclaim; in the second Lorenzo il Magnifico receives the ambassadors in the company of a dignified giraffe; the third and fourth are dedicated to the Medici popes, while the fifth, naturally, is for Cosimo I, who gets the most elaborate treatment of all.

Upstairs the next series of rooms is known as the **Quartiere degli Elementi**, with more by Vasari and co, depicting allegories of the elements. Beyond these are several rooms used to display works pilfered by the Nazis during the war and since recovered (*closed at the time of writing*). Many of the paintings were personally selected by Goering and Hitler, who were apparently quite fond of *Leda and the Swan* and other mild mythological erotica. In a small room is the original of Verrocchio's boy with the dolphin, from the courtyard fountain.

A balcony across the Salone dei Cinquecento leads to the **Quartiere di Eleonora di Toledo**, Mrs Cosimo I's private apartments. Of special note here is her chapel, one of the masterpieces of Bronzino, who seemed to relish the opportunity to paint something besides Medici portraits. The next room, the **Sala dell'Udienza**, has a quattrocento coffered ceiling by Benedetto and Giuliano da Maiano, and walls painted with a rather fine romp by Mannerist Francesco Salviati (1550–60).

The last room, the **Sala dei Gigli** ('of the lilies') boasts another fine ceiling by the da Maiano brothers; it contains Donatello's bronze *Judith and Holofernes*, a late and rather gruesome work of 1455; the warning to tyrants inscribed on its base was added when the statue was abducted from the Medici palace and placed in the Piazza della Signoria. Off the Sala dei Gigli are two small rooms of interest: the **Guardaroba**, a unique 'wardrobe' adorned with 57 maps painted by Fra Egnazio Danti in 1563, depicting all the world known at the time. The **Cancelleria** was Machiavelli's office from 1498 to 1512, when he served the republic as secretary and diplomat. He is commemorated with a bust and a portrait. Poor Machiavelli died bitter and unaware of the notoriety that his works would one day bring him, and he would be amazed to learn that his name had become synonymous with cunning, amoral intrigue. After losing his job upon the return of the Medici, and at one point tortured and imprisoned on a false suspicion of conspiracy, Machiavelli lived in forced idleness in the country, where he wrote his political works and two fine plays, feverishly trying to return to favour, even dedicating his most famous book, *The Prince*, to Lorenzo, Duke of Urbino (a nonentity further glorified by Michelangelo's Medici tombs); his concern throughout was to advise realistically, without mincing words, the fractious and increasingly weak Italians on how to create a strong state. His evil reputation came from openly stating what rulers do, rather than what they would like other people to think they do.

Two collections long housed in the Palazzo Vecchio, the excellent **Collection of Old Musical Instruments**, and the **Collezione Loeser**, a fine assortment of Renaissance art left to the city in 1928 by Charles Loeser, the Macy's department-store heir, have at the time of writing tumbled into Italian museum limbo. The violins and cellos (several by Cremona greats like Stradivarius and Guarneri) have been earmarked for a new destination; the tourist office can give you a status report.

> *After the pomposity of the Palazzo Vecchio and a Campari cure at the Piazza della Signoria's landmark **Café Rivoire**, you may be in the mood to reconsider the 20th century. The best place to do this in Florence is at its only gallery of modern art, the **Collezione della Ragione**, located on the Piazza della Signoria, above the Cassa di Risparmio bank (open Sat 9–2 and sometimes during the week; information ℂ 217305).*

There are typical still lifes by De Pisis; equally still landscapes by Carlo Carra; mysterious baths by De Chirico; Tuscan landscapes by Mario Mafai, Antonio Donghi and Ottone Rosai; a speedy Futurist horse by Fortunato Depero and a window with doves by Gino Severini; a number of richly coloured canvases by Renato Guttuso and paintings after Tintoretto by Emilio Vedova, and many others, surprises, perhaps, for those unfamiliar with living Italians as opposed to dead ones.

> *Just south of the Palazzo Vecchio is the entrance to the **Uffizi**; enormous queues in the summer are very common; try to arrive early, or book a ticket in advance by credit card on ℂ 234 7941; you pay an extra L2,500 booking fee, and pick up the tickets at the gallery at the time of your visit (open daily exc Mon 8.30–6.50, Sun 8.30–1.50; adm L12,000).*

Florence has the most fabulous art museum in Italy, and as usual we have the Medici to thank; for the building that holds these treasures, however, credit goes to Grand Duke Cosimo's much maligned court painter. Poor Giorgio Vasari! His roosterish boastfulness and the conviction that his was the best of all possible artistic worlds, set next to his very modest talents, have made him a comic figure in most art criticism. Even the Florentines don't like him. On one of the rare occasions when he tried his hand as an architect, though, he gave Florence something to be proud of. The Uffizi ('offices') were built as Cosimo's secretariat, incorporating the old mint (producer of the first gold florins in 1252), the archives, and the large church of San Pier Scheraggio, with plenty of room for the bureaucrats needed to run Cosimo's efficient, modern state. The matched pair of arcaded buildings have cold elegant façades that conceal Vasari's surprising innovation: iron reinforcements that make the huge amount of window area possible and keep the building stable on the soft sandy ground. It was a trick that would be almost forgotten until the Crystal Palace and the first American skyscrapers.

Almost from the start the Medici began to store some of their huge art collection in parts of the building. There are galleries in the world with more works of art— the Uffizi counts a mere 1800—but the Uffizi overwhelms by the fact that every one of its paintings is worth looking at.

Near the ticket counter are the remains of the church of San Pier Scheraggio. This is now decorated with Andrea del Castagno's stately **Frescoes of Illustrious Men** (1450), including the Cumaean Sibyl(!) as well as Dante and Boccaccio, both of whom attended political debates in this very church. From here you can take the lift or sweeping grand stair up to the second floor, where the Medici once had a huge theatre, now home to the **Cabinet of Drawings and Prints**. Although the bulk of this extensive and renowned collection is only open to scholars with special permission, a roomful of tempting samples gives a hint at what they have a chance to see.

Nowadays one thinks of the Uffizi as primarily a gallery of paintings, but for some hundred years after its opening, visitors came almost exclusively for the fine collection of Hellenistic and Roman marbles. Most of these were collected in Rome by Medici cardinals, and not a few were sources of Renaissance inspiration. The **Vestibule** at the top of the stair contains some of the best, together with Flemish and Tuscan tapestries made for Cosimo I and his successors. **Room 1**, usually shut, contains excellent early Roman sculpture.

Rooms 2–6: 13th and 14th centuries

The Uffizi's paintings are arranged chronologically. The roots of the Early Renaissance are strikingly revealed in **Room 2**, dedicated to the three great **Maestà** altarpieces by the masters of the 13th century. All portray the same subject of the Madonna and Child enthroned with angels. The one on the right, by Cimabue, was painted in around the year 1285 and represents a breaking away from the flat, stylized Byzantine tradition. To the left is the so-called *Rucellai Madonna*, painted in the same period by the Sienese Duccio di Buoninsegna for Santa Maria Novella. It resembles Cimabue's in many ways, but has a more advanced technique for creating depth, and the bright colouring that characterizes the Sienese school. Giotto's altarpiece, painted some 25 years later, takes a great leap forward, not only in his use of 'false' perspective, but in the arrangement of the angels, standing naturally, and in the portrayal of the Virgin, gently smiling, with real fingers and breasts.

To the left, **Room 3** contains representative Sienese works of the 14th century, with a beautiful Gothic *Annunciation* (1333) by Simone Martini and the brothers Pietro and Ambrogio Lorenzetti. **Room 4** is dedicated to 14th-century Florentines: Bernardo Daddi, Nardo di Cione, and the delicately coloured *San Remigio Pietà* by Giottino. **Rooms 5 and 6** portray Italian contributions to the International Gothic school, most dazzlingly Gentile da Fabriano's *Adoration of the Magi* (1423), two good works by Lorenzo Monaco, and the *Thebaid* of Gherardo Starnina, depicting the rather unusual activities of the 4th-century monks of St Pancratius of Thebes, in Egypt—a composition strikingly like Chinese scroll scenes of hermits.

Rooms 7–9: Early Renaissance

In the Uffizi, at least, it's but a few short steps from the superbly decorative International Gothic to the masters of the Early Renaissance. **Room 7** contains minor works by Fra Angelico, Masaccio and Masolino, and three masterpieces. Domenico Veneziano's pastel *Madonna and Child with Saints* (1448) is one of the rare pictures by this Venetian master who died a pauper in Florence. It is a new departure not only for its soft colours but for the subject matter, unifying the enthroned Virgin and saints in one panel, in what is known as a *Sacra Conversazione*. Piero della Francesca's famous *Double Portrait of the Duke Federigo da Montefeltro and his Duchess Battista Sforza of Urbino* (1465) depicts one of Italy's noblest Renaissance princes—and surely the one with the most distinctive nose. Piero's ability to create perfectly still, timeless worlds is even more evident in the allegorical 'Triumphs' of the Duke and Duchess painted on the back of their portraits. A similar stillness and fascination floats over into the surreal in Uccello's *Rout of San Romano* (1456), or at least the third of it still present (the other two panels are in the Louvre and London's National Gallery; all three once decorated the bedroom of Lorenzo il Magnifico in the Medici palace). Both Piero and

Uccello were deep students of perspective, but Uccello went half-crazy; applying his principles to a violent battle scene has left us one of the most provocative works of all time—a vision of warfare in suspended animation, with pink, white and blue toy horses, robot-like knights, and rabbits bouncing in the background.

Room 8 is devoted to the works of the rascally romantic Fra Filippo Lippi, whose ethereally lovely Madonnas were modelled after his brown-eyed nun. In his *Coronation of the Virgin* (1447) she kneels in the foreground with two children, while the artist, dressed in a brown habit, looks dreamily towards her; in his celebrated *Madonna and Child with Two Angels* (1445) she plays the lead before the kind of mysterious landscape Leonardo would later perfect. Lippi taught the art of enchanting Madonnas to his student Botticelli, who has some lovely works in this room and the next; Alesso Baldovinetti, a pupil of the far more holy Fra Angelico, painted the room's beautiful *Annunciation* (1447). **Room 9** has two small scenes from the *Labours of Hercules* (1470) by Antonio Pollaiuolo, whose interest in anatomy, muscular expressiveness and violence presages a strain in Florentine art that would culminate in the great Mannerists. He worked with his younger brother Piero on the refined, elegant *SS. Vincent, James and Eustace*, transferred here from San Miniato. This room also contains the Uffizi's best-known forgery: *The Young Man in a Red Hat* or self-portrait of Filippino Lippi, is believed to have been the work of a clever 18th-century English art dealer who palmed it off on the Grand Dukes.

Botticelli: Rooms 10–14

To accommodate the bewitching art of 'Little Barrels' and his throngs of 20th-century admirers, the Uffizi converted four small rooms into one great Botticellian shrine. Although his masterpieces displayed here have become almost synonymous with the Florentine Renaissance at its most spring-like and charming, they were not publicly displayed until the beginning of the 19th century, nor given much consideration outside Florence until the turn of the century.

Botticelli's best works date from the days when he was a darling of the Medici—family members crop up most noticeably in the *Adoration of the Magi* (1476), where you can pick out Cosimo il Vecchio, Lorenzo il Magnifico and Botticelli himself (in the right foreground, in a yellow robe, gazing at the spectator). His *Annunciation* is a graceful, cosmic dance between the Virgin and the Angel Gabriel. In the *Tondo of the Virgin of the Pomegranate* the lovely melancholy goddess who was to become his Venus makes her first appearance.

Botticelli is best known for his sublime mythological allegories, nearly all painted for the Medici and inspired by the Neoplatonic, humanistic and hermetic currents that pervaded the Florentine intelligentsia of the late 15th century. Perhaps no painting has been debated so fervently as *La Primavera* (1478). Commissioned by Lorenzo di Pierfrancesco, this hung for years in the Medici Villa at Castello. The subject of the Allegory of Spring may have been suggested by Marsilio Ficino, the great natural magician of the Renaissance; the figures supposedly represent the 'beneficial' planets able to dispel sadness. *Pallas and the Centaur* has been called another subtle allegory of Medici triumph—the rings of Athene's gown were a family device. Other interpretations see the taming of the sorrowful centaur as a melancholy comment on reason and civilization. Botticelli's last great mythology, *The Birth of Venus*, was also commissioned by Lorenzo di Pierfrancesco and inspired by a poem by Poliziano, Lorenzo il Magnifico's Latin and Greek scholar, who described how Zephyr and Chloris blew the newborn goddess to shore on a scallop shell, while Hora hastened to robe her, a scene Botticelli portrays once again with dance-like rhythm and delicacy of line. Yet the goddess of love floats towards the spectator with an expression of wistfulness—perhaps reflecting the artist's own feelings of regret, for artistically, the poetic, decorative style he perfected in this painting would be disdained and forgotten in his own lifetime. Spiritually, too, Botticelli turned a corner after creating this haunting, uncanny beauty—his, and Florence's, farewell to a road not taken. Although Vasari's biography of Botticelli portrays him as a prankster rather than a sensitive soul, the painter absorbed more than any other artist the *fin-de-siècle* neuroticism that beset the city with the rise of Savonarola. So thoroughly did he reject his Neoplatonism that he would only accept commissions of sacred subjects or supposedly edifying allegories like his *Calumny*, a small but disturbing work, and a fitting introduction to the dark side of the quattrocento psyche.

This large room also contains works by Botticelli's contemporaries. Two paintings of the *Adoration of the Magi*, one by Ghirlandaio and one by Filippino Lippi, show the influence of Leonardo's unfinished but radical work in pyramidal composition (in the next room); Leonardo himself got the idea from the large *Portinari Altarpiece* (1471) by Hugo Van der Goes in the centre of the room, a work brought back from Bruges by Medici agent Tommaso Portinari. Behind it hangs Lorenzo di Credi's *Venus*, a charmer inspired by Botticelli.

Rooms 15–24: More Renaissance

Room 15 is dedicated to Leonardo da Vinci's early career in Florence. Here are works by his master Andrea Verrocchio, including the *Baptism of Christ*, in which the young Leonardo painted the angel on the left. Modern art critics believe the large *Annunciation* (1475) is almost entirely by Leonardo's hand—the soft faces, the botanical details, the misty, watery background would become the trademarks of his magical brush. Most influential, however, was his unfinished *Adoration of the Magi* (1481), a highly unconventional composition that

Leonardo abandoned when he left Florence for Milan. Although at first glance it's hard to make out much more than a mass of reddish chiaroscuro, the longer you stare, the better you'll see the serene Madonna and Child surrounded by a crowd of anxious, troubled humanity, with an exotic background of ruins, trees and horsemen, all charged with expressive energy. Other artists in Room 15 include Leonardo's peers: Lorenzo di Credi, whose religious works have eerie garden-like backgrounds, and the nutty Piero di Cosimo, whose dreamy *Perseus Liberating Andromeda* includes an endearing mongrel of a dragon that gives even the most reserved Japanese tourist fits of giggles. Tuscan maps adorn **Room 16**, as well as scenes by Hans Memling.

The octagonal **Tribuna** (Room 18) with its mother-of-pearl dome and *pietra dura* floor and table was built by Buontalenti in 1584 for Francesco I, and like the Studiolo in the Palazzo Vecchio, it was designed to hold Medici treasures. For centuries the best-known of these was the *Venus de' Medici*, a 2nd-century BC Greek sculpture, farcically claimed as a copy of Praxiteles' celebrated Aphrodite of Cnidos, the most erotic statue in antiquity. In the 18th century, amazingly, this rather ordinary girl was considered the greatest sculpture in Florence; today most visitors walk right past, snubbing her without a second glance. Other antique works include the *Wrestlers* and the *Knife Grinder*, both copies of Pergamese originals, the *Dancing Faun*, the *Young Apollo*, and the *Sleeping Hermaphrodite* in the adjacent room, which sounds fascinating but is usually curtained off.

The real stars of the Tribuna are the Medici court portraits, many by Bronzino, who could not only catch the likeness of Cosimo I, Eleanor of Toledo and their children, but aptly portrayed the spirit of the day—these are people who took themselves very seriously indeed. They have for company Vasari's posthumous portrait of *Lorenzo il Magnifico* and Pontormo's *Cosimo il Vecchio*, Andrea del Sarto's *Girl with a Book by Petrarch*, and Rosso Fiorentino's *Angel Musician*, an enchanting work entirely out of place in this stodgy temple.

Two followers of Piero della Francesca, Perugino and Luca Signorelli, hold pride of place in **Room 19**; Perugino's *Portrait of a Young Man* is believed to be modelled on his pupil Raphael. Signorelli's *Tondo of the Holy Family* was to become the inspiration for Michelangelo's (*see* p.125). The Germans appear in **Room 20**, led by Dürer and his earliest known work, the *Portrait of his Father* (1490), done at age 19, and *The Adoration of the Magi* (1504), painted after his first trip to Italy. Also here are Lucas Cranach's Teutonic *Adam and Eve* and *Portrait of Martin Luther* (1543), not someone you'd expect to see in Florence. **Room 21** is dedicated to the great Venetians, most famously Bellini and his uncanny *Sacred Allegory* (1490s), the meaning of which has never been satisfactorily explained. There are two minor works by the elusive Giorgione, and a typically weird

St Dominic by Cosmè Tura. Later Flemish and German artists appear in **Room 22**, works by Gerard David and proto-Romantic Albrecht Altdorfer, and a portrait attributed to Hans Holbein of *Sir Thomas More*. **Room 23** is dedicated to non-Tuscans Correggio of Parma and Mantegna of the Veneto, as well as Boltraffio's strange *Narcissus* with an eerie background reminiscent of Leonardo.

Rooms 25–27: Mannerism

The window-filled **South Corridor**, with its views over the city and fine display of antique sculpture, marks only the halfway point in the Uffizi but nearly the end of Florence's contribution. In the first three rooms, however, local talent rallies to produce a brilliantly coloured twilight in Florentine Mannerism. By most accounts, Michelangelo's only completed oil painting, the *Tondo Doni* (1506), was the spark that ignited Mannerism's flaming orange and turquoise hues. Michelangelo was 30 when he painted this unconventional work, in a medium he disliked (sculpture and fresco being the only fit occupations for a man, or so he believed). It is a typical Michelangelo story that when the purchaser complained that the artist was asking too much for it, Michelangelo promptly doubled the price. As shocking as the colours are the spiralling poses of the Holy Family, sharply delineated against a background of five nude, slightly out-of-focus young men of uncertain purpose (are they pagans? angels? boyfriends? or just filler?)—an ambiguity that was to become a hallmark of Mannerism and the Sistine Chapel ceiling. In itself, the *Tondo Doni* is more provocative than immediately appealing; the violent canvas in **Room 27**, Rosso Fiorentino's *Moses Defending the Children of Jethro*, was painted some 20 years later and at least in its intention to shock the viewer puts a cap on what Michelangelo began.

Room 26 is dedicated mainly to Raphael, who was in and out of Florence 1504–8. Never temperamental or eccentric like his contemporaries, the good-natured Raphael was the sweetheart of the High Renaissance. His Madonnas, like *The Madonna of the Goldfinch*, a luminous work painted in Florence, have a tenderness that was soon to be over-popularized by others and turned into holy cards, a cloying sentimentality added like layers of varnish over the centuries. It's easier, perhaps, to see Raphael's genius in non-sacred subjects, like *Leo X with Two Cardinals*, a perceptive portrait study of the first Medici pope with his nephew Giulio de' Medici, later Clement VII. The same room contains Andrea del Sarto's most original work, the fluorescent *Madonna of the Harpies* (1517), named after the figures on the Virgin's pedestal. Of the works by Pontormo, the best is in **Room 27**, *Supper at Emmaus* (1525), a strange canvas with peasant-faced monks emerging out of the darkness, brightly clad diners with dirty feet, and the Masonic symbol of the Eye of God hovering over Christ's head.

Rooms 28–45

Although we now bid a fond farewell to the Florentines, the Uffizi fairly bristles with masterpieces from other parts of Italy and abroad. Titian's delicious nudes, especially the incomparably voluptuous *Venus of Urbino*, raise the temperature in **Room 28**; Parmigianino's hyper-elegant *Madonna with the Long Neck* (1536) in **Room 30** is a fascinating Mannerist evolutionary dead-end, possessing all the weird beauty of a foot-long dragonfly. Sebastiano del Piombo's *Death of Adonis*, in **Room 32**, is notable for its melancholy, lagoony, autumn atmosphere and the annoyed look on Venus' face. **Room 34** holds Paolo Veronese's *Holy Family with St Barbara*, a late work bathed in a golden Venetian light, with a gorgeously opulent Barbara gazing on. In **Room 35** his contemporary Tintoretto is represented by a shadowy *Leda* languidly pretending to restrain the lusty swan; the Uffizi's El Greco is here as well, reminding us that this most Mannerist of Mannerists learned how to do it in Venice.

Room 41 is Flemish domain, with brand-name art by Rubens and Van Dyck; the former's *Baccanale* may be the most grotesque canvas in Florence. Struggle on gamely to **Room 43** to see three striking Caravaggios. His *Bacchus* and *The Head of Medusa* are believed to be self-portraits; in its day the fleshy and heavy-eyed Bacchus, half portrait and half still life, but lacking the usual mythological appurtenances, was considered highly iconoclastic. Here, too, is one of the best versions of *Judith and Holofernes* by Artemisia Gentileschi; after she was allegedly raped by a fellow artist (who was acquitted in court), the subject of a woman slicing off a man's head became her favourite theme. There are three portraits by Rembrandt in **Room 44**, including two of himself, young and old, and landscapes by Ruysdael. **Room 45** is given over to some fine 18th-century works, including two charming portraits of children by Chardin, and others by Goya and Longhi, and Venetian landscapes by Guardi and Canaletto. Even more welcome by this time is the bar at the end of the corridor, with a lovely summer terrace.

Corridoio Vasariano

In 1565, when Francesco I married Joanna of Austria, the Medici commissioned Vasari to link their new digs in the Pitti Palace with the Uffizi and the Palazzo Vecchio in such a manner that the archdukes could make their daily rounds without having to rub elbows with their subjects. With a patina of 400 years, Florence wouldn't look quite right without this covered catwalk, leapfrogging on rounded arches from the back of the Uffizi, over the Ponte Vecchio, daintily skirting a medieval tower, and darting past the façade of Santa Felicità to the Pitti Palace. The Corridoio (*reopened in September 1997 after restoration of bomb damage*) is open according to availability of staff. At the moment it is closed, and nobody seems to know when it will next open. The entrance system also varies; the ticket has been incorporated into the Uffizi ticket, with no special booking required. Just one of those Italian vagueries; check with the tourist office. It not only offers interesting views of Florence, but has been hung with a celebrated collection of artists' self-portraits, beginning with Vasari himself before continuing in chronological order, past the Gaddis and Raphael to Rembrandt, Van Dyck, Velazquez, Hogarth, Reynolds, Delacroix, Corot and scores in between.

For all that Florence and Tuscany contributed to the birth of science, it is only fitting that the **Museum of the History of Science** *should be in the centre of the city, behind the Uffizi in Piazza Giudici* (open Mon–Sat 9.30–1, Mon, Wed and Fri 2–5 also; closed Sun; adm exp).

Much of the ground floor is devoted to instruments measuring time and distance that are often works of art in themselves: Arabian astrolabes and pocket sundials, Tuscan sundials in the shape of Platonic solids, enormous elaborate armillary spheres and a small reliquary holding the bone of Galileo's finger, erect, like a final gesture to the city that until 1737 denied him a Christian burial. Here, too, are two of his original telescopes and the lens with which he discovered the four moons of Jupiter. Other scientific instruments come from the Accademia del Cimento (of 'trial', or 'experiment'), founded in 1657 by Cardinal Leopoldo de' Medici, the world's first scientific organization, dedicated to Galileo's principle of inquiry and proof by experimentation. 'Try and try again' was its motto.

Upstairs, there's a large room filled with machines used to demonstrate principles of physics, which the ladies who run the museum will operate if you ask. Two unusual ones are the 18th-century automatic writer and the instrument of perpetual motion. The rooms devoted to medicine contain a collection of 18th-century wax anatomical models, designed to teach budding obstetricians about unfortunate foetal positions, as well as a fine display of surgical instruments from the period.

From the museum, head back along the Arno towards the Uffizi, peering over the stone balustrade to Florence's beautifully situated rowing club. Follow the river west, in the shadow of the Vasari Corridor; on the right, they are still repairing the damage from the 1993 bomb. Ahead, of course, stretches the **Ponte Vecchio.**

> *Bent bridges seeming to strain like bows*
> *And tremble with arrowy undertide . . .*

'Casa Guidi Windows', Elizabeth Barrett Browning

Often at sunset the Arno becomes a stream of molten gold, confined in its walls of stone and laced into its bed with the curving arches of its spans. That is, during those months when it has a respectable flow of water. But even in the torrid days of August, when the Arno shrivels into muck and spittle, its two famous bridges retain their distinctive beauty. The most famous of these, the Ponte Vecchio, the 'Old Bridge', crosses the Arno at its narrowest point; the present bridge, with its three stone arches, was built in 1345, and replaces a wooden construction from the 970s, the successor to a span that may well have dated back to the Romans.

On this bridge, at the foot of the Marzocco, or statue of Mars, Buondelmonte dei Buondelmonti was murdered in 1215, setting off the wars of the Guelphs and Ghibellines. The original Marzocco was washed away in a 14th-century flood, and Donatello's later leonine version has been carted off to the Bargello.

Like old London Bridge, the Ponte Vecchio is covered with shops and houses. By the 1500s, for hygienic reasons, it had become the street of hog butchers, though after Vasari built Cosimo's secret passage on top, the Grand Duke, for personal hygienic reasons, evicted the butchers and replaced them with goldsmiths. They have been there ever since, and shoppers from around the world descend on it each year to scrutinize the traditional Florentine talent for jewellery—many of the city's great artists began their careers as goldsmiths, from Ghiberti and Donatello, to Cellini, who never gave up the craft, and whose bust adorns the middle of the bridge. In the 1966 flood the shops did not prove as resilient as the Ponte Vecchio itself, and a fortune of gold was washed down the Arno. All is since restored.

> *In the summer of 1944, the river briefly became a German defensive line during the slow painful retreat across Italy. Before leaving Florence, the Nazis blew up every one of the city's bridges, saving only, on Hitler's special orders, the Ponte Vecchio, though they blasted a large number of ancient buildings on each side of the span to create piles of rubble to block the approaches. Florence's most beautiful span, the **Ponte Santa Trínita** was the most tragic victim.*

Immediately after the war the Florentines set about replacing the bridges exactly as they were: for Santa Trínita, old quarries had to be reopened to duplicate the stone, and old methods revived to cut it (modern power saws would have done it too cleanly). The graceful curve of the three arches was a problem; they could not be constructed geometrically, and considerable speculation went on over how the architect (Ammannati, in 1567) did it. Finally, recalling that Michelangelo had advised Ammannati on the project, someone noticed that the same form of arch could be seen on the decoration of Michelangelo's tombs in the Medici Chapel, constructed most likely by pure artistic imagination. Fortune lent a hand in the reconstruction; of the original statues of the 'Four Seasons', almost all the pieces were fished out of the Arno and rebuilt. Spring's head was eventually found by divers completely by accident in 1961.

*The German bombs damaged **Via Por S. Maria**, the main street leading to the Ponte Vecchio, although just to the west you'll find some of the oldest, best-preserved lanes in Florence. Near the Mercato Nuovo at the top of the street (see p.108) stands the **Palazzo di Parte Guelfa**, the 13th-century headquarters of the Guelph party, and often the real seat of power in the city, paid for by property confiscated from the Ghibellines; in the 15th century Brunelleschi added a hall on the top floor and an extension. Next door is the guildhall of the silk makers, the 14th-century **Palazzo dell'Arte della Seta**, still bearing its bas-relief emblem, or 'stemma', of a closed door, the age-old guild symbol. Continue around the Guelph Palace to Via Pellicceria to see the fine ensemble of medievall buildings on the tiny square near Via delle Terme, named after the old Roman baths.*

*To get an idea of what day-to-day life was like inside these sombre palaces some 600 years ago, stroll over to nearby Via Porta Rossa, site of the elegant **Palazzo Davanzati**, arranged as the **Museo della Casa Fiorentina Antica**, a delightful museum unfortunately closed indefinitely for extensive restoration. There is an exhibition of what you would see were it open on the ground floor* (open 8.30–1.50; closed alternative Sundays and Mondays).

Originally built in the mid-14th century for the Davizzi family, the house was purchased by merchant Bernardo Davanzati in 1578 and stayed in the family until the 1900s. Restored by an antique collector in 1904, it is the best-preserved medieval-Renaissance house in Florence and filled with period furnishings.

The façade is basically as it was, except for a 16th-century addition of a fifth-floor loggia, replacing the battlements—in the rough-and-tumble 14th century, a man's home literally had to be a castle. But it was also a showroom for his prosperity, and by the standards of the day, the dwellers of this huge palace were multi-millionaires. Below the grand loggia, used for sumptuous public entertainment, the palace is entered by way of a striking vertical **Courtyard**, which was cut off from the street in times of danger. No family would feel safe without a year's store of grain and oil—against famine, siege, plagues or inflation. One storeroom is now used for an audio-visual history of the house. The well in the corner served all the floors of the house, and there is a medieval dumb waiter to transport the shopping up to the kitchen. Until the rest of the museum reopens, you'll have to imagine the formal **Sala Grande**, the bright **Sala dei Pappagalli**, frescoed with parrots, a rare en suite bedroom, and another, the **Sala dei Pavoni**, topped by a frieze of peacocks and other exotic birds flitting among the trees, the **Salone** with its 15th-century Flemish tapestries and a portrait of Giovanni di Bicci de' Medici, the **Sala Piccola** with its *cassoni*, or elaborately painted wedding chests, the **Camera della Castellana di Vergi**, decorated with a lovely fresco from a medieval French romance, and the **kitchen**, as usual on the top floor in the hope that in case of fire, only that part of the palace would burn.

Start: *north of Piazza della Signoria*
Finish: *Santa Maria Nuova*
Walking time: *a morning for Dante's Florence,*
an afternoon for Florence as It Was

III: Medieval Florence

Between the Piazza del Duomo and Piazza della Signoria lies the medieval kernel from which the Florentine Renaissance emerged like a hot-house flower; here too, is the Bargello, home to some of the finest sculpture in the world.

Lunch/Cafés

Antico Noe, Volta di San Piero 6r. A dive of a wine bar in a dubious arcade, but next door there is a trattoria serving Tuscan fare at reasonable prices.

Cantinetta da Verazzano, Via dei Tavolini 18–20r. A wine bar and bakery which serves inventive filled foccaccia and other appetizing snacks to go with their own wine.

Cima, Borgo degli Albizi 37r. Florence's first bookshop café where you can enjoy a snack while browsing through the stacks.

Enoteca, Via Giraldi (off Via Ghibellina). This wine bar, open 11am–1am (closed Sun) is housed in what was once an open loggia of Palazzo Borghese, hence the high vaulted ceilings and columns. The speciality is Tuscan wine from lesser-known producers. To accompany these, a choice of hearty soups (in winter), wooden platters of cheeses, meats or marinated fish, salads, savoury flans, terrines and so on.

Enoteca Birreria Centrale, Piazza dei Cimatori 1r, ✆ 211915. Draught beer and an extensive wine and grappa selection are on offer in this smart, stylish bar. Seasonal dishes are prepared and there is a garden with tables outdoors (closed Sun, around L25,000).

La Loggia degli Albizi, Borgo degli Albizi 19r. Melt-in-the-mouth cakes and pastries in an unpretentious bar. Try the *tortina della nonna*; a *crème pâtissière*-filled buttery pastry tart topped with almonds.

Le Mosacce, Via del Proconsolo 55r, ✆ 294361. Here you can eat one course or all three—good quality regional food, lively atmosphere (closed Sat, Sun, Mon and evenings).

Da Pennello, Via Dante Alighieri 4r, ✆ 294848. Aside from the usual Tuscan menu, this trattoria has a groaning table of antipasti (about L40,000).

Vineria, Via dei Cimatori 18r. A hole-in-the-wall sandwich bar and wine counter.

In 1265 Dante Alighieri was born in the quarter just to the north of the Piazza della Signoria; he was nine, attending Candlemas, 'when first the glorious Lady of my mind was made manifest to mine eyes; even she who was called Beatrice by many who know not wherefore'. Beatrice went on to wed another, and died suddenly in 1290; Dante tried to forget his disappointment and grief in battle, fighting in the wars against Arezzo and Pisa, then in writing his 'autopsychology' *La Vita Nuova*. In 1302, as a White Guelph, he was exiled. A friend just managed to rescue the manuscript of the *Inferno* from the crowds who came to sack and pillage his home. Dante died in Ravenna in 1321, and although he was never allowed to return home, the Florentines have belatedly tried to make amends to

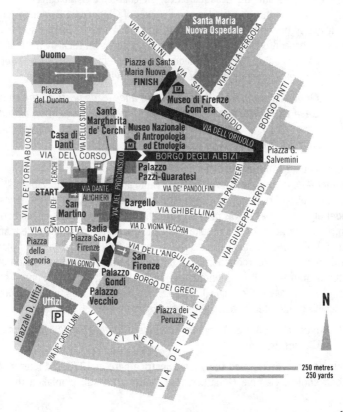

Florence Walk III: Medieval Florence

their poet. Yet the memorials fall curiously flat. His grand tomb in Santa Croce is empty and his huge statue in front of the church a glowering failure.

> *The best place to summon the shade of Italy's greatest poet is in the narrow medieval lanes of Florence, especially in his old haunts just to the north of Piazza della Signoria. Most scholars believe Dante was born on what is now* **Via Dante Alighieri**. *A modern bas-relief on one of the buildings shows the sights that would have been familiar to Dante, one of which would have been the sturdy well-preserved* **Torre del Castagno** *on Piazza San Martino, used as the residence of the* priori *before the construction of the Palazzo Vecchio—in the 13th century Florence had scores of similar tower houses. Here, too, is the tiny* **San Martino del Vescovo**, *Dante's parish church.*

Founded in 986, San Martino (*open 10–12 and 3–5; closed Sun*) was rebuilt in 1479 when it became the headquarters of the charitable Compagnia dei Buonuomini. The Compagnia commissioned a follower of Ghirlandaio to paint a series of colourful frescoes on the Life of St Martin and the Works of Charity, scenes acted out by quattrocento Florentines, in their own fashions on their own streets. The church also has a fine Byzantine Madonna, and one by Perugino, the latter by a *finestra a tromba*, a window used to distribute bread during the plague.

> *Opposite, from Via S. Margherita an alley leads north to the so-called* **Casa di Dante**, *actually built in 1911 over the ruins of an amputated tower house of the Giuochi family, although scholars all agree that the Alighieri lived somewhere close by.*

Since 1960, a museum dedicated to Dante (*open winter 10–4, Sun 10–2, summer 9–6, closed Tues; adm*) makes a game attempt to evoke Dante's life and times, in spite of neglect and stingy Florentine low-watt light bulbs. There is a model of Florence as it was in the 13th century, and mock-ups of the battle of Campaldino, where Dante as a soldier fought Arezzo. Near the entrance is an edition of *The Divine Comedy*, printed in tiny letters on a poster by a mad Milanese; of the manuscript reproductions, the most interesting is an illumination of the infamous murder of Buondelmonte dei Buondelmonti, with the Ponte Vecchio and a statue of Mars, the original *Marzocco*, in place. Upstairs there are copies of Botticelli's beautiful line illustrations for the *Commedia*.

> *From there, Via S. Margherita continues to little* **Santa Margherita de' Cerchi**, *built in 1032.*

Dante as a boy first espied the young Beatrice here in 1273 and later wed his second choice, Gemma Donati, whose family arms still emblazon the 13th-century porch. Both Beatrice and Gemma were buried here in their family tombs; no trace remains today although you can still see the tombstone of Monna Tessa, Beatrice's nurse.

> *From here, continue up to Via del Corso and turn right to Via Procon-solo. Here at No. 10 the elegant **Palazzo Pazzi-Quaratesi**, built in 1472 by Giuliano da Maiano for Jacopo de' Pazzi, was the headquarters of the banking family that organized the murder conspiracy against Lorenzo and Giuliano de' Medici. No. 12, the Palazzo Nonfinito—begun in 1593 but never completed—is now the home of the **Museo Nazionale di Antropologia ed Etnologia** (open Thurs–Sat 9–1 and one Sun in the month (variable); free adm).*

Founded in 1869, the first ethnological museum in Italy, this has a collection of Peruvian mummies, musical instruments collected by Galileo Chini (who deco-rated the Liberty-style extravaganzas at Viareggio), lovely and unusual items of Japan's Ainu and Pakistan's Kafiri, and a number of skulls from all over the world.

> *Dante would also recognize the two great towers in Piazza San Firenze, just to the south: the looming Bargello and the beautiful Romanesque campanile of the ancient Benedictine abbey, or **Badia**, which he cited in the Paradiso (entrance in Via Dante, open Mon–Sat 5–7, Sun 7.30–11.30). Or, that is to say, he will recognize the campanile again, once they take off the giant condom it's been wearing during restoration.*

The abbey was founded at the end of the 10th century by the widow of Umberto, the Margrave of Tuscany, and further endowed by their son Ugo, 'the Good Mar-grave'. Dante would come here to gaze upon Beatrice, and some 50 years after the poet's death, Dante's first biographer, Boccaccio, used the Badia as his forum for innovative public lectures on the text of *The Divine Comedy*. Curiously, Boc-caccio's (and later, the Renaissance's) principal criticism of the work is that Dante chose to write about lofty, sacred things in the vulgar tongue of Tuscany.

Except for the campanile, the Badia has become a hotchpotch from too many remodellings. Inside, however, are two beautiful things from the Renaissance: the *Tomb of Count Ugo* (1481) by Mino da Fiesole and the *Madonna Appearing to St Bernard* (1485), a large painting by Filippino Lippi. Through an unmarked door to the right of the choir, you can reach the upper loggia of the **Chiostro degli Aranci**, where the Benedictines grew oranges. Built in the 1430s, it is embell-ished with a fine if anonymous series of frescoes on the life of St Bernard.

> *Across from the Badia looms the **Bargello**, a battlemented urban fortress, well proportioned yet of forbidding grace; for centuries it saw duty as*

Florence's police station and prison. Today its only inmates are men of marble, gathered together to form Italy's finest collection of sculpture, a fitting complement to the paintings in the Uffizi (open 8.30–1.50, Tues, Thurs, Fri 8.30–4, closed the second and fourth Mon of the month, and the first and third Sun; adm L8,000). Note the iron lion scaling the flag pole.

The Bargello is 'stone Florence' squared to the sixth degree, rugged *pietra forte*, the model for the even grander Palazzo Vecchio. Even the treasures it houses are hard, definite—and almost unremittingly masculine. The Bargello offers the best insight available into Florence's golden age, and it was a man's world indeed.

Completed in 1255, the Bargello was intended as Florence's Palazzo del Popolo, though by 1271 it served instead as the residence of the foreign *podestà*, or chief magistrate, installed by Guelph leader Charles of Anjou. The Medici made it the headquarters of the captain of police (the *Bargello*), torture chamber and city jail, a function it served until 1859. In the Renaissance it was the peculiar custom to paint portraits of the condemned on the exterior walls of the fortress; Andrea del Castagno was so good at it that he was nicknamed Andrea of the Hanged Men. All of these ghoulish souvenirs have long since disappeared, as have the torture instruments—burned in 1786, when Grand Duke Peter Leopold abolished torture and the death sentence in Tuscany, only a few months behind the Venetians, who were the first in the world to do so. Today the **Gothic courtyard**, former site of the gallows and chopping block, is a delightful place, owing much to an imaginative restoration in the 1860s. The encrustation of centuries of *podestà* armorial devices and plaques in a wild vocabulary of symbols, the shadowy arcades and stately stairs, the big cowardly lions of Oz with rusting crowns, all combine to create one of Florence's most romantic corners.

*The main ground-floor gallery is dedicated to **Michelangelo** and his century, although it's an oddly decaffeinated Michelangelo on display here, low on his trademark angst and ecstasy.*

His *Bacchus* (1496), a youthful work inspired by bad Roman sculpture, has all the personality of a cocktail-party bore. Better to invite his noble *Brutus* (1540), even if he's just a bust—the only one the sculptor ever made, in a fit of republican fervour after the assassination of Duke Alessandro de' Medici. Also by Michelangelo is the lovely *Pitti Tondo* and the unfinished *Apollo/David*. From Michelangelo's followers there's a tippling *Bacchus* by Sansovino, and Ammannati's *Leda and the Swan* (a work inspired by a famous but lost erotic drawing by Michelangelo).

The real star of the room is Benvenuto Cellini, who was, besides many other things, an exquisite craftsman and daring innovator. His large bust of *Cosimo I*

(1548), with its fabulously detailed armour, was his first work cast in bronze; the unidealized features did not curry favour with the boss that poor Cellini worked so avidly to please. Here, too, is a preliminary model of the *Perseus*, as well as four small statuettes and the relief panel from the original in the Loggia dei Lanzi.

The last great work in the room is by Medici court sculptor Giambologna, now again enjoying a measure of the fashionableness he possessed during his lifetime; art historians consider him the key Mannerist figure between Michelangelo and Bernini. Giambologna's most famous work, the bronze *Mercury* (1564), has certainly seeped into popular consciousness as the representation of the way the god should look. The stairway from the courtyard leads up to the shady **Loggia**, now converted into an aviary for Giambologna's charming bronze birds, made for the animal grotto at the Medici's Villa di Castello.

> *Upstairs the **Salone del Consiglio Generale** is dedicated to the greatest works of Donatello.*

This magnificent hall, formerly the courtroom of the *podestà*, contains the greatest masterpieces of Early Renaissance sculpture. And when Michelangelo's maudlin self-absorption and the Mannerists' empty virtuosity begin to seem tiresome, a visit to this room, to the profound clarity of the greatest of Renaissance sculptors, will prove a welcome antidote. Donatello's originality and vision are strikingly modern—and mysterious. Unlike Michelangelo, who went so far as to commission his own biography when Vasari's didn't please him, Donatello left few traces, not only of his long life, but of what may have been the sources of inspiration behind his three celebrated works displayed here. The chivalric young *St George* (1416) is from the façade of Orsanmichele; his alert watchfulness, or *prontezza*, created new possibilities in expressing movement, emotion and depth of character in stone. Note the accompanying bas-relief of the gallant saint slaying the dragon, a masterful work in perspective. Donatello's fascinatingly androgynous bronze *David*, obviously not from the same planet as Michelangelo's David, is young, cool and suave, and conquers his Goliath more by his charming enigmatic smile than by his muscles. Cast for Cosimo il Vecchio in 1430, this was the first free-standing nude figure since antiquity, and one of the most erotic, exploring depths of the Florentine psyche that the Florentines probably didn't know they had.

The same erotic energy and mystery surrounds the laughing, dangerous-looking, precocious boy Cupid, or *Atys Amor*; with its poppies, serpents and winged sandals, it could easily be the ancient idol people mistook it for in the 1700s. Like Botticelli's mythological paintings, Cupid is part of the artistic and intellectual undercurrents of the period, full of pagan philosophy, a possibility rooted out in the terror of the Counter-Reformation and quite forgotten soon after.

Other Donatellos in the *salone* further display the sculptor's amazing diversity. The small, rather haughty marble *David* (1408) was his earliest known work—he was about 20 at the time. In the centre of the hall, his *Marzocco*, the symbol of Florence, long stood on the Ponte Vecchio. Although the two versions of Florence's patron saint, *John the Baptist*, are no longer attributed to Donatello, they show his influence in their striving to express the saint's spiritual character physically rather than by merely adding his usual holy accessories. The *Dancing Putto* and two busts are Donatello's; his workshop produced the gilded bas-relief of the *Crucifixion*.

On the wall hang the two famous trial reliefs for the second set of baptistry doors, by Ghiberti and Brunelleschi, both depicting the *Sacrifice of Isaac.* Between the panels, the vigorous relief of a tumultuous *Battle Scene* is by the little-known Bertoldo di Giovanni, Donatello's pupil and Michelangelo's teacher. There are a number of other excellent reliefs and busts along the walls, by Agostino di Duccio and Desiderio da Settignano, and Luca della Robbia's sweet Madonnas.

> *The remainder of the first floor houses fascinating collections of* ***decorative arts*** *donated to the Bargello in the last century.*

The **Sala della Torre** is devoted to Islamic art. The **Sala Carrand** named after the French donator of works in this room contains splendiferous Byzantine and Renaissance jewellery, watches and clocks, and a Venetian astrolabe. Off this room is the **Cappella del Podestà** where the condemned were given their last rites, their eyes filled with a damaged fresco of the Last Judgement by the school of Giotto, discovered under the plaster in the 1840s; note the scene of Paradise, with the earliest known portrait of Dante, with his piercing gaze and eagle's beak nose.

A stairway from the ivory collection leads up to the **Second Floor**. It houses fine enamelled terracottas of the della Robbia family workshop, a room of portrait busts, beautiful works by Antonio Pollaiuolo and Verrocchio, including his *David* and bust of the lovely *Young Lady with a Nosegay*, with her hint of a smile and long, sensitive fingers. There is also a collection of armour, and the most important collection of small Renaissance bronzes in Italy.

> ***Piazza San Firenze***, *the strangely shaped square that both the Badia and the Bargello call home, is named after the large church of* ***San Firenze***, *an imposing ensemble, now partially used as Florence's law courts. Opposite, the* ***Palazzo Gondi*** *is a fine Renaissance merchants' palace built by Giuliano da Sangallo in 1489 but completed only in 1884; it's not easy to pick out the discreet 19th-century additions. In 1994,*

during roadworks, a section of Roman Florentia's walls and a tower were discovered under the Piazza's pavement.

*Via Ghibellina, flanking the Bargello, leads to the **Palazzo Borghese** (No.110), one of the finest neoclassical buildings in the city, erected in 1822—for a party in honour of Habsburg Grand Duke Ferdinand III. The host of this famous affair was one of the wealthiest men of his day, the Roman prince Camillo Borghese, husband of Pauline Bonaparte and the man responsible for shipping so many of Italy's artistic treasures off to the Louvre. Note the Borghese dragons balancing precariously on the cornice.*

*From here, backtrack a bit and turn right up Via Giralda to **Borgo degli Albizi**, the fine old street that in ancient times was the Via Cassia, linking Rome with Bologna; it deserves a leisurely stroll for its palaces and perhaps even its boutiques. **Palazzo Ramirez di Montalvo** built by Ammannati in 1568 for Cosimo I's favourite, Antonio Moltalvo, is decorated with elaborate graffito and a de luxe model of Cosimo's coat of arms, although the whole is rather worse for wear, sheltering auctioneers and Jehovah's Witnesses. You can't miss No.18, the cinquecento **Palazzo Valori**, nicknamed 'Palazzo dei Visacci' or 'Funny Face Palace' for its owner's curious desire to immortalize Florence's great men (Dante, Boccaccio, Vespucci, Alberti, etc) with surreal, semi-relief herm-busts in blue draperies on three floors of the façade. Borgo degli Albizi ends up in one of Florence's most picturesque little squares, **Piazza San Pier Maggiore**; only the arched portico remains of the church that once stood here and had to be destroyed in 1784 because of its decided lean; the rooms on top look like one of the cosiest addresses in the city.*

*If it, too, fails to answer to the Florence you've been seeking, take Via dell'Oriuolo just around to the left (with a fine view of the Duomo closing off the end of the street), for the **Museo di Firenze Com'Era** (Museum of Florence as It Was), located by the big garden at No.24 (open 9–2, Sun 9–1, closed Thurs; adm).*

The museum is not large at present it contains only a number of plans and maps, as well as a collection of amateurish watercolours of Florence's sights from the last century, and paintings of Florence's surroundings by Ottone Rosai, a local favourite who died in 1957. Today's Florentines seem much less interested in the Renaissance than in the city of their grandparents. For some further evidence, look around the corner of Via S. Egidio, where some recent remodelling has uncovered posters over the street from 1925, announcing plans for paving the war debt and a coming visit of the Folies Bergère. The Florentines have restored them and put them under glass.

The jewel of this museum is right out in front, the nearly room-sized *Pianta della Catena*, most beautiful of the early views of Florence. It is a copy, as the original made in 1490 by an unknown artist—that handsome fellow pictured in the lower right-hand corner—was lost in a Berlin museum during the last war. This fascinating painting captures Florence at the height of the Renaissance, a city of buildings in bright white, pink and tan; the great churches are without their façades, the Uffizi and Medici chapels have not yet appeared, and the Medici and Pitti palaces are without their later extensions.

> *From Via dell'Oriuolo, Via Folco Portinari takes you to Florence's oldest and busiest hospital,* **Santa Maria Nuova**, *founded in 1286 by the father of Dante's Beatrice, Folco Portinari. Readers of Iris Origo's* The Merchant of Prato *will recognize it as the work-place of the good notary, Ser Lapo Mazzei. The portico of the hospital, by Buontalenti, was finished in 1612.*

Start: *Piazza Santa Trínita*
Finish: *Ognissanti*
Walking time: *2 hours*

IV: Piazza Santa Trínita

Florence has always been a city of merchants and bankers; this walk takes in what has been their fashionable high rent district since the days of the Renaissance.

Lunch/Cafés

Amon, Via Pallazuolo 26–28r, ℂ 293146. Closed Sun. This takeaway prepares fresh Egyptian food, including excellent felafel.

Belle Donne, Via delle Belle Donne 16r, ℂ 2382609. A small, almost hidden entrance leads into this colourful trattoria serving Tuscan fare with flare. About L40,000.

Cantinetta Antinori, Piazza Antinori 3, ℂ 292234. Closed Sat and Sun. This chic little wine bar, occupying a corner of Palazzo Antinori, is much frequented by well-heeled tourists, and serves Tuscan fare accompanied by wines from the Antinori estates.

Giacosa, Via Tornabuoni 83r, ℂ 2396226. An elegant bar which serves good sandwiches, cakes, pastries and ice cream. The Negroni (a deliciously lethal mixture of gin, campari and vermouth) was reputedly invented here.

Latte and Company, Via del Parione 46r, closed Sun. This new, sunny milk bar has a range of freshly baked American goodies, unusual sandwiches (from L3,500) and salads (from L5,000 to eat in or to take away).

Il Procacci, Via Tornabuoni 64r. Many of the locals who frequent this high-quality grocers-cum-bar do so to sample the famous *panini tartufati* (truffle sandwiches) and to sip a glass of prosecco.

Rose's, Via del Parione 26r, ℂ 287090. A modern, lively bar which serves light lunches, home-made cakes, sandwiches and even sushi from 8 to 11pm (except Sun and Mon).

Three old Roman roads—Via Porta Rossa, Via delle Terme and Borgo SS. Apostoli—converge in the irregularly shaped **Piazza Santa Trínita**. *Borgo SS. Apostoli is named after one of Florence's oldest churches, the little Romanesque Santi Apostoli (11th century), which is located just off the crossroads in the sunken Piazzetta del Limbo, former cemetery of unbaptized babies.*

Piazza Santa Trínita itself boasts an exceptionally fine architectural ensemble, grouped around the 'Column of Justice' from the Roman Baths of Caracalla, given by Pius IV to Cosimo I, and later topped with a red statue of Justice by Francesco del Tadda. Its pale granite is set off by the palaces of the piazza: the High Renaissance-Roman **Palazzo Bartolini-Salimbeni** by Baccio d'Agnolo (1520) on the corner of Via Porta Rossa, formerly the fashionable Hôtel du Nord where Herman Melville stayed; the medieval **Palazzo Buondelmonti**, with a 1530 façade by Baccio d'Agnolo, once home to the reading room and favourite haunt of such literati in Florence in the 19th century as Dumas, Browning, Manzoni and Stendhal; and the magnificent curving **Palazzo Spini-Feroni** (or Feroni-Spini) to the right of Borgo SS. Apostoli, the largest private medieval palace in Florence, built in 1289 and still retaining its original battlements, now occupied by Salvatore Ferragamo, with a museum displaying 60 years of fashion designs (*open 9–1 and 2–6 Mon–Fri; closed in August; adm free*).

Around the corner on Lungarno Corsini, the British Consulate occupies the **Palazzo Masetti**, ironically once home to the flamboyant Countess of Albany, wife of Bonnie Prince Charlie, who found happiness by leaving the Pretender for

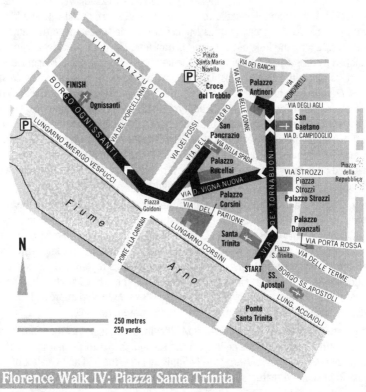

Florence Walk IV: Piazza Santa Trinita

Italian dramatist Vittorio Alfieri, but insisted to the end that she was England's rightful Queen Louise.

> The church of **Santa Trínita** has stood on the west side of the piazza, in one form or another, since the 12th century; its unusual accent on the first syllable (from the Latin Trinitas) is considered to be proof of its ancient foundation.

Although the pedestrian façade added by Buontalenti in 1593 isn't especially welcoming, step into its shadowy 14th-century interior for several artistic reasons, beginning with the **Bartolini-Salimbeni Chapel** (fourth on the right), frescoed in 1422 by the Sienese Lorenzo Monaco; his *Receiving of the Virgin* on the left takes place in a Tuscan fantasy backdrop of pink towers. He also painted the chapel's graceful, ethereally coloured altarpiece of the *Annunciation* (currently under restoration).

The **Sassetti Chapel**, the second to the right of the high altar, is one of the masterpieces of Domenico Ghirlandaio, completed in 1495 for wealthy merchant Francesco Sassetti and dedicated to the *Life of St Francis*, but also to the life of Francesco Sassetti, the city and his Medici circle: the scene above the altar, of Francis receiving the Rule of the Order, is transferred to the Piazza della Signoria, watched by Sassetti (to the right, with the fat purse) and Lorenzo il Magnifico; on the steps stands the great Latinist Poliziano with Lorenzo's three sons. The *Death of St Francis* pays homage to Giotto's similar composition in Santa Croce. The altarpiece, the *Adoration of the Shepherds* (1485), is one of Ghirlandaio's best-known works, often described as the archetypal Renaissance painting, a contrived but charming classical treatment; the Magi arrive through a triumphal arch, a Roman sarcophagus is used as manger and a ruined temple for a stable—all matched by the sibyls on the vault; the sibyl on the outer arch is the one who supposedly announced the birth of Christ to Augustus.

Santa Trínita is a Vallombrosan church and the first chapel to the right of the altar holds the Order's holy of holies, a **painted crucifix** formerly located up in San Miniato. The story goes that on a Good Friday, a young noble named Giovanni Gualberto was on his way to Mass when he happened upon the man who had recently murdered his brother. But rather than take his revenge, Gualberto pardoned the assassin in honour of the holy day. When he arrived at church to pray, this crucifix nodded in approval of his mercy. Giovanni was so impressed that he went on to found the Vallombrosan order in the Casentino.

The Sanctuary was frescoed by Alesso Baldovinetti, though only four Old Testament figures survive on the ceiling. In the second chapel to the left the marble *Tomb of Bishop Benozzo Federighi* (1454) is by Luca, the first and greatest of the della Robbias, and features his trademark enamelled terracotta in bouquets of flowers. On the north side of the nave, in the fourth chapel, a detached fresco by Neri di Bicci portrays San Giovanni Gualberto and his fellow Vallombrosan saints; over the arch you can see him forgiving the murderer of his brother, although it's not easy to make out. Lastly, in the third chapel on the left, there's a gold-ground altarpiece of the *Coronation of the Virgin*, by Bicci di Lorenzo (1430).

> *The streets north of Piazza Santa Trínita have always been the choicest district of Florence, and* **Via de' Tornabuoni** *the city's smartest shopping street. Milan's current status as headquarters of Italy's fashion industry is a sore point with Florence, which used to be top dog and lost its position in the 1970s for lack of a large international airport. Florence, in a few words, wants its business back. Pitti Uomo, the biannual men's ready-to-wear trade fair, is now the most important event of its kind in Italy, and the increase in traffic at the local airport has made the city considerably more accessible. Via Tournabuoni and environs sport window displays that could hold their own in Milan.*

In the bright and ambitious 1400s, when Florence was the centre of European high finance, Via de' Tornabuoni and its environs was the area the new merchant élite chose for their palaces. Today's bankers build great skyscrapers for the firm and settle for modest mansions for themselves; in Florence's heyday, things were reversed. Bankers and wool tycoons really owned their businesses. While their places of work were quite simple, their homes were imposing city palaces, all built in the same conservative style and competing with each other in size like some Millionaires' Row in 19th-century America.

> *The champion among these was the* **Palazzo Strozzi**, *a long block up Via de' Tornabuoni from Piazza Trínita; note the Gucci boutique, where George Eliot lived in 1860 turn right in Via Strozzi for Piazza Strozzi.*

This rusticated stone cube of fearful dimensions squats in its piazza like the inscrutable monolith in *2001: A Space Odyssey*, radiating almost visible waves of megalomania. The palazzo was begun by Benedetto da Maiano in 1489 for the extraordinarily wealthy Filippo Strozzi, head of one of Florence's greatest banking clans and adviser to Lorenzo il Magnifico. When he died in 1491, the façade facing Piazza Strozzi was almost complete; future generations had neither the money nor the interest to finish the massive cornice. And one wonders whether his son, also called Filippo, ever took much pleasure in it; though at first a Medici ally like his father and wed to Piero de' Medici's daughter, Filippo attempted to lead a band of anti-Medici exiles against Florence; captured and imprisoned in the Fortezza da Basso, he stabbed himself, while many other Strozzi managed to escape to Paris to become bankers and advisers to the king of France.

There are few architectural innovations in the Palazzo Strozzi, but here the typical Florentine palace is blown up to the level of the absurd: although of three storeys like other palaces, each floor is as tall as three or four normal ones; even the rings for tying up horses are big enough for elephants. Like Michelangelo's *David*, Florence's other beautiful monster, it emits the unpleasant sensation of what Mary McCarthy called the 'giganticism of the human ego', the will to surpass not only antiquity but nature herself. But the Strozzi, it turns out, were only pikers in the ego stakes; in spite of its enormous dimensions, their Ponderosa could fit neatly into the courtyard of the Pitti Palace (*see* p. 193–7). Nowadays, at least, the Strozzi palace is moderately useful as a space to hold temporary exhibitions.

> *There are two other exceptional palaces in the quarter. At the north end of Via de' Tornabuoni stands the beautiful golden **Palazzo Antinori** (1465, architect unknown), home to one of Tuscany's most prolific wine-producing families; it has the city's grandest Baroque church **San Gaetano** (1648, by Gherardo Silvani) as its equally golden companion, its façade decorated with statues that would fit alright in Rome but look like bad actors in Florence. The second palace, the most celebrated example of domestic architecture in Florence, is the **Palazzo Rucellai**, in Via della Vigna Nuova (undergoing major restoration work since 1995; the façade should be finished by the end of 1998, but the rest of the building will take much longer).*

Its original owner, Giovanni Rucellai, was a quattrocento tycoon like Filippo Strozzi, but an intellectual as well, whose *Zibaldone* or commonplace book is one of the best sources available on the life and tastes of the educated Renaissance merchant. In 1446 Rucellai chose his favourite architect, Leon Battista Alberti, to design his palace. Actually built by Bernardo Rossellino, it follows Alberti's precepts and theories in its use of the three classical orders; instead of the usual rusticated stone, the façade has a far more delicate decoration of incised irregular blocks and a frieze, elements influential in subsequent Italian architecture—though far more noticeably in Rome than Florence itself. Originally the palace was only five bays wide, and when another two bays were added later the edge was left ragged, unfinished, a nice touch, as if the builders could return at any moment and pick up where they left off. The frieze, like that on Santa Maria Novella, portrays the devices of the Medici and Rucellai families (Giovanni's son married another daughter of Piero de' Medici), a wedding believed to have been fêted in the **Loggia dei Rucellai** across the street, also designed by Alberti.

Since 1987, the Palazzo Rucellai (it's still belongs to the family) has housed the **Museo di Storia della Fotografia Fratelli Alinari** (*open 10–7.30; closed Wed; adm*) devoted to the history of photography. Exhibits come from the fascinating archives of the Alinari brothers, who founded the world's first photography society in 1852. Keep an eye out for posters concerning special shows.

> *Behind the Rucellai palace (on Via della Spada) stands the ancient church of **San Pancrazio**, with an antique-style porch by Alberti, guarded by two of the mossiest, most mouldering lions in Italy: one looks like a St Bernard, and the other a muffin. At one point in its up-and-down career the church served as a tobacco factory. Now it's been given a new life as the **Museo Marino Marini**, © 219432 (open Sun 10–5, 10–1, plus Thurs 10–11pm in summer; closed Tues; adm), containing 180 works by Marini, one of the greatest Italian sculptors of this century (1901–80). Marini also worked as a painter and lithographer, and his portraits and favourite subjects (especially the Horse and Rider) are known for their sensuous surfaces and uncanny psychological intensity. If you come on a Saturday at 5.30 (but not in July, August, or September), the **Rucellai Chapel** behind San Pancrazio at 18 Via della Spada should be open for Mass, your only chance to see this minor Renaissance gem designed in 1467 by Alberti, housing a unique model of the Sanctuary of the Holy Sepulchre in Jerusalem that is Giovanni Rucellai's funerary monument. Via della Spada is very different from nearby chic Via Tournabuoni and Via della Vigna. This is a real neighbourhood with busy grocers, butchers and a baker's shop.*

> *Before taking leave of old Florence's west end, head back to the Arno and **Piazza Goldoni**, named after the great comic playwright from Venice.*

The most important building on the piazza, the **Palazzo Ricasoli**, was built in the 15th century but bears the name of one of unified Italy's first prime ministers, Bettino 'Iron Baron' Ricasoli. The bridge here, the **Ponte alla Carraia**, is new and nondescript, but its 1304 version played a leading role in that year's most memorable disaster: a company staging a water pageant of the *Inferno*, complete with monsters, devils and tortured souls, attracted such a large crowd that the bridge collapsed under the weight, and all were drowned. Later it was drily commented that all the Florentines who went to see Hell that day found what they were looking for.

> *Just to the east on Lungarno Corsini looms the enormous **Palazzo Corsini**, the city's most flamboyant piece of Roman Baroque extravagance, begun in 1650 and crowned with a bevy of statues.*

The Corsini, the most prominent family of 17th- and 18th-century Florence, were reputedly so wealthy that they could ride from Florence to Rome entirely on their own property. The **Galleria Corsini** is considered the finest private gallery in the city (*adm by appointment only, © 218994 between 9 and 12, Mon, Wed, Fri; enter from Via Parione*), with paintings by Giovanni Bellini, Signorelli, Filippino

Lippi and Pontormo, and *Muses* from the ducal palace of Urbino, painted by Raphael's first master, Timoteo Viti. It also has the rarest of Florentine amenities: a garden, a 17th-century oasis of box hedges, Roman statues, lemon trees and tortoises, surrounded by large trees once used as *ragnaie*, strung with nets to trap small birds for the spit. Further east on Lungarno Corsini stood the Libreria Orioli, which published the first edition of *Lady Chatterley's Lover* in 1927.

> *While walking along the Lungarno Corsini, stop to enjoy the hugely varied Florence skyline from this vantage point. Lining the river, the palaces themselves are of all shapes and sizes, contrasting with the cluster of red rooftops near San Frediano. Add to these the various bell towers, the Ponte Vecchio, the near hills with San Miniato and Forte Belvedere surrounded by lofty cypresses to the east, and the higher ground of the Valombrosa beyond that. If you happen to be doing this at midday, you will assailed by bell ringing from all directions.*

> *To the west of Piazza Goldoni lies the old neighbourhood of the only Florentine to have a continent named after him. Amerigo Vespucci, or Americus Vespucius in Latin (1451–1512), was a Medici agent in Seville, and made two voyages from there to the New World on the heels of Columbus. His parish church,* **Ognissanti** *(All Saints, open Sat 9–12, Mon and Tues; you may have to ring), is set back from the river behind a dingy Baroque façade, on property donated in 1256 by the Umiliati, a religious order that specialized in wool-working.*

The Vespucci family tomb is below the second altar to the right, and little Amerigo himself is said to be pictured next to the Madonna in the fresco of the Madonna della Misericordia, which is probably another Florentine tall story. Also buried in Ognissanti was the Filipepi family, one of whom was Botticelli.

The best art is in the **Convent**, just to the left of the church at no.42. Frescoed in the refectory is the great *Last Supper*, or *Cenacolo*, painted by Domenico Ghirlandaio in 1480. It's hard to think of a more serene and elegant Last Supper, almost like a garden party with its background of fruit trees and exotic birds; a peacock sits in the window, cherries and peaches litter the lovely tablecloth. On either side of the fresco are two scholarly saints moved here from the church itself: Ghirlandaio's *St Jerome in his Study*, and on the right, young Botticelli's *St Augustine in his Study*.

As you leave, note the extraordinary Art Deco building at No. 60r Borgo Ognissanti, quite an unexpected sight in this very sober street. Piazza d'Ognissanti is dominated by the two five-star hotels which face each other, but the most notable building is the **Palazzo Lenzi**, from the first half of the 15th century and lavishly covered with graffiti; it now houses the French Consulate.

Start: *Santa Maria Novella*
Finish: *Palazzo Medici-Riccardi*
Walking time: *a morning or afternoon*

V: Santa Maria Novella

This walk includes two of Florence's greatest art churches and the stomping grounds of its merchant family whose members through luck, pluck and bucks hit the jackpot and became Grand Dukes.

Lunch/Cafés

Mario, Via Rosina 2r, ℘ 218550. Only open for lunch and closed Sun, this bustling trattoria serves wonderful home-made food at rock-bottom prices. On Fridays, it's worth making a special trip for the fish. (Around L20,000).

Da Nerbone, Mercato Centrale di San Lorenzo, ℘ 219949. Open 7–2, closed Sun. In the heart of Florence's bustling covered market, this food counter with a few formica-topped tables (although many of the locals eat standing up) has been dishing out such traditional fare as tripe sandwiches and boiled beef with *salsa verde* since 1872. For those who are not so keen on offal, there are also hearty soups and the odd salad. A definite bargain.

Palle d'Oro, Via Sant' Antonino 43r, ℘ 288383. This popular and inexpensive restaurant is always crowded at luchtimes—always a good sign. You can eat at the counter, take food away or sit down at the back. About L20,000, closed Sun).

Peking, Via Melarancio 21r, ℘ 282922. If you just can't face another plate of pasta, this popular Chinese restaurant is one of the better of the many in Florence. Don't expect New York or London Chinatown standards. (about L25,000).

Da Sergio, Piazza San Lorenzo 8r. Just by the church of San Lorenzo, and crowded with stall owners from the market. Excellent local dishes and very reasonable prices.

As in Venice and so many other Italian cities, the two churches of the preaching orders—the Dominicans' Santa Maria Novella and the Franciscans' Santa Croce—became the largest and most prestigious in the city, where wealthy families vied to create the most beautiful chapels and tombs. In Florence, by some twitch of city planning, both of these sacred art galleries dominate broad, stale squares that do not invite you to linger; in the irregular **Piazza Santa Maria Novella** *you may find yourself looking over your shoulder for the ghosts of the carriages that once raced madly around the two stout obelisks set on turtles, just as in a*

*Roman circus, in the fashionable carriage races of the 1700s. The arcade on the south side, the **Loggia di San Paolo**, is very much like Brunelleschi's Spedale degli Innocenti, although it suffers somewhat from its use as a busy bus shelter; the lunette over the door, by Andrea della Robbia, shows the* Meeting of SS. Francis and Dominic.

Santa Maria Novella *redeems the anomie of its square with its stupendous black and white marble* **façade**, *the finest in Florence.*

The lower part of the façade, with its looping arcades, is Romanesque work in the typical Tuscan mode, finished before 1360. In 1456 Giovanni Rucellai commissioned Alberti to complete it, a remarkably fortunate choice. Alberti's half not only perfectly harmonizes with the original, but perfects it with geometrical harmonies to create a kind of Renaissance sun temple. The original builders started it off by orienting the church to the south instead of west, so that at noon the sun streams through the 14th-century rose window. The only symbol Alberti put on

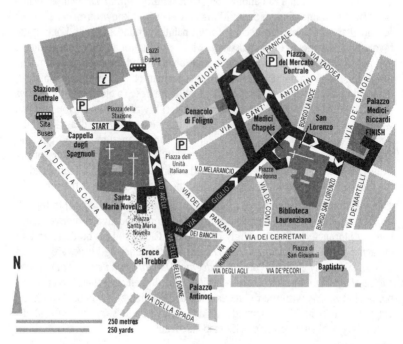

Florence Walk V: Santa Maria Novella

the façade is a blazing sun; the unusual sundials, over the arches on the extreme right and left, were added by Cosimo I's court astronomer Egnazio Danti. Note how the base of the façade is also the base of an equilateral triangle, with Alberti's sun at the apex.

The beautiful frieze depicts the Rucellai emblem (a billowing sail), as on the Palazzo Rucellai. The wall of Gothic recesses to the right, enclosing the old cemetery, are *avelli*, or family tombs.

> The **interior** is vast, lofty and more 'Gothic' in feel than any other church in Florence.

No thanks to Vasari, who was set loose to remodel the church to 16th-century taste, painting over the original frescoes, removing the rood screen and Dominicans' choir from the nave, and remodelling the altars; in the 1800s restorers did their best to de-Vasari Santa Maria with neo-Gothic details. Neither party, however, could touch two of the interior's most distinctive features—the striking stone vaulting of the nave and the perspective created by the columns marching down the aisles, each pair placed a little closer together as they approach the altar.

Over the portal at the entrance is a fresco lunette by Botticelli that has recently been restored, as well as an anonymous 14th-century *Annunciation* in an elaborate 'Tuscan' frame. One of Santa Maria Novella's best-known frescoes is at the second altar on the left: Masaccio's *Trinity*, painted around 1425, and one of the revolutionary works of the Renaissance. Masaccio's use of architectural elements and perspective gives his composition both physical and intellectual depth. The flat wall becomes a deeply recessed Brunelleschian chapel, calm and classical, enclosed in a coffered barrel vault; at the foot of the fresco a bleak skeleton decays in its tomb, bearing a favourite Tuscan reminder: 'I was that which you are, you will be that which I am.' Above this morbid suggestion of physical death kneel the two donors; within the celestially rational inner sanctum the Virgin and St John stand at the foot of the Cross, humanity's link with the mystery of the Trinity. In the nearby Brunelleschi-designed pulpit Galileo was first denounced by the Inquisition for presuming to believe that the earth went around the sun.

There is little else to detain you in the aisles, but the elevated chapel in the left transept, the **Cappella Strozzi**, is one of the most evocative corners of 14th-century Florence, frescoed entirely by Nardo di Cione and his brother, Andrea Orcagna; on the vault pictures of *St Thomas Aquinas and the Virtues* are echoed in Andrea's lovely altarpiece of *The Redeemer Donating the Keys to St Peter and the Book of Wisdom to St Thomas Aquinas*; on the left wall there's a crowded scene of *Paradise*, with the righteous lined up in a medieval school class photograph. On the right, Nardo painted a striking view of Dante's *Inferno*, with all of a Tuscan's special attention to precise map-like detail.

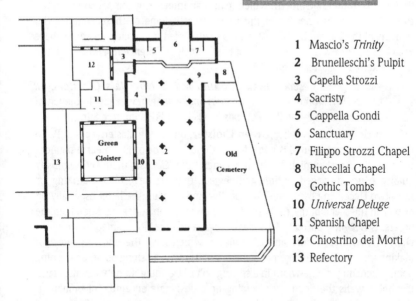

1 Mascio's *Trinity*
2 Brunelleschi's Pulpit
3 Capella Strozzi
4 Sacristy
5 Cappella Gondi
6 Sanctuary
7 Filippo Strozzi Chapel
8 Ruccellai Chapel
9 Gothic Tombs
10 *Universal Deluge*
11 Spanish Chapel
12 Chiostrino dei Morti
13 Refectory

In the richly decorated **Sacristy** hangs Giotto's recently restored *Crucifix* (*c.* 1300), one of the artist's first works; compare it to the famous *Crucifix,* in the **Gondi Chapel**, carved in wood by Brunelleschi, which, according to Vasari, so astonished his friend Donatello that he dropped all the eggs he was carrying in his apron for their lunch when he first set eyes upon it.

The charming fresco cycle in the **Sanctuary** (1485–90), painted by Domenico Ghirlandaio, portrays the *Lives of the Virgin, St John the Baptist and the Dominican Saints* in magnificent architectural settings; little Michelangelo was among the students who helped him complete it. Nearly all of the bystanders are portraits of Florentine quattrocento VIPs, including the artist himself (in the red hat, in the scene of the *Expulsion of St Joachim from the Temple*), but most prominent are the ladies and gents of the Tornabuoni house. More excellent frescoes (currently being restored) adorn the **Filippo Strozzi Chapel**, the finest work ever to come from the brush of Filippino Lippi, painted in 1502 near the end of his life; the exaggerated, dark and violent scenes portray the lives of *St Philip* (his crucifixion and his subduing of the dragon before the Temple of Mars, which creates such a stench it kills the heathen prince) and of *St John the Evangelist* (raising Drusiana from the dead and being martyred in boiling oil). The chapel's beautifully carved tomb of Filippo Strozzi is by Benedetto da Maiano. The

Rucellai Chapel contains a marble statue of the *Madonna* by Nino Pisano and a fine bronze tomb by Ghiberti, which makes an interesting comparison with the three Gothic tombs nearby in the right transept. One of these contains the remains of the Patriarch of Constantinople, who died in the city, an end perhaps hastened by sorrow after the failure of the Council of Florence in 1439 to reunite the Western and Eastern Churches.

> *More great frescoes await in **Santa Maria Novella's Cloisters**, all recently restored and open as a city museum* (entrance just to the left of the church; open 9–2, weekends 8–1; closed Fri; adm; free Sun).

The first cloister, the so-called **Green Cloister**, one of the masterpieces of Paolo Uccello and his assistants, is named after the *terraverde* or green earth pigment used by the artist, which lends the scenes from *Genesis* their eerie, ghostly quality. Much damaged by time and neglect, they are nevertheless striking for their two Uccellian obsessions—perspective and animals, the latter especially on display in the scene of the *Creation*. Best known, and in better condition than the others, is Uccello's surreal *Universal Deluge*, a composition framed by the steep walls of two arks, before and after views, which have the uncanny effect of making the scene seem to come racing out of its own vanishing point, a vanishing point touched by divine wrath in a searing bolt of lightning. In between the claustrophobic walls the flood rises, tossing up a desperate ensemble of humanity, waterlogged bodies, naked men bearing clubs, crowded in a jam of flotsam and jetsam and islets rapidly receding in the dark waters. In the right foreground, amidst the panic, stands a tall robed man, seemingly a visionary, perhaps even Noah himself, looking heavenward while a flood victim seizes him by the ankles. Some of Uccello's favourite perspective studies were of headgear, especially the wooden hoops called *mazzocchi* which he puts around the necks and on the heads of his figures.

The **Spanish Chapel** opens up at the far end of the cloisters, taking its name from the Spanish court followers of Eleonora di Toledo who worshipped here; the Inquisition had earlier made the chapel its headquarters in Florence. The chapel is, again, famous for its frescoes, the masterpiece of a little-known 14th-century artist named Andrea di Buonaiuto, whose subject was the Dominican cosmology, perhaps not something we have much empathy for these days, but here beautifully portrayed so that even the *Hounds of the Lord* (a pun on the Order's name, the 'Domini canes') on the right wall seem more like pets than militant bloodhounds sniffing out heresy. The church behind the scene with the hounds is a fairy pink confection of what Buonaiuto imagined the Duomo would look like when finished; it may well be Arnolfo di Cambio's original conception. Famous Florentines, including Giotto, Dante, Boccaccio and Petrarch, stand to the right of the dais supporting the pope, emperor and various sour-faced hierophants. Off to the right the artist has portrayed four rather urbane Vices with dancing girls, while the Dominicans lead stray sheep back to the fold. On the left wall, *St Thomas Aquinas* dominates the portrayal of the Contemplative Life, surrounded by Virtues and Doctors of the Church.

The oldest part of the monastery, the **Chiostrino dei Morti** (1270s), contains some 14th-century frescoes, while the **Great Cloister** beyond is now off limits, the property of the Carabinieri, the new men in black charged with keeping the Italians orthodox. Off the Green Cloister, the **Refectory** is a striking hall with cross vaulting and frescoes by Alessandro Allori, now serving as a museum.

*Just behind, but a world apart from Santa Maria Novella, another large, amorphous square detracts from one of Italy's finest modern buildings—Florence's **Stazione Centrale**, designed by the architect Michelucci in 1935. Adorned by only a glass block canopy at the entrance (and an early model of that great Italian invention, the digital clock), the station is nevertheless remarkable for its clean lines and impeccable practicality; form following function in a way that even Brunelleschi would have appreciated.*

*One of the medieval lanes leading south from Piazza Santa Maria Novella, Via delle Belle Donne was once known for its excellent brothels. Today it is worth a short stroll to see one of the very few crossroads in Italy marked by a cross, a Celtic custom that never really caught on here—Italians are far more fond of corner shrines to the Madonna or some lucky saint. According to legend, **Croce del Trebbio** (from a corruption of 'trivium') marks the spot of a massacre of Patarene heretics in the 1240s, after the masses had been excited by a sermon delivered by the fire-eating Inquisitor St Peter Martyr from the pulpit of Santa Maria Novella.*

*The walk back from Via delle Belle Donne, along Via del' Giglio, brings you into the beginnings of **San Lorenzo**'s outdoor market stalls, with the Medici Chapels looming up in the foreground.*

The lively quarter just east of Santa Maria Novella has been associated with the Medici ever since Giovanni di Bicci de' Medici commissioned Brunelleschi to rebuild the ancient church of San Lorenzo in 1420; subsequent members of the dynasty lavished bushels of florins on its decoration and Medici pantheon, and on several projects commissioned from Michelangelo. The mixed result of all their efforts could be held up as an archetype of the Renaissance, and one which Walter Pater described as 'great rather by what it designed or aspired to do, than by what it actually achieved'. One can begin with San Lorenzo's façade of corrugated brick, the most *nonfinito* of all of Michelangelo's unfinished projects; commmissioned by Medici Pope Leo X in 1516, the project never got further than Michelangelo's scale model, which may be seen in the Casa Buonarroti. To complete the church's dingy aspect, the piazza in front contains a universally detested 19th-century statue of Cosimo I's dashing father, Giovanni delle Bande Nere, who died at the age of 28 of wounds received fighting against Emperor Charles V.

The **interior**, although completed after Brunelleschi's death, is true to his design, classically calm in good grey *pietra serena*. The artistic treasures it contains are few but choice, beginning with the second chapel on the right housing *The Marriage of the Virgin*, a 1523 work by the Mannerist Rosso Fiorentino. Joseph, usually portrayed as an old man, according to Rosso is a Greek god with golden curls in a flowing scene of hot reds and oranges—a powerful contrast to the chapel's haunting, hollow-eyed tomb slab of the Ray Charles of the Renaissance, Francesco Landini (died 1397), the blind organist whose madrigals were immensely popular and influential in Italian music. At the end of the right aisle, there's a lovely delicately worked tabernacle by Desiderio da Settignano.

Most riveting of all, however, are **Donatello's pulpits**, the sculptor's last works, completed by his pupils after his death in 1466. Cast in bronze, the pulpits were commissioned by Donatello's friend and patron Cosimo il Vecchio, some think to keep the sculptor busy in his old age. Little in Donatello's previous work prepares the viewer for these scenes of Christ's Passion and Resurrection with their rough, distorted, and impressionistic details, their unbalanced, highly emotional and overcrowded compositions, more reminiscent of Rodin than anything Florentine; one critic believes they represent 'the first style of old age in the history of art'. Unfortunately they were set up on columns in the 17th century, just above eye level, like so many things in Florence, a fault somewhat redeemed by a new lighting system. Nearby, directly beneath the dome, lies buried Donatello's patron and Florence's original godfather, Cosimo il Vecchio; the grille over his grave bears the Medici arms and the simple inscription, *Pater Patriae*, 'the Father of his Country'.

It was the godfather's father, Giovanni di Bicci de' Medici, who in 1420 commissioned Brunelleschi to build the **Old Sacristy** *off the left transept.*

Often cited as one of the first and finest works of the early Renaissance, Brunelleschi designed this cube of a sacristy according to carefully calculated mathematical proportions, emphasized with a colour scheme of white walls, articulated in soft grey *pietra serena* pilasters and cornices; a dignified decoration that would become his trademark, something Florentine architects would borrow for centuries. Donatello contributed the terracotta tondi and lunettes, as well as the bronze doors, embellished with lively Apostles. The Sacristy was built to hold the sarcophagi of Giovanni di Bicci de' Medici and his wife; in 1472 Lorenzo il Magnifico and his brother Giuliano had Verrocchio design the beautiful bronze and red porphyry wall tomb for their father Piero the Gouty and their uncle Giovanni. Unfortunately Verrocchio saw fit to place this in front of Brunelleschi's original door, upsetting the careful balance.

The **chapel** across the transept from the entrance to the Old Sacristy houses a 19th-century monument to Donatello, who was buried here at his request near Cosimo il Vecchio. The lovely *Annunciation* is by Filippo Lippi; the large, colourful fresco of the *Martyrdom of St Lawrence* around the corner in the aisle is by Bronzino and has just been restored.

> *Just beyond the Bronzino a door leads into the 15th-century **Cloister**, and from there a stair leads up to Michelangelo's celebrated **Biblioteca Laurenziana** (open Mon–Sat 9–1).*

If Brunelleschi's Old Sacristy heralded the Renaissance, Michelangelo's library is Mannerism's prototype, or Brunelleschi gone haywire, no longer serene and mathematically perfect, but complicated and restless, the architectural elements stuck on with an eye for effect rather than for any structural purpose. The vestibule barely contains the remarkable stair, flowing down from the library like a stone cascade, built by Ammannati after a drawing by Michelangelo. This grand entrance leads into a collection that includes a very rare 5th-century Virgil and other Greek and Latin codices, beautifully illuminated manuscripts, and the original manuscript of Cellini's autobiography; ask for a look around.

> *San Lorenzo is most famous, however, for the **Medici Chapels**, which lie outside and behind the church (open Tues, Thurs, Fri, 8.30–2, 8.30–4; closed first, third and fifth Mon in month; adm exp).*

The entrance leads through the crypt, a dark and austere place where many of the Medici are actually buried. Their main monument, the family obsession, is just up the steps, and has long been known as the **Chapel of the Princes**, a stupefying, fabulously costly octagon of death that, as much as the Grand Dukes fussed over it, lends their memory an unpleasant aftertaste of cancerous bric-a-brac that grew and grew. Perhaps only a genuine Medici could love its insane, trashy opulence; all of Grand Duke Cosimo's descendants, down to the last, Anna Maria Ludovica, worked like beavers to finish it according to the plans left by Cosimo's illegitimate son, dilettante architect Giovanni de' Medici. Yet even today it is only partially completed, the *pietre dure* extending only part of the way up the walls. The 19th-century frescoes in the cupola are a poor substitute for the originally planned *Apotheosis of the Medici* in lapis lazuli, and the two statues in gilded bronze in the niches over the sarcophagi (each niche large enough to hold a hippopotamus) are nothing like the intended figures to be carved in semi-precious stone. The most interesting feature is the inlaid *pietra dura* arms of Tuscan towns and the large Medici arms above, with their familiar six red boluses blown up as big as beachballs. These balls probably derive from the family's origins as pharmacists (*medici*), and opponents sneeringly called them 'the pills'. Medici supporters, however, made them their battle cry in street fights: 'Balls! Balls! Balls!'

> *A passageway leads to Michelangelo's **New Sacristy**, commissioned by Leo X to occupy an unfinished room originally built to balance Brunelleschi's Old Sacristy.*

Michelangelo's first idea was to turn it into a new version of his unfinished, overly ambitious Pope Julius tomb, an idea quickly quashed by his Medici patrons, who requested instead four wall tombs. Michelangelo only worked on two of the monuments, but managed to finish the New Sacristy itself, creating a silent and gloomy mausoleum, closed in and grey, a chilly introspective cocoon calculated to depress even the most chatty tour groups.

Nor are the famous tombs guaranteed to cheer. Both honour nonentities: that of *Night and Day* belongs to Lorenzo il Magnifico's son, Giuliano, the Duke of Nemours, and symbolizes the Active Life, while the *Dawn and Dusk* is of Guiliano's nephew, Lorenzo, Duke of Urbino (and dedicatee of *The Prince*), who symbolizes the Contemplative Life (true to life in one respect—Lorenzo was a disappointment to Machiavelli and everyone else, passively obeying the dictates of his uncle Pope Leo X). Idealized statues of the two men, in Roman patrician gear, represent these states of mind, while draped on their sarcophagi are Michelangelo's four allegorical figures of the *Times of Day*, so heavy with weariness and grief they seem ready to slide off on to the floor. The most finished figure, *Night*, has always impressed the critics; she is almost a personification of despair, the mouthpiece of Michelangelo's most bitter verse:

> *Sweet to me is sleep, and even more to be like stone*
> *While wrong and shame endure;*
> *Not to see, nor to feel, is my good fortune.*
> *Therefore, do not wake me; speak softly here.*

Both statues of the dukes look towards the back wall, where a large double tomb for Lorenzo il Magnifico and his brother Giuliano was originally planned, to be decorated with river gods. The only part of this tomb ever completed is the statue of the *Madonna and Child* now in place, accompanied by the Medici family patrons, the doctor saints *Cosmas and Damian*.

In 1975, charcoal drawings were discovered on the walls of the little room off the altar. They were attributed to Michelangelo, who may have hidden here in 1530, when the Medici had regained Florence and would only forgive the artist for aiding the republicans if he would finish their tombs. But Michelangelo had had enough of their ducal pretences and went to Rome, never to return to Florence. Ask at the cash desk for a permit to see the drawings, as only twelve people can enter at one time

What makes the neighbourhood around San Lorenzo so lively is its **street market**, *which the Florentines run with an almost Neapolitan flamboyance every day except Sunday and Monday. Stalls selling clothes and leather extend from the square up Via dell'Ariento and vicinity (nicknamed 'Shanghai') towards the* **Mercato Centrale**, *Florence's main food market, a cast-iron and glass confection of the 1870s, brimful of fresh fruit and vegetables upstairs, and leering boars' heads and mounds of tripe on the ground floor* (open daily).

Beyond the market, at Via Faenza 42, is the entrance to Perugino's **Cenacolo di Foligno** *fresco, housed in the ex-convent of the Tertiary Franciscans of Foligno. This 1490s Umbrian version of the Last Supper was discovered in the 1850s and has recently been restored* (visit by appointment only, © 284272, Sun and holidays at 10.30).

A block from San Lorenzo and the Piazza del Duomo stands the **Palazzo Medici-Riccardi**, *once home to Florence's unofficial court, where ambassadors would call, kings would lodge, and important decisions would be made.*

Built in 1444 by Michelozzo for Cosimo il Vecchio, it was the principal address of the Medici for a hundred years, until Cosimo I abandoned it in favour of larger quarters in the Palazzo Vecchio and the Pitti Palace. In 1659 the Riccardi purchased the palace, added to it and did everything to keep it glittering until Napoleon and his debts drove them to bankruptcy in 1809. The palace is now used as the city's prefecture.

In its day, though, it was the largest private address in the city, where the family lived with the likes of Donatello's *David* and *Judith and Holofernes*, Uccello's *Battle of San Romano* and other masterpieces now in the Uffizi and Bargello. Frescoes are much harder to move, however, and the Palazzo Medici is worth visiting to see the most charming one in Italy, Benozzo Gozzoli's 1459 *Procession of the Magi*, located in the **Cappella dei Magi** upstairs (*open 9–12.45 and 3–5.15; Sun 9–12.45; closed Wed; adm L6000. Only a few people allowed in at once; in summer you can reserve a time*, © 2760340).

Painting in a delightful, decorative manner more reminiscent of International Gothic than the awakening Renaissance style of his contemporaries, Gozzoli took a religious subject and turned it into a merry, brilliantly coloured pageant of beautifully dressed kings, knights and pages, accompanied by greyhounds and a giraffe, who travel through a springtime landscape of jewel-like trees and castles. This is a largely secular painting, representing less the original Three Kings than the annual pageant of the *Compagnia dei Magi*, Florence's richest confraternity. The scene is wrapped around three walls of the small chapel—you feel as if you had walked straight into a glowing fairytale world. Most of the faces are those of the Medici and other local celebrities (the young Lorenzo il Magnifico posed for the young king dressed in gold); Gozzoli certainly had no qualms about putting himself among the crowd of figures on the right wall, with his name written on his red cap. In the foreground, note the black man carrying a bow. Blacks, as well as Turks, Circassians, Tartars and others, were common enough in Renaissance Florence, originally brought as slaves. By the 1400s, however, contemporary writers mention them as artisans, fencing masters, soldiers and one famous archery instructor, who may be the man pictured here.

The altarpiece, a copy of a *Madonna* by Filippo Lippi, has been moved into the other room of the palace opened to visitors, the **Gallery**, up the second flight of stairs on the right, from the courtyard. It's hard to imagine a more striking contrast than that between Gozzoli and the Neapolitan Luca Giordano (nicknamed *Luca fa presto* or 'Quick-draw Luke'), who painted this hilarious ceiling for the Riccardi in 1683, as a left-handed compliment to the Medici for selling them the palace. No longer mere players in a religious pageant, the Medici, or at least the overstuffed Grand Duke Cosimo III and his unspeakable heir Gian Gastone, take the leading roles, defying the laws of gravity and good taste in an apotheosis of marshmallow clouds.

Start: *San Marco*
Finish: *Opificio delle Pietre Dure*
Walking time: *one full day*

VI: San Marco

Centred around Piazza San Marco on Florence's north side, this walk takes in two mighty opposites of the Florentine Renaissance —the gentle spiritual masterpieces of Fra Angelico and the overweening *David* of Michelangelo in the Accademia.

Lunch/Cafés

Badiani, Via dei Mille 20. Worth a detour for the fantastic ice cream, especially the *buontalenti* with an egg-rich secret recipe.

Bar Genius, Via San Gallo. Good local snack-coffee bar.

Buffet Freddo, Via degli Alfani 70r. It's always a tight squeeze in this little wine shop which has a huge selection of sandwiches plus pastas (L6000), crostini and vegetable flans. A good choice of wines to wash it all down.

Gran Caffè San Marco, Piazza S. Marco. A big bar with home-made cakes, pastries and ice cream. There is a self-service restaurant at the back with a garden.

Il Micio, Via Fra Bartolomeo 52r, ✆ 573257. As well as the full menu (around L35,000), the young owners also serve express single dishes at lunch— a *primo* and two veg or a *secondo* and two veg for L15,000 all in (closed Sun).

Mirò, Via San Gallo 57r, ✆ 481030. This restaurant, a pleasant, airy room with columns and a painted ceiling, serves interesting light lunches (from L15,000; closed Sun).

Rostcceria Alfio e Beppe, Via Martelli 118r. A mouthwatering selection of take-away cooked food. Try the *spiedino arrosto di pollo, tacchino e maiale*— kebabs of chicken, turkey, pork and garlic bread roasted on the spit.

*On the northern edge of the Renaissance city, **Piazza San Marco** is a lively square full of art students from the nearby Accademia. The north side of the square is occupied by the **Church and Dominican Convent of San Marco.***

The convent was Cosimo il Vecchio's favourite pious project; in 1437 he commissioned Michelozzo to enlarge and rebuild it, and to add to it Europe's first public library, where Florentine scholars and humanists rediscovered the ancient classics collected by Cosimo's agents (now in the Biblioteca Laurenziana). A later prior of San Marco, Savonarola, had little use for the Medici, although he owed his position to the influence of Lorenzo il Magnifico in 1491.

San Marco is best known for the works of the other-worldly Fra Angelico (1387–1455). His spiritual qualities were endorsed in 1982 when he was beatified by John Paul II; in 1984 the Pope declared him the patron of artists, taking over St Luke's old job. In residence here between 1436 and 1447, Angelico was put in charge of decorating the new convent constructed by Cosimo. His paintings and frescoes in San Marco, itself unchanged from the 1400s, offer a unique opportunity to see his works in the peaceful, contemplative environment in which they were meant to be seen (*open Tues, Thurs, Fri, 8.30–4, other days 8.30–1.50; closed first, third, fifth Sun and second and fourth Mon in month; adm. Church open 7–12 and 4–7 daily*).

Every painter in the 15th century earned his living painting sacred subjects, but none painted them with the deep conviction and faith of Beato Angelico, who communicated his biblical visions in soft angelic pastels, bright playroom colours and an ethereal blondness, so clear and limpid that they just had to be true. 'Immured in his quiet convent', wrote Henry James, 'he apparently never

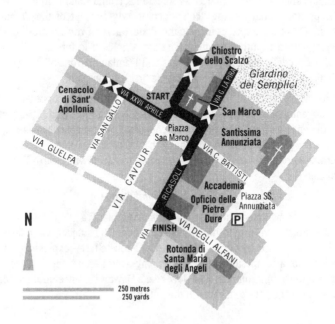

Florence Walk VI: San Marco

received an intelligible impression of evil; and his conception of human life was a perpetual sense of sacredly loving and being loved.' Yet the gentle friar was certainly not artistically naive, and adopted many of his contemporaries' innovations, especially artificial perspective, in his technique.

> *A visit to San Marco begins with Michelozzo's harmonious **Cloister of Sant'Antonino** in which Fra Angelico painted the frescoes in the corners. Just off the cloister, the **Pilgrims' Hospice**, also by Michelozzo, has been arranged as a gallery of Fra Angelico's paintings, which have been gathered from all over Florence.*

Here you'll find his great *Last Judgement* altarpiece (1430), a serenely confident work in which all the saved are well-dressed Italians holding hands, led by an angel in a celestial dance. They are allowed to keep their beautiful clothes in heaven, while the bad (mostly princes and prelates) are stripped of their garments to receive their interesting tortures.

One of the most charming works is the *Thirty-five Scenes from the Life of Christ*, acted out before strikingly bare, brown Tuscan backgrounds, painted as cupboard doors for Santissima Annunziata. Three of the scenes are by Fra Angelico's talented apprentice, Alesso Baldovinetti. The noble, gracefully lamenting figures in the magnificent *Deposition* altarpiece from Santa Trínita stand before an elegant townscape dominated by Angelico's ziggurat-style concept of the Temple in Jerusalem. Other masterpieces include the **Tabernacle of the Linaioli** (the flax-workers), with a beautiful predella. The same holds true for the *Pala di San Marco*, the predella picturing SS. Cosmas and Damian, patrons of medicine and the Medici, in the act of performing history's first leg transplant.

Other rooms off the cloister contain works by Fra Bartolommeo, another resident of the convent whose portraits capture some of the most sincere spirituality of the late 15th century. The **Chapter House** contains Beato Angelico's over-restored fresco of *Crucifixion and Saints*, a painting that lacks his accustomed grace; in the **Refectory** there's a more pleasing *Last Supper* by the down-to-earth Domenico Ghirlandaio.

> *Stairs lead up to Michelozzo's beautiful **Convent**.*

At the top your eyes meet the Angelic Friar's masterpiece, a miraculous *Annunciation* that must have earned him his beatification. The subject was a favourite with Florentine artists, not only because it was a severe test—expressing a divine revelation with a composition of strict economy—but because the Annunciation, falling near the spring equinox, was New Year's Day for Florence until the Medici finally adopted the pope's calendar in the 1600s.

The monks of San Marco each had a small white cell with a window and a fresco to serve as a focal point for their meditations. Angelico and his assistants painted 44 of these; those believed to have been done by the master are along the outer wall (cells 1–9, the *Noli me Tangere*, another *Annunciation*, a *Transfiguration*, a *Harrowing of Hell*, a *Coronation of the Virgin*, and others). He also painted the scene in the large cell used occasionally by Cosimo il Vecchio and other visiting celebrities. One corridor is entirely painted with scenes of the Crucifixion, all the same but for some slight difference in the pose of the Dominican monk at the foot of the Cross; walking past and glancing in the cells successively gives the impression of an animated cartoon. The **Prior's cell** at the end belonged to Savonarola; it has simple furniture of the period and a *Portrait of Savonarola* in the guise of St Peter Martyr (with an axe in his brain) by his friend Fra Bartolomeo. In a nearby corridor hangs a copy of the anonymous painting in the Corsini Gallery, of Savonarola and two of his followers being burned at the stake in the Piazza della Signoria. The **Library**, entered off the corridor, is as light and airy as the cloisters below, and contains a collection of beautiful choir books. Architecturally the library was one of Michelozzo's greatest works, radiating a wonderful spirit of serenity, church-like with its vaulted nave and aisles.

The **church of San Marco** was rebuilt, along with the convent, in the 15th century, though the interior was rearranged by Giambologna and the Baroque façade added in 1780. The right aisle has an 8th-century mosaic from Constantinople, reminiscent of works from Ravenna. There's a painting by Fra Bartolommeo nearby of a *Madonna and Six Saints*; the theatre-like chapel of Sant'Antonio to the left of the altar is by Giambologna; there's a *Resurrection* by Allori (1584), and in the left aisle, behind a statue of Savonarola, the tomb of the great linguist, humanist, and poet Poliziano, a member of Lorenzo il Magnfico's inner circle. Also have a look at the *Annunciation* on the back wall by Jacopo di Cione (1371).

> *Near San Marco, at Via G. La Pira 4, the **University of Florence** runs several small museums; nearly all the collections were begun by the indefatigable Medici.*

The **Geology and Palaeontology Museum** has one of Italy's best collections of fossils, many uncovered in Tuscany, including antiquated elephants from the Valdarno (*open Mon 2–6; Tues–Sat 9–1, 2–8 and first Sun of the month 9.30–12.30; adm L5000, L8000 Sun*). The **Mineralogy and Lithology Museum** houses strange and beautiful rocks, especially from Elba, the treasure island of minerals; there's a topaz weighing in at 151kg, meteorites, and a bright collection of Medici trinkets, worked from stones in rainbow hues (*open Mon–Fri 9–1, first Sun of the month 9.30–12.30; adm free on weekdays, L5000 Sun*). The **Botanical Museum** is of less interest to the casual visitor, though it houses one of the most extensive herbariums in the world; most impressive here are the exquisite wax models of plants made in the early 1800s (*open Mon, Wed, Fri 9–12. Call for information © 2757462; adm free*). Also on Via La Pira is the entrance to the University's **Giardino dei Semplici**, the botanical garden created for Cosimo I. The garden maintains its original layout, with medicinal herbs, Tuscan plants, flowers and tropical plants in its greenhouses (*open Wed 9–12, Mon and Fri 9–12 and 2.30–5 ; adm free*).

> *Backtrack to Piazza San Marco and then continue down Via XXVII Aprile to the Renaissance convent of* **Sant'Apollonia** (*open daily 8.30–1.50, closed the second and fourth Mon and the first, third and fifth Sun of the month*).

Cenacoli, or frescoes of the Last Supper, became almost *de rigueur* in monastic refectories; in several cases the Last Supper fresco is all that remains of a convent. Until 1860, the Renaissance convent of Sant'Apollonia was the abode of cloistered nuns, and their *cenacolo* was a secret. When the convent was suppressed, and the painting discovered under the whitewash, the critics believed it to be the work of Paolo Uccello, but lately have unanimously attributed it to Andrea del Castagno, painted 1445–50. The other walls have *sinopie* of the *Crucifixion*, *Entombment* and *Resurrection* by Castagno; in the vestibule there are good works by Neri di Bicci and Paolo Schiavo

> *Not far away you can enter a radically different artistic world in the* **Chiostro dello Scalzo**, *again off Piazza S. Marco at Via Cavour 69* (open Mon and Thurs 9–1).

Of the Confraternity of San Giovanni Battista, all that has survived is this cloister, frescoed (1514–24) with scenes of the *Life of St John the Baptist* by Andrea del Sarto and his pupil Franciabigio. Del Sarto, Browning's 'perfect painter', painted these in monochrome grisaille, and while the scene of the *Baptism of Christ* is a beautiful work, some of the other panels are the most unintentionally funny things in Florence—the scene of Herod's banquet is reduced to a meagre breakfast where the king and queen look up indignantly at the man bringing in the platter of the Baptist's head as if he were a waiter who had made a mistake with their order.

> *From here backtrack to Piazza San Marco and Via Ricasoli, site of the* **Accademia** *school of art and architecture, founded by Cosimo I in 1562. In 1935 the building was graced with the loggia from the former hospital of San Matteo, a work inspired by the Spedali degli Innocenti complete with della Robbia lunettes. Via Ricasoli makes a beeline for the Duomo. On most days, the view is obstructed by the crowds milling*

In the summer the queues are as long as those at the Uffizi, everyone anxious to get a look at Michelangelo's *David.* Just over a hundred years ago Florence decided to take this precocious symbol of republican liberty out of the rain and install it, with much pomp, in a specially built classical exedra in this gallery.

Michelangelo completed the *David* for the city in 1504, when he was 29, and it was the work that established the overwhelming reputation he had in his own time. The monstrous block of marble—16ft high but unusually shallow—had been quarried 40 years earlier by the Cathedral Works and spoiled by other hands. The block was offered to other artists, including Leonardo da Vinci, before young Michelangelo decided to take up the challenge of carving the largest statue since Roman times. And it is the dimensions of the *David* that remain the biggest surprise in these days of endless reproductions. Certainly as a political symbol of the Republic, he is excessive—the irony of a David the size of a Goliath is disconcerting—but as a symbol of the artistic and intellectual aspirations of the Renaissance he is unsurpassed.

And it's hard to deny, after gazing at this enormous beefcake *alla fiorentina*, that these same Renaissance aspirations by the 1500s began snuggling uncomfortably close to the frontiers of kitsch. Disproportionate size is one symptom; the calculated intention to excite a strong emotional response is another. In the *David*, virtuosity eclipses vision, and commits the even deadlier kitsch sin of seeking the sterile empyrean of perfect beauty—most would argue that Michelangelo here achieves it, perhaps capturing his own feelings about the work in the *David*'s chillingly vain, self-satisfied expression. This is also one of the few statues to have actually injured someone. During a political disturbance in the Piazza della Signoria, its arm broke off and fell on a farmer's toe. In 1991 it was David's toe which fell victim when a madman chopped it off. Since then, the rest of his anatomy has been shielded by glass.

In the Galleria next to the *David* are four of Michelangelo's famous *nonfiniti*, the *Prisoners* or Slaves, worked on between 1519 and 1536, sculpted for Pope Julius' tomb and left in various stages of completion, although it is endlessly argued whether this is by design or through lack of time. Whatever the case, they illustrate Michelangelo's view of sculpture as a prisoner in stone just as the soul is a prisoner of the body.

The Gallery was founded by Grand Duke Pietro Leopold in 1784 to provide students with examples of art from every period. The big busy Mannerist paintings around the *David* are by Michelangelo's contemporaries, among them Pontormo's *Venus and Cupid*, with a Michelangelesque Venus among theatre masks. Other rooms contain a good selection of quattrocento painting, including the *Madonna del Mare* by Botticelli, a damaged Baldovinetti, the *Thebaid* by a follower of Uccello, and Perugino's *Deposition*. The painted frontal of the **Adimari chest** shows a delightful wedding scene of the 1450s with the Baptistry in the background that has been reproduced in half the books ever written about the Renaissance.

The hall off to the left of the *David* was formerly the women's ward of a hospital, depicted in a greenish painting by Pontormo. Now it is used as a gallery of plaster models by 19th-century members of the Accademia, a surreal, bright white neoclassical crowd.

> *Around the corner from the Accademia, in Via degli Alfani 78, is the workshop of* pietre dure, *(inlaid 'hard stones' or semi-precious stones), the* **Opificio delle Pietre Dure** (open 9–2; closed Sun; adm).

Cosimo I was the first to actively promote what was to become Florence's special craft, and it was Ferdinando I who founded the Opificio in 1588 as a centre for craftsmen, mainly to supply the *pietre dure* by the square yard for the Medici chapels. In the late 18th century, the Lorraine dukes made this rather plain fomer convent of San Nicoló into their workshop and museum, and they've been here ever since, creating their 'paintings in stones'; some, like the *Veduta del Pantheon* by Ferdinando Partini are extraordinarily detailed, catching light and shadow in their cold meticulous perfection

> *Still on Via degli Alfani, across Via dei Servi, stands the* **Rotonda di Santa Maria degli Angeli,** *an octagonal building begun by Brunelleschi in 1434, one of his last works and one of the first centralized buildings of the Renaissance.*

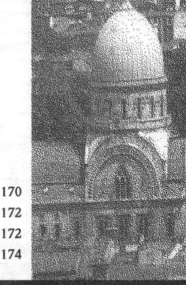

VII: Piazza Santissima Annunziata

Start: *Piazza Santissima Annunziata*

Finish: *Casa Buonarroti*

Walking time: *one day*

This mightily eclectic walk runs the gauntlet from Brunelleschi's serene foundlings' hospital to an Etruscan chimera to Florence's funky flea market, with the odd forays into Tuscan Baroque in between, before ending up at Michelangelo's house.

Caffè Cibreo, Via del Verrochio. There are various bits to Cibreo, and this is the elegant bar where, apart from coffee or aperitivi, you can eat lunch. Try the *polpettone con patate e maionese*, a divine meat loaf with tangy mayonnaise and potato salad.

Cibreo, 2 Via del Verrocchio 5r, ✆ 2345853. Here is the entrance to the poor man's Cibreo serving a limited menu at cheaper prices (around L25,000).

Gelateria Pagetti, Borgo Pinti 69r, closed Sat. This small, modest milk bar makes wonderful ice cream; there's not a huge choice, but it's all delicious.

La Pentola dell' Oro, Via di Mezzo 24r, ✆ 241821. Closed Sun. Officially a club: you may have to pay (a small amount) to join before you can eat here. It's worth it; the menu is very varied and there's lots of unusual dishes. About L35,000.

Il Pizzaiuolo, Via dei Macci 113r, ✆ 241171. Closed Tues. 'They' say that the best pizza in town is to be had here. There's lots more besides...

Ruth's, Via Farini 2/A, ✆ 2480888. This new kosher vegetarian restaurant also serves fish and Middle Eastern food. The menu at lunchtime is somewhat reduced (about L20,000).

Robiglio, Via dei Servi 112. A classic, old-fashioned bar with excellent cakes and pastries, good for the mid-morning cappuccino and brioche. They also do sandwiches and savouries.

Tavola Calda Sant'Ambrogio. Appetizing snacks and meals for cheap prices (around L20,000).

*This walk begins very near to where Walk VI ends, in **Piazza Santissima Annunziata**.*

This lovely square, really the only Renaissance attempt at a unified ensemble in Florence, is surrounded on three sides by arcades. In its centre, gazing down the splendid vista of Via dei Servi towards the Duomo, stands the equestrian statue of Ferdinand I (1607) by Giambologna and his pupil Pietro Tacca, made of bronze

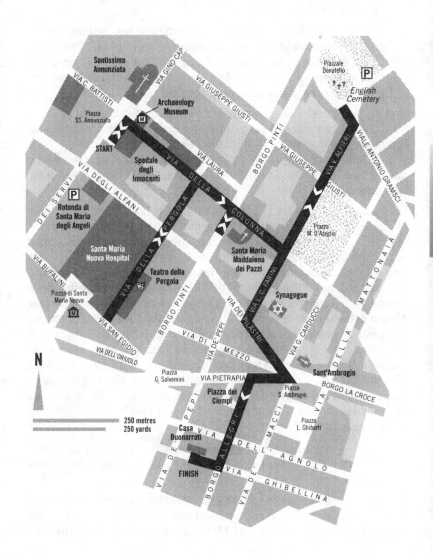

Santissima
Annunziata

Piazzale
Donatello

P

English
Cemetery

VIA C. BATTISTI

VIA GINO CAP

VIA GIUSEPPE GIUSTI

BORGO PINTI

VIA GIUSEPPE

VIALE ANTONIO GRAMSCI

VIA V. ALFIERI

Piazza
SS. Annunziata

Archaeology
Museum

M

START

VIA LAURA

VIA DELLA PERGOLA

VIA DELLA COLONNA

GIUSTI

Spedale
degli
Innocenti

VIA DEGLI ALFANI

Piazza
M. D'Azeglio

DEI SERVI

Rotonda di
Santa Maria
degli Angeli

P

MATTONAIA

VIA BUFALINI

Santa Maria
Nuova Hospital

Santa Maria
Maddalena
dei Pazzi

Teatro della
Pergola

Piazza di Santa
Maria Nuova

M

BORGO PINTI

VIA L. C. FARINI

Synagogue

VIA G. CARDUCCI

VIA DELLA

VIA SAN EGIDIO

VIA DEI PILASTRI

VIA DELL'ORIUOLO

VIA DI DE PEPI

VIA DI MEZZO

N

Piazza
G. Salvemini

VIA PIETRAPIANA

Sant'Ambrogio

BORGO LA CROCE

Piazza
S. Ambrogio

VIA

DELLA

250 metres
250 yards

DE PEPI

Piazza dei
Ciompi

MACCI

Piazza
L. Ghiberti

Casa
Buonarroti

VIA DELL' AGNOLO

BORGO ALLEGRI

VIA DE'

FINISH

VIA GHIBELLINA

from Turkish cannons captured during the Battle of Lepanto. More fascinating than Ferdinand is the pair of bizarre Baroque fountains, also by Tacca, that share the square. Recently restored and possessed of a nominally marine theme, they resemble overflowing tureens of bouillabaisse that any ogre would be proud to serve, presided over by pairs of winged monkeys.

> *In the 1420s Filippo Brunelleschi struck the first blow for classical calm in this piazza when he built the celebrated* **Spedale degli Innocenti** *and its famous portico—an architectural landmark, but also a monument to Renaissance Italy's long, hard and ultimately unsuccessful struggle towards some kind of social consciousness.*

Even in the best of times, Florence's poor were treated like dirt, although babies, at least, were treated a little better. The Spedale degli Innocenti was the first hospital for foundlings in Italy and the world (at the left end of the loggia you can still see the original window-wheel, where babies were left anonymously, until 1875). The place still serves as an orphanage today, as well as the local nursery school.

The Spedale was Brunelleschi's first completed work and demonstrates his use of geometrical proportions adapted to traditional Tuscan Romanesque architecture. His lovely portico is adorned with the famous blue and white tondi of infants in swaddling clothes by Andrea della Robbia, added as an appeal to charity in the 1480s after several children died of malnutrition. Brunelleschi also designed the two beautiful cloisters of the convent; the **Chiostro delle Donne**, reserved for the hospital's wet nurses, is especially fine. Upstairs, the **Museo dello Spedale** (*open 8.30–2, Sun 8–1; closed Wed; adm*) contains a number of detached frescoes from Ognissanti and other churches, among them an unusual series of red and orange prophets by Alessandro Allori; other works include a *Madonna and Saints* by Piero di Cosimo, a *Madonna and Child* by Luca della Robbia, and the brilliant *Adoration of the Magi* (1488) painted by Domenico Ghirlandaio for the hospital's church, a crowded, colourful composition featuring portraits of members of the Arte della Lana, or Wool Guild, who funded the Spedale.

> *The second portico (currently being restored) on the piazza was built in 1600 in front of Florence's high society church,* **Santissima Annunziata,** *named for a miraculous picture of the Virgin.*

Founded in 1250, the church was rebuilt by Michelozzo beginning in 1444 and funded by the Medici, in response to the crowds of pilgrims attracted to the famous icon. To shelter the crowds, Michelozzo designed the **Chiostrino dei**

Voti, a glass-roofed atrium in front of the church that was originally packed with ex-votos that the Florentines have since tidied away. Most of the Chiostrino's frescoes are by Andrea del Sarto and his students but the most enchanting work is Alesso Baldovinetti's *Nativity* (1462)—sadly faded, with the ghost of a transcendent landscape. Also present are two youthful works: Pontormo's *Visitation* and Rosso Fiorentino's Mannerist *Assumption*.

The interior is the most gaudy and lush Baroque creation in the city, the only one the Florentines ever spent much money on during the Counter-Reformation. Michelozzo's design includes an unusual polygonal **Tribune** around the sanctuary, derived from antique buildings and entered by way of a triumphal arch designed by Leon Battista Alberti. Directly to the left as you enter is Michelozzo's marble **Tempietto**, hung with lamps and candles, built to house the miraculous *Annunciation*, painted by a monk with the help of an angel who painted the Virgin's face. Its construction was funded by the Medici, who couldn't resist adding an inscription on the floor that 'The marble alone cost 4000 florins'! The ornate canopy over the *tempietto* was added in the 17th century.

The next two chapels on the left side contain frescoes by Andrea del Castagno, painted in the 1450s but whitewashed over by the Church when it read Vasari's phoney story that Castagno murdered his fellow painter Domenico Veneziano—a difficult feat, since Veneziano outlived his supposed murderer by several years. Rediscovered in 1864, Castagno's fresco of *St Julian and the Saviour* in the first chapel has some strange Baroque bedfellows by Giambattista Foggini; the next chapel contains his highly unusual *Holy Trinity with St Jerome*. The right aisle's fifth chapel contains a fine example of an early Renaissance tomb, that of the obscure Orlando de' Medici by Bernardo Rossellino. The neighbouring chapel in the transept has a painted crucifix by Baldovinetti, while in the next one the *Pietà* is the funerary monument of Cosimo I's court sculptor and Cellini's arch-rival Baccio Bandinelli; in this *Pietà* he put his own features on Nicodemus, as Michelangelo did in the *Pietà* in the Museo del Duomo. Bandinelli's most lasting contribution (or piece of mischief) was his collusion with Cosimo in creating the first 'Accademia' of art in 1562, which eventually did away with the old artist-pupil relationship in favour of the more impersonal approach of the art school.

Nine semicircular chapels radiate from the Tribune. The one at the rear contains the sarcophagus of Giambologna, a far more successful follower of Michelangelo; his pupil Pietro Tacca is buried with him, in this chapel designed by Giambologna before his death. The next chapel to the left contains the fine *Resurrection* by Bronzino, one of his finest religious paintings. On the left side of Alberti's triumphal arch, under a statue of St Peter, is the grave of Andrea del Sarto; next to it is the tomb of bishop Angelo Marzi Medici (1546), one of Florence's loudest Counter-Reformation blasts.

The **Chiostro dei Morti**, off the left transept, is most notable for Andrea del Sarto's rather original fresco, the *Madonna del Sacco* (1525), named after the sacks of grain on which St Joseph leans. The **Cappella di San Luca** off the cloister belongs to the Accademia and contains the graves of Cellini, Pontormo, Franciabigio and other artists (*open 7–12.30 and 4–7*).

> *From Piazza SS. Annunziata, Via della Colonna leads to Florence's* **Museo Archeologico** (open 9–2, Sun 9–1, closed first, third and fifth Sun of the month and open Mon following these days; adm), *housed in the 17th-century Palazzo della Crocetta, originally built for Grand Duchess Maria Maddalena of Austria.*

Just like nearly every other museum in Florence, this impressive collection was begun by the Medici, beginning with Cosimo il Vecchio and accelerating with the insatiable Cosimo I and his heirs. The Medici were especially fond of Etruscan things, while the impressive Egyptian collection was begun by Leopold II in the 1830s. At the time of writing the museum is undergoing rearrangement, but with a little luck you'll be able to find your way around.

The ground floor is devoted to Greek and Etruscan art, including the famous bronze *Chimera*, a remarkable beast with the three heads of a lion, goat and snake. This Etruscan work of the 5th century BC, dug up near Arezzo in 1555 and immediately snatched by Cosimo I, had a great influence on Mannerist artists. There is no Mannerist fancy about its origins, though; like all such composite monsters, it is a religious icon, a calendar beast symbolizing the three seasons of the ancient Mediterranean agricultural year. In the same hall stands the *Arringa-tore*, or Orator, a monumental bronze of the Hellenistic period, a civilized-looking gentleman, dedicated to Aulus Metellus.

Among the beautiful, often strange Etruscan urns and alabaster sarcophagi, mirrors and small bronzes, there is plenty of Greek art; Etruscan noble families were wont to buy up all they could afford. The beautiful Hellenistic horse's head once adorned the Palazzo Medici-Riccardi. The *Idolino*, a bronze of a young athlete, is believed to be a Roman copy of a 5th-century BC Greek original. There is an excellent *Kouros*, a young man in the archaic style from 6th-century BC Sicily, and some beautiful vases. An unusual, recent find, the silver *Baratti Amphora*, was made in the 4th century BC in Antioch and covered with scores of small medallions showing mythological figures. Scholars believe that the images and their arrangement may encode an entire system of belief, the secret teaching of one of the mystic-philosophical cults common in Hellenistic times, and they hope some day to decipher it.

The Egyptian collection has recently been modernized; there are some interesting small statuettes, mummies, canopic vases, and a unique wood-and-bone chariot, nearly completely preserved, found in a 14th-century BC tomb in Thebes. Out in the garden are several reconstructed Etruscan tombs (usually closed). A magnificent collection of precious stones and cameos, coins, and sculpture is kept under wraps and may only be visited by scholars with special permission.

> *East of the Archaeological Museum, Via della Colonna becomes one of Florence's typical straight, boring Renaissance streets. On the right, Via della Pergola houses a perfect example of 17th-century theatre at No.12/32.* **Teatro della Pergola** *are generally acknowledged to be the oldest theatre in Italy and is a superb example of its kind. Prose, chamber music concerts and opera is regularly staged here, and visits are possible by appointment only, generally in the mornings (© 2631807 for information). It's worth detouring down Borgo Pinti, to No.58, to visit one of the city's least known but most intriguing churches,* **Santa Maria Maddalena dei Pazzi**, *a fine example of architectural syncretism* (open 9–12 and 5–7).

The church itself was founded in the 13th century, rebuilt in classically Renaissance style by Giuliano da Sangallo, then given a full dose of Baroque when the church was rededicated to the Counter-Reformation saint of the Pazzi family. Inside it's all high theatre, with a gaudy *trompe-l'oeil* ceiling, paintings by Luca Giordano, florid chapels, and a wild marble chancel. From the Sacristy a door leads down into a labyrinth-crypt to the **Chapter House** (*token adm*) which contains a fresco of the *Crucifixion* (1496), one of Perugino's masterpieces. Despite the symmetry and quiet, contemplative grief of the five figures at the foot of the Cross and the magic stillness of the luminous Tuscan-Umbrian landscape, the fresco has a powerful impact, giving the viewer the uncanny sensation of being able to walk right into the scene. The fresco has never been restored; in the 1966 flood, the water came within 4 inches of the scenes, and stopped. There's also a sinopia of Christ coming down from the Cross to comfort St Francis.

> *Florence's Jewish community, although today only 1200 strong, has long been one of the most important in Italy, invited to Florence by the Republic in 1430, but repeatedly exiled and readmitted until Cosimo I founded Florence's Ghetto in 1551. When the Ghetto was opened up in 1848 and demolished soon after, a new* **Synagogue** *(1874–82) was built in Via L.C. Farini (turn right from Via della Colonna).*

This is a tall, charming Mozarabic Pre-Raphaelite hybrid inspired by the Hagia Sophia and the Transito Synagogue of Toledo. Although seriously damaged by the Nazis in August 1944—and later by the Arno in 1966—it has been lovingly restored. *Security is tight, but the synagogue may be toured Sun–Thurs 10–1 and 2–5 and Fri 10–1 in winter; Sun–Thurs 10–1 and 2–4, Fri 10–1 in summer (men must cover their heads)*. There's a small **Jewish Museum** upstairs, with a documentary history of Florentine Jews as well as ritual and ceremonial items from the synagogue's treasure (*same hours, ℡ 2346654 for information*).

> *From the synagogue walk north to Piazzale Donatello, past shady elegant* **Piazza d'Azeglio***, Florence's experiment with a London square. No.35 on the left bears a plaque in memory of Pellegrino Artusi, (d 1911) renowned cook and author of* La Scienza in Cucina e L'Arte di Mangiar Bene*, the Tuscan cookbook regarded as a culinary bible by many. Donatello's name has suffered terrible indignities of late (many people under the age of 20 only know him as a Teenage Mutant Ninja Turtle) but the Florentines, at least, could spare their greatest sculptor something more dignified than* **Piazzale Donatello***, a swollen artery in the city's frenetic system of* viali *that take traffic around the centre. Pity, too, Elizabeth Barrett Browning (1809–61) and the other expatriates buried in the piazza's* **English Cemetery***—now a traffic island choked in eternal fumes.*

> *South of the synagogue the streets of Sant'Ambrogio are among the most dusty and piquant in the city centre, a neighbourhood where tourists seldom tread. Life revolves around* **Sant'Ambrogio,** *one of the oldest churches in Florence and its neighbouring food market made of cast iron in 1873; the church (rebuilt in the 13th century, simple 19th-century façade) is of interest for its artwork.*

The second chapel on the right has a lovely fresco of the *Madonna Enthroned with Saints* by Orcagna (or Gaddi), and the **Cappella del Miracolo**, just left of the high altar, where a priest in 1230 found drops of blood in the chalice rather than wine, contains Mino da Fiesole's celebrated marble *Tabernacle* (1481) and his own tomb. The chapel has a beautiful fresco of a procession bearing the chalice by Cosimo Rosselli, with depictions of 15th-century Florentine celebrities, including Pico della Mirandola and Rosselli himself (in a black hat, in the group on the left). Andrea Verrocchio is buried in the fourth chapel on the left; on the wall by the second altar, there's a beautiful painting of the *Nativity with angels and saints* by Alesso Baldovinetti. The deteriorated fresco of an atypical

St Sebastian on the entrance wall is by Agnolo Gaddi, along with a *Deposition* by Niccoló di Piero Gerini.

> *From Sant'Ambrogio take Via Pietrapiana to the bustling **Piazza dei Ciompi**, named after the wool-workers' revolt of 1378.*

In the morning, Florence's flea market or **Mercatino** takes place here, the best place in town to buy that 1940s radio or outdated ball gown you've always wanted. One side of the square is graced with the **Loggia del Pesce**, built by Vasari in 1568 for the fishmongers of the Mercato Vecchio and decorated with terracotta seafood; when the Mercato Vecchio was demolished the loggia was salvaged and re-erected here.

> *From Piazza dei Ciompi walk down Borgo Allegri and turn right at Via Ghibellina for No.70, the **Casa Buonarroti**.*

Michelangelo never lived in this house, although he purchased it in 1508. That wasn't the point, especially to an artist who had no thought for his own personal comfort, or anyone else's—he never washed, and never took off his boots, even in bed. Real estate was an obsession of his, as he struggled to restore the status of the semi-noble but impoverished Buonarroti family. His nephew Leonardo inherited the house and several works of art in 1564; later he bought the two houses next door to create a memorial to his uncle, hiring artists to paint scenes from Michelangelo's life. In the mid-19th century, the house was opened to the public as a Michelangelo museum (*open 9.30–1.30; closed Tues; adm*).

The ground floor is dedicated to mostly imaginary portraits of the artist, and works of art collected by his nephew's descendants, including an eclectic Etruscan and Roman collection and a lovely predella of the *Life of St Nicolas of Bari* by Giovanni di Francesco. The main attractions, however, are upstairs, beginning with Michelangelo's earliest known piece, the beautiful bas-relief of *The Madonna of the Steps* (1490–1), the precocious work of a 16-year-old influenced by Donatello and studying in the household of Lorenzo il Magnifico; the relief of a *Battle Scene*, inspired by classical models, dates from the same period. Small models and drawings of potential projects that never came off line the walls; there's the wooden model for the façade of San Lorenzo, with designs for some of the statuary Michelangelo intended to fill in its austere blank spaces—as was often the case, his ideas were far too grand for his patron's purse and patience.

The next four rooms were painted in the 17th century to illustrate Michelangelo's life, virtues and apotheosis, depicting a polite, deferential and pleasant Michelangelo hobnobbing with popes. Those who know the artist best from

The Agony and the Ecstasy may think they painted the wrong man by mistake. One of the best sections is a frieze of famous Florentines in the library. Other exhibits include a painted wooden *Crucifix* discovered in Santo Spirito in 1963 and believed by most scholars to be a documented one by Michelangelo, long thought to be lost; the *contrapposto* position of the slender body, and the fact that only Michelangelo would carve a nude Christ weigh in favour of the attribution.

Start: *Santa Croce*
Finish: *the Horne Museum*
Walking time: *half a day*

VIII: Santa Croce

179

The grand temple of Florentine contradiction, Franciscan Santa Croce is both the city's pantheon and one its greatest galleries of 14th-century frescoes.

Lunch/Cafés

Baldovino, Via San Giuseppe 22r, ℗ 241773. Pizzeria and osteria with a wood oven; there is a wide choice, a Friday fish-based menu and no one will bat an eye if you order just a starter (closed Tues, around L25,000).

Caffé Le Colonnine, Borgo La Croce, where it meets Via de' Benci. A big bar with seats outside in the summer which serves anything from a coffee to pizza and steak.

Osteria dei Benci, Via de' Benci 13r, ℗ 2344923. Closed Sun. A small, rustic trattoria with a young, cheerful staff which serves interesting seasonal dishes on colourful ceramic plates. You can go for something light—a soup in winter or a salad in summer, or for the full works. Their home-made pesto is delicious. (About L30,000.)

Da Benvenuto, Via de' Neri 47r. A lively trattoria serving traditional Tuscan food at reasonable prices.

Buffet Freddo, Via de' Neri at the corner of Via de' Benci. This popular self-service wine bar has a good selection of snack food—cheeses, salamis, prosciutto, *crostini*, etc.—as well as pastas, hot dishes of the day, roast meats, and vegetables.

Il Francescano, Largo Bargellini, Via San Giuseppe 26. Good food, comprehensive wine list and yuppie atmosphere (closed Wed, around L50,000).

La Maremmana, Via de' Macci 77r, ℗ 241226. Reasonably priced set menus, just near the Sant'Ambrogio market (closed Sun, around L25,000).

Vivoli, Via Isola delle Stinche 7r. Considered by Florentines to serve the best ice cream in the whole of Italy.

Enoteca Baldovino, Via S. Giuseppe (on the corner of Borgo Allegri), ℗ 2347 220. Just across the road from the restaurant of the same name, this new wine bar serves coffee, a selection of cold dishes and pastas at lunchtime, accompanied by a good choice of wines and cheer from the Scottish owner.

No place in Florence so feeds the urge to dispute as the church of Santa Croce, Tuscany's 'Westminster Abbey', the largest Franciscan basilica in Italy, a must-see

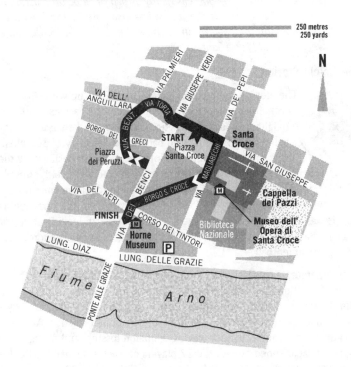

250 metres
250 yards

N

for every tour group. It was here that Stendhal had his revelation: 'I had attained to that supreme degree of sensibility where the divine intimations of art merge with the impassioned sensuality of emotion. As I emerged from the port of Santa Croce, I was seized with a fierce palpitation of the heart; I walked in constant fear of falling to the ground.' But don't be put off; most people manage to emerge from a visit without tripping over themselves.

> *The contradictions begin in the **Piazza Santa Croce**, which has its interesting points—the row of medieval houses with projecting upper storeys, supported by stone brackets; the faded bloom of dancing nymphs on the **Palazzo dell'Antella**; the curious 14th-century **Palazzo Serristori-Cocchi**, opposite the church; a grim 19th-century statue of Dante (if Dante really looked like that, it's no wonder Beatrice married someone else). Because this piazza is the lowest-lying in the city, it suffered the worst in the 1966 flood, when 5m of oily water poured in: note*

the small plaque way high up on the corner of the Piazza and Via Verdi. It's hard to visualize—but was nearly as bad once before; just under it another plaque records that the water also rose in 1557. Notice the watermark on the palazzo on the opposite side of Via Verdi, and elsewhere around Piazza Santa Croce.

The Calcio Storico

The eternal argument of Santa Croce heats up with rib-crunching violence every year, when the various neighbourhoods of Florence compete in a Renaissance football match. Its origins go back to 17 February 1530, when the friendless republic of Florence had been besieged by the army of Charles V for three months. People were cold, hungry and miserable, but they were grimly determined to repel the emperor's troops, who could look down on Piazza Santa Croce from the surrounding hills. It was then decided to give them something worth looking at, to show exactly what the Florentines thought of their siege: they played a rowdy, noisy game of football.

To commemorate this last great thumbing-of-the-communal-nose at the forces of reaction that would smother Florence for centuries, young bloods from the four quarters of the city don hose, baggy doublets and brightly plumed hats every year around the time of the summer solstice. After a good deal of pageantry, banner waving, gonfalon tossing, and a magnificent display of caparisoned horses, the 27 players on each side take the field—an immense rectangle of sand laid in the centre of the piazza. A cannon is fired, and the two sides charge at each other, butting heads, swinging fists, kicking, and grappling in a mix of no-holds-barred rugby, football, and Roman wrestling, anything to get the ball into the adversaries' goal. The prize: a pure white calf.

*As a backdrop to all this sweat and dirt rises **Santa Croce's** neo-Gothic façade, built in 1857–63 and financed by Sir Francis Sloane, whose Sloane Square in London has more admirers than this white with green and pink stripes design, derived from Orcagna's Tabernacle in Orsanmichele. Yet of all the modern façades grafted on to Italy's churches in order to atone for the chronic Renaissance inability to finish any project, this is one of the least offensive. The church is undergoing a major millennial rehauling and roof repair at the time of writing, and any of the many monuments and chapels may be either covered up or closed for restoration.*

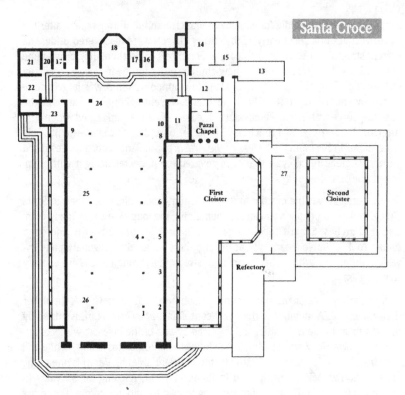

1 Madonna del Latte	**15** Rinuccini Chapel
2 Tomb of Michelangelo	**16** Peruzzi Chapel
3 Monument to Dante	**17** Bardi Chapel
4 Benedetto da Maiano's Pulpit	**18** Sanctuary
5 Vittorio Alfieri's Tomb	**19** Bardi di Libertà Chapel
6 Tomb of Machiavelli	**20** Bardi di Vernio Chapel
7 Donatello's *Annunciation*	**21** Niccolini Chapel
8 Tomb of Leonardo Bruni	**22** Bardi Chapel
9 Tomb of Carlo Marsuppini	**23** Salviati Chapel
10 Tomb of Rossini	**24** Monument to Alberti
11 Castellani Chapel	**25** Tomb of Lorenzo Ghiberti
12 Baroncelli Chapel	**26** Galileo's Tomb
13 Medici Chapel	**27** Museo dell'Opera di S. Croce
14 Sacristy	

Santa Croce was reputedly founded by St Francis himself; during repairs after the flood, vestiges of a small early 13th-century church were discovered under the present structure. It went by the board in Florence's colossal building programme of the 1290s. The great size of the new church speaks for the immense popularity of Franciscan preaching. Arnolfo di Cambio planned it, and it was largely completed by the 1450s, but as in Santa Maria Novella, Giorgio Vasari and the blinding forces of High Renaissance mediocrity were unleashed upon the **interior**. Vasari never had much use for the art of Andrea Orcagna—he not only left him out of his influential *Lives of the Artists* but in Santa Croce he destroyed Orcagna's great fresco cycle that once covered the nave, replacing it with uninspired side altars.

For centuries it was the custom to install monuments to illustrious men in Santa Croce, and as you enter, you can see them lining the long aisles. Like many Franciscan churches, Santa Croce's large size, its architectural austerity and open timber roof resemble a barn, but at the end there's a lovely polygonal sanctuary, which shimmers with light and colour streaming through the 14th-century stained glass.

Perversely, the greater the status of the person buried in Santa Croce, the uglier their memorial. A member of the Pazzi conspiracy, Francesco Nori, is buried by the first pillar in the right aisle, and is graced by one of the loveliest works of art, the *Madonna del Latte* (1478), a bas-relief by Antonio Rossellino, while the **Tomb of Michelangelo** (1570, the first in the right aisle) by Vasari is one of the least attractive. Michelangelo died in Rome in 1564, refusing for 35 years to return to Florence while alive, but agreeing to give the city his corpse. Dante has fared even worse, with an 1829 neoclassical monument that's as disappointing as the fact (to the Florentines) that Dante is buried in Ravenna, where he died in exile in 1321.

Facing the nave, Benedetto da Maiano's **marble pulpit** (1476) is one of the most beautiful that the Renaissance ever produced. Behind it, the **Vittorio Alfieri Monument** (1809) was sculpted by neoclassical master Antonio Canova and paid for by Alfieri's lover, the Countess of Albany. Next is the nondescript 18th-century **Monument of Niccolò Machiavelli**, and then Donatello's restored and pristine *Annunciation* (1430s?), a tabernacle in gilded limestone, the angel wearing a remarkably sweet expression as he gently breaks the news to a grave, thoughtful Madonna.

Bernardo Rossellino's **Tomb of Leonardo Bruni** (1447), another masterpiece of the Renaissance, is perhaps the one monument that best fits the man it honours. Bruni was a Greek scholar, a humanist, and the author of the first major historical work of the period, *The History of Florence*, a copy of which his tranquil effigy holds. The tomb, with its Brunelleschian architectural setting, proved a great inspiration to other artists, most obviously Desiderio da Settignano and his equally beautiful **Tomb of Carlo Marsuppini** (1453) directly across the nave, and the less inspired, more imitative **Monument to Rossini** crowded in to the left. The last tomb in the aisle belongs to Greek-Italian poet and patriot Ugo Foscolo.

Santa Croce is especially rich in trecento frescoes, which provides the unique opportunity to compare the work of Giotto with his followers. The south transept's **Castellani Chapel** has some of the later, more decorative compositions by Agnolo Gaddi (*Scenes from the Lives of Saints*, 1380s). The beautiful **Baroncelli Chapel** was painted with *Scenes from the Life of the Virgin* by Agnolo's father Taddeo, Giotto's assistant in the 1330s, and includes a bright gilded altarpiece, the *Coronation of the Virgin* by Giotto and his workshop.

The next portal gives on to a **Corridor** and the **Medici Chapel** (open for Mass at 6pm daily), both designed by Michelozzo, containing one of Andrea della Robbia's finest altarpieces and a 19th-century fake Donatello, a relief of the *Madonna and Child* that fooled the experts for decades. From the corridor a door leads to the **Sacristy**, its walls frescoed by Taddeo Gaddi (*The Crucifixion*), Spinello Aretino and Niccolò di Pietro Gerini. Behind the 14th-century grille, the **Rinuccini Chapel** was frescoed by one of Giotto's most talented followers, the Lombard Giovanni da Milano, in the 1360s.

> *The frescoes in the two chapels to the right of the sanctuary, the* **Peruzzi Chapel** *and the* **Bardi Chapel***, were painted by the legendary Giotto in the 1330s, towards the end of his life when the artist returned from Padua and his work in the Arena chapel.*

The frescoes have not fared well during the subsequent 660 years. Firstly Giotto painted large parts of the walls *a secco* (on dry plaster) instead of *affresco* (on wet plaster), presenting the same kind of preservation problems that bedevil Leonardo's *Last Supper;* secondly, the 18th century thought so little of the frescoes that they were whitewashed over as eyesores. Rediscovered some 150 years later and finally restored in 1959, the frescoes now, even though fragmentary, may be seen more or less as Giotto painted them. The Peruzzi Chapel contains scenes from the *Lives of St John the Evangelist and the Baptist*. In the Bardi Chapel the subject is the *Life of St Francis*, which makes an interesting comparison with the frescoes in Assisi. The contrast between Giotto's frescoes and the chapel's 13th-century altarpiece, also showing scenes of the *Life of St Francis*, is a fair yardstick for measuring the breadth of the Giottesque revolution. Ruskin, in his *Mornings in Florence*, fixed his attention on St Louis, and spent breathless page upon page praising it as the perfect example of Giotto's style, never suspecting that the entire figure had been added only a few years previously by the frescoes' restorer.

Agnolo Gaddi designed the stained glass around the **Sanctuary**, as well as the fascinating series of frescoes on the *Legend of the True Cross*.

The Legend of the True Cross

This popular medieval story begins with Noah's son, Seth, as an old man, asking for the essence of mercy. The Angel Gabriel replies by giving Seth a branch, saying that 5000 years must pass before mankind may know true redemption. Seth plants the branch over Adam's grave on Mount Sinai, and it grows into a magnificent tree. King Solomon orders the tree cut, but as it is too large to move, the trunk stays where it is and is used as the main beam of a bridge. The Queen of Sheba is about to cross the bridge when she has a vision that the saviour of the world will be suspended from its wood, and that his death will mark the end of the Kingdom of the Jews. She refuses to cross the bridge, and writes of her dream to Solomon, who has the beam buried deep underground. Nevertheless, it is dug up and used to make the cross of Christ.

The cross next appears in the dream of Emperor Constantine before the Battle of Milvian Bridge, when he hears a voice saying that under this sign he will conquer. When it proves true, he sends his mother Helen to find the cross in Jerusalem. There she meets Judas Cyriacus, a pious Jew who knows where Golgotha is, but won't tell until Helen has him thrown in a well and nearly starved to death. When at last he agrees to dig, a sweet scent fills the air, and Judas Cyriacus is immediately converted. To discover which of the three crosses they find is Christ's, each is held over the coffin of a youth; the True Cross brings him back to life. After all this trouble in finding it, Helen leaves the cross in Jerusalem, where it is stolen by the Persians. Their King Chosroes thinks its power will bring him a great victory, but instead he loses the battle, and Persia, to Emperor Heraclius, who decides to return the holy relic to Jerusalem. But the gate is blocked by the Angel Gabriel, who reminds the proud Heraclius that Jesus entered the city humbly, on the back of an ass. And so, in a similar manner, the emperor returns the cross to Jerusalem.

Further to the left are two more chapels frescoed by followers of Giotto: the fourth, the **Bardi di Libertà Chapel**, by Bernardo Daddi and the last, the **Bardi**

di Vernio Chapel, by Maso di Banco, one of the most innovative and mysterious artists of the trecento. The frescoes illustrate the little-known *Life of St Sylvester*—his baptism of Emperor Constantine, the resurrection of the bull, the closing of the dragon's mouth and resurrection of two sorcerers; on the other wall of the chapel are a *Dream of Constantine* and *Vision of SS. Peter and Paul.* In the corner of the transept, the richly marbled **Niccolini Chapel** offers a Mannerist-Baroque change of pace, built by Antonio Dossi in 1584 and decorated with paintings by Allori. Next, the second **Bardi Chapel** houses the famous *Crucifix* by Donatello that Brunelleschi called 'a peasant on the Cross'. The last of the funeral monuments, near the door, belonging to Lorenzo Ghiberti and Galileo, the latter an 18th-century work. For falling foul of the Inquisition, Galileo was not permitted a Christian burial until 1737.

> *Santa Croce's **Pazzi Chapel** carries an entrance fee, but it's well worth it* (open 10–12.30 and 3–5, until 6.30 in the summer; closed Wed; adm).

Brunelleschi, who could excel on the monumental scale of the cathedral dome, saved some of his best work for small places. Unless you know something of the architect and the austere religious tendencies of the Florentines, the Pazzi Chapel is inexplicable, a Protestant reformation in architecture unlike anything ever built before. The 'vocabulary' is essential Brunelleschi, the geometric forms emphasized by the simplicity of the decoration: *pietra serena* pilasters and rosettes on white walls, arches, 12 terracotta tondi of the Apostles by Luca della Robbia, coloured rondels of the Evangelists in the pendentives by Donatello, and a small stained-glass window by Baldovinetti. Even so, that is enough. The contemplative repetition of elements makes for an aesthetic that posed a direct challenge to the International Gothic of the time.

Leaving the Pazzi Chapel (notice Luca della Robbia's terracotta decorations on the portico), a doorway on the left of the cloister leads to another work of Brunelleschi, the **Second Cloister**, designed with the same subtlety and one of the quietest spots in Florence.

> *The old monastic buildings off the first cloister now house the **Museo dell'Opera di Santa Croce** (open 10–12.30 and 3–5, until 6.30 in the summer; closed Wed; adm).*

Here you can see Cimabue's celebrated *Crucifix*, devastated by the flood, and partly restored after one of Florence's perennial restoration controversies. The refectory wall has another fine fresco by Taddeo Gaddi, of the *Tree of the Cross* and the *Last Supper*; fragments of Orcagna's frescoes salvaged from Vasari's obliteration squads offer powerful, nightmarish vignettes of *The Triumph of Death and Hell.* Donatello's huge gilded bronze statue of *St Louis of Toulouse* (1423)—a flawed work representing a flawed character, according to Donatello—was made for the façade of Orsanmichele. The museum also contains works by Andrea della Robbia, and a painting of Mayor Bargellini with a melancholy Santa Croce submerged in the 1966 flood for a backdrop; under the colonnade there's a statue of *Florence Nightingale*, born in and named after the city in 1820.

> *The east end of Florence, which is a rambling district packed with arti-sans and small manufacturers, traditionally served as the artists' quarter in Renaissance times. Still one of the livelier neighbourhoods, with a few lingering artists lodged in the upper storeys, hoping to breathe inspiration from the very stones where Michelangelo walked, it is a good place to observe the workaday Florence behind the glossy façade. Just west of Piazza Santa Croce is a series of streets—**Via Bentaccordi** (where a plaque marks Michelangelo's boyhood home), **Via Torta** and **Piazza dei Peruzzi**—which makes an almost complete ellipse. These mark the course of the inner arcade of the Roman amphitheatre, some stones of which can still be seen among the foundations of the palaces.*

> *One of the things that rather spoils Santa Croce is the predominance of leather and gold shops, even in the narrow back streets. While walking down Borgo La Croce, take time to look at the decorated façade of No. 10, Palazzo Spinelli, which now houses a restoration school. If the heavy wooden door is open, go in and look at the arched courtyard and quiet little garden at the back.*

> *From Santa Croce, canyon-like Borgo Santa Croce leads towards the Arno and the delightful **Horne Museum**, housed in a Renaissance palace.* (Entrance at Via de' Benci 6; open Mon–Sat 9–1; adm L8000).

Herbert Percy Horne (1844–1916) was an English art historian, biographer of Botticelli, and Florentinophile, who bequeathed his collection to the nation. A large *Deposition*, the last work of Gozzoli, sadly darkened with age, a painting by the great Sienese Pietro Lorenzetti, and a tondo by Piero di Cosimo hang on the first floor. The next room contains Horne's prize, Giotto's golden painting of young *St Stephen*; other works include Signorelli's *Redeemer*, a beardless, girlish youth, Beccafumi's *Decalione e Pirra*, and a saccharine *St Sebastian* by Carlo Dolci. Room 3 has a rousing quattrocento battle scene, taken from a marriage chest, good 15th-century wood inlays, and a relief of the head of *St John the Baptist* by Desiderio da Settignano. Upstairs a diptych attributed to Barna da Siena holds pride of place, together with an impressive array of Renaissance furniture and household objects.

IX: The Oltrarno

Start: *Santa Felicità*
Finish: *Porta San Niccolò/*
  Porta San Miniato
Walking time: *at least one full day*

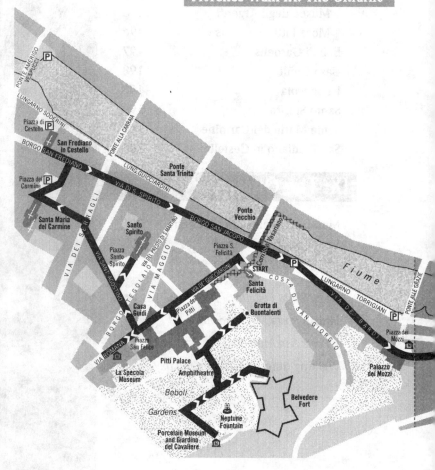

The Oltrarno—the 'beyond' the Arno—is both Florence's populist left bank and the stage for the biggest chunk of Medici megalomania of them all, the Pitti Palace, not to mention several small churches each housing a gem.

Lunch/Cafés

Borgo Antico, Piazza Santo Spirito 6r, ℗ 210437. This lively pizzeria is usually not too crowded at lunchtime, and also serves imaginative pastas and salads.

Cabiria, Piazza Santo Spirito. A café/pub which also serves good-value meals and sandwiches. Pleasant and bustling by day, packed out and noisy at night.

Caffé Ricchi, Piazza Santo Spirito 9r, ℗ 215864. Closed Sun. Apart from making wonderful ice cream, this bar serves a good selection of hot and cold dishes at lunch time. Tables in the piazza in warm weather.

La Casalinga, Via Michelozzi 9r, ℗ 218624. Closed Sun. Now a famous neighbourhood trattoria, the Casalinga is always crowded with locals, students and tourists interested in good-value traditional home cooking.

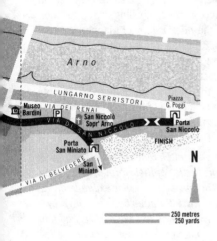

Fuori Porta, Via Monte alle Croce 10r, near the Porta San Niccolò, ✆ 2342483. Closed Sun. A wine bar with a superb selection of bottles which serves pastas and hot and cold sandwiches. Try the excellent *crostini*—toasted bread with various toppings.

Osteria del Cinghiale Bianco, Borgo San Jacopo 43r, ✆ 215706. This cozy restaurant does a special lunch menu for L12,000 *(closed Tues and Wed)*.

Sabatino, Borgo San Frediano 39r, ✆ 284625. Old-fashioned, family-run trattoria serving simple but good Florentine dishes at big wooden tables. Very modest prices *(closed Sat and Sun)*.

Once over the Ponte Vecchio, a different Florence reveals itself: greener, quieter, and less burdened with traffic. The Oltrarno is not a large district. A chain of hills squeezes it against the river, and their summits afford some of the best views over the city.

*Once across the Arno, the Medici's catwalk becomes part of the upper façade of **Santa Felicità**. Its dome was destroyed to make way for the Vasari Corridor in the mid-16th century.*

One of Florence's most ancient churches, rebuilt in the 18th century, Santa Felicità is believed to have been founded by the Syrian Greek traders who introduced Christianity to the city, and established the first Christian cemetery in the small square in front of the church. There is one compelling reason to enter, for here, in the first chapel on the right, is the *ne plus ultra* of Mannerism: Pontormo's weirdly luminous *Deposition* (1528), painted in jarring pinks, oranges and blues that cut through the darkness of the little chapel. The composition itself is highly unconventional, with an effect that derives entirely from the use of figures in unusual, exaggerated poses; there is no sign of a cross, the only background is a single cloud. Sharing the chapel is Pontormo's *Annunciation* fresco, a less idiosyncratic work, as well as four tondi of the Evangelists in the cupola, partly the work of Pontormo's pupil and adopted son, Bronzino.

*As the Medici consolidated their power in Florence, they made a point of buying up the most important properties of their former rivals, especially their proud family palaces. The most spectacular example of this was Cosimo I's acquisition of the **Pitti Palace**, built in 1457 by a powerful banker named Luca Pitti who seems to have had vague ambitions of toppling the Medici and becoming the big boss himself. Follow* *the Vasari Corrodorio down Via de' Guicciardini to the palace, looking up to note the bomb damage to surrounding buildings. Machiavelli died at No. 110/r in 1527. The very smart new forecourt sloping from Via de' Guicciardini to Piazza Pitti was completed for the European Summit in June 1996.*

With its extensive grounds, now the Boboli Gardens, the palace was much more pleasant than the medieval Palazzo Vecchio, and in the 1540s Cosimo I and his wife Eleanor of Toledo moved in for good. The palace remained the residence of the Medici, and later the House of Lorraine, until 1868. The original building, probably designed by Brunelleschi, was only as wide as the seven central windows of the façade. Succeeding generations found it too small for their burgeoning hoards of bric-a-brac, and added several stages of symmetrical additions, resulting in a long bulky profile, resembling a rusticated Stalinist ministry .

There are eight separate museums in the Pitti, including collections dedicated to clothes, ceramics and carriages—a tribute to Medici acquisitiveness in the centuries of decadence, a period from which, in the words of Mary McCarthy, 'flowed a torrent of bad taste that has not yet dried up . . . if there had been Toby jugs and Swiss weather clocks available, the Grand Dukes would certainly have collected them'. For the diligent visitor who wants to see everything, the Pitti is pitiless; it is impossible to see all in one day.

*The Pitti museum that most people see is the **Galleria Palatina**, containing the Grand Dukes' famous collection of 16th–18th-century paintings, stacked on the walls in enormous gilt frames under the berserk opulence of frescoed ceilings celebrating planets, mythology, and of course, the Medici. The gallery is on the first floor of the right half of the palace (ticket office on the ground floor, off Ammannati's exaggerated rustic courtyard, a Mannerist masterpiece. The size of it was determined by the Pitti, who, out of spite for the Strozzi family, made their courtyard large enough to contain the whole Palazzo Strozzi; open 8.30–6.50, Sun 8.30–2, Fri 8.30–11.30; closed Mon; adm L12,000).*

A monumental staircase leads you into the Sala degli Staffieri (with a marble statue of Bacchus by Baccio Bandinelli), through the Gallerie delle Statue, to the neoclassical **Sala Castagnoli**, with the *Tavola delle Muse* in its centre, itself an excellent introduction to the Florentine 'decorative arts'; the table, a paragon of the intricate art of *pietra dura*, was made in the 1870s. The Galleria's best paintings are in the five former reception rooms off to the left, with colourful ceilings painted in the 1640s by Pietro da Cortona, one of the most interesting Italian

Baroque artists. In the **Sala di Prometeo** don't miss Filippo Lippi's lovely *Tondo of the Madonna and Child*, Rubens' *Three Graces*, and Baldassare Peruzzi's unusual *Dance of Apollo*. Some more interesting paintings to ferret out include Filippino Lippi's *Death of Lucrezia* and Raphael's *Madonna dell'Impannata*, both in the adjacent **Sala di Ulisse**. In the next room down you can peek into the Empire bathroom of Elisa Baciocchi, Napoleon's sister, who ruled the Département de l'Arno between 1809 and 1814, and spent most of those years busily redecorating the Pitti.

Caravaggio's *Sleeping Cupid* is in the next room, the **Sala dell'Educazione di Giove**. Just off this room lies the pretty **Sala della Stufa**, frescoed with the *Four Ages of the World* by Pietro da Cortona. Another reception room, the **Sala dell'Iliade** (frescoed in the 19th century), has some fine portraits by the Medici court painter and Rubens' friend, Justus Sustermans. Two *Assumptions* by Andrea del Sarto, *Philip II* by Titian, *La Maddalena* by Artemisia Gentileschi and a Velázquez equestrian *Portrait of Philip IV* share the room with one of the most unexpected residents of the gallery, *Queen Elizabeth*, who seems uncomfortable in such company.

In the **Sala di Saturno** Raphael dominates, with several paintings done in his early Florence days: *Maddalena and Agnolo Doni* (1506) and the *Madonna 'del Granduca'*, influenced by the paintings of Leonardo. Some 10 years later, Raphael had found his own style, beautifully evident in his famous *Madonna della Seggiola* ('of the chair'), perhaps the most popular work he ever painted, and one that is far more complex and subtle than it appears. The rounded, intertwining figures of the Madonna and Child are seen as if through a slightly convex mirror, bulging out—one of the first examples of conscious illusionism in the Renaissance. The **Sala di Giove**, used as the Medici throne room, contains one of Raphael's best-known portraits, the lovely and serene *Donna Velata* (1516). The small painting of *The Three Ages of Man* is usually attributed to Giorgione. Salviati, Perugino, Fra Bartolommeo and Andrea del Sarto are also represented here.

The **Sala di Marte** has two works by Rubens, *The Four Philosophers* and the *Consequences of War*, as well as some excellent portraits by Tintoretto and Van Dyck (*Cardinal Bentivoglio*), and Titian's rather dashing *Cardinal Ippolito de' Medici* in Hungarian costume. Ippolito, despite being destined for the Church, was one of the more high-spirited Medici, and helped to defend Vienna from the Ottoman Turks before being poisoned at the age of 24.

In the **Sala di Apollo** there's more Titian—his *Portrait of a Grey-eyed Gentleman*, the perfect 16th-century English gentleman, a romantic character with an intense gaze, and his more sensuous than penitent *Mary Magdalene*—as well as works by Andrea del Sarto and Van Dyck.

The last room is the **Sala di Venere**, with several works by Titian, including his early *Concert*, a work perhaps partly painted by Giorgione and a powerful *Portrait of Pietro Aretino*, Titian's close and caustic friend, who complained to the artist that it was all too accurate and gave it to Cosimo I. There are two beautiful, optimistic landscapes by Rubens, painted at the end of his life, and an uncanny self-portrait, entitled *La Menzogna* (the Falsehood), by Neapolitan Salvator Rosa. The centrepiece statue, the *Venus Italica*, was commissioned by Napoleon from neoclassical master Antonio Canova in 1812 to replace the Venus de' Medici which he 'centralized' off to Paris—a rare case of the itchy-fingered Corsican trying to pay for something he took.

> *Proceed through the Sala delle Nicchie to the* **State Apartments** (open Jan–Mar by appointment only, ℃ 2388614; April–Dec 8.30–6.45; closed Mon), *situated in the right half of the Pitti.*

These were last redone in the 19th century by the Dukes of Lorraine, with touches by the Kings of Savoy, who occupied them during Florence's interlude as national capital. Among the heavy garish expensive furnishings, there is a fine series of Gobelin tapestries ordered from Paris by Elisa Baciocchi.

> *On the second floor above the Galleria Palatina has been installed Florence's modern* **Galleria d'Arte Moderna** *with works from the late 18th and 19th centuries* (tickets from the office in the courtyard, same hours as the Galleria Palatina; adm exp).

Though the monumental stair may leave you breathless (the Medici negotiated it with sedan chairs and strong-shouldered servants), consider a visit for some sunny painting of the Italy of your great-grandparents. The 'Splatterers' or *Macchiaioli* (Tuscan Impressionists) illuminate **Room 16** and the rest of the museum, forming an excellent introduction to the works by Silvestro Lega, Giovanni Fattori, Nicolo Cannicci, Francesco Gioli, Federigo Zandomeneghi and Telemaco Signorini, with an interval of enormous Risorgimento battle scenes. What comes as a shock, especially if you've been touring Florence for a while now, is that the marriage between painting and sculpture that characterizes most of Italian art history seems to have resulted in a nasty divorce in the late 1800s: while the canvases radiate light, statuary becomes disturbingly kitsch, morbidly, stupefyingly obsessed with death and beauty, culminating on one level with the *Pregnant Nun* and the *Suicide*, by Antonio Ciseri in **Room 19**.

*The ground floor on the left flank of the Pitti was used as the Medici summer apartments and now contains the **Museo degli Argenti**, the family's incredible collection of jewellery, vases, trinkets and pricey curiosities (open 9–7; closed Mon; adm L12,000 valid for Costume and Porcelain Museums).*

The Grand Duke's guests would be received in four of the most delightfully frescoed rooms in Florence, beginning with the **Sala di Giovanni di San Giovanni**, named after the artist who painted it in the 1630s. The theme is the usual Medici tooting their own horns—but nowhere does such dubious material achieve such flamboyant treatment. Here the Muses, chased from Paradise, find refuge with Lorenzo il Magnifico; Lorenzo smiles as he studies a bust of Pan by Michelangelo. His real passion, a collection of antique vases carved of semi-precious stones or crystal, is displayed in a room off to the left; the vases were dispersed with the rise of Savonarola, but Lorenzo's nephew Cardinal Giulio had no trouble in relocating them, as Lorenzo had his initials LAUR.MED. deeply incised into each. The three **Reception rooms** were painted in shadowy blue *trompe l'oeil* by two masterly Bolognese illusionists, Agostino Michele and Angelo Colonna.

The Grand Dukes' treasure hoard is up on the mezzanine. These golden toys are only a small fraction of what the Medici had accumulated; despite the terms of Anna Maria's will, leaving everything to Florence, the Lorraines sold off the most valuable pieces and jewels to finance Austria's wars. Among the leftovers here, however, is a veritable apoplexy of fantastical bric-a-brac: jewelled bugs, cameos, sea monster pendants, interlaced ivory cubes, carved cherry pits, gilt nautilus shells, chalices made of ostrich eggs, enough ceramic plates to serve an army, a Mexican mitre made of feathers, intricate paper cut-outs, cups carved from buffalo horns, and 17th-century busts and figurines made of seashells that would not shame the souvenir stand of any seaside resort.

*The **Museum of Costumes** (open 8.30–1.50; weekly closing alternates between Sun and Mon; adm L8000) is housed in the Meridiana pavilion, the south extension of the Pitti, a dull addition added by the Lorraines; its prize exhibit is the reconstructed dress that Eleanor of Toledo was buried in—the same one that she wears in Bronzino's famous portrait. The **Porcelain Museum** (visits by appointment, © 287096) is housed in the airy casino of Cosimo III, out in the Giardino del Cavaliere in the Boboli Gardens (follow the signs). The **Museo delle Carrozze**, with a collection of Medici and Lorraine carriages and sedan chairs, has recently been reopened.*

> *Finally, the hardest part of the Pitti to get into may be worth the trouble if you're fond of Spanish painting. Until it finds a more permanent home, the **Contini Bonacossi Collection** resides in the Meridiana pavilion.*

This recent bequest includes works of Cimabue, Duccio and Giovanni Bellini, some sculpture and china, and also paintings by El Greco, Goya and Velázquez—the last represented by an exceptional work, *The Water Carrier of Seville* (*open for tours at 10am, Tues, Thurs and Sat—you must make an appointment with the secretary of the Uffizi Gallery*).

> *Stretching back invitingly from the Pitti, the shady green of the **Boboli Gardens**, Florence's largest (and only) central garden, is an irresistible oasis in the middle of a stone-hard city—only now here too you have to pay to get in* (open 9am until one hour before sunset; adm).

Originally laid out by Buontalenti, the Boboli reigns as queen of all formal Tuscan gardens, the most elaborate and theatrical, a Mannerist–Baroque co-production of Nature and Artifice laid out over a steep hill, full of shady nooks and pretty walks and beautifully kept. The park is populated by a platoon of statuary, many of them copies of Roman works, while others are absurd Mannerist pieces like Cosimo I's court dwarf Morgante posing as a chubby Bacchus astride a turtle (near the left-hand entrance, next to Vasari's Corridor).

Just beyond this lies the remarkable **Grotta di Buontalenti** which is one of the architect's most imaginative works, anticipating Gaudì with his dripping, stalactite-like stone, from which fantastic limestone animals struggle to emerge. Casts of Michelangelo's *nonfiniti* slaves stand in the corners, replacing the originals put there by the Medici, while back in the shadowy depths stands a luscious statue of Venus coming from her bath by Giambologna. At the time of writing, the interior of the Grotta is being restored, and after a drought of centuries, it should soon gush again, along with Buontalenti's other *jeux d'eaux.*

The **Amphitheatre**, ascending in regular tiers from the palace, was designed like a small Roman circus to hold Medici court spectacles. It has a genuine obelisk, of Rameses II from Heliopolis, snatched by the ancient Romans and shipped here by the Medici branch in Rome. The granite basin, large enough to submerge an elephant, came from the Roman Baths of Caracalla. Straight up the terrace is the **Neptune Fountain**; a path leads from there to the pretty **Kaffeehaus**, a boat-like pavilion with a prow and deck offering a fine view of Florence and drinks in the summer. From here the path continues up to the **Belvedere Fort** (*see* p.206). Other signs from the Neptune Fountain point the way up to the secluded **Giardino del Cavaliere**, located on a bastion on Michelangelo's fortifications (*open same hours as the Porcelain Museum*). Cosimo III built the casino here to escape the summer heat in the Pitti Palace; the view over the ancient villas, vineyards and olives is pure Tuscan enchantment.

> *In the old days the neighbourhood around the Pitti was a fashionable address, but in the 19th century rents for a furnished palace were incredibly low. Shortly after their secret marriage, the Brownings found one of these, the* **Casa Guidi** *at Piazza San Felice 8, the perfect place to settle; during their 13 years here they wrote their best poetry. It is now owned by the Browning Institute and can be visited weekdays* (open 3–6). *Dostoevsky wrote* The Idiot *while living nearby, at No.21 Piazza Pitti. Note the doorbells at No.13, ten little wrought-iron gargoyles waiting to have their heads pulled. Past the Pitti on Via Romana 17 are two of Florence's great oddball attractions, both part of the* **La Specola** *museum.*

The **Zoological Section** (*open 9–1; closed Wed; adm L6000*) has a charmingly old-fashioned collection of nearly everything that walks, flies or swims, from the humble sea worm to the rare Madagascar aye-aye or the swordfish, with an accessory case of different blades. Some trophies bagged by the hunt-crazy House of Savoy are displayed, and near the end come small wax models of human and animal anatomy, wax eggs, a wax peeled chicken and wax skinned cat. The real horror show stuff, however, is kept hidden away in the **Museum of Waxes** (*open 9–1; closed Wed; adm L6000*). Dotty, prudish old Cosimo III was a hypochondriac and morbidly obsessed with diseases, which his favourite artist, a Sicilian priest named Gaetano Zumbo, was able to portray with revolting realism. His macabre anatomical models were one of the main sights for Grand Tourists in the 18th century.

> *From La Specola walk back to Piazza San Felice, turn left briefly up Via Mazzetta then right in Borgo Tegolaio into Piazza Santa Spirito, the centre of the Oltrarno. In the morning you'll usually find a few markett stalls under the plane trees as well as a quiet café or two. In the evening, however, the bars fill until the early hours with people who meet and chat in the piazza and on the steps of* **Santo Spirito**.

The plain 18th-century façade hides Brunelleschi's last, and perhaps greatest church. He designed Santo Spirito in 1440 and lived to see only one column erected, but subsequent architects were faithful to his elegant plan for the interior. This is done in Brunelleschi's favourite pale grey *pietra serena* articulation, a rhythmic forest of columns with semicircular chapels gracefully recessed into the transepts and the three arms of the crossing. The effect is somewhat spoiled by the ornate 17th-century *baldacchino*, which sits in this enchanted garden of architecture like a 19th-century bandstand.

Most of the good paintings were sold off over the years. The best that remain include Filippino Lippi's beautiful *Madonna and Saints* in the right transept and Verrocchio's jewel-like *St Monica and Nuns*, an unusual composition and certainly one of the blackest paintings of the Renaissance, pervaded with a dusky, mysterious quality; Verrocchio, who taught both Leonardo and Botticelli, was a Hermetic alchemist on the side. The fine marble altarpiece and decoration in the next chapel is by Sansovino; the elaborate barrel-vaulted **Vestibule** and octagonal **Sacristy**, entered from the left aisle, are by Giuliano da Sangallo, inspired by Brunelleschi.

To the left of the church, in the **refectory** (*open 9–2, Sun 8–1, closed Mon; adm L4000*) of the long gone 14th-century convent are the scanty remains of a *Last Supper* and a well-preserved, highly dramatic *Crucifixion* by Andrea Orcagna, in which Christ is seen alone against an enormous dark sky, with humanity ranged below and angels like white swallows swirling around in a cosmic whirlwind. The refectory also contains an interesting collection of Romanesque odds and ends, including 13th-century stone sea-lions from Naples.

> *Retrace your steps down Borgo Tegolaio turning right in Via Sant'Agostino. This becomes Via S. Monaca en route to Piazza Carmine, now, unfortunately a large car park. However, some of its mellow, ochre-coloured buildings are impressive: look through the closed, wrought-iron gate at No.2 to a beautiful garden and huge palazzo which extends all the way to Via dei Serragli. The main attraction is the Oltrarno's other great church,* **Santa Maria del Carmine**.

There is little to say, however, about the rough stone façade, or the interior of Santa Maria del Carmine, which burned in 1771 and was reconstructed shortly after. Miraculously, the **Cappella Brancacci**, one of the landmarks in Florentine art, survived both the flames and attempts by the authorities to replace it with something more fashionable (*open 10–5—last adm 4.45, Sun and hols 1–5; closed Tues; adm L5000; only 30 people admitted at a time for 15 minutes; you can usually avoid waiting if you go at lunch time*). Three artists worked on the Brancacci's frescoes: Masolino, who began them in 1425, and who designed the cycle, his pupil Masaccio, who worked on them alone for a year before following his master to Rome, where he died at the age of 27, and Filippino Lippi, who finished them 50 years later. Filippino took care to imitate Masaccio as closely as possible, and the frescoes have an appearance of stylistic unity. Between 1981 and 1988 they were subject to one of Italy's most publicized restorations, cleansed of 550 years of dirt and overpainting, including the controversial removal of Adam and Eve's fig leaves, enabling us to see what so thrilled the painters of the Renaissance.

Masaccio in his day was a revolution and a revelation in his solid, convincing naturalism; his figures stand in space, without any fussy ornamentation or Gothic grace, and were very much inspired by Donatello's sculptures. Masaccio conveyed emotion with broad, quick brush strokes and with his use of light, most striking in *Expulsion of Adam and Eve*—two first humans in despair at the wilderness of the world, one of the most memorable and harrowing images created in the Renaissance. Next to it, in the *Tribute Money*, the young artist displays his mastery of Brunelleschian artificial perspective and light effects. The three episodes in the fresco show an official demanding tribute from the city (in the centre), St Peter fetching it on Christ's direction, from the mouth of a fish (on the left) and lastly, his handing over of the money to the official. Other works by 'Shabby Tom' include *St Peter Baptizing* and *St Peter Healing with his Shadow* both on the upper register, and *St Peter Enthroned and Resurrecting the Son of the King of Antioch* from a shroud filled with bones, the right half of which was finished by Filippino Lippi. The more elegant and unearthly Masolino is responsible for the remainder, except for the lower register's *Release of St Peter from Prison*, *St Peter Crucified* and *St Paul Visiting St Peter in Prison*, all by Filippino Lippi, based on Masaccio's sketches.

Among the detached frescoes displayed in the cloister and refectory is a good one by Filippino's dad, Fra Filippo Lippi, who was born nearby in Via dell'Ardiglione.

> *Those with the time or inclination to stroll the streets of the Oltrarno can discover one of the city's last real residential neighbourhoods, the streets lined with bakeries and barber shops instead of boutiques and restaurants. The westernmost quarter within the medieval walls, Borgo San Frediano just off Piazza del Carmine, is known for its workshops and unpretentious antique dealers. The **Porta San Frediano**, a tall tower gate guarding the Pisa road, has its old wooden door and locks still in place. The domed 17th-century church of **San Frediano in Cestello**, with its blank poker face, is the landmark along this stretch of the Arno.*
>
> *The neighbourhoods get trendier as you head east, especially along Via di Santo Spirito, its extension Borgo San Jacopo, and wide Via Maggio, leading inland from the Ponte Santa Trínita.*

Via Santo Spirito in particular is lined with fine palaces and medieval towers pruned by the Republic, belonging to some of the oldest noble families in

Florence, embellished with coats of arms above doorways, and some marvellous internal gardens if you are lucky enough to find doors open. Note the little carved arches at waist level, built into the buildings. Some have been blocked up, are used as postboxes or simply as decoration, but they were originally used to dispense wine to thisty passers-by. At No.23 the R painted on the wall indicated a refuge during the war. Note the terracotta Madonna on the right-hand corner before crossing Via Maggio, and the fountain with its Medici crest under the triangular room on the corner of Borgo San Jacopo. The pretty façade of the church of San Jacopo on the left sports a series of delightful little gargoyles above its triple arches.

> Many great medieval bankers also erected their palaces in the Oltrarno. Several may still be seen along Via de' Bardi, east of the Ponte Vecchio. John Pope Henessy lived in No.28 until his death in 1994. Palazzo Capponi (No.36) has a ghoulish gargoyle incorporated into its stone crest above the door. On the right, now a garden, a little plaque commemorates a stay by St Francis in 1211. The church of Santa Lucia dei Magnoli on the left has a della Robbia-like relief above the door, and on the next right-hand corner is the 'Smallest Art Gallery in the World'.

> In Piazza dei Mozzi you'll find the **Museo Bardini/Galleria Corsi** (open 9–2, Sun 8–1; closed Wed; adm L6000), an eclectic collection of art and architectural fragments left to the city in 1922 by the great antique dealer and Risorgimento veteran Stefano Bardini.

Bardini built this rather lugubrious palace, reusing bits of the church of San Gregorio della Pace that originally stood on the site, incorporating the doorways, ceilings and stairs that he salvaged from the demolition of the Mercato Vecchio and other buildings in central Florence, and using the crypt to install his tombs and funereal altarpieces (there's an especially fine one by Andrea della Robbia). Also outstanding are Tino di Camaino's trecento *Charity*, a *Madonna* attributed to Donatello, a panel painting of *St Michael* by Antonio Pollaiuolo, and a magnificent set of Persian carpets, old musical instruments, a cardinal's hat that may have belonged to Silvio Piccolomini, 15th-century papier-mâché dummies, a wooden model of Pisa Baptistry, furniture and armour. More of the Bardini collection, recently left to the city by Stefano's son, will soon be open in the elegant 13th–14th-century **Palazzo dei Mozzi**, also in the piazza. The bridge here, the nondescript postwar **Ponte alle Grazie**, replaced a famous medieval bridge with seven chapels on it, home to seven nuns, who one imagines spent much of their time praying that the Arno wouldn't flood.

Further east, narrow Via di San Niccolò leads to **San Niccolò sopr'Arno**, a church rebuilt in the 14th century, with a lovely fresco in the sacristy of the *Madonna della Cintola* ('of the girdle') by Baldovinetti. The street ends with a bang at **Porta San Niccolò**, an impressively looming gate of 1340 that has recently been restored. A smaller gate just to the south, the **Porta San Miniato**, stands near the walkway up to San Miniato (*see* pp.207–8).

Peripheral Attractions

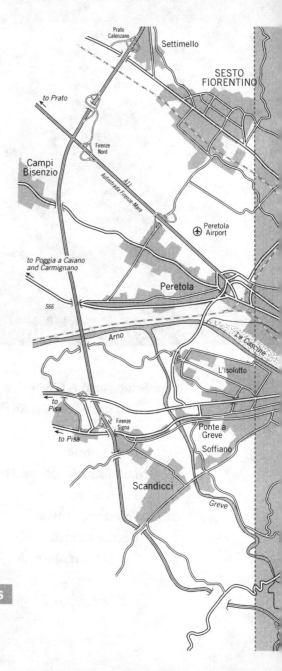

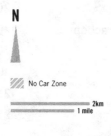

N

No Car Zone

2km
1 mile

Florence Environs

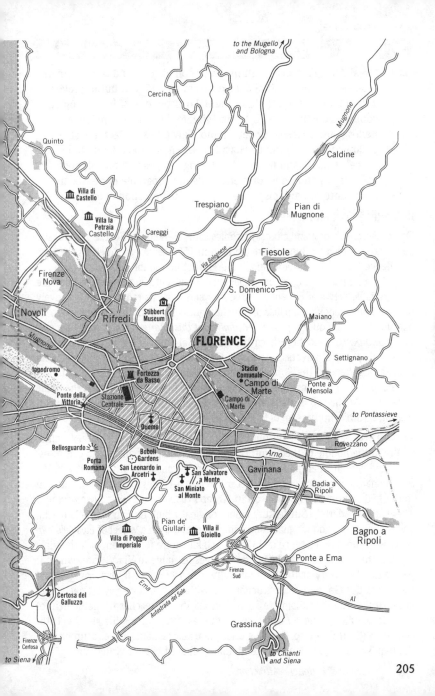

to the Mugello and Bologna

Cercina

Quinto

Villa di Castello

Villa la Petraia Castello

Trespiano

Careggi

Caldine

Pian di Mugnone

Fiesole

Via Bolognese

S. Domenico

Firenze Nova

Novoli

Rifredi

Stibbert Museum

FLORENCE

Maiano

Settignano

Ippodromo

Mugnone

Fortezza da Basso

Stadio Comunale

Campo di Marte

Ponte a Mensola

Ponte della Vittoria

Stazione Centrale

Campo di Marte

to Pontassieve

Duomo

Bellosguardo

Boboli Gardens

Arno

Rovezzano

Porta Romana

San Leonardo in Arcetri

San Salvatore a Monte

Gavinana

San Miniato al Monte

Badia a Ripoli

Pian de' Giullari

Villa il Gioiello

Villa di Poggio Imperiale

Bagno a Ripoli

Firenze Sud

Ponte a Ema

Ema

Autostrada del Sole

A1

Certosa del Galluzzo

Grassina

Firenze Certosa

to Siena

to Chianti and Siena

Great Aunt Florence, with her dour complexion and severe, lined face, never was much of a looker from street level, but improves with a bit of distance, either mental or from one of her hilltop balconies: the Belvedere Fort, San Miniato, Piazzale Michelangelo, Bellosguardo, Fiesole or Settignano. Few cities, in fact, are so endowed with stunning vistas; and when you look down on Florence's palaces and towers, her loping bridges and red tile roofs and famous churches, Brunelleschi's incomparable dome seems even more remarkable, hovering like a benediction over the city.

Belvedere Fort and Arcetri

One of Florence's best and closest balconies is the **Belvedere Fort**, a graceful six-point star designed by Buontalenti and built in 1590–5, not so much for the sake of defence but to remind any remaining Florentine republicans who was boss. Since 1958, it has been used for special exhibitions, but you can always enjoy the unforgettable views of Florence and countryside from its ramparts. It is a lovely place to bring a book for a pause in frenetic sightseeing, and there is a big lawn on one side to stretch out on (*open 9–6 daily, but this changes when there are special exhibitions*). Get there from the Boboli Gardens, or by ascending one of Florence's prettiest streets, **Costa San Giorgio**, which begins in Piazza Santa Felicità, just beyond the Ponte Vecchio, and winds up the hill, lined with old villas and walled gardens. The villa at No.19 was, from 1610 to 1631, the home of Galileo. At the top of the street stands the arch of the **Porta San Giorgio**, bearing a 13th-century relief of St George and the dragon.

Above Porta San Giorgio, yet only 10 minutes' walk from the Ponte Vecchio, you're in the middle of the country, a rolling landscape of olives and cypresses, villas and gardens: here, at least, rural Tuscany begins right at the city wall. Via San Leonardo winds its way out towards Arcetri; a 10-minute walk will take you to the 11th-century **San Leonardo in Arcetri** (*usually open Sunday mornings*). There is a wonderful 13th-century pulpit, originally built for San Pier Scheraggio, and a small rose window, made according to legend from a wheel of Fiesole's *carroccio*, captured by Florence in 1125. A half-kilometre further on, past the Viale Galileo crossroads, Via San Leonardo changes its name to Via Viviani, where it passes the **Astrophysical Observatory** (which you can visit, day or night) and the **Torre del Gallo**, a reconstruction of a 14th-century tower by art dealer Stefano Bardini. Another kilometre further on Via Viviani reaches the settlement of Pian de' Giullari, where Galileo spent the last years of his life, in the 16th-century **Villa il Gioiello**, virtually under house arrest after his encounter with the Inquisition in 1631, and where Milton is believed to have visited him.

San Miniato

From Porta San Miniato you can walk up to San Miniato church on the stepped Via di San Salvatore al Monte, complete with the Stations of the Cross, or take the less pious bus 13 up the scenic Viale dei Colli from the station or Piazza del Duomo. High atop its monumental steps, San Miniato's distinctive and beautiful façade can be seen from almost anywhere in Florence, although relatively few visitors take the time to visit one of the finest Romanesque churches in Italy (*open 8–12.30 and 2–6, all day Sun*).

San Miniato was built in 1015, over an earlier church that marked the spot where the head of St Minias, a 3rd-century Roman soldier, bounced when the Romans axed it off. Despite its distance from the centre San Miniato has always been one of the churches dearest to the Florentines' hearts. The remarkable geometric pattern of green, black and white marble that adorns its façade was begun in 1090, though funds only permitted the embellishment of the lower, simpler half of the front; the upper half, full of curious astrological symbolism (someone has just written a whole book about it), was added in the 12th century, paid for by the Arte di Calimala, the guild that made a fortune buying bolts of fine wool, dyeing them a deep red or scarlet that no one else in Europe could imitate, then selling them back for twice the price; their proud gold eagle stands at the top of the roof. The glittering mosaic of Christ, the Virgin and St Minias, came slightly later.

The Calimala was also responsible for decorating the interior; as in many Romanesque churches with an important martyr's tomb, the crypt gets centre stage, and the presbytery is raised above it. As the Calimala became richer, so did the fittings; the delicate intarsia **marble floor** of animals and zodiac symbols dates from 1207. The lower walls were frescoed in the 14th and 15th centuries, and include an enormous St Christopher. At the end of the nave stands Michelozzo's unique, free-standing **Cappella del Crocifisso**, built in 1448 to hold the crucifix that spoke to St John Gualberto (now in Santa Trínita); it is magnificently carved and adorned with terracottas by Luca della Robbia. To enhance a visit to San Miniato, go at 4.30pm to hear Gregorian chanting by the monks.

Off the left nave is one of Florence's Renaissance showcases, the **Chapel of the Cardinal of Portugal** (1461–6). The 25-year-old cardinal, a member of the Portuguese royal family, happened to die in Florence at an auspicious moment, when the Medici couldn't spend enough on publicly prominent art, and when some of the greatest artists of the quattrocento were at the height of their careers. The chapel was designed by Manetti, Brunelleschi's pupil; the ceiling was exquisitely decorated with enamelled terracotta and medallions by Luca della Robbia; the tomb of the Cardinal was beautifully carved by Antonio Rossellino; the fresco of the *Annunciation* was charmingly painted by Alesso Baldovinetti; the altarpiece of *Three Saints* is a copy of the original by Piero Pollaiuolo.

Up the steps of the choir more treasures await. The marble transenna and pulpit were carved in 1207, with art and a touch of medieval humour. Playful geometric patterns frame the mosaic in the apse, *Christ between the Virgin and St Minias*, made in 1297 by artists imported from Ravenna, and later restored by Baldovinetti. The colourful **Sacristy** on the right was frescoed by Spinello Aretino in 1387, but made rather flat by subsequent restoration. In the **Crypt** an 11th-century altar holds the relics of St Minias; the columns are topped by ancient capitals. The **cloister** has frescoes of the *Holy Fathers* by Paolo Uccello, remarkable works in painstaking and fantastical perspective, rediscovered in 1925.

The panorama of Florence from San Miniato is lovely to behold, but such thoughts were hardly foremost in Michelangelo's mind during the Siege of Florence. The hill was vulnerable, and to defend it he hastily erected the fortress (now surrounding the cemetery to the left of the church), placed cannons in the unfinished 16th-century campanile (built to replace an original which fell over), and shielded the tower from artillery with mattresses. He grew fond of the small church below San Miniato, **San Salvatore al Monte**, built by Cronaca in the late 1400s, which he called his 'pretty country lass'.

With these associations in mind, perhaps, the city named the vast, square terrace car park below, **Piazzale Michelangelo**, the most popular viewpoint only because it is the only one capable of accommodating an unlimited number of tour buses. On Sunday afternoons, crowds of Florentines habitually make a stop here as well during their afternoon *passeggiata* (stroll). Besides another copy of the *David* and a fun, tacky carnival atmosphere rampant with souvenirs, balloons and ice cream, the Piazzale offers views that can reach as far as Pistoia on a clear day.

Bellosguardo

Many would argue that the finest of all views over Florence is to be had from Bellosguardo, located almost straight up from Porta Romana at the end of the Boboli Gardens or Piazza Torquato Tasso. Non-mountaineers may want to take a taxi; the famous viewpoint, from where you can see every church façade in the city, is just before Piazza Bellosguardo. The area is a peaceful little oasis of superb villas and houses gathered round a square—there are no shops, bars or indeed anything commercial. The grandest villa, Villa Bellosguardo, was built in 1780 for Marquis Orazio Pucci, ancestor of the late Florentine fashion designer Emilio Pucci. The great tenor Enrico Caruso bought it for his retirement, although he lived there for only three years before he died, in 1921; he wanted his villa to become an academy of *bel canto*, and apparently he's about to get his wish.

If you are anywhere near the centre of the city it is easy to take the bus to see Florence's riverside park, its pretty Russian church or its quirkiest museum.

The Cascine

Bus 17 from the station or Duomo will take you through the congestion to the Cascine, which is the long (3.5km), narrow public park lining this bank of the Arno. This was originally used as the Medici's dairy farm, or cascina, *and later as a Grand Ducal hunting park and theatre for public spectacles.*

The newer sections of the city are irredeemably dull. Much of Florence's traffic problem is channelled through its ring of avenues, or *viali*, laid out in the 1860s by Giuseppe Poggi to replace the demolished walls. On and along them are scattered points of interest, including some of the old city gates; the distances involved and danger of carbon monoxide poisoning on the *viali* make the idea of walking insane.

A windy autumn day here in 1819 inspired Shelley to compose the 'Ode to the West Wind'. Three years later Shelley's drowned body was burnt on a pyre in Viareggio, by his friend Trelawny; curiously, a similar incineration took place in the Cascine in 1870 when the Maharaja of Kohlapur died in Florence. According to ritual his body had to be burned near the confluence of two rivers, in this case, the Arno and Mugnone at the far end of the park, on a spot now marked by the *Ponte all'Indiano* (the Indian's Bridge), a modern, bright rust-coloured road bridge which can be seen for miles around. Florentines come to the Cascine to play; it contains a riding school, race tracks, a small amusement park and zoo for the children, tennis courts, and a swimming-pool; the Grand Ducal railway terminus, Stazione Leopolda, is about to be converted into a concert hall. At night, the *viale* which runs parallel to the river and the Cascine is the favourite hang-out for transvestites and the car drivers that ogle them.

Fortezza da Basso

The same bus continues to the train station, just beyond which cars and buses hurtle around the **Fortezza da Basso**, an enormous bulk built by Antonio da Sangallo on orders from Alessandro de' Medici in 1534. It immediately became the most hated symbol of Medici tyranny. Ironically, the duke who built the Fortezza da Basso was one of very few people to meet his end within its ramparts—stabbed by his relative and bosom companion Lorenzaccio' de' Medici. As a fortress, the place never saw any action which was as thrilling or vicious as the Pitti fashion shows that take place behind the walls in its 1978 exhibition hall.

Russian Church

Just east of the Fortezza, at the corner of Via Leone X and Viale Milton, there's an unexpected sight rising above the sleepy residential neighbourhood—the five graceful and very lofty colour-tiled onion domes of the **Russian Church**, made even more exotic by the palm tree tickling its side. In the 19th century, Florence was a popular winter retreat for Russians who could afford it, among them Dostoievsky and Maxim Gorki. Completed by Russian architects in 1904, it is a pretty jewel box of brick and majolica decoration, open on the third Sunday of the month at 10.30 am when the priest from Nice comes to hold services in Russian.

The Stibbert Museum

From Piazza della Libertà, dull Via Vittorio Emanuele heads a kilometre north to Via Stibbert and the Stibbert Museum (alternatively, take bus 31 or 32 from the station). Those who make the journey to see the lifetime's accumulations of Frederick Stibbert (1838–1906), who fought with Garibaldi and hobnobbed with Queen Victoria, can savour Florence's most bizarre museum, and one of the city's most pleasant small parks, laid out by Stibbert with a mouldering Egyptian temple sinking in a pond (*open for tours on the hour, 9–1—when you may wander at will, bank holidays 9–12.30; closed Thurs; adm L5000*; and just try to obey the sign on the door: 'Comply with the Forbidden Admittances!').

Stibbert's Italian mother left him a 14th-century house, which he enlarged, joining it to another house to create a sumptuous Victorian version of what a medieval Florentine house should have looked like—64 rooms to contain a pack-rat's treasure hoard of all things brilliant and useless, from an attributed Botticelli to snuff boxes, to what a local guide intriguingly describes as 'brass and silver basins, used daily by Stibbert'. Stibbert's serious passion, however, was armour, and he amassed a magnificent collection from all times and places. The best pieces are not arranged in dusty cases, but with a touch of Hollywood, on grim knightly mannequins ranked ready for battle.

Day Trips

The outskirts of the city have long lured the Florentines out of their streets of history into some of Tuscany's loveliest countryside. Lofty Fiesole, Florence's grandmother, and a set of Medici villas are all easily reached by public transport.

Fiesole

Florence liked to look at itself as the daughter of Rome, and in its fractious heyday explained its quarrelsome nature by the fact that its population from the beginning was of mixed race, of Romans and 'that ungrateful and malignant people who of old came down from Fiesole', according to Dante. First settled in the 2nd millennium BC, it grew to become the most important Etruscan city in the region. Yet from the start Etruscan *Faesulae*'s relationship with Rome was rocky, especially after sheltering Catiline and his conspirators in 65 BC. Because of its lofty position, Fiesole was too difficult to capture, so the Romans built a camp below on the Arno to cut off its supplies. Eventually Fiesole was taken, and it dwindled as the Roman camp below grew into Florentia, growth the Romans encouraged to spite the feisty old Etruscans on their hill. This easily defended summit, however, ensured Fiesole's survival in the Dark Ages. When times became safer, families began to move back down to the Arno to rebuild Florence. They returned to smash up most of Fiesole after defeating it in 1125; since then the little town has remained aloof, letting Florence dominate and choke in its own juices far, far below.

But ever since the days of the *Decameron*, whose storytellers retreated to its garden villas to escape the plague, Fiesole has played the role of Florence's aristocratic suburb; its cool breezes, beautiful landscapes and belvedere views make it the perfect refuge from the torrid Florentine summers. There's no escaping the tourists, however; we foreigners have been tramping up and down Fiesole's hill since the days of Shelley. A day trip has become an obligatory part of a stay in Florence, and although Fiesole has proudly retained its status as an independent *comune*, you can make the 20-minute trip up on Florence city bus 7 from the station or Piazza San Marco. If you have the time, walk up (or perhaps better, down) the old lanes bordered with villas and gardens to absorb some of the world's most civilized scenery.

Around Piazza Mino

The long sloping stage of Piazza Mino is Fiesole's centre, with the bus stop, the local tourist office, the cafés, and the **Palazzo Pretorio**, its loggia and façade emblazoned with coats of arms. The square is named after a favourite son, the quattrocento sculptor Mino da Fiesole, whom Ruskin preferred to all others. An example of his work may be seen in the **Duomo**, whose plain façade dominates the north side of the piazza. Built in 1028, it was the only building spared by the vindictive Florentines in 1125. It was subsequently enlarged and given a scouring 19th-century restoration, leaving the tall, crenellated campanile as its sole distinguishing feature. Still, the interior has an austere charm, with a raised choir over the crypt similar to San Miniato. Up the steps to the right are two beautiful works by Mino da Fiesole: the *Tomb of Bishop Leonardo Salutati* and an altar front. The main altarpiece in the choir, of the Madonna and saints, is by Lorenzo di Bicci, from 1440. Note the two saints frescoed on the columns; it was a north Italian custom to paint holy people as if they were members of the congregation. The crypt, holding the remains of Fiesole's patron, St Romulus, is supported by ancient columns bearing doves, spirals and other early Christian symbols.

Behind the Cathedral, on Via Dupré, the **Bandini Museum** contains more sacred works, including numerous della Robbia terracottas, some good trecento paintings by Lorenzo Monaco, Neri di Bicci and Taddeo Gaddi (*open winter 9.30–5, summer 9–7, exc Tues; adm*).

Archaeological Zone

Behind the cathedral and museum is the entrance to what remains of *Faesulae*. Because Fiesole stayed out of trouble in the Dark Ages, its Roman-era monuments have survived in much better shape than those of Florence; although hardly spectacular, the ruins are charmingly set amid olive groves and cypresses. The small **Roman Theatre** has survived well enough to host plays and concerts in the summer; Fiesole would like to gently remind you that in ancient times it had the theatre and plays while Florence had the amphitheatre and wild beast shows. Close by are the rather confusing remains of two superimposed temples, the baths, and an impressive stretch of Etruscan walls (best seen from Via delle Mure Etrusche, below) that proved their worth against Hannibal's siege (*open summer 9–7, winter 10–4; closed Tues; adm*). The **Archaeology Museum** is housed in a small 20th-century Ionic temple, displaying some very early small bronze figurines with flapper wing arms, Etruscan funerary urns and stelae, including the interesting 'stele Fiesolana' with a banquet scene (*open summer 9–7, winter 10–4, closed Tues; adm*).

Walking Around Fiesole

From Piazza Mino, Via S. Francesco ascends steeply (at first) to the hill that served as the Etruscan and Roman acropolis. Halfway up is a terrace with extraordinary views of Florence and the Arno sprawl, with a monument to the three gallant *carabinieri* who gave themselves up to be shot by the Nazis in 1944 to prevent them from taking civilian reprisals. The church nearby, the **Basilica di**

Sant'Alessandro, was constructed over an Etruscan/Roman temple in the 6th century, reusing its lovely *cipollino* (onion marble) columns and Ionic capitals, one still inscribed with an invocation to Venus. At the top of the hill, square on the ancient acropolis, stands the monastery of **San Francesco**, its church containing a famous early cinquecento *Annunciation* by Raffaellino del Garbo and an *Immaculate Conception* by Piero di Cosimo. A grab-bag of odds and ends collected from the four corners of the world, especially from Egypt and China, is displayed in the quaint **Franciscan Missionary Museum** in the cloister; it also has an Etruscan collection (*open summer 9–12 and 3–6, winter 10–12 and 3–5*). There are much longer walks along the hill behind the Palazzo Pretorio. The panoramic Via Belvedere leads back to Via Adriano Mari, and in a couple of kilometres to the bucolic **Montecéceri**, a wooded park where Leonardo da Vinci performed his flight experiments, and where the Florentine architects once quarried their dark *pietra serena* from quarries which are now abandoned but open for exploration. In Borgunto, as this part of Fiesole is called, there are two 3rd-century BC **Etruscan tombs** on Via Bargellino; east of Borgunto scenic Via Francesco Ferrucci and Via di Vincigliata pass by Fiesole's castles, the **Castel di Poggio**, site of summer concerts, and the **Castel di Vincigliata**, built on the site of a ruin dating back to 1031, while further down is American critic Bernard Berenson's famous **Villa I Tatti**, which he left, along with a distinguished collection of Florentine art, to Harvard University as the Centre of Italian Renaissance Studies. The road continues down towards Ponte a Mensola (6km from Fiesole; and Settignano, with buses back to Florence.

San Domenico di Fiesole

Located between Fiesole and Florence, San Domenico is a pleasant walk down from Fiesole by way of Via Vecchia Fiesolana, the steep and narrow old road that passes, on the left, the **Villa Medici**, built by Michelozzo for Cosimo il Vecchio; in its lovely garden on the hillside, Lorenzo and his friends of the Platonic Academy would come to get away from the world; it was also the lucky Iris Origo's childhood home (*no adm*). San Domenico, at the bottom of the lane, is the convent where Giovanni da Fiesole first entered his monkish world as Fra Angelico. The 15th-century church of **San Domenico** contains his lovely *Madonna with Angels and Saints*, in the first chapel on the left, as well as a photograph of his *Coronation of the Virgin*, which Napoleon snapped up in 1809 and sent to the Louvre. Across the nave there's a *Crucifixion* by the school of Botticelli, an unusual composition of verticals highlighted by the cypresses in the background. In the chapterhouse (*ring the bell at No.4*) Beato Angelico left a fine fresco of the *Crucifixion* before moving down to Florence and San Marco.

Badia Fiesolana

The lane in front of San Domenico leads down in five minutes to the Badia Fiesolana, the ancient cathedral of Fiesole, built in the 9th century by Fiesole's bishop, an Irishman named Donatus, with a fine view over the rolling countryside and Florence in the background. Though later enlarged, perhaps by Brunelleschi, it has preserved the elegant façade of the older church, a charming example of the geometric black and white marble inlay decoration that characterizes Tuscan Romanesque churches. The interior (*open only on Sunday mornings*) is adorned with *pietra serena* very much in the style of Brunelleschi. The convent buildings next door are now the home of the European University Institute.

Settignano

The least touristic hilltop balcony above Florence sits under the village of Settignano (bus 10 from the station or from Piazza San Marco). The road passes by way of **Ponte a Mensola**, where Boccaccio spent his childhood, and where it is believed he set the first scenes of the *Decameron*, in the Villa Poggio Gherardo. A Scottish Benedictine named Andrew founded its church of **San Martino a Mensola** in the 9th century and was later canonized. Rebuilt in the 1400s, it has three good trecento works: Taddeo Gaddi's *Triptych*, his son Agnolo's panel paintings on St Andrew's casket, and on the high altar another triptych by the school of Orcagna. From the quattrocento there's a *Madonna and Saints* by Neri di Bicci and an *Annunciation* by a follower of Beato Angelico.

Settignano is one of Tuscany's great cradles of sculptors, producing Desiderio da Settignano and the brothers Antonio and Bernardo Rossellino; Michelangelo spent his childhood here as well, in the Villa Buonarroti. Strangely enough, not one of them left any examples of his work; the good art which is in the central church of **Santa Maria** is by Andrea della Robbia (an enamelled terracotta of the Madonna and Child) and Buontalenti (the pulpit). There are, however, splendid views of Florence from Piazza Desiderio, and a couple of places to quaff a glass of Chianti.

Medici Villas

Like their Bourbon cousins in France, the Medici dukes liked to pass the time acquiring new palaces for themselves. In their case, however, the reason was less self-exaltation than simple property speculation; one secret of Medici success was that they always thought several generations ahead. As a result the countryside is littered with Medici villas, most of them privately owned, although some are partly open to the public.

Villa Careggi

Perhaps the best-known Medici villa is Careggi (Viale Pieraccini 17, bus 14C from the station), a fortified farmhouse that was enlarged for Cosimo il Vecchio by Michelozzo in 1434. In the 1460s, the became synonymous with the birth of humanism. The greatest Latin and Greek scholars of the day, Ficino, Poliziano, Pico della Mirandola and Argyropoulos, would meet here with Lorenzo il Magnifico and hold philosophical discussions in imitation of a Platonic symposium, calling their informal society the Platonic Academy. It fizzled out when Lorenzo died. Cosimo il Vecchio and Piero had both died at Careggi, and when he felt the end was near, Lorenzo had himself carried out to the villa, with Poliziano and Pico della Mirandola to bear him company. After Lorenzo died, the villa was burned by Florentine republicans, though Cosimo I later had it rebuilt, and Francis Sloane had it restored. It is now used as a nursing home, and can only be visited by request, © 4279981 (*ask inside at the office of the Unità Operativa Affari Generali of USL*), but you can stroll through its gardens and woods.

Villa la Petraia

Further east, amid the almost continuous conurbation of power lines and industrial landscapes that blight the Prato road, the Villa la Petraia manages to remain Arcadian on its steeply sloping hill (it's very hard to reach if you're on your own; take a taxi or, if you are adventurous, bus 28 from the station, and get off after the wastelands, by Via Reginaldo Giuliano). La Petraia was purchased by Grand Duke Ferdinando I in 1557 and rebuilt by Buontalenti, keeping the tower of the original country castle intact. Unfortunately Vittorio Emanuele II liked it as much as the Medici, and redesigned it to suit his relentlessly bad taste. Still, a tour of the villa's interior (*open 9–4.30, closed the second and fourth Monday of the month; in spring and summer, the hours extend in the evening; adm*) is worthwhile for the ornate Baroque court, frescoed with a pastel history of the Medici by 17th-century masters Volterrano and Giovanni di San Giovanni; Vittorio Emanuele II added the glass roof so that he could use the space as a ballroom. Of the remainder of the palace, you're likely to remember best the Chinese painting of Canton and the games room, with billiard tables as large as football fields and perhaps the world's first pinball machine, made of wood. A small room contains one of Giambologna's most endearing statues, *Venus Wringing Water from Her Hair*. La Petraia's beautiful garden and park, shaded by ancient cypresses, is open throughout the afternoon.

Villa di Castello

One of Tuscany's most famous gardens is just down the hill from La Petraia, at Villa di Castello (turn right at Via di Castello and walk 450 metres). The villa was bought in 1477 by Lorenzo di Pierfrancesco and Giovanni de' Medici, cousins of Lorenzo il Magnifico who were Botticelli's patrons, and they hung the walls of this villa with his mythological paintings, now the big stars in the Uffizi. The villa was sacked in the 1530 siege, restored by Cosimo I, and today is the headquarters of the Accademia della Crusca, founded in 1582 and dedicated to maintaing the purity of Italian language, rather like the more recent Academie Française, but far less stuffy and pedantic; members, who are currently compiling a historical diction-ary, look at their task as linguistic 'baking'; one room has all their names carefully preserved, not on the usual coats of arms, but on bakers' shovels (*no adm*).

The **Garden** (*open 9–4.30, closed the second and fourth Monday of the month; in spring and summer, the hours extend in the evening*) was laid out for Cosimo I by Tribolo, who also designed the fountain in the centre, with a statue of *Her-cules and Antenaeus* by Ammannati. Directly behind the fountain is the garden's main attraction, a fascinating example of the Medici penchant for the offbeat and excessive, an artificial cavern known as the **Grotto degli Animali**, filled by Ammannati and Giambologna with marvellous, true-to-life statues of every animal, fish and bird known to man (some of them are copies of Giambologna's originals in the Bargello), and lined with mosaics of pebbles and seashells. The shady terrace above offers the best view over the geometric patterns of the garden below; a large statue by Ammannati of January, or *Gennaio*, emerges shivering from a pool of water among the trees.

A 20-minute walk north from Villa di Castello to Quinto takes you to two unusual 7th-century BC **Etruscan tombs**: La Montagnola, Via Filli Rosselli 95 (*open Tues, Thurs, Sat and Sun 9–12, and an hour later in summer; free adm*); La Mula, Via della Mula 2 (*open Sat 10–12, also in summer Tues 10–12 and Sat 3–6.30*). Neither has any art, but the chambers under their 8-metre artificial hills bear an odd relationship to ancient cultures elsewhere in the Mediterranean—domed tholos tombs as in Mycenaean Greece, corbelled passages like the navetas of Majorca, and entrances that look like the sacred wells of Sardinia.

Sesto Fiorentino

You can change gears again by heading out a little further in the sprawl to Sesto Fiorentino, a suburb that since 1954 has been home to the famous Richard-Ginori china and porcelain firm. Founded in Doccia in 1735, the firm has opened the **Doccia Museum** on Via Pratese 31 (*signposted*) to display a neat chronology of its production of Doccia ware, including many Medici commissions (a ceramic Venus de' Medici), fine painted porcelain, and some pretty Art Nouveau works (*open Tues, Thurs and Sat 9.30–1 and 3.30–6.30; adm*).

Villa Demidoff at Pratolino

The village of Pratolino lies 12km north of Florence along Via Bolognese (*take bus 25A or a Sita bus from Piazza Stazione*) and it was here that the infatuated Duke Francesco I bought a villa in the 1568 as a gift to his mistress, the Venetian Bianca Capello. Francesco commissioned Buontalenti—artist, architect, and hydraulics engineer, nicknamed 'delle Girandole' for the fantastic fireworks he made (*girandola* is the Italian for Catherine wheel)—to design the enormous gardens, and he made Pratolino the marvel of its day, full of water tricks, ingenious automata and a famous menagerie. Sadly, none of Buontalenti's marvels has survived, but the largest-ever example of this play between art and environment has (perhaps because it is impossible to move)—Giambologna's massive *Appennino*, a giant rising from stone, part stalactite, part fountain himself, conquering the dragon, said to be symbolic of the Medici's origins in the Mugello just north of here. The rest of the park was made into an English garden by the Lorena family and named for Prince Paolo Demidoff who bought it in 1872 and restored Francesco's servants' quarters as his villa; today it is an invitingly cool refuge from a Florentine summer afternoon (*open March–April, Sun 10–6; May–Sept, Thurs–Sun 10–8; closed in winter; adm*).

Poggio a Caiano

Of all the Medici villas, Poggio a Caiano is the most evocative of the country idylls so delightfully described in the verses of Lorenzo il Magnifico; this was not only his favourite retreat, but is generally considered the very first Italian Renaissance villa. Lorenzo purchased a farmhouse here in 1480, and commissioned Giuliano da Sangallo to rebuild it in a classical style. It was Lorenzo's sole architectural commission, and its classicism matched the mythological nature poems he composed here, most famously *L'Ambra*, inspired by the stream Ombrone that flows nearby. (COPIT buses, © 877012, go past every half-hour, departing from the front of McDonalds on the north side of the station.)

Sangallo designed the villa according to Alberti's description of the perfect country house in a style that presages Palladio, and added a classical frieze on the façade, sculpted with the assistance of Andrea Sansovino (now replaced with a copy). Some of the other features—the clock, the curved stair and central loggia—were later additions. In the **interior** (*open 9–1.30, closed second and third Mon; adm*) Sangallo designed an airy, two-storey **Salone**, which the two Medici popes had frescoed by 16th-century masters Pontormo, Andrea del Sarto, Franciabigio and Allori. The subject, as usual, is Medici self-glorification, and depicts family members dressed as Romans in historical scenes that parallel events in their lives. In the right lunette, around a large circular window, Pontormo painted the lovely *Vertumnus and Pomona* (1521), a languid summer scene under a willow tree, beautifully coloured. In another room, Francesco I and Bianca Cappello his wife died in 1587, only 11 hours apart; Francesco was always messing about with poisons but a nasty virus seems to have been the probable killer. The pleasant **grounds** (*open 9–6.30, winter till 4.30; Sun 9–12.30*) contain fine old trees and a 19th-century statue celebrating Lorenzo's *L'Ambra*.

Carmignano and Villa Artimino

A local bus continues 5km southwest of Poggia a Caiano to the village of **Carmignano**, which possesses, in its church of San Michele, Pontormo's uncanny painting of *The Visitation* (1530s), one of the masterpieces of Florentine Mannerism. There are no concessions to naturalism here—the four soulful, ethereal women, draped in Pontormo's accustomed startling colours, barely touch the ground, standing before a scene as substantial as a stage backdrop. The result is one of the most unforgettable images produced in the 16th century. (*Guided tours by appointment only, ✆ 8792030 or 8718081.*)

Also south of Poggio a Caiano, at **Comeana** (3km, signposted) is the well-preserved Etruscan **Tomba di Montefortini**, a 7th-century BC burial mound, 11m high and 80m in diameter, covering two burial chambers. A long hall leads down to the vestibule and rectangular tomb chamber, both carefully covered with false vaulting, the latter preserving a wide shelf, believed to have been used for gifts for the afterlife. An equally impressive tomb nearby, the **Tomba dei Boschetti**, was seriously damaged over the centuries by local farmers (*Montefortini open 9–1, closed Mon, Boschetti always open*).

The Etruscan city of Artimino, 4km west, was destroyed by the Romans and is now occupied by a small town and yet another Medici property, the **Villa Artimino** ('La Ferdinanda'), built as a hunting lodge for Ferdinando I by Buontalenti. Buontalenti gave it a semi-fortified air with buttresses to fit its sporting purpose, but the total effect is simple and charming, the long roofline punctuated by innumerable chimneys; the graceful stair was added in the last century from a drawing by the architect in the Uffizi. An **Etruscan Archaeological Museum** has been installed in the basement, containing items found in the tombs; among them a unique censer with two basins and a boat, bronze vases, and a red figured krater painted with initiation scenes, found in a 3rd-century tomb (*villa open Tues 9–12.30 and 3–6, winter 8.30–12 and 2–4, guided tours only by appointment, ✆ 8718072; museum open Mon–Sat 9–1, Sun 9–12.30; closed Wed; adm*). There's a convenient place for lunch in the grounds. Also in Artimino is an attractive Romanesque church, **San Leonardo**, built of stones salvaged from earlier buildings.

Poggio Imperiale and the Certosa del Galluzzo

One last villa that is open for visits, the **Villa di Poggio Imperiale**, lies south of Florence, at the summit of Viale del Poggio Imperiale, which leaves Porta Romana with a stately escort of cypress sentinels. Cosimo I grabbed this huge villa from the Salviati family in 1565, and it remained a ducal property until there were no longer any dukes to duke. Its neoclassical façade was added in 1808, and the audience chamber was decorated in the 17th century by the under-rated Rutilio Manetti and others. Much of the villa is now used as a girls' school (*open Wed 10–12 by request, © 220151*).

The **Certosa del Galluzzo** (also known as the Certosa di Firenze) lies further south, scenically located on a hill off the Siena road (take bus 36 or 37 from the station). Founded as a Carthusian monastery by 14th-century tycoon Niccolò Acciaiuoli, the monastery has been inhabited since 1958 by Cistercians; there are twelve now living there, one of whom takes visitors around (*open 9–12 and 3–6; closed Mon*). The Certosa has a fine 16th-century courtyard and an uninteresting church, though the crypt-chapel of the lay choir contains some impressive tombs. The **Chiostro Grande**, surrounded by the monks' cells, is decorated with 66 majolica tondi of prophets and saints by Giovanni della Robbia and assistants; one cell is opened for visits, and it seems almost cosy. The Gothic **Palazzo degli Studi**, intended by the founder as a school, contains five lunettes by Pontormo, painted while he and his pupil Bronzino hid out here from the plague in 1522.

Siena

Draped on its three hills, Siena (pop. 61,400) is the most beautiful city in Tuscany, a flamboyant medieval ensemble of palaces and towers cast in warm, brown, *Siena*-coloured brick. Its soaring skyline is its pride, dominated by the blazing black and white banner of the cathedral and the taut needle of the Torre di Mangia; and yet the Campo, the very centre of Siena, is only four streets away from olive groves and orchards. The contrast is part of the city's charm; densely built-up brick urbanity, and round the corner a fine stretch of long Tuscan farmland that fills the valleys within the city's walls.

Here art went hand in hand with a fierce civic pride to make Siena a world of its own, and historians go so far as to speak of 'Sienese civilization' in summing up the achievements of this unique little city.

Ancient Rivals

Few rivalries have been more enduring than that between Florence and Siena; to understand Tuscany, take a moment to compare the two. Long ago, while Florence was off at university, busily studying her optics and geometry, Lady Siena spent her time dancing and dropping her scarf for knights at the tournament. Florence thought she had the last laugh in 1555, when Duke Cosimo and his black-hearted Spanish pals wiped out the Sienese Republic and put this proud maiden in chains. It's frustrating enough today, though, when Florence looks up in the hills and sees Siena, an unfaded beauty with a faraway smile, sitting in her tower like the Lady of Shalott.

For two towns built by bankers and wool tycoons, they could not have less in common. Siena may not possess an Uffizi or a David, but neither does it have to bear the marble antimacassars and general stuffiness of its sister on the Arno, nor her smog, traffic, tourist hordes and suburban squalor. Florence never goes over the top. Siena loves to, especially in the week around the race of the Palio, the wildest party in Tuscany, a worthy successor to the fabulous masques and carnivals, the bullfights and bloody free-for-alls of the Sienese Middle Ages. In fact, Florence has been clicking its tongue at Siena since the time of Dante, who inserted in his *Inferno* a sarcastic reference to a famous club called the *Brigata*— twelve noble Sienese youths who put up 250,000 florins for a year of nightly feasting; every night they had three sumptuously laid tables, one for eating, one for drinking, and the third to throw out the window. 'A people even more vain than the French,' sneered Dante. Another story goes that a Florentine prince was approached by the Sienese, who asked him to build a madhouse in their city. The prince replied that it was easy: all the Sienese had to do was close all their gates and they'd have the biggest madhouse of all.

But there's more to Siena than that. This is a city with its own artistic tradition; in the 1300s, Sienese painters were giving lessons to the Florentines. Always more decorative, less intellectual than Florence, Siena fell behind in the quattrocento. By then, fortunately, the greatest achievement of Sienese art was already nearing completion—Siena itself

History

Everywhere in Siena you'll see the familiar Roman symbol of the she-wolf suckling the twins. This is Siena's symbol as well; according to legend, the city was founded by the sons of Remus, Senius and Ascius. One rode a black horse, the other a white, and the simple comunal shield of black and white halves (the *balzana*) has been the other most enduring symbol of Siena over the centuries. It is most likely that somebody was living on these three hills long before this mythological pair. Excavations have found traces of Etruscan and even Celtic habitation. The almost impregnable site, dominating most of southern Tuscany, would always have been of great interest. Roman-era *Sena Julia* which was refounded by Augustus as a colony for his veterans, never achieved much importance, and we know little about the place until the early 12th century, when the emerging *comune* began keeping written records. In 1125, an increasingly independent Siena elected its first consuls. By 1169, the *comune* wrested political control away from the bishop, and some ten years later Siena developed its own written constitution.

The political development is complex, and with good reason. Twelfth-century Siena was a booming new city; control over its rich countryside, supplying some of the best wool in Italy, helped start an important cloth industry, and a small silver mine, acquired from Volterra in the 1160s, provided seed capital for what was to become one of the leading banking towns of Europe. Like so many other Italian cities, Siena was able early on to force its troublesome rural nobles to live within its walls, where they built scores of tall defence towers, fought pitched battles in the streets and usually kept the city divided into armed camps; in the narrowest part of the city, the *comune* once had to lay out new streets parallel to Via Camollia because of one particularly boisterous nobleman whose palace most Sienese were afraid to pass. Yet Siena was never completely able to bring its titled hoodlums under control. The businessmen made the money, and gradually formed their city into a sophisticated self-governing republic, but the nobles held on to many of their privileges for centuries, giving an anachronistically feudal tinge to Siena's life and art.

Like its brawling neighbours, medieval Siena enjoyed looking for trouble; in the endless wars of the 13th century they never had to look very far. Originally a Guelph town, Siena changed sides early to avoid being in the same camp as arch-rival Florence. Along with Pisa, Siena carried the Ghibelline banner through the Tuscan wars with varying fortunes. Its finest hour came in 1260, when a Florentine herald arrived with the arrogant demand that Siena demolish its walls and deliver up its large population of Ghibelline exiles from Florence. If not, the armies of Florence and the entire Guelph League—some 40,000 men—were waiting outside to raze the city to the ground. Despite the overwhelming odds, the Sienese determined to resist. They threw the keys of the city on the altar of the yet unfinished cathedral, dedicating Siena to the Virgin Mary (a custom repeated ever since when the city is endangered, most recently just before the battle for liberation in 1944). In the morning, they marched out to the **Battle of Monteaperti** and beat the Florentines so badly that they captured their *carroccio*.

After the battle Siena had Florence entirely at her mercy and naturally was anxious to level the city and sow the ground with salt. One of the famous episodes in the *Inferno* relates how the Florentine exiles, who made up a substantial part of the Sienese forces, refused to allow it. Unfortunately for Siena, within a few years Florence and the Tuscan Guelphs had the situation back under control and Siena was never again to come so close to dominating Tuscan affairs. Nevertheless the city would be a constant headache to Florence for the next three centuries. When things were quiet at the front, the Sienese had to settle for bashing each other. The constant stream of anti-Siena propaganda in Dante isn't just Florentine bile; medieval Siena had a thoroughly earned reputation for violence and contentiousness. The impressive forms and rituals of the Sienese Republic were merely a façade concealing endless, pointless struggles between the various factions of the élite. Early on, Siena's merchants and nobles divided themselves into five *monti*, syndicates of self-interest that worked like political parties only without any pretence of principle. At one point, this Tuscan banana republic had 10 constitutions in 27 years, and more often than not its political affairs were settled in the streets. Before the Palio was invented, Siena's favourite civic sport was the *Gioco del Pugno*, a general fist-fight in the Campo with 300 on a side. Sometimes tempers flared, and the boys would bring out the axes and crossbows.

Siena's Golden Age

The historical record leaves us with a glaring paradox. For all its troubles and bad intentions, Siena often managed to run city business with disinterest and intelligence. An intangible factor of civic pride always made the Sienese do the right thing when something important was at hand, like battling with the Florentines or selecting a new artist to work on the cathedral. The Battle of Monteaperti may have proved a disappointment in terms of territorial ambitions, but it inaugurated the most brilliant period of Sienese culture, and saw the transformation of the hilltop fortress town into the beautiful city we see today. In 1287, under pressure from the

Guelphs and their Angevin protectors, Siena actually allied itself with Florence and instituted a new form of government: the **'Council of the Nine'**. Excluding nobles from office, as Florence would do six years later, the rule of the Nine was to last until 1355, and it gave Siena a more stable regime than it knew at any other period.

Business was better than ever. The city's bankers came to rival Florence's, with offices in all the trading centres and capitals of Europe. A sustained peace, and increasing cultural contacts with France and Naples, brought new ideas and influences into Siena's art and architecture, just in time to embellish massive new building programmes like the **Cathedral** (begun 1186, but not substantially completed until the 1380s) and the **Palazzo Pubblico** (1295–1310). Beginning with Duccio di Buoninsegna (1260–1319) Sienese artists took the lead in exploring new concepts in painting and sculpture and throughout the 1300s they contributed as much as or more than the Florentines in laying the foundations for the Renaissance. Contemporary records betray an obsessive concern on the part of bankers and merchants for decorating Siena and impressing outsiders. At the height of its fortunes, in the early 14th century, Siena ruled most of southern Tuscany. Its bankers were known in London, in the Baltic and in Constantinople, and its reputation for beauty and culture was matched by few cities in Europe.

The very pinnacle of civic pride and ambition came in 1339, with the fantastical plan to expand the as yet unfinished cathedral into the largest in all Christendom. The walls of that great effort, a nave that would have been longer than St Peter's in Rome, stand today as a monument to the dramatic event that snapped off Siena's career in full bloom. The **Black Death** of 1348 carried off three-fifths of the population—a mortality not greater than some other Italian cities, perhaps, but the plague hit Siena at a moment when its economy was particularly vulnerable, and started a slow but irreversible decline that was to continue for centuries. Economic troubles led to political instability, and in 1355 a revolt of the nobles, egged on by Emperor Charles IV, who was then in Tuscany, overthrew the Council of the Nine. Then in 1371, seven years before the Ciompi revolt in Florence, the wool-workers staged a genuine revolution. Organized in a sort of trade union, the **Compagnìa del Bruco**, they seized the Palazzo Pubblico and instituted a new government with greater popular representation.

The decades that followed saw Siena devote more and more of its diminishing resources to buying off the marauding mercenary companies that infested much of Italy at this time. By 1399 the city was in such straits that it surrendered its independence to **Giangaleazzo Visconti**, the tyrant of Milan, who was then attempting to surround and conquer Florence. After his death Siena reclaimed its freedom. Political confusion continued throughout the century, with only two periods of relative stability. One came with the pontificate (1458–63) of Pius II,

the great Sienese scholar **Aeneas Silvius Piccolomini**, who exerted a dominating influence over his native city while he ruled at Rome. In 1487, a nobleman
named **Pandolfo Petrucci** took over the government; as an honest broker, regu-
lating the often murderous ambitions of the *monti*, he and his sons kept control of
the republic until 1524.

The Fall of the Republic

Florence was always waiting in the wings to swallow up Siena, and finally had its
chance in the 1500s. The real villain of the piece, however, was not Florence but
that most imperious emperor, **Charles V**. After the fall of the Petrucci, the
factional struggles resumed immediately, with frequent assassinations and riots,
and constitutions changing with the spring fashions. Charles, who had bigger prey
in his sights, cared little for the fate of the perverse little republic; he feared,
though, that its disorders, religious toleration, and wretched financial condition
were a disease that might spread beyond its borders. In 1530, he took advantage
of riots in the city to install an imperial garrison. Yet even the emperor's representatives, usually Spaniards, could not keep Siena from sliding further into anarchy
and bankruptcy on several occasions, largely thanks to Charles's war taxes. Cultural life was stifled as the Spaniards introduced the Inquisition and the Index.
Scholars and artists fled, while poverty and political disruptions made Siena's once
proud university cease to function.

In 1550, Charles announced that he was going to build a fortress within the city's
walls, and that the Sienese were going to pay for it. Realizing that even the trifling
liberty still left to them would soon be extinguished, the Sienese ruling class
began intrigues with Charles' great enemy, France. A French army which was led
by a Piccolomini, arrived in July 1552. Inside the walls the people revolted and
locked the Spanish garrison up in its own new fortress. The empire was slow to
react, but inevitably, in late 1554, a huge force of imperial troops, along with
those of Florence, entered Sienese territory. The siege was prosecuted with
remarkable brutality by Charles's commander, the **Marquis of Marignano**, who
laid waste much of the Sienese countryside (which did not entirely recover until
this century), tortured prisoners and even hired agents to start fires inside the
walls. After a brave resistance, led by a republican Florentine exile named **Piero
Strozzi** and assisted by France, Siena was starved into surrendering in April 1555.
Two years later, Charles's son Philip II sold Siena to Duke Cosimo of Florence,
and the ancient republic disappeared into the new Grand Duchy of Tuscany.

If nothing else, Siena went out with a flourish. After the capture of the city, some
2000 republican bitter-enders escaped to make a last stand at Montalcino.
Declaring 'Where the *Comune* is, there is the City', they established what must
be the world's first republican government-in-exile. With control over much of

the old Sienese territory, the **'Republic of Siena at Montalcino'** held out against the Medici for another four years.

With its independence lost and its economy irrevocably ruined, Siena withdrew into itself. For centuries there was to be no recovery, little art or scholarship, and no movements towards reform. The Sienese aristocracy, already decayed into a parasitic *rentier* class, made its peace with the Medici dukes early on; in return for their support, the Medici allowed them to keep much of their power and privileges. The once great capital of trade and finance shrank rapidly into an overbuilt farmers' market, its population dropping from a 14th-century high of 60–80,000 to around a mere 15,000 by the year 1700. This does much to explain why medieval and Renaissance Siena is so well preserved today—for better or worse, nothing at all has happened to change it.

By the 'Age of Enlightenment', with its disparaging of everything medieval, the Sienese seem to have quite forgotten their own history and art, and it is no surprise that the rest of Europe forgot them too. During the first years of the Grand Tour, no self-respecting northern European would think of visiting Siena. Few had probably ever heard of it, and the ones who stopped overnight on the way to Rome were usually dismayed at the 'inelegance' of its medieval buildings and art. It was not until the 1830s that Siena was rediscovered, with the help of literati like the Brownings, who spent several summers here, and that truly Gothic American, Henry James. The Sienese were not far behind in rediscovering it themselves. The old civic pride that had lain dormant for centuries yawned and stretched like Sleeping Beauty and went diligently back to work. Before the century was out, everything that could still be salvaged of the city's ancient glory was refurbished and restored. More than ever fascinated by its own image and eccentricities, and more than ever without any kind of an economic base, Siena was ready for its present career as a cultural attraction, a tourist town.

Highlights of Siena

The **Campo** with the Palazzo Pubblico and Fonte Gaia, the **Cathedral** complex and the **Pinacoteca** offer the culmination of Sienese civilization and art and should not be missed. But in Siena the cream is spread evenly on the top of its three hills, if not in famous monuments, in the beauty of the streets and squares, the little *contrade* fountains and private houses—even a place that sounds as dry and dusty as the state archives (in the **Palazzo Piccolomini**) is well worth a visit. Every church has at least one fine work of art; among the best are **Santa Maria dei Servi**, **Sant'Agostino**, and the **Oratorio di San Bernardino**, while the **Enoteca Nazionale** in the Fortezza Medicea contains Italy's finest works of art from the vine. Don't miss the new museum in the **Ospedale Santa Maria della Scala**.

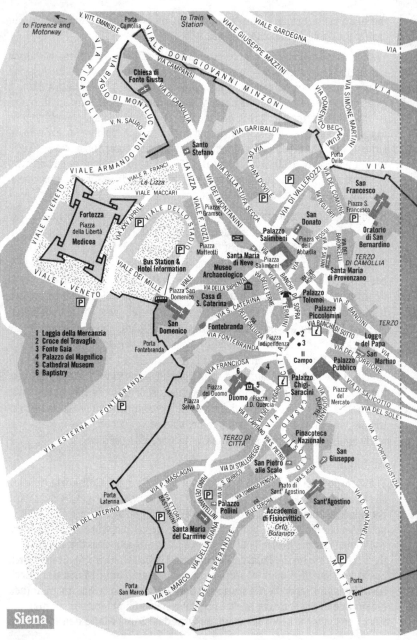

to Florence and
Motorway

to Train
Station

V. VITT. EMANUELE

Porta
Camollia

VIALE GIUSEPPE MAZZINI

VIALE SARDEGNA

VIA

VIALE DON GIOVANNI MINZONI

VIA RICASOLI

VIA B. PERUZZI

VIA DI CAMOLLIA

VIA CAMPANSI

Chiesa di
Fonte Giusta

VIA BIAGIO DI MONTLUC

V. N. SAURO

VIA GARIBALDI

VIA SIMONE MARTINI

VIA DOMENICO BEC

CUM

VIA

VIALE ARMANDO DIAZ

VIALE R. FRANCI

Le Lizza

VIALE MACCARI

LA LIZZA

Santo
Stefano

VIA DEL PIAN D'OVILE

Porta
Ovile

VIA

VIALE V. VENETO

VIA XXV APRILE

VIALE DELLO STADIO

Fortezza
Piazza
della Libertà
Medicea

VIALE DEI MILLE

VIALE V. VENETO

VIALE DEL MONTANINI

VIALE DEI TOZZI

Piazza
Gramsci

Piazza
Matteotti

VIA DELLA STUFA SECCA

VIA DI VALLEROZZI

VIA DEL COMUNE

VIA DEGLI ORTI

VIA DEI ROSSI

VIA BARONCELLI

P

San
Francesco

Piazza S.
Francesco

P

Oratorio
di San
Bernardino

San
Donato

Palazzo
Salimbeni

Piazza
dell'
Abbadia

TERZO
DI CAMOLLIA

Bus Station &
Hotel Information

Santa Maria
di Neve

Museo
Archeologico

Piazza San
Domenico

Casa di
S. Caterina

Piazza
Salimbeni

VIA DELLA SAPIENZA

VIA DELLE TERME

VIA DEI TERMINI

VIA BANCHI DI SOPRA

VIA DEI PELLEGRINI

Santa Maria
di Provenzano

San
Domenico

Fontebranda

VIA FONTEBRANDA

VIA DI CITTÀ

Palazzo
Tolomei

Palazzo
Piccolomini

VIA BANCHI DI SOTTO

VIA S. BANDINI

TERZO

Logge
del Papa

San
Martino

VIA

Porta
Fontebranda

Piazza
Indipendenza

1 2
3

Il
Campo

Palazzo
Pubblico

VIA DEL PORRIONE

Piazza
del
Mercato

VIA DI SALICOTTO

1 Loggia della Mercanzia
2 Croce del Travaglio
3 Fonte Gaia
4 Palazzo del Magnifico
5 Cathedral Museum
6 Baptistry

VIA FRANCIOSA

6

4

5

Piazza
del Duomo

Piazza
Selva D.

Duomo

Piazza
J.D. Quercia

VIA DEL CAPITANO

Palazzo
Chigi-
Saracini

VIA DEL CASATO

VIA GIOVANNI DUPRÈ

VIA DEL SOLE

VIA DI PORTA GIUSTIZIA

VIA ESTERNA DI FONTEBRANDA

Pinacoteca
Nazionale

San
Giuseppe

VIA DI STALLOREGGI

VIA S. PIETRO

San Pietro
alle Scale

VIA S. AGATA

VIA DI SAN QUIRICO

VIA P. MASCAGNI

VIA DI DIANA

Porta
Laterina

VIA DEL LATERINO

VIA ETTORE BASTIANINI

Palazzo
Pollini

VIA DI TOMMASO PENDOLA

VIA DELLE CERCHIA

Prato di
Sant'Agostino

Accademia
di Fisiocvittici

Sant'Agostino

VIA DELLE SPERANDIE

VIA P.A. MATTIOLI

VIA D. FONTANELLA

Santa Maria
del Carmine

VIA DELLA DIANA

Orto
Botanico

P

P

Porta
San Marco

VIA S. MARCO

Porta
Tufi

TERZO
DI
CITTÀ

Siena

228

The fastest route from Florence to Siena (68km) is the unnumbered toll-free Superstrada del Palio (1hr); the most scenic are the Chiantigiana SS222 through the heart of Chianti and the Via Cassia (SS2), which weave amongst the hills the Superstrada avoids. Both take about 2 hours. From the south, there are two possible approaches from the A1: the SS326 by way of Sinalunga (50km) or the more scenic, winding S73 by way of Monte San Savino (44km). Cars are forbidden to enter the centre, but there are clearly defined parking areas along all entrances to the city, especially around Piazza San Domenico, the Fortezza and along Viale del Stadio. Two places to **hire a car** are General Cars, in Via Vittorio Toselli 26, ✆ 40518, and Avis, in Via Simone Martini 36, ✆ 270305.

by train

Siena's station is located below the city, 1.5km from the centre down Viale G. Mazzini and is linked to the centre by frequent buses. Siena's main line runs from Empoli (on the Florence–Pisa line) to Chiusi (Florence–Rome). There are trains roughly every hour, with frequent connections to Florence from Empoli (97km, 1hr), less frequently to Pisa from Empoli (125km, 2hrs) and to Chiusi towards Umbria and Rome (65km to Chiusi, 1hr). A secondary line runs towards Grosseto (70km, 1hr), with eight trains a day; three continue to Orbetello. To save a trip to the station, all rail information/tickets are available at the SETI travel agency, No.56 on the Campo.

by bus

Almost every town in southern Tuscany can be reached by bus from **Piazza San Domenico**, the big transport node on the western edge of Siena, with tourist information and hotel information booths. A board lists departure times and the location of stops; the ticket office (with a fancy, computer-operated information dispenser) is in the little building next to San Domenico church. The name of the company serving the whole of Siena province is TRA-IN, ✆ 202245, causing endless difficulties, according to the local tourist authorities, with English tourists looking for TRA-INs in the train station. Other companies depart for other cities like Florence (SITA, about once every hour, Rome, Perugia, Pisa, etc.), but all leave from San Domenico. Within the walls, there is now a bus service run by the TRA-IN, using what they call the *pollicini* or Tom Thumbs: little buses designed to get around narrow streets; and regular buses run to the **train station** and everywhere else in the modern suburbs, departing from **Piazza Matteotti** north of the Campo.

Tourist Information

Piazza del Campo 56, ✆ 280551. Via di Città 43, ✆ (0577) 42 209. **Post Office**: Piazza Matteotti 37. **Hotel Reservations**: Piazza San Domenico, ✆ 288084.

Orientation: Terzi and the Contrade

The centre of Siena and the site of the Palio is the famous piazza called simply **Il Campo**. From here, the city unfolds like a three-petalled flower along three ridges. It has been a natural division since medieval times, with the oldest quarter, the **Terzo di Città**, including the cathedral, to the southwest; the **Terzo di San Martino** to the southeast; and the **Terzo di Camollia** to the north.

Siena is tiny, barely over a square mile. The density, and the hills, make it seem much bigger. There are no short cuts across the valleys between the three *terzi*. Although there are no cars in the centre, taxis and motor scooters will occasionally try to run you down.

Contrade

The Sienese have taken the *contrade* for granted so long that their history is almost impossible to trace. Basically, the word denotes the 17 neighbourhoods into which Siena is divided. Like the *rioni* of Rome, they were once the original wards of the ancient city—not merely geographical boundaries, but self-governing entities; the ancients often referred to them as the city's 'tribes'. In Siena, the *contrade* survived and prospered all through classical times and the Middle Ages. More than anything else, they maintained the city's traditions and sense of identity through the dark years after 1552. Incredibly enough, they're still there now, unique in Italy and perhaps all Europe. Once Siena counted over 60 *contrade*. Now there are 17, each with a sort of totem animal for its symbol:

Aquila (eagle), *Onda* (dolphin), *Tartuca* (turtle), *Pantera* (panther), *Selva* (rhinoceros) and *Chiocciola* (snail); all southwest of the Campo in Terzo di Città.

Leocorno (unicorn), *Torre* (elephant), *Nicchio* (mussel shell), *Civetta* (owl) and *Valdimontone* (ram); in Terzo di San Martino southeast of the Campo.

Oca (goose), *Drago* (dragon), *Giraffa* (giraffe), *Lupa* (wolf), *Bruco* (caterpillar) and *Istrice* (porcupine); all in the north in the Terzo di Camollia.

Sienese and Italian law recognize each of these as being legally chartered communities; today a *contrada* functions as a combination social and dining club, neighbourhood improvement organization, religious confraternity and mutual assistance fund. Each elects its own officials annually in May. Each has its own chapel, museum and fountain, its own flag and colours, and its own patron saint who pulls all the strings he can in Heaven to help his beloved district win the Palio.

Sociologists, and not only in Italy, are becoming ever more intrigued with this ancient yet very useful system, with its built-in community solidarity and tacit social control. (Siena has almost no crime and no social problems, except of course for a lack of jobs.) The *contrade* probably function much as they did in Roman or medieval times, but it's surprising just what up-to-date, progressive and adaptable institutions they can be. Anyone born in a *contrada* area, for example, is automatically a member; besides their baptism into the Church, they also receive a sort of 'baptism' into the *contrada*. This ritual isn't very old, and it is conducted in the pretty new fountains which the *contrade* have constructed all over Siena in recent years as centrepieces for their neighbourhoods.

To learn more about the *contrade*, the best place to go is one of the 17 little *contrada* museums. The tourist office has a list of addresses. One of the best is that of the Goose in the Terzo di Camollia. Though the caretakers usually live close by, most of them ask visitors to contact them a week in advance. The tourist office also has details of the dates of the annual *contrada* festivals, and the other shows and dinners they are wont to put on; visitors are always very welcome.

The Palio

The thousands of tourists who come twice a year to see the Palio, Siena's famous horse race around the Campo, probably think the Sienese are doing it all just for them. Yet like the *contrade* which contest it, the Palio is an essential part of Sienese culture, something that means as much to the city as it did centuries ago. The oldest recorded Palio was run in 1283, though no one can say how far the custom goes back. In the Middle Ages, besides horse races there were violent street battles, bloody games of primeval rugby and even bullfights. At present, the course is three times around the periphery of the Campo, though earlier it was run on various routes through the city's main streets.

The *palio* (Latin *pallium*) is an embroidered banner, the prize offered for winning the race. Two races are held each year, on 2 July and 16 August, and the *palio* of each is decorated with an image of the Virgin Mary; after political violence the city's greatest passion was always Mariolatry. The course has room for only ten horses in each race. Some of the 17 *contrade* are chosen by lot each race to ensure that everyone has a fair chance. The horses are also selected by lot, but the *contrade* are free to select their own jockeys. Although the race itself only lasts a minute and a half, there's a good hour or two of pageantry preceding the event; the famous flag-throwers or *alfieri* of each participating *contrada* put on a dazzling show, while the medieval *carroccio*, drawn by a yoke of white oxen, is pressed into service to circle the Campo, bearing the prized *palio* itself.

The Palio is no joke; baskets of money ride on each race, not to mention the sacred honour of the district. To obtain divine favour, each *contrada* brings its horse into its chapel on race morning for a special blessing (and if a little horse manure drops during the ceremony, it's a sign of good luck). The only rule stipulates that you can't seize the reins of an opponent. There are no rules against bribing opposing jockeys, making alliances with other *contrade*, or ambushing jockeys before the race. The course around the Campo has two right angles. Anything can happen; recent Palii have featured not only jockeys but *horses* flying through the air. The Sienese say no one has ever been killed at a Palio. There's no reason to believe them. They wouldn't believe it themselves; it is an article of faith among the Sienese that fatalities are prevented by special intervention of the Virgin Mary. The post-Palio carousing, while not up to medieval standards, is still impressive; in the winning *contrada* the party might go on for days.

No event in Italy is as infectiously exhilarating as the Palio. There are two ways to see it, either from the centre of the Campo, which is packed tight and always very hot, or from an expensive (L250,000–400,000) seat in a viewing stand, which you must book well in advance. Several travel agencies offer special Palio tours; otherwise book by April.

Siena Walks

If you keep your eyes open while walking the back streets of Siena you'll see the city's entire history laid out for you in signs, symbols and a hundred other clues. You usually won't have trouble guessing which *contrada* you're in. Little ceramic plaques with the *contrada* symbol appear on many buildings and street corners, not to mention flags in the neighbourhood colours, bumper stickers on the cars and the fountains, each with a modern sculptural work, usually representing the *contrada's* animal.

Look for noblemen's coats of arms above the doorways; aristo-cratic, archaic Siena will show you more of these than almost any Italian city. In many cases they are still the homes of the original families, and often the same device is on a dozen houses on one block, a reminder of how medieval Siena was largely divided into separate compounds, each under the protection (or intimidation) of a noble family. One common symbol is formed from the letters IHS in a radiant sun. Siena's famous 15th-century preacher, San Bernardino, was always pestering the nobles to forget their con-tentiousness and enormous vanity; he proposed that they should replace their heraldic symbols with the monogram of Christ. The limited success his idealism met with can be read on the buildings of Siena today.

They don't take down old signs in Siena. One, dated 1641, informs prostitutes that the Most Serene Prince Matthias (the Florentine governor) forbids them to live on his street (Via di Salicotto). Another, a huge 19th-century marble plaque on the Banchi di Sotto, reminds us that 'In this house, before modern restorations reclaimed it from squalidness, was born Giovanni Caselli, inventor of the pantograph'. A favourite, on Via del Giglio, announces a stroke of the rope and a 16-lira fine for anyone throwing trash in the street, with proceeds to go to the accuser.

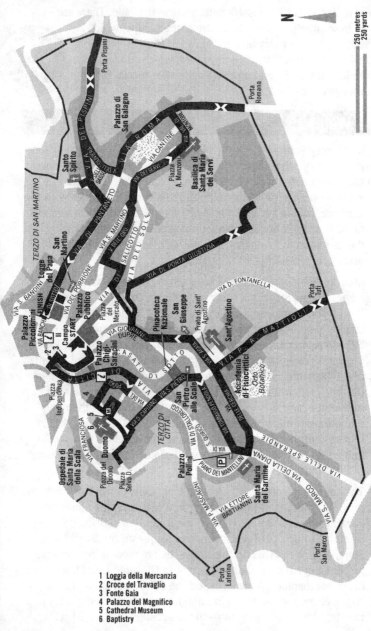

Siena Walk I: Around the Campo

1 Loggia della Mercanzia
2 Croce del Travaglio
3 Fonte Gaia
4 Palazzo del Magnifico
5 Cathedral Museum
6 Baptistry

Start: *the Campo*
Finish: *Palazzo Piccolomini*
Walking time: *one day*

I: Around the Campo

This walk through the Campo, Terzo di Città and Terzo Sa Martino takes in the shrines of Sienese civilization: the Palazzo Pubblico, the Cathedral and the masterpieces of Sienese art in the Pinacoteca.

Lunch/Cafés

Compagnia di S. Martino, Via del Porrione 25/27, ✆ 49306. Next to the delightful (and rather expensive) Osteria Le Logge (*see* Restaurants), this Tavola Calda is just off the Campo and good value (closed Sun, about L20,000).

La Costarella, Via di Città 33. An excellent ice-cream parlour near the Campo with tables overlooking the Square.

Enoteca Le Bollicine, Via G. Dupre 64, ✆ 42650. Large chalices of the best Tuscan and Italian wine and plates of Italian cheeses and salamis.

Mariotti da Mugalone, Via dei Pellegrini 8/12, ✆ 283235. Typical Sienese trattoria (closed Thurs, around L40,000).

Osteria del Ficomezzo, Via dei Termini 71, ✆ 222384. Just north of the Campo, this simple and rustic trattoria is bustling at luchtime, and offers menus at L15,000–L20,000. In the evenings, it is a little more upmarket (closed Sun).

Papei, Piazza del Mercato 6, ✆ 280894. Right on the market place with tables outside, this trattoria serves hearty traditional Sienese dishes (closed Mon, about L40,000).

La Torre, Via Salicotto 7–9, ✆ 287548. Just behind the Campo, this good little trattoria is always jam-packed (closed Thurs, around L30,000).

There is no lovelier square in Tuscany than the **Campo**, and none more beloved by its city. The Forum of ancient *Sena Julia* was on this spot, and in the Middle Ages it evolved into its present fan shape, rather like a scallop shell or a classical theatre. The Campo was paved in brick as early as 1340; the nine sections into which the fan is divided are in honour of the Council of the Nine, rulers of the city at the time. Thousands crowd over the bricks here every year to see the Palio, run on the periphery.

> For a worthy embellishment to their Campo, the Sienese commissioned for its curved north end the **Fonte Gaia** from Jacopo della Quercia who was their greatest sculptor, though what you see now is an uninspired copy of 1868.

Della Quercia worked on it from 1408 to 1419, creating the broad rectangle of marble with reliefs of Adam and Eve and allegorical virtues. It was to be the opening salvo of Siena's Renaissance, an answer to the Baptistry doors of Ghiberti in Florence (for which della Quercia himself had been one of the contestants). Perhaps it was a poor choice of stone, but the years have been incredibly unkind to this fountain; the badly eroded remains of the original can be seen up on the loggia of the Palazzo Pubblico. Piazza del Campo is less polluted with tourist tat than many other sights in Tuscany (Campo dei Miracoli in Pisa and Piazza del Duomo in Florence, for example).

No one can spend much time in Siena without noticing its fountains. The Republic always made sure each part of the city had access to good water; medieval Siena created the most elaborate engineering works since ancient Rome to bring the water in. Fonte Gaia, and others such as Fontebranda, are fed by underground aqueducts that stretch for miles across the Tuscan countryside. Charles V, when he visited the city, is reported to have said that Siena is 'even more marvellous underground than it is on the surface'. The original Fonte Gaia was completed in the early 1300s; there's a story that soon after, some citizens dug up a beautiful Greek statue of Venus, signed by Praxiteles himself. The delighted Sienese carried it in procession through the city and installed it on top of their new fountain. With the devastation of the Black Death, however, the preachers were quick to blame God's wrath on the indecent pagan on the Fonte Gaia. Throughout history, the Sienese have always been ready to be shocked by their own sins; in this case, with their neighbours dropping like flies around them, they proved only too eager to make poor Venus the scapegoat. They chopped her into little bits, and a party of Sienese disguised as peasants smuggled the pieces over the border and buried them in Florentine territory to pass the bad luck on to their enemies.

On the southeastern side of the Campo stands the **Palazzo Pubblico***.*

If the Campo is like a Roman theatre, the main attraction on stage since 1310 has been this brick and stone palace, the enduring symbol of the Sienese Republic and still the town hall today. Its façade is the face of Siena's history, with the she-wolf of Senius and Ascanius, Medici balls, the IHS of San Bernardino, and squared Guelph crenellations, all in the shadow of the tremendous **Torre di Mangia** (*open daily 10–6, winter until 3.30, but times very according to daylight hours*), the graceful, needle-like tower that Henry James called 'Siena's Declaration of Independence'. At 335ft, the tower was the second tallest ever raised in medieval Italy (only the campanile in Cremona beats it). At the time, the cathedral tower up on its hill completely dominated Siena's skyline; the Council of the Nine wouldn't accept that the symbol of religious authority or any of the nobility's fortress-skyscrapers should be taller than the symbol of the republic, so its Perugian architects, Muccio and Francesco di Rinaldo, made sure its height would be hard to surpass.

There was a practical side to it, too. At the top hung the *comune*'s great bell, which had to be heard in every corner of the city tolling the hours and announcing the curfew, or calling the citizens to assemble in case of war or emergency. One of the first men to hold the job of bell-ringer gave the tower its name, a fat, sleepy fellow named *Mangiaguadagni* ('eat the profits') or just Mangia for short; there is a statue of him in one of the courtyards.

> *Climb the tower's endless staircase for the definitive view of Siena—on the clearest days you will also be able to see about half of the medieval republic's territory, a view that is absolutely, positively worth the slight risk of cardiac arrest (open daily 9–5.30; winter until 2.15pm; adm). At the foot of the tower, the marble* **Cappella della Piazza**, *with its graceful rounded arches, stands out clearly from the Gothic earnestness of the rest of the building. It was begun in 1352, in thanks for deliverance from the Black Death, but not finally completed until the mid-15th century.*

> *Most of the Palazzo Pubblico's ground floor is still used for city offices, but the* **upper floors** *have been made into the* **city's museum** (open 9–7.30, Sun 9–1.30; winter until 1.30, but times very according to daylight hours; adm. L8000).

Here the main attraction is the series of state rooms done in frescoes, a sampling of the best of Sienese art throughout the centuries. The first, the historical frescoes in the **Sala del Risorgimento**, were done by an artist named A. G. Cassioli only in 1886: the meeting of Vittorio Emanuele II with Garibaldi, his coronation, portraits and epigrams of past patriots, and an 'allegory of Italian Liberty', all in a colourful and photographically precise style. If anything, it is a tribute to Sienese artistic conservatism; finally liberated after 300 years of Florentine rule, they immediately went back to their good old medieval habits.

Next on the same floor is the **Sala di Badia** with frescoes depicting the story of Alessandro VII and some vigorous battle scenes by the Sienese Spinello Aretino (1300s) and the *Sixteen Virtues* by Martino di Bartolomeo. The adjoining **anticamera del Concistoro** has a lovely *Madonna and Child* by Matteo di Giovanni. In the **Sala del Concistoro**, Gobelin tapestries adorn the walls while the great Sienese Mannerist Beccafumi contributed a ceiling of frescoes in the 1530s celebrating the political virtues of antiquity; that theme is continued in the vestibule to the **Chapel**, with portraits of ancient heroes from Cicero to Judas Maccabeus, all by Taddeo di Bartolo. These portrayals, along with more portraits of the classical gods and goddesses and an interesting view of ancient Rome, show clearly just how widespread was the fascination with antiquity even in the 1300s. Intruding among the classical crew, there's also a king-sized St Christopher covering an entire wall. Before setting out on a journey it was good luck to catch a glimpse of this saint, and in Italy and Spain he is often painted extra large so you won't miss him. In a display case in the hall, some of the oldest treasures of the Sienese Republic are kept: the war helmet of the Captain of the People, and a delicate **golden rose**, a gift to the city from the Sienese pope, Pius II.

The **Chapel** (*Cappella del Consiglio*) is surrounded by a lovely wrought-iron grille designed by Jacopo della Quercia; when it is open you can see more frescoes by Taddeo di Bartolo, an altarpiece by Il Sodoma, and some exceptional carved wood seats, by Domenico di Nicolò (*c.*1415–28). In the adjacent chamber (the **Sala del Mappamondo**), only the outline is left of Lorenzetti's cosmological fresco, a diagram of the universe including all the celestial and angelic spheres, much like the one in the Campo Santo at Pisa. Above it, there is a very famous fresco by Simone Martini (*c.*1330), showing the redoubtable condottiere **Guidoriccio da Fogliano** on his way to attack the castle of Montemassi, during a revolt against Siena. Also by Martini is an enthroned Virgin, or *Maestà*, that is believed to be his earliest work (1315).

The Allegories of Good and Bad Government

When you enter the **Sala dei Nove** (or Sala della Pace), meeting room of the Council of the Nine, you'll understand at a glance why they ruled Siena so well. Whenever one of the councillors had the temptation to skim some cream off the top, or pass a fat contract over to his brother-in-law the paving contractor, or tighten the screws on the poor by raising the salt tax, he had only to look up at Ambrogio Lorenzetti's great frescoes to really feel like a worm. There are two complementary sets, with scenes of Siena under good government and bad, and allegorical councils of virtues or vices for each. Enthroned Justice rules the good Siena, with such counsellors as Peace, Prudence and Magnanimity; bad Siena groans under the thumb of one nasty piece of work, sneering, fanged Tyranny and his cronies: Pride, Vainglory, Avarice and Wrath among others. The good Siena is a happy place, with buildings in good repair, well-dressed folk who are dancing in the streets, and well-stocked shops where the merchants appear to be making a nice profit. Bad Siena is almost a mirror image, only the effects of the Tyrant's rule are plain to see: urban blight, crime in broad daylight, buildings crumbling and abandoned, and business bad for everybody—a landscape which for many of us modern city dwellers will seem all too familiar.

Lorenzetti finished his work around 1338, probably the most ambitious secular painting ever attempted up to that time. The work has been recently cleaned and restored; fittingly, Good Government has survived more or less intact, while Bad Government has not aged so well and many parts have been lost. In the next room is Guido da Siena's large *Madonna and Child* (mid-1200s), the earliest masterpiece of the Sienese school. If you're not up to climbing the tower, at least take the long, unmarked stairway by the Sala del Risorgimento that leads up to the **loggia**, with the second-best view over Siena and the disassembled bits and pieces of della Quercia's reliefs from the Fonte Gaia, not particularly impressive in their worn and damaged state, although *The Expulsion from Paradise* retains something of its power.

> *Part of the beauty of the Campo lies in the element of surprise; one usu-ally enters from narrow arcades between austere medieval palaces that give no hint of what lies on the other side. Two of Siena's three main streets form a graceful curve around the back of the Campo; where they meet the third, behind the Fonte Gaia, is the corner the Sienese call the* **Croce del Travaglio** *(a mysterious nickname: the 'cross of affliction').*

Here, the three-arched **Loggia della Mercanzia**, in a sense Siena's Royal Exchange, was the place where the Republic's merchants made their deals and settled their differences before the city's famed commercial tribunal. The Loggia marks the transition from Sienese Gothic to the early Renaissance style—begun in 1417, it was probably influenced by Florence's Loggia dei Lanzi. The five statues of saints around the columns are the work of Antonio Federighi and Vecchietta, the leading Sienese sculptor after della Quercia.

> *The three streets that meet here lead directly into the* **three terzi** *of Siena. All three are among the city's most beautiful streets.*
>
> *Southwest from the Croce del Travaglio, Via di Città climbs up to the highest and oldest part of Siena, the natural fortress of the Terzo di Città. On the way it passes the grandiose* **Palazzo Chigi-Saracini**.

This is the grandiose Gothic palace with mullioned windows that follows the curve of the street and has a wretched, barely alive old tree hanging over the courtyard wall. The tower dates from the 13th century; the rest beautifully com-bines stone and brick, and no one minds if you enter to see the lovely courtyard with its gallery, frescoed vaulting and old well. The palace contains an interna-tionally important music school, the Accademia Musicale Chigiana, and a large collection of instruments (Liszt's piano, Stradivarius violins, etc. are not really available for view—the school needs a written request or will only accept groups) and Sienese and Florentine art, that can be seen, along with its lavish concert chamber, by appointment, ✆ 46152. Next door is yet another reminder of the Piccolomini, the **Palazzo delle Papesse**. The family, along with the Colonna of Rome and the Correr of Venice, was one of the first really to exploit the fiscal pos-sibilities of the papacy; Aeneas Silvius (Pius II) built this palace, designed by Rossellino, for his sister, Caterina Piccolomini.

*All approaches from Via di Città to Siena's glorious Cathedral, spilling over the highest point in the city, are somewhat oblique. Backtrack a bit down Via di Città and turn left on Via dei Pellegrini, which winds around the back, past the Cathedral's **Baptistry** (open daily 10–1 and 2.30–5 winter; summer 9–7.30; adm L3000) tucked underneath.*

In this unusual but prominent setting the Office of Works architects squeezed in perhaps the only baptistry in Italy situated directly under a cathedral apse. Behind its unfinished 1390s Gothic façade, this baptistry contains some of the finest art in Siena. It's hard to see anything in this gloomy cellar, though; bring plenty of coins for the lighting machines.

Frescoes by Vecchietta, restored to death in the 19th century, decorate much of the interior. The crown jewel, however, is the **baptismal font**, a king-sized work embellished with some of the finest sculpture of the quattrocento. Of the gilded reliefs around the sides, *Herod's Feast* is by Donatello, and the *Baptism of Christ* and *St John in Prison* by Ghiberti. The first relief, with the *Annunciation of the Baptist's Birth*, is the work of Jacopo della Quercia, who also added the five statues of prophets above. Two of the statues at the corners of the font, the ones representing the virtues Hope and Charity, are also by Donatello.

To the right of the Baptistry, the banal-looking Renaissance **Palazzo del Magnifico** by Cozzarelli was the family headquarters of the Petrucci, Sienese power-brokers (and perhaps would-be tyrants) in the late 15th and early 16th centuries.

*Continue up the steps to the left of the Baptistry, and through a portal in a huge, free-standing wall of striped marble arches, a memorial to that incredible ill-starred 1339 rebuilding plan confounded by the plague. The **Cathedral** the Sienese had to settle for may not be a transcendent expression of faith, nor an important landmark in architecture, but it is certainly one of the most delightful, decorative ornaments in Christendom.*

Begun around 1200, it was one of the first Gothic cathedrals in central Italy. It started in good Gothic tradition as a communal effort and was not really a project of the Church. There doesn't seem to have been very much voluntary labour. Even in the Middle Ages Italians were a little too blasé for that—but every citizen with a cart was expected to bring two loads of marble from the quarries each year, earning him a special indulgence from the bishop. One load must have been white and the other black, for under the influence of Pisa, the Sienese built themselves one thoroughly striped cathedral—stripes darker and bolder than Pisa's or Lucca's. The campanile, with its distinctive fenestration, narrowing in size down six levels, rises over the city like a giant ice-cream parfait. Most of the body of the church was finished by 1270, and 14 years later

Giovanni Pisano was called in to create the sculpture for the lavish **façade**, with statues of biblical prophets and pagan philosophers. The upper half was not begun until the 1390s, and the glittering mosaics in the gables are, like Orvieto's, the work of Venetian artists of the late 19th century.

> The **interior** is a treasure-box (open 7.30–1.30 and 2.30–sunset). Perhaps the cathedral is the only church in Italy that could keep a serious visitor busy for an entire day. Upon entering the main portal, the ferociously striped pilasters and the Gothic vaulting, a blue firmament painted with golden stars, inevitably draw the eye upwards. However, the most spectacular feature is at your very feet—the **marble pavement**, where the peculiar figure smiling up at you is Hermes Trismegistus, the legendary Egyptian father of alchemy (see **Topics, p.58–9**), depicted in elegant sgraffito work of white and coloured marble.

In fact, the entire floor of the cathedral is covered with almost 12,000 square metres of virtuoso *sgraffito* in 56 scenes which include portraits, mystical allegories and events from the Old Testament. Like the Biccherna covers in the Palazzo Piccolomini, they are a tradition carried on over centuries. Many of Siena's best artists worked on them, beginning in 1369 and continuing into the 1600s; Giorgio Vasari claimed that Duccio di Buoninsegna himself first worked in this medium, though none of the pictures here is his.

Even in a building with so many marvels—the Piccolomini Library, Nicola Pisano's pulpit, Duccio's stained glass, works by Donatello, della Quercia, Pinturicchio, Michelangelo, Bernini and many others—this pavement perhaps takes pride of place. The greatest limitation of Sienese art was always the conservatism of its patrons, accustomed to demanding the same old images in the same old styles. Commissions from the Office of Cathedral Works, controlled by the state, were usually more liberal, allowing the artists to create such unique, and in some cases startling images, one of the greatest achievements of Renaissance Siena.

The *Hermes* on the cathedral pavement, by Giovanni di Stefano, was completed in the 1480s, a decade after Ficino's translation; it shows him together with Moses, holding a book with the inscription 'Take up thy letters and laws, O Egyptians'. Hermes is covered over, along with many of the other stonework figures, for much of the time. On either side, all 10 prophetic *Sibyls* done by various artists at the same time decorate the aisles of the church. Nor are Hermes and the sibyls the only peculiar thing on this floor. Directly behind him begins a series of large scenes, including a *Wheel of Fortune*, with men hanging on to it for dear life, another wheel of uncertain symbolism, and emblems of Siena and other Tuscan and Latin cities. Oddest of all is a work by Pinturicchio, variously titled the *Allegory of Virtue* or the *Allegory of Fortune*; on a rocky island full of

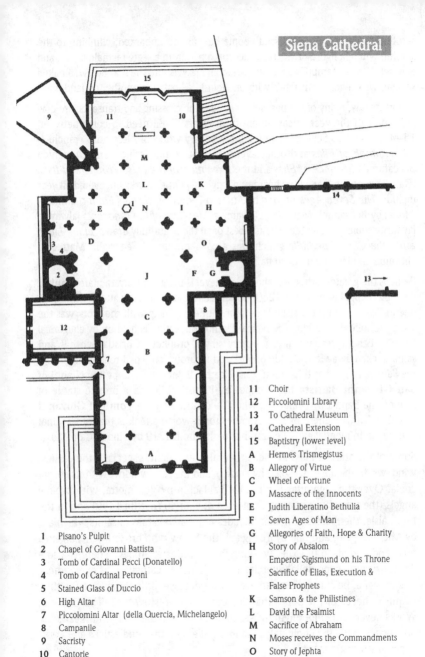

Siena Cathedral

15
5
11   10
9
6
M
L
K
E   1 N   I   H
D   O
3
4   F   G
2   J
13 →
12   C
8
B
7
A

1   Pisano's Pulpit
2   Chapel of Giovanni Battista
3   Tomb of Cardinal Pecci (Donatello)
4   Tomb of Cardinal Petroni
5   Stained Glass of Duccio
6   High Altar
7   Piccolomini Altar (della Quercia, Michelangelo)
8   Campanile
9   Sacristy
10 Cantorie

11 Choir
12 Piccolomini Library
13 To Cathedral Museum
14 Cathedral Extension
15 Baptistry (lower level)
A   Hermes Trismegistus
B   Allegory of Virtue
C   Wheel of Fortune
D   Massacre of the Innocents
E   Judith Liberatino Bethulia
F   Seven Ages of Man
G   Allegories of Faith, Hope & Charity
H   Story of Absalom
I   Emperor Sigismund on his Throne
J   Sacrifice of Elias, Execution &
    False Prophets
K   Samson & the Philistines
L   David the Psalmist
M   Sacrifice of Abraham
N   Moses receives the Commandments
O   Story of Jephta

243

serpents, a party of well-dressed people has just disembarked, climbing to the summit where a figure of 'Socrates' accepts a pen from a seated female figure, and another, 'Crates', empties a basket of gold and jewels into the sea. Below, a naked woman with a gonfalon stands with one foot in a boat, and another on land.

Unfortunately, many of the best scenes, under the crossing and transepts, are covered most of the year to save them from wear. You'll need to come between 15 August and 15 September to see the visionary works of Alessandro Franchi—the *Triumph of Elias* and other events in that prophet's life—and Domenico Beccafumi's *Sacrifice of Elias* and the *Execution of the False Prophets of Baal.* (Hasn't anyone in Siena ever heard of plexiglass?) Other works uncovered all year include *The Seven Ages of Man* by Antonio Federighi, *Scenes From the Life of Moses* by Beccafumi, Matteo di Giovanni's *Massacre of the Innocents* (always a favourite subject in Sienese art), and best of all the beautifully drawn *Judith Liberating the City of Bethulia* which was a collaboration of Federighi, Matteo di Giovanni and Urbano da Cortona.

Perhaps the greatest attraction above floor level is the great Carrara marble **pulpit** done by Nicola Pisano in the 1280s. Pisano started on it directly after finishing the one in Pisa; one of the assistants he brought here to help with the work was the young Arnolfo di Cambio. The typical Pisano conception is held up by allegorical figures of the seven liberal arts—more sibyls, prophets, Christian virtues and saints tucked away in the odd corners, and vigorous, crowded relief panels from the Passion as good as the ones in Pisa. Nearby, in the left transept, the **chapel of San Giovanni Battista** has frescoes by Pinturicchio and a bronze statue of St John the Baptist by Donatello, who also contributed the **Tomb of Giovanni Pecci**, a 1400s Sienese bishop. Another tomb worth a look is that of Cardinal Petroni, an influential early Renaissance design from 1310 by Tino di Camaino.

Some of the stained glass in the cathedral is excellent, especially the earliest windows, in the apse, designed by Duccio, and the rose window with its cornucopia. Over the high altar is a bronze baldachin by Vecchietta, with bronze angels (the two lower ones by Francesco di Giorgio Martini,1499) and in the north aisle, the Piccolomini altar includes four early statues of saints which are by Michelangelo, and one by Torrigiani, the fellow who broke Michelangelo's nose and ended up in exile, working in Westminster Abbey. There is also a *Madonna* by Jacopo della Quercia. Throughout the cathedral, as everywhere else in Siena, be sure to keep an eye out for details—little things like the tiny, exquisite heads of the popes that decorate the clerestory wall. The Office of Works never settled for anything less than the best, and even such trifles as the holy water fonts, the choir stalls, the iron grilles and the candlesticks are works of genuine artistic merit.

*The **Piccolomini Library** contains the famous frescoes by Pinturicchio maintained as part of the cathedral complex. It was built to hold the library of Aeneas Silvius, the greatest member of Siena's greatest noble family. The entrance is off the left aisle, near the Piccolomini Altar (open 10–1 and 2.30–4.45 daily; summer 9–7.15; adm L2000).*

Siena's Renaissance Man

Aeneas Silvius Piccolomini (1405–64), eventually to become Pope Pius II, was the very definition of a Renaissance man. One of 18 children who were born into a branch of the mighty Piccolomini family, little Aeneas's quick intelligence soon attracted a great deal of attention, and he received the finest humanist education Siena could offer. To this he added natural charm, good looks, excellent Latin and an innate sense of diplomacy that soon earned him posts of responsibility with the leading ecclesiastics of the day.

Aeneas Silvius' interests ranged wide, and his keen observations and objective point of view on all aspects of life were invaluable to the scholarship of the day, especially in geography and topography. His *On Europe*, *On Asia* and *An Account of Bohemia* were among the most important works since ancient times; *On Asia* was closely studied by Columbus. Aeneas had enough time left over to write weighty tomes on history, on the lives of great men, on education and on antiquities; he was gifted enough in literature (he wrote poetry, a comedy and an erotic novella) to be crowned Poet Laureate. In politics, he worked fitfully to reform the Church of Rome and the constitution of Siena. He was the first to detail and describe the beauties of the Italian landscape, in which he found the greatest delight, as well as the little scenes of daily life that struck him. These, along with his thoughts and ambitions, even the unseemly, unflattering ones, went into his *Commentaries*, the most vivid and personal autobiography until Benvenuto Cellini's, and the only one ever published by a pope.

Aeneas Silvius took holy orders in 1446, marking a new serious turn in his life. Thanks to his service to popes Eugenius IV, Nicholas V and Calixtus III he became a bishop and cardinal, and was elected pope in 1458, in a corrupt conclave that he described in frank detail. His election hardly put an end to his womanizing, although his peers, who thought they had elected a worldly humanist, were astonished at Pius II's dedicated efforts to promote the papacy and defend the faith by preaching a Crusade against the Turks who had just captured Constantinople. His chief memorial is the little Renaissance city of Pienza, southeast of Siena, which Bernardo Rossellino created out of the humble village of his birth, Corsignano. But because of the honesty of his autobiography, Pius II has never been considered a very good pope, although 15th-century historians praised his honesty, courage and consistency. The irony is that other Renaissance popes were surely just as conniving and ambitious if not worse (for one thing, Pius II was one of the first who didn't believe in magic or astrology); the difference is they never wrote down their thoughts.

In 1495, 31 years after his death, Cardinal Francesco Piccolomini, a man who would become Pope Pius III, decided his celebrated uncle's life would make a fine subject for a series of frescoes. He gave the job to Pinturicchio, his last major commission; among his assistants was the young, still impressionable Raphael—anyone who knows his *Betrothal of the Virgin* will find these paintings eerily familiar. The 10 scenes include Aeneas Silvius' attendance at the court of James I in Scotland—a Scotland with a Tuscan landscape—where he served with an embassy. Later he is shown accepting a poet laureate's crown from his friend Emperor Frederick III, and presiding over the meeting of Frederick and his bride-to-be, Eleanor of Aragon. Another fresco depicts him canonizing St Catherine of Siena. The last, poignant one portrays a view of Ancona, and its cathedral on Monte Guasco, where Pius II went in 1464, planning a crusade against the Turks. While waiting for the help promised by the European powers, help that never came, he fell ill and died.

Art historians and critics, following the sniping biography of the artist by Vasari, are not always kind to Pinturicchio. As with Gozzoli's frescoes for the Medici Palace in Florence, the consensus seems to be that this is a less challenging sort of art, or perhaps just a very elevated approach to interior decoration. Certainly Pinturicchio seems extremely concerned with the latest styles in court dress and coiffure. However, the incandescent colour, fairy-tale backgrounds and beautifully drawn figures prove irresistible. These are among the brightest and best-preserved of all quattrocento frescoes; the total effect is that of a serenely confident art, concerned above all with beauty for beauty's sake, even when chronicling the life of a pope. Aeneas Silvius' books have all been carted away somewhere but one of his favourite things remains, a marble statue of the *Three Graces*, a copy of the work by Praxiteles that was much studied by the artists of the 1400s.

> *Around the side of the cathedral, off the right transept, Piazza Jacopo della Quercia is the name the Sienese have given to the doomed nave of their 1330s* **cathedral extension***. All around the square, the heroic pilasters and arches rise, some incorporated into the walls of later buildings. Beyond the big, blank façade, a little door on the right gives entrance to the* **Museo Metropolitana***, built into what would have been one of the cathedral transepts (open Nov–mid-March 9–1; 9–7.30 till end Sept; 9–6 Oct; adm).*

This is the place to go to inspect the cathedral façade at close range. Most of the statues now on the façade are modern copies, replacing the works of great sculptors like Nicola Pisano, Urbano da Cortona and Jacopo della Quercia. The originals have been moved to the museum for preservation, and you can look the cathedral's marble saints right in the eye (many of these remarkable statues, fairly alive with early Renaissance *prontezza* (alertness), seem ready to hop off their pedestals and start declaiming if they suspect for a minute you've been skipping Sunday Mass).

Besides these, there are some architectural fragments and leftover pinnacles, as well as some bits of the marble pavement that had to be replaced. On the first floor, a collection of Sienese paintings includes Duccio di Buoninsegna's masterpiece, the *Maestà* that hung behind the cathedral's high altar from 1311 until 1505. Painted on both sides, the main composition is a familiar Sienese favourite, the enthroned Virgin flanked by neat rows of adoring saints—expressive faces and fancy clothes with a glittering gold background. Among the other paintings and sculptures are works by Pietro and Ambrogio Lorenzetti, Simone Martini, Beccafumi and Vecchietta.

Among the works on the top floor is the *Madonna dagli Occhi Grossi* ('of the Big Eyes') by an anonymous artist of the 1210s, a landmark in the development of Sienese painting and the original cathedral altarpiece. There's a hoard of golden croziers, reliquaries, and crucifixes from the Cathedral Treasure, including another lovely golden rose from the Vatican; this was probably a gift from Aeneas Silvius. A stairway leads up to the top of the **Facciatone**, the 'big façade' of the unfinished nave, where you can enjoy a view over the city.

> *Opposite the old cathedral façade, one entire side of the piazza is occupied by the great* **Ospedale di Santa Maria della Scala**, *believed to have been founded in the 9th century. For centuries one of the largest and finest hospitals in the world, this is now Italy's biggest and most exciting museum project* (open daily; the hours change every few weeks but if you come between 10.30 and 4:30 (open later in summer) you're sure to get in; adm).

According to legend, the hospital had its beginnings with a pious cobbler named Sorore, who opened a hostel and infirmary for pilgrims who were on their way to Rome. (Siena was an important stop on medieval Europe's busiest pilgrimage route, the Via Francigiana.) Sorore's mother, it is said, later had a vision here—of babies ascending a ladder into heaven, and being received into the arms of the Virgin Mary—and consequently a foundling hospital was soon added. A meticulous attention to the health of its citizens was always one of the most praiseworthy features of Siena; in the 14th century it insisted on such revolutionary practices as the washing of hands by doctors and nurses, meals adapted to each patient's illness, and the use of iron beds (to prevent the spread of bedbugs). To encourage donations, laws were passed allowing wealthy Sienese to deduct gifts from their taxes (remember, this is the 14th century) and not a few left huge sums in their wills; after the plague of 1348, the hospital was up to its ears in gold. Even in the decadence of the 1700s advances in such things as inoculations were being made here.

In recent years, the hospital functions have been gradually moved out to more accessible locations (one of the last to die here was novelist and folktale compiler, Italo Calvino). As the place closed up, there was talk of converting it into a museum. Now they're doing it, and in a big way. The Sienese say that their new museum, dedicated to all the arts of the city's history, will be one of the largest in the world, with three times the exhibition space of the Pompidou Centre. Don't ask when it will be finished; the point of this innovative exercise is that it will *never* be finished. An international competition was held to plan the new complex; the winner, Professor Guido Canali of Parma, came up with the idea of a *cantiere didattico*, an 'educational construction site' so to speak, where the process of museum-building itself is part of the attraction. Nevertheless, they should have much of the permanent exhibits in place in ten years or so, along with shops, temporary exhibits and restoration workshops. In a typical gesture of Sienese civic pride, the comune declined to ask for state help in getting this project done; they mean to keep control of it by paying the whole bill themselves.

For now, it's definitely worth the price of admission just to see the big frescoes in the **Sala dei Pellegrini**, the hospital's main reception hall. Another pioneering fresco cycle devoted to a secular subject, like those in the Palazzo Pubblico, this is a tribute to old Siena's advanced, humanistic outlook; all the scenes are devoted to the history of the hospital, including the vision of Sorore's mother, and everyday views of the hospital's activities. In the best of them, Domenico di Bartolo shows how Sienese art was still keeping up with the Florentines in 1441 with his *Reception, Education and Marriage of a Daughter of the Hospital*; care of abandoned children, the *getatelli* (literally, 'little ones thrown away'), was one of the hospital's important functions. Other frescoes, by different Sienese artists, portray in loving detail the care of the sick, the distribution of alms to the poor, and the paying of the wetnurses of the *getatelli.* All are lively, crowded scenes of life in a unique institution, and an insight into a side of old Siena you might not have thought to exist.

Already, there is plenty more to see, including a collection of precious golden reliquaries and other church paraphernalia, some of it from medieval Constantinople, in refurbished chambers cheerfully marked *isolamento dei contagiosi.* Some other original features of the hospital include the **Capella del Sacro Chiodo**, with damaged frescoes by Vecchietta, the elaborate **Capella SS. Annunziata**, and the thoroughly spooky **Capella di Santa Caterina**, which begins with a leering skull and ends with an altarpiece by Taddeo di Bartolo. Old views and relics of the hospital are displayed in many of the long hallways of the complex; in some of the oldest, you can see how the façade was originally covered with frescoes, a colourful counterpoint to the cathedral façade across the way.

Another part of the complex now houses the **Museo Archeologico**, with an Etruscan and Roman collection (*open 9–2, Sun 9–1; closed 2nd and 4th Sun of the month; adm L4000*).

> *For a short detour, take almost-hidden Vicolo di San Girolamo, which leads down from the right side of Santa Maria della Scala into an ancient quarter of steep narrow streets below the hospital, all part of the **contrada** of the Selva.*

Tucked away in a corner to the left, little Piazza della Selva has one of the most charming of the new *contrade* fountains, topped by a bronze statue of the neighbourhood's rhinoceros symbol. Here too is Selva's pretty parish church, Renaissance **San Sebastiano** *(often open Saturday afternoons)*, built in the form of a Greek cross in 1507, chock-full of interesting paintings (including an *Assumption* by Lorenzo Sabbatini), frescoes and reliquaries.

> *Leaving the cathedral in the opposite direction, climb back up the steep steps and cross Piazza del Duomo to walk south down Via del Capitano, leading you into the haunts of the dolphin and turtle (Onda and Tartuga). Where the street meets Via di Città, it changes its name to Via San Pietro, passing the 14th-century Palazzo Buonsignori, one of the most harmonious of the city's noble palaces, now restored as the home of the **Pinacoteca Nazionale** (open 9–7; Sun 8–1; Mon 8.30–1; adm).*

This is the temple of Sienese art, a representative sampling of this inimitable city's style; many of the works have been recently restored. The collection is arranged roughly chronologically, beginning on the ground floor with Guido da Siena and his school in the mid-13th century (**Room 2**), continuing through an entire room of delicate, melancholy Virgins by Duccio and his followers, reaching a climax with Duccio's luminous though damaged *Madonna dei Francescani* in **Room 4**. More Madonnas and saints fill room after room, including important works by Siena's greatest 14th-century artists. One of the most famous is Simone Martini's *Madonna and Child*; the story goes that this Madonna was a great Palio fan. When everyone had gathered in the Campo for the event, she would wander out in the empty streets and tiptoe over for a look. One day, she lingered too long in the Campo and had to run back home, losing her veil in her haste. She has yet to find it, and according to the Sienese, she weeps sweetly during the Palio, probably because she can't get through the Pinacoteca's security system. Other Madonnas that stand out are those of Pietro and Ambrogio Lorenzetti (*Madonna Enthroned* and the *Annunciation*, both in **Room 7**) and Taddeo di Bartolo (*Triptych*, in **Room 9**), with their rosy blooming faces and brilliant colour, a remarkable counterpoint to the relative austerity of contemporary painting in Florence. One element that is clearly evident in many of these paintings is Sienese civic pride; the artists take obvious delight in including the city's skyline and landmarks in the background of their works—even in nativities.

Sienese Renaissance painters are well represented, often betraying the essential conservatism of their art and resisting the new approaches of Florence: Domenico di Bartolo's 1433 *Madonna* in **Room 9**; Nerocchio and Matteo di Giovanni of the 1470s (**Room 14**); Sano di Pietro, the leading painter of the 1440s (**Rooms 16–18**). The first floor displays some of Il Sodoma's most important works, especially the great *Scourging of Christ* which is in **Room 31** (1514); in **Room 37** the *Descent into Hell* is one of the finest works by Siena's great Mannerist, Beccafumi.

> *Next to the Pinacoteca, the church of **San Pietro alle Scale** contains* The Flight into Egypt, *an altarpiece by Rutilio Manetti, the only significant Sienese painter of the Baroque era and a follower of Caravaggio. From here, turn right into Via Tommaso Pendola and left at Via di San Quirico.*

Here in the centre of the *contrada* of the *Chiocciola* (snail) is a work by Baldassare Peruzzi: **Santa Maria del Carmine**, a 14th-century church remodelled by Peruzzi in 1517. It houses a painting of *St Michael*, one of Beccafumi's masterpieces, and a grimly Cavaraggiesque *Last Judgement* by an anonymous 16th-century artist.

> *Via delle Cerchia will take you back towards the centre, past Via Piero Andrea Mattioli which leads to Siena's small **Botanical Gardens** (open Mon–Fri 8–5, Sat 8–12; book in advance for a guided tour, ✆ 298874). Via delle Cerchia continues to the panoramic Prato Sant'Agostino and the church of **Sant'Agostino**.*

This gloomy bulk conceals a happy rococo interior of 1749 by Vanvitelli, a Dutchman born Van Wittel who was the chief architect of the kings of Naples. Most of the building dates back to the 13th century, however, and there are surviving bits of trecento frescoes and altarpieces all around. On the right, seek out Perugino's *Crucifixion*, a rare non-Sienese painting. After the war, the other works of art were gathered together in the nearby Piccolomini chapel: a fine painting of the *Epiphany* by Il Sodoma, with a background reminiscent of Leonardo da Vinci, a horrific *Massacre of the Innocents* by Matteo di Giovanni, one of his favourite subjects, and a lovely *Madonna and Saints*, frescoed in the lunette by Ambrogio Lorenzetti. In the Cappella Bichi, frescoes were uncovered in 1978, believed to be by Francesco di Giorgio Martini, an artist who went on to become more famous for his military engineering.

At Prato de Sant'Agostino 4 is one of Siena's Old Curiosity Shops, the **Accademia di Fisiocritici** *(open 9–1 and 3–6; closed Sat, Sun and Thurs afternoons; check at the tourist office).*

Founded in 1691, the academy of Fisiocritici made important contributions to the study of the natural sciences in the Enlightenment. Today it holds a delightfully dusty, old-fashioned science museum, with 2000 terracotta mushrooms, meteorites that fell near Siena in 1794, stuffed birds and a beautiful collection of minerals.

Via Piero Andrea Mattioli will take you on a long detour to the city walls and the **Porta Tufi;** *instead, head down pretty Via Sant'Agata/Via Giovanni Dupré, past* **San Giuseppe.**

This church marks Siena's uneasy compromise with the new world of the 1600s. One of the city's first Baroque churches, it was nevertheless built not in Baroque marble or travertine but in Siena brown brick. It is in the parish of the *Onda* district.

Turn right off the end of Via Giovanni Dupré to reach Piazza del Mercato, Siena's market square, directly under the Palazzo Pubblico; cross this to enter the populous eastern third of the city, the **Terzo San Martino.**

The most intriguing parts of this neighbourhood are here on the hillside behind Piazza del Mercato, old streets on slopes and stairs in the *contrada* of the *Torre*—one of the 'unlucky' *contrade* that hasn't won a Palio in decades. If you have time, take a stroll down **Via Porta Giustizia** for a country ramble within the city walls and down into the valley that separates Terzo di San Martino from Terzo di Città.

Alternatively, take Via Malcontenti from Piazza del Mercato, turn right in Via Salicotta, left at steep Vicolo di Coda, go up to the top and then right again at Via del Rialto which becomes **Vicolo dell'Oro,** *an alley of overhanging medieval houses, much like the ones in the Palazzo Pubblico's frescoes of Good and Bad Government. Bearing right, Via S. Girolamo leads around to Via dei Servi and* **Santa Maria dei Servi,** *its massive campanile looming over Piazza Alessandro Manzoni, the heart of the* contrada *of the* Valdimontone *(ram).*

Here, in the north transept, is one of the earliest and best Sienese nativities, the altarpiece in the second north chapel by Taddeo di Bartolo. Among the many other good paintings in this church is a *Madonna* by Coppo di Marcovaldo and the *Madonna del Popolo* by Lippo Memmi. An interesting comparison can be made between two versions of that favourite Sienese subject, the *Massacre of the Innocents*: one from the early trecento by Pietro Lorenzetti, and another from 1491 by Matteo di Giovanni.

Just east of Piazza Alessandro Manzoni, Via Val di Montone and Via Roma descend to one of Siena's best surviving city gates, the double-fortified **Porta Romana** *of 1327; in the opposite direction, it leads up to the* **Società Esecutori Pie Disposizioni** *(best to call ahead, ✆ 284300; open Mon–Fri 9–12, also Tues and Thurs 3–5) at No.71, which keeps an oratory and a small but choice collection of paintings by Il Sodoma and other Sienese masters. At No.47 is the 15th-century* **Palazzo di San Galgano**, *sometimes attributed to Giuliano da Maiano. From Via Roma turn right in Via Oliviera, then left in Vicolo del Sasso for* **Santo Spirito**.

Not many visitors make it to this little domed church with its pure Renaissance portal. It holds another set of frescoes by Il Sodoma in the Spanish chapel on the right, with a figure of *St James of Compostela* on horseback, slicing up hapless Moors with his sword and a virile *St Sebastian*.

Via Pispini, which passes in front of the church, is the road to Perugia, and at the end is the elegant fortified **Porta Pispini**, *embellished by Il Sodoma with a fine* Nativity, *although only traces of it remain today. After Porta Pispini, double back and follow Via Pispini until it meets Via Pantaneto. Turn right, and this will return you to the Croce del Travaglio by way of the* **Loggia del Papa**.

This Renaissance ornament, designed by Federighi and decorated by Francesco di Giorgio Martini, was given to Siena by Aeneas Silvius Piccolomini in 1462. Nearby, the single-naved church of **San Martino** was given a new façade in 1613 and holds a *Nativity* by Beccafumi in the left aisle, and in the right aisle, a recently restored *Circumcision* by Guido Reni.

Continue a short way down the graceful curve of Via Banchi di Sotto to Siena's most imposing palazzo privato, *the* **Palazzo Piccolomini** *(open daily 9–1, Sat 9–12.30; closed Sun), done in the Florentine style by Rossellino in the 1460s.*

This palace now houses the old Sienese state archive—not a place you might consider visiting but for the presence of the famous *Tavolette della Biccherna* (the account books of the *Biccherna*, or state treasury). Beginning in the 1200s, the Republic's custom was to commission the best local artists to decorate the covers of the *tavolette*; the most interesting show such prosaic subjects as medieval citizens coming in to pay their taxes, city employees counting their pay and earnest monks trying to make the figures square—all are Cistercians from San Galgano, the only people medieval Siena trusted to do the job. Among the other manuscripts and documents you'll find Boccaccio's will.

Start: *Via Banchi di Sopra*
Finish: *Porta Camollia*
Walking time: *half a day*

II: Around the Terzo di Camollia

This walk explores medieval palaces, frescoed parish churches, city gates and delightful *contrade* fountains in Siena's third 'petal'— The Terzo di Camollia.

Lunch/Cafés

Antico Sghengero, Via di Città 13. A tiny but welcoming stand-up bar just off the Campo selling interesting sandwiches and drinks.

Gastronomia Morbidi, Banchi di Sopra 75, ☎ 280268. Founded in 1925, four floors of national and Sienese culinary specialities and a wine section selling all the best wines in Italy.

Gelateria Nannini, Piazza Salimbeni. Bar and ice-cream parlour with a wide choice (closed Fri); also bar gelateria in Piazza Matteotti 32.

Nannini, Banchi di Sopra 41. Big old-fashioned bar serving cakes and sandwiches, coffee and cocktails. You can also buy a wide selection of Sienese goodies here including panforte sold by weight.

Osteria la Chiacchera, Costa di S. Antonio 4, ☎ 280631. Near the Casa di S. Caterina, this tiny trattoria offers simple and traditional Sienese dishes served at marble-topped tables. About L25,000 (closed Sun).

Il Salotto, Via Camollia 31–32. A selection of pizzas, crepes and pastas at reasonable prices are served at this trendy bar, conveniently placed near the end of the walk.

Leading north from the Campo, Via Banchi di Sopra, a most aristocratic thoroughfare, is lined with the palaces of the medieval Sienese élite. It forms the spine of the **Terzo di Camollia***, the largest and most populous of the terzi.*

The first important palace is also one of the oldest, that of the Tolomei family, a proud clan of noble bankers who liked to trace their ancestry back to the Greek Ptolemies of Hellenistic-era Egypt. The **Palazzo Tolomei**, begun in 1208, is the very soul of Sienese Gothic; it gave its name to Piazza Tolomei in front, the space used by the Republic for its assembly meetings before the construction of the Palazzo Pubblico and is now, appropriately, a bank.

In front note Siena's she-wolf (1610); opposite, the church of **San Cristoforo** is one of the oldest in the city; two galleries of the cloister remain off to the left.

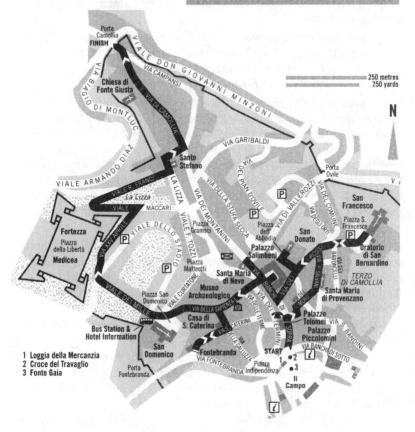

250 metres
250 yards

N

1 Loggia della Mercanzia
2 Croce del Travaglio
3 Fonte Gaia

The remaining bit of cloister of the church of San Cristoforo is to be found through a little wooden door which faces you as you turn right down Via del Moro which will take you down to the 1594 proto-Baroque **Santa Maria di Provenzano**.

Parish church of the *contrada* of the Giraffe, this is one of the last important churches erected in Siena, built by Flaminio del Turco, with the most imposing interior after the Cathedral itself; lofty pillars support a daring dome. This particular Virgin Mary, a terracotta image said to be left by St Catherine (*see* p.258), has had one of the most popular devotional cults in Siena since the 1590s; the Palio of 2 July is in her honour, and the banner is usually kept here along with a vast array of ex-votos.

> *The quiet streets behind the church were Siena's red light district in Renaissance times. Walk north of Santa Maria on Via Provenzano Salvani, and turn right at Via dei Rossi, to bring you out at one of the city's largest churches,* **San Francesco,** *begun in 1326.*

It's a sad tale; after a big fire in the 17th century, this great Franciscan barn was used for centuries as a warehouse and barracks. Restorations were begun in the 1880s, and the 'medieval' brick façade was completed only in 1913. The striped interior is still one of the most impressive in Siena, a monolithic rectangle with vivid stained glass (especially so in the late afternoon) and good transept chapels in the Florentine manner. A few bits of art have survived, including damaged frescoes by both Lorenzettis in the north transept, a *Crucifixion* by Pietro, and two fine works by Ambrogio—the strangely-coloured *Martyrdom of the Franciscans at Ceuta* and *St Louis d'Anjou at the Feet of Boniface VIII.*

Next to San Francesco is the equally simple **Oratorio di San Bernardino**, begun in the late 1400s to hold the heart of Siena's famous Franciscan (1380–1444), considered the foremost and most persuasive Italian preacher of the 15th century (*open between mid-March and end Oct*). If Bernardino wasn't entirely successful in taming the worldly pride of Siena's nobles, his motto 'Make it clear, make it short, and keep it to the point' has earned him a difficult posthumous job as the patron saint of advertising.

The upper chapel of the oratory *(not usually open, but ring for the doorkeeper)* is one of the monuments of the Sienese Renaissance, containing fine frescoes by Beccafumi, Il Sodoma, and the almost forgotten High Renaissance master Girolamo del Pacchia, few of whose works survive.

> *After San Francesco, you need to backtrack down Via dei Rossi to see the fountain of the* Bruco (caterpillar) contrada; *it's built into the wall under the road on your right as you walk away from San Francesco (not under the steps). Go down to the fountain, and look behind you; on the wall of the house opposite is a curious marble bas-relief of a woman at a window peering at a pomegranate from behind half-closed curtains. There are caterpillars everywhere!*

Bruco's name recalls the famous Compagnìa del Bruco, the trade union that initiated the revolt of 1371 and temporarily reformed Siena's faction-ridden government. The workers paid a terrible price for it; while the revolution was under way, some young noble *provocateurs* started a fire that consumed almost the entire *contrada*. Today *Bruco* is the worst of the 'unlucky' neighbourhoods; it hasn't won a Palio since 1955.

> *Midway down Via dei Rossi, turn right for one of Siena's most delightful squares, Piazza dell'Abbadia, home to the simple little church of **San Donato**, with a delicate rose window. It enjoys a fine view over the magnificent Gothic windows of the rear façade of **Palazzo Salimbeni**; to see the front, continue down Via dei Rossi and turn right.*

This was the compound of the Tolomeis' mortal enemies, and their centuries-long vendetta dragged Sienese politics into chaos on more than a few occasions. Together with the two adjacent palaces on the square, the Salimbeni is now home of the **Monte dei Paschi di Siena**, the oldest bank in Italy, founded in 1472. This remarkable savings bank, with a medieval air, has a tremendous influence over everything that happens in southern Tuscany. Ultra-modern inside, the bank holds a good art collection, sometimes open to the public with special exhibitions.

> *Continue up Via Banchi di Sopra to **Santa Maria della Neve**.*

You may be lucky enough to find this suavely elegant oratory, attributed to Francesco di Giorgio Martini (1470), open; if so, go inside to see the altarpiece, *Our Lady of the Snows*, the masterpiece of Matteo di Giovanni.

> *With Palazzo Salimbeni at your back, walk along Costa Incrociata to Via Sapienza. The **Biblioteca Comunale Intronati** next door has a precious collection of manuscripts—among them, some of St Catherine's 400 letters and a copy of the* Divine Comedy *with illustrations by Botticelli (open 9–7, Sat 9–2, closed Sun; adm free). From the archaeology museum, turn down Costa Sant'Antonio and turn right in Via Santa Caterina, the main street of the* contrada *of the* Oca, *which stretches down steeply to the western city walls. In contrast to poor caterpillar, the equally proletarian **Oca** (goose) seems to have always been the best organized and most successful of the* contrade. *During the Napoleonic Wars when the Tuscan and city governments were in disarray, the Oca's men temporarily took charge of the city. The goose's most famous daughter, Caterina Benincasa, was born here, on Vicolo del Tiratoio, in 1347.*

> *Off Via Santa Caterina, in Vicolo di Tiratoio, St Catherine's house is preserved as a shrine, the **Santuario e Casa di Santa Caterina** (open daily winter 9–12.30 and 3.30–6, summer 9–12.30 and 2.30–6; free adm) The entrance is on Costa Sant' Antonio. Then turn right in Via Santa Caterina.*

St Catherine

St Catherine was the last but one of the 25 children born into the family of a wool dyer. At an early age, the visions started. By her teens she had turned her room at home into a cell, and while she never became a nun, she lived like a hermit, a solitary ascetic in her own house, sleeping with a stone for a pillow. After she received the stigmata, like St Francis, her reputation as a holy woman spread across Tuscany. But Catherine was quite a different kettle of fish. Unlike the charming, other-worldly Francis, she was tremendously political and involved in the temporal affairs of her day. The records say she never smiled. Completely illiterate, she corresponded through a secretary with popes, emperors and towns that asked her to settle disputes, and her letters are powerful masterpieces of direct, simple, righteous prose, although it has been noted that her favourite words were 'fire' and 'blood'. So complete was the moral authority conferred by her saintliness and humility that she could say: 'What I want, I order.' She wasn't always obeyed: her letter to the *condottiere* Sir John Hawkwood (of the equestrian fresco in Florence cathedral) asking him to lead a Crusade, met with a polite 'No, thank you'.

In 1378, Florence was under a papal interdict, and the city asked Catherine to plead its case at the papal court in Avignon. She went, but with an agenda of her own—convincing Pope Gregory XI (whom in her 'holy insolence' she addressed as *Babbo mio* or 'Daddy') to move the papacy back to Rome where it belonged. As a woman, and a holy woman to boot, she was able to tell the pope to his face what a corrupt and worldly Church he was running, without ending up dangling from the palace wall.

Talking the pope (a French pope, mind you) into leaving the civilized life in Provence for turbulent, barbaric 14th-century Rome is only one of the miracles with which Catherine was credited. Political expediency probably helped more than divine intervention—much of Italy, including anathemized Florence, was in revolt against the absentee popes. She followed them back, and died in Rome in 1380, at the age of only 33, her heart broken when she heard that an anti-pope had been enthroned in Avignon, beginning the Great Schism. Canonization came in 1460 and in our own century she has been declared co-patron of Italy (along with St Francis) and one of the Doctors of the Church. She and St Teresa of Avila are the only women to hold this honour, both of them for their inspired devotional writings and practical, incisive letters enouraging church reform.

The sanctuary, behind a grand portico donated in the 1940s by the cities of Italy, occupies the whole of the Benincasa home and the dyer's workshop, each room converted into a chapel, many with ceiling frescoes by 15th- and 16th-century Sienese artists, although oddly none was inspired to paint his best. There are four oratories in the house, and relics such as St Catherine's rock-pillow. The old kitchen, now the upper oratory, has a beautiful 17th-century tile floor; another oratory now serves as the *Oca's contrada* chapel (note the goose in the detail of the façade).

> *Via Santa Caterina slopes down towards the city walls and to the* **Fontebranda**, *a simple, pointed-arched fountain of the 13th century, topped by lion gargoyles.*

It doesn't seem much now, but medieval and Renaissance travellers always remarked on it, as an important part of Siena's advanced system of fountains and aqueducts. On the hill above the Fontebranda, however, the bold Gothic lines of the apse and transepts of San Domenico give a great insight into the straightforward, strangely modern character of much of Sienese religious architecture.

> *From here you get the best view of* **San Domenico** (open winter 9–1 and 3–6; summer 7–1 and 3–6.30); *for a closer look it's a long climb. The easiest way up is to retrace your steps to St Catherine's house and Costa Sant'Antonio, turning left in Via della Sapienza for Piazza San Domenico, which doubles as the bus depot.*

Inside, the church is as big and empty as San Francesco; among the relatively few works of art is the only portrait from the life of *St Catherine*, on the west wall, done by her friend, the artist Andrea Vanni. This church was the scene of many incidents in the saint's life—she was known to go into ecstasy in the Cappella della Volte, where many Sienese watched the Host go flying from the hand of the priest directly into her mouth. Her head is ensconced in a golden reliquary (the Romans, suspecting she would be canonized one day, cut her body into bits when she died—the Venetians made off with a foot). The real attraction, though, is the wonderfully hysterical set of frescoes by Il Sodoma in the **Cappella Santa Caterina**, representing the girl in various states of serious exaltation. The lateral fresco on the left depicts one of the more disturbing scenes from her letters: a Sienese, Niccolo di Tuldo, was condemned to death for some misdemeanour and in rage filled his prison cell with curses. Catherine arrived to calm him down and succeeded so well in convincing him to submit to his own sacrifice that the two of them went off to the site of execution as if going to a party; Catherine undid his collar for him, and let his head drop on her own lap after the chop. The saint wrote: 'When the cadaver was taken away, my soul rested in such delicious peace and I rejoiced so in the perfume of that blood that I did not wish them to take away that thing that lay upon my clothes.'

> *The open, relatively modern quarter around San Domenico offers a welcome change from the dark and treeless streets of this brick city. From Piazza San Domenico, walk down Via dei Mille and turn right at Via XXV Aprile for the shady park of **La Lizza**, and down Via C. Maccari for the **Fortezza Medicea.***

Though the site is the same, this is not the hated fortress Charles V compelled the Sienese to build in 1552; as soon as the Sienese chased the imperial troops out, they razed it to the ground. Cosimo I forced its rebuilding after annexing Siena, but to make the bitter pill easier to swallow he employed a Sienese architect, Baldassare Lanci, and let him create what must be the most elegant and civilized, least threatening fortress in Italy. The Fortezza, a long, low rectangle of Siena brick profusely decorated with Medici balls, seems more like a setting for garden parties or summer opera than anything designed to intimidate a sullen populace. The Sienese weren't completely won over; right after Italian reunification they renamed the central space of the fortress **Piazza della Libertà**. The grounds are now a city park, and the vaults of the munition cellars have become the **Enoteca Nazionale**, the 'Permanent Exhibition of Italian Wines'. Almost every variety of wine Italy produces can be bought here—by the glass or by the bottle; the Enoteca's purpose is to promote Italian wines, and it ships thousands of bottles overseas each year (*open Tues–Sat noon–1am, Mon noon–8; closed Sun*).

> *From the Fortezza walk up Viale Franci, and then turn left, passing Santo Stefano and turn left in Via di Camollia for the charming little Renaissance church of **Fonte Giusta**, in Vicolo Fontegiusta.*

Designed in 1482 by Urbano da Cortona, Fonte Giusta has a square plan, divided into three short naves. There is an elaborate marble altar, and a lovely painting of *The Sibyl Announcing to Augustus the Coming of Christ* by architect and stage designer Baldassare Peruzzi (1481–1536), a native of Siena who spent most of his career in Rome—where he built the Villa Farnesina for Sienese banker Agostino Chigi, a building generally considered the finest secular building of the High Renaissance. He later worked as architect of St Peter's after the death of Raphael in 1520. His architectural style was more delicate and graceful than any other of his age, and his services were always in demand, but according to Vasari he never made any money because he was too good-natured to demand any from his wealthy patrons.

*From here it is a short walk along the Via di Camollia to the **Porta Camollia** in the northernmost corner of Siena, which underwent the Baroque treatment in the 1600s.*

Here you will see the famous inscription 'Wider than her gates Siena opens her heart to you'. Old Siena was never that sentimental. The whole thing was added in 1604—undoubtedly under the orders of the Florentine governor—to mark the visit of Grand Duke Francesco I, who wasn't really welcome at all.

Peripheral Attractions

From Porta Camollia, Viale Vittorio Emanuele leads through some of the modern quarters outside the walls. Soon after the Camollia gate it passes a pretty stone column, commemorating the meeting of Emperor Frederick III and his bride-to-be Eleanor of Aragon in 1451—the event captured in one of the Pinturicchio frescoes in the Piccolomini Library. Next looms a great brick defence tower, the **Antiporto**, erected just before the Siege of Siena, and rebuilt in 1675. Further down, the **Palazzo dei Diavoli**, built in 1460, was the headquarters of the Marquis of Marignano during that siege.

There isn't much to see on the outskirts of the city—thanks largely to Marignano, who laid waste lovely and productive lands for miles around. Some 2km east of the city (take Via Simone Martini from the Porta Ovile), in the hills above the railway station, the basilica and monastery of **L'Osservanza** has been carefully restored after serious damage in the last war. Begun in 1422, a foundation of San Bernardino, the monastery retains much of its collection of 13th- and 14th-century Sienese art.

To the west of the city, the road to Massa Marittima passes through the hills of the Montagnola Sienese which was an important centre of monasticism in the Middle Ages. Near the village of Montecchio (6km), the hermitage of **Lecceto**, one of the oldest in Tuscany, has been much changed over the centuries but retains some Renaissance frescoes in the church and a 12th-century cloister; nearby, the hermitage of **San Leonardo al Lago** is mostly in ruins; the 14th-century church survives, with masterly frescoes (c. 1360) by Pietro Lorenzetti's star pupil, Lippo Vanni. Just outside the village of Sovicille (13km), there is a Romanesque church of the 12th century, the **Pieve di Ponte alla Spina**. The village of Rosia (17km) has another Romanesque church, and just to the south the Vallombrosan **Abbey of Torri** has much to show from its original foundation in the 1200s; there is a rare three-storey cloister, with three different types of columns (*open Mon–Fri 9–12*).

Excursions from Siena

TRA-IN buses from Piazza San Domenico will take you to two of Tuscany's most distinctive hill towns, Etruscan **Volterra** and **San Gimignano** with its medieval skyscrapers intact; both have enough sights to occupy a full day. You need a car, however, for the great monastery of **Monte Oliveto Maggiore** with its delightful frescoes by Il Sodoma. **Chianti** begins just north of Siena: TRA-IN buses will take you to most of the villages.

Pisa

Pisa (pop. 104,000) is at once the best-known and the most mysterious of Tuscan cities. Its most celebrated attraction has become, along with the Colosseum, gondolas and spaghetti a symbol for the entire Italian republic; even the least informed recognize the 'Leaning Tower of Pizza' even if they've never heard of Florence or Siena. Tour buses disgorge thousands every day into the Field of Miracles, who spend a couple of hours, by a plastic tower, and leave again for places more tangible, like Florence, Elba or Rome. At night even the Pisani make a mass exodus into the suburbs, as if they sense that the city is too big for them, not physically, but in terms of unfulfilled ambitions, of past greatness nipped in the bud.

Yet go back to about 1100, when according to the chroniclers, precocious Pisa was 'the city of marvels', the 'city of ten thousand towers', with a population of 300,000—or so it seemed to the awed writers of that century, who, at least outside Venice, had never seen such an enormous, cosmopolitan and exotic city in Christian Europe since the fall of Rome. Pisan merchants made themselves at home all over the Mediterranean, bringing back new ideas and new styles in art in addition to their fat bags of profit; Pisa contributed as much to the rebirth of Western culture as any city. Pisan Romanesque, with its stripes and blind arcades, which had such a wide influence in Tuscany, was inspired by the great Moorish architecture of Andalucía; Nicola Pisano, first of a long line of great sculptors, is as important to the renaissance of sculpture as Giotto is to painting.

Like a Middle Eastern city, Pisa has put all its efforts into one fabulous spiritual monument, while the rest of the city wears a decidedly undemonstrative, almost anonymous face, a little run down. It is a subtle place, a little sad perhaps, and a little grotty, but strangely seductive if you give it a chance. After all, one can't create a Field of Miracles in a void.

History

In the Middle Ages, Pisa liked to claim that it began as a Greek city, founded by colonists from Elis. Most historians, however, won't give them credit for anything earlier than 100 BC or so, when a Roman veterans' colony was settled there. Records of what followed are scarce, but Pisa, like Amalfi and Venice, must have had an early start in building a navy and establishing trade connections. By the

11th century, the effort had blossomed into opulence; Pisa built itself a small empire, including Corsica, Sardinia, and for a while the Balearics. Around 1060, work was begun on the great cathedral complex, inaugurating the Pisan Romanesque. The city was a wonder to all who saw it: the great traveller Benjamin Tudela wrote that it had 10,000 towers. No wonder they made one or two lean, just to stand out.

The First Crusade (1090s), when Pisa's battling archbishop led the entire fleet in support of the Christian knights, turned out to be an economic windfall for the city. Unlike its greatest rival in the Western Mediterranean, Amalfi, Pisa from the start had adopted a course of combat with the states of the Moslem world, less from religious bigotry than a clear eye on the main chance; the same attitude led the city to capture and sack Amalfi itself in 1135. When the Pisans weren't battling with the Moslems of Spain and Africa, they were learning from them. A steady exchange of ideas brought much of medieval Arab science, philosophy and architecture into Europe through Pisa's port. Pisa's architecture, the highest development of the Romanesque in Italy, saw its influence spread from Sardinia to Apulia in southern Italy; when Gothic arrived in Italy Pisa was one of the few cities to take it seriously, and the city's accomplishments in that style rank with Siena's. In science, Pisa contributed a great though shadowy figure, that most excellent mathematician Leonardo Fibonacci, who either rediscovered the principle of the Golden Section or learned it from the Arabs, and also introduced Arabic numerals to Europe. Pisa's scholarly traditions over the centuries would be crowned in the 1600s by its most famous son, Galileo Galilei.

Pisa was always a Ghibelline city, the greatest ally of the emperors in Tuscany if only for expediency's sake. When a real threat came, however, it was not from Florence or any of the other Tuscan cities, but from the rising mercantile port of Genoa. After years of constant warfare, the Genoese devastated the Pisan navy at the Battle of Meloria (an islet off Livorno) in 1284. It signalled the end of Pisan supremacy, but all chance of recovery was quashed by an even more implacable enemy: the Arno. Pisa's port was gradually silting up, and when the cost of dredging became greater than the traffic could bear, the city's fate was sealed. The Visconti of Milan seized the economically enfeebled city in 1396, and nine years later Florence snatched it from them. Excepting the period 1494–1505, when the city rebelled and kept the Florentines out despite an almost constant siege, Pisa's history was ended. The Medici dukes did the city one big favour, supporting the university and even removing Florence's own university to Pisa. In the last 500 years of Pisa's long, pleasant twilight, this institution has helped the city stay alive and vital, and in touch with the modern world; one of its students was the nuclear physicist Enrico Fermi.

The airport is linked to Pisa by train or city bus no. 7, departing from Piazza Stazione, in front of the main station, which lies south of the Arno, © 28 546; train information © 1478 88 088. Many trains (Florence–Pisa or Genoa–Rome lines) also stop at Stazione San Rossore; if you're making Pisa a day trip you may want to get off there, as it's only a few blocks from the cathedral and Leaning Tower—or else bus no. 1 will take you there from the central station.

by bus

All intercity buses depart from near Piazza Vittorio Emanuele II, the big roundabout just north of the central station: APT buses for Volterra, Livorno and the coastal resorts (to the left on Via Nino Bixio, © 505 511/883 111) and LAZZI buses to Florence, Lucca, La Spezia (on Via d'Azeglio, © 46 288). Many of these buses also stop at Piazza D. Manin, just outside the walls of the cathedral. The Natural Park Migliarino San Rossore Massaciuccoli may be reached by city bus no. 11 from Piazza Vittorio Emmanuele. Pisa lends itself well to **bicycles**; you can hire one at Via Nino Bixio, near the station.

Tourist Information

Piazza Duomo, near the Leaning Tower, © (050) 560 464, or Via Benedetto Croce 26, © 40 096. Just outside the central station, there's an accommodation/information office, © 42 291.

Highlights of Pisa

There's a lot more to Pisa besides the **Leaning Tower**, beginning with the extraordinary set of monuments and museums just near the big tipster on and around the emerald lawn of the **Campo dei Miracoli**, all covered in Walk I.

Most tourists get no further; the rest of Pisa seems remarkably calm compared to Florence and Siena, and makes for delightful walking. Don't miss the fine art and sculpture collection in the **Museo Nazionale di San Matteo**, the monuments around **Piazza Cavalieri** and the churches of **San Nicola**, **San Francesco**, **Santa Maria della Spina** and **Santa Caterina**, nor the attractive **medieval market core** around Borgo Stretto, Via dei Sette Volte and Piazza Vettovaglie.

Start: *The Field of Miracles*
Finish: *train station*
Walking time: *a day*

*Truly one might as well try to describe
the face of one's angel as those holy
places of Pisa.*

Edward Hutton

Walk I: The Field of Miracles

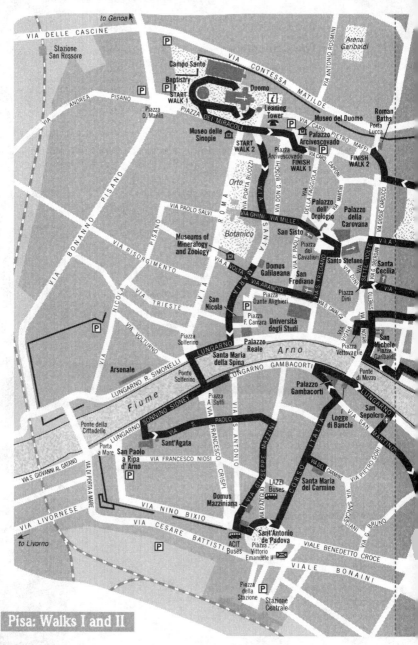

Pisa: Walks I and II

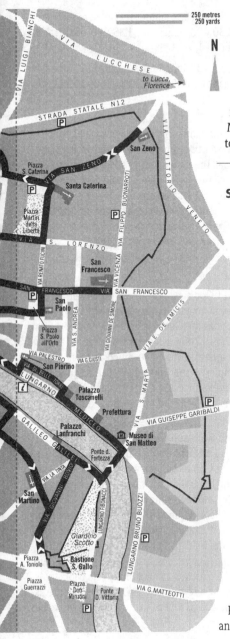

We have divided Pisa into two walks, each of which takes a leisurely day: this first one could be called the essential day tripper's walk: if you arrive be train or bus, it involves taking a city bus No1 from the station to the Campo dei Miracoli, while seeing what there is to see on the way back to the station.

Lunch/Cafés

Santa Maria, Via Santa Maria, ℂ 561881. Not far from the leaning tower this typical trattoria offers good mixed roasts and home made *tiramisù*. Self-service (closed Wed, around L35,000).

Emilio, Via Carlo Cammeo 44, ℂ 562141. Just outside the walls a family-run friendly place serving good quality food and fresh seafood (closed Fri, around L30,000).

Da Bruno, Via Luigi Bianchi 10, ℂ 560818. There's not many places to eat a decent meal near touristy Campo dei Miracoli, but try this traditional trattoria just outside the city walls. (About L40,000; closed Tues.)

Just outside the walls are two handy, if run-of-the-mill, *tavola calda* food counters: **Asmara**, Via C. Cammeo 27 (closed Fri); **Giardino**, Piazza Manin 1 (closed Mon).

Osteria dei Cavalieri, Via S. Frediano 16, ℂ 580858, closed Sun and Sat lunch. Old fashioned white table cloths in an old palazzo, with an à la carte menu or choice of four set-price meals: L18,000 quick, L30,000 vegetarin, L35,000 meat, and L40,000 for seafood, all well prepared.

Nuraghe, Via Mazzini 58, ✆ 56 125, closed Mon. Sunny Sardinian cuisine for a change of pace, and very popular too. Get there early; around L35,000.

Almost from the time of its conception, the Field of Miracles was the nickname given to medieval Italy's most ambitious building programme. As with Florence's cathedral, too many changes were made over two centuries of work to tell exactly what the original intentions were. But of all the unique things about this complex, the location strikes one first—a broad expanse of green lawn at the northern edge of town, just inside the walls. The cathedral was begun in 1063, the famous Leaning Tower and the baptistry in the middle 1100s, at the height of Pisa's fortunes, and the Campo Santo in 1278. (*For the museums and monuments on the Field of Miracles, you can save by getting the joint ticket, for L15,000*).

> The **Baptistry** *(open 9–sunset; 8–7.40 in summer) is the biggest of its kind in Italy; those of many other cities would fit neatly inside.*

The original architect, Master Diotisalvi ('God save you'), saw the lower half of the building done in the typical stripes-and-arcades Pisan style. A second colonnade was intended to go over the first, but as the Genoese gradually muscled Pisa out of trade routes, funds ran short. In the 1260s, Nicola and Giovanni Pisano, members of that remarkable family of artists who did so much to re-establish sculpture in Italy, redesigned and completed the upper half in a harmonious Gothic crown of gables and pinnacles. The Pisanos also added the dome over Diotisalvi's original prismatic dome, still visible from the inside. Both domes were impressive achievements, among the largest attempted in the Middle Ages.

Inside, the austerity of the simple, striped walls and heavy columns of grey Elban granite is broken by two superb works of art. The great **baptismal font** is the work of Guido Bigarelli, the 13th-century Como sculptor who decorated it with 16 exquisite marble panels. These are finely carved in floral and geometrical patterns of inlaid stones, a northern, almost monochrome variant on the Cosmati work of medieval Rome and Campania. Nicola Pisano's **pulpit** (1260) was one of the first of that family's masterpieces, and established the form for their later pulpits, the columns resting on fierce lions, the relief panels crowded with intricately carved figures in impassioned New Testament episodes, a style that seems to owe much to the reliefs on old Roman triumphal arches and columns. The baptistry is famous for its uncanny acoustics; try singing a few notes from as near to centre as they will allow you. If there's a crowd the guards will be just waiting for someone to bribe them to do it.

> *One of the first and finest works of the Pisan Romanesque, the **cathedral façade**, with four levels of colonnades, turned out to be a little more ornate than Buscheto, the architect, had planned back in 1063.*

These columns, with similar colonnades around the apse and the Gothic frills later added around the unique elliptical dome, are the only showy features on the calm, restrained exterior. On the south transept, the late 12th-century **Porte San Ranieri** has a fine pair of bronze doors by Bonanno, one of the architects of the Leaning Tower. The Biblical scenes are enacted among real palms and acacia trees; naturally, the well-travelled Pisans would have known what such things looked like.

> *Of the **interior**, little of the original art survived a fire in 1595 (open open winter 7.45–1, 3–sunset; April–Oct 10–7.40 and 1–7.40 Sun; the cathedral is often closed to tourists for most of the day).*

The roof went, as well as the Cosmati pavement, of which only a few patches still remain. A coffered Baroque ceiling and lots of bad painting were contributed during the reconstruction, but some fine work survives. The triumphal arch still has its fresco of the *Madonna and Child* by the Maestro di San Torpè (St Tropez) and the great mosaic of Christ Pantocrator in the apse by Cimabue, and there are portraits of the saints by Andrea del Sarto framed on the entrance pier (the charming *St Agnes*), in the choir and his *Madonna della Grazia* in the right nave. Giambologna's bronze angels stand at the entrance to the choir, and in the right transept note the sarcophagus carved by Tino di Camaino for Emperor Henry VII, who enjoyed his election for less than a year before he died near Siena in 1313.

The **pulpit** (*c.* 1300), by Giovanni Pisano, is the acknowledged masterpiece of the family. The men of 1595 used the fire as an opportunity to get rid of this nasty old medieval relic, and the greatest achievement of Pisan sculpture sat disassembled in crates, quite forgotten until this century. Works of genuine inspiration often prove profoundly disturbing to ages of certainty and good taste. Pisano's pulpit is startling, mixing classical and Christian elements with a fluency never seen before his time. St Michael, as a telamon, shares the honour of supporting the pulpit with Hercules and the Fates, while prophets, saints and sibyls look on from their appointed places. The relief panels, jammed with expressive faces, diffuse an electric immediacy equal to the best work of the Renaissance. Notice particularly the *Nativity*, the *Massacre of the Innocents*, the *Flight into Egypt*, and the *Last Judgement.* Next to the pulpit is a 16th-century bronze lamp known as the **Lamp of Galileo**, which Galileo observed when it was newly hung on its long rope. It swung for a long time, and Galileo noticed that although the swings shortened, they didn't seem to go any slower or faster; it formed the basis for his calculations on oscillations and his discovery of the principle of the pendulum.

*The stories claiming the tilt of the **Leaning Tower** was accidental were most likely pure fabrications, desperate tales woven to account for what, before mass tourism, must have seemed a great civic embarrassment. The argument isn't very convincing. It seems hard to believe that the tower would start to lean when only 33ft tall; half the weight would still be in the foundations. The argument then insists that the Pisans doggedly kept building it after the lean commenced. The architects who measured the stones in the last century to get to the bottom of the mystery concluded that the tower's odd state was absolutely intentional from the day it was begun in 1173. Mention this to a Pisan, and he will be as offended as if you had suggested lunacy is a problem in his family. The tower is now closed and will probably remain so for ever.*

The leaning campanile is hardly the only strange thing in the Field of Miracles. The more time you spend here, the more you will notice: little monster-griffins, dragons and such, peeking out of every corner of the oldest sculptural work, skilfully hidden where you have to look twice to see them, or the big bronze griffin sitting on a column atop the cathedral apse (a copy) and a rhinoceros by the door, Moslem arabesques in the Campo Santo, perfectly classical Corinthian capitals in the cathedral nave and pagan images on the pulpit. The elliptical cathedral dome, in its time the only one in Europe, shows that the Pisans had not only the audacity but the mathematical skills to back it up. You may have noticed that the baptistry too is leaning—about 4ft, in the opposite direction. And the cathedral façade leans outwards about a foot, disconcerting from the right angle. This could hardly be accidental. So much in the Field of Miracles gives evidence of a sophisticated, strangely modern taste for the outlandish. Perhaps the medieval master masons simply thought that perpendicular buildings were becoming a little trite.

Whatever, the campanile is beautiful and something unique in the world—also an expensive bit of whimsy, with its 190 marble and granite columns. At the moment, it's also proving expensive to the local and national governments as they try to decide how best to shore up the tower. Until 1995, the tilt has been increasing by a millimetre a year; some experts blame the construction of the enceinte in 1838, which seriously altered the water table, and say the 1934 injection of a hundred tons of cement in the footing of the wall has only made matters worse. In 1989, the sudden collapse of the medieval (and perpendicular) Torre Civica in Pavia decided the diligent doctors of the campanile, now 16.5ft off perpendicular, that it had become too precarious to withstand the traffic and it was closed indefinitely.

A flood of screwball proposals to stabilize the 15,000-ton tower poured into Pisa; among them, tying it to a blimp, planting sequoias all around it, propping it up with the world's largest bottle of Coke. Many engineers would simply lighten the tower by knocking off the upper bell chamber, added in the 1300s. What has actually happened so far seems modest in comparison: counterweights (800 tonnes of lead ingots) were stacked at the base of the tower's leaning side, stopping the tilt. The next stage, replacing the lead ingots with an underground support, is rather trickier. A ring of cement will be laid around the foundations, anchored to ten steel cables attached to the bedrock 164ft underground. But digging under the tower is perilous; in September 1995, while workers were freezing the ground to mute vibrations, they hit an undocumented ring of cement from the last century, when suddenly to their horror the tower heaved a groan and tipped another tenth of an inch. To prevent similar scares, engineers in the spring of 1998 are going to give the tower a rather unsightly girdle of plastic coated steel braces, attached by a pair of 72ft steel cables to a counterweight system hidden among the building on the north end of the Campo dei Miracoli, capable of increasing the tension to 100 tonnes if the tower starts to sag again during the digging. Work is supposed to be finished by autumn 1998—but expect the Field of Miracles to look like the Field of Hard Hats for a while yet.

> *If one more marvel in the Campo dei Miracoli is not excessive, there is the **Campo Santo,** a remarkable cloister and graveyard as unique in its way as the Leaning Tower (open 9–sunset; 8–7.40 in summer; adm). Basically, the cemetery is a rectangle of gleaming white marble, unadorned save for the blind arcading around the façade and the beautiful Gothic tabernacle of the enthroned Virgin Mary over the entrance. With its uncluttered, simple lines, the Campo Santo seems more like a work of our own century than the 1300s.*

The cemetery began, according to legend, when Archbishop Lanfranchi, who led the Pisan fleet into the first Crusade, came back with boatloads of soil from the Holy Land for extra-blessed burials. Over the centuries, thousands of dead Pisans and an exceptional hoard of frescoes and sculpture accumulated here. Much of it went up in flames on a terrible night in July 1944, when an Allied incendiary bomb hit the roof and set it on fire. Many priceless works of art were destroyed and others, including most of the frescoes, damaged beyond hope of ever being perfectly restored. The biggest loss was the set of frescoes by Benozzo Gozzoli— the *Tower of Babylon, Solomon and Sheba, Life of Moses* and the *Grape Harvest* and others; in their original state they must have been as fresh and colourful as his famous frescoes in Florence's Medici Palace. Even better known, and better preserved, are two 14th-century frescoes of the *Triumph of Death* and the *Last Judgement* by an unknown artist (perhaps Andrea Orcagna of Florence) whose failure to sign his work has passed him down to posterity with an unfortunate

Halloween name, the 'Master of the Triumph of Death'. In this memento of the century of plagues and trouble, Death (in Italian, feminine: *La Morte*) swoops down on frolicking nobles, while in the *Last Judgement* (which has very little heaven) the damned are variously cooked, wrapped up in snakes, poked, disembowelled, banged up and chewed on; still, they are some of the best paintings of the trecento, and somehow seem less gruesome and paranoid than similar works of centuries to come (though good enough to have inspired that pop classic, Lizst's *Totentanz*).

For another curiosity, there's the *Theological Cosmography* of Piero di Puccio, a vertiginous diagram of 22 spheres of the planets and stars, angels, archangels, thrones and dominations, cherubim and seraphim, etc; in the centre, the small circle trisected by a 'T' was a common medieval map pattern for the known earth. The three sides represent Asia, Europe and Africa, and the three lines the Mediterranean, the Black Sea and the Nile. Among the sculpture in the Campo Santo, there are sarcophagi and Roman bath tubs, and in the gallery of prewar photographs of the lost frescoes, a famous Hellenistic marble vase with bas-reliefs.

> *There are two museums surrounding the Campo dei Miracoli: opposite the cathedral, the **Museo delle Sinopie** (open 9–sunset; 8–7.40 in summer; adm).*

Housed in the 13th-century Ospedale Nuovo di Misericordia, this contains the pre-painted sketches on plaster of the frescoes lost in the Campo Santo fire. The name *sinopia* comes from Sinope, a Turkish port on the Black Sea, from where the reddish pigment originally derived; once the *sinopia* was drawn, the artist would cover the area he meant to paint in one day with wet plaster (*grasello*). When a fresco is detached from the wall, it is often possible to save the sinopia. During the restoration of the Campo Santo, these works of art in their own right were brought here—*The Triumph of Death* and the *Last Judgement* and others that were lost in the bombing.

> *The second museum, **Museo del Duomo**, in Piazza Arcivescovado (open 9–sunset; 8–7.40 in summer; adm exp), is arranged in the old Chapter House, with descriptions in English available for each room.*

The first rooms contain the oldest works—beautiful fragments from the cathedral façade and altar and two Islamic works, the very strange, original **Griffin** from the top of the cathedral, believed to have come from Egypt in the 11th century, and a 12th-century bronze basin with an intricate decoration. Statues by the Pisanos from the baptistry were brought in from the elements too late; worn and bleached, they resemble a convention of mummies. Other sculptures in the next room survived better: Giovanni Pisano's grotesque faces, his gaunt but noble *St*

John the Baptist and the lovely *Madonna del Colloquio*, so named because she speaks to her child with her eyes; in the next room are fine works by Tino di Camaino, including the tomb of San Ranieri and his sculptures from the tomb of Emperor Henry VII, sitting among his court like some exotic oriental potentate. In **Room 9** are works by Nino Pisano and in **Rooms 10–11**, containing the Cathedral Treasure, Giovanni Pisano's lovely ivory *Madonna and Child* steals the show, curving to the shape of the elephant's tusk; there's an ivory coffer and the cross that led the Pisans on the First Crusade. Upstairs are some extremely big angels used as candlesticks, intarsia and two rare illuminated 12th- and 13th-century scrolls (called exultet rolls), perhaps the original visual aids; the deacon would unroll them from the pulpit as he read so the congregation could follow the story with the pictures. The remaining rooms have some Etruscan and Roman odds and ends (including a good bust of Caesar) and prints and engravings of the original Campo Santo frescoes made in the 19th century. The courtyard has a unique view of the Leaning Tower, which seems to be bending over to spy inside.

Near the museum the **Palazzo Arcivescovale** is now the university faculty of Theology, pop in to see the disarmingly lovely 15th-century courtyard, a classic Tuscan arrangement of arcades and statues in traditional Tuscan colours.

> *For centuries the main artery between the Campo dei Miracoli and the Arno has been the gracefully curving Via Santa Maria, one of Pisa's finest streets, lined with elegant palaces and old towerhouses, some half hidden by fast fooderies and pizzerias.*

This is the only street in Pisa where you'll see many tourists outside of the Field of Miracles, but few ever pause to poke their heads in the doors for a look at the secret gardens and courtyards, or the curiosities of the façades. At Via L. Ghini, you can turn right for the enormous **Orto Botanico**, the botanical gardens created by Ferdinando I de Medici for the university in 1595; the institute in the gardens has a façade, entirely covered with shells and mother-of-pearl (*open Mon–Fri 8–1 and 2–5.30; Sat 8–1*).

> *Turn left at Via dei Mille, which broadens into a square at the foot of* **San Sisto***, a simple 11th-century church in brick, containing a handful of good Romanesque columns and a pretty 13th-century Madonna. From San Sisto, continue on and you hit vast* **Piazza dei Cavalieri***, encircled by beautiful palaces. In the old days this was Piazza delle Sette, where the medieval Pisans clobbered each other in the* Gioco del Mazzascudo *'Club and Shield Game', the precursor of today's somewhat more civilized* Gioco del Ponte (see *p.19*).

Duke Cosimo I started what was probably the last crusading order of knights, the Cavalieri di Santo Stefano, in 1562. The crusading urge had ended long before, but the duke found the order a useful tool for placating the anachronistic fantasies of the Tuscan nobility—most of them newly titled bankers—and for licensing out freebooting expeditions against the Turks. Cosimo had Vasari build the **Palazzo della Carovana** for the order, conveniently demolishing the old Palazzo del Popolo, the symbol of Pisa's lost independence. Vasari gave the palace an outlandishly ornate *sgrafitto* façade; the building now holds the prestigious Scuola Normale Superiore, founded by Napoleon in 1810. In front of it stands a statue of Cosimo I by Francavilla.

Next to the palace is the order's church, **Santo Stefano**, built by Vasari in 1565, although the façade was designed by a young Medici dilettante. The history of the order is told on the lavish coffered ceiling, and its pirate trophies are on display—eight gilded leather lanterns and long, fantastical pennants snatched by the order's pirates from defeated Turkish and North African galleys; one is claimed to have been captured from the flagship of Ali Pasha in the Battle of Lepanto. On the left hangs a *Nativity* by Bronzino and a *Holy Family* by Orazio Gentileschi.

Also on the Piazza, the **Palazzo dell'Orologio** was built around the 'Hunger Tower' (left of the big clock—see plaque), famous in Dante's story of Count Ugolino della Gherardesca, the Pisan podestà who was walled in here with his sons and grandsons after the fickle city began to suspect him of intrigues with the Genoese after Pisa's defeat at Meloria in 1284. If the intent was to kill off the family and its progeny, the cruel punishment failed: the Gherardeschi ruled as *signori* from 1316 to 1341, and in 1330 founded Pisa's university.

*Via San Frediano leads to the church of **San Frediano**.*

Usually half hidden by the ambulances of the Misericordia di Pisa parked in front, San Frediano has a typical if dingy Pisan façade. It houses two of the most elaborate marble confessionals in Italy: parishoners can choose to whisper their sins with pensive skeletons and other reminders of mortality, or opt for the more worldly confessional decorated with arms and armour–and not a religious symbol in sight. Note, too, an *Adoration of the Magi* by Aurelio Lomi, immediately on your right.

> *To the left, Piazza Dante Alighieri is the site of aformentioned **Università degli Studi**, founded by the Gherardeschi, and revived in 1472 by Lorenzo de' Medici. Via L'Arancio will take you back to Via Santa Maria, where no. 26 is the **Domus Galilaeana**, Galileo's house (open by appointment, © 050 501116), with a library of his books, and other works that recall the accomplishments of Pisa's genius (see **Topics**, pp.56–8); in the next house was born Antonio Pacinotti, the physicist who came up with the prototype of the dynamo.*

*Continue across Via Santa Maria to Via Volta, appropriately the site of Pisa's two university science museums. Via Santa Maria then continues to the Arno and the 12th-century church of **San Nicola**, conserving part of its original façade; the rest looks as if it had been scoured off.*

Take a good look at the belltower, cylindrical at the bottom, octagonal in the middle, and hexagonal on top. Designed by Nicola Pisano, it has exactly the same kind of tilt as the Leaning Tower itself, built to lean forward before curving back again towards perpendicular. Ask the sacristan to show you the famous spiral stair inside, which Vasari claimed inspired Bramante's Belvedere stair in the Vatican. The church itself, patched together here and there over the centuries, shelters a fine painting of the *Madonna* by Traini, a wooden sculpture of the same by Nino Pisano in the fourth chapel on the left, a quattrocento painting of *St Nicholas of Tolentino* shielding Pisa from the plague (fourth chapel on the right), and just to the left of the presbytery, a *Crucifixion* attributed to Giovanni Pisano.

*The neighbouring royal palace was begun in 1559 by Cosimo I and has recently from a new life as the **Museo Nazionale di Palazzo Reale**.*

This now functions as an annexe to the Museo Nazionale di San Matteo, (*entrance Lunargno Pacinotti 46, open Mon–Sat 9–2, free*), housing a fine collection of old armour dusted off every June for the annual Gioco del Ponte as well as some 900 other pieces from the 15th to the 17th centuries. Another section soon to be installed (at least a year from now) will concentrate paintings, sculptures and collectables (mostly from the 15th–18th centuries) from lay collections–from the Medici and Lorraine archducal hoards,

*Beyond lies the **Arno**, the river that first made the city great before forsaking it in silt.*

After the Campo dei Miracoli, the thing that has most impressed Pisa's visitors is its languidly curving, completely tree-less river front, an exercise in Tuscan gravity. Two mirror image lines of blank-faced yellow and ochre buildings, all the same height, with no remarkable bridges (they were all blown up in the last war, but never were very showy), with none of the picturesque quality of Florence. 'The lung'Arno is so beautiful a sight, so wide and magnificent, so gay and smiling, that one falls in love with it,' wrote poet Giacomo Leopardi in the last century, while Norman Douglas on a winter's evening found that 'In Pisa, at such an hour, the Arno is the emblem of Despair...So may Lethe look or Styx: the nightmare of a flood'. The Lung'Arno is particularly impressive during the Festa di San Ranieri in mid-June when all the buildings along the river are illuminated with thousands of candles (*see* p.19).

*The uncanny monotony is broken by only one landmark, but it is something special. Cross the Ponte Solferino and turn left for **Santa Maria***

della Spina, *sitting on the south bank like a precious jewel-box (albeit swathed in scaffolding for the foreseeable future).*

A reliquary for one of the thorns from Christ's crown of thorns brought back from the Crusades, Santa Maria della Spina is one of the few outstanding achievements of Italian Gothic. Originally it wasn't Gothic at all, but when partially rebuilt in 1323, the new architect—perhaps one of the Pisanos—turned it into an extravaganza of pointed gables and blooming pinnacles. All the sculptural works are first class, especially the figures of Christ and the Apostles in the 13 niches facing the streets. Although its placement on the Lungarno Gambacorti is perfect, it was not originally here at all, but located at the mouth of the Arno, where it suffered so many floods that it was at the point of vanishing in 1871, when the city decided to dismantle and rebuild it on this new site. Inside the luminous zebra interior, the statues of the *Madonna and Child, SS Peter and John* are by Andrea and Nino Pisano.

Continue downriver along Lungarno Sidney Sonnino, passing the ex-Convento San Benedetto, prettily decorated with terracotta tiles and intricate relief work in terracotta. Looking ahead, you can see remains of the old brick **Citadel,** *built by the Florentines in the 15th century, and the* **Arsenals** *(1588) of the galleys of Cavalieri di Santo Stefano, marking the site of the famous 'Golden Gate'—medieval Pisa's door to the sea. The Decorations on the façade of San Paolo a Ripa continue round the side of the building. Just before the Pontedella Cittadella is* **San Paolo a Ripa del Arno.**

San Paolo stands in a small park, and curiously enough is believed to have been built over the site of Pisa's oldest church and original cathedral; perhaps building cathedrals in open fields was an old custom in these parts. It has a ravishing 11th-century (but not tilting) façade believed to have been the prototype for the Duomo itself. Behind it, don't miss the little octagonal brick chapel of **Sant'Agata**, crowned with a prismatic roof like an Ottoman tomb.

Via San Paolo leads back towards the centre; turn right at Via Mazzini where at no. 71 (bearing right when the road divides) you can pay your respects to the original romantic revolutionary at the **Domus Mazziniana,** *in a newish house; the original was bombed in the war (open 8.30–1.30, Sat 8.30–12, closed Sun).*

The Man who Sacrificed Everything

Giuseppe Mazzini was born in Genoa in 1805, the son of a doctor enamoured of the French Revolution and a mother who, even more than the typical Italian mamma, thought her son was the Messiah. At age 16, the young Giuseppe witnessed a tide of refugees passing through Genoa hoping to escape to Spain after the failed Piedmont revolution of 1821. The sight of people suffering so much for political ideals moved him deeply. He started wearing black, as if in mourning for freedom; he continued to dress in mournful monochrome for the rest of his life.

His career as an active revolutionary began in 1827 when he joined the Carbonari, a strict, hierarchical secret society which plotted armed revolution in Italy. He was however not one to obey orders blindly , and in 1830 he was betrayed to the police by his own local leader and sent to prison for three months. During that time, Mazzini developed a political philosophy that never wavered: a belief in the unity and perfect equality of humanity (including even women and workers) and in humanity's ability to progress thanks to education. Not only did every individual have equal rights, but duties and obligations to the public good. He believed in God, but a God incarnate in the will of the people: his religion was democracy.

To make all this possible, Mazzini thought that the first goal of revolution should be an independent, unified Italy. From exile in Switzerland, he founded his own semi-secret society called *La Giovine Italia*, 'Young Italy', with the goal of instilling a sense of national identity in the Italian people and helping them to lead the revolution that would make Italy a democratic republic. Italy, Mazzini reasoned, could then lead a great democratic revolution across Europe. The society was called 'Young Italy' because one of its initial concerns was avoiding what Mazzini called 'middle-aged scepticism'; at first no one over age 40 was allowed to join, although Mazzini realized he was cutting out too many essential people. One of the first recruits was a sailor named Garibaldi.

Mazzini's sense of mission meant he spent most of his life writing and plotting in exile, under the threat of the death penalty back home in Genoa. His first insurrection in 1834 was a fiasco after his commander, entrusted with Young Italy's funds, lost all the money gambling in Paris. It led, however, to over a decade of exile for Mazzini in London, where he kept the flame of revolt alive by making contacts and writing, earning a pitiful income from journalism. Accounts of Mazzini in London (where the only thing he loved was the fog) tell of him giving most of his money to beggars, who soon learned that the affable Italian in black could never say no. He lived in a cramped book-filled room, where canaries flew about everywhere because he could not bear to confine them in cages. He founded a free evening school in the city in order to teach poor Italian immigrant children to read and write.

Mazzini next returned to Italy in 1849 when the Roman Republic was declared. Thanks to his reputation and integrity, he was acclaimed its natural leader, and gave the city the most tolerant, enlightened government it ever had in its entire history—while working for no pay and dining every day in a workers' canteen. The experiment, however, lasted only three months before the French troops summoned by Pius IX arrived and squashed the heroic defence of the Republic by the people of Rome, led by the dashing Garibaldi.

Hopelessly romantic republican insurrections supported by Mazzini in 1853 and 1857 went down to tragic defeat in Milan and Naples. Ironically, it was an equally hopeless insurrection in 1860, in which Mazzini had no direct part, that finally succeeded when Garibaldi and his Thousand volunteers took Sicily. But Mazzini declared that what actually resulted from all of Garibaldi's noble efforts–the kingdom of Italy of Vittorio Emanuele II–was not the real Italy either, not the tolerant democracy of his dreams, and he refused to live in it.

Although Mazzini helped in the organization of the First International in London, his beliefs in private property and his insistence on a social as well as political revolution saw his influence quickly lose out to Marx, especially when he failed to support the Paris commune in 1871 (because French republicans had crushed his Republic of Rome, he could not bring himself to trust them). In 1872, he returned clandestinely to Italy under the alias of John Brown, the firey American abolitionist, only to die on this spot in Pisa. His other chief memorial in Italy is the nice big apologetic tomb they gave him in Genoa, although his epitaph by poet Giosuè Carducci tells the bitter truth: 'The man/who sacrificed everything/who loved much/and forgave much and never hated/GIUSEPPE MAZZINI/after forty years of exile/today passes freely on Italian soil/now that he is dead/O Italy/such glory and such baseness/and such a debt for the future.'

*From Mazzini's last address, continue south past **Sant'Antonio de Padova**, to the vast oval of Piazza Vittorio Emanuele (with a big statue of the king Mazzini disdained. The station is just behind.*

Start: *Station*
Finish: *Roman Baths*
Walking time: a leisurely day

Walk II: North/South of the Arno

281

With or without a map you can get lost in a jiffy. With the cathedral on the very edge of town, Pisa has no real centre. Still, the Pisans are very conscious of the division made by the Arno; every year in June the north and south sides fight it out on the Ponte di Mezzo in the *Gioco del Ponte*. The prime attraction on this walk is the Museo di San Matteo; the remainder explores some of the city's little known by-ways, where you may well be the only visitor in sight.

Lunch/Cafés

La Fo'acina, Via del Carmine. Closed Fri. A tiny and cheerful place in which to enjoy a slice of hot pizza or filled foccaccia.

Pergoletta, Via delle Belle Torri 36, ✆ 5432 458. Closed Mon, Aug. In an old towerhouse, with a pretty garden, Pergoletta serves some of the best prepared Tuscan classics in Pisa (including the trendy *minestra di farro*–spelt soup) and succulent grills; around L40,000.

Osteria La Mescita, Via Cavalca 2, ✆ 544 294, closed Mon. A very pleasant trattoria with a rustic feel to it. There is a huge choice of wines, and cheeses, salamis, and a choice of hot and cold dishes which change daily. Average L35,000.

Numero 11, Via Cavalca 11, closed Sat lunch and Sun. Just behind the market, this tiny eating place offers no frills but exceptional value. Queue up to be served savoury flans, filled foccaccia, hot and cold dish of the day or salad; lay your own place at one of the few outside tables, and clear away when you have finished.

Federico Salza, Borgo Stretto 46 ✆ 580 244. A spectacular cake shop-and much more-which is a feast for the eyes as much as for the palate. Excellent pastries and sandwiches; at lunchtime, hot dishes are served in an adjacent room.

Pizzeria Montino, Via del Monte, ✆ 598 595. Tiny place tucked by the Cassa di Risparmo, with a handful of outdoor tables. Inexpensive pizza, *frittelle*, meat and salad.

From the station, start down to Pisa's main shopping street, pedestrian-only Corso Italia. Here too are some palaces of note, many sprouting heavy coats-of-arms as if they were inflicted with tree fungus. Note especially No. 89, a pink Neo-Venetian confection, and No. 46, with a *remarkable coffered 'beehive' ceiling that the owners often illuminate after dark. Midway along the Corso a piazza opens to the right with a very grim and grimy statue of Nicola Pisano (who as the father of Italian sculpture deserves a bit better) and **Santa Maria del Carmine**, with a blank barn of a façade housing a pretty 17th-century organ (not in working order unfortunately) and an Ascension by Alessandro Allori.*

*The Corso is closed off by the lofty arcades of the wool and silk market, the **Logge di Banchi**, built in 1603 perhaps on a design by Buontalenti, and emblazoned with their balls—here the size of beach balls. The Logge is linked by 'a bridge of sighs' to the handsome 14th-century Gothic **Palazzo Gambacorti** now used as the offices of the mayor, its main front facing Via San Martino. Walk past the building and peer into the high ground floor windows for a look at the usually illuminated painted, vaulted ceilings. The Palazzo overlooks the **Ponte di Mezzo**.*

This disappointingly new and ugly bridge is the site of the fiercely contested Gioco del Ponte on June 27, a custom dating from the days of Cosimo I that replaces the bloody Club and Shield fun of the past. The Gioco commences with a parade of 800 Pisans in 16th-century costume with all the swish pageantry that the Tuscans do so well, and climaxes in a rowdy tug of war match with a seven ton cart over the bridge, pitting the Parte di Tramontana (neighbourhoods north of the Arno) against the Parte di Mezzogiorno (neighbourhoods to the south).

*Upstream from the Logge di Banchi, along the Lungarno Galileo Galilei stands the octagonal pink stone church of **San Sepolcro**, sunken below the modern pavement; a pair of good moustachioed lions guard the back door.*

Built in 1150 by Diotisalvi for the Knights Templars, who were fond of such geometric shapes, it has a marble arcade around the floor, a *Madonna* by Gozzuoli's workshop, and tombs, one of which contains Maria Mancini, one of the few women to have a brand of cigars named after her. The niece of Cardinal Mazarin and wife of powerful Prince Colonna, the beautiful Maria was the great love of the young Louis XIV—so great that Mazarin thought she was driving his royal charge to distraction and sent her back to Italy.

*Behind San Sepolcro runs **Via San Martino**, an attractive street of palazzi with tiny alleys running into it from all sides. In the Middle Ages this was Pisa's Casbah—the main street of the Chinizica, the quarter of Arab and Turkish merchants. At no. 19 a Roman relief was incorporated into the building, known since the Middle Ages as Kinzica, a maiden who saved Pisa when the Saracens sailed up to the Golden Gate. Continue east to **San Martino** (usually locked).*

A big brick hulk built over and around a 14th-century church, San Martino has a white marble façade that seems austere by Pisan ice-cream parfait standards, although adorned with an excellent relief by Andrea Pisano of *St Martin and the Beggar* (actually a copy—the original is inside).

> *After the church, Via San Martino becomes Via Ceci, passing the* **Piazzetta della Crocifisso**—*named for the Crucifix that saw a miracle that greatly impressed the Pisans in 1837; a stone (in the glass case) was thrown at it, but hovered in the air and did no harm. From here, take Via Latinta to the Arno; shade, benches and drinks may be had to the right in the* **Giardino Scotto**, *in the creeper-covered remains of the city wall extending from the 16th-century* **Bastione Sangallo***.*

The gardens once belonged to the **Palazzo Scotto**, where Shelley lived in 1820–2 and wrote *Adonais*, *Epipsychidion* and 'Evening: Ponte al Mare, Pisa':

> *Within the surface of the fleeting river*
> *The wrinkled image of the city lay,*
> *Immovably unquiet, and forever*
> *It trembles, but it never fades away.*

> *Cross back to the right bank, over the Ponte di Fortezza, reconstructed in 1958; just to the left is the church of* **San Matteo***.*

Built in the 11th century, San Matteo was lavishly Baroqued with fake marbles and gold in the 17th century. The ceiling over the single nave is one huge *trompe l'oeil* painting on *The Glory of God* and the holy-water stoups, covered with angels and *putti*, are good enough to eat.

> *The old convent attached to the church later served as prison for many years; now it immures much of the best of Pisan art from the Middle Ages and Renaissance in the* **Museo di San Matteo** *(open 9–7, 9–2 Sun, closed Mon; adm L8000).*

The ground floor contains a fine collection of medieval ceramic plates from the Middle East, brought home by old Pisan sea dogs, and some of the local efforts to imitate the same, starting in the 13th century; a large cache of jugs were found right under the Hunger Tower. Upstairs, is a well-arranged collection of 12th- and 13th-century works gathered from the city's churches, including Byzantine-style *Crucifixions* by Giunta di Capitinio (or Pisano), possibly of Greek origin, and believed to be the first artist ever to sign his work (early 1200s), and another signed by Berlighiero (d. 1236), whose family worked around Lucca: they mark the beginning of more 'humanized' representations of Christ in response to the preaching of St Francis. Other fine works are by the conservative Maestro di San

Martino, one of the leading Pisan painters of the day, and by Ranieri di Ugolino, who was inspired by the then avant-garde Cimabue in the Duomo.

From the 14th century—not a good time for Pisa, after its defeat at Meloria—there's a superb golden polyptych by Simone Martini (1319), and paintings from the brush of the excellent Francesco di Traini, Taddeo di Bartolo, Agnolo Gaddi, Antonio Veneziano and Turino Vanni. Pisa found its best expression in sculpture; the marble polychrome *Madonna del Latte* by Andrea and Nino Pisano (father and son) is often pointed out as a key work in the translation of Giotto's revolution into three dimensions. Note the fine bas-relief of the *Nativity* by Tino di Camaino (d. 1337), the star pupil of Giovanni Pisano who worked directly with Giotto.

After all the trecento works, the Early Renaissance comes as a startling revelation, as it must have been for the people of the 15th century: here is Neri di Bicci's wonderfully festive *Coronation of the Virgin*, bright with ribbons, a *Madonna* from the decorative Gentile da Fabriano, a recently restored *Madonna* and saints by Ghirlandaio, a sorrowful *St Paul* by Masaccio, whose features and draperies are softly moulded, an anonymous *Madonna with Angel Musicians*, and a beautifully coloured *Crucifixion* by Gozzoli that looks more like a party than an execution. The last great work is Donatello's gilded bronze reliquary bust of *San Lussorio*, who could pass for Don Quixote.

> *Next to the museum on the Lungarno is the* **Prefettura**, *housed in the lovely 13th-century stone brick and marble Palazzo Medici, decorated with slender twin and triple columns; it was a favoured residence of the magnificent Lorenzo. Continue up the Lungarno Mediceo to the corner of Via delle Belle Torri, and the 16th-century* **Palazzo Toscanelli***, once attributed to Michelangelo. Byron lived there in 1821–2 and wrote six cantos of* Don Giovanni—*just a short swim up the Arno from his friend Shelley. The palace now houses the state archive. From here, turn up picturesque* **Via delle Belle Torri***, lined with houses from the 12th and 13th centuries, which rub shoulders with a lot of new constructions that fill in the gaps left by bombs. At Piazza Cairoli, there's another 11th century church,* **San Pierino** *just to the right, turn back to Lungarno Mediceo and continue straight on to lively Piazza Garibaldi, located between the Ponte di Mezzo and a web of little arcaded market streets; Vicolo delle Donzelle, an unmarked lane at the top left corner of the Piazza, will take you into Pisa's arcaded market square,* **Piazza Vettovaglie** *('victuals square') where every morning except Sunday the city's ancient mercantile traditions are renewed over stands of olives and cheese.*

*Leave Piazza Vettovaglie by way of Via Sant'Orsola, then turn right in old arcaded **Borgo Stretto**, its porticoes supported by capitals from the 11th century. Amid them rises the church of **San Michele in Borgo**.*

Begun in 990—just as Pisa was beginning to feel its oats as a maritime republic—San Michele has one of the most gorgeous façades in the city, redone in the 14th century, with three tiers of arcades and little faces tucked in between them. Note the elaborate, faded red graffiti, nearly impossible to read, similar to the names one sometimes sees on Spanish churches, written in bull's blood letters. Much of the interior collapsed during bombing raids in 1944 and had to be rebuilt, although a 13th-century fresco of St Michael survives inside, in the lunette over the left door.

*Continuing along the Borgo Stretto, turn right at Via Mercanti for the striking 12th-century façade of **San Paolo all'Orto**. Turn right at the far end of Piazza San Paolo all'Orto into Via San Francesco, and walk 5 minutes to **San Francesco**, begun in 1270.*

Built in three stages between the 13th and 17th centuries, San Francesco is essentially Gothic behind a plain marble façade that Ferdinand DUX de' Medici financed in order to write his name in big letters on top. The vast interior (as always a testimony to the extraordinary religious revival inspired by the preaching orders) was 'restored to its primitive splendour in year XI' according to the Fascist-era plaque at the back. It contains some fine art: a marble 15th-century high altarpiece by Tomaso Pisano and frescoes from 1342 in the vault by Taddeo Gaddi. The altar is incongruously illuminated with an almost fluorescent light, clashing with the otherwise dim and restful interior. Flanking the altar, the second chapel on the right is shared by a beautiful 14th-century Florentine polyptych and the tomb of the unfortunate Count Ugolino, his sons and grandsons. A case of reliquaries in the transept contains a cassock of St Francis. In the last chapel on the left, look up to see the *sinopie*, also by Taddeo Gaddi. The sacristy was frescoed with *Scenes from the Life of the Virgin* by Taddeo di Bartolo in 1397; in the Chapterhouse are more frescoes, this time by Niccolò di Pietro Gerini. After seeing the church, take a minute to look into the cloisters.

*Backtrack along Via San Francesco, passing the 12th-century **Santa Cecilia**, whose façade and campanile are decorated with round majolica tiles. At the end, cross Via Oberdan for **Piazza San Felice** where the bank, the **Cassa di Risparmio di Pisa** occupies one of the prettiest 12th-century buildings in the city, with a crenellated tower house tucked around back. Backtrack to Piazza Dini and turn up narrow and slightly scruffy **Via delle Sette Volte**, lined with medieval buildings, covered with vaults and the opinions of the Pisans (the grafitti* *champs of Tuscany) and very romantic, if rather smelly, after dark. At the top of the lane, turn right down Via San Lorenzo for Piazza Martiri della Libertà, where the plane trees create a shady oasis in the summer and there's a large statue dedicated to Grand Duke Peter Leopold I. Cut across this for the church of **Santa Caterina**.*

Pisa's Dominican headquarters, Santa Caterina has a beautiful, typically Pisan marble façade of 1330 in two tiers, with a lovely spoked rose window. The equally attractive interior, with one enormous assymetrical nave, is decorated with liquorice candystripes; there's a sculptural group of the *Annunciation* on its high altar and the *tomb of Archbishop Saltarelli* on the left, all the work of Nino Pisano. On the left there's a *Madonna and Saints* by Fra Bartolommeo, a pietà by Santi ti Tito and a large painting from the 1340s attributed to Francesco Traini and Francesco Memmi, of the *Apotheosis of Saint Thomas Aquinas*, with Plato and Aristotle in attendance and the defeated infidel philospher Averroes below.

*From Santa Caterina, turn right in Via San Zeno for **San Zeno**, a deconsecrated Romanesque chapel, in parts as old as the 5th century, near the 13th-century **Porta San Zeno** and a good section of medieval walls. Turn right into the piazza and Via Santa Caterina which will bring you to the vestiges of Pisa's **Roman baths** from the 2nd century AD, near the medieval **Porta di Lucca**. From here, Via Cardinale Pietro Maffi leads west back to the Campo dei Miracoli.*

Peripheral Attractions

A couple of kilometres up river to the east stands 'Pisa's second leaning tower', the campanile of the Romanesque **San Michele dei Scalzi**. **Calci**, under the slopes of Monte Pisano, has a good 11th-century church and an eroded giant of a campanile, while 11km from Calci, in a prominent site overlooking the Arno, is the ornate **Certosa di Pisa**, founded in 1366, but completely Baroqued in the 18th century, in a kind of 1920s Spanish-California exhibition style with three fine cloisters (*open 9–4, summer 9–6*). There are lavish pastel frescoes by Florentine Baroque artist Bernardo Poccetti and his school, and a giraffe skeleton, stuffed penguins, Tuscan minerals, wax intestines—all part of the university's **Natural History Collections**, founded by the Medici, housed in the Certosa since 1981 (*guided visits, May–Oct 9–7; Nov–April 9–4; closed Mon; adm; for the natural history collections, by appointment © 937 092*).

Towards the coast, 6km from Pisa, is the beautifully isolated basilica of **San Piero a Grado**. According to tradition it was founded in the 1st century by St Peter himself when he shipwrecked here, and in the Middle Ages was a popular pilgrimage destination. Although first documented in 375, the current buildings date from the 11th century, embellished with blind arcades and ceramic *tondi*. Like many very early churches and basilicas, it has an apse on either end, though in different sizes; the columns were brought in from a variety of ancient buildings. The altar stone, which was believed to have been set there by Peter himself, was found in recent excavations that also uncovered the remains of several previous churches. Frescoes which were in the nave, by a 14th-century Lucchese, Deodato Orlandi, tell the *Story of St Peter* with effigies of the popes up to the millennium (John XVIII) and a view of heaven.

In 1822, a strange ceremony took place on the wide, sandy beach of **Gombo**, near the mouth of the Arno, described in morbid detail by Edward Trelawny: 'the brains literally seethed, bubbled, and boiled as in a cauldron, for a very long time. Byron could not face this scene, he withdrew to the beach and swam off to the *Bolivar*.' Such was Shelley's fiery end, after he drowned while sailing from Livorno. Gombo, and Pisa's other beaches, the **Marina di Pisa** and **Tirrenia**, are more often plagued by pollution than cremations, although Marina di Pisa makes a pretty place to stroll, with its Liberty-style homes and pine forests.

Since 1979, 21,000 hectares of coast between Viareggio and Livorno has been set aside as the **Parco Naturale di Migliarino, San Rossore, Massacùccoli**—a wild landscape of wetlands and marshes, pines and beaches, with several zones open to public access; the headquarters is at Via Aurelia Nord 4, © (050) 525211 (*open daily 8–2*), where you can book a guided tour. The **Tenuta di San Rossore**, a hunting estate intact since the 11th-century, once owned by the Medici and Lorraine dukes, the kings of Savoy, is now held by the President of the Republic, who lets visitors in on Sundays and holidays (*open winter 8.30–5.30, summer 8.30–7.30; guided tours on Tues, Thurs, Sat and Sun, © 050 539111*). Get there on Viale delle Cascine and Via delle Lenze.

Excursions from Pisa

From Pisa you can catch a morning train down to Piombino and sail in an hour to **Elba**, with its lovely beaches. APT buses north of the Stazione Centrale will take you south to the haunting hilltown of **Volterra** or north to Puccini's old haunts around **Torre del Lago**; **Viareggio**, just to the north, may have lost some of its fashionable cachet but still has a good beach and some wonderful Liberty villas.

Catch a morning train to the **Cinque Terre** (changing at La Spezia), one of the loveliest and most dramatic coastlines in Italy. Five charming fishing villages, perilously perched on high cliffs, are linked only by a railway line and footpath.

Catch a bus north to **Carrara** to see one of the world centres of the marble industry. If you have a car, you can drive up into the mountains (the Apuan Alps), and visit the quarries from which Michelangelo ripped his marble.

Lucca

Nowhere in Lucca
will you see the face of a Philistine.

Travels in Lucca, Heine

Of all Tuscany's great cities, Lucca (pop. 92,500) is the most cosy, sane and domestic, a tidy gem of a town encased within its famous walls. Yet even these hardly seem formidable, more like garden walls than something that would keep the Florentines at bay. The old ramparts and surrounding areas, once the outworks of the fortifications, are now full of lawns and trees, forming a miniature green belt; on the walls, where the little city's soldiers once patrolled, now the citizens ride their bicycles and walk their dogs, and often stop to admire the view.

Like paradise, Lucca is entered by way of St Peter's Gate. Once inside you'll find tidy, well-preserved Romanesque churches and medieval towers that destroyed Ruskin's romantic notion that a medieval building had to be half-ruined to be beautiful, a revelation that initiated his study of architecture. Nor do Lucca's numerous Liberty-style shop signs show any sign of rust; even the mandatory, peeling ochre paint and green shutters of the houses seem part of some great municipal housekeeping plan. Bicycles have largely replaced cars within the walls. At first glance it seems too bijou, a good burgher's daydream. But after its long and brave history it has certainly earned the right to a little quiet. The annual hordes of Tuscan tourists leave Lucca alone for the most part, though there seems to be a small number of discreet visitors, many of them German and Swedish, who come back every year. They don't spread the word, apparently trying to keep one of Italy's most beautiful cities to themselves.

History

Lucca's rigid grid of streets betrays its Roman origins; it was founded as a colony in 180 BC as *Luca*, and in 56 BC entered the annals of history when Caesar, Pompey and Crassus met here to form the ill-fated First Triumvirate. It was converted to Christianity early on by St Peter's disciple Paulinus, who became first bishop of Lucca. The city did especially well in the Dark Ages; in late Roman times it was the administrative capital of Tuscany, and under the Goths managed to repulse the murderous Lombards; its extensive archives were begun in the 8th century, and many of its churches were founded shortly after. By the 11th and 12th centuries Lucca emerged as one of the leading trading towns of Tuscany, specializing in the production of silk, sold by colonies of merchants in the East and West, who earned enough to make sizeable loans to Mediterranean potentates. A Lucchese school of painting developed, such as it is, and beautiful Romanesque churches were erected, influenced by nearby Pisa. Ghibellines and Guelphs, and then Black and White Guelphs made nuisances of themselves as they did everywhere else, and Lucca often found itself pressed to maintain its independence from Pisa and Florence.

In 1314, at the height of the city's wealth and power, the Pisans and Ghibellines finally managed to seize Lucca. But Lucca had a trump card up a secret sleeve: a remarkable adventurer named Castruccio Castracani. Castracani, an ambitious noble who for years had lived in exile—part of it in England—heard the bad news and at once set forth to rescue his hometown. Within a year he had chased the Pisans out and seized power for himself, leading Lucca into its most heroic age, capturing most of Western Tuscany to form a little Luccan empire, subjugating even big fish like Pisa and Pistoia. After routing the Florentines at Altopascio in 1325, Castracani was planning to snatch Florence too, but died of malaria just before the siege was to begin—another example of Florence's famous good luck. Internal bickering between the powerful families soon put an end to Lucca's glory days, though in 1369 the city managed to convince Emperor Charles IV to grant it independence as a republic, albeit a republic ruled by oligarchs like Paolo Guinigi, the sole big boss between 1400 and 1430.

But Lucca continued somehow to escape being gobbled up by its voracious neighbours, functioning with enough tact and tenacity to survive even after the arrival of the Spaniards—a fact one can attribute not so much to its great walls as to its relative insignificance. Amazingly enough, after the Treaty of Câteau-Cambrésis, Lucca found itself standing together with Venice as the only truly independent states in Italy. And like Venice, the city was an island of relative tolerance and enlightenment during the Counter-Reformation, its garden walls in this case proving stout enough to deflect the viperous Inquisition. In 1805 Lucca's independence ended when Napoleon gave the republic to his sister Elisa Baciocchi, who ruled as its princess; it was given later to Marie Louise, Napoleon's widow, who governed well enough to become Lucca's favourite ruler and earn a statue in the main Piazza Napoleone. Her son sold it to Leopold II of Tuscany in 1847, just in time for it to join the Kingdom of Italy.

The railway station is just south of the walls on Piazza Ricasoli, with lots of trains on the Viareggio–Lucca–Florence line, ✆ 47013. Buses leave from Piazzale Verdi, just inside the walls on the western end: LAZZI buses to Florence, Pistoia, Pisa, Prato, Abetone, Bagni di Lucca, Montecatini and Viareggio, ✆ 584876, and CLAP (that's right, CLAP) buses to towns in Lucca province, including Collodi, Marlia, and Segromigno, and the Serchio valley, ✆ 587897. Get around Lucca itself like a Lucchese by hiring a bicycle from the tourist office in Piazzale Verdi or from **Barbetti,** Via Anfiteatro 23, ✆ 954444.

Tourist Information

Vecchia Porta San Donato, Piazzale Verdi, ✆ (0583) 419689.

Lunch/Cafés

Antico Caffè della Mura, Piazzale Vittorio Emanuele 2, ✆ 47962. This elegant café/restaurant/bar, convenient for the beginning and end of the walk, is the only place to eat and drink right on the walls. Its privileged position comes at a price (*expensive*).

Gelateria Veneta, Via Veneto 7 and Chaisso Barletti 23. The best ice cream in Lucca, this family-run establishment has over 150 years of experience and they use only fresh ingredients without any additives (*closed Tues*).

Gli Orti di Via Elisa, Via Elisa 17, ✆ 491 241. Good value pizzeria/trattoria which also has a self-service salad bar.

Guido Cimino, Piazza dell' Anfiteatro. This highly original bar/restaurant has jazzy decor and seats on the piazza in the summer. You can snack or eat a full meal from the menu of the day from noon until the early hours (*closed Tues and Mon in winter*).

The two best take-away pizzerias are **La Sbragia** in Via Fillungo, so popular that it has a ticket number system, or else **Da Felice** round the corner in Via Buia.

Highlights of Lucca

Although Lucca has two museums of paintings, its finest art, sculpture and architecture are concentrated in the **Cathedral**, **San Michele in Foro** and **San Frediano**. Don't miss atmospheric **Piazza dell'Anfiteatro**, a climb up to the top of the **Torre Guinigi** and a stroll down delightful **Via del Fosso**, the main street **Via Fillungo** and a climb up to the **Walls**.

Start: *Porta San Pietro*
Finish: *Baluardo San Paolino*
Walking time: *one day*

Lucca Walk

The charming little universe of Lucca is made on a scale for pedestrians; it doesn't even have the hills that can make Siena a sweat in the summer. Few cars penetrate its *cordon sanitaire* of walls—you're more likely to be knocked over by a bicycle. Lucca is to be savoured; make this walk a whole day. A stroll around the walls themselves makes a delicious second helping.

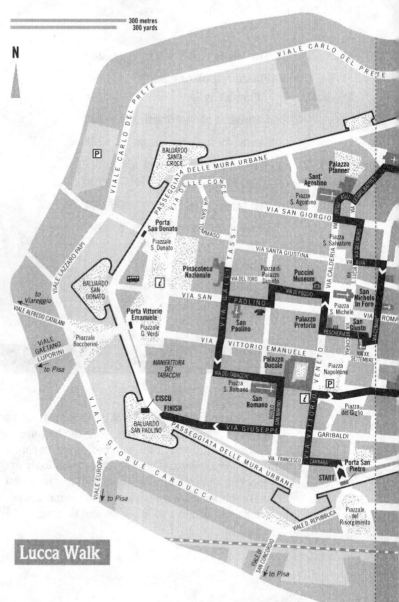

N

300 metres
300 yards

VIALE CARLO DEL PRETE

VIALE CARLO DEL PRETE

BALUARDO SANTA CROCE

PASSEGGIATA DELLE MURA URBANE

VIA DELLE CON

Palazzo Pfanner

Sant' Agostino

Piazza S. Agostino

VIA SAN GIORGIO

VIA CALDERIA

VIA SANTA GIUSTINA

Piazza S. Salvatore

Porta San Donato

Piazzale S. Donato

VIA SAN TOMMASO

Pinacoteca Nazionale

Piazza di Palazzo Dipinto

Puccini Museum

VIA BUIA

VIA DEL TORO

VIA DI POGGIO

San Michele In Foro

VIA SAN PAOLINO

VIA GALLI TASSI

Piazza S. Michele

VIA ROMA

VIALE LAZZARO PAPI

BALUARDO SAN DONATO

Porta Vittorio Emanuele

Piazzale G. Verdi

San Paolino

Palazzo Pretoria

San Giusto

VIA PESCHERIA

to Viareggio

VIALE ALFREDO CATALANI

VIALE GAETANO LUPORINI

Piazzale Boccherini

VIA

VITTORIO EMANUELE

VIA VENETO

VIA XX SETTEMBRE

to Pisa

MANIFATTURA DEI TABACCHI

Palazzo Ducale

Piazza Napoleone

CISCU FINISH

VIA DEI TABACCHI

Piazza S. Romano

San Romano

VICOLO SAN MARINO

P

Piazza del Giglio

BALUARDO SAN PAOLINO

PASSEGGIATA DELLE MURA URBANE

VIA GIUSEPPE

GARIBALDI

VIALE EUROPA

VIA FRANCESCO

CARRARA

Porta San Pietro

VIALE GIOSUE CARDUCCI

START

to Pisa

VIALE D. REPUBBLICA

Piazzale del Risorgimento

VIALE DI SAN CONCORDIO

to Pisa

Lucca Walk

294

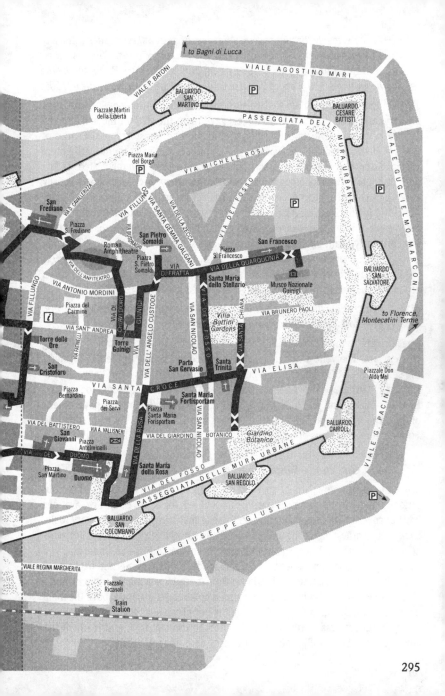

*Lucca's lovely bastions evoke images of the walled rose gardens of chivalric romance, enclosing a smaller, perfect cosmos. They owe their charm to Renaissance advances in military technology. Prompted by the beginning of the Wars of Italy, Lucca began to construct the **walls** in 1500.*

The councillors wanted up-to-date fortifications to counter new advances in artillery, and their (unknown) architects gave them the state of the art, a model for the new style of fortification that would soon be transforming the cities of Europe. Being Renaissance Tuscans, the architects also gave them a little more elegance than was strictly necessary. The walls were never severely tested. Today, with the outer ravelins, fosses and salients cleared away (such earthworks usually took up more space than the city itself), Lucca's walls are just for decoration; under the peace-loving Duchess Marie Louise they were planted with a double row of plane trees to create a splendid elevated garden boulevard that extends around the city for nearly 4km, offering a continuous bird's-eye view over Lucca. They are among the best preserved in Italy. Of the gates, the most elaborate and flowery is the **Porta San Pietro** (1566) near the station, its portcullis still intact, with Lucca's proud motto of independence, LIBERTAS, inscribed over the top.

Inside the gate, turn left at Via Carrara, and then right onto Via Vittorio Veneto for Piazza Napoleone and Piazza Giglio.

These shady twin squares are Lucca's civic centre and the focus of its evening *passeggiata*. The yellow hodgepodge of a palace in Piazza Napoleone, formerly the seat of the lords of Lucca and the republican council, has been known as the **Palazzo Ducale** ever since it was used by Lucca's queens for a day, Elisa Bonaparte and Duchess Marie Louise; now it contains local government offices. The most important architect to have a crack at it was Ammannati in the 16th century, and signs of his Mannerist handiwork survive in the courtyard.

*From Piazza del Giglio, Via del Duomo leads past the church of **San Giovanni e Santa Reparata**, Lucca's original cathedral.*

The exterior has only parts of an 1187 portal to show for its old distinction, but inside there are some surprises (*open daily 9.30–3.15; adm*). Recent excavations have uncovered a series of buildings on this site that bring the city's history to life back to the earliest days. The church covers the site of a 5th-century basilica; adjacent to it stands the huge, square Baptistry from the 1300s, and under this you can see the original Roman font—a walk-in model for total-immersion baptisms—with bits of its mosaics, as well as later Romanesque pavements and a bishop's chair. San Giovanni also has a superb painted coffered ceiling and, above the main door, an attractive organ case. The organ is not playable as the pipes have been removed. Lucca was a city of organ builders in the old days, and many of the churches have beautifully crafted instruments with elaborate cases.

*Past San Giovanni are another pair of squares, Piazzas San Martino and Antelminelli; the former sees an **Antiques Market** every third Sat and Sun of each month, watched over by Lucca's **San Martino Cathedral**, begun by Pope Alexander II in 1070 and completed in the 15th century.*

This is perhaps the outstanding work of the Pisan style outside Pisa, begun in the 11th century and completed only in the 15th. Above the singular **porch**, with three different sized arches, are stacked three levels of colonnades, with pillars arranged like candy sticks, while behind and on the arches are exquisite 12th- and 13th-century reliefs and sculpture—the best work Lucca has to offer. See especially the *Adoration of the Magi* by Nicola Pisano over the left doorway, the two highly elaborated organ cases facing each other across the aisle, the column carved with the Tree of Life, with Adam and Eve crouched at the bottom and Christ on top, and a host of fantastical animals and hunting scenes, the months and their occupations, mermaids and dragons, a man embracing a bear, even *Roland at Roncevalles*, all by unknown masters. On the right side of the portico, there's also a medieval maze, which you can trace with your finger. Walk round the back, where the splendidly ornate apse and transepts are set off by the green lawn. The **Campanile**, crenellated like a battle tower, dates from 1060–1261.

*The dark **interior** offers a good introduction to the works of Lucca's only great artist, Matteo Civitali (1435–1501), who worked as a barber until his mid-30s, when he decided he'd rather be a sculptor. He deserves to be better known, but may never be since everything he made is still in Lucca.*

His most famous work is the octagonal **Tempietto** (1484), a marble tabernacle in the middle of the left aisle, containing Lucca's most precious holy relic, the world-weary *Volto Santo* ('Holy Image'), a cedar-wood crucifix said to be a true portrait of Jesus, sculpted by Nicodemus, an eyewitness to the crucifixion. Saved from the iconoclasts, it was set adrift in an empty boat and floated to Luni, where the bishop was instructed by an angel to place it in a cart drawn by two white oxen; where the oxen should halt, there too should the image remain. They made a lumbering beeline for Lucca, where the *Volto Santo* has remained ever since. Its likeness appeared on the republic's coins, and there was a devoted cult of the image in medieval England; Lucca's merchant colony in London cared for a replica of the *Volto Santo* in old St Thomas's, and according to William of Malmesbury, King William Rufus always swore by it, '*per sanctum vultum de Lucca*'. Long an object of pilgrimage, the image goes out for a night on the town in a candlelight procession each 13 September.

Further up the left aisle a chapel contains Fra Bartolommeo's *Virgin and Child Enthroned*. Here, too, is an altar by Giambologna, of *Christ with Saints Peter and Paul*. Civitali carved the cathedral's high altar, and also two expressive tombs in the south transept. A door from the right aisle leads to the sacristy (*adm*), where you can see Lucca's real icon, the remarkable **Tomb of Ilaria del Carretto** (1408), perhaps Jacopo della Quercia's most beautiful work, a tender, tranquil effigy of the young bride of boss Paolo Guinigi, complete with the family dog at her feet, waiting for his mistress to awaken. Ilaria may not be here for long; they're contemplating moving her to the new cathedral museum, or somewhere else. In fact the city has always had a strange love-hate relationship with this lovely statue. Right after her husband was overthrown they hustled her out of the cathedral, and she didn't come back for centuries. Near the statue is a *Madonna Enthroned with Saints* by Domenico Ghirlandaio. A side altar near the sacristy has a typically strange composition from the Venetian Tintoretto, a *Last Supper* with a nursing mother in the foreground and cherubs floating around Christ. In the centre, unfortunately often covered up, is a particularly fine section of the inlaid marble floor; on the entrance wall, a 13th-century sculpture of St Martin has been brought in from the façade.

> Next to the cathedral is the newly opened **Museo della Cattedrale** *(open daily, 10–6, 10–3 and 10–6 Sat and Sun winter; adm L5000).*

This displays more of the cathedral's treasures, including the ornaments (the crown and garments) of the *Volto Santo*, della Quercia's *St John the Baptist* and tapestries and paintings from San Giovanni.

> *Walk along the flank and behind the Duomo towards the walls, then turn left up Via della Rosa, passing the sweet little oratory of* **Santa Maria della Rosa** *(© 48287 for visits, or wait for Mass at 4pm on the first Thurs of the month), built in 1309 in the Pisan Gothic style. Via della Rosa follows the outer line of the old Roman enceinte. Even if it's closed, you can see the gothic carving on the side of the building as you continue down Via delle Rose. Note that the Madonna on the corner of the church is holding a rose. In the early 12th century, when the first church was built outside the gates, it took the name* **Santa Maria Forisportam** *('outside the gates'); it's just ahead, to your right, set in a charming square with a column, once used as a turning post in Lucca's medieval palio. Its marble façade is topped off by brick, and inside, there is yet another carved organ case.*

A pretty church with blind arcades in the Pisan style, it was Santa Maria Forisportam that converted Ruskin (and through Ruskin, millions of others) to medieval architecture: 'Here in Lucca I found myself suddenly in the presence of twelfth-century buildings, originally set in such balance of masonry that they could all stand without mortar; and in material so incorruptible, that after six hundred years of sunshine and rain, a lancet could not now be put between their joins. Absolutely for the first time I now saw what medieval builders were and what they meant. I took the simplest of façades for analysis, that of Santa Maria

Foris-Portam, and thereon literally *began* the study of architecture.' Inside, it not only looks but smells terribly old. The font is made from a Palaeo-Christian sarcophagus and there are two paintings by Guercino, by the fourth altar on the right and in the left transept; near the latter is a remarkable 14th-century painting on wood on the *Dormition and Assumption of the Virgin.*

> *From Piazza Santa Maria Forisportam, turn right in Via Santa Croce, where* **Porta San Gervasio** *is the best preserved gate from Lucca's second set of walls, built in 1260; it gives onto the former moat, now a picturesque little canal running alongside Via del Fosso. Just over this, beyond the gate, is* **Santa Trinità**, *home of Civitali's* **Madonna della Tosse** *(Our Lady of the Cough), a bit too syrupy sweet, but perhaps that helped the cure (if closed, ask for the key in the convent next door). If you need to have a break at this point, continue briefly along Via Elisa; the next lane to the right after Santa Trinità will take you into the* **Botanical Gardens**, *and a left into the gardens of the* **Villa Bottini** *(open 9–1.30), the only two oases of green inside the city walls.*

> *Otherwise, backtrack a few paces and turn right (north) up Via del Fosso, with its fine perspective of the 17th-century column of* **Santa Maria dello Stellario***. At the column turn right in Via della Quarquonia, where a long piazza opens up on your left, named after its 13th-century church,* **San Francesco***.*

Adorned with a shabby marble font and rose window, San Francesco is a typical church of the preaching order, with the tombs of Castruccio Castricani (d. 1328) and the Lucchese composer of the famous minuet, Luigi Boccherini (1743–1805). To the right of the high altar are fine, detached 15th-century frescoes of the Florentine school. There are more frescoes in the cloister, and a good 13th-century tomb.

> *From San Francesco, continue down Via Quarquonia for the palatial brick Villa Guinigi, built in 1418 by the big boss Paolo Guinigi in his glory days. It now houses the* **Museo Nazionale Guinigi** *(open 9–7, Sun, 9–2 closed Mon; adm L4000).*

Its ground floor houses an interesting collection of Romanesque reliefs, capitals and transennas, some of which are charmingly primitive—St Michael slaying the dragon, Samson killing the lion, a 9th-century transenna with birds and beasts, spirals and daggers. **Room IV** has a lovely *Annunciation* by Civitali, and beyond, a set of neoclassical reliefs from the Palazzo Ducale of the *Triumphs of Duchess Maria Luisa*. The painting gallery upstairs contains intarsia panels from the cathedral, each with scenes of Lucca as seen from town windows, some trecento works by the Lucca school and a charming quattrocento *Madonna and Child* by the

'Maestro della Vita di Maria'. Other rooms contain a miasma of oversize 16th-century canvases, some by Vasari.

> Backtrack down Via della Quarquonia and Via D. Fratta to **San Pietro Somaldi**, a 12th-century church with a grey and white striped façade; the relief over the door is by Guido da Como and dated 1203. From here turn south briefly down the street of the Guardian Angel (Via dell'Angelo Custode) to Via Guinigi, into a neighbourhood of Lucca that has scarcely changed in the past 500 years. Here the medieval ancestors of the Guinigi had their stronghold in a block of 14th-century houses and the **Torre Guinigi** (open winter 10–4.30, summer 8.30–7.30; adm L4500).

This is one of Lucca's landmarks, with a tree sprouting out of the top—the best example of this quaint Italian fancy that you'll see here and there throughout the country. One of the most elaborate of medieval family fortresses, the tower has recently been restored, and it's worth the slight risk of cardiac arrest to climb the 230 steps for the view over the city and the marbly Apuan Alps.

> From the tower, follow Via Sant'Andrea to Via di Chiavi d'Oro (golden key street). This leads to Via dell'Anfiteatro and into the most remarkable relic of Roman Lucca, the **Piazza dell'Anfiteatro**—the Roman amphitheatre.

Like a fossil, only outlines of its arches are still traceable in the outer walls, while within the inner ring only the form remains—the marble was probably carted off to build San Michele and the cathedral—but Lucca is a city that changes so gradually and organically that the outline has been perfectly preserved. The foundations of the grandstands now support a perfect ellipse of medieval houses. Duchess Marie Louise cleared out the old buildings in the former arena, and now, where gladiators once slugged it out, there is a wonderfully atmospheric piazza, where the boys play football and the less active sit musing in sleepy cafés. The amphitheatre is also home to some great shops.

> Walk directly across the amphitheatre and out the other side. Turn right onto Via Fillungo for 50 metres and then into Piazza San Frediano with its tall church and even taller campanile of **San Frediano**, built in the early 1100s and shimmering with the colours of the large 13th-century mosaic on its upper façade, showing Christ and the Apostles in an elegant flowing style, often attributed to Berlinghiero Berlinghieri.

The 11th-century bronze Arabian falcon at the top is a copy—the original is so valuable that it's locked away. The palatial **interior** houses Tuscany's most remarkable baptismal font, the 12th-century *Fontana lustrale*, covered with reliefs; behind is an equally beautiful terracotta lunette of the *Annunciation* by Andrea della Robbia. The chapels are richly decorated—the fourth on the left has an altarpiece in the form of a Gothic polyptych by Jacopo della Quercia, who also sculpted the two tombstones. The second on the left, when walking down the church, has frescoes painted by Amico Aspertini in 1508 (*currently under restoration*).

The bedecked mummy is St Zita, patroness of domestic servants; born in 1218, she entered the service of a family in Lucca at the age of 12 and remained with them until her death. She would not only give her clothes and food to the poor, but that of her masters, which at first caused her to be maltreated. Ever since her canonization in 1696 she has been greatly venerated, not only in Italy, but in England, where maids belonged to the Guild of St Zita. The Lucchesi are very fond of her, and on 26 April they bring her uncorrupted body out to caress.

> *Follow the church along to Via Cesare Battista and turn right in Via degli Asili for the* **Palazzo Pfanner**.

An 18th-century palace with a delicious, statue-filled garden (for a look into it and at San Frediano's handsome apse, climb up the city wall beyond), it has a famous grand stairway of white marble, and is used to display a collection of silks made in Lucca, and 17th–19th-century costumes (*the costumes are no longer on display; the statue-filled garden is open summer 9–7, winter 10–4; by appointment only, ✆ 48524*). Just behind Palazzo Pfanner is **Sant'Agostino** (1300s), with a campanile sitting on the ruins of the Roman theatre.

> *South of Sant'Agostino, turn left in Via San Giorgio, and right in* **Via del Moro**, *lined with medieval houses. Turn left again in Via Buia (meaning 'dark street'), and right in Lucca's main street, medieval* **Via Fillungo**. *In this area, don't just keep your eyes at eye-level; the streets are narrow, and if you don't look up, you will miss some wonderful stone carving above doors and windows.*

Via Fillungo and its surrounding lanes make up the busy shopping district, packed on Saturday and Sunday afternoons when the Lucchese are out for their afternoon *passeggiata*. It is a tidy nest of straight and narrow alleys where the contented cheerfulness that distinguishes Lucca from many of its neighbours seems somehow magnified. A number of shopfronts have remained unchanged for over a century— one of the most charming is the jeweller's at No.20. Even older are the loggias of the 14th-century palaces, now bricked in, and the ancient **Torre dell' Ore**, which since 1471 has striven to keep the Lucchesi on time, and perhaps now suggests that it's time for a coffee in Lucca's historic **Caffè di Simo** at No.58. There's of course a church to be seen, 13th-century **San Cristoforo**, now used for exhibitions. It is also Lucca's war memorial, with the names of the dead all along the walls.

> *Where Via Fillungo becomes Via Cenami, turn right in Via Pescheria and right again onto Via Vittorio Veneto for the* **Palazzo Pretorio**, *built in*

*1492 by Matteo Civitali, whose statue stands in the portico (at the time of writing, much of the portico (including Civitali's statue) is closed off for work). Beyond the palazzo turn right in Via Vittorio Emanuele for handsome Piazza San Michele, Lucca's Roman forum and site of **San Michele in Foro**, a masterpiece of Pisan Gothic and a church so grand that many people mistake it for the cathedral.*

The ambitious façade rises high above the level of the roof, to make the building look even grander (the Italians call the style 'wind-breaker'). Every column in the five levels of Pisan arcading is different: some doubled, some twisted like corkscrews, inlaid with mosaic Cosmati work or carved with monsters, while in between are friezes richly carved with animals. The whole is crowned by a giant statue of the Archangel, and on the corner of the façade is a *Madonna* by Civitali, paid for by the city in gratitude for deliverance from a plague in 1480; the graceful, rectangular campanile is Lucca's tallest and loveliest. The interior is more austere, but there's a glazed terracotta *Madonna and Child* attributed to Luca della Robbia, a striking 13th-century *Crucifixion* hanging over the high altar, and a painting of plague saints by Filippino Lippi. Giacomo Puccini began his musical career here as a choirboy (his father and grandfather had been organists in the cathedral).

*Young Puccini didn't have far to walk; he lived in narrow Via di Poggio 30, just opposite San Michele's façade. His house is now a little **Puccini Museum** (entrance in Corte San Lorenzo 9, open summer 10–1 and 3–6; closed Jan–mid-March, other winter months reduced hours—check before you go—and closed Mon).*

The museum has a few odds and ends left by Puccini (1858–1924), including manuscripts, letters, mementoes, his overcoat and other bits and pieces, as well as his piano. Once his operas had made him famous, he bought a villa at Torre del Lago, just south of Viareggio, where he said, 'I can practise my second favourite instrument, my rifle' on the coots and ducks in Lake Massaciuccoli; he was famous for terrorizing the local peasants by tearing around like a demon in his motorcar. His villa is also a museum, rather more extensive than the one here, and the maestro is buried in the adjacent chapel—he died just after having run through his last opera, *Turandot,* with Toscanini. In August, Torre del Lago hosts an opera festival in Puccini's honour.

*At the end of Via di Poggio, turn left in Piazza del Palazzo Dipinto for Via San Paolino (the Roman decumanus major, or main east–west street) and the church of **San Paolino** (1539) where little Puccini played the organ to earn his pin-money.*

Dedicated to the native of Antioch who converted Lucca and made it the first Christian city of Tuscany around the year 65, San Paolino contains two beautiful works: a 13th-century French *Virgin and Child* carved in stone brought back by Lucchese silk merchants from Paris, and an anonymous quattrocento Florentine *Coronation of the Virgin*, with Mary hovering over a city of pink towers; she is crowned by God the Father instead of Christ, who usually does the honours.

> *Walk past the church and turn right in Via Galli Tassi. At No.43 stands the 17th-century **Palazzo Mansi**, home of the Pinacoteca Nazionale (open 9–7, Sun 9–4, closed Mon; adm L8000).*

Most of the art, as well as the rich furnishings in several of the rooms, dates from the 17th century; the few paintings which might be interesting, portraits by Pontormo and Bronzino, are all indefinitely at the restorer's. In the study hangs a dark and damaged Veronese, and Tintoretto's *Miracle of St Mark Freeing the Slave*, showing, with typical Tintorettian flamboyance, Venice's patron saint dive-bombing from heaven to save the day. The 1600s frescoes are more fun than the paintings, especially the *Judgement of Paris*, which Venus wins by showing a little leg. And one can't help but wonder what rococo dreams tickled the fancy of the sleeping occupants of the amazing bedroom.

> *From the picture gallery, backtrack across Via S. Paolino, and continue along Via Galli Tassi towards the state tobacco company, which perfumes the whole quarter with a fine aroma that disguises the fact that it produces Toscanelli cigars, one of the world's vilest smokes. Turn left in Via dei Tabacchi for **San Romano**, a rarely opened Dominican church that preserves the Tomb of San Romano (1490), one of Civitali's finest works. Turn right in Vicolo San Romano, and right at Via Guiseppe Garibaldi, where you can climb up to the city walls and to **Baluardo San Paolino**.*

So this walk through Lucca ends where it begins, at the walls—where another walk can easily begin. Baluardo San Paolino is the site of the headquarters of the 'International Institute for the Study of City Walls' (CISCU), © 478978, which will get you in for a tour of the bastion's interior (*open 10–12.30 and 3.30–6*).

Excursions from Lucca

Villas around Lucca

In 16th-century Lucca, as elsewhere in Italy, trade began to flounder, and once-plucky, daring merchants, or at least those sufficiently well-upholstered, turned to the more certain joys of real estate, where they could genteelly decline in a little country palace and garden. For the Lucchesi, the favourite area to construct such pleasure domes was in the soft, rolling countryside to the north and northeast of the city. Three of these villas or their grounds are open for visits. In Segromigno, 10km from Lucca in the direction of Pescia, there's the charming, mid 16th-century but often modified **Villa Mansi**, embellished with a lovely half-Italian (i.e. geometric) and half-English (i.e. not geometric) garden laid out by the great Sicilian architect Juvarra (*② 920234, open summer 10–12.30, 3–7 ; winter 10–12.30, 3–5 , closed Mon adm. L9000*). Nearby in Camigliano, the even more elaborate **Villa Torrigiani**, also begun in the 16th century, was long celebrated for its fabulous parties and entertainments. Set in a lush park of pools and trees, it has 16th–18th-century furnishings (*② 928008, villa open Mar–Oct 3–6, summer 10–1 and 3–7 closed Tues; park open same hours all year; adm exp*). Elisa Bonaparte Baciocchi combined a villa and a summer palace to make her country retreat, now called the **Villa Pecci-Blunt ex-Villa Reale** in Marlia. Only the park and the Giardino Orsetti are open, but they are lovely (*guided tours by appointment, ② 30108, open Mar–end Nov 10–12 and 3–6 exc Mon; adm*).

The Lucchese Plain

East and west of Lucca, what was swampland in the Middle Ages has been reclaimed to form a rich agricultural plain. One of its features are its 'courts'—farm hamlets not constructed around a central piazza, but with houses in neat rows. At one time there were 1100 such 'courts' on the plain. Among the highlights of the area is curious **Castello di Nozzano** just to the west, built by Matilda of Tuscany on a hill, its pretty tower now incongruously topped by a large clock. To the east, one of the first villages, **Capannori**, is the head town of several 'courts' and has a couple of interesting Romanesque churches, especially the 13th-century **Pieve San Paolo**, around which a small village incorporated itself, using the campanile for defence. The most imposing monument near Capannori is the 19th-century **Acquedotto del Nottolini**, which is also visible from the autostrada. Just south is the pretty hilltop village of **Castelvecchio**, its tall houses forming an effective circular wall. **Altopàscio**, on the Lucca–Empoli road, was built around an 11th-century hospice run by an obscure chivalric order called the Hospitaller Knights of the Order of Altopàscio, who originally occupied themselves with rescuing travellers from the swamps. Only the campanile of their church remains in the village today. **Montecarlo** gives its name to a very good dry white wine produced in the immediate area.

Further east of Lucca you can take the waters at **Montecatini Terme** (LAZZI buses), one of Italy's biggest and most elegant spas; or to the north, visit the charming, older spa of **Bagni di Lucca** on the Serchio river, popular in the early 19th century. CLAP buses go to **Collodi**, where there's a Pinocchio park for the kids and the magnificent 17th-century Castello Garzoni with its superb gardens for the adults; **Barga**, further north, is a hilltown overlooking the marble mountains of Carrara, with a great cathedral begun in 1000. Lucca is also convenient for **Viareggio**, Puccini's **Torre del Lago**, and the coastal resorts (LAZZI buses).

Food and Drink

In Italy, the three Ms (the Madonna, Mamma and *Mangiare*) are still a force to be reckoned with, and in a country where millions of otherwise sane people spend much of their waking hours worrying about their digestion, standards both at home and in the restaurants are understandably high. Everybody is a gourmet, or at least they think they are, and food is not only something to eat, but a subject approaching the heights of philosophy—two Umbrian businessmen were once overheard on a train heatedly discussing mushrooms for over four hours. Although ready-made pasta, tinned minestrone and frozen pizza in the *supermercato* tempt the virtue of the Italian cook, few give in (although many a working mother wishes she could at times).

Regional traditions are strong in Italy, not only in dialect but in the kitchen. Tuscany is no exception and firmly maintains its distinctive cuisine, although it does not rank among the great culinary regions of Italy; it offers good, honest, traditional dishes, often humble, rarely elaborate. The Medici may have put on some magnificent feeds, but the modern Tuscan is known by his fellow Italians as a *mangiafagioli*, or bean-eater. Some observers hold it as part of the austere Tuscan character, others as another sign of their famous alleged miserliness.

The truth is that, although beans and tripe often appear on the menu, most people when dining out want to try something different, from other regions, perhaps, or the recent concoctions of Italian *nouvelle cuisine*, or *cucina nuova*, or perhaps a recipe from the Middle Ages or Renaissance. Some of the country's finest restaurants are in Tuscany; and, in practice, the diversity of dishes, from traditional to bizarre, is almost endless.

Eating trends in Italy are changing with changes in lifestyles. These days, many more women work and therefore have less time to devote to dishes requiring lengthy preparation. Many of the supermarkets have ready-prepared fresh food, and more women are taking advantage of it. It's usually left up to Grandma to tackle the *pasta fatta in casa* (home-made pasta) and other such time-consuming endeavour. First, though, a few general comments on eating out.

Eating Out

In Italy the various types of restaurants—*ristorante, trattoria* or *osteria*—have been confused. A *trattoria* or *osteria* can be just as elaborate as a restaurant, though rarely is a *ristorante* as informal as a traditional *trattoria.* Unfortunately the old habit of posting menus and prices in the windows has fallen from fashion, so it's often difficult to judge variety or prices. Invariably the least expensive restaurant-type place is the increasingly rare *vino e cucina*, a simple place serving simple cuisine for simple everyday prices. It is essential to remember that the fancier the fittings, the fancier the bill, though neither of these points has anything at all to do with the quality of the food. If you're uncertain, do as you would at home—look for lots of locals.

Prices

When you eat out, mentally add to the bill (*conto*) the bread and cover charge (*pane e coperto*, L2000–4000) and a 10 per cent service charge. This is often included in the bill (*servizio compreso*); if not, it will say *servizio non compreso*, and you'll have to do your own arithmetic. Additional tipping is at your discretion, but never do it in family-owned and -run places. Prices quoted for meals in this book are for an average complete meal Italian-style, with wine, for one person. We have divided restaurants into the following price categories.

very expensive	over L90,000
expensive	L60,000–90,000
moderate	L40,000–60,000
inexpensive	below L40,000

People who haven't visited Italy for years and have fond memories of eating full meals for under a pound will be amazed at how much prices have risen; though in some respects eating out in Italy is still a bargain, especially when you figure out how much all that wine would have cost you at home. In many places you'll often find restaurants offering a *menu turistico*—full, set meals of usually meagre inspiration for L20–25,000. Good, imaginative chefs often offer a *menu degustazione*—a set-price gourmet meal that allows you to taste their daily specialities and seasonal dishes. Both of these are cheaper than if you had ordered the same food à la carte. When you leave a restaurant you will be given a receipt (*ricevuto fiscale*) which according to Italian law you must take with you out of the door and carry for at least 300m. If you aren't given one, it means the restaurant is probably fudging on its taxes and thus offering you lower prices. There is a slim chance the tax police may have their eye on you and the restaurant, and if you don't have a receipt they could slap you with a heavy fine.

Eating on the Hoof

There are several alternatives to sit-down meals. The 'hot table' (*tavola calda*) is a buffet which sells hot and cold foods, where you can choose a simple prepared dish or a whole meal, depending on your appetite. The food in these can be truly impressive, though many offer only a few hot dishes, pizza and sandwiches. Try to avoid the tavola calda in the most obviously tourist areas as these will most probably produce cardboard imitations of what should be on offer. Shops selling pizza by the slice (*pizza a taglio*) tend to sell only pizza and foccaccias plus drinks. Again, it's worth looking for these down a side street. *Gastronomia* and *pizzicheria* are both types of delicatessen although the former tend to have more prepared dishes to take away. The *rosticceria* is another convenient alternative. These shops are open at lunch and dinner time and always make a feature of roast dishes (particularly delicious are the chickens roast on a spit). They will have the wherewithall for a complete meal—hot or cold—from *antipasto* to *dolce*, wine and bread at reasonable prices. Most people take food out, but some places have a few tables as well. Many bars in cities now serve a choice of hot and cold dishes at lunchtime, again at very moderate prices. For really elegant picnics, have a *tavola calda* pack up something nice for you. And if everywhere else is closed, there are always the railway station bars—these will at least have sandwiches and drinks, and perhaps some surprisingly good snacks you've never heard of before. Common snacks you'll encounter include *panini* of prosciutto, cheese and tomatoes, or other meats; *tramezzini*, little sandwiches on plain, square white bread that are always much better than they look; pizza, of course, or the traditional sandwich of Tuscany, a hard roll filled with warm *porchetta* (roast whole pig stuffed with fennel and garlic).

The Meals

Breakfast (*prima colazione*) in Italy is no lingering affair, but an early morning wake-up shot to the brain: a *cappuccino*, a *caffè latte* (white coffee), or a *caffè lungo* (a generous portion of espresso), accompanied by a croissant-type roll, called a *cornetto* or *briosce*. This can be consumed in nearly any bar, and repeated during the morning as often as necessary, which is why breakfast in most Italian hotels is no big deal and seldom worth the price charged. If you have breakfast in a bar, do try to choose one which says *pasticceria* (pastry shop) or *produzione propria* (home-produced). This more or less guarantees that your brioche will be at least decent or at best, melt-in-the-mouth divine. The alternatives are mass-produced, dry and usually tasteless.

Lunch or *pranzo*, is generally served around 1pm. Times are changing, even when it comes to Italian eating habits. A combination of less rigid working hours (the three-hour break in the middle of the day is no longer *de rigeur*), and health considerations (it seems to be sinking in that a daily four course meal at lunch is counter-productive to health and efficient manpower) means that less people are making a big fuss of lunch. Weekends are an exception when you will find restaurants full of families and friends tucking into mountains of food, and meals lasting three hours. Lunch is the most important meal of the day for the Italians, with a minimum of a first course (*primo*—any kind of pasta dish, broth or soup, or rice dish or pizza), a second course (*secondo*—a meat or fish dish, accompanied by a *contorno* or side dish—a vegetable, salad or potatoes usually), followed by fruit or dessert and coffee. You can, however, begin with a platter of *antipasti*—the appetizers Italians do so brilliantly, ranging from warm seafood delicacies, to raw ham (*prosciutto crudo*), salami in a hundred varieties, lovely vegetables, savoury toasts, olives, pâté, and many, many more. There are restaurants that specialize in *antipasti*, and they usually don't take it amiss if you decide to forget the pasta and meat and just nibble on these scrumptious *hors d'oeuvres* (though in the end it will probably cost as much as a full meal). Most Italians accompany their meal with wine and mineral water (*acqua minerale*, with or without bubbles, *con* or *senza gas*, which supposedly aids digestion), concluding with a *digestivo* (liqueur).

Evening meal, *cena*, is usually eaten at around 8pm. This is much the same as *pranzo* although lighter, without the pasta: a pizza and beer, eggs, or a fish dish. In restaurants, however, Italians often order all the courses, so if you have only a sandwich for lunch you can have a full meal in the evening.

Some Regional Specialities

The Tuscans will tell you that the basic simplicity of their cooking is calculated to bring out the glories of their wine, which may well be true, as it tends to be the perfect complement to a glass of Chianti or Vino Nobile. Nearly all their specialities are born of thrift, like *bruschetta*, a Tuscan and Umbrian favourite that uses sliced stale bread, roasted over the fire, covered with olive oil and rubbed with garlic. *Acqua cotta*, popular in southern Tuscany, is *bruschetta* with an egg; another version adds mashed tomatoes. The other traditional Tusco-Umbrian *antipasto* is *crostini*, thin slices of toast with a piquant pâté spread of chicken livers, anchovies, capers and lemons, or other variations.

For *primo*, the traditional Tuscan relies mostly on soups. Perhaps most traditional is *ribollita* ('reboiled'), a hearty mushy vegetable soup with beans, cabbage, carrots and chunks of boiled bread. Another is *pappa col pomodoro*, which, while being bread-based, is very different to *ribollita* as its only ingredients, apart from the bread, are tomatoes, garlic, basil and olive oil. It's a very pure dish.

Panzanella, a bread-based summer salad of quite solid consistency made from day-old bread, tomatoes, red onions, cucumber and olive oil, can be a godsend on a hot summer's day. Other first courses you'll find are *fagioli al fiasco* (beans with oil and black pepper simmered in an earthenware pot) or *fagioli all'uccelletto* (beans with garlic and tomatoes). The most Tuscan of pasta dishes is *pappardelle alla lepre* (wide noodles with a sauce of stewed hare); others are the simple but delicious *spaghetti con briciolata* (with olive oil, breadcrumbs and parsley); *nastri alla borracina* (ribbons of pasta served with a 'moss' of freshly chopped spinach and marjoram, basil, rosemary, mint and sage); and, most splendid of all, *turtui cu la cua* (*tortellini* with tails), filled with mascarpone, ricotta and spinach, with a butter and basil sauce.

Another great Tuscan soup is the hearty *pasta e fagioli*, (pasta and beans), a thick broth of cannelini beans flavoured with garlic and rosemary in which pasta is cooked.

The local bread is often a subject of controversy among the uninitiated who cannot deal with its total lack of salt. This peculiar characteristic dates way back to medieval times when salt was highly taxed (there are very few natural salt deposits in the area), and Tuscany was a poor region. *Pane toscano* has, however, many devoted fans who are addicted to its crusty outside and spongy crumb. It is this latter quality which makes it so appropriate for all those bread-based soups; try making them with an English cottage loaf, and you will end up with mush.

Tuscany does not offer exceptional *secondi*. There is the famous steak, *bistecca alla fiorentina* (cooked over coals, charred on the outside and pink in the middle, and seasoned with salt and pepper); otherwise Tuscans are content with grilled chops—lamb, pork or veal. *Fritto misto* is an interesting alternative, where lamb chops, liver, sweetbreads, artichokes and courgettes (*zucchini* are dipped in batter and deep fried. Otherwise, look for *arista di maiale* (pork loin with rosemary and garlic), *francesina* (meat, onion and tomato stew in Vernaccia di San Gimignano wine), *anatra* (duck), *piccione* (stuffed wild pigeon), *cinghiale* (boar), either roasted or in sausages or *stufato* (stewed). Tuscans are rather too fond of their *girarrosto*, a great spit of tiny birds and pork livers. It's fairly easy to find seafood as far inland as Florence—one traditional dish is *seppie in zimino*, or cuttlefish simmered with beets. Hardy souls in Florence can try *cibreo* (cockscombs with chicken livers, beans and egg yolks).

Tuscany's tastiest cheese is tangy *pecorino* made from ewe's milk; the best is made around Pienza. When it's aged it becomes quite sharp and is grated over pasta dishes. Typical desserts, to be washed down with a glass of Vinsanto, include Siena's *panforte* (a rich, spicy dense cake full of nuts and candied fruit), *cenci,* a carnival sweet (deep-fried strips of dough), *castagnaccio* (chestnut cake, with pine nuts, raisins and rosemary), Florentine *zuccotto* (a cake of chocolate, nuts and candied fruits) and *crostate* (fruit tarts). A traditional accompaniment to Vinsanto are the hard, almond and egg *biscotti di Prato,* originally from the town just west of Florence. Dunking them in Vinsanto softens them enough to avoid putting your latest dental work at risk.

Tuscan Wines

Quaffing glass after glass of Chianti inspired Elizabeth Barrett Browning to write her best poetry, and the wines of Tuscany may bring out the best in you as well. The first really to celebrate Tuscan wines was a naturalist by the name of Francesco Redi in the 1600s, who, like many of us today, made a wine tour of the region, then composed a dithyrambic eulogy called 'Bacchus in Tuscany'. Modern Bacchuses in Tuscany will find quite a few treats, some famous and some less well known, and plenty of cellars and *enoteche* (wine bars) where you can do your own survey—there's a famous one in Siena with every wine produced in Tuscany, and the rest of Italy as well.

Most Italian wines are named after the grape and the district they come from. If the label says DOC (*Denominazione di Origine Controllata*) it means that the wine comes from a specially defined area and was produced according to a certain traditional method; DOCG (the G stands for *Garantita*) means that a high quality is also guaranteed, a badge worn only by the noblest wines. *Classico* means that a wine comes from the oldest part of the zone of production; *Riserva,* or *Superiore,* means a wine has been aged longer. Most Tuscan farmers also make a cask of *Vinsanto,* a dessert wine that can be sweet or almost dry, and which according to tradition is holy only because priests are so fond of it.

Tuscany produces 19 DOC and DOCG wines, including some of Italy's noblest reds: the dry, ruby red **Brunello di Montalcino** and the garnet **Vino Nobile di Montepulciano**, deep red with the fragrance of violets. Chianti may be drunk young or as a *Riserva,* especially the higher octane Chianti Classico. There are seven other DOC Chianti wines (Montalbano, Rufina, Colli Fiorentini, Colli Senesi, Colli Aretini, Colline Pisa and simple Chianti). Sangiovese is the chief grape of all Chianti as well as all the classified red wines of Tuscany. Lesser known DOC reds include dry, bright red **Rosso delle Colline Lucchesi**, from the hills north of Lucca; hearty **Pomino Rosso**, from a small area east of Rufina in the Mugello; **Carmignano**, a consistently fine ruby red that can take considerable ageing, produced just west of Florence; and **Morellino di Scansano**, from the hills south of Grosseto, a dry red to be drunk young or old. The three other DOC reds from the coast are **Parrina Rosso**, from Parrina which is near Orbetello;

Montescudaio Rosso; and **Elba Rosso**, a happy island wine, little of which makes it to the mainland. All three have good white versions as well.

Of the Tuscan whites, the most notable is **Vernaccia di San Gimignano** (also a *Riserva*), dry and golden in colour, the perfect complement to seafood; delicious, but more difficult to find, are dry, straw-coloured **Montecarlo** from the hills east of Lucca and **Candia dei Colli Apuani**, a light wine from the mountains of marble near Carrara. From the coast comes **Bolgheri**, white or rosé, both fairly dry. Cortona and its valley produce **Bianco Vergine Valdichiana**, a fresh and lively wine; from the hills around Montecatini comes the golden, dry **Bianco della Valdinievole**. **Bianco di Pitigliano**, of a yellow straw colour, is a celebrated accompaniment to lobster.

Eating Out in Florence ✆ (055-)

Florence in its loftier moods likes to call itself the 'birthplace of international haute cuisine', a claim that has very much to do with Catherine de' Medici, a renowned trencherwoman, who brought a brigade of Florentine chefs with her to Paris and taught the Frenchies how to eat artichokes, but has little to do with the city's contribution to the Italian kitchen. Florentine food is on the whole extremely simple, with the emphasis on the individual flavours and fresh ingredients. A typical primo could be *pappardelle*, a type of wide tagliatelle egg-pasta, served usually with a meat sauce, or game such as wild boar, rabbit and duck. Soups are also popular: try the *minestrone toscano* with a base of *cavolo nero*, a kind of black cabbage with long, slim crinkly leaves and peculiar to Tuscany, borlotti beans and potatoes. The most famous main course in Florence is the *bistecca alla fiorentina*, a large steak on the bone, 2 inches thick, cut from loin of beef and cooked on charcoal simply seasoned with salt and pepper. As for the vegetables, you could try *piselli alla fiorentina*, peas cooked with oil, parsley and diced bacon, or *tortino di carciofi*, a delicious omelette with fried artichokes, *fagioli all' uccelletto*, cannellini beans stewed with tomatoes, garlic and sage and *spinaci saltati*,-fresh spinach sautéd with garlic and olive oil. Florentine desserts tend to be sweet and fattening: *bomboloni alla crema* are vanilla-filled doughnuts and *le fritelle di San Giuseppe* are bits of deep-fried batter covered in sugar. If you prefer cheese, try the sturdy *pecorino toscano*. For better or worse, the real Florentine specialities rarely turn up on many restaurant menus, and you'll probably never learn what a Florentine cook can do with cockscombs, calves' feet and tripe.

Like any sophisticated city with lots of visitors, Florence has plenty of fine restaurants; even in the cheaper places standards are high, and if you don't care for anything fancier, there will be lots of good red Chianti to wash down your meal. Central Florence, by popular demand, is full of *tavole calde*, pizzerias, cafeterias and snack bars, where you can grab a sandwich or a salad instead of a full sit-down meal (one of the best pizza-by-the-slice places is just across from the Medici Chapels). Note that many of the best places are likely to close for all of August; you would also be wise to call ahead and reserve, even a day or two in advance.

Restaurants

very expensive

The Bristol, Via dei Pescioni 2, © 287814. *Open for lunch and dinner daily.* On the whole, hotel restaurants are not the best bet in Florence, but the Bristol (at the Helvetia & Bristol hotel) is a notable exception, featuring Tuscan or international dishes, all well pre-pared and impeccably served. Surroundings are intimate and elegant with lots of dark velvet and antique paintings.

Cibreo, Via dei Macci 118/r, © 2341100. *Open for lunch and dinner, closed Sun and Mon Easter, mid-July–mid-Sept.* One of the most Florentine of Florentine restaurants, Cibreo overlooks the lively market of Sant'Ambrogio. The decor is simple—food is the main concern, and all of it is market-fresh. You can go native and order tripe antipasto, pumpkin soup, and cockscombs and kidneys, or play it safe with prosciutto from the Casentino, a fragrant soup (no pasta here) of tomatoes, mussels and bell-pepper, leg of lamb stuffed with artichokes or duck with sultanas and pine nuts. Top it off with a delicious lemon *crostata* or cheese-cake; accompany it with an excellent choice of Italian or French wines, or a prized bottle of Armagnac. Their chocolate cake is the answer to every chocaholic's dreams

Alle Murate, Via Ghibellina 52r, © 240618. *Open for dinner, closed Mon.* This elegant but relaxed restaurant is very popular for its 'creative traditional' food. There are two set menus, one of Tuscan dishes and the other offering something a little different. Even when old friends such as lasagne and *bistecca* appear, they are given an innovative touch. There is plenty of fish—recommended dishes include spaghetti with sea bass, steamed octopus on a bed of mashed potato, and squid and mangetout. Meat lovers might try lamb's brain salad, pigeon stuffed with peppers and potatoes, or duck's livers with ceps and rosemary.

Enoteca Pinchiorri, Via Ghibellina 87, near the Casa Buonarroti, © 242777. *Open for lunch and dinner, closed Sun, Mon and Wed lunch. and Aug.* One of the finest gourmet restaurants in Italy; the owners inherited the building, a wine shop, some 10 years ago, and converted it into a beautifully appointed restaurant, with meals served in a garden court in the summer. They've also increased what was already in the cellars to an astonishing collection of some 80,000 bottles of the best Italy and France have to offer. The cooking, a mixture of nouvelle cuisine and traditional Tuscan recipes, wins prizes every year. They also do a series of set menus; you can choose between Tuscan, fish or the day's menu based on market avail-ability. Italians tend to complain about the minute portions; it is a standard joke in Flo-rence that you go to eat at Pinchiorri, and then to fill up on a pizza afterwards. Prices are reckoned to be L150,000 excluding wine, but the sky's the limit if you go for a more interesting bottle.

Sabatini, Via Panzani 9a, behind S. Maria Novella, © 282802. *Closed Mon and first two weeks July.* With a branch in Tokyo,

Sabatini has been a favourite with tourists and locals for decades. It's a little old-fashioned, but you may find the sober elegance the perfect setting for enjoying their big Florentine steaks, the flamboyant *spaghetti alla lampada* and *pappardelle con lepre*, herb-strewn leg of lamb, and a decadent *semifreddo al croccantino* with hot chocolate sauce.

Da Stefano, Via Senese 271, Galuzzo, ℭ 2049105. *Open for dinner only, closed Sun.* Now generally acknowledged to be the best fish restaurant in town, Stefano's message is *solo pesce, solo fresco a solo la sera* (only fish, only fresh and only in the evening). His fish is extraordinarily fresh; how else could he dare to serve it raw on an impressive platter of ice with tangy mayonnaise. Another visually impressive dish that doesn't fail to satisfy the palate is the *spaghetti alla Stefano*—a mountainous pile of steamy spaghetti brimful of shellfish. Worth the 10-minute drive out of town.

expensive

l'Bambino, Via del Parione 74-76r (off Piazza Goldini), ℭ 214005. *Open for lunch and dinner, closed Wed.* This new, lively and trendy restaurant is run by one of Florence's cult figures. The decor is unusual, and the food interesting. Try the spaghetti with lobster.

Buca Lapi, Via del Trebbio 1r, ℭ 213768. Another traditional Florentine restaurant, located since 1800 in the old wine cellar of the lovely Palazzo Antinori. Experiment with *pappardelle al cinghiale* (wide pasta with boar), which tastes better than it sounds; the *bistecca fiorentina con fagioli* here is hard to beat, downed with many different Tuscan wines.

Caffè Concerto, Lungarno C. Colombo 7, ℭ 677377. *Open for lunch and dinner,*

closed Sun and three weeks in August. The setting on the north bank of the Arno to the east of the centre is lovely, and the interior is warm wood and glass with good lighting and lots of greenery. The creative cooking features hearty portions of traditional ingredients, yet prepared with a different twist.

Coco Lezzone, Via del Parioncino 26r, off Lungarno Corsini, ℭ 287178. In old Florentine dialect, the name means big, smelly cook, but this shouldn't put you off. The food here—Tuscan classics using ingredients of the highest quality—is excellent, the ambience is informal.

Don Chisciotte, Via C. Ridolfi 4r (between the Fortezza Basso and Piazza dell'Indipendenza), ℭ 475430. *Open for lunch and dinner, closed Sun and Mon lunch.* A small restaurant serving inventive Italian food with a particular emphasis on fish and vegetables. Let yourself be tempted by baked baby squid, delicate warm vegetable and fish salad or green tagliatelle with scampi and courgettes.

Oliviero, Via delle Terme 51r, 5 minutes from the Piazza della Signoria, ℭ 212421. *Open for lunch and dinner, closed Sun.* Don't be put off by the rather sleazy decor (red velvet seating, pink candles), and the slightly bizarre clientele; the food is excellent. Feast on such curiosities as *gnudi di fiori di zucchina e ricotta* (ravioli stripped of its pasta coating with ricotta cheese and courgette flowers) and boned pigeon stuffed with chestnuts.

Pane e Vino, Via San Niccolò 70r (in the Oltrarno, just in from Ponte alla Grazie), ℭ 2476956. *Open for lunch and dinner, closed Sun.* This pleasant and informal restaurant started life as an *enoteca* and still has a superb wine list and very knowledgeable staff to go with it. If you are happy to trust the chef's choice, go for the *menu degustazione*; it changes daily, has seven small courses and is very good value. With any luck, the porcini mushroom flan will be available—it is superb.

Taverna del Bronzino, Via delle Route 25–27r, ✆ 495220. *Open for lunch and dinner, closed Sun.* An elegant, traditional restaurant in a residential area north of the Duomo. The menu features plenty of traditional and less traditional Tuscan dishes—the *bistecca alla fiorentina* is succulent and tender, and the truffle-flavoured tortellini famous; there are also several fish choices for each course.

moderate

Angiolino, Via Santo Spirito 57r, ✆ 2398976. *Open for lunch and dinner, closed Mon.* Although it has lost some of its genuinely 'characteristic' qualities after recent renovation, Angiolino is still a fairly reliable place to eat Tuscan standards. The vegetable antipasti are especially good, and the simple *pollastrina sulla griglia* (grilled spring chicken) is mouthwateringly tasty.

Baldovino, Via Giuseppe 22r (Piazza S. Croce), ✆ 241773. *Open for lunch and dinner daily.* This excellent trattoria/pizzeria has been given a complete face lift by a young Scotsman, who offers anything from a big salad, a filled foccaccia or a pizza (baked in a wood-burning oven) to a full menu of pastas, fish and meat. The steaks served in various ways, originate from the Val di Chiana (where all good steaks should come from). The wine list is interesting: the same owner runs a wine bar just across the road.

Il Cantinone Gallo Nero, Via S. Spirito 5, ✆ 218898. Housed in a subterranean wine cellar, it specializes in Chianti Classico and country cooking—*pappa al pomodoro* (thick tomato soup), polenta with boar, beans and sausage. One room is devoted to wine tasting and antipasti.

Il Latini, Via dei Palchetti 6r (by Palazzo Rucellai), ✆ 210916. *Open for lunch and dinner, closed Mon and August.* Latini is an institution in Florence, among both Italians and tourists. It is crowded (be prepared to queue–the don't accept bookings) and noisy but fun. You sit at long tables and are served huge portions of Florentine classics. The *primi* aren't great; this place is for serious carnivores in need of a fix, a *bistecca* or, more unusual, the *gran pezzo*—a vast rib roast of beef. The house wine (the family have a large estate) is good—try one of the *riservas.*

Ristoro di Cambi, Via Sant'Onofrio 1/r, ✆ 217134. *Open for lunch and dinner, Closed Sun.* In the Oltrarno, some way to the west of the centre, this is a very popular place with the Florentine intelligentsia. The food is genuinely Florentine, the decor rustic. The soups—classic *ribollita* and *pappa al pomodoro*—are tasty and warming, and the *bistecca alla fiorentina* the real McCoy.

lla Vecchia Bettola, west of the Carmine in Viale Ariosto 32–34/r, ✆ 224158. *Open for lunch and dinner, closed Sun.* Marble-topped tables, wooden stools and benches and tiled walls make up the interior of this noisy trattoria. The food is great; the menu changes daily, but you can nearly always find their classic *tagliolini con funghi porcini* (egg pasta with ceps). The grilled meats are tasty and succulent, and the ice cream comes from Vivoli.

Sostanza, Via della Porcellana 25r (just west of Santa Maria Novella), ✆ 212691. *Open for lunch and dinner, closed Sat and Sun.* One of the few remaining authentic Florentine trattorias, this is a good place to eat *bistecca.* One of their most famous dishes is the simple, but delectable *petto di pollo* al *burro,* chicken breast sautéed in butter.

inexpensive

Aquacotta, Via dei Pilastri 51r (north of Piazza S. Ambrogio), ✆ 242907. *Open for lunch and dinner, closed Tues evening and Wed.* The bread soup which lends this trattoria its name is a simple but delicious dish; you can, of course, sample it here. You could follow that by deep-fried rabbit accompanied by crisply fried courgette flowers.

Borgo Antico, Piazza Santo Spirito 6, ✆ 210437. *Open for lunch and dinner daily.* This pizzeria is popular with a young trendy crowd, and you may have to wait, especially in summer for a table in the square. Inside, the background music can be loud. But the pizza is good, and there are plenty of other choices—interesting pastas, big salads and more substantial meat and fish dishes.

Osteria Santo Spirito, Piazza Santo Spirito 16r, ✆ 2382383. *Open for lunch and dinner daily.* If there is no room at Borgo Antico (above), walk across the piazza to this osteria where there is a choice of cold dishes, pastas (try the gnocchi with melted cheese infused with truffle oil), and more. The decor is unusual for Florence—warm red paintwork with contemporary lighting.

La Casalinga, Via Michelozzi 9r. *Open for lunch and dinner, closed Sun.* This family-run trattoria near Piazza Santo Spirito is always busy, and it's not surprising given the quality of the simple home cooking and the low prices. The *ribollita* (a hearty bread-based soup) is excellent.

Trattoria Cibreo, at the back of Cibreo, Via de' Macci 118r. *Open for lunch and dinner, closed Sun and Mon.* This little annexe to smart Cibreo (*see* above) is a real find. The food is exactly the same (excluding the odd more extravagant dish), but it is served at marble-topped tables on less expensive porcelain. So you can still eat the exquisite yellow pepper soup, cockscombs, stuffed rabbit and superb chocolate cake while gloating over the fact that your bill will be a third of that of your neighbours across the kitchen.

Di Vinus, Via del' Orto 35/A *Open 6–2am daily.* This brand-new wine bar in the Oltrarno (near Piazza Carmine) with its white walls, bricked arches, wooden tables and good music is a very pleasant place to do anything from sipping a glass of wine with a nibble of cheese, choosing a full meal from the short daily menu, to indulging in an exotic cocktail.

Al Tranvai, Piazza Torquato Tasso 14r (just south of the Carmine), ✆ 225197. *Open lunch and dinner, closed Sat and Sun.* The two rows of tables in this cheerful little trattoria are always full, and you may not get much elbow room. The varied menu changes daily, but the *crostini misti* (little rounds of toast with various toppings) are always on offer. Offal features strongly—tripe, *lampredotto* (intestines), chicken gizzards and other mysterious bits and pieces.

Le Belle Donne, Via delle Belle Donne 16r, ✆ 2382609. *Open for lunch and dinner, closed Sat and Sun.* It's easy to miss the entrance to this small trattoria just off Via Tournabuoni. Once you find it, an eye-catching display of seasonal fruit and vegetables greets you, indicative of the emphasis on vegetable dishes (although it is not exclusively vegetarian). It's always crowded, so do book.

Il Pizzaiuolo, Via dei Macci 113r, near Sant'Ambrogio, ✆ 241171. *Open for lunch and dinner, closed Tues and Aug.* A relatively new pizzeria, but one of the best. The *pizzaiuolo* (pizza maker) is Neapolitan, and his creations are puffy and light. There's lots more to choose from as well if you can get past the queues.

La Pentola dell' Oro, Via di Mezzo 24, north of Piazza Salvemini, ℂ 241821. *Open for lunch and dinner, closed Sun.* Also known as Da Alessi after the mythical owner, this is one of the best value-for-money places in Florence. The menu is long and varied, and many of the superb dishes are based on ancient recipes. There are a number of vegetable and salad choices. It is technically a club, so you may be asked to pay a small membership fee.

Sabatino, Borgo San Frediano 39/r, ℂ 284625. *Open for lunch and dinner, closed Sat and Sun.* The interior of this simple, family-run trattoria in the heart of the San Frediano district feels as if it has always been that way. Cooking methods, too, are of the old-fashioned variety, and prices are similarly retro. Hearty soups, tripe and kidneys are usually on the menu. Not to be confused with (very up-market) Sabatini; *see* above.

Santa Lucia, Via Ponte alle Mosse 102r (north of the Cascine), ℂ 353255. *Open for lunch and dinner, closed Wed.* There are three pizzerias in town where the pizza is genuinely Neapolitan, and this noisy, steamy, unromantic place, run by Neapolitans, is possibly the best (and the cheapest). They are topped with the sweetest tomatoes and the creamiest *mozzarella di buffala.* There are also some good seafood antipasti.

vegetarian

Gaugin, Via degli Alfani 24/r, ℂ 2340616. *Open for dinner daily.* A mixture of Italian and Middle Eastern dishes in this arty restaurant. And you don't have to stick to the traditional *primo, secondo, dolce* formula.

Ruth's, Via Farini 2/A, ℂ 2480888 (*inexpensive*). *Open for lunch and dinner, closed Fri dinner and Sat lunch.* With a bright and modern interior, this new kosher vegetarian restaurant next to the synagogue also serves

fish and Middle Eastern dishes. One of their specialities is the brick, which tastes better than it sounds: a kind of savoury pastry, filled with fish, potatoes or cheese, and fried. In the evenings there is a spicy fish couscous.

Centro Vegetariano Fiorentino, Via delle Ruote 30/r, ℂ 47030 (*inexpensive*). *Open for lunch and dinner, closed Sun lunch and Mon.* One-year membership (L2000) is required for entrance to the centre which has excellent fresh food with a wide choice of soups, salads and more substantial dishes in pleasant surroundings.

Restaurants around Florence

Biagio Pignatta, near the Medici villa in Artimino, ℂ 8718080 (*moderate*). *Open for lunch and dinner, closed Wed and lunch Thurs (in winter).* Named after a celebrated Medici chef, the menu here is pure Tuscan with particular attention to dishes with a Rennaissance flavour. *Papperdelle sul coniglio* (with rabbit sauce), *ribollita, crepes alla Catherina de' Medici* are all regulars. There is an olive-wood grill for meat, and a terrace overlooking vines and olives.

Bibé, Via delle Bagnese 1r, ℂ 2049085 (*moderate*). *Open for lunch and dinner, closed Sun.* This old farmhouse is situated a couple of kms south of Porta Romana. It has a lovely garden (somewhat marred by its proximity to the road and mosquitos), although the inside is very pleasant, too. The food is basically Tuscan, but with the odd twist. The ceps soup with chick peas is a good way to follow the classic *crostini* (toast topped with chicken livers), or try the *crespelle alla fiorentina*—light crepes filled with ricotta cheese and spinach. The roasts are good, as is the fried chicken and rabbit. Desserts here are creative and divine.

Da Delfina, Via della Chiesa, Artimino, near Carmignano, ℂ 8718074 (*expensive*).

Worth the drive out for its enchanting surroundings, lovely views, the charming atmosphere and sublime cooking—home-made tagliatelle with a sauce made from greens, risotto with garden vegetables, wild asparagus, succulent kid and lamb dishes.

Osteria al Ponte Rotto, Via Certaldese 8, San Casciano, ℡ 828090 (*inexpensive*). *Open for lunch, closed Tues*. Once a little trattoria at the back of the family-run grocery, things here have been smartened up, but the Osteria is still a simple place serving home-cooked food. The *zuppa lombarda* (a warming bean and bread soup) is excellent as are the grilled meats, or try the rabbit stewed with black olives. From San Casciano (a few kms down the Siena superstrada) follow the signs to Montespertoli-Certaldo.

La Panacea del Bartolini, Via Bosconi, Olmo, ℡ 548972 (*expensive*). *Open for lunch and dinner, closed Mon in winter*. In a panoramic position above Fiesole (head north and follow the signs), the food at this restaurant is elegant and sophisticated, but based on the traditions of Tuscan cooking. The antipasti are exquisite, from a rabbit and Vinsanto terrine to a duck breast and orange salad. Variations on the traditional Florentine steak include a sauce of *aceto balsamica etrusca*.

Cafés and Bars

Cabiria Café, Piazza Santo Spirito. One of Florence's most recherché terraces for a Campari. Pleasant by day, noisy and trendy at night.

Caffè Cibreo, Via del Verrocchio 5r. Next to the Sant' Ambrogio food market; bustling at market times, more elegant in the evening.

Caffè Italiano, Via Condotta 56r. On two levels; downstairs for standing at the bar,

upstairs for a longer sit. Coffee, tea and cakes are great, and you can also enjoy a light lunch here.

Dolce Vita, Piazza del Carmine. The place where fashionable young Florentines strut their latest togs—a favourite pastime since the 14th century (*closed Sun and two weeks in Aug*).

Dolci e Dolcezze, Piazza Cesare Beccaria 8r, at the top of Ponte San Niccolò, ℡ 2345438. The most delicious cakes, pastries and marmalades in the city—the *crostate*, *torte* and *bavarese* are expensive but worth every lira. It now has another shop in Via del Corso 41r (*closed Mon*).

Fiaschettieria Vecchio Casentino, Via dei Neri 5. A welcoming little wine bar, serving Tuscan vintages and charcuterie (*closed Mon and Aug*).

Giacosa, Via Tornabuoni 83. Has a certain sparkle, good sandwiches and ice cream, and a reputation for having invented the Negroni (gin, Campari and vermouth).

Gilli, Piazza della Repubblica 13–14r. Dates back to 1733, when the Mercato Vecchio still occupied this area; its two panelled back rooms are especially pleasant in the winter.

Giubbe Rosse, Piazza della Repubblica. Another famous café, rendezvous of Florence's literati at the turn of the century; the chandelier-lit interior has changed little since.

Hemmingway, Piazza Piattellina 9r. The beautiful and restful decor makes this a delightful place for tea, coffee, apéritifs and snacks. *Open from 4pm–1am*.

Rivoire, Piazza della Signoria 5r. Florence's most elegant and classy watering hole is, with a marble-detailed interior, as lovely as the piazza itself.

La Via del' Té, Piazza Ghiberti 22r. Looking onto the Sant' Ambrogio food market, with a huge range of teas to choose from plus sweet and savoury snacks.

Gelaterie

Festival del Gelato, Via del Corso 75r. Over 100 variations of ice cream.

Il Granduca, Via dei Calzaiuoli 57r. Creamy concoctions that challenge those of nearby rival Perché No (*closed Wed*).

Dei Neri, Via dei Neri 20/22r, near Santa Croce. Tasty cones, but no seats (*closed Wed*).

L'Oasi, 5 Via dell'Oriuolo, near the Duomo. A sophisticated flavour and a choice of cakes.

Perché No, Via Tavolini 194, near Via Calzaiuoli. Another challenger for the *gelato* throne with wonderful ice cream in 1940s surroundings.

Ricchi, Piazza Santo Spirito. A huge choice and a scrumptious *tiramisú* (*closed Sun and first half of August*).

Il Triangulo delle Bermude, Via Nazionale 61r. Has a superb choice.

Vivoli, Via Isola delle Stinche 7r (between the Bargello and S. Croce). Florence's claim to being the ice-cream capital of the world owes much to the decadently delicious confections and rich *semifreddi* served here (*closed Mon*).

Eating Out in Siena ✆ (0577–)

Sitting between three of Italy's greatest wine-producing areas, the Chianti, the Brunello of Montalcino and the Vino Nobile of Montepulciano, there is always something distinguished to wash down the simple dishes of the Sienese table. This city's real speciality is sweets, and quite a few visitors to Siena find they have no room for lunch or dinner after repeated visits to the pastry shops for slices of *panforte* (an alarmingly heavy but indecently tasty cake laced with fruits, nuts, orange peel and secret Sienese ingredients), or *panpepato* (similar but with pepper in it). They are all artists—shop windows flaunt gargantuan creations of cakes and crystallized fruit, metres high, and as colourful as a Lorenzetti fresco, set out for all to admire before they are carted off to some wedding party. The **Enoteca** inside the Medici fortress (*see* p.260) is another distraction; sometimes they organize special wine tastings, concentrating on one particular region of Italy. Siena being a university town, snacks and fast food of all kinds are common; a *cioccina* is Siena's special variation on pizza; *pici* (thick south Tuscan spaghetti) with a sauce prepared from ground fresh pork, *pancetta*, sausages and chicken breasts, added to tomatoes cooked with Brunello wine, is the city's favourite pasta dish.

Siena's Salami

Buristo is a cooked salami made from the blood and fatty leftovers of sausages and heavily spiced; *finocchiona* is peppered sausage meat seasoned with fennel seeds and stuffed into the sausage skin; *soppressata* is a boiled salami made from a mixture of rind and gristle; the alternative version, *soppressata in cuffia*, is made in the same way and stuffed into a boned pig's head. The *salsiccioli secchi* are perhaps the most appetising salami of all, made from the leanest cuts of pork or wild boar, enhanced with garlic and black or red pepper.

Restaurants

very expensive

Certosa di Maggiano, Via di Certosa 82 (1km southeast of Porta Romana), © 288 180. *Open for lunch and dinner daily.* Part of a luxury hotel housed in a former Carthusian monastery, the setting of this restaurant, be it the pretty dining room, the 14th-century cloisters or by the swimming pool, is exquisite. Modern, haute cuisine dishes are served with some pomp, and the overall decor is, perhaps, rather precious. Prices are outrageously high, but remember you are paying for the surroundings.

expensive

Antica Trattoria Botteganova, Via Chiantigiana 29, © 284230. *Open for lunch and dinner, closed Sun and Mon lunch.* A few kms northeast of Siena on the SS408 to Montevarchi. Traditional dishes are well-prepared and beautifully presented. Meats such as the stuffed rabbit are earthy, or go for the more delicate fish choices such as the tomato flan with basil-flavoured sturgeon fillets and black tagliolini with scallops and courgette. There is an extensive wine list.

Cane e Gatto, Via Pagliaresi 6, © 287 545. *Open for dinner, closed Thurs.* The food is creative and interesting in this little restaurant near Porta Romana. For those with hearty appetites, the menu degustazione has some seven or eight courses and is good value. Alternatively, you can eat à la carte.

Da Enzo, Via Camollia 49, © 281277. *Open for lunch and dinner, closed Tues.* The menu in this traditional restaurant is long and varied with plenty of choice between fish and meat. The classic garlicky spaghetti with clams (*vongole*) is good, and there is a roast fish of the day.

moderate

Ai Marsili, Via del' Castoro 3, © 47 154. *Open for lunch and dinner, closed Mon.* An elegant setting for a large choice of excellent Sienese dishes, some based on ancient recipes. The green gnocchi with duck sauce is an unusual starter, or, to make a change, try the delicate Risotto al Limone. Among the meat courses is Wild boar alla Cacciatora, an earthy stew with black olives, veal escalope sautéed with fresh tarragon, or Catherine de' Medici's famous dish Faraona alla Medici, guinea fowl roasted with pine nuts, almonds and plums.

Osteria di Castelvecchio, Via Castelvecchio 65, © 49 586. *Open for lunch and* *dinner, closed Tues*. The decor is original and modern, but this building was once the stable block of one of Siena's oldest Palazzi. Mauro and Simone cook and serve up reworkings of traditional recipes with an emphasis on vegetarian dishes (Wednesdays are, in particular, dedicated to non-meat eaters, but not exclusively so). The *menu degustazione* is good value, and the wine list is long and varied.

Osteria Le Logge, Via del Porrione 33, ✆ 48013. Open for lunch and dinner, closed Sun. The high-ceilinged and airy main room of this restaurant must be one of the most pleasant places to eat in Siena, and lone eaters are treated with respect. The food also makes a visit worthwhile. A tempting choice of antipasti precedes such primi as home-made ravioli stuffed with artichokes, or *malfatti al' osteria*, a delicate concoction of spinach and ricotta baked with bechamel. There are always several fish dishes (a sizzling plate of sardines cooked with pine nuts comes straight from the oven), or go for the more robust capon cooked with chestnuts and Brunello wine.

Guido, Vicolo Pier Pettinato 7, ✆ 280042. *Open for lunch and dinner daily*. This central, traditional Sienese restaurant has a somewhat medieval feel to its dark brick walls, high, vaulted ceilings, stone arches and flags hung in the corners. The grilled meats—lamb, veal and the traditional *bistecca* are excellent here.

L'Angolo, Via Garibaldi 15, ✆ 289295. A large traditional trattoria where osso buco and green gnocchi are the specialities *(closed Sat)*.

Osteria dell'Artista, Via Stalloreggi 11, ✆ 280 306. Typical Sienese food—a small and quiet place not usually inundated with tourists *(closed Thurs)*.

Taverna di Cecco, Via Cecco Angioleri 19, near the Campo, ✆ 288518. Specializes in pasta dishes, meats and nearly everything else done up with either truffles or porcini mushrooms in season *(closed Sun)*.

Tullio ai Tre Cristi, Vicolo Provenzano, ✆ 280608. On this site since about 1830, this is perhaps the most authentic of Sienese restaurants; its menu includes things like *ribollita*, tripe with sausages and roast boar from the Maremma. The *pici* are home made. There are tables outside in the summer *(closed Mon)*.

inexpensive

Less expensive places—and there are many good ones—are usually found a little further away from the Campo.

Osteria La Chiacchiera, Via Costa Sant' Antonio 4, ✆ 280631. *Open for lunch and dinner daily*. This little trattoria, on a steeply sloping side street near Santa Caterina's birth place, is a friendly place to taste traditional Sienese cooking. Two small rooms, worn cotto floors, and wooden or marble-topped tables provide the setting for excellent *pici*, *ribollita*, kidneys, cockscombs (*cibreo*), tripe, hearty stews or a simple *bistecca*. Highly recommended.

Osteria di Ficomezzo, Via dei Termini 71, ✆ 222384. *Open for lunch and dinner, closed Sun*. One of those trattorias where lunch is a simpler (and cheaper) affair than dinner; prices here are nonetheless very reasonable. The ambiance is rustic Tuscan, and the food is along the sames lines although, in the evening, some more inventive dishes such as guinea fowl cooked with tarragon or chicken livers in balsamic vinegar and peppers appear alongside the more traditional pici, hearty soups, grilled meats and stews.

Il Grattacielo, Via dei Pontani 8, ✆ 289326. *Open 8–2 and 5–8, closed Sun*. A popular student hangout. If you want a snack at this simple, central eatery, avoid the lunchtime rush. There are few tables, so you may well end up eating on the hoof, but the roast pork and other simple dishes are good, the wine flows freely and prices are rock bottom.

Pizzeria Carlo e Franca, Via Pantaneto 138, ℗ 284385. *Open for lunch and dinner, closed Wed.* Antipasti and pizzas at reasonable prices not far from the centre.

La Torre, Via Salicotto 17, ℗ 287548. *Open for lunch and dinner, closed Thurs.* A fun, family-run trattoria just below the Torre di Mangia, La Torre is often full of students who appreciate the home cooking at reasonable prices. The pasta is homemade, and there is a wide choice of roast meats and poultry-try the pigeon.

Trattoria da Dino, Casato di Sopra 71, ℗ 49331. *Open for lunch and dinner, closed Wed.* The food here is Casalinga—

simple and homemade- with grilled meats and a good *Spiedino alla Sienese*, a kind of meat kebab.

Da Trombicche, Via delle Terme 66, ℗ 288089. *Open for lunch and dinner, closed Sun.* A small, simple and friendly wine bar which serves complete meals or snacks. Wine is doled out from a 50-litre flask on the counter by way of a tube...

Gelaterie

Siena isn't as obsessed with ice cream as Florence is, but there are a couple of central places to cool off with a cone. Both have a wide choice of luscious homemade flavours.

Gelateria Costarella, Via di Città 33 (*closed Tues*).

Fonte Gaia, Piazza del Campo 21 (*open daily*).

Eating Out in Pisa ℗ (050–)

In Pisa you will find eating out difficult on a Sunday night. At other times, walks on the wild side of the Tuscan kitchen seem more common than in other towns—eels and squid, *baccalà*, tripe, wild mushrooms, 'twice-boiled soup' and dishes that waiters cannot satisfactorily explain. Don't be intimidated; there's always more common fare on the menu, and occasionally the more outlandish items turn into surprising treats.

Restaurants

expensive

Al Ristoro dei Vecchi Macelli, Via Volturno 49, ℗ 20424. Open for lunch and dinner, closed Sun lunch and Wed. A 15th century slaughter house provides the setting for this sophisticated and popular restaurant. A must for pasta lovers: the menu at L50,000 lire offers only pasta (home-made, of course), dishes like green spaghetti with seafood,

pasta with sardines, ravioli flavoured with wild herbs, tortelli stuffed with duck and flavoured with truffles. If you can't face this, the carte offers meat and seafood choices.

Cagliostro, Via del Castelletto 26/30, ℗ 575413. Open for lunch and dinner, closed Tues and Sun. The décor in this elegant restaurant/caffé/enoteca/art gallery/night club and general trendy hang out is extraordinary, and it is hard to believe that you are in Italy. The cooking is 'Tuscan Creative' with other dishes thrown in from around Italy. Try tagliolini with truffles, filet of ostrich with orange sauce, or one of the ever-present vegetable sformati (a kind of flan without pastry). People come from miles around to taste the steamed chocolate soufflé, and there is a long and interesting cheese list with cheeses from all over Europe. The wine list is also worthy of note. Lunch is a more modest (and cheaper) affair.

moderate

Pisa is well endowed with unpretentious trattorie, many of them near the centre around the university.

Da Bruno, Via Luigi Bianchi, ✆ 560818. *Open for lunch and dinner, closed Tues.* Outside the walls a few blocks east of the Campo dei Miracoli, this is another place to see how well you like simple Pisan cooking—things like polenta with mushrooms and baccalà (dried cod)

La Mescita, Via D. Cavalca 2, ✆ 544294. *Open for lunch andf dinner, closed Mon.* At the heart of the busy Vettovaglie market area, the Mescita is an attractive trattoria with a huge wine list. Wine takes the centre stage here, and the hot and cold dishes are designed to enhance it.

Il Nuraghe, Via Mazzini 58, ✆ 44368. A traditional trattoria which has specialities such as ricotta ravioli and snails. The chef here is Sardinian, so Tuscan and Sarde specialities rub shoulders. Maialino Sardo—roast suckling piglet—is one such dish (*closed Mon*).

Osteria La Grotta, Via San Francesco 103, ✆ 578105. *Open for lunch and dinner, closed Sun.* The atmosphere in this osteria is decidedly cosy, not least because the walls in one of the rooms were built in the 1920s to simulate a grotto. The food is also comforting; traditional dishes, imaginatively prepared and without pretentions. Meat lovers should do well here; try the Gran Padellata del Maremmano, a rich stew of three different kinds of meat cooked with spicy sausage and vegetables.

Osteria dei Cavalieri, Via San Frediano 16, ✆ 580858. *Open for lunch and dinner, closed Sat lunch and Sun.* There are several set menus in this modern, airy osteria near Piazza dei Cavalieri-vegetarian, meat and fish although you can, of course, eat à la carte. Food is basically Tuscan, but prepared with some degree of innovation; there is a good wine list. If you want to finish your meal with the Grand Marnier soufflé, remember to order it in advance.

Lo Schiaccianoci, Via Vespucci 104, east of the station, ✆ 21024. Those eels from Lake Massaciuccoli and other fresh seafood delicacies hold pride of place. It only serves seafood (not fresh water fish) (*open lunch and dinner, closed Sun*).

Taverna Kostas, Via del Borghetto 39, ✆ 571467. *Open for lunch and dinner, closed Mon.* As the name suggests, the sophisticated menu here has a Greek bias, and you can eat an excellent moussaka as well as Italian dishes: cabbage-stuffed ravioli with a cheese sauce or red tagliolini with fish sauce, move on to rabbit cooked in aromatic herbs or the interesting 'tiella' di mare (a hearty fish stew). Leave room for the excellent desserts.

inexpensive

Numero Undici, Via Cavalca 11, ✆ 544294. *Open for lunch and dinner, closed Sat lunch and Sun.* This diminutive trattoria has no frills in terms of service; you order from the counter, and take your plate etc. to the table. You clear away after yourself. But prices are rock bottom and the food delicious. There are filled focaccias, cheese and vegetable flans, salads and a few hot dishes which change daily. It's fun to sit outside at lunchtime and watch the market packing up.

Re di Puglia, Via Aurelia Sud 7, Loc. Mortellini, ✆ 960157. *Open for dinner, also lunch on Sun. Closed Mon and Tues in winter.* Another carnivor's dream, this converted farmhouse (1 km from the Pisa Sud autostrada exit) primarily uses produce fresh from the farm. Tuck into homemade pasta with mutton, rabbit or goat, and follow this with meat cooked on the huge grill which, in winter, takes centre stage in the dining room. To finish off, go for the delicious pears cooked in wine with almond sauce. Prices here border on the moderate, but it is still excellent value.

Lo Spuntino, Vicolo dei Tinti, ✆ 580240. Open for lunch and dinner, closed Fri. A rather touristy choice and a bit difficult to find (it's in an alley just off Via Oberdan), but the pizzas, primi and secondi are good value.

outside Pisa

Da Gino, loc. Marina di Pisa, Via Curzoli 2, ✆ 35408. *Open for lunch and dinner, closed Mon dinner and Tues.* 11 kms out of town and near the sea, Gino's serves predominantly fish, and super-fresh it is too. A typical meal might include baby squid with rocket and pine nuts, spinach and ricotta-filled ravioli with shrimp and asparagus, or

Cacciucco, the local hearty fish stew (but you must order it in advance; expensive).

Cafés and Gelaterie

Bar La Loggia, Piazza Vittorio Emmanuele. Here they have an above average selection of sandwiches and seats under the loggia.

Al Banco della Berlina, Piazza della Berlina 9 (between Piazza Garibaldi and Piazza Mazzini). As warm and welcoming as an Italian café can get in a charming little piazza. Serves tasty cocktails.

Bar Moderno Gelateria, Via Corsica 10, near the Piazza dei Cavalieri. For stylish postmodern ice cream.

Bottega del Gelato, Piazza Garibaldi 11. For a delicious cone, even late at night, with a wide choice and heavenly frozen yoghurts.

Caffè Gambrinus, Piazza Vittorio Emmanuele. One of the more pleasant bars in which to wait for your train in spite of the pink decor.

Pasticceria Federico Salza, Borgo Stretto 46 (off Piazza Garibaldi). The best cakes in Pisa await, and a lovely large terrace for lingering (*closed Mon*).

Pick a Flower, Via Serafini 14. A popular student bar located in a handsome old palazzo (*closed Sun*).

Antico Caffè dell'Ussero, Lungarno Pacinotti 27. Pisa's oldest coffee-house.

Eating Out in Lucca ✆ (0583–)

expensive

Giglio, Piazza del Giglio, ✆ 494058. *Open for lunch and dinner, closed Tues dinner and Wed.* A big open fireplace heats the elegant and sober dining room in winter,

and, in summer, tables are set outside looking onto the piazza. Fish is the speciality here.

Puccini, Corte S. Lorenzo 1/3, ✆ 316116. *Open for lunch and dinner, closed Wed lunch and Tues (in winter).* Just opposite

Casa Puccini, this modern and elegant restaurant is one of the best in Lucca. Fish (always very fresh) predominates, and it is prepared carefully and presented beautifully.

moderate

Antica Locanda dell' Angelo, Via Pescheria 21, ✆ 47711. *Open for lunch and dinner, closed Sun dinner and Mon.* You can taste such unusual dishes as risotto with shrimps and green apples flavoured with curry, black tagliatelle with tomato, basil and pecorino, or go for classics like lamb roasted with fresh thyme and duck breast with marjoram. In this rustically elegant restaurant. The desserts are special here, and are all home-made.

La Buca di Sant' Antonio, Via della Cervia 1, ✆ 55881. *Open for lunch and dinner, closed Sun dinner and Mon.* There has been some kind of restaurant on this site since 1782, and today La Buca (as it is known locally) is justly popular-booking is advisable. The menu features both old, traditional dishes and those with a contemporary twist. Try the artichoke omelette or the salmon trout with marinated anchovies to start, follow this with fettucine with pigeon sauce, pappardelle with hare sauce or the traditional Zuppa di Farro. Guinea fowl stewed with rgaisins might follow, or a simple, but delicious, spit-roasted capretto (kid).

Canuleia, Via Canuleia, ✆ 47470. Situated near the amphitheatre in a medieval workshop, this serves local food with some surprises and usually a choice of vegetarian dishes *(closed Sat and Sun)*.

inexpensive

Buatino, Via del Borgo Giannotti 508, ✆ 343207. *Open for lunch and dinner, closed Sun.* This trattoria, just outside Porta Santa Maria, serves classic Lucchese dishes using the freshest of ingredients. Try the tasty and succulent roast pork (Arista di Maiale), simple grilled chicken and, of course, Zuppa di Farro. A couple of evenings a week, music (usually jazz or a cabaret) may accompany your meal, and there is interesting artwork on the walls. Buatino is good value anyway, but prices are even lower at lunchtime.

Da Giulio in Pelleria, Via Conce, ✆ 55948. In the northwest corner within the walls, here you can enjoy some surprising dishes at rock-bottom prices. Popular enough to warrant reservations, with top-quality 'peasant' fare, *(closed Sun and Mon)*.

Da Guido, Via Cesare Battisti 28, ✆ 47219. *Open for lunch and dinner, closed Sun.* You are unlikely to enjoy a peaceful meal in this basic but popular trattoria, as the TV will almost certainly be on. However, it's full of character and the food is wholesome and portions generous. Try the home-made tortelli.

Da Leo, Via Tegrini 1, ✆ 492236. *Open for lunch and dinner, closed Sun.* This traditional trattoria, near San Michele, is often pretty chaotic, and full of locals and tourists alike. The menu features both meat and fish; spaghetti alle vongole (with baby clams), tordelli (a kind of fat ravioli) with ragou, salt cod (baccala) with chick peas, squid (seppie) stewed with swiss chard, tripe or deep fried chicken and rabbit.

Gli Orti di Via Elisa, Via Elisa 17, ✆ 491241. *Open for lunch and dinner, closed Wed, Thurs.* Run by the son of the owner of La Buca (*see* above), this cheerful trattoria with its rows of tables and black and white checked floors is great for a cheap and cheerful meal. Pizzas, salads (from the help-yourself buffet) plus good pastas etc.

Around Lucca

Lucca does especially well at table if you have the horsepower to reach its immediate surroundings.

Il Gazebo della Locanda Elisa, loc. Massa Pisana, ☎ 379737. Part of the impressive Relais & Chateaux hotel Villa La Principessa Elisa (*see* hotels), this elegant restaurant is housed in a beautiful round 19th century conservatory. Views are of the immaculate gardens and pool. The menu is interesting and inventive-quail terrine with onion marmalade, aubergine ravioli with shrimp sauce, roast guinea fowl with onion and mustard. An expensive treat for a special occaision (*very expensive*).

Locanda Maiola, loc. Maiola di Sotto, ☎ 86296. *Open for dinner and Sun lunch by arrangement. Closed Tues.* 27km N of Lucca, just beyond Bagni di Lucca. It is well worth the beautiful drive up into the hills on a fine summer evening to eat at this small trattoria, once lived in by the owners' grandparents. Raw ingredients of the highest quality are prepared by his wife, and the pasta is all home-made. There are three set menus, all of them excellent value. Antipasti of grilled vegetables, farro salad, baby river trout whet the appetite for papardelle with ceps mushrooms, tagliatelle with trout and tortelli. On to roast suckling pig or lamb and rabbit cooked with olives. Try and leave enough room for the excellent puddings. Exceptional value (*moderate*).

La Mora, Via Sesto di Moriano 1748, Ponte a Moriano, ☎ 406402. 8km N of Lucca on the Bagni di Lucca road. *Open for lunch and dinner, closed Wed.* This restaurant must surely be one of the 'musts' of the region, and prices are reasonable to boot. Housed in an old post house, now gentrified, there has been hostelry on the site since 1867. The superb food, faithful to the Lucchese traditions, features hearty local soups (The Gran Farro is unbeatable), pastas both classic (pappardelle with hara sauce) and unexpected (tagliolini with eels, risotto with partridge), and robustly-tasty meat dishes such as casseroled pidgeon, duck breast with green pepper, pheasant and wild boar. There are also several fresh water fish options. The wine list is extensive and the hosts charming and helpful. In summer, eat on the terrace (*expensive*).

Solferino, Via delle Gavine 50, ☎ 59118. *Open for lunch and dinner, closed Wed and lunch Thurs.* Situated 6km west of Lucca on the Viareggio road in San Macario in Piano, Il Solferino has been run by the same family for four generations and famous throughout Tuscany for almost as long. It operates on two levels. The main, more expensive, restaurant has an extensive menu offering regional dishes and a bit more; duck with truffles, wild boar and grilled seafood are a few of the treats on which one could splurge. There is also an Osteria, a room where a fixed-price menu of Lucchese dishes is on offer, and the inexpensive prices here include local wine. In olive oil season (from mid-November), try the *zuppa alla frantoiana*—a rich vegetable soup with a swirl of pungent new oil on top.

Where to Stay

Florence, Siena, Pisa and Lucca are endowed with hotels (*alberghi*) of every description, from the spectacular to the mighty humble. These are rated by the government's tourism bureaucracy, from five stars at the luxurious top end to one star at the bottom. The ratings take into account such things as a restaurant on the premises, plumbing, air conditioning, etc., but not character, style or charm. Use the stars, which we include in this book, as a quick reference for prices and general amenities only. Another thing to remember about government ratings is that a hotel can stay at a lower rating than it has earned, so you may find a hotel with three stars as comfortable as one with four.

Breakfast is optional only in some hotels, and in pensions it is mandatory. And you may as well expect to face half-board (breakfast and lunch or dinner) if the hotel has a restaurant. Otherwise, meal arrangements are optional. Although eating in the hotel restaurant can be a genuine gourmet experience, in the majority of cases hotel food is bland, just as it is anywhere else.

Prices

There's no inflation in Italy, if you believe the government; the prices just go up by themselves. With the holiday business booming, this curious paradox is well expressed in hotel prices; every year they rise by 6–8 per cent across the board, and are often more expensive than for hotels in northern Europe. The prices listed in this book are for double rooms only. For a single room, count on paying two-thirds of a double; to add an extra bed in a double will add 35 per cent to the bill. (A *camera matrimoniale* is a room with a double bed, a *camera doppia* has twin beds, a *camera singola* is a single.) Taxes and service charges are included in the given rate. Some establishments charge L10–25,000 for air-conditioning. Also note that if rooms are listed without bath, it simply means the shower and lavatory are in the corridor. Prices are by law listed on the door of each room and will be printed in the hotel lists available from the local tourist office; any discrepancies should be reported to the tourist office. Most rooms have two or three different rates, depending on the season. Costs are often a third less if you travel in the low season.

Throughout this book, prices listed are for a double room in high season; and, unless otherwise stated, including a private bath. Here is the range of prices you are likely to encounter for hotels in the various classifications in 1998–9; for rooms without bath, subtract 20–30 per cent.

Category	Double with Bath
***** luxury	L500,000 and up
**** very expensive	L350–500,000
*** expensive	L220–350,000
** moderate	L100–220,000
* inexpensive	up to L100,000

If you have a certain place in mind, it is essential to book in advance as soon as possible (considering the slowpoke Italian post, preferably by fax or phone, or increasingly through the Internet). If your Italian is non-existent, the National Tourist Office's Travellers' Handbook has a sample letter and list of useful terms. Under Italian law, a booking is valid once a deposit has been paid. If you have to cancel your reservation, the hotel will keep the deposit unless another agreement has been reached. If you're coming in the summer without reservations, start calling around for a place in the morning.

One Italian institution, the **albergo diurno** (day hotel), may prove handy, though there seem to be fewer of them all the time. Located in the centre of the largest cities and at the railway stations, these are places where you can take a shower, a shave, have your hair done, etc. They are open 6am–midnight.

Inexpensive Accommodation

Bargains are few and far between in Italy. The cheapest kind of hotel is an inn, or *pensione*; some provinces treat these as one-star hotels or list them separately (or not at all). The majority of inexpensive places will always be around the railway station, though in the large cities you'll often find it worth your while to seek out some more pleasant location in the historic centre. You're likely to find anything in a one-star Italian hotel. Often they will be practically perfect, sometimes almost luxurious; memorably bad experiences will be few. Besides the youth hostels (*see* below), there are several city-run hostels, with dormitory-style rooms open to all. In Florence religious institutions often rent out extra rooms.

Self-catering Holidays: Villas and Flats

Renting a villa or flat has always been the best way to visit Tuscany. If you're travelling with a family it is the most economic alternative. One place to look for holiday lets is in the Sunday paper; or write to the area's tourist office for a list of local rental agencies. These ought to provide photos of the accommodation to give you an idea of what to expect. Make sure all pertinent details are written down in your rental agreement to avoid misunderstandings later. In general, minimum lets are for two weeks; rental prices usually include insurance, water and electricity, and sometimes linen and maid service. Don't be surprised if upon arrival the owner 'denounces' (*denunciare*) you to the police; according to Italian law, all visitors must be registered upon arrival. Many of the companies listed below offer savings on charter flights, ferry crossings or fly-drive schemes to sweeten the deal. Try to book as far in advance as possible for the summer season.

Holiday Rental Companies

in the UK

International Chapters, 102 St John's Wood Terrace, London NW8 6PR, ✆ (071) 722 9560, ✆ (071) 722 9140, has apartments and villas in all four cities, and handles bookings for the major Italian holiday-home companies. The largest of these is **Cuendet** which publishes an extensive illustrated catalogue of holiday villas, flats and farmhouses. Its headquarters are at Il Cerreto, 53030 Strove, Siena. It also has the listings of **Tuscan Enterprises**, a company with headquarters in Castellina in Chianti, and their own listings called **Italian Chapters**. Other firms include:

Citalia, 3–5 Marco Polo House, Lansdowne Road, Croydon CR9 9EQ, ✆ (081) 686 5533.

Continental Villas, 3 Paxton Walk, Phoenix St, London WC2H 8PW, ✆ (071) 497 0444.

Hoseasons Holidays Abroad Ltd, Sunway House, Lowestoft, Suffolk NR32 3LT, ✆ (0502) 500 555.

Interhome, 383 Richmond Rd, Twickenham TW1 2EF, ✆ (081) 891 1294.

Magic of Italy, 227 Shepherds Bush Rd, London W6 7AS, ✆ (081) 748 7575.

David Newman's European Collection, PO Box 733, 40 Upperton Rd, Eastbourne, ✆ (0323) 410 347.

Perrymead Properties Overseas, 55 Perrymead Street, London SW6, ✆ (081) 878 5788.

Sovereign, Astral Towers, Betts Way, Crawley, West Sussex RH10 2GX, ✆ 0293 599 988.

Vacanze in Italia, Bignor, Pulborough, West Sussex RH20 1QD; call for brochure ✆ (07987) 421.

in the USA

At Home Abroad, 405 East 56th St, New York, NY 10022, ✆ (212) 421 9165.

CUENDET: Posarelli Vacations, Suzanne T. Pidduck, 1742 Calle Corva, Camarillo, CA93010, ✆ (805) 987 5278.

Hideaways International, PO Box 4433, Portsmouth, New Hampshire 03801, ✆ (603) 430 4433.

Homeowners International, 1133 Broadway, New York, NY 10010, ✆ (212) 691 2361 or (800) 367 4668.

Italian Villa Rentals, 550 Kirkland Way, Suite 100, Kirkland, Washington 98033, ✆ (206) 827 3694.

Overseas Connection, 70 West 71st St, Suite 1C, New York, NY 10023, ✆ (212) 769 1170.

RAVE (Rent-a-Vacation-Everywhere), 383 Park Ave, Rochester, NY 14607, ✆ (716) 256 0760.

Rent in Italy, Elaine Muoio, 3801 Ingomar St N.W., Washington, DC 20015,

✆ (202) 244 5345, @ (202) 362 0520. Specialist in Italian villa rentals.

in Italy

The Best in Italy, Via Ugo Foscolo 72, Firenze, ✆ (055) 223 064, which specializes in posh villas with domestic staff.

Casaclub, Via Termini 83, Siena, ✆ (0577) 44041 (villas throughout Tuscany, Umbria and Lazio).

Toscana Vacanze, Via XX Settembre 6, 52047 Marciano della Chiana, ✆ (0575) 845 348 (villas in Chianti and environs).

Toscanamare Villas, Via W della Gheradesca 5, Castagneto Carducci (LI), ✆ (0565) 744012, @ 744339 (villas on the Versilia coast).

Tuscan Enterprises, for houses in Chianti; write to Casella Postale 34, Via delle Mura 22, Castellina in Chianti, 53011 Siena, ✆ (0577) 740623.

Vela, Via Colombo 16, Castiglione della Pescaia, ✆ (0564) 933 495 (villas and flats on the seaside and in panoramic locations).

Camping

Florence ✆ (055–)

Camping di Fiesole, on top of the hill. Lovely, but packed and expensive in the summer.

Camping Internazionale, Via S. Cristofano 2, south of the city in Bottai Tavarnuzze, ✆ 237 4704, near the A1 exit of the Autostrada Firenze–Certosa; convenient for motorists (*open end of March to mid-Oct*).

Camping Muncipale Olivades, Viale Michelangelo 80, ✆ 6531089. Has fine views over the city and free hot showers;

arrive early to get a spot. On the other hand, there's no shade and a disco until 1am. Bus 13 will take you there from the station.

Mugello Verde International Camping, 25km north of Florence on the road to Bologna, at Via Masso Rondinaio 2, in San Piero a Sieve, ✆ 848511. Very pleasant setting among hills and forests, and frequent buses down to Florence. *Open all year.*

Camping La Camerata, Viale Righi 2/4, ✆ 600315, 20 mins by no.17 bus out of the centre of town, this fully wheelchair-accessible campsite is in the spacious and pleasant grounds of the youth hostel. *Open all year.*

Campeggio Panoramico, Via Peramonda, Fiesole, ✆ 599069. *Open all year.*

Campeggio Italiani e Stranieri, Viale Michelangelo 80, ✆ 6811977, bus 12 or 13.

Siena ✆ (0577–)

Camping Colleverde, Via Scacciapensieri 47, ✆ 280044. 3km north of the city, bus 8 or 12 from Piazza Gramsci (open mid-March–mid-Nov).

Camping Luxor, near Castellina in Chianti on the SS2, ✆ 743047. Well kept and set in the woods, free pool.

Pisa ✆ (050–)

Camping Internazionale, Via Litoreana, ✆ 35211. 15km away near the beach at Marina di Pisa (*open May to end Sept*).

Camping San Mikael, Via Bigattiera, Tirrenia, ✆ 33103. Nice and shady (*open June–mid-Sept*).

Campeggio Torre Pendente, Via delle Cascine 86, ✆ 561704. 1km from the Leaning Tower (bus 5 from the station); the closest, if not amazingly atmospheric (*open 1 April–mid-Oct*).

Florence has some exceptionally lovely hotels, and not all of them at Grand Ducal prices, although base rates here are the highest in Tuscany. In this town historic old palace-hotels are the rule rather than the exception; those listed below are some of the more atmospheric and charming, but to be honest few are secrets, so reserve as far in advance as possible. Some hotels with a restaurant will require half-board, and many will lay down a heavy breakfast charge as well that is supposed to be optional.

There are almost 400 hotels in Florence, but not enough for anyone who arrives in July and August without a reservation. Don't despair: there are several hotel consortia that can help you find a room in nearly any price range for a small commission. If you're arriving by car or train, the most useful will be ITA.

ITA: in Santa Maria Novella station, ✆ 282 893, open 9–9; in the AGIP service station at Peretola, to the west of Florence on A11, ✆ 4211800. Between March and November there's an office in the Chianti-Est service plaza on the A1, ✆ 621349, and another in the Fortezza da Basso, ✆ 471960. No bookings can be made over the telephone and a booking fee of between L3000 and L10,000 is charged, according to the category of hotel.

Florence Promhotels: Viale A. Volta 72, ✆ 570481. Free booking service in Florence.

luxury

★★★★★ **Excelsior**, Piazza Ognissanti 3, ✆ 624201/✆ 210278. Napoleon's sister Caroline once lived in the building which is now one of Florence's top hotels. Recently renovated, the huge dimensions and neo-classical lines feature tons of marble, lots of dark mahogany and stained glass to create an old-fashioned and luxurious atmosphere. Bedrooms are all that you would expect for the prices with antiques, heavy drapes and marble bathrooms. Some have a view of the Arno.

★★★★★ **Grand Hotel**, Piazza Ognissanti 1, ✆ 288781/✆ 217400. You can't really mention one without the other; sister hotel to the Excelsior, and facing it over the piazza, the Grand is equally plush. It was fully renovated some four years ago and no expense was spared. An immense hall with stained-glass ceiling, columns, marble floors, and lofty potted plants combines lounge, cocktail bar and restaurant. The more expensive bedrooms (regularly inhabited by the rich and famous) are decorated in early Florentine style with hand-crafted wood and paintwork. Carpets are thick and fabrics rich.

★★★★ **Helvetia & Bristol**, Via dei Pescioni 2, ✆ 287814/✆ 288353 If you prefer luxury on a smaller scale, this hotel is the obvious choice. There are only 52 bedrooms and each one is different, all exquisitely furnished with rich fabrics adorning windows, walls and beds; service is discreet and the atmosphere understated. Many illustrious names have appeared in the hotel's register, including Stravinsky, D'Annunzio, Bertrand Russell and Pirandello. There are many superb antiques in both pulic rooms and bedrooms, and a superb restaurant.

★★★★★ **Regency**, Piazza d'Azeglio 3, ✆ 245247, ✆ 2346735. In Florence's plane-tree shaded 'London Square', there's the even smaller Regency, charming and intimate with only 33 air-conditioned rooms; between the two wings there's an elegant town garden. The public rooms are beautifully panelled, and the fare in the dining room superb; there's a private garage for your car.

★★★★ **J&J**, Via di Mezzo 20, ☎ 2345005, 🖂 240282. A completely different type of luxury hotel than the above, the J&J occupies an unassuming building, an ex-convent in a quiet residential street near Sant' Ambrogio. In spite of its 16th-century origins, the interiors are fresh and new, combining original features and antique furniture with chic contemporary design. Each room is totally different. The suites are enormous with sitting areas and luxurious bathrooms; one even has a bathtub in the room.

very expensive

★★★★ **Astoria**, Via del Giglio 9, ☎ 2398095, 🖂 214632. This comfortable hotel has more character than many of those located near the station. Recently refurbished, it is in a grand 16th-century palazzo near San Lorenzo market. Public rooms are suitably impressive and some of the bedrooms likewise. Avoid those on the lower floors on the street. Frequently used by up-market tour goups.

★★★★ **Kraft**, Via Solferino 2, ☎ 284273, 🖂 2398267. In a useful location if you are in Florence for the opera season (it is 2 minutes' walk from the Teatro Comunale), the Kraft has the added advantage of a small rooftop pool. Bedrooms are light and sunny, comfortably furbished with cheerful fabrics. The suites on the top floor have great views. There is a restaurant.

★★★★ **Lungarno**, Borgo San Jacopo 14, ☎ 264211, 🖂 268437. This discreet hotel enjoys a marvellous location on the river,

only 2 minutes' walk from the Ponte Vecchio. The ground-floor sitting/breakfast room and bar take full advantage of this with picture windows looking onto the water. The building is fairly modern, but incorporates a medieval tower. The whole hotel has just been refurbished; the small-ish bedrooms are decorated in smart blue and cream and the best have balconies with 'The View'. You need to book way ahead if you want one of these.

★★★★ **Mona Lisa**, Borgo Pinti 27, ☎ 247 9751, 🖂 247 9755. A Renaissance palace now owned by the descendants of sculptor Giovanni Dupre, this is one of the most charming small hotels in Florence, hiding behind its stern façade. The palazzo is well preserved, the furnishings are family heirlooms, as are the many works of art. Try to reserve one of the tranquil rooms that overlook the garden; all are air-conditioned and have frigo-bars. The Mona Lisa has no restaurant, though breakfast is available; it has private parking.

★★★★ **Principe**, Lungarno Vespucci 34, ☎ 284848. Among the many hotels along the Arno, this is one of the most pleasant—a small, comfortable hotel, centrally air-conditioned and sound-proofed, with a little garden at the back; the nicer rooms have terraces over the Arno.

★★★★ **Rivoli**, Via della Scala 33, ☎ 50123, 282853, 🖂 294041. An elegant and refined 15th-century building with air conditioning and TV in all rooms.

★★★★ **Villa Carlotta**, Via Michele di Lando 3, ☎ 220501. This Tuscan-Edwardian hotel is in a quiet residential district in the upper Oltrarno, close to the Porta Romana. The 26 sophisticated rooms have recently been tastefully refurnished and have every mod con. There's a garden and glassed-in veranda, where the large breakfasts are served; a private garage offers safe parking.

★★★★ Villa Belvedere, Via Benedetto Castelli 3, ✆ 222501, ✉ 223163. Not one of the more interesting buildings to be found in this part of peripheral Florence (a kilometre above Porta Romana), but the Belvedere offers a very pleasant alternative to central accommodation with a beautiful garden, tennis court, a nice pool and good views (as befit its name). Rooms are modern and comfortable with lots of wood and plenty of space. For trips into town, you can leave your car and catch a nearby bus. Light meals are served in the restaurant.

expensive

★★★ Aprile, Via della Scala 6, ✆ 216237, ✉ 280947. Convenient for the station, and appropriately there is a bust of Cosimo I above the door of what was once a Medici palace. Vaulted ceilings and frescoes remain intact, and the bedrooms all have period furniture although some are on the gloomy side. The breakfast room, however, is very pleasant, and there is the added advantage of a shady courtyard.

★★★ Beacci Tornabuoni, Via Tornabuoni 3, ✆ 212645. Another excellent small hotel, which puts you in the centre of fashionable Florence, on the top three floors of an elegant Renaissance palace. The rooms are comfortable, air-conditioned and equipped with mini-bars, though it's more fun to sit over your drink on the panoramic roof terrace.

★★★ Hermitage, very near the Ponte Vecchio in Vicolo Marzio 1, ✆ 287216. You have to look hard to find this little hotel tucked away behind the Ponte Vecchio on the north side of the river. It is built upside down; the lift takes you to the fifth floor with its ravishing roof garden, reception and ele-

gant blue and yellow sitting room. From here you go down to the bedrooms which are on the small side, but charmingly furnished with antiques and tasteful fabrics. Some have river views.

★★★ Hotel Calzaiuoli, Via Calzaiuoli 6, ✆ 212456, ✉ 268310. Just a few steps from Piazza Signoria and on a traffic-free street, this is a comfortable hotel with modern, nicely decorated rooms and wonderful views from the top floor.

★★★ Mario's, Via Faenza 89, ✆ 216801, ✉ 212039. In a street with more than its fair share of hotels, many of them of dubious quality, Mario's is a haven. Convenient for the station and a block ar two from the central market, the atmosphere is friendly and the decor rustic Florentine. A generous breakfast is served in a pretty room at long tables and guests are pampered with fresh flowers and fruit on arrival. If you don't want to sleep with your windows closed, ask for a room at the back; the street can be noisy.

★★★ Morandi alla Crocetta, Via Laura 50, ✆ 2344747, ✉ 2480954. This small, popular hotel (it has only 10 rooms), is situated in the university area northeast of Piazza San Marco. Run by an Irish woman and her family, the building was a convent in the 16th century, and some of the comfortable and pleasant rooms still have the odd fresco. Two have private terraces.

★★★ Porta Faenza, Via Faenza 77, ✆ 217 975, ✉ 210101. Tony's Inn was, for many years, a cheerful and friendly budget hotel run by an Italian photographer and his Canadian wife, popular with students. In 1997, the whole place was gutted, and a smart new hotel was opened under the same management. Porta Faenza (the building is near the old gate to the city) is now equipped with air conditioning, sound proofing and all the usual facilities found in a three-star hotel. The character of the old building has been preserved with stone arches and beamed ceilings, and bedrooms are comfortable. There is a private garage. Obviously, prices have gone up considerably, but the welcome is still friendly.

★★★ **Silla**, Via dei Renai 5, ✆ 234 2888, @ 2341437. Ten minutes' walk east of the Ponte Vecchio on the south bank of the river, the Silla's location is central, yet in a quiet and relatively green neighbourhood. The old-fashioned *pensione* is on the first floor of a 16th-century palazzo (there is no lift up the two flights of external steps), and the spacious breakfast terrace has great views over the Arno and beyond. The interior decor may be a little over the top, but rooms are spotless and spacious.

★★★ **Torre Guelfa**, Borgo SS Apostoli 8, ✆ 2396338/@ 2398577. Boasting the tallest privately owned tower in Florence from whence you can sip an aperitivo and marvel at the 360° view, this small hotel is bang in the middle of the *centro storico*. The grand double salon, a sunny breakfast room, stylish bedrooms in pastel shades with wrought-iron and hand-painted furniture plus, of course, the tower, make this a very pleasant place to stay.

moderate

★★ **Alessandra**, Borgo SS Apostoli 17, ✆ 283438, @ 210619. This modest hotel on a central, but quiet, back street has 25 rooms of varying standards, and not all have private baths. The best have waxed parquet floors and antique furniture and prices are reasonable.

★★ **Belletini**, Via de' Conti 7, ✆ 213561, @ 282980. The rooms in this friendly hotel near to the Medici chapels are decorated in traditional Florentine style; a couple have

stunning views of the nearby domes. Breakfasts are generous and good.

★★★ **Casci**, Via Cavour 13, ✆ 211686, @ 2396461. The Lombardis, who run the Casci in this 15th-century palazzo (once home to Rossini), emphasize that it is very much a family hotel. The atmosphere is relaxed and cheerful, the reception area is full of helpful information, the breakfast room sports a frescoed ceiling while the recently refurbished bedrooms are bright and modern. The choice few look onto a garden at the back. Good value.

★★★ **Classic Hotel**, Viale Machiavelli 25, ✆ 229351, @ 229353. If you are travelling by a car, staying in the centre of town is more trouble (and expense) than it's worth. Even if you are not, the Classic offers excellent value for money, and a very pleasant location just above Porta Romana on the way to Piazzale Michelangelo. A 5-minute walk will take you to a bus stop for downtown. The pink-washed villa stands in a shady garden (a welcome respite from the heat of the city), and breakfast is served in the conservatory in summer. Rooms are furnished with a mixture of old and new, walls are white, parquet floors are polished and plaster work has been recently restored. There is even the odd fresco.

★★ **Hotel Delle Tele**, Via Panzani 10, ✆/@ 2382419. On the busy street which runs from the station to the Duomo, bedrooms at the front of this hotel are well double-glazed. Recently renovated. Trompe l'oeil decorations add character.

★★ **Residence Johanna Cinque Giornate**, Via Cinque Gionate 12, ✆/@ 473377. Like the Residence Johanna (*see* below), this new home-from-home offers good value for money in a city where bargains are few and far between. Some way from the centre (near the Fortezza da Basso), the villa stands in its own garden which also offers car parking. The six bedrooms are prettily and comfortably furnished, and a breakfast tray and electric kettle is provided in each room, and there is a sitting room with plenty of reading material. This is not really a hotel (hence the lack of official star rating) in that there is no night porter, and guests are very much left to themselves, but other facilities are of a three-star standard.

★★ **La Scaletta**, Via Guicciardini 13, ✆ 283028, @ 289562. Between the Ponte Vecchio and the Pitti Palace, this friendly *pensione* also has the advantage of a roof garden and great views into Boboli. The 12 bedrooms (not all with bathrooms and some of which sleep up to four) are decently furnished, the nicest with some antique pieces. Public rooms maintain a feel of the 15th-century origins of the building, and a very moderately priced dinner is served in a vaulted dining room.

★ **Sorelle Bandini**, Piazza Santo Spirito 9, ✆ 215308, @ 282761. In spite of its state of disrepair and relatively high prices, the Sorelle Bandini remains popular. This is partly due to the romantic loggia which runs along one side of the fourth-storey hotel, but also to its location on fascinating Piazza Santo Spirito, bustling by day and lively (and noisy) at night. Expect uncomfortable beds, cavernous rooms, heavy Florentine furniture and a certain shabby charm.

★★★ **Splendor**, Via San Gallo 30, ✆ 483 427, @ 461276. This little 19th-century palazzo is near Piazza San Marco in the university district. The public rooms are quite grand with frescoed ceilings and chandeliers. The bedrooms are plain in comparison, but perfectly adequate. Not all have private baths. There is a pretty terrace.

inexpensive

The obvious place to look is the seedy, crowded, tourist-student inferno that surrounds the central station, especially in Via Nazionale, Via Fiume, Via Guelfa and Via Faenza down to Piazza Indipendenza. Many of the cheapest places post minions in the station to snatch up weary backpackers. Although convenient if you arrive by train, few of these hotels will brighten your stay in Florence; grouchy owners who lock the door at midnight seem to be the rule. Some of the hotels in this category are a little over the L100,000 limit, but are included for the type of accommodation they offer (fairly basic), rather than the price.

★ **Il Granduca**, Via Pier Capponi 13, ✆ 572803. One of the nicest hotels in this category, with a garden and garage, although a bit out of the centre, between Piazza Donatello and Piazza della Libertà. Not all rooms en suite.

★ **Ausonia e Rmini**, Via Nazionale 24, ✆ 496547. A basic hotel near the station.

★ **Bavaria**, Borgo degli Albizi 26, ✆ 234 0313. The 16th-century palazzo in which this *pensione* is housed is most impressive—the facade is said to be frescoed by Vasari—but don't get your hopes up. The accommodation is decidedly spartan with minimal formica furniture, but the rooms (some of them vast) are clean and cheap. Some have splendid views of the city.

★ **Maxim**, Via dei Medici 4, ✆ 217474. Although there are better bargains to be had, this simple friendly hotel is very central. The basic rooms, from two to four people, all have the same bright green linoleum, and the bathrooms are new.

Residenza Johanna, Via Bonifacio Lupi 14, ✆ 481896, @ 482721. Only a tiny brass plaque over the bell gives away the location of this 'non-hotel'. There are no TVs or phones in the room, no doorman (guests are given their own keys), and not all rooms have private baths, but furnishings are comfortable, bedrooms prettily decorated with floral papers and there's lots of reading material supplied. Breakfast is not served, so there is a do-it-yourself tray in each room, and kettles in the corridor. Great value if you are prepared to be a little way from the centre of town, north of Piazza San Marco.

★ **Scoti**, Via Tournabuoni 7, ✆ 292128. A surprisingly up-market address for this simple and cheap *pensione* which could be ideal if you would rather splurge on the wonderful clothes in the surrounding shops than on your hotel. Facilities are basic—large rooms of up to four beds (there is a couple of more intimate singles), no private bathrooms, simple furniture, but there is bags of atmosphere starting with the floor-to-ceiling frescoes in the sitting room. The new, friendly owners (Doreen is Australian) have given the place a new coat of paint.

★ **La Mia Casa**, Piazza S. Maria Novella 20, ✆ 213061. Within spitting distance of the station. It is almost impossible to find a room in this *pensione* which is housed in a crumbling 17th-century palazzo, and they don't like to take bookings; phone up on the day and see what the situation is. Another case of 'a certain shabby charm': the walls are covered in fabric, and rooms are clean. The owner shows free videos in English every night.

★ **Firenze**, Piazza dei Donati 4, ✆ 214203, ◉ 212370. The location of this newly renovated *pensione*, between Piazza Signoria and the Duomo, is excellent. The rather unimaginative rooms all now have bathrooms.

★ **Orchidea**, Borgo degli Albizi 11, ✆/◉ 2480346. Dante's in-laws once lived in the 12th-century building where the Anglo-Italian family who run the Orchidea offer seven cheerful rooms. Only one (a triple) has a private shower, and the best look onto a garden at the back. It is cosier than many similar establishments.

★ **La Romagnola**, Via della Scala 40, ✆ 211597. Another cheap option 5 minutes' walk from the station. Simple, spacious rooms (some are a bit dark), bits of frescoed ceiling, and some carved beds. The owners are very friendly.

Rooms to Let

Besides hotels, a number of institutions and private homes let rooms—there's a complete list in the back of the annual provincial hotel book. Many take women only, and fill up with students in the spring when Italian schools make their annual field trips.

Youth Hostels

There are four youth hostels to choose from in Florence. The purpose-built and fully wheelchair-accessible **Archi Rossi**, Via Faenza 94r, ✆ 290804, is the nearest hostel to the station, spanking new and well-equipped. Book a place after 6am; rooms can be occupied after 2.30. Phone bookings are accepted and there is a 12.30am curfew. **Ostello Europa Villa Camerata**, Viale A. Righe 2/4 (bus 17B from the station), ✆ 601451, has 500 beds for people with IYHF cards. Located in an old palazzo with gardens, it is a popular place, and you'd be wise to show up at 2pm to get a spot in the summer; maximum stay three days. **Ostello Santa Monaca**, Via Santa Monaca 6, ✆ 268338, has 111 beds near the Carmine church; sign up for a place in the morning. **Istituto Gould**, Via dei Serragli 44, is so popular that you must book well in advance, ✆ 212576.

In Fiesole

Many frequent visitors to Florence wouldn't stay anywhere else: it's cooler, quieter, and at night the city far below twinkles as if made of fairy lights. If money is no object, the superb choice is:

***** **Villa San Michele**, Via Doccia 4, ✆ 59451. In a breathtaking location just below Fiesole with a façade and loggia reputedly designed by Michelangelo himself. Originally a monastery in the 14th century, it has been carefully reconstructed after bomb damage in the Second World War to create one of the most beautiful hotels in Italy, set in a lovely Tuscan garden, complete with a pool. Each of its 29 rooms is richly and elegantly furnished and air-conditioned; the more plush suites have jacuzzis. The food is delicious, and the reasons to go down to Florence begin to seem insignificant; a stay here is complete in itself. Paradise, however, comes at a stratospheric price. One of the better suites will cost around L2,000,000. A lot of VIPs stay here.

**** **Villa Aurora**, Piazza Mino 38, Fiesole, ✆ 59100, @ 59587 (*expensive*). This agreeable 19th-century villa is located right on Fiesole's famous piazza from where the no. 7 bus will whisk you down to central Florence in 20 minutes. There are 25 bedrooms—the best have rustic antiques and splendid views over the city. Some of the bathrooms are pokey. There is a restaurant on a terrace overlooking Florence in the summer, and the bar next door (noisy at times) is under the same ownership.

*** **Pensione Bencistà**, Via Benedetto di Maiano 4, Fiesole, ✆/@ 59163 (*expensive*). The views offered from the Bencista's fragrant, flower-decked terrace are every bit as good as those at Villa San Michele (above), and the welcome will be more friendly. This

former monastery has been added to over the years, and a complicated series of stairs and passageways lead to the bedrooms, each one different from the next, but all comfortably furnished with solid antique pieces. Obviously, those with a view of the city are most sought after, and two even have terraces. The three little sitting rooms are particularly inviting in cooler weather when fires are lit. Half-board—breakfast and either lunch or dinner—is obligatory here, but prices are reasonable.

*** **Villa Fiesole**, Via Beato Angelico 35, Fiesole, ✆ 597252, @ 599133. This new hotel was once part of the San Michele convent, indeed it shares part of its driveway with the hotel of the same name. It's a lot cheaper, however. The smart, neoclassical-style interiors are variations on a fresh blue and yellow colour scheme. Bedrooms are extremely comfortable with thick carpeting, rich fabrics and gleaming new paintwork. Light meals are served in a sunny dining room or on the adjacent terrace, and there is a pool. The hotel (and pool) is fully wheelchair accessible. Don't be misled by the three-star rating. The facilities (and prices) here are of a four-star standard.

* **Villa Baccano**, Via Bosconi 4, ✆ 59341 (*low moderate*). In the hills, 2km out of the centre of Fiesole. Simple rooms in a lovely garden setting.

* **Villa Sorriso**, Via Gramsci 21, ✆ 59027 (*inexpensive*). In the centre, an unpretentious, comfortable hotel with a terrace overlooking Florence.

Villa Hotels in the Hills

If you're driving, you may consider lodging outside the city where parking is hassle free and the summer heat is less intense. Some places are within very few kms of the city.

luxury

***** **Grand Hotel Villa Cora**, Viale Machiavelli 18–20, ℰ 2298451. A luxurious choice near Piazzale Michelangelo, this opulent 19th-century mansion is set in a beautiful formal garden overlooking the Oltrarno. Built by the Baron Oppenheim, it later served as the residence of the wife of Napoleon III, Empress Eugénie. Its conversion to a hotel has dimmed little of its splendour; some of the bedrooms have frescoed ceilings and lavish 19th-century furnishings—all are air-conditioned and have frigo-bars, and there's a pretty pool. In the summer meals are served in the garden, and there's a fine view of Florence from the roof terrace.

very expensive

***** **Villa La Massa**, Via La Massa 6, ℰ 6510101, ℰ 6510109. Another lovely choice, located up the Arno some 6km from Florence at Candeli. The former 15th-century villa of Count Giraldi, the hotel retains the old dungeon (now one of two restaurants), the family chapel (now a bar), and other early-Renaissance amenities, combined with 20th-century features like tennis courts, a pool and air conditioning. The furnishings are fit for a Renaissance princeling, there's dining and dancing by the Arno in the summer, a shady garden, and a hotel bus to whizz you into the city. The food is, however, pricey and not always up to scratch.

**** **Torre di Bellosguardo**, Via Roti Michelozzi 2, ℰ 2298145. In the 12th century a tower was built at Bellosguardo, enjoying one of the most breathtaking views over the city. It was later purchased by the Cavalcanti, friends of Dante, and a villa was added below the tower; Cosimo I confiscated it; the Michelozzi purchased it from the Medici; Elizabeth Barrett Browning wrote about it. In 1988 it opened its doors as a small hotel. Frescoes by Baroque master Poccetti adorn the entrance hall, fine antiques adorn the rooms, each unique and fitted out with a modern bath. The large and beautiful terraced garden has a pool. For a splurge, reserve the two-level tower suite, with fabulous views in four directions. The superb formal gardens look down to the city below, and light lunches are served around the pool in summer.

**** **Villa Villoresi**, Via Campi 2, Colonnata di Sesto Fiorentino, ℰ 443692, ℰ 442 063. A lovely oasis in the middle of one of Florence's more unlovely suburbs. One of its charms is that it hasn't been too pristinely restored, and Contessa Cristina Villoresi's family home has retained much of its slightly faded appeal as well as its frescoed ceilings, antiques and chandeliers. The villa boasts the longest loggia in Tuscany, and five of the best, and grandest, bedrooms have direct access to this. Other rooms are much plainer—and cheaper.

expensive

**** **Paggeria Medicea**, Viale Papa Giovanni XXIII 3, Artimino, near Carmignano, ℰ 8718081. You can play the Medici in the refurbished outbuildings of Grand Duke Ferdinand's villa. It has some unusual amenities—a hunting reserve and a lake stocked with fish, also a pool and tennis court, and pleasant modern rooms, many with balconies, all air-conditioned. A short walk accross the gardens brings you to the restaurant Biagio Pignatta, housed in what was once the butcher's quarters, and where the menu is Tuscan.

*** **Villa le Rondini**, Via Vecchia Bolognese 224, ℰ 400081, ℰ 268212. In a pleasant setting about 7km north of Florence, this hotel has several separate buildings and is surrounded by olives and cyprus trees. The most interesting rooms are in the original 16th-century villa. There is a very pleasant pool.

★★★ **Il Trebbiolo**, Via del Trebbiolo 8, Molin del Piano, Fiesole, ✆ 8300098, @ 830 0583. This small and elegant hotel is situated about 7km north of Fiesole in open country-side surrounded by olives and vines. The bedrooms are furnished with taste and flair, and the public rooms are equally inviting with antique furniture and modern art on the walls. The peaceful garden has wonderful hill views, and there is a restaurant serving dinner.

moderate

★★★ **Hermitage**, Via Gineparia 112, Bonistallo, ✆ 877040. Further afield, near Poggio a Caiano, this is a fine affordable choice for families; there's a pool in the grounds, air-conditioned rooms, not to mention gallons of fresh air and quiet.

★★ **Villa Natalia**, Via Bolognese 106, ✆ 490773, @ 470773. A rather faded villa in a convenient setting with a bus stop near by for the short journey into Florence. The bedrooms are filled with antiques, but the atmosphere downstairs in the public rooms is a little institutional. Book well ahead, as several American universities make block bookings throughout the year.

Where to Stay in Siena (✉ 53100) ✆ (0577–)

Many of Siena's finest and most interesting hotels are outside the walls—out in the lovely countryside, or near the city gates, as close to the centre as cars can logically penetrate. What's left, in the centre, is simple but comfortable enough. In the summer, rooms are in short supply and it would be a good idea to book ahead. If you come without a reservation, your first stop should be the Hotel Information Centre run by the city's innkeepers, ✆ 288084. It's conveniently located in Piazza San Domenico, the terminus of all intercity bus routes (*open 9–7 Mon–Sat*). If you arrive by train, take the city bus up from the station to Piazza Matteotti, and walk a block down Via Curtatone. Even at the worst of times, they should be able to find you something—except during the Palio, of course, when you should make your bookings several months in advance.

If you have a car, a number of hotels outside the walls have a rural Tuscan charm and views of the city that more than make up for the slight inconvenience.

luxury–very expensive

★★★★ **La Certosa di Maggiano**, near the Porta Romana, ✆ 288180, @ 288189. About 1km southeast of the city, this is one of the most remarkable establishments in Italy, a restored 14th-century Carthusian monastery. There are only 14 rooms, and the luxuries

include a heated pool, air conditioning that works, a quiet chapel and cloister, a salon for backgammon and chess, tennis courts, an excellent restaurant, and a library that would be an antiquarian's dream. Of course, all this doesn't come cheap.

very expensive

★★★★ Park Hotel, Via Marciano 18, ✆ 448 03, 🖹 49020. Situated on the hill that dominates Siena with stunning views of the Tuscan landscape, the 16th-century building designed by Peruzzi offers 69 rooms with all the comforts of a class 1 hotel.

★★★★ Villa Patrizia, Via Fiorentina 58, ✆ 50431, 🖹 50431, is a large old villa north of the town with air conditioning, tennis, parking and a pool.

expensive

★★★★ Villa Scacciapensieri, Strada Scacciapensieri 10, 3km north of the city, ✆ 41441. There are sunset views over Siena from this quiet country house divided into 29 spacious rooms; besides the view, it features a pool and a good restaurant with an outdoor terrace.

★★★ Santa Caterina, Via Enea Silvio Piccolomini 7, ✆ 221105, 🖹 271087. An 18th-century house not far from Porta Romana, with 19 attractive rooms which are double glazed and air-conditioned.

expensive–moderate

Many of Siena's two- and three-star hotels cluster around the entrances to the city.

★★★ Garden, Via Custoza 2, ✆ 47056. Has a swimmimg pool.

★★★ Palazzo Ravizza, Pian dei Mantellini, near the Porta Laterina, just inside the walls, ✆ 280462. Its 30 rooms occupy an old town house, the restaurant isn't anything special, but the rooms are cosy and there is a pretty terrace.

moderate

★★★ Chiusarelli, Via Curtatone 15, ✆ 280 562, 🖹 271177. An attractive villa in a pretty garden, with the bonus of a car park. Conveniently near the bus station.

★★★ Continentale, Via Banchi di Sopra 85, ✆ 41451. A very central location in a 16th-century palace complete with faded frescoes and grand stairway.

★★★ Duomo, Via Stalloreggi 34, south of the Duomo, ✆ 289088. A comfortably old-fashioned choice close to the centre.

★★★ Minerva, Via Garibaldi 72, ✆ 284 474, 🖹 284474. Situated on a busy road but all the rooms are ranged round an inner courtyard; there is a also a lift and facilities for the disabled.

★★★ Moderno, Via B. Peruzzi 19, ✆ 270 596, 🖹 270596. A large hotel in a central location with a garden and parking.

★★ Lea, Viale XXIV Maggio 10, ✆ 283207. Centrally located at the end of the pedestrian zone.

moderate–inexpensive

★★ Canon d'Oro, Via Montanini 28, near the bus station, ✆ 44321. A well-run establishment and a good bargain.

★★ Centrale, Via Cecco Angolieri 26, ✆ 280379.

★★ Piccolo Hotel Il Palio, Piazza del Sale 19, ✆ 281131. A little way from the centre, but it has the advantages of a quiet location and a friendly, English-speaking proprietress.

★ Tre Donzelle, Via delle Donzelle, ✆ 280 358. Quite genteel.

inexpensive

Inexpensive places are a little hard to find—especially before term when they're full of students looking for a permanent place.

★★ Piccolo Hotel Etruria, 3 Via delle Donzelle off Via Banchi di Sotto near the

Campo, ✆ 283685, ✉ 288461. Friendly, recently remodelled and a good bargain.

** **Il Giardino**, Via Baldassare Peruzzi 43, ✆ 220090. Highly recommended in readers' letters, situated near the Porta Pispini, with good views and a swimming pool.

★ **La Perla**, Via delle Terme, ✆ 288088.

Youth Hostel

The city of Siena runs its own youth hostel, the **Ostello della Gioventù Guidoriccio**, Via Fiorentina 17, ✆ 52212, in Lo Stellino, 2km from the city (bus no. 15 from Piazza Gramsci). No cards required; arrive early in July and August.

Where to Stay in Pisa (✉ 56100)   ✆ (050–)

Capital of day trippers, Pisa isn't known for fine hotels, but there's usually enough room for the relatively few visitors who elect to stay overnight.

luxury–expensive

**** **Grand Hotel Duomo**, Via S. Maria 94, ✆ 561894, ✉ 560418. The best, very close to the Campo dei Miracoli, a modern though richly appointed luxury hotel with a roof garden and a garage; all the rooms are air-conditioned.

*** **Royal Victoria**, Lungarno Pacinotti, ✆ 940111, ✉ 940180. A tasteful and modern establishment, its best features are rooms overlooking the Arno and its own garage; parking can be a problem in Pisa (L70,000 without bath, L115,000 with).

**** **D'Azeglio**, Piazza Vittorio Emanuele II 18/B, ✆ 500310, ✉ 28017. Near the station, comfortable, modern, air-conditioned rooms.

moderate

*** **Verdi**, Piazza Repubblica 5, ✆ 598 947, ✉ 598944. In a well-restored historic palace in the centre, Verdi has 32 comfortable modern rooms, but no restaurant.

*** **Terminus e Plaza**, Via Colombo 45, ✆/✉ 500303. Like many middle-range hotels south of the Arno, near the train station (L58–115,000 depending on the plumbing).

*** **Villa Corliano**, Loc. Rigoli, ✆ 818 193. A rather faded 15th-century villa halfway between Lucca and Pisa with Baroque frescoes and antique furniture, set in beautiful grounds.

*** **Villa Kinzica**, Piazza Arcivescovado 2, ✆ 560419, ✉ 551204. In a marvellous location, with air conditioning.

*** **California Park Hotel**, Loc. Madonna dell'Acqua, San Giuliano Terme, just outside the city on the SS1 (Via Aurelia), ✆ 890726, ✉ 890727. A good place to stay if you're driving—a large hotel with a park and a pool (*open Mar–Oct*).

inexpensive

Inexpensive places are spread throughout town, and most of them are often full of students; it's always best to call first.

** **Amalfitana**, Via Roma 44, ✆ 29000, ✉ 25218. Small and cheap, but on a busy road.

★ **Giardino**, in Piazza Manin, just outside the walls, near the Campo dei Miracoli, ✆ 562101.

** **Di Stefano**, Via Sant'Apollonia 35, ✆ 553559, ✆ 556038. Central, recently upgraded, with TVs in each room.

* **Gronchi**, Piazza Arcivesovado 1, ✆ 561 823. The nicest in this category; tidy, with a touch of class, tucked in a quiet corner near the Campo dei Miracoli.

* **Helvetia**, Via Don Boschi 31, ✆ 553 084. Also near the Campo dei Miracoli.

*There's also a **Youth Hostel** at Via Pietrasantina 15, ✆ 890622; bus no. 3 from the station will take you there.*

Where to Stay in Lucca (✉ 55100)　　　✆ (0583–)

Lucca can be less than charm city if you arrive without booking ahead; there simply aren't enough rooms (especially inexpensive ones) to meet demand, and the Lucchesi aren't in any hurry to do anything about it.

luxury–very expensive

***** **Principessa Elisa**, outside the city, at Massa Pisana on Via SS del Brennero, ✆ 379737. Here you can bed down in Castruccio Castracani's own palace, built for the great Lucchese warlord in 1321. Often rebuilt since, it currently wears the façade of a stately rococo mansion, and is surrounded by acres of 18th-century gardens and a pool. Thoroughly modern inside, amenities include air conditioning, TVs and minibars in the rooms (*open Mar–Nov*).

moderate

*** **La Luna**, Corte Compagni 12, ✆ 493 634. In a quiet part of the centre, this is a cosy place, with a private garage.

*** **Piccolo Hotel Puccini**, Via di Poggio 9, ✆ 55421, ✆ 53487. A small and comfortable hotel right in the heart of things, with 14 rooms.

*** **Rex**, Piazza Ricasoli 19, ✆ 955443, ✆ 954348. A good hotel with 25 rooms, all but one with a bathroom.

*** **Universo**, Piazza Puccini, ✆ 493678. Inside the walls you cannot do better than

this slightly frayed, green-shuttered and thoroughly delightful place, although some rooms are nicer than others; Ruskin and nearly everyone else who followed him to Lucca slept here.

*** **Villa Rinascimento**, Santa Maria del Giudice, 9km along the S12 from Lucca to Pisa, ✆ 378292, ✆ 378292. Large, clean and simply decorated rooms in a 15th-century villa, with the added attractions of a rustic dining room and swimming pool.

moderate–inexpensive

** **Ilaria**, Via del Fosso 20, ✆ 47558. Offers 14 quaint rooms on Lucca's baby canal.

inexpensive

** **Diana**, Via del Molinetto 11, near the cathedral, ✆ 490368. Friendly and well-run with some of the nicest inexpensive rooms in Tuscany, some with bath.

** **Moderno**, Via V. Civitalli 38, ✆ 55 840, a central location. Modern, comfortable and rarely crowded.

** **Villa Casanova**, Via Casanova, Balbano, just outside the city (city bus 5 and then a 2.5km uphill walk, or take a taxi), © 548429. Simple rooms but a pleasant garden, tennis and a swimming pool to lounge by.

★ **Cinzia**, Via della Dogana 9, © 491323. One of the cheapest inside the walls.

Youth Hostel

The youth hostel is 2km north of town on Via del Brennero, in Salicchi (bus 7 from the station), © 341811 (*open 10 Mar–10 Oct*).

Nightlife with Great Aunt Florence is still awaiting its Renaissance; according to the Florentines she's conservative, somewhat deaf and retires early—1am is very, very late in this city. However, there are plenty of people who wish it weren't so, and slowly, slowly, Florence by night is beginning to mean more than the old *passeggiata* over the Ponte Vecchio and an ice cream, and perhaps a late trip up to Fiesole to contemplate the lights.

Look for listings of concerts and events in Florence's daily, *La Nazione*; the tourist office's free *Florence Today* contains bilingual monthly information and a calendar, as does a booklet called *Florence Concierge Information*, available in hotels and tourist offices; the monthly *Firenze Spettacolo*, sold in newsstands, is published only in Italian but fills you in on ecology and trekking activities, film societies, bar music and the latest New Age mumbo jumbo to rock Florence. The annual guide *Guida locali di Firenze* also gives listings. For a listing of all current films being shown in Florence (Italian and dubbed in Italian), call © 198.

In Siena, Pisa and Lucca classical music lovers are the most likely to be rewarded. Take note of the cities' festivals, which can be great fun (*see* pp.17–20).

Entertainment and Nightlife

Pubs

The city has exploded with Irish pubs; there's also the odd English and Scottish version.

The Fiddler's Elbow, Piazza Santa Maria Novella. One of the original ones, some live music and an ex-pat atmosphere. A handy place to wait for a train, but a bit grim.

The Lion's Fountain, Borgo degli Albizi 34/r. A nice place which also serves food.

The William, Via Magliabechi, pastiche of an English pub.

The Old Stove, Via Pelliccceria.

Robin Hood Pub, Via dell'Oriuolo, as above.

Meeting Places

The evening in Florence will usually begin by meeting up in a piazza. For typical crowds, head to **Piazza Michelangelo**, where local lads and lasses perch on their scooters eating ice cream. Or stroll along to the central **Piazza della Repubblica** then down **Via Calzaiuoli** to the **Ponte Vecchio** and back again.

For the more alternative and trendy crowd, head for **Piazza Santo Spirito**, especially in the summer months when the piazza and the church steps are packed with young people served by the surrounding pubs and bars. You could meet in Il Cabiria or on **Piazza del Carmine** in front of La Dolce Vita disco bar. Other meeting places include Parterre and Le Cascine.

Opera, Ballet and Music

The opera and ballet season runs from September to Christmas, concerts from January to April at the **Teatro Comunale**, and the **Maggio Musicale** festival, which features all three, from May until the end of June. There is usually more opera in July. Big-name jazz performers, classical artists and others are brought to Florence by **Musicus Concentus**, Piazza del Carmine 14, ✆ 287 347; rock and jazz tours happen in the big **Palasport**, Campo di Marte, Viale Paoli.

Classsical concerts are held in the church of Santa Croce; Teatro Comunale, Corso Italia 16, ✆ 211158; Teatro della Pergola, Via della Pergola 12–32, ✆ 2479651; and Teatro Verdi, Via Ghibellina 99, ✆ 212320. The following **orchestras** or organisations put on concerts regularly: **ORT Orchestra Regionale Toscana**, Via dei Benci 20, ✆ 242767; **Amici della Musica**, Via G Sirtori 49, ✆ 608420; **Orchestra da Camera Fiorentina**, Via E. Poggi 6, ✆ 7877322.

Rock and jazz venues: **Teatro Puccini**, Via delle Cascine 41; **Auditorium Flo**, Via M. Mercati 24b, ✆ 490437; **Teatro Verdi**, Via Ghibellina 101, ✆ 212320. Concerts are arranged by **Toscana Music Pool**, ✆ 243 280; Box Office, Via Faenza 139r, ✆ 210804.

Cinemas

Original language (usually English) films are shown on Mondays (and occasionally Tuesdays) at the following cinemas: **Goldoni**, Via de' Serragli 109, ✆ 222437 and **Odeon**, Via Sassetti 1, ✆ 214068. These two show latest releases whereas the **Cinema Astro**, Piazza San Simone near Santa Croce (no tel; *closed Mon and July*) shows films that have been around for a while. Arty **Spazio Uno** in Via del Sole 10, ✆ 215634 and the **LunediClub** (on Mondays, at the Istituto Stensen, L2000 membership), Viale Don Minzoni 251, ✆ 576551, often have films in their original language, but it isn't always English

Clubs

Check out each club's offerings as many places have themed evenings. Or head to one of the squares listed below and ask around to find out what is going on.

Caffedecò, Piazza della Libertà 45–46r. If you want to join Florence's swells, put on the dog and head out to this elegant place done up in tasteful art deco, with live jazz (*closed Mon*).

Cafè Cabiria, Piazza Santo Spirito 4r. Small, quiet by day, trendy and heaving at night.

Central Park, Parco delle Cascine. Summer club with live music, three dance floors, shows and snacks. Possibly the trendiest place in Florence, full of serious clubbers.

Dolce Vita, Piazza del Carmine. One of the most popular places in the Oltrarno, a bar to see and be seen in.

Du Monde, Via San Niccolò 103r. A cocktail bar offering food, drink and music for the elegant Florentine which stays open until 5 in the morning.

Flog Concerti, Via Michele Mercati 24b. Dance music and live concerts (especially the more alternative Italian 'ragamuffin' bands such as 99 Posse and Mano Negra). (*Every Thurs–Sun, summer only.*)

Full-Up, Via della Vigna Nuova 25r. Closed Sun and Mon and June-Sept. Mirrored walls and disco lighting. Dated music.

Jazz Café, Via Nuova de' Caccini 3. *Closed Sun and Mon.* A pleasant but smokey atmosphere with live jazz on Friday and Saturday nights, and a free jam session on Tuesdays.

Lido, Lungarno Pecori Giraldi 1. *Closed Mon.* A pretty setting on the Arno. Small, with mixed music and a mixed crowd.

Mago Merlino, Via dei Pilastri 31r. A relaxed tea-room/bar with live music, theatre, shows and games.

Maracanà, Via Faenza 4. For live samba, mambo and bossanova.

Maramao, Via dei Macci 79r, *closed Mon.* The music in this slick, cool venue is often Latin-American.

The Mood, Corso dei Tintori 4, *closed Mon.* An underground venue with a good mix of music. Young and energetic.

Parterre, Piazza della Libertà, outdoors. Two bars, concerts and video screens.

Rex Café, Via Fiesolana 23r. Currently number one hotspot, popular in winter. Unusual decor, tapas, music and dancing.

Riflessi d'Epoca, Via dei Renai 13r. Frequently has live jazz in a smoky ambience. It stays open later than the average club (i.e. after 1am).

Rifrullo, Via S. Niccolò 55r. An older pub/wine bar, probably the most popular of all and one of the first to attract people to the Oltrarno. There's no word for 'cosy' in Italian, but the Rifrullo does the best it can.

Stonehenge, Via dell'Amorino 16r, near S. Lorenzo. Rock and cocktails from 10pm until after 1am.

Gay Clubs

There are two **gay clubs** in Florence: **Satanassa**, Via Pandolfini 26r (*closed Mon*), with cocktail bar and disco, and **Tabasco**, Piazza Santa Cecilia 3r, Italy's first gay bar, opened in the '70s.

Discos

Andromeda, Via dei Climatori 13, ✆ 292002. Particularly popular with young foreigners. *Closed Sun.*

Auditorium Flog, Via M.Mercanti 24b, ✆ 490437. Student venue—packed.

Jackie 'O, Via Erta Canina 24. An old favourite, early 30s age group. *Closed Mon, Tues, Wed.* Includes piano bar.

Kasar, Lungarno Colombo 23, ℭ 676912, *closed Mon and Wed.*

Rock Caffè, Borgo degli Albizi 66r, ℭ 244662. A theme every night. *Closed Sun.*

Tenax, out near the airport in Via Pratese 47, ℭ 293082. Lots of live music—the current place to go in Florence. Always busy. *Open daily.*

Space Electronic, Via Palazzuolo 37 ℭ 293 082. A high-tech noise box. *Open daily.*

Meccanó, Viale degli Olmi 1, ℭ 331371. Where the younger crowd get their kicks—a different music policy each night.

Siena

One of the loveliest things to do on a summer evening is to attend a free concert given by the students and teachers at the **Accademia Musicale Chigiana**, Via de la Città 85, ℭ 46152; the tourist office has the programme as well. From the end of April until early September, the *contrade* hold their annual festivals: the Dragon, Turtle, Giraffe, Owl, Unicorn, Snail and Dolphin in June; the Caterpillar, Elephant, Mussel Shell, Rhinoceros, Porcupine and Panther in July–August.

Pisa

Associazione di Cultura Cinematografica, Vicolo Scaramucci 4, ℭ 502640, on the south bank near Piazza San Martino, shows an excellent selection of films from around the world. Concerts take place at **Teatro Comunale Verdi** in Via Palestro, more off-beat shows at a former church at the end of Via San Zeno.

Lucca

On the third weekend of every month there is an enormous **antiques market** in and around Piazza San Martino. There are markets on Wednesdays and Saturdays in Via dei Bacchettoni. The summer **Festival de Malia** (at the Villa Neale, 8km towards Pistoia) and September's **Settembre Lucchese** (in the city's Teatro Comunale) centre around classical music and ballet.

Shopping

'Made in Italy' has long been a byword for style and quality, especially in fashion and leather, but also in home design, ceramics, kitchenware, jewellery, lace and linens, glassware and crystal, chocolates, hats, straw-work, art books, engravings, hand-made stationery, gold and silverware, a hundred kinds of liqueurs, wine, aperitifs, coffee machines, gastronomic specialities, antique reproductions, as well as the antiques themselves. Florence, which increasingly resembles a glittering medieval shopping mall, has the biggest choices, and holds a major monthly antique fair every last Sunday, while Lucca holds one every third Sunday. If you are looking for art or antiques and are spending a lot of money, be sure to demand a certificate of authenticity—reproductions can be very, very good. To get your antique or modern art purchases home, you will have to apply to the Export Department of the Italian Ministry of Education—a possible hassle. You will have to pay an export tax as well; your seller should know the details.

Italians don't like department stores, but there are a few chains— COIN stores often have good buys in almost the latest fashions. Standa is more like Woolworth's, with a reasonable selection of clothes, houseware, etc., often with a supermarket in the base-ment. UPIM in the centre of Florence has closed down (although there are two branches in the suburbs), and been replaced by La Rinascente, possibly the most upmarket department store in Italy with men's and women's clothes, household goods, cosmetics etc. Most stay open throughout the day, but some take the same break as other Italian shops—from 1pm to 3 or 4pm. Non-EU nationals should make sure to save their receipts for Customs on the way home. Shipping goods is a risky business unless you do it through a very reputable shop. Note that the attraction of shopping in Italy is strictly limited to luxury items; for less expensive clothes and household items you'll always, always do better in Britain or America. Prices for clothes, even in street markets, are often ridiculously high. Bargains of any kind are rare, and the cheaper goods are often very poor quality.

Italian clothes are lovely, but if you have a large-boned Anglo-American build, you may find it hard to get a good fit, especially on trousers or skirts (Italians are a long-waisted, slim-hipped bunch). Shoes are often narrower than the sizes at home.

Sizes

Women's Shirts/Dresses

UK	10	12	14	16	18
US	8	10	12	14	16
Italy	40	42	44	46	48

Sweaters

	10	12	14	16
	8	10	12	14
	46	48	50	52

Women's Shoes

	3	4	5	6	7	8
	4	5	6	7	8	9
	36	37	38	39	40	41

Men's Shirts

UK/US	14	14½	15	15 ½	16	16 ½	17	17½
Italy	36	37	38	39	40	41	42	43

Men's Suits

UK/US	36	38	40	42	44	46
Italy	46	48	50	52	54	56

Men's Shoes

UK	2	3	4	5	6	7	8	9	10	11	12
US	5	6	7	7½	8	9	10	10½	11	12	13
Italy	34	36	37	38	39	40	41	42	43	44	45

Weights and Measures

1 kilogramme (1000 g)—2.2 lb1 lb—0.45 kg
1 etto (100 g)— 1/4 lb (approx)
1 litre—1.76 pints

1 pint—0.568 litres
1 quart—1.136 litres
1 imperial gallon—4.546 litres
1 US gallon—3.785 litres

1 metre—39.37 inches
1 kilometre—0.621 miles

1 foot—0.3048 metres
1 mile—1.61 kilometres

Shopping in Florence

Antiques and Art Galleries

Via Maggio, Borgo Ognissanti and the various Lungarni are the places to look for antiques and art galleries.

Antica Maraviglia, Borgo San Jacopo 6r, ✆ 2381489. Antique toys and games, objects and porcelain.

Atelier Alice, Via Faenza 12, and I Mascheroni Atelier, Via dei Tavolini 13r. Both sell Italian carnival masks.

P. Bazzanti e Figli, Lungarno Corsini 44. Where you can pick up an exact replica of the bronze pig in the Mercato Nuovo.

La Bottega di Marino, Via Santo Spirito 8r, ✆ 213184. Family restorers and antiques merchants.

Casa dei Tessuti, Via de' Pecori 20–24r. Keeps Florence's ancient cloth trade alive with lovely linens, silks and woollens.

Auction Houses

Serious collectors may want to check Florence's busy auction houses.

Casa d'Aste Pandolfini, Borgo degli Albizi 26, ℰ 2340888.

Casa d'Aste Pitti, Via Maggio 15, ℰ 239 6382.

Palazzo Internazionale delle Aste ed Esposizioni, Via Maggio 11, ℰ 282905.

Sotheby's (Associate Office), Via Verdi 1 ℰ 2479021.

Books

Bookworms do better in Florence than most Italian cities, although the prices of books in English will make you weep.

After Dark, Via Del Moro 86r. New and second-hand English books.

Cima, Borgo Albizi 37r. One of Florence's biggest, and the first to have a coffee shop and Internet service.

BM Bookshop, Borgo Ognissanti 4r. Books in English and an excellent selection of art books.

Feltrinelli, Via Cavour 12–20r. The English department is on the first floor and there is also a good selection of art books.

Franco Maria Ricci, Via delle Belle Donne 41r. A fabulous collection of art books.

For the widest selections in English, with many books about Florence:

The Paperback Exchange, Via Fiesolana 31r.

Seeber, Via Tornabuoni 70r.

Children

Caponi, Borgo Ognissanti 12r. Has a fairytale selection of dresses if you happen to know the kind of little girl who can wear white.

Città del Sole, Borgo Ognissanti, near Piazza Goldoni. The best toy shop in Florence.

Menicucci, Via Guicciardini 5. Their window is always full of the most wonderful stuffed toys.

Department Stores

COIN, Via dei Calzaiuoli 56r.

La Rinascente, Piazza della Repubblica 1.

Standa, Via Panzani 31r.

Fashion and Accessories

With the expansion of Peretola Airport in Florence, and the important bi-annual menswear show, Pitti Uomo, Florence is winning back some of its kudos as a fashion centre, after a mass exodus of the big designers to Milan. Many of the big names of the 1960s and '70s, which turned into the international chain stores of the 1980s and '90s, are represented in smart Via Tornabuoni and in the streets around the Duomo. Clothes shops generally are to be found in Via Roma and Via Calzaiuoli.

Giorgio Armani, Via della Vigna Nuova 51r.

Emporio Armani, Piazza Strozzi 14–16r.

Enrico Coveri, Via Tornabuoni 81r.

Gucci, Via Tournabuoni 73r.

Oliver, Via Vacchereccia 15r. Fashionable casual men's wear.

Prada, Via Vaccheraccia 26r.

Principe, Via degli Strozzi 21–19r. Classical men's and women's wear.

Valentino, Via della Vigna Nuova 47r.

Borsellino Hat, Via dei Cimatori 22r. Classic hat makers.

La Nuova Modisteria, Via Chiara 15r. The best for men's women's and children's hats, with a remarkable choice of style and colours.

Beltrami, Via Tornabuoni. Shoes.

Ferragamo, Via Tornabuoni 14r. Best boots in town.

Madova, Via Guicciardini 1r. An incredible selection of gloves made at their own factory.

Food and Wine

There is a number of speciality food shops around the Mercato Centrale, or you can try the following:

Allrientar Gastronomia, in Borgo SS. Apostoli. Where you can pick up items like truffle creams.

La Bolognese, Via de' Serragli 24. For delicious fresh pasta. Try their *ravioli al tartufo* —truffle-flavoured ravioli.

Il Fornaio, Via Guicciardini 6r and Via Faenza 39r. For a huge choice of breads, foccaccias, pizza by the slice and cakes.

La Bottega del Brunello, Via Ricasoli 81r. Shop divided in two parts—for display and for tasting the wine and specialities on sale.

Old English Stores, Via Vecchietti 28r. For that pot of Marmite or Worcester sauce you've been craving.

Il Procacci, Via Tornabuoni 64r. This is a high-quality *alimentari* (food shop) selling regional specialities as well as foreign foods.

La Porta del Tartufo, Borgo Ognissanti 133r. Concentrates on different types of truffles or 'truffled' foods ranging from grappa to salmon paste. Also good wines and other typical products.

Vivimarket, Via del Melarancio 17/r. For the best selection of Asian food in town.

Cantina e Gola, Piazza Pitti 16. A good selction of wines, oils and vinegars, and cookery books (in both English and Italian) to go with them.

Casa del Vino, Via dell' Ariento 16r. Wine to taste and to buy plus snacks in the San Lorenzo street market.

Enoteca, Via Giraldi. Specializes exclusively in Tuscan wines from lesser-known producers. Over 140 labels; you can also eat there.

Enoteca Murgia, Via dei Banchi 57, off Piazza S. Maria Novella. Wines and spirits.

Marchesi de' Frescobaldi, Via di S Spirito 11. One of the largest wine suppliers in Italy; visit their ancient cellars.

Le Volpi e L'Uva, Piazza de' Rossi 1 (just south of the Ponte Vecchio), great selection of interesting wines and very helpful staff.

Jewellery

Florence is famous for its jewellery, and the shops on and around the Ponte Vecchio are forced by the nature of their location into wide-open competition. Good prices for Florentine brushed gold (although much of it is now made in Arezzo) and antique jewellery are more common than you may think.

Cibola, Via XXVII Aprile 47r, ✆ 499113. Halfway between a shop and an art gallery—interesting artistic jewellery.

Pietro Agnoletti, Via de'Pepi 18, ✆ 240 810. Handmade gold jewellery, but you must book for an appointment.

La Fibula, Via Guelfa 106r. Goldsmiths who help you design your own creations.

Kitchenware

Bartolini, Via dei Servi 30r. A large shop that stocks just about everything.

Open House, Via Barbadori 40r. For contemporary design.

Il Tegame, Piazza Gaetano Salvemini 7.

Leather

Florence is still known for its leather, and you'll see plenty of it in the centre, around Via della Vigna Nuova and Via del Parione, and less expensively at an unusual institution called the Leather School, which occupies part of Santa Croce's cloister (entrance at Piazza Santa Croce 16 or Via S. Giuseppe 5r). Some of the cheapest places for leather jackets are the stalls and shops around San Lorenzo market, but be prepared to bargain.

Giulio Giannini e Figlio, Piazza Pitti 37, ✆ 212621. Originally book binders, now they also produce leather albums and leather desk-top objects as well as handmade paper following a 17th-century technique.

Gucci, Via Tornabuoni 73–75.

Fratelli Rossetti, Piazza Repubblica 43/45. One of the largest and best.

Linen

Ghezzi, Via Calzaiuoli 110r. Fashionable towels and bed linens.

Marbled Paper

Florence is one of the few places in the world to make marbled paper, an art brought over from the Orient by Venice in the 12th century. Each sheet is hand-dipped in a bath of colours to create a delicate, lightly coloured, clouded design— no two sheets are alike. Stationery items or just sheets of marbled paper are available at:

La Bottega, Artigiana del Libro, Lungarno Corsini 40r.

Giulio Giannini e Figlio, Piazza Pitti 37r.

Il Papiro, the oldest manufacturer, has three shops at Via Cavour 55r, Piazza del Duomo 24r, and Lungarno Acciaiuoli 42r.

Il Torchio, Via dei Bardi 17, ✆ 2342862. Sells all types of coloured paper. The workbench is in the shop so you can see the artisans in action.

These shops (and many others) also carry Florentine paper with its colourful Gothic patterns.

Perfumes and Medieval Cures

Lorenzo Villoresi, Via de' Bardi 14, ✆ 234 1187. If you've always wanted to have a perfume designed especially for you, make an appointment; he also has some exotic ready-made perfumes, sold only here, in Florence.

Farmaceutica di Santa Maria Novella, Via della Scala 16n. Hasn't changed much since 1612 and still sells medieval cures and Dominican remedies.

Silver, Crystal, Mosaics, Porcelain

Ceramiche Gambone, Via della Robbia 82. Ceramics, crystal, glass and bronze.

Paci, Viuzzo delle Case Nuove 1, ✆ 732 2624. A father and son make and restore hard stone mosaic objects. Ronald Reagan shopped here!

A. Poggi, Via Calzaiuoli 105r and 116r. Has one of the city's widest selections of silver, crystal and porcelain (including Florence's own Richard-Ginori).

Sbigoli Terrecotte, Via Sant'Egidio 4r. In business for over 150 years.

Street Markets

Florence's lively street markets offer good bargains, fake designer glad rags and even some authentic labels. The huge **San Lorenzo market** is the largest and most boisterous, where many Florentines buy their clothes; **Sant'Ambrogio** is a bustling food market; the **Mercato Nuovo** or Straw Market is the most touristic, but not flagrantly so. There's a small market every morning except Sundays where stalls sell food, clothes and shoes in **Piazza Santo Spirito**. Every second Sunday of the month, there's a big craft and flea market and every third Sunday, an organic food market there. There's an extensive clothes and shoes market every Tuesday morning in the Cascine, but perhaps the most fun is the **Mercato delle Pulci** (Flea Market) on Sundays in Piazza dei Ciompi, offering all kinds of desirable junk.

Shopping in Siena

Siena, with its population of only 60,000, is blissfully short of designer boutiques and so on. Even the usual tourist trinkets seem lacking—illuminated plastic models of the cathedral are harder to find every year! Nevertheless, a thorough search of the back streets will turn up plenty of unpretentious artisan workshops—almost all of them so unconcerned with tourism they don't even bother hanging out a sign.

Vetrate Artistiche Toscane, Via della Gallozza 5. Glass workers and restorers, also selling small objects and mirrors, lampshades, etc.

Via di Città 94. Sells interesting ceramic pieces.

Via Galuzza 5, just off Piazza Independenza. An artist with a distinctive modern style creates works in stained glass here (most of them portable).

Via San Girolamo 15. Brass and pewter shields of the *contrade*, and other paraphernalia of Siena's great obsession, are sold here.

Books

Libreria Senese, Via di Città 64. Siena's best bookshop.

Food

Antica Drogheria Manganelli, Via di Città 71–73. Hundred-year-old original wooden shelving and a beautiful display of delicious regional foods and wines.

L'Enoteca San Domenico, Via del Paradiso 56. A good selection of wine, Tuscan and otherwise, and other edible goodies.

Forno dei Galli, Via dei Termini 45. Historic Sienese bakers selling bread, fresh pasta and pasticceria.

Gastronomia Morbidi, Banchi di Sopra 75, ✆ 280268. Founded in 1925, this wonderful shop has four floors of national and Sienese culinary specialities and a wine section selling all the best wines in Italy.

La Nuova Pasticceria di Iasevoli, Via Dupré 37. This uninteresting-looking bakers produces some of the best Sienese biscuits and cakes (*cantucci, pan di santi, panforte* and *ricciarelli*) in the city.

Pasticceria Nannini, Via F. Tozzi 2. Typical Sienese sweets and pastries.

Accessories

Furla, Banchi di Sopra 21. For expensive designer handbags.

Il Papiro, Via di Città 37. For marbled paper goods, pens, inks and cards.

Pisa is the best place in Tuscany to purchase bizarre and tacky **souvenirs**, and the best selection is crowded around the Campo dei Miracoli. Light-up Leaning Towers in pink and yellow come in all sizes and are an amazingly good buy; some have a pen and pencil set attached for the scholar, or grinning plastic kittens for the kids' room, or naked ladies for your favourite uncle. The other specialities are medieval weapons—crossbows, cudgels, maces, whips—and plastic skulls, reptiles and insects. If you'd prefer a **book** in English, try Feltrinelli at Corso Italia 117.

Books

The Bookshop, Via Rigattieri 39. The only English-language book shop in Pisa; a good stock of titles plus cards etc.

Clothes

If it is the boutiques you're after, head down Via Oberdan and Corso Italia. Borgo Stretto is good for boutiques and smart clothes shops, for example:

Casa del Guanto, Via di Borgo Stretto 48. All types of gloves.

Nazareno Gabrielli, Via di Borgo Stretto 25. Sells clothes, leather wear, accessories.

Food

L'altra Roba, Piazza delle Vettovaglie 3. Sells dried fruit, vegetables preserved in oil as well as conserves, oil and wine.

Enogastronomia F.lli Simi, Via San Martino 6. Pasta, cheeses, wines, olive oil and homemade cakes are what the Simi family have been selling for over 100 years.

Gastronomia Gratin, Via Crispi 66. A smart general food store with a good selection of salami, ham, oil and wine.

Piazza delle Vettovaglie. Food market in a pretty medieval square.

La Badiola, Via del Parco 10, località San Pancrazio. Produces and sells good-quality reasonably priced wines in a beautiful setting, an old villa in a large park.

La Bottega di Mamma, Piazza del Anfiteatro 4. Kitchen shop crammed full of colourful up-market ceramics and fabrics.

La Botteghina del Vipore, loc. Pieve Santo Stefano. All the most delicious Tuscan products are on sale here, including some exclusively made for the Botteghina such as butter made from pure buffalo milk.

Bulthaup, Piazza del Anfiteatro 45. Contemporary kitchen design.

Caniparoli, Via San Paolino. Chocolate to make you swoon.

Enoteca Petroni, Via Beccheria. Stocks a huge selection of wines, Italian and otherwise.

Pasticceria Taddeucci, Piazza San Michele 34. Pastries both savoury and sweet, as well as homemade ricotta tart and other local specialities.

Sports and Activities

Boats and Sailing

The sailing is beautiful among the coves of the Tuscan archipelago and around the Argentario; if you want to learn how, there's a good sailing school in **Torre del Lago Puccini**, ✆ (0584) 342084.

Golf

The nearest golf course to Florence is the 18-hole **Golf Club Ugolino**, in Gràssina, 7km southeast of the city, on the Chiantigiana–Impruneta, ✆ 2301085; a lovely course laid out among olives and cypresses.

Medieval Sports

Some ancient sports like the annual horse races, or **palios** (two in Siena) are still popular, and not entirely as a tourist attraction: the rivalries between neighbourhoods and cities are intense. The Florentines play three games of **Renaissance football** a year (*calcio in costume*); in Lucca **crossbow archers** compete from different city quarters. In Pisa it's medieval **tug-of-war**.

Racing and Riding

Horse riding is increasingly popular, and Agriturist has a number of villa and riding holidays on offer in Tuscany. **The National Association of Equestrian Tourism** (ANTE) is probably more active here than anywhere in Italy. **Centro Ippico Cintoia**, Via Cintoia Bassa, Strada in Chianti, ✆ 854 7973, provides lessons, guided walks and excursions. The Cascine has Florence's race course (**Ippodromo Le Cascine**, ✆ 360 598) and trotting course (**Ippodromo della Mulina**, ✆ 411107). The nearest place to go riding in the Tuscan hills is the **Country Riding Club**, Via di Grioli, at Badia a Settimo in Scandicci, 6km southwest of Florence, ✆ 790277. In Pisa you can go

riding at the **Cooperativa Agrituristica** in Via Tre Colli in Calci. For more information, write directly to the local **Agriturist** office: Via della Sapienza 39, 53100 Siena, ✆ (0577) 46194; Via B. Croce 62, 56100 Pisa, ✆ (050) 26221; Viale Barsanti e Matteucci, 55100 Lucca, ✆ (0583) 332044.

Rowing

There is an annual rowing race between the four old maritime republics of Venice, Amalfi, Genoa and Pisa, which alternates between the cities. If there's enough water in the Arno, you can try rowing or canoeing; contact the **Società Canottieri Comunali**, Lungarno Ferrucci 6, ✆ 681 2151, or the **Società Canottieri Firenze**, Lungarno dei Medici 8, ✆ 282130 (membership only).

Squash

Centro Squash, Viale Piombino 24/29, Florence ✆ 7323055.

Swimming

The one activity most summertime visitors begin to crave after tramping through the sights is a dip in a pool. The prettiest one in Florence is the **Piscina le Pavoniere**, in the Cascine, open June–Sept 10–6.30; others are **Bellariva**, up the Arno at Lungarno Colombo 2, open June–Sept 11–5. There are two covered, year-round pools: **Amici del Nuoto**, Via del Romito 38, ✆ 483951, and **Costoli**, Via Paoli, near Campo di Marte, ✆ 669744. In Pisa you can swim in the pool in **Via Andrea Pisano**.

Tennis

Tennis-courts are nearly everywhere. In Florence try the **Circolo Tennis alle Cascine**, ✆ 356651.

The fathers of modern Italian were Dante, Manzoni, and television. Each did their part in creating a national language from an infinity of regional and local dialects; the Florentine Dante, the first 'immortal' to write in the vernacular, did much to put the Tuscan dialect in the foreground of Italian literature. Manzoni's revolutionary novel, *I Promessi Sposi* (The Betrothed), heightened national consciousness by using an everyday language all could understand in the 19th century. Television in the last few decades is performing an even more spectacular linguistic unification; although the majority of Italians still speak a dialect at home, school, and work, their TV idols insist on proper Italian.

Perhaps because they are so busy learning their own beautiful but grammatically complex language, Italians are not especially apt at learning others. English lessons, however, have been the rage for years, and at most hotels and restaurants there will be someone who speaks some English. In small towns and out of the way places, finding an Anglophone may prove more difficult. The words and phrases below should help you out in most situations, but the ideal way to come to Italy is with some Italian under your belt; your visit will be richer, and you're much more likely to make some Italian friends.

Pronunciation

Italian words are pronounced phonetically. Every vowel and consonant (except *h*) is sounded. Consonants are the same as in English, except the *c* which, when followed by an 'e' or 'i', is pronounced like the English 'ch' (*cinque* thus becomes cheenquay). Italian *g* is also soft before 'i' or 'e' as in *gira*, pronounced jee-ra. *H* is never sounded; *z* is pronounced like 'ts'. The consonants *sc* before the vowels 'i' or 'e' become like the English 'sh' as in *sci*, pronounced shee; *ch* is pronounced like a 'k' as in *Chianti*, kee-an-tee; *gn* as 'ny' in English (*bagno*, pronounced banyo; while *gli* is pronounced like the middle of the word million (*Castiglione*, pronounced Ca-steely-oh-nay).

Vowel pronunciation is: *a* as in English father; *e* when unstressed is pronounced like 'a' in fate, as in *mele*, when stressed can be the same or like the 'e' in pet

Language

(*bello*); *i* is like the 'i' in machine; *o*, like *e*, has two sounds: 'o' as in hope when unstressed (*tacchino*), and usually 'o' as in rock when stressed (*morte*); *u* is pronounced like the 'u' in June.

The accent usually (but not always!) falls on the penultimate syllable. Also note that in the big northern cities, the informal way of addressing someone as you, *tu*, is widely used; the more formal *lei* or *voi* is commonly used in provincial districts.

Useful Words and Phrases

yes/no/maybe	*sì/ no/ forse*
I don't know	*Non lo so*
I don't understand (Italian)	*Non capisco (italiano)*
Does someone here	*C'è qualcuno qui*
speak English?	*che parla inglese?*
Speak slowly	*Parla lentamente*
Could you assist me?	*Potrebbe aiutarmi?*
Help!	*Aiuto!*
Please	*per favore*
Thank you (very much)	*(Molte) grazie*
You're welcome	*Prego*
It doesn't matter	*Non importa*
All right	*Va bene*
Excuse me	*Mi scusi*
Be careful!	*Attenzione!*
Nothing	*Niente*
It is urgent!	*È urgente!*
How are you?	*Come sta?*
Well, and you?	*Bene, e Lei?*
What is your name?	*Come si chiama?*
Hello	*Salve* or *ciao* (both informal)
Good morning	*Buongiorno* (formal hello)
Good afternoon, evening	*Buonasera* (also formal hello)
Good night	*Buona notte*
Goodbye	*ArrivederLa* (formal), *arrivederci*, *ciao* (informal)
What do you call this in Italian?	*Come si chiama questo in italiano?*
What?	*Che?*
Who?	*Chi?*
Where?	*Dove?*
When?	*Quando?*
Why?	*Perché?*
How?	*Come?*
How much?	*Quanto?*
I am lost	*Mi sono smarrito*
I am hungry	*Ho fame*

I am thirsty	*Ho sete*
I am sorry	*Mi dispiace*
I am tired	*Sono stanco*
I am sleepy	*Ho sonno*
I am ill	*Mi sento male*
Leave me alone	*Lasciami in pace*
good	*buono/ bravo*
bad	*male/ cattivo*
slow	*lento*
fast	*rapido*
big	*grande*
small	*piccolo*
hot	*caldo*
cold	*freddo*
up	*su*
down	*giù*
here	*qui*
there	*lì*

Shopping, Service, Sightseeing

I would like...	*Vorrei...*
Where is/are...	*Dov'è/ Dove sono...*
How much is it?	*Quanto viene questo?/ Quant'è/ Quanto costa questo?*
open	*aperto*
closed	*chiuso*
cheap/expensive	*a buon prezzo/ caro*
bank	*banca*
beach	*spiaggia*
bed	*letto*
church	*chiesa*
entrance	*entrata*
exit	*uscita*
hospital	*ospedale*
money	*soldi*
museum	*museo*
newspaper (foreign)	*giornale (straniero)*
pharmacy	*farmacia*
police station	*commissariato*
policeman	*poliziotto*
post office	*ufficio postale*
sea	*mare*
shop	*negozio*
room	*camera*
telephone	*telefono*
tobacco shop	*tabaccaio*

WC	*toilette/ bagno*
men	*Signori/ Uomini*
women	*Signore/ Donne*

Time

What time is it?	*Che ore sono?*
month	*mese*
week	*settimana*
day	*giorno*
morning	*mattina*
afternoon	*pomeriggio*
evening	*sera*
today	*oggi*
yesterday	*ieri*
tomorrow	*domani*
soon	*fra poco*
later	*dopo/ più tardi*
It is too early	*È troppo presto*
It is too late	*È troppo tardi*

Days

Monday	*lunedì*
Tuesday	*martedì*
Wednesday	*mercoledì*
Thursday	*giovedì*
Friday	*venerdì*
Saturday	*sabato*
Sunday	*domenica*

Numbers

one	*uno/ una*
two	*due*
three	*tre*
four	*quattro*
five	*cinque*
six	*sei*
seven	*sette*
eight	*otto*
nine	*nove*
ten	*dieci*
eleven	*undici*
twelve	*dodici*
thirteen	*tredici*
fourteen	*quattordici*
fifteen	*quindici*

sixteen	*sedici*
seventeen	*diciassette*
eighteen	*diciotto*
nineteen	*diciannove*
twenty	*venti*
twenty-one	*ventuno*
twenty-two	*ventidue*
thirty	*trenta*
thirty-one	*trentuno*
forty	*quaranta*
fifty	*cinquanta*
sixty	*sessanta*
seventy	*settanta*
eighty	*ottanta*
ninety	*novanta*
hundred	*cento*
one hundred and one	*cent'uno*
two hundred	*duecento*
one thousand	*mille*
two thousand	*duemila*
million	*milione*
a thousand million	*miliardo*

Transport

airport	*aeroporto*
bus stop	*fermata*
bus/coach	*autobus/pullman*
railway station	*stazione ferroviaria*
train	*treno*
platform	*binario*
port	*porto*
port station	*stazione marittima*
ship	*nave*
automobile	*macchina*
taxi	*tassì*
ticket	*biglietto*
customs	*dogana*
seat (reserved)	*posto (prenotato)*

Travel Directions

I want to go to...	*Desidero andare a...*
How can I get to...?	*Come posso andare a...?*
Do you stop at...?	*Ferma a...?*
Where is...?	*Dov'è...?*
How far is it to...?	*Quanto siamo lontani da...?*

What is the name of this station?	*Come si chiama questa stazione?*
When does the next ... leave?	*Quando parte il prossimo...?*
From where does it leave?	*Da dove parte?*
How long does the trip take...?	*Quanto tempo dura il viaggio?*
How much is the fare?	*Quant' è il biglietto?*
Have a good trip	*Buon viaggio!*
near	*vicino*
far	*lontano*
left	*sinistra*
right	*destra*
straight ahead	*sempre diritto*
forward	*avanti*
backwards	*indietro*
north	*nord*
south	*sud*
east	*est/ oriente*
west	*ovest/ occidente*
round the corner	*dietro l'angolo*
crossroads	*bivio*
street/road	*strada*
square	*piazza*

Driving

car hire	*noleggio macchina*
motorbike/scooter	*motocicletta/ Vespa*
bicycle	*bicicletta*
petrol/diesel	*benzina/ gasolio*
garage	*garage*
This doesn't work	*Questo non funziona*
mechanic	*meccanico*
map/town plan	*carta/ pianta*
Where is the road to...?	*Dov' è la strada per...?*
breakdown	*guasto or panna*
driving licence	*patente di guida*
driver	*guidatore*
speed	*velocità*
danger	*pericolo*
parking	*parcheggio*
no parking	*sosta vietata*
narrow	*stretto*
bridge	*ponte*
toll	*pedaggio*
slow down	*rallentare*

Italian Menu Vocabulary

Antipasti

These before-meal treats can include almost anything; among the most common are:

Antipasto misto	mixed antipasto
Bruschetta	garlic toast (sometimes with tomatoes)
Carciofi (sott'olio)	artichokes (in oil)
Crostini	liver pâté on toast
Frutti di mare	seafood
Funghi (trifolati)	mushrooms (with anchovies, garlic, and lemon)
Gamberi ai fagioli	prawns (shrimps) with white beans
Mozzarella (in carrozza)	cow or buffalo cheese (fried with bread in batter)
Olive	olives
Prosciutto (con melone)	raw ham (with melon)
Salami	cured pork
Salsicce	sausages

Minestre (Soups) and Pasta

These dishes are the principal typical first courses (*primi*) served throughout Italy.

Agnolotti	ravioli with meat
Cacciucco	spiced fish soup
Cannelloni	meat and cheese rolled in pasta tubes
Cappelletti	small ravioli, often in broth
Crespelle	crêpes
Fettuccine	long strips of pasta
Frittata	omelette
Gnocchi	potato dumplings
Lasagne	sheets of pasta baked with meat and cheese sauce
Minestra di verdura	thick vegetable soup
Minestrone	soup with meat, vegetables, and pasta
Orecchiette	ear-shaped pasta, often served with turnip greens
Panzerotti	ravioli filled with mozzarella, anchovies, and egg
Pappardelle alla lepre	pasta with hare sauce
Pasta e fagioli	soup with beans, bacon, and tomatoes
Pastina in brodo	tiny pasta in broth
Penne all'arrabbiata	quill-shaped pasta with tomatoes and hot peppers
Polenta	cake or pudding of corn semolina
Risotto (alla Milanese)	Italian rice (with stock, saffron and wine)

Spaghetti all'amatriciana	with spicy sauce of salt pork, tomatoes, onions, and chili pepper
Spaghetti alla Bolognese	with ground meat, ham, mushrooms, etc.
Spaghetti alla carbonara	with bacon, eggs, and black pepper
Spaghetti al pomodoro	with tomato sauce
Spaghetti al sugo/ ragù	with meat sauce
Spaghetti alle vongole	with clam sauce
Stracciatella	broth with eggs and cheese
Tagliatelle	flat egg noodles
Tortellini al pomodoro/ panna/ in brodo	pasta caps filled with meat and cheese, served with tomato sauce/with cream/in broth
Vermicelli	very thin spaghetti

Carne (Meat)

Abbacchio	milk-fed lamb
Agnello	lamb
Animelle	sweetbreads
Anatra	duck
Arista	pork loin
Arrosto misto	mixed roast meats
Bistecca alla fiorentina	Florentine beef steak
Bocconcini	veal mixed with ham and cheese and fried
Bollito misto	stew of boiled meats
Braciola	chop
Brasato di manzo	braised beef with vegetables
Bresaola	dried raw meat similar to ham
Capretto	kid
Capriolo	roe-buck
Carne di castrato/ suino	mutton/pork
Carpaccio	thin slices of raw beef served with a piquant sauce
Cassoeula	winter stew with pork and cabbage
Cervello (al burro nero)	brains (in black butter sauce)
Cervo	venison
Cinghiale	boar
Coniglio	rabbit
Cotoletta (alla Milanese/alla Bolognese)	veal cutlet (fried in breadcrumbs/with ham and cheese)
Fagiano	pheasant
Faraona (alla creta)	guinea fowl (in earthenware pot)
Fegato alla veneziana	liver (usually of veal) with filling
Lepre (in salmi)	hare (marinated in wine)
Lombo di maiale	pork loin

Lumache	snails
Maiale (al latte)	pork (cooked in milk)
Manzo	beef
Osso buco	braised veal knuckle with herbs
Pancetta	rolled pork
Pernice	partridge
Petto di pollo (alla fiorentina/bolognese/ sorpresa)	boned chicken breast (fried in butter/ with ham and cheese/stuffed and deep fried)
Piccione	pigeon
Pizzaiola	beef steak with tomato and oregano sauce
Pollo (alla cacciatora/alla diavola/ alla Marengo)	chicken (with tomatoes and mushrooms cooked in wine/grilled/ fried with tomatoes, garlic and wine)
Polpette	meatballs
Quaglie	quails
Rane	frogs
Rognoni	kidneys
Saltimbocca	veal scallop with *prosciutto* and sage, cooked in wine and butter
Scaloppine	thin slices of veal sautéed in butter
Spezzatino	pieces of beef or veal, usually stewed
Spiedino	meat on a skewer or stick
Stufato	beef braised in white wine with vegetables
Tacchino	turkey
Trippa	tripe
Uccelletti	small birds on a skewer
Vitello	veal

Pesce (Fish)

Acciughe or *Alici*	anchovies
Anguilla	eel
Aragosta	lobster
Aringa	herring
Baccalà	dried salt cod
Bonito	small tuna
Branzino	sea bass
Calamari	squid
Cappe sante	scallops
Cefalo	grey mullet
Coda di rospo	angler fish
Cozze	mussels
Datteri di mare	razor (or date) mussels
Dentice	dentex (perch-like fish)

Dorato	gilt head
Fritto misto	mixed fried delicacies, usually fish
Gamberetto	shrimp
Gamberi (di fiume)	prawns (crayfish)
Granchio	crab
Insalata di mare	seafood salad
Lampreda	lamprey
Merluzzo	cod
Nasello	hake
Orata	bream
Ostriche	oysters
Pesce spada	swordfish
Polipi/ polpi	octopus
Pesce azzurro	various types of small fish
Pesce di San Pietro	John Dory
Rombo	turbot
Sarde	sardines
Seppie	cuttlefish
Sgombro	mackerel
Sogliola	sole
Squadro	monkfish
Stoccafisso	wind-dried cod
Tonno	tuna
Triglia	red mullet (*rouget*)
Trota	trout
Trota salmonata	salmon trout
Vongole	small clams
Zuppa di pesce	mixed fish in sauce or stew

Contorni (Side Dishes, Vegetables)

Asparagi (alla fiorentina)	asparagus (with fried eggs)
Broccoli (calabrese, romana)	broccoli (green, spiral)
Carciofi (alla giudia)	artichokes (deep fried)
Cardi	cardoons, thistles
Carote	carrots
Cavolfiore	cauliflower
Cavolo	cabbage
Ceci	chickpeas
Cetriolo	cucumber
Cipolla	onion
Fagioli	white beans
Fagiolini	French (green) beans
Fave	broad beans
Finocchio	fennel
Funghi (porcini)	mushrooms (boletus)
Insalata (mista, verde)	salad (mixed, green)

Lattuga	lettuce
Lenticchie	lentils
Melanzane (al forno)	aubergine/eggplant (filled and baked)
Patate (fritte)	potatoes (fried)
Peperoni	sweet peppers
Peperonata	stewed peppers, onions, etc. similar to ratatouille
Piselli (al prosciutto)	peas (with ham)
Pomodoro(i)	tomato(es)
Porri	leeks
Radicchio	red chicory
Radice	radish
Rapa	turnip
Sedano	celery
Spinaci	spinach
Verdure	greens
Zucca	pumpkin
Zucchini	courgettes

Formaggio (Cheese)

Bel Paese	a soft white cow's cheese
Cacio/ Caciocavallo	pale yellow, often sharp cheese
Fontina	rich cow's milk cheese
Groviera	mild cheese (gruyère)
Gorgonzola	soft blue cheese
Parmigiano	Parmesan cheese
Pecorino	sharp sheep's cheese
Provolone	sharp, tangy cheese; *dolce* is less strong
Stracchino	soft white cheese

Frutta (Fruit, Nuts)

Albicocche	apricots
Ananas	pineapple
Arance	oranges
Banane	bananas
Cachi	persimmon
Ciliege	cherries
Cocomero	watermelon
Composta di frutta	stewed fruit
Datteri	dates
Fichi	figs
Fragole (con panna)	strawberries (with cream)
Frutta di stagione	fruit in season
Lamponi	raspberries
Macedonia di frutta	fruit salad

Mandarino	tangerine
Mandorle	almonds
Melagrana	pomegranate
Mele	apples
Melone	melon
Mirtilli	bilberries
More	blackberries
Nespola	medlar fruit
Nocciole	hazelnuts
Noci	walnuts
Pera	pear
Pesca	peach
Pesca noce	nectarine
Pignoli/ pinoli	pine nuts
Pompelmo	grapefruit
Prugna/ susina	prune/plum
Uva	grapes

Dolci (Desserts)

Amaretti	macaroons
Cannoli	crisp pastry tubes filled with ricotta, cream, chocolate or fruit
Coppa gelato	assorted ice cream
Crema caramella	caramel-topped custard
Crostata	fruit flan
Gelato (produzione propria)	ice-cream (homemade)
Granita	flavoured ice, usually lemon or coffee
Monte Bianco	chestnut pudding with whipped cream
Panettone	sponge cake with candied fruit and raisins
Panforte	dense cake of chocolate, almonds, and preserved fruit
Saint Honoré	meringue cake
Semifreddo	refrigerated cake
Sorbetto	sorbet/sherbet
Spumone	a soft ice cream
Tiramisù	layers of sponge fingers and Mascarpone, coffee and chocolate
Torrone	nougat
Torta	cake, tart
Torta millefoglie	layered pastry with custard cream
Zabaglione	whipped eggs and Marsala wine, served hot
Zuppa inglese	trifle

Bevande (Beverages)

Acqua minerale con/ senza gas	mineral water with/without fizz
Aranciata	orange soda
Birra (alla spina)	beer (draught)
Caffè (freddo)	coffee (iced)
Cioccolata (con panna)	chocolate (with cream)
Gassosa	lemon-flavoured soda
Latte	milk
Limonata	lemon soda
Succo di frutta	fruit juice
Tè	tea
Vino (rosso, bianco, rosato)	wine (red, white, rosé)

Cooking Terms, Miscellaneous

Aceto (balsamico)	vinegar (balsamic)
Affumicato	smoked
Aglio	garlic
Alla brace	on embers
Bicchiere	glass
Burro	butter
Cacciagione	game
Conto	bill
Costoletta/ Cotoletta	chop
Coltello	knife
Cucchiaio	spoon
Filetto	fillet
Forchetta	fork
Forno	oven
Fritto	fried
Ghiaccio	ice
Griglia	grill
In bianco	without tomato
Limone	lemon
Magro	lean meat/or pasta without meat
Marmellata	jam
Menta	mint
Miele	honey
Mostarda	candied mustard sauce, eaten with boiled meats
Olio	oil
Pane (tostato)	bread (toasted)
Panini	sandwiches
Panna	cream
Pepe	pepper
Peperoncini	hot chili peppers

Piatto	plate
Prezzemolo	parsley
Ripieno	stuffed
Rosmarino	rosemary
Sale	salt
Salmi	wine marinade
Salsa	sauce
Salvia	sage
Senape	mustard
Tartufi	truffles
Tazza	cup
Tavola	table
Tovagliolo	napkin
Tramezzini	finger sandwiches
Umido	cooked in sauce
Uovo	egg
Zucchero	sugar

Useful Hotel Vocabulary

Vorrei una camera doppia, per favore	I'd like a double room, please
Vorrei una camera singola, per favore	I'd like a single room, please
con bagno, senza bagno	with bath, without bath
per due notti	for two nights
Partiamo domani mattina	We are leaving tomorrow morning
C'è una camera con balcone?	Is there a room with a balcony?
Mancano acqua calda, sapone, luce,	There isn't (aren't) any hot water,
carta igienica, asciugamani, coperte,	soap, light, toilet paper, towels,
cuscini, gruccie	blankets, pillows, coathangers
Posso pagare con carta di credito?	May I pay by credit card?
Per favore, potrei vedere un' altra camera?	May I see another room, please?
Sì, va bene, grazie	Yes, that's fine, thank you
È compresa la prima colazione?	Is breakfast included?
Come posso raggiungere il centro città?	How do I get to the town centre?

Note: Page numbers in *italics* refer to maps and plans. Page numbers in **bold** indicate main references.

Index

Answers to 'A Florentine Puzzle' (pp.54/55)

1 Façade, San Miniato.
2 Baptistry, interior apse.
3 Windows at the rear of San Iacopo sopr'Arno, visible from Santa Trínita.
4 Windows, Orsanmichele.
5 Façade, Santa Croce (inspired by Orcagna's tabernacle in Orsanichele)
6 Baptistry doors (Pisano's and Ghiberti's first set); Portico of the Bigallo, interior apse, Santa Croce.
7 Loggia dei Lanzi.
8 Rucellai Chapel, San Pancrazio.